PROCEEDINGS OF THE
17TH ANNUAL INTERNATIONAL
SYMPOSIUM ON

High Performance Computing Systems and Applications

and the

OSCAR Symposium

COMPTES RENDUS DU
17IÈME SYMPOSIUM ANNUEL
INTERNATIONAL SUR LES

Systèmes et applications du calcul de haute performance

et le

Symposium OSCAR

Program Sponsors

Commanditaires

PROCEEDINGS OF THE
17TH ANNUAL INTERNATIONAL
SYMPOSIUM ON

High Performance Computing Systems and Applications
and the
OSCAR Symposium

May 11-14, 2003, Sherbrooke, Québec, Canada

COMPTES RENDUS DU
17IÈME SYMPOSIUM ANNUEL
INTERNATIONAL SUR LES

Systèmes et applications du calcul de haute performance
et le
Symposium OSCAR

11-14 mai 2003, Sherbrooke, Québec, Canada

Editor/Éditeur
D. Sénéchal

Department of Physics
Université de Sherbrooke
Shrerbrooke, QC J1K 2R1
Canada

Département de physique
Université de Sherbrooke
Sherbrooke, QC J1K 2R1
Canada

NRC·CNRC
NRC Research Press
Presses scientifiques du CNRC
Ottawa 2003

Printed in Canada on acid-free paper.

Publisher's Note: This book has been prepared from camera ready copy provided by the editor in order to make the books available for the conference.

ISBN 0–660–19028–1
NRC No. 46320

National Library of Canada Cataloguing in Publication

International Symposium on High Performance Computing Systems and Applications (17th : 2003 : Sherbrooke, Quebec)
Proceedings of the 17th Annual International Symposium on High Performance Computing Systems and Applications and the OSCAR Symposium : May 11-14, 2003, Sherbrooke, Quebec, Canada / editor, D. Sénéchal = Comptes rendus du 17ième Symposium annuel international sur les systèmes et applications du calcul de haute performance et le Symposium OSCAR : 11-14 mai 2003, Sherbrooke, Québec, Canada / éditeur, D. Sénéchal.

Issued by the National Research Council of Canada.
"NRC no. 46320"--T.p. verso
Includes bibliographical references.
Text in English only; includes prefatory material in French.
ISBN 0-660-19028-1
Cat. No. NR15-67/2003E

1. High performance computing--Congresses. I. Sénéchal, David, 1963- II. National Research Council Canada III. OSCAR Symposium (2003 : Sherbrooke, Quebec) IV. Title. V. Title: Comptes rendus du 17ième Symposium annuel international sur les systèmes et applications du calcul de haute performance et le Symposium OSCAR.

QA76.88.I58 2003 004.1'1 C2003-902343-5

Inquiries: Proceedings Program, NRC Research Press, National Research Council of Canada, Ottawa, Ontario K1A 0R6, Canada.

Correct citation for this publication: Sénéchal, D. (*Editor/Éditeur*). 2003. *Proceedings of the 17th International Symposium on High Performance Computing Systems and Applications and OSCAR Symposium/ Comptes rendus du 17ième symposium annuel international sur les Systèmes et applications du calcul de haute performance et le Symposium OSCAR.* NRC Research Press/Les Presses scientifique du CNRC, National Research Council of Canada/Conseil national de recherches Canada, Ottawa, ON K1A 0R6, Canada, 318 pages.

Table of Contents
Table des matières

Preface

This volume contains the proceedings of the 17th annual International Symposium on High Performance Systems and Applications (HPCS 2003), held at the Delta Hotel in Sherbrooke (Québec) Canada, from May 11 to May 14 2003. The symposium covers various areas of High-Performance Computing, from specific scientific applications to computer architecture. This year, the HPC symposium joins with the first OSCAR symposium, and this gives this year's edition a special *clustering* flavor. OSCAR is an Open Source clustering software suite for building, maintaining, and using high performance clusters.

This volume is divided into three parts : (I) Various applications of HPC, from Mathematics to Engineering, with a special emphasis on Condensed Matter Physics and Chemistry. (II) Systems papers, covering computer architectures, grids, networking and scheduling. (III) OSCAR papers, covering building, installation and maintenance of computer clusters. Finally, two tutorials close the volume. Additional contributions to the symposium could not be included in this volume, for lack of time.

We would like to acknowledge the symposium's sponsors. First of all, the *Ministère des Finances, de l'Économie et de la Recherche* of the Québec government, for its financial support within its program dedicated to scientific conferences in Québec. Then, the various corportations involved in High-Performance Computing : Intel, IBM, SGI, HP and Sun. These companies have supported the HPCS conferences in the past and they all contribute to the growth of HPC in Canada. We also thank the Université de Sherbrooke for its support, both financial and in kind, through many of its employees. The staff of the *Réseau Québécois de Calcul de Haute Performance* (RQCHP) has contributed to the organization of the symposium. We thank the C3.ca association, especially Andrew Pollard, Bruce Attfield and Claudette Tourigny, for its financial support and its help and guidance. We also thank Mrs L. Généreux of the Sherbrooke Economic Development Corporation for initial help. Finally, we are grateful to the NRC Press and its Staff (especially Gerald J. Neville and Robert Forrest) for the production of this volume.

This symposium would not have taken place without the patient labor of the local organizing committee. In particular, I thank Benoit des Ligneris, Carol Gauthier, Brahim Tighiouart and Alain Veilleux for their sustained effort.

David Sénéchal, *Université de Sherbrooke*
Program Chair

Préface

Ce volume contient les comptes-rendus du $17^{\text{ème}}$ sympoisum annuel sur les systèmes et applications du calcul de haute performance (HPCS 2003), qui s'est tenu à l'Hôtel Delta de Sherbrooke (Québec), Canada, du 11 au 14 mai 2003. Le sympoisum couvre plusieurs domaines reliés au calcul de haute performance (CHP), des applications scientifiques à l'architecture des ordinateurs. Cette année, le symposium s'est adjoint le premier symposium OSCAR, ce qui lui donne une saveur particulière, avec une certaine emphase sur les grappes de calcul. OSCAR est une suite logicielle à code source libre pour l'installation, l'entretien et l'utilisation de grappes de calcul de haute performance.

Ce volume est divisé en trois parties : (I) Applications diverses du CHP, des mathématiques au génie, avec un accent particulier sur la physique de la matière condensée et la chimie. (II) Articles de systèmes, portant sur l'architecture, le *grid*, les réseaux et la gestion des tâches. (III) Les articles OSCAR, portant sur l'assemblage, l'installation et l'administration de grappes de calcul. Enfin, deux tutoriels ferment la marche. D'autres contributions au symposium n'ont pu être incluses dans le volume, par manque de temps au moment de mettre sous presse.

Nous tenons à remercier les commanditaires du symposium. En premier lieu, le Ministère des Finances, de l'Économie et de la Recherche du Québec, pour son aide à travers son programme de soutien à la tenue de congrès scientifiques. Ensuite, les entreprises impliquées dans le CHP : Intel, IBM, SGI, HP et Sun. Ces compagnies ont soutenu les conférences HPCS dans le passé et contribuent à l'essor du calcul de haute performance au Canada. Nous remercions aussi l'Université de Sherbrooke pour son soutien, à la fois financier et à travers le temps de ses employés. Le personnel du Réseau Québécois de Calcul de Haute Performance (RQCHP) a aussi été mis à contribution. Nous remercions l'association C3.ca pour son soutien financier, et en particulier Andrew Pollard, Bruce Attfield and Claudette Tourigny pour les conseils prodigués. Nous remercions Mme L. Généreux de la Société de Développement Économique de Sherbrooke pour son aide initiale dans le projet. Enfin, nous sommes reconnaissants envers les Presses scientifiques du CNRC et son personnel (en particulier Gerald J. Neville and Robert Forrest) pour la production de ce volume.

Ce symposium n'aurait pas eu lieu sans le travail patient et soutenu du comité organisateur. En particulier, nous remercions Benoit des Ligneris, Carol Gauthier, Brahim Tighiouart et Alain Veilleux de l'effort soutenu qu'ils ont consenti.

David Sénéchal, *Université de Sherbrooke*
Président du symposium

Local Organizing Committee / *Comité organisateur*

Benoit des Ligneris
(CCS, Université de Sherbrooke)
Carol Gauthier
(RQCHP, CCS, Université de Sherbrooke)
Kaan Inal
(Génie, Université de Sherbrooke)
Marcel Lacroix
(Génie, Université de Sherbrooke)
Makan Pourzandi
(Ericsson)
David Sénéchal
(Sciences, Université de Sherbrooke)
Brahim Tighiouart
(IMSI, Université de Sherbrooke)
André-Marie Tremblay
(Sciences, Université de Sherbrooke)
Alain Veilleux
(CCS, Université de Sherbrooke)

Program Committee / *Comité scientifique*

S. Akl *(Queen's University)*
J. Almhana *(Université de Moncton)*
S. Arunkumar *(Indian Institute of Technology)*
E. Aubanel *(University of New Brunswick)*
A. Bandrauk *(Université de Sherbrooke)*
V. Bhavsar *(University of New Brunswick)*
Benoit des Ligneris *(Université de Sherbrooke)*
M. Côté *(Université de Montréal)*
M. Dagenais *(École Polytechnique, Montréal)*
B. d'Auriol *(University of Texas at El Paso)*
K. Gallivan *(Florida State University)*
P.C.J. Graham *(University of Manitoba)*
W. Habashi *(McGill University)*
I. Haddad *(Ericsson)*
E.V. Krishnamurthy *(Australian National University)*
M. Lacroix *(Université de Sherbrooke)*
L. Lefèvre *(INRIA, France)*
A. Louri *(University of Arizona)*
P. Lu *(University of Alberta)*
F. Major *(Université de Montréal)*
E. Moreno *(Euripides Foundation of Marilia, Brazil)*
V. Murthy *(University of New South Wales)*
K. Neale *(Université de Sherbrooke)*
L. Nelson *(Bishop's University)*
E. Nobile *(INMA, Trieste)*
M. Ould-Khaoua *(University of Glasgow)*
G. Peslherbe *(Concordia University)*
G. Qian-Ping *(Simon Fraser University)*
A. Rau-Chaplin *(Dahousie University)*
S. Scott *(Oak Ridge National Laboratory)*
D. Sénéchal *(Université de Sherbrooke)*
R. Shaw *(University of New Brunswick)*
A. Skorek *(UQTR)*
G. Slater *(University of Ottawa)*
A. Sodan *(University of Windsor)*
A. Soldera *(Université de Sherbrooke)*
D. Stacey *(University of Guelph)*
L. Tao *(Pace University, NY)*
A.-M. Tremblay *(Université de Sherbrooke)*
J.-Y. Trépanier *(École polytechnique, Montréal)*

Part I : Applications
Partie I : applications

Concurrent Computation and Time Complexity Bounds for Algebraic Fractals

F. Chris MacPhee[a] and Virendrakumar C. Bhavsar[b]

[a,b]Advanced Computational Research Laboratory, Faculty of Computer Science,
University of New Brunswick, Fredericton, NB, E3B 5A3, Canada
http://www.cs.unb.ca/acrl/

[a] *Chris.Macphee@unb.ca*

[b] *bhavsar@unb.ca*

This paper considers various parallelization schemes and applies them to concurrent computation of algebraic fractals on IBM SP3 and SGI Onyx 3400 systems. We adapt the time complexity bounds of parallel Monte Carlo methods to predict the execution time behavior of these schemes.

Nous étudions plusieurs méthodes de parallélisation appliquées au calcul simultané de plusieurs objets fractals algébriques sur un IBM SP3 et sur un SGI Onyx 3400. Nous adaptons les bornes de complexité temporelles des calculs Monte-Carlo parallèles afin de prédire le comportement du temps d'exécution de ces méthodes.

1. Introduction

The generation of fractal images from the self-squared function $z \leftarrow z^2 + c$ is widely discussed in the literature (for example, see [1]). The superset $z \leftarrow z^\alpha + c$ proposed by Gujar and Bhavsar [2] allows the exponent of z to be positive and negative, integer as well as real. Some techniques for the vectorization [4] and parallelization [chap. 3, 6; 7; 9] of fractal computations are given in the literature.

In the following section, we brielfly describe the computational aspects of algebraic fractals. Subsequently, we analyze the visual characteristics of the fractals. In §3, we consider the parallelization schemes proposed by MacPhee and Bhavsar [7] for fractal generation. Assuming independent and identically distributed (i.i.d.) execution times for pixel computations, we apply the time complexity bounds for parallel Monte Carlo methods in §4. We present the computational results of our experiments on IBM SP3 and SGI Onyx 3400 systems in §5. We investigate if the bounds could be used to describe the execution time behavior of these schemes. Finally, we conclude the paper with our findings.

2. Computational and Visual Characteristics

We consider the following parameters for algebraic fractal computations: the pixels map is 1024×1024 with $|\Re(z)| \leq 1.5$ and $|\Im(z)| \leq 1.5$, the maximum allowable number of iterations per pixel is 100, and z is said to diverge if $|z| > 10$.

We use the Open Visualization Data Explorer (OpenDX) package for visualizing fractals. The colour scheme used is intentionally skewed to provide more resolution in the [1, 10] and [91, 100] ranges, due to their higher concentration. Figure 1 shows sample images of various α; see http://www.cs.unb.ca/acrl/fractal/ for additional images.

Table 1 provides a statistical summary for various values of α. Algebraic fractals discussed within this paper have a bimodal distribution, with over 90% of the points having a value of [1, 10] or [91, 100], as seen in Figure 2.

As discussed in [7], as $|\alpha|$ increases, the number of nodes and satellites increase for $\alpha \geq 2$ and $\alpha \leq -2$, respectively. The rightmost images of Figure 1 shows that fractal images tend toward a unit circle centered on the origin as $|\alpha|$ tends toward infinity, approximated by $\alpha = \pm 100000$.

Table 1. Statistical summary of number of iterations in fractal images

	pixel		*column*	
α	***mean***	***std dev***	***mean***	***std dev***
-100000	65.7859	46.7158	67364.8	27608.5
-10	71.3106	44.1683	73022.1	23831.1
-2	83.2948	34.8595	85293.9	17162.6
2	22.2449	35.9684	22778.8	19381.1
10	29.4801	43.4767	30187.6	24781.6
100000	36.2092	46.7143	37078.2	27607.2

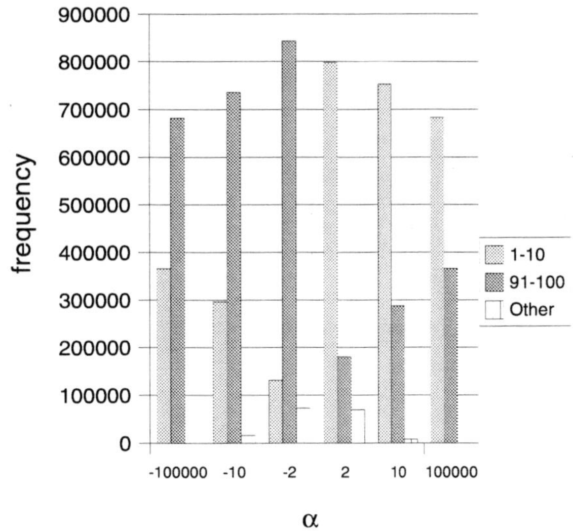

Figure 2. Distribution of number of iterations for pixel computations for various α

The unit circle forms due to the interior or exterior of the circle quickly diverging. We see that z^{α} can be defined by

$$\begin{aligned} z^{\alpha} &= |z|^{\alpha}\left[\cos(\alpha\Theta)+i\sin(\alpha\Theta)\right] \\ &= \sqrt{\Re(z)^2+\Im(z)^2}^{\,\alpha}\left[\cos(\alpha\Theta)+i\sin(\alpha\Theta)\right] \end{aligned}$$

(1)

where $\Theta = \arctan(\frac{y}{x})$. Therefore, the divergence of the pixel as $|\alpha|$ tends toward infinity is dependent upon $\Re(z)^2+\Im(z)^2$, as seen in Table 2.

Table 2. Iterations of pixels as $|\alpha|$ tends toward infinity

	α	*Iterations of pixel*
$\Re(z)^2+\Im(z)^2>1$	∞	2*
$\Re(z)^2+\Im(z)^2\le 1$	∞	100
$\Re(z)^2+\Im(z)^2>1$	$-\infty$	100
$\Re(z)^2+\Im(z)^2\le 1$	$-\infty$	2*
** Note: z is initialized to* $0+i0$ *for* α>0 *and* $1+i1$ *for* α≤0, *so the first iteration sets z=c. z exceeds the limit during the second iteration, when* z^{α} *(i.e.* c^{α}*) occurs.*		

3. Parallelization Schemes

The three fractal programs with message passing given in [7, 9], static, smart static, and dynamic work assignments, are used to conduct the experiments. Note that the computation of each pixel is independent.

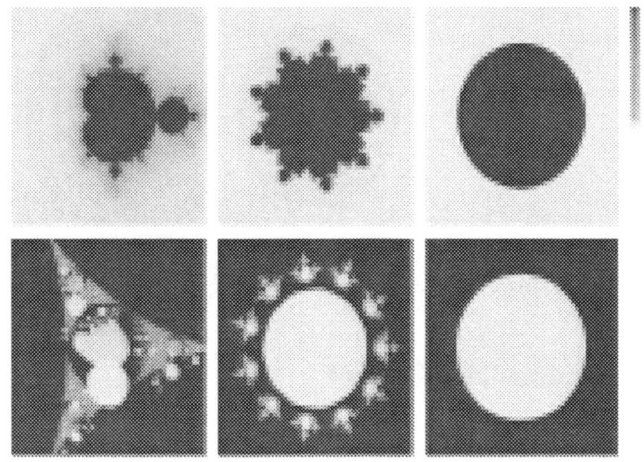

Figure 1. Various fractal images
Top row: α = 2, 10, 100000
Bottom row: α = -2, -10, -100000

In the static work assignment program, column groups are divided evenly among processors. This assignment scheme creates a load balancing problem, where either the inner or outer processors receive more computationally intensive columns for α ≥ 2 and α ≤ -2, respectively.

In the smart static work assignment program, the workload is approximated by calculating the area under an approximation curve and dividing the workload, rather than columns, evenly over the processors.

In the dynamic work assignment program, the master passes work to the slaves in a block size of 2 columns. The block size of 2 columns was determined through experimentation with the machines discussed in §5 and, based upon these machines, approximating for larger numbers of processors.

4. Time Complexity Analysis

As stated earlier, the computation of each pixel is independent. Further, when pixel computations are carried out on a multiprocessor machine, the execution time depends on many factors, including scheduling by the operating system, shared memory conflicts, nondeterminism in I/O and interprocessor communication, and the work assignment scheme. In this context, we hypothesize that the execution times of pixels are i.i.d. random variables. Therefore, we believe that the time complexity bounds given by Bhavsar and Isaac [8] for parallel Monte Carlo methods could be applied to parallel algebraic fractal generation schemes discussed in the previous section.

Bhavsar and Isaac [8] proposed two basic static and dynamic computational assignment schemes for parallel Monte Carlo algorithms based on renewal theory and order statistics. These schemes assign the primary estimate computations to processors. For the fractal generation, the same schemes could be applied to pixel computations (PICs).

Table 3. PIC-time distribution-free time complexity results for the various schemes for parallel Monte Carlo algorithms

Scheme	***Expected time complexity***
SCA-1 $(P \ll K)$	$\frac{K\mu}{P} \le E[T(P,K)] \le \frac{K\mu}{P} + \frac{\sqrt{K}\cdot\sigma}{2}$
SCA-2 $(\frac{P}{K} \sim 10)$	$\frac{K\mu}{P} \le E[T(P,K)] \le \frac{K\mu}{P} + \frac{(P-1)\sqrt{K}}{\sqrt{(2P-1)P}} \cdot \sigma$
SCA-3 $(P = K)$	$\frac{\mu}{P} \le E[T(P,K)] \le \mu + \frac{(K-1)}{\sqrt{2K-1}} \cdot \sigma$
SCA-4 $(P > K)$	*PIC-time distribution-free time complexity results are not possible.*
DCA-1	$E[T(P,K)] etd \frac{K\mu}{P} + \frac{(P-1)(\mu^2+\sigma^2)}{2P\mu}$
DCA-2	$\tau \leqslant E[T(P,K)] \leqslant \tau + \frac{(P-1)}{\sqrt{2P-1}} \cdot \sigma$ $where\, \tau\; etd\, \frac{K\mu}{P} + \frac{(P-1)(\mu^2-\sigma^2)}{2P\mu}$

K = desired total number of primary estimates of a problem variable.
μ = mean of i.i.d. PIC times
σ = standard deviation of i.i.d. PIC times
P = number of processors

Table 3 provides a list of the PIC time complexity results for the assignment schemes based on results given in [8]. The number of PICs to be calculated, *K*, is the total number of rows in the fractal image. For fractals within this paper, we have set *K*=1024.

In the static computation assignment (SCA) schemes, a fixed number of PICs are assigned to the processors before any computations are initiated. The SCA time complexity bounds are composed of multiple SCA schemes, determined by the relationship of *P* to *K*.

In SCA-1 and 2, *K* PICs are assigned over *P* processors, such that each processor is assigned the same number of PICs. In SCA-3, one PIC is assigned to each processor. In SCA-4, one PIC is assigned to each processor, but computations are terminated once *K* PICs are completed. Only SCA-1, 2, and 3 are used for the purposes of algebraic fractal computation.

In the dynamic computation assignment (DCA) schemes, PICs are farmed out to the processors; the decision to initiate further PICs is based on a preset criteria. In DCA-1, PICs are farmed to processors until *K* PICs have been completed; any incomplete PICs on the remaining processors are aborted. In DCA-2, only *K* PICs are farmed to the processors; unlike DCA-1, no PICs are aborted. Only DCA-2 is used for the purpose of algebraic fractal computation, as all PICs must be completed.

The means and standard deviations of the algebraic fractals found in Table 1 are used to obtain the bounds of the speedup defined by Table 3. Figures 3 and 4 depict the upper and lower bounds of the speedup for the generation of α = 10, along with the estimated performance of the static, smart static, and dynamic assignment schemes.

4.1 SCA Schemes

The makeup of the SCA time complexity bounds are considered to be as follows:

SCA-1 $(P\, trèssupérieuràn\, K)$: for *P* = 2, 4, 8, .:. , 64.

SCA-2 $(P/K \sim 10)$: for *P* = 128, 256, and 512.

SCA-3 $(P = K)$: for *P* = 1024.

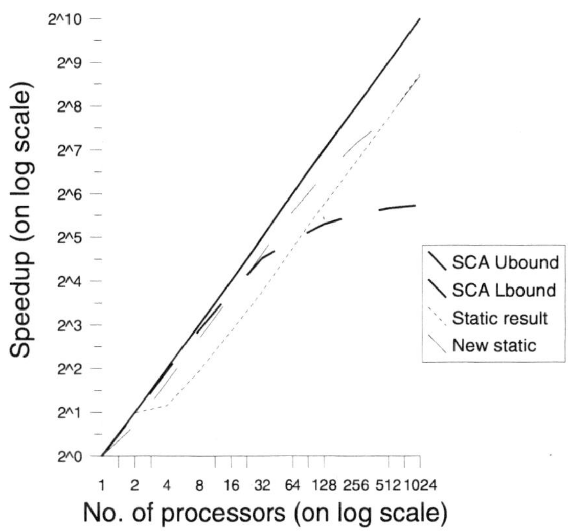

Figure 3. Theoretical and estimated performance of static schemes for parallel Monte Carlo algorithms for generating a fractal image with α = 10

As seen in Figure 3, neither static assignment scheme follows the lower bound at α = 10 for small values of *P*. SCA-1 requires i.i.d. random variables to satisfy a normal distribution through the application of the Central Limit theorem, but in this case the PIC times do not uphold our assumption of being i.i.d. random variables.

As α increases, the smart static assignment scheme distributes PICs more efficiently to the processors, which emulates the normal distribution required by SCA-1. For large α, the smart static assignment scheme results are within the upper and lower bounds given by SCA-1.

Both static assignment schemes are within the SCA-2 and 3 bounds, as the lower bound is not dependent on i.i.d. random variables.

4.2 DCA-2 Scheme

As seen in Figure 4, the dynamic assignment scheme results are within the bounds given by DCA-2. Due to the low standard deviation of processor execution times, the dynamic assignment scheme achieves a high efficiency, only slightly below the upper bound given by DCA-2.

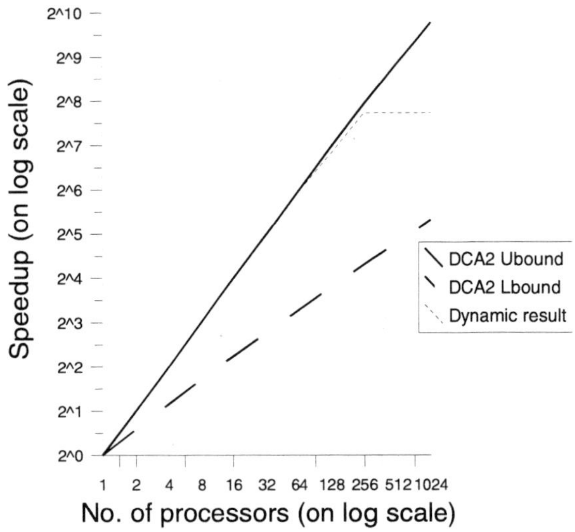

Figure 4. Theoretical and estimated performance of various dynamic schemes for parallel Monte Carlo algorithms for generating a fractal image with row division = 2 and α = 10

5. Experimental Results

Experiments were performed on the IBM SP3 in the Advanced Computational Research Laboratory of the University of New Brunswick (http://www.cs.unb.ca/acrl/) and the SGI Onyx 3400 in the Computation and Visualization Centre of the Memorial University of Newfoundland (http://www.cvc.mun.ca/).

The IBM SP3 is configured with 4 compute nodes, with each node containing 2 x 2-way 375 MHz POWER3 64-bit Winterhawk II Processor cards and 1 GB of memory. The SGI Onyx 3400 is configured with 28 compute nodes with each node containing one 400MHz IP35 MIPS R12000 processor and 0.5 GB of memory.

A total of 9 processors were used during the experiments, configured as 1 master and 8 slaves.

5.1 IBM SP

Figures 5 and 6 show the DCA-2 bounds and experimental performance of the dynamic assignment scheme for various α on the IBM SP3.

While α ≤ -2 are within the DCA-2 bounds, α ≥ 2 falls below the DCA-2 lower bound. Due to the higher mean of the pixels and rows of α ≤ -2 fractals, more time is spent on computation rather than communication. This allows α ≤ -2 fractals to achieve a larger speedup than their α ≥ 2 counterparts.

5.2 SGI Onyx 3400

Figures 7 and 8 show the DCA-2 bounds and experimental performance of the dynamic assignment scheme for various α on the SGI Onyx 3400.

Both α ≥ 2 and α ≤ -2 results are within the DCA-2 bounds on the SGI Onyx 3400. This is due to its improved interconnection network and the higher computation time required to complete results on the SGI Onyx 3400. Both factors increase the computation-to-communication ratio, which increases speedup.

6. Conclusion

The computation and visualization characteristics of algebraic fractals were discussed and a bimodal distribution of the pixel values was observed for α ≥ 2 and α ≤ -2. As |α| tends toward infinity, the distribution of the number of iterations for each pixel of the fractals focuses almost exclusively on the two local maxima of [1, 10] and [91, 100], due to pixels either quickly diverging or converging.

The assumption of i.i.d. pixel execution times is used to apply time complexity bounds of parallel Monte Carlo methods. For the static assignment scheme, the execution time was found to be below the lower bound of the SCA-1 scheme, as it is dependent upon a normal distribution, which the assignment scheme does not provide. The execution time for the smart static assignment scheme was found to be below the lower bound of the SCA-1 scheme when |α| is small, but as |α| increases, which increases the assignment schemes efficiency, a normal distribution is achieved and both bounds apply. Both static assignment schemes are within both of the SCA-2 and SCA-3 bounds. The dynamic assignment scheme is within the DCA-2 bounds and is only slightly below the given upper bound.

Experimental results on the IBM SP and SGI Onyx 3400 show that the DCA-2 bounds hold in practice, although a lower computation-to-communication ratio may pull the speedup below the DCA-2 lower bound.

In conclusion, the time complexity bounds given in this paper can be used to predict the execution time behavior of concurrent computation of algebraic fractals.

References

[1] H. O. Peitgen and P. Richter, *The Beauty of Fractals*, Springer-Verlag, Berlin, 1996.

[2] U. G. Gujar and V. C. Bhavsar, "Fractals from $z \leftarrow z^{\alpha} + c$ in the Complex z-plane", *Comp. and Graph.*, 16(1), pp. 45-49, 1992.

[3] S. V. Dhurandhar, V. C. Bhavsar, and U. G. Gujar, "Analysis of z-plane fractal images from $z \leftarrow z^{\alpha} + c$ for $\alpha < 0$", *Comp. and Graph.*, 17(1), pp. 89-94, 1993.

[4] V. C. Bhavsar, U. G. Gujar, N. Vangala, "Vectorization of generation of fractals from $z \leftarrow z^{\alpha} + c$ on IBM 3090 / 180VF", *Comp. and Graph.*, 17(2), pp. 169-174, 1993.

[5] E. Aubanel, "Parallel Programming with Generalized Fractals," Faculty of Computer Science, University of New Brunswick, , February 2002, http://www.cs.unb.ca/profs/aubanel/aubanel_fractals.html.

[6] B. Wilkinson and M. Allen, *Parallel Programming*, Prentice Hall, Upper Saddle River, 1999.

[7] F. Chris MacPhee and V. C. Bhavsar, Efficient Parallelization of Algebraic Fractals, Technical Report, Faculty of Computer Science, University of New Brunswick, Fredericton, N.B., Canada, March 2002.

[8] V. C. Bhavsar and J. R. Isaac, "Design and Analysis of Parallel Monte Carlo Algorithms," *SIAM J. Stat. Comput.*, 8(1), pp. 73-95, 1987.

[9] F. Chris MacPhee and V. C. Bhavsar, "An Efficient Static Assignment scheme for Algebraic Fractals," *Proceedings of High Performance Computing Systems & Applications*, J. Almhana and V. Bhavsar (Eds.), IEEE, Los Alamitos, CA, pp. 232-233, June 2002.

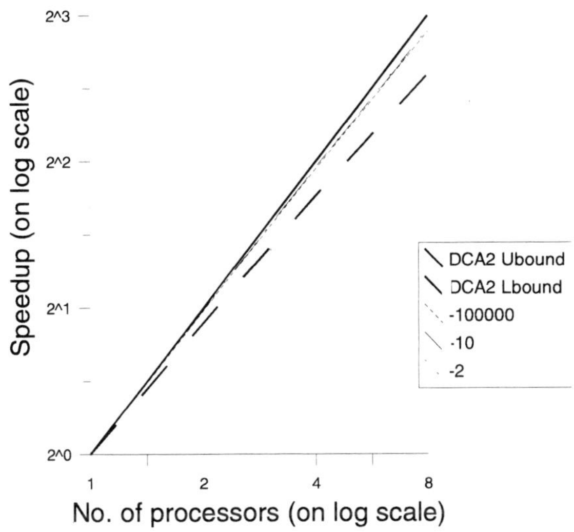

Figure 5. Experimental performance of the dynamic assignment scheme for various $\alpha \leq -2$ on the IBM SP3

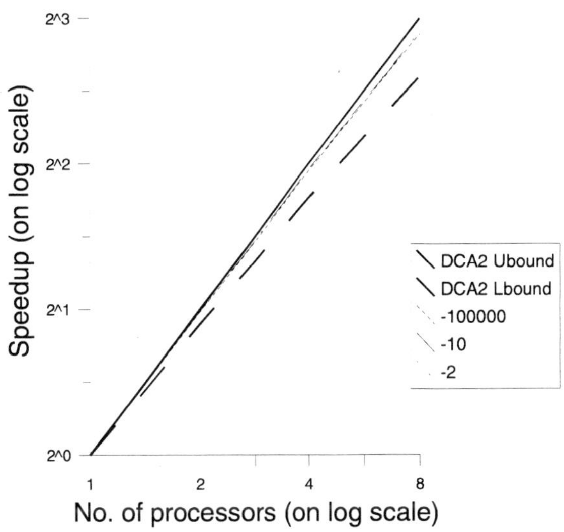

Figure 7. Experimental performance of the dynamic assignment scheme for various $\alpha \leq -2$ on the SGI Onyx 3400

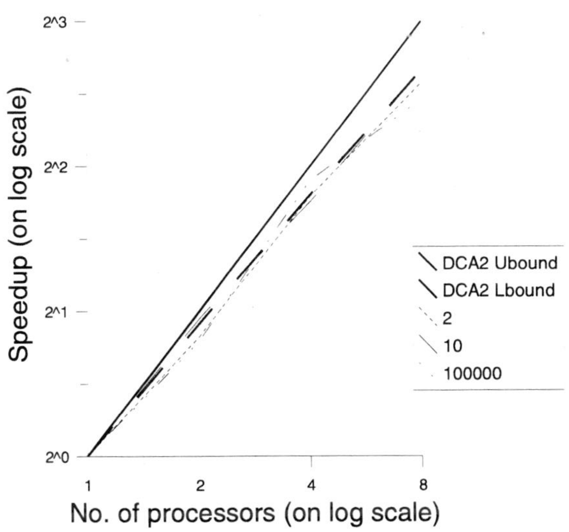

Figure 6. Experimental performance of the dynamic assignment scheme for various $\alpha \geq 2$ on the IBM SP3

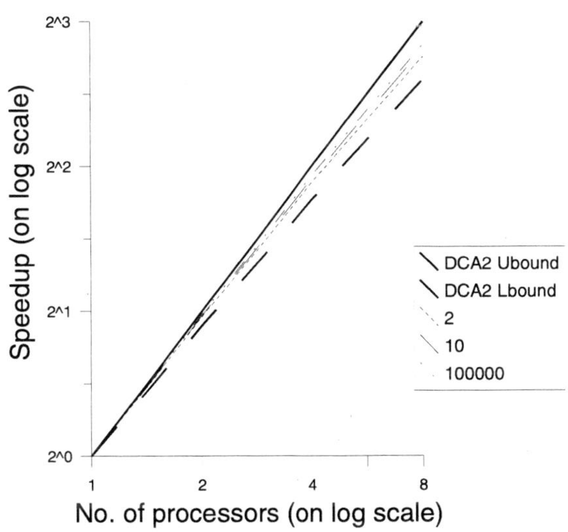

Figure 8. Experimental performance of the dynamic assignment scheme for various $\alpha \geq -2$ on the SGI Onyx 3400

Fast Algorithm to Estimate Dense Disparity Fields

M. Kardouchi[a], E. Hervet

[a]University of Moncton, Computer Science Dept., Moncton, N.B., Canada
{kardoum,hervete}@umoncton.ca

This paper describes a method to compute dense correspondences (disparity map) between two images in a stereo pair in case of significant displacements. In order to deal with large amplitude disparity fields, a multi-resolution technique called block matching have been used in the past[1,2]. Although quite successful, this technique cannot easily cope with disparity discontinuities as it does not explicitly exploit image structure. Additionally, its computational complexity is high and thus take time to achieve; block matching requires examination of numerous vectors. In this paper, we propose a faster approach which combines feature matching with Delaunay triangulation, resulting in reliable long range correspondences with a low computational complexity (sparse representation). First, the proposed method computes feature points by using a simple intensity corner detector. Then, correspondence pairs are found between the two images by maximizing a cross-correlation measure over small windows. Finally, a Delaunay triangulation is applied to the resulting points, and a dense vector field is computed by adaptive interpolation over Delaunay triangles. In order to reduce the computation time, we propose an algorithm to parallel the adaptive interpolation. The method has been tested on stereoscopic images. The results are very encouraging, especially at object boundaries, and the computational complexity is lower than the one of multi-resolution block matching.

Cet article décrit une méthode pour estimer des champs de correspondances denses (cartes de disparités) entre deux images stéréoscopiques, dans le cas de déplacements significatifs. Pour pouvoir extraire des champs de disparités à large amplitude, une technique appelée appariement par bloc a déjà été utilisée. Bien que très satisfaisante, cette technique est peu efficace pour des disparités discontinues car elle n'exploite pas explicitement la structure des images. De plus, sa complexité calculatoire est élevée car elle requiert l'analyse de nombreux vecteurs. Nous proposons dans cet article une approche plus rapide qui combine appariement et triangulation de Delaunay et qui donne des correspondances fiables avec une faible complexité. Dans un premier temps, la méthode proposée calcule des points d'intérêt en utilisant un simple détecteur de coins basé sur l'intensité. Puis on cherche à mettre en correspondance les points détectés entre les deux images en maximisant un coefficient de corrélation entre deux fenêtres centrées en ces points. Enfin, on applique une triangulation de Delaunay aux coins extraits puis une interpolation adaptative aux triangles de Delaunay pour obtenir un champ de disparités dense. Afin de réduire les temps de calcul, nous proposons une parallélisation de notre algorithme d'interpolation adaptative. La méthode a été testée sur des images stéréoscopiques. Les résultats sont très encourageants, spécialement aux frontières entre objets, et la complexité calculatoire est plus faible que celle de l'appariement par bloc.

1 Introduction

In a pair of stereoscopic images representing a scene shot at different times or from different points of view, we call disparity the displacement between two image points, each from one image, that corresponds to the same real 3D point in the scene. When processing digital images made of pixels, the estimation of disparities for most or all pixels yield a so-called disparity map or field.

Estimation of dense correspondences, such as disparity fields in stereoscopic image pairs, is a difficult problem in the presence of large displacements. Methods based on block matching can handle large displacements but they are computationally involved. Moreover, they cannot reliably disambiguate among candidate blocks since simple cumulative error criteria are typically used.

In this paper we propose a new method that addresses these issues. It consists of four main components: computation of sparse correspondences based on feature points, computation of dense vector fields based on these sparse correspondences by means of Delaunay triangulation, adaptive refinement of the triangulation and finally parallelization of the method. These four components are described next.

We apply our method on stereoscopic images to estimate disparity fields. Experimental results are shown in Sect. 4.

2 Estimating Disparity Fields

2.1 Detecting and matching feature points

A feature point detector's purpose is to locate significant intensity structures in an image. Often, points of abrupt intensity changes are characterized by large intensity gradient and are used as an indication of a significant image structure. In this work, we opt for a signal-based method, the so-called Harris Detector[3]. We apply it to each image of a stereo image pair (I_0, I_1). The Harris detector's threshold is fixed depending on the average image gradient. In our application, this threshold is selected so that 800-1,200 corner points are recovered from a 720×480-pixel image. The final results are not especially sensitive to the number of corner points detected.

Correspondences for extracted corners are performed by evaluating similarity between small windows around two feature points, one from each image. To measure this similarity, we use a statistical method based on cross-correlation[5–7]. For each matched corner, the disparity estimate is computed. Typically, we found $\sim$700 acceptable matches for $\sim$1000 feature points detected in a 720×480-pixel image. The cross-correlation eliminates almost all false matches, however a small number of them may be undetected, affecting the final results. We remove the remaining unreliable matches by a post-processing described in Sect. 2.2.2. As a result, we obtain a set of feature point pairs (correspondences) that can be used as control points for dense vector fields interpolation.

2.2 Computing dense vector fields

In this section, we present a method to generate dense vector fields from the computed correspondence pairs. First, a Delaunay triangulation is performed, then the triangles nodes are post-processed to eliminate potential outliers, and finally a dense vector field is computed by low-order spatial interpolation within each Delaunay triangle.

2.2.1 *Delaunay triangulation*

The Delaunay triangulation can be described as follows. Let $\mathcal{P}$ be the set of all points in a two-dimensional plane to be triangulated. The Delaunay triangulation of $\mathcal{P}$, denoted $DT(\mathcal{P})$, is the unique triangulation based on the concept of empty overlap with circles, i.e.,

$$DT(\mathcal{P}) = \Big\{(p,q,r) \in \mathcal{P}^3, C(p,q,r) \cap \mathcal{P} = \emptyset\Big\},$$

where $C(p,q,r)$ is a circle circumscribed on the three points p, q, and r.

In the case considered here, $\mathcal{P}$ is the set of correspondence points in image I_0. Clearly, more feature points exist in "active" image areas, i.e., at object boundaries or in textured regions. Thus, smaller triangles will result in these "active" areas, and larger triangles will appear in homogeneous regions.

2.2.2 *Eliminating potential outliers*

As mentioned in Sect. 2.1, unreliable correspondence points may be found and removed by the Delaunay triangulation. Such unreliable points may adversely affect the dense field interpolation described in the next section. In order to eliminate them, we use the following procedure: (i) for each correspondence point p in image I_0, identify its neighborhood $\eta(p)$, i.e., all vertices of triangles containing p, except p (Fig. 1); (ii) remove unreliable correspondence points; a correspondence point p is considered unreliable if $\|\overrightarrow{d_p} - \bar{d_p}\| > \rho$, where $\overrightarrow{d_p}$ is the correspondence vector at p, $\bar{d_p}$ is the average correspondence vector over $\eta(p)$, and ρ is an adjustable threshold. Using this simple procedure, we are able to remove significant number of outlying correspondences (although a few correct matches are also removed) at very low computational cost. We tested the proposed procedure on several natural stereoscopic images. Results obtained with the cross-correlation matching and the above post-processing step are presented in Sect. 4. Typically, at least 16% of the total number of correspondence points are removed by this post-processing step.

2.2.3 *Adaptive interpolation of vectors*

Given the triangulation and the correspondence vectors at triangles nodes, we compute a dense vector field under the assumption that, in spatial coordinates, motion/disparity varies linearly within each triangle. Given the three vertices of a triangle, a vector $\overrightarrow{d} = [d_1, d_2]^T$ at each pixel within the triangle is computed from a linear model.

Let p_1, p_2, and p_3 be the three nodes of a triangle (Fig. 2). If $\overrightarrow{d_{p_1}}$, $\overrightarrow{d_{p_2}}$ and $\overrightarrow{d_{p_3}}$ are the correspondence vectors associated with p_1, p_2 and p_3, respectively, then the vector $\overrightarrow{d_x}$ for image point x within the triangle formed by the triplet of corners p_1, p_2, and p_3 is given by:

$$\overrightarrow{d_x} = (1-i-j)\overrightarrow{d_{p_1}} + i\overrightarrow{d_{p_2}} + j\overrightarrow{d_{p_3}}, \qquad (1)$$

where i and j relate the coordinates of point x to those of the node points p_1, p_2, and p_3. Referring to Fig. 2, the equations for the values of i and j are:

$$i = \frac{(|\overrightarrow{p_1x}|^2 - |\overrightarrow{p_1n}|^2)^{\frac{1}{2}}}{|\overrightarrow{p_1p_2}|\cos(\frac{\pi}{2}-\Theta)}, \quad j = \frac{(|\overrightarrow{p_1x}|^2 - |\overrightarrow{p_1m}|^2)^{\frac{1}{2}}}{|\overrightarrow{p_1p_3}|\cos(\frac{\pi}{2}-\Theta)}, \qquad (2)$$

where

$$\Theta = \arccos\left(\frac{\overrightarrow{p_1p_2}\cdot\overrightarrow{p_1p_3}}{|\overrightarrow{p_1p_2}|\cdot|\overrightarrow{p_1p_3}|}\right), \quad |\overrightarrow{p_1m}| = \frac{\overrightarrow{p_1p_3}\cdot\overrightarrow{p_1x}}{|\overrightarrow{p_1p_3}|},$$

$$|\overrightarrow{p_1n}| = \frac{\overrightarrow{p_1p_2}\cdot\overrightarrow{p_1x}}{|\overrightarrow{p_1p_2}|},$$

with $\overrightarrow{p_1p_2}$ denoting a vector joining points p_1 and p_2, while m and n are orthogonal projections of x onto $\overrightarrow{p_1p_3}$ and $\overrightarrow{p_1p_2}$.

The resulting disparity fields obtained with this approach are continuous everywhere. This interpolation estimates correctly the disparities in the areas delimited by triangles if all the nodes of these triangles belong either to an object or to background. However, it does not work well when, for example, the three nodes of a triangle straddle the object/background boundary. To solve this problem, int the past we proposed to refine those triangles that exhibit excessive prediction error between stereo image pairs. Very encouraging results were obtained with this approach, however this refinement does not always work reliably, particularly when, for example, one side of a triangle is small compared to the two other sides. In this situation, the small triangle side is a limiting factor in the division into subtriangles.

To address this problem, we propose an adaptive interpolation over Delaunay triangles. This adaptation is based on two parameters: the first one, as before, accounts for the Euclidian distance between the position of disparity under interpolation, within a given triangle, and the three vertices of this triangle; the second parameter, that we introduce now, allows to weigh the interpolation depending (indirectly) on the reliability of disparity vectors at triangle vertices. We assume disparity vector's reliability is high if the associated disparity-compensated prediction error is low.

In particular, let p_1, p_2, and p_3 be the three vertices (nodes) of a triangle to which the disparity under interpolation belongs. For each pixel x belonging to this triangle (Fig. 3) we compute three prediction errors as follows:

$$\epsilon_j(x) = \sum_{y \in \xi(x) \cup \{x\}} \left(I_0(y) - I_1\left(y + \overrightarrow{d_{p_j}}\right)\right)^2, \quad (3)$$

with $j = 1, 2, 3$ and where, again, I_0 is the left image and I_1 is the right image, while $\xi(x)$ is a small neighborhood of point x. Note that $\xi(x)$ is a pixel-based and not a vertex-based neighborhood.

The disparity vector $\overrightarrow{d_x}$ for the image point x is computed using the following interpolation:

$$\overrightarrow{d_x} = \beta_1 \overrightarrow{d_{p_1}} + \beta_2 \overrightarrow{d_{p_2}} + \beta_3 \overrightarrow{d_{p_3}} \quad (4)$$

with

$$\beta_i = \left(\frac{\frac{\lambda_i}{(1+\epsilon_i)}}{\frac{\lambda_1}{(1+\epsilon_1)} + \frac{\lambda_2}{(1+\epsilon_2)} + \frac{\lambda_3}{(1+\epsilon_3)}} \right), \quad (5)$$

where we note $\lambda_1 = (1 - i - j)$, $\lambda_2 = i$, and $\lambda_3 = j$ from Eq. 1 which was the case for non-adaptive interpolation. λ_1, λ_2, λ_3 relate the coordinates of point x to those of the nodes p_1, p_2, and p_3. However, they are weighted by the corresponding prediction errors ϵ_1, ϵ_2, and ϵ_3. In consequence, the new weights β_i become adaptive; their values depend on how well the disparities at triangle vertices can match intensities in the two views, as explained in more detail.

Interpretation

Two cases of interpolation can be distinguished according to the positioning of a Delaunay triangle with respect to object boundaries:

a) *all nodes of a triangle belong either to an object or to the background:* in this case, the disparity vectors $\overrightarrow{d_{p_1}}$, $\overrightarrow{d_{p_2}}$, and $\overrightarrow{d_{p_3}}$, estimated at nodes p_1, p_2, and p_3, are likely to be similar since all nodes belong either to an object or to the background. Therefore, the prediction errors $\epsilon_j(x)$ should be nearly the same for $j = 1, 2, 3$. We deduce from Eq. 5 that the components β_j, $j = 1, 2, 3$, may be approximated as follows: $\beta_j \simeq \lambda_j$, $j = 1, 2, 3$. The Eq. 4 becomes equivalent to Eq. 1; a linear interpolation is sufficient in this situation;

b) *triangle overlaps both an object and the background:* in this case, for a point x which belongs to a given triangle, two cases can occur:
(i) *point x belongs to the object (Fig. 3):* in this case, it is very likely that the prediction errors $\epsilon_2(x)$ and $\epsilon_3(x)$ are smaller than $\epsilon_1(x)$. Indeed, as x belongs to the object, the prediction error in the neighborhood of point x should be small, and therefore in the limit (as $\epsilon_2(x)$ and $\epsilon_3(x)$ become very small, and $\epsilon_1(x)$ gets very large), we should have $\beta_2 >> \beta_1$ and $\beta_3 >> \beta_1$. Then from Eq. 4 we can deduce that only the disparities at points p_2 and p_3 will contribute significantly to the estimation of the disparity vector at point x. The contribution of the disparity vector at point p_1 should be negligible.
(ii) *point x belongs to the background:* in this case, the prediction errors $\epsilon_2(x)$ and $\epsilon_3(x)$ are expected to be larger than $\epsilon_1(x)$, and therefore in the limit (as $\epsilon_2(x)$ and $\epsilon_3(x)$ become very small, and $\epsilon_1(x)$ gets very large), we should have $\beta_2 << \beta_1$ and $\beta_3 << \beta_1$. From this relationship, we can deduce that in Eq. 4, the contribution of disparity vectors at points p_2 and p_3 should be reduced while the one of the disparity vector at p_1 should be increased.

The above discussion shows that the adaptive interpolation proposed can take into account discontinuities in the disparity field; parameters β_j, $j = 1, 2, 3$, smooth out disparity field through the parameters λ_j, $j = 1, 2, 3$, but at the same time takes into account discontinuities through the prediction energy $\epsilon_j(x)$, $j = 1, 2, 3$.

3 Parallelization

In this section we present a method to parallel and so speed up the computation for the adaptive delaunay interpolation (Sect. 2.2.3). First we do it theoretically (Sect. 3.1), obtaining a linear equation for the distribution of points to be processed upon a multi-processor cluster, according to the speed of each processor. But the Delaunay triangulation deals with a number of triangles that must each be processed entirely or not, so in Sect. 3.2 we give an algorithm to distribute equally the computation for all triangles on cluster.

3.1 Balancing computation

Let us consider a cluster with N processors, each processor being able to compute p_i elementary operations in a second. Then we can assign to each processor the relative weight $w_i = p_i / \sum_{i=1}^{N} p_i$, $i = 1, \ldots, N$, such that $\sum_{i=1}^{N} w_i = 1$. Let us also introduce: N_t the total number of triangles to be processed; N_p the total number of points; t_k the number of points in triangle k, $k = 1, \ldots, N_t$; and finally n_i the number of points given to processor i, $i = 1, \ldots, N$, knowing that we want the computation for all the triangles being balanced at best upon the N processors, i.e., each processor must have as close as possible the same amount of computation as the others.

Using the previous notations, we also have the relationship: $\sum_{i=1}^{N} t_i = N_p$. Ideally, the distribution of the entire set of points upon the processors, according to the speed of each processor, would give: $\frac{n_i}{w_i} = \lambda$, where λ is a constant depending on the characteristics of the cluster.

Finally we obtain a linear system to solve:

$$\begin{bmatrix} 1 & 0 & \dots & 0 & 0 \\ 0 & 1 & \dots & 0 & 0 \\ \vdots & \vdots & \ddots & \vdots & \vdots \\ 0 & \dots & \dots & 1 & 0 \\ 1 & 1 & \dots & 1 & 1 \end{bmatrix} \begin{pmatrix} n_1/\lambda \\ \vdots \\ n_n/\lambda \\ -N_p/\lambda \end{pmatrix} = \begin{pmatrix} w_1 \\ \vdots \\ w_n \\ 0 \end{pmatrix} \quad (6)$$

3.2 Distributing computation

Practically, we do not apply directly Eq. 6 because the processing of one triangle can not be split into two or more processors. First of all we sort the triangles according to their number of points, then we use the following algorithm: (i) From Eq. 6 we compute the number of points n_1 to be processed by processor #1. Most often this gives an integer number t of triangles plus a few more points. More precisely, we have the relationship:

$$\sum_{k=1}^{t} t_k \leq n_1 \leq \sum_{k=1}^{t+1} t_k \quad (7)$$

(ii) Then we have to choose to give either t or $t+1$ triangles to processor #1 since the $(t+1)$-th triangle can not be split. The choice is made by a simple majority rule. (iii) While not all the triangles are affected to a processor, repeat step (i) and (ii) for processors #2, ..., #N.

4 Experimental Results

4.1 Disparity fields

We have tested the proposed method on real stereoscopic images pair *Flowerpot* (see Acknowledgments) shown in Fig. 4.

First, feature points were extracted from the two images using the Harris corner point detector. Then, correspondence pairs were found by maximizing a cross-correlation measure. Fig. 5 shows correspondence vectors before and after post-processing. We notice that most of the false matches have been eliminated. The set of resulting correspondence points was then used to compute dense disparity fields. Fig. 6 shows the dense fields obtained with linear interpolation before and after refinement. Although the vector fields before and after look very similar, many local differences exist that can be better seen in enlarged sub-windows, or by simulating a camera translation from reconstruction of intermediate images between I_0 and I_1[8]. In a sequence reconstructed from disparity fields with no refinement, errors appeared at some object boundaries, especially around the flower pot where discontinuities are significant. Most of these errors were eliminated with refined disparities and the overall perception of the simulated camera translation was very natural.

4.2 Parallel configurations

Tables 1 and 2 give the number of triangles, the % of points and the computation times for the adaptive Delaunay triangulation upon each processor, respectively for a 4-node and a 8-node cluster. The images used for these experiments are the same as in Sect. 4.1 (*Flowerpot*). The total number of triangles for this pair of images is $N_t = 347$ and the total number of points $N_p = 306,530$. The computation times were obtained on a cluster we dispose in the computer science department of the University of Moncton. It is composed of a 2 GHz processor-speed Pentium IV server with 512 Mb RAM connected to 12 nodes, of which 8 are 500 MHz speed with 128 Mb RAM and 4 are 400 MHz speed with 128 Mb RAM. The server and the nodes are running under a Mandrake 9.0 Linux system and the program we used for the adaptive Delaunay triangulation was compiled with full optimization options for this system.

Run on one node, the adaptive Delaunay triangulation gave us a 414 ms time computation. Now suppose we want to be able to process stereo image pairs from a pair of real-time videos. With the 24 images per second standard, i.e., one image every 41.67 milliseconds, we could only process one pair out of 10 from the videos. It is clearly not enough if the videos contain some fast moving objects.

Tables 1 and 2 show the execution times upon 4 and 8 processors. We can see that for example for the 4-node execution, each processor does not process exactly 25% of the total number of points since our algorithm is designed not to split triangles. Moreover, as explained in Sect. 3.2, a necessary previous step to distributing of triangles is their sorting according to their number of points. That is why the first processors must compute high numbers of triangles with small numbers of points, while the last processors have to process a few number of triangles with high numbers of points. And that also explains why it is often the last or the last but one processor which take more time to achieve: due to the majority rule we use in our algorithm (see Sect. 3.2), for each processor we have to choose whether it will process one more triangle or not. If so and if the triangles are big, then a processor can be assigned a few more calculations than the others.

For the 4-node and the 8-node parallel configurations, we considered the most time-consuming processor and measured the gain in time compared to a single execution that gave us 414 ms:

- For the 4-node execution, the most time-consuming processor takes 120 ms, then we speeded up our execution by a 3.45 ratio (instead of ideally 4). Then for 24 images/s videos, we would be able to process one image out of 3, that is much better than one out of 10;
- For the 8-node execution, the most time-consuming processor takes 67 ms, then we speeded up our execution by a 6.18 ratio (instead of ideally 8). Thus

we could process one image out of 2 from stereoscopic videos. For most videos it is highly sufficient, considering there is no drastic changes between three successive images.

In conclusion the parallelization of the adaptive Delaunay triangulation leads to very fast computations, allowing us to be able to estimate reliable disparity fields from a pair of videos in real time.

5 Conclusions

We have presented a fast, parallel method for the estimation of large-amplitude disparity fields. This method is based on three main components. First, sparse correspondences are computed by means of feature-point extraction and cross-validation. Then, dense disparity fields are estimated using adaptive interpolation over triangles obtained from Delaunay triangulation. The interpolation algorithm accounts for the fidelity of sparse correspondence vectors at triangle vertices by means of prediction error, i.e., the ability of the vectors to match intensities in the two views. Finally, we proposed an algorithm to distribute the adaptive processing of triangles on a multiple processors cluster according to the computation speed of each processor.

This approach is very efficient computationally compared to classical methods, allowing us to process video streams. For example this could very useful for real-time object tracking or to real-time 3D reconstruction in a near future.

References

1. M. Bober and J. Jittler, "Robust motion analysis", *Proc. IEEE Conf. on Computer Vision and Pattern Recognition*, pp. 947-952, 1994.
2. E. Memin and P. Perez, "Dense estimation and object-based segmentation of optical flow with robust technique", *IEEE Trans. Image Processing*, vol. 7, no. 5, pp. 703-719, 1998.
3. C. Harris and M. Stephens, "A combined corner and edge detector", *Proc. Alvey Vision Conference*, pp. 147 151, 1988.
4. P. Beaudet, "Rotationally invariant image operators", *Proc. of 4-th Int. Joint Conference on Pattern Recognition*, Tokyo, pp. 579-583, 1978.
5. V.S. Nalwa, "A guided tour of computer vision", Addison-Wesley, 1993.
6. Z. Puzicha, T. Hofmann and J.M. Buhmann, "Non-parametric similarity measures for unsupervised texture segmentation and image retrieval", *Proc. IEEE Conf. on Computer Vision and Pattern Recognition*, pp. 267-272, June 1997.
7. P. Pritchett and A. Zisserman, "Wide baseline stereo matching", *Proc. 6-th International Conference on Computer Vision*, pp. 754-760, 1998.
8. M. Kardouchi, J. Konrad and C. Vazquez, "Estimation of large amplitude motion: Application to intermediate view image reconstruction", *Proceedings of the International Society of Optical Engineering*, Vol. 4310, pp. 340-351, 2001.
9. W. Cheney, and D. Kincaid, "Numerical Mathematics and Computing", *third edition*, Brooks/Cole Publishing Company.
10. S. F. McGinn and R. E. Shaw, "Parallel Gaussian Elimination Using OpenMP and MPI", *Proc. HPCS'2002*, pp. 169-173, June 2002.

Figures and Tables

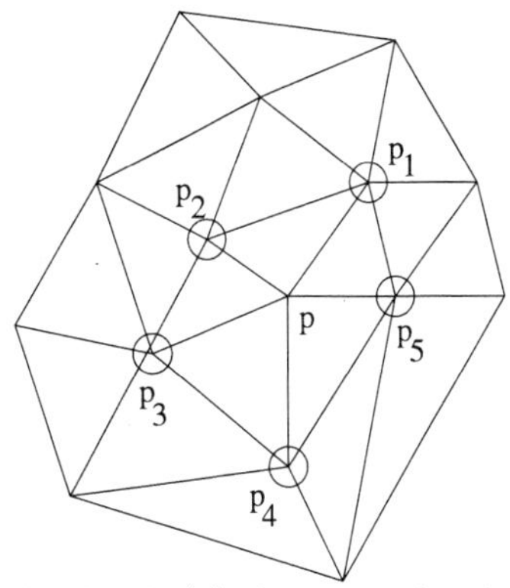

Figure 1. Neighborhood $\eta(p)$ of correspondence point p.

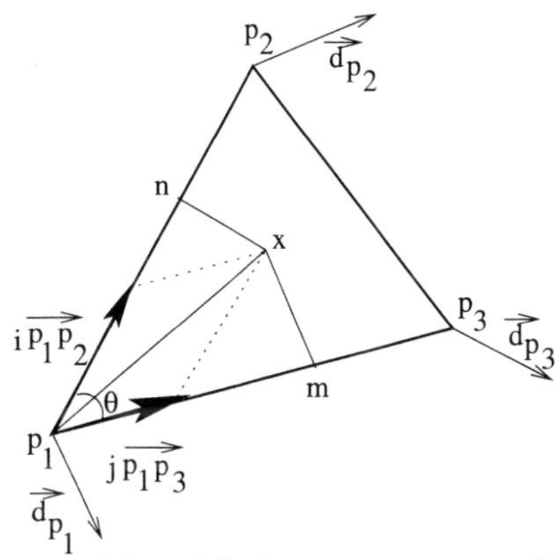

Figure 2. Interpolation of displacement vector at x within triangle with nodes p_1, p_2 and p_3.

Proc.	# triangles	% points	Time (ms)
#1	271	24.96	111
#2	44	25.27	110
#3	21	24.06	104
#4	11	25.71	120
Total	347	100.0	max.: 120

Table 1
Computation times for adaptive interpolation of Delaunay upon 4 processors.

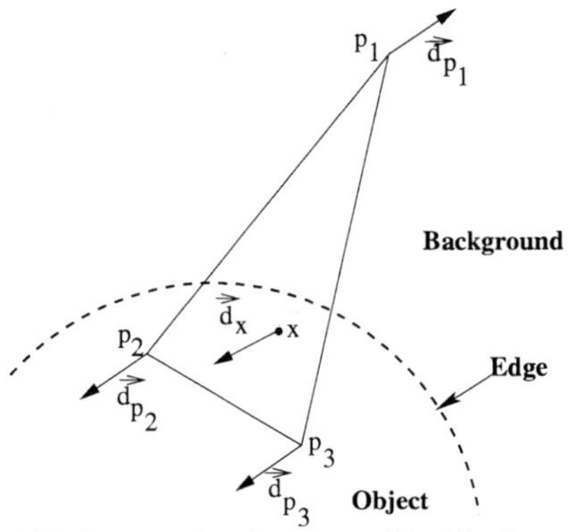

Figure 3. A Delaunay triangle across object/background boundary. In order to accurately interpolate the disparity at position x, higher weights for vectors, $\vec{d_{p_2}}$ and $\vec{d_{p_3}}$, and a lower weight for vector $\vec{d_{p_1}}$ need to be used.

Figure 4. A stereo pair of images we used for experimental results: *Flowerpot.*

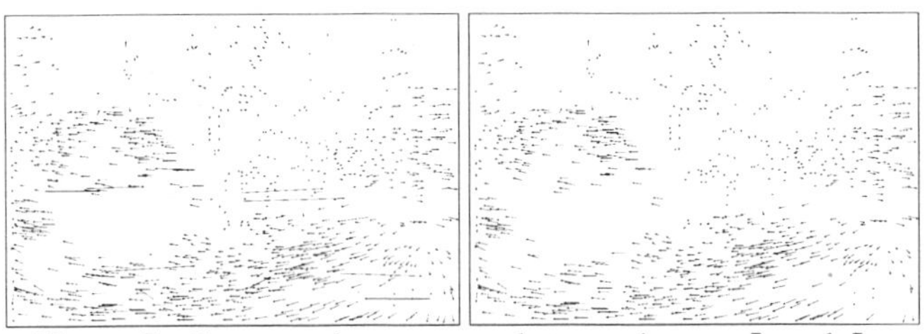

Figure 5. Correspondence vectors between images I_0 and I_1. Left: before post-processing; Right: after post-processing to remove outliers (Sect. 2.2.3).

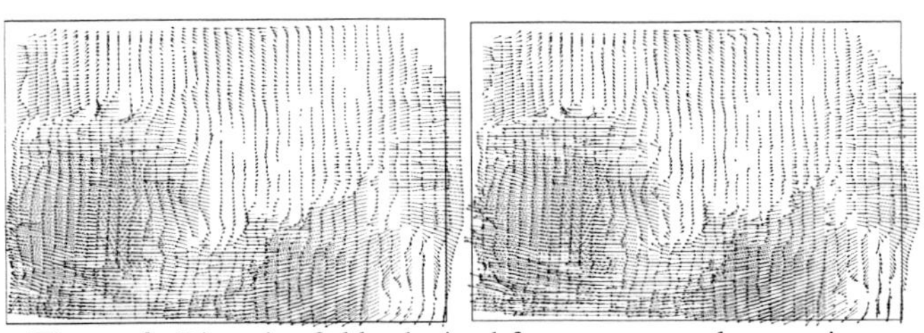

Figure 6. Disparity fields obtained from correspondence points by the proposed method. Left: without mesh refinement; Right: with mesh refinement. For clarity, both vector fields have been horizontally and vertically subsampled by 18 and 6, respectively.

Proc.	# triangles	% points	Time (ms)
#1	221	12.54	61
#2	50	12.42	61
#3	26	12.28	59
#4	18	12.99	62
#5	12	11.66	56
#6	9	12.40	58
#7	7	14.18	64
#8	4	11.53	67
Total	347	100.0	max.: 67

Table 2
Computation times for adaptive interpolation of Delaunay upon 8 processors.

Acknowledgements

We thank NHK (Japan) for the stereoscopic test sequence *Flowerpot* used in experiments.

Evolutionary Grids of Interacting Stellar Binaries Containing Neutron Star Accretors

Lorne Nelson, Ernest Dubeau, and Jonathan Benjamin[a]

[a]Physics Department, Bishop's University, Lennoxville, Québec, Canada J1M 1Z7
lnelson@ubishops.ca

High-performance computing has enabled astrophysicists to carry out detailed calculations of enormously complex systems. In this paper we describe the implementation of one such calculation involving the evolution of close, interacting binary stellar systems. In particular, we examine the evolution of systems containing an ordinary low-mass star that is being cannibalized by its compact companion (neutron star). Since there are many dimensions of parameter space associated with this problem (i.e., chemical composition, angular momentum dissipation, initial masses of the donor and the companion, chemical profile of the donor at the onset of mass transfer), using a highly efficient stellar evolution code that incorporates all of the salient physics (e.g., nuclear burning, hydrodynamics, radiative and convective transfer, tidal and rotational distortion) is essential. The results of the current investigation are briefly presented and future objectives for this research are also discussed.

Le calcul de haute performance a permis aux astrophysiciens de simuler des systèmes extrêmement complexes. Dans ce travail, nous décrivons la simulation de l'évolution d'un système binaire rapproché. Plus précisément, nous étudions l'évolution d'un système comportant une étoile ordinaire de faible masse cannibalisée par un compagnon compact (une étoile à neutrons). Puisque l'espace des paramètres associés à ce problème est vaste (composition chimique, dissipation du moment cinétique, masses initiales du donneur et de son compagnon, profil chimique du donneur au moment du transfert de masse), il est crucial d'appliquer un code d'évolution efficace qui incorpore toute la physique pertinente (combustion nucléaire, hydrodynamique, transport par rayonnement et convectif, distortions dues aux marées et à la rotation). Les résultats de notre recherche actuelle sont présentés, et les objectifs futurs sont discutés.

1 Introduction

Before the advent of computers, stellar structure and evolution was studied by purely analytic (and semi-analytic) methods ([1] [2]). However, due to the inherent nonlinearity of the equations of stellar structure and evolution, these approaches were extremely limited and it became necessary to use sophisticated numerical methods to obtain detailed quantitative information. In the modern era of stellar evolution, stellar codes are designed to be either: (i) highly efficient so as to accommodate analyses requiring large numbers of computations; or, (ii) extremely accurate so that stellar observations can be used to infer precise details concerning the physical properties of stars. In the latter case, helioseismology requires extremely precise theoretical models describing the modes of vibration of the Sun so that its internal structure can be deduced (e.g., the location of the boundary between the radiative core and the convective envelope [3]). These techniques have also been extended to the study of the interior properties of white dwarf stars. On the other hand, very efficient codes are needed to carry out population syntheses and to investigate problems whose 'parameter space' is extensive. In a typical population synthesis, the main objective is to follow the evolution of a population of stars that is generated using Monte Carlo techniques. For example, the evolution of a globular cluster containing a million stars can be followed by calculating the evolution of each star individually and taking into account its possible interactions with other stars in the cluster. Parameter space analyses are conducted so that the widest spectrum of results corresponding to a physically realistic range of parameters (e.g., the initial chemical composition of star) can be generated. This type of analysis can also be used to develop a general picture of a particular physical phenomenon associated with the evolution of stars for which certain physical parameters are not well known.

1.1 Interacting Binaries

Interacting binary systems are some of the most exotic and intriguing astronomical objects in the Galaxy. They are composed of two stars that are in such close proximity that at least one of them is affecting the evolution of the other. In most cases this interaction is manifested in the form of mass transfer (e.g., hydrogen-rich gas from the atmosphere of the donor star can be pulled off by its accreting companion). If the stars are very close to each other then the donor star will be very tidally and rotationally distorted. The actual shape of the donor depends on the geometry of the equipotential surfaces (i.e., Roche geometry [4]). When the donor fills its critical Roche lobe, matter will flow from its atmosphere through the inner Lagrange point and eventually settle on the surface of the accretor (the inner Lagrange point is a point of unstable gravitational equilibrium that is located directly between the centers of the two stars).

The most important subclass of these interacting binaries contains an accreting compact object (e.g., a white dwarf, neutron star, or black hole). Since the gas that flows through the inner Lagrange point has non-zero angular momentum, it cannot fall directly onto the surface of the accretor. Instead it spirals in towards the accretor in the form of an accretion disk (see Figure 1). Strongly magnetic white dwarfs are the only exceptions to this mode of mass trans-

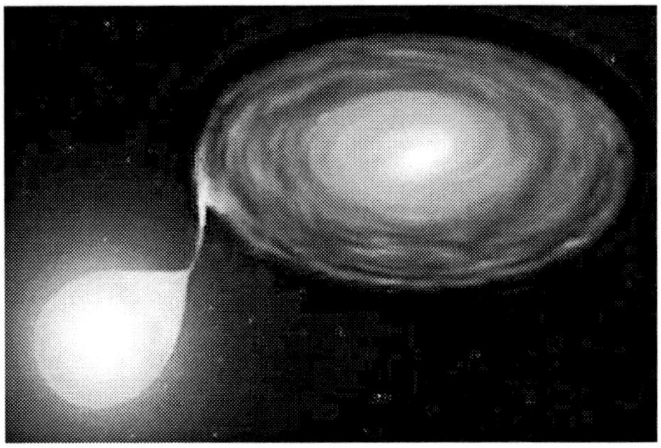

Figure 1. Artist's depiction of an interacting binary. Note the tear-drop shape of the donor star resulting from tidal and rotational distortion. Gas stripped from the donor forms an accretion disk. The neutron star at the center of the accretion disk is too small to be seen.

fer.

Interacting binaries containing compact objects are intrinsically bright because of the great depth of their gravitational potential wells (this is due to the fact that much of the gravitational potential energy of the infalling matter is converted to electromagnetic radiation). Partial eclipses and disk instabilities lead to changes in the intensity of the light observed from these systems and hence they are often referred to as "Variable Stars". Periodicities in the light curves allow astronomers to deduce certain properties such as their orbital periods. Systems composed of white dwarf accretors (about the same size as the Earth but extremely dense) that are cannibalizing ordinary stars (similar to our Sun), are known as Cataclysmic Variables. They are of particular interest because they may be the progenitors of Type Ia supernovae (extremely violent and bright cosmic explosions). These supernovae are used extensively by astronomers to determine the distance scale to the farthest observable points in the Universe. In conjunction with other observations, the supernova measurements have only recently allowed astronomers to conclude that the expansion of the Universe is presently accelerating! This conclusion has profound implications for our understanding of what dominates the evolution of the Universe (i.e., the 'dark energy' problem [5]).

1.2 Low-Mass X-Ray Binaries (LMXB's)

Low-Mass X-ray Binaries are interacting systems wherein a low mass star ($< 3M_{\odot}$) is being cannibalized by a neutron-star accretor (see [6], and references therein). Because of the depth of the gravitational potential well of the neutron star, the photons emitted from these systems are very energetic and thus these systems are typically discovered at X-ray frequencies. LMXB's can be formed if one of the stars in the progenitor binary undergoes a supernova explosion (assuming that the explosion does not disrupt the binary). The star that explodes leaves behind a neutron star remnant and it becomes the compact accretor. Once the donor star attaches to its (critical) Roche lobe, mass transfer ensues and an accretion disk forms around the neutron star. According to the conventional model, the neutron star is spun up by accretion torques causing it to become a pulsar.

Depending on the timescales for orbital angular momentum dissipation (e.g., gravitational radiation reaction, or magnetic stellar wind braking) and nuclear evolution (i.e., nuclear burning in the core of the donor star), the binary can either evolve to extremely short orbital periods (perhaps even as small as several minutes) or evolve to very long periods (thousands of days). Nuclear evolution causes the donor star to expand and become a red giant (with concomitantly long orbital periods) while angular momentum losses tend to enhance mass transfer which leads to an attenuation in nuclear burning. The dividing line between LMXB's that evolve to extremely short periods and those that evolve to long periods is known as the *bifurcation limit* and is very sensitive to the assumed input physics ([7]). Above the bifurcation limit, the physical radius of the donor is largely governed by its core mass; that is, the mass of the nearly pure helium core created as the result of hydrogen being fused into helium (i.e., hydrogen burning). As the donor evolves (simultaneously losing mass and growing larger in radius) it reaches a point where so much mass has been transferred that only a small amount of hydrogen surrounds its core. At this juncture, the donor collapses (i.e., detaches from its Roche lobe) and mass transfer ceases. What remains is a low-mass helium degenerate dwarf [HeDD] in orbit with a (recycled) pulsar. In the past decade more than fifty of these systems have been discovered ([8]). It is now clear that LMXB's that evolve above the bifurcation limit are the progenitors of many of these binary millisecond pulsar systems.

But what about LMXB's that evolve below the bifurcation limit? Only very recently have pulsars been discovered in accreting binary systems (i.e., SAX J1808.4-3658[9]; XTE J0929-314 [10]; XTE J1751-305[11]; XTE J1807-294 [12]), and all have ultrashort orbital periods (between 35 minutes and 2 hours). These discoveries fill in the 'missing link' in terms of our understanding of the origin of recycled pulsars and seem to confirm our theoretical models of the evolution of LMXB's. The calculations that are presented in this paper verify the basic model (over a very large portion of parameter space) while providing us with a detailed picture of the physical phenomena associated with the evolution of LMXB's (e.g., hydrogen shell flashes in the envelope of the donor).

2 Methodology

The evolution of interacting binaries containing compact objects is largely governed by the response of the donor to the orbital dynamics of the binary. Solving for this response is the difficult part of the computation. Based on semi-analytic hydrodynamic rules for the rate of mass transfer as a function of the location of the Roche lobe relative to the surface of the donor, it is possible to decouple the evolution of the orbit (and accretion of a matter onto the compact object) from the evolution of the donor itself.

2.1 Evolution of the Donor

Ignoring the effects of magnetic fields, the equations of stellar structure can be expressed in terms of four partial differential equations that describe the hydrodynamic evolution, mass continuity, energy conservation, and mode of energy transfer (radiative, conductive, and/or convective transfer) inside the donor star. A Lagrangian approach is adopted such that the variable m_r defines the mass contained inside a sphere of radius r, and t denotes the elapsed time. These equations can be expressed as:

$$\begin{aligned}
\frac{\partial P}{\partial m_r} &= -\left(\frac{G}{4\pi}\right)\frac{m_r}{r^4} - \frac{1}{4\pi r^2}\left(\frac{\partial^2 r}{\partial t^2}\right) \\
\frac{\partial r}{\partial m_r} &= \frac{1}{4\pi r^2 \rho} \\
\frac{\partial L}{\partial m_r} &= \varepsilon_{nuc} - \varepsilon_{\nu} - T\left(\frac{\partial S}{\partial t}\right) \\
\frac{\partial T}{\partial m_r} &= -\left(\frac{3}{64\pi^2 ac}\right)\frac{L\kappa}{r^4 T^3} \quad \text{[Rad/Cond]} \\
\frac{\partial T}{\partial m_r} &= \left(\frac{T}{P}\right)\left(\frac{\partial P}{\partial m_r}\right)\nabla_{ad} \quad \text{[Convective]} \qquad (1)
\end{aligned}$$

where P is the pressure, ρ is the mass density, T is the temperature, S is the specific entropy, L is the luminosity, ϵ_{nuc} is the rate of nuclear energy generation (per unit mass), ϵ_{ν} is the rate of energy losses due to neutrinos (per unit mass), κ is the opacity (for radiative/conductive transfer), and ∇_{ad} is the adiabatic temperature gradient (for convective transfer). Note that G, a, and c are physical constants.

2.1.1 Input Physics

In order to solve the equations of stellar evolution, the input physics must be specified. An equation of state (EOS) must be adopted, and the dependence of nuclear energy generation (ε_{nuc}), neutrino losses (ε_{ν}), and the radiative/conductive opacities on the density, temperature and chemical composition must be specified. These can be stated (respectively) as:

$$\begin{aligned}
P &= P(\rho, T, X_i) \\
\varepsilon_{nuc} &= \varepsilon_{nuc}(\rho, T, X_i) \\
\varepsilon_{\nu} &= \varepsilon_{\nu}(\rho, T, X_i) \\
\kappa &= \kappa(\rho, T, X_i) \qquad (2)
\end{aligned}$$

where X_i is the abundance vector (i.e., the abundance of the ith chemical constituent). Additional constraints associated with the creation and destruction of the chemical elements due to nuclear burning and particle decays must also be specified.

The input physics that was used in these computations is described extensively in a paper by Nelson, MacCannell, & Dubeau ([13]; and references therein). Specifically, we implemented the OPAL radiative opacities ([14]) in conjunction with the low-temperature opacities of Alexander & Ferguson ([15]), and the Hubbard & Lampe ([16]) conductive opacities. Great care was taken to ensure that each of these opacities blends smoothly across their respective boundaries of validity. Our treatment enforces continuity of the respective first-order partial derivatives over the enormous range of the independent variables (i.e., ρ, T, and X_i) that are needed to fully describe the properties of the donors. The equation of state is a combination of an analytic EOS for arbitrary mixtures of hydrogen, helium, and heavier elements that is matched to the Magni & Mazzitelli ([17]) EOS for pure helium. The analytic EOS includes the effects of molecular hydrogen formation, radiation, arbitrarily relativistic electron degeneracy, and an approximate treatment of pressure ionization. The effects of plasma neutrino cooling are calculated according to the prescription of Itoh ([18]). Nuclear energy generation rates are calculated based on the work of Fowler et al. ([19]).

2.1.2 Method of Solution

The four equations of stellar structure are solved using a variant of the Henyey method ([20]). In essence, a mesh is superimposed on the star that effectively divides it into a number of zones (typically between several hundred to nearly 5,000 depending on the run of the physical variables). The differential equations are then written in finite difference form and solved using a 'relaxation technique' under the constraints imposed by the four (central and surface) boundary conditions. In order to avoid numerical singularities at the center ($r = 0$ and $L = 0$), the differential equations of the central zone are solved using high-order series solutions. To increase global accuracy, a small outer zone containing the stellar atmosphere and approximately $\sim 0.01\%$ of the stellar mass is calculated *a priori* and is used to provide the outer boundary conditions (in terms of T and P) for the solution of the linearized system of difference equations.

This technique requires an initial guess for the internal structure of the star (i.e., a 'block start'). The values of the physical variables must be specified at the edges of each zone and midzone values are interpolated. Once a set of approximate solutions has been applied, corrections to the physical variables can be computed thereby producing a more exact solution. This process is repeated through many successive iterations until the desired level of accuracy is obtained. An adaptive mesh is employed so that mass transfer can be handled smoothly. Since a temporal sequence of models is being calculated, the results from the previously computed model (at $t = t_o$) can be used as an initial approximation for the structure of the new model ($t_o + \delta t$). The physical structure is then allowed to relax to an arbitrarily precise solution.

2.2 Parameter Space

The parameter space needed to fully investigate the evolution of this type of binary system is inherently five dimensional. The vector of parameter space contains the following elements: (i) the initial mass of the donor (M_2); (ii) the initial mass of the accretor (M_1); (iii) the initial chemical profile of the interior of the donor star; (iv) the metallicity of the donor (i.e., the concentration of elements heavier than helium [Z]); and, (v) the mode of angular momentum losses that drives mass transfer. Thus a grid of representative initial conditions needs to be created and each individual case must be evolved. The resolution of the grid is simply constrained by the available computing power. A minimal grid, however, should comprise at least 120 unique cases (using the five dimensional vector defined above, this number is calculated as $2 \times 2 \times 10 \times 3 \times 1$, respectively). Each time sequence (track) in the evolution requires that between 10^5 and 5×10^5 models be calculated. Time steps as small as several minutes or as large as one million years are employed. The actual value of the time step depends on the physical timescales that are relevant for each phase of the evolution. For example, long phases of slow cooling can be calculated using large time steps while nuclear shell flashes near the surface of the donor star require very short time steps. Since there are several physical variables that are defined at each of the internal mesh points, our 'minimal grid' generates approximately 10 terabytes of data of which only approximately 1% is saved.

Because the calculation is characterized by many unique initial conditions, our computational strategy is to assign a different set of initial conditions to each individual processor. We have carried out these calculations in a number of different ways in order to optimize the available computing resources. Originally we used PVM and our own distribution and retrieval software to carry out computations on approximately 100 NT-based Intel platforms (200 - 1800 MHz) that are located in various labs located throughout Bishop's University. We have also used a Beowulf cluster (36 Intel CPU's running at 1.8 to 2.4 GHz) that is located at the Université de Sherbrooke (Centre de Calcul Scientifique). At 1.8 GHz, a single evolutionary sequence can generally be completed within a month of dedicated CPU time. We are in the process of constructing a 128 node cluster that will be combined with the existing cluster. This increase in computing power should allow us to easily enlarge the grid size by at least an order of magnitude.

3 Results

Stars are born as the result of the fragmentation of giant interstellar molecular cloud complexes (composed mostly of hydrogen). Each fragment can collapse under its own gravity and this causes the hydrogen gas to heat up. Once the temperature is sufficiently high ($\sim 10^7$ K), nuclear fusion of hydrogen into helium will commence. A star that has just started to burn hydrogen and is in approximate thermal equilibrium is said to be a Zero Age Main Sequence (ZAMS) star. Its hydrogen abundance is approximately uniform throughout its stellar interior. For the calculations presented in this paper, the initial mass fraction of hydrogen of stars on the ZAMS is taken to be $X = 0.71$. As the star evolves, its hydrogen abundance decreases most quickly at its center where temperatures and densities are highest. When its central hydrogen abundance reaches zero (i.e., $X_c = 0$), the star is said to be on the Terminal Age Main Sequence (TAMS). Past this point, a low mass star develops a helium core and enters the subgiant phase. Once the core has attained a mass of $M_c \simeq 0.20 M_\odot$, it becomes a red giant and its radius grows very quickly.

In order to investigate the effects of different chemical profiles on the evolution of these interacting binary systems, we allowed single stars to evolve from the ZAMS to the tip of the red giant branch (i.e., just before the ignition of helium burning). The star (i.e., the donor) was then brought into contact with its Roche lobe at various points during its chemical evolution (expressed in terms of X_c and M_c). At the *onset of mass transfer*, the initial conditions corresponded to $X_c = 0.71, 0.3, 0.1$ for stars without cores and $M_c = 0$ to $0.35 M_\odot$ (in increments of $0.05 M_\odot$) for stars that had developed cores. Note that if the neutron star and donor are very close to each other after the binary has been formed, the donor will not have had much time to evolve before filling its (critical) Roche lobe and thus its value of X_c will be very large when mass transfer first occurs. However if they are formed with a relatively wide separation, the donor may have to become a giant (with a large core mass) by the time that it fills its Roche lobe. Thus the initial chemical profile of the donor is correlated with the initial orbital separation of the two stars.

We calculated approximately 120 evolutionary tracks for the parameter space described in §2.2. The initial masses of the donors corresponded to values of $M_2 = 1$ and $1.5 M_\odot$, while the masses of the accretors were taken to be $M_1 = 0.7$ and $1.4 M_\odot$ (the latter value being regarded as the 'canonical' neutron star mass). The initial chemical profile of the donor was parameterized in terms of either X_c or M_c, while the donor's metallicity was chosen to be representative of Population I and II stars. Specifically we adopted values of $Z = 0.0001$, 0.004, and 0.02. Note that $Z = 0.02$ is approximately equal to the (Population I) solar value.

With regard to the final dimension of parameter space, it was assumed that gravitational radiation and magnetic stellar wind (MSW) braking were responsible for orbital angular momentum losses. We used the RVJ ([21]) parameterization of the Verbunt-Zwaan MSW braking law (i.e., $\dot{J}_{orb} \propto R^\gamma$ where $\dot{J}_{orb}$ is the time derivative of the orbital angular momentum, R is the radius of the donor star and γ is a dimensionless number). For the present investigation, we set $\gamma = 3$. Mass transfer was assumed to be completely non-conservative. We thus set the mass-capture fraction (i.e., $|\dot{M}_1|/|\dot{M}_2|$) equal to zero, and assumed that the matter lost from the system carried away a specific an-

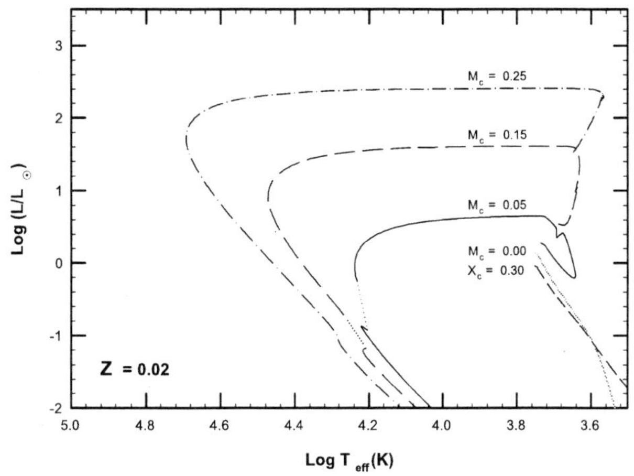

Figure 2. Evolutionary tracks of various interacting binary systems plotted on an HR diagram. For each track, the initial mass of the donor is $1.0M_{\odot}$, its metallicity is $Z = 0.02$, and the mass of the accreting neutron star is $1.4M_{\odot}$. The symbols X_c and M_c denote the values of the central hydrogen content and the helium core mass (in solar masses) of the donor at the onset of mass transfer, respectively. Note that $M_c = 0.0$ is equivalent to $X_c = 0$.

gular momentum equal to that of the neutron star (i.e., fast Jeans' mode). There are several other possible scenarios that we plan to investigate, including conservative mass transfer ($|\dot{M}_1| = 0$), and using other values of γ.

3.1 Evolutionary Tracks

Many physical variables are needed to fully describe the properties of evolving binary systems. These include the orbital period (P_{orb}), mass transfer rate, masses of the two stars, chemical profile of the interior of the donor, and its surface luminosity (L) and effective surface temperature (T_e). The luminosity and effective temperature are very important quantities in stellar astronomy since both can, in principle, be measured if the distance to the star is known. Moreover, the radius can be related to these quantities using the blackbody relation $L = 4\pi\sigma R^2 {T_e}^4$. A plot of $\log L$ versus $\log T_e$ is known as the Hertzsprung-Russell (HR) diagram and the path that a star follows in this diagram is known as its evolutionary track. In Figure 2 we present the evolutionary tracks of a $1.0M_{\odot}$ metal-rich ($Z = 0.02$) donor and a $1.4M_{\odot}$ accretor in the HR diagram for various initial states of chemical evolution. The donors having initial values of $X_c = 0.3$ and 0 (the latter being equivalent to $M_c = 0$) exhibit very different evolutionary tracks compared to donors that have developed helium cores. The dividing line between these two types of evolution is known as the bifurcation limit. For these two cases (below the limit), the donors lose mass and evolve towards increasingly lower luminosities and effective temperatures. Their radii continuously decrease leading to a decrease in P_{orb} (this behavior changes when their masses are $< 0.1M_{\odot}$ and electron degeneracy dominates the EOS). For the two systems, the initial value of P_{orb} is $\sim$ 10 hours and it decreases to values of < 1 hour. Even though the $X_c = 0$ donor is trying to build a core, mass is lost at a sufficiently high rate that nuclear burning (and further growth of the core) is stymied.

For larger core masses ($\geq 0.05M_{\odot}$) the donor does evolve through the subgiant phase and becomes a red giant (this corresponds to the somewhat vertical parts of the tracks seen in Figure 2). For many of these donors, their luminosities increase by more than an order of magnitude while simultaneously losing more than one-half of their mass. Eventually so much mass is stripped away from the donor that its mass becomes comparable to the mass of the core itself. The remaining hydrogen-rich envelope contains so little mass that it can no longer provide sufficient pressure to sustain hydrogen burning. Thus the envelope collapses and the radius of the donor star decreases substantially. This critical juncture in the evolution corresponds to the nearly horizontal parts of the tracks seen in Figure 2. During this phase their radii can drop between one to two orders of magnitude. This isoluminous phase has a very short duration ($< 10^6$ years) compared with the billions that it took for the donors to reach this stage. Once a donor reaches its maximum effective temperature, there is a precipitous decrease in the (surface) luminosity. The donor subsequently consists largely of a helium core ($0.15 \leq (M/M_{\odot}) \leq 0.45$) on top of which exists an extremely thin hydrogen envelope ($< 10^{-3}M_{\odot}$). As the donor continues to collapse, the hydrogen is reheated and a "thermonuclear flash" ensues. Depending on the mass of the core, the ignition of hydrogen burning can be quiescent or extremely violent (hydrodynamic) ([22]). Moreover, once the hydrogen re-ignites, the donor can expand and fill its Roche lobe causing further mass transfer. Eventually the thermonuclear runaway is quenched and the donor's envelope collapses. It is possible for the donor to go through several cycles like this before nuclear burning is permanently extinguished. After the final flash, the donor is destined to cool and approach its zero-temperature configuration (i.e., become completely electronic degenerate). Such a star is referred to as a helium degenerate dwarf [HeDD]. The typical radii of these very cool and faint dwarfs is only a few hundredths of a solar radius. The cooling tracks are nearly straight lines corresponding to approximately constant radii (but decreasing luminosities and temperatures). Also note in Figure 2 that the dotted lines denote the portions of a particular evolutionary track *between* which violent thermonuclear flashes occur (e.g., the 0.05 and $0.15M_{\odot}$ cases).

An example of a two cycle hydrogen shell flash is shown in Figure 3. The initial conditions correspond to a $1M_{\odot}$ donor with an initial core mass of $0.1M_{\odot}$ that is losing mass to a $1.4M_{\odot}$ accretor ($Z = 0.02$). Once the donor climbs the red giant branch, it reaches the isoluminous phase and then contracts until the hydrogen envelope is sufficiently hot causing nuclear burning to be re-ignited. The luminosity of the donor rises temporarily and then eventually returns to a point where the process begins again.

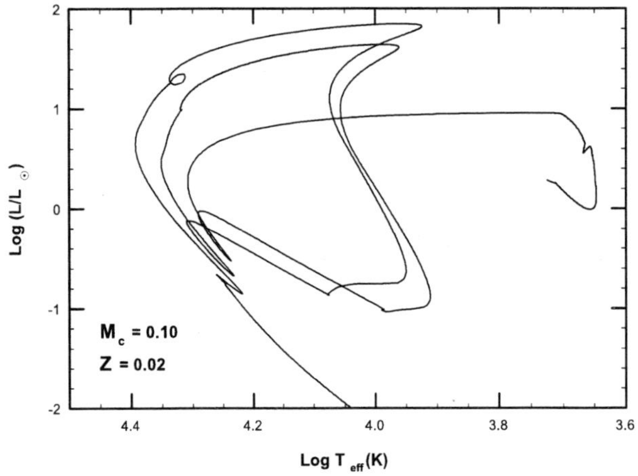

Figure 3. The evolution of an initial $1.0M_\odot$ donor ($Z = 0.02$) in orbit with a $1.4M_\odot$ accreting neutron star plotted on the HR diagram. The presence of two violent hydrogen shell flashes is evident from the two large loops that occupy the left-hand side of the diagram.

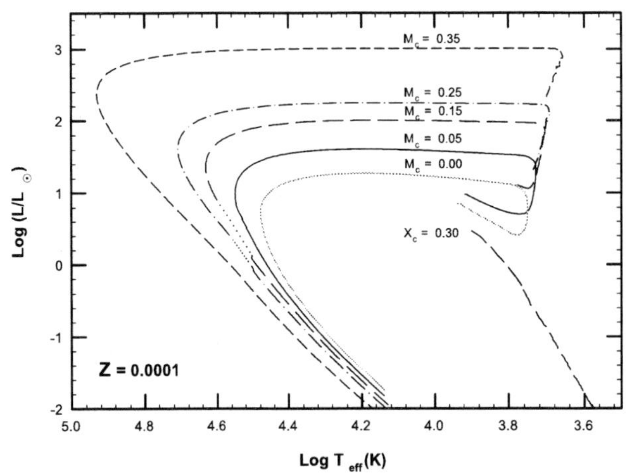

Figure 4. Evolutionary tracks of various interacting binary systems plotted on an HR diagram. For each track, the initial mass of the donor is $1.0M_\odot$, its metallicity is $Z = 0.0001$, and the mass of the accreting neutron star is $1.4M_\odot$. The symbols X_c and M_c denote the values of the central hydrogen content and the helium core mass (in solar masses) of the donor at the onset of mass transfer, respectively. Note that $M_c = 0.0$ is equivalent to $X_c = 0$.

The third time that the donor reaches this point, the density of the hydrogen in the shell is sufficiently low that only a small flash occurs and then the donor settles into a very long stage of cooling.

In Figure 4 we present the evolutionary tracks of extremely metal-poor donors ($Z = 0.0001$). These stars are associated with the very first generation of stars that was formed in our galaxy (the hydrogen gas clouds from which they formed had not yet been contaminated by heavy elements produced by supernova explosions). The behavior of the evolutionary tracks is very similar to that seen for $Z = 0.02$ but we notice that, unlike the previous case, a donor with an initially zero core mass can become a giant and ultimately produce a HeDD. Thus the location of the bifurcation limit is different. Stars with lower metallicities are more luminous and burn their supplies of hydrogen faster. Consequently they have a higher probability of forming a helium core before mass loss can extinguish nuclear burning. Note the existence of violent thermonuclear runaways for $M_c = 0.15$ and $0.25M_\odot$.

4 Conclusion

The large-scale numerical computations presented in this paper have provided us with realistic models describing the evolution of interacting binary systems containing neutron star accretors. Although parameter space is five dimensional, we have been able to explore a large slice of it. The grid of initial conditions was chosen so as to cover the most realistic range of physical parameters. The models allow us to conclude that there is an extremely sharp bifurcation between systems for which the donors evolve to become giants and then subsequently cool as HeDD's, and those leading to continuous mass loss wherein the donors are eventually reduced to Jupiter-sized objects ($\sim 0.001M_\odot$). Astronomers have observed the end-products of both evolutionary outcomes. The binary pulsar system PSR B1855+09 is a typical example of a LMXB that has evolved to yield a millisecond pulsar in orbit with a HeDD. Using a radio telescope to measure the Shapiro delay of the pulsar signal, the mass of the HeDD has been measured to be $0.258M_\odot$ to within $\sim 0.02M_\odot$ ([23]). The observational results are in the good agreement with our evolutionary models and we can conclude that, based on their estimate of the effective temperature (4800 K), the HeDD is likely to have a luminosity of $\approx 2 \times 10^{-4}L_\odot$ and an age (after the onset of mass transfer) of $\approx 2.5 \times 10^9$ years. On the other side of the bifurcation limit, X-ray pulsars in accreting binary systems have just recently been discovered. These systems (e.g., XTE J0929-314) have very short orbital periods and this is exactly what the theoretical models predict for binary systems just below the bifurcation limit (more detailed results concerning accreting binary millisecond pulsar systems can be found in the work of Nelson and Rappaport ([24]).

To make more progress in understanding the evolution of these systems we must first fully explore parameter space and then conduct the appropriate population synthesis analysis. The population synthesis is an enormous undertaking since the first stage of the synthesis may produce thousands of LMXB's and all of their evolutions will have to be computed. A sufficiently large population synthesis should allow us to determine the probabilities of the formation of the various types of binary pulsars that are observed in the galaxy, and this in turn should allow us to constrain the mode of angular momentum dissipation in these systems. We are currently in the process of undertaking this investigation.

Acknowledgments

This work was supported in part by a grant from the Canada Research Chairs program and NSERC (Canada). We would also like to thank Drew MacCannell and the Centre de Calcul Scientifique (Université de Sherbrooke) for their technical assistance.

References

1. S. Chandrasekhar. *An Introduction to the Study of Stellar Structure*. New York: Dover, 1938.
2. M. Schwarzschild. *Structure and Evolution of the Stars*. New York: Dover, 1958.
3. J.N. Bahcall, M.H. Pinsonneault, and S. Basu. *Astrophysical Journal*, 555:990, 2001.
4. Z. Kopal. *Close Binary Systems*. New York: Chapman & Hall, 1959.
5. S. Perlmutter et al. *Astrophysical Journal*, 516:565, 1999.
6. P.C. Joss and S.A. Rappaport. *Annual Reviews of Astronomy and Astrophysics*, 22:537, 1984.
7. E. Pylyser and G.-J. Savonije. *Astronomy and Astrophysics*, 191:57, 1988.
8. F. Camillo, D.R. Lorimer, P Friere, A.G. Lyne, and R.N. Manchester. *Astrophysical Journal*, 535:975, 2000.
9. D. Chakrabarty and E.H. Morgan. *Nature*, 394:346, 1998.
10. D.K. Galloway, D. Chakrabarty, E.H. Morgan, and R.A. Remillard. *Astrophysical Journal (Letters)*.
11. C.B. Markwardt and J.H. Swank. *I.A.U. Circulars*, # 7867, 2002.
12. C.B. Markwardt, E. Smith, and J.H. Swank. *I.A.U. Circulars*, # 8080, 2003.
13. L.A. Nelson, K. MacCannell, and E. Dubeau. *Astrophysical Journal*, (submitted), 2003.
14. C. A. Iglesias and F. J. Rogers. *Astrophysical Journal*, 464:943, 1996.
15. D.R. Alexander and J.W. Ferguson. *Astrophysical Journal*, 437:879, 1994.
16. W. B. Hubbard and M. Lampe. *Astrophysical Journal (Supplement)*, 18:163, 1969
17. G. Magni and I. Mazzitelli. *Astronomy and Astrophysics*, 72:134, 1979.
18. N. Itoh. Neutrino energy loss in stellar interiors. In T. Kajino, editor, *Proceedings of International Conference on Origin and Evolution of the Elements*. World Scientific, 1993.
19. W. Fowler, W.A. Caughlin, and B. Zimmermann. *Annual Reviews of Astronomy and Astrophysics*, 13:69, 1975.
20. R. Kippenhahn & A. Weigert. *Stellar Structure and Evolution*. Berlin: Springer-Verlag, 1991.
21. S. Rappaport, F. Verbunt, and P.C. Joss. *Astrophysical Journal*, 275:713, 1993.
22. Ph. Podsiadlowski, S. Rappaport, and E.D. Pfahl. *Astrophysical Journal*, 565:1107, 2002.
23. M.H. van Kerkwijk, J.F. Bell, V.M. Kaspi, and S.R. Kulkarni. *Astrophysical Journal (Letters)*, 530:37, 2000.
24. L.A. Nelson and S. Rappaport. *Astrophysical Journal*, (submitted), 2003.

HYDRA-MPI: An Adaptive Particle-Particle, Particle-Mesh code for conducting Cosmological Simulations on MPP Architectures

Robert Thacker[a], Gavin Pringle[b], H. M. P. Couchman[a], Stephen Booth[b]

[a]Department of Physics and Astronomy, McMaster University, 1280 Main St. West, Hamilton, Ontario, L8S 4M1, Canada
thacker@physics.mcmaster.ca

[b]Edinburgh Parallel Computing Center, Edinburgh University, James Clerk Maxwell Building, Mayfield Road, Edinburgh EH9 3JZ, UK

We discuss the design and implementation of a parallel adaptive P^3M code, for massively parallel architectures. The code, although primarily designed for conducting gravitational simulations in a cosmological context, also includes a Smoothed Particle Hydrodynamics solver. The code is written in a combination of C, FORTRAN 77 and FORTRAN 90. The MPI-2 remote memory access standard is used for one-sided message passing thereby enabling more time to be spent in raw computation. The design decision has lead to a number of interesting problems and circumstances, which we discuss in detail. Raw performance figures are presented in terms of numbers of particles per second to compare to alternative codes.

Nous discutons de la conception et de l'implémentation d'un code P^3M parallèle et adaptif pour les architectures massivement parallèles. Le code, quoique conçu principalement pour les simulations gravitationnelles dans le contexte de la cosmologie, comprend aussi un code hydrodynamique basé sur des particules. Le code est écrit en C, FORTRAN 77 et FORTRAN 90. Le standard MPI-2 est utilisé pour le passage unidirectionnel des messages, ce qui permet de laisser plus de temps aux calculs proprement dits. La plan adopté a mené à certains problèmes et circonstances, que nous discutons en détail. Les performances sont présentées en fonction du nombre de particules par seconde, dans le but de comparer à d'autres codes existants.

1 Introduction

The current generation of surveys of the Cosmic Microwave Background (CMB) radiation (*e.g.* MAXIMA [1]) and large scale structure (*e.g.* DEEP2 [2]) are providing an unpredented amount of highly accurate data about the Universe: the era of 'Precision Cosmology' has truely begun. While solving many long standing questions, the new data pose new and tougher challenges. The enormous volumes surveyed by modern galaxy surveys require highly accurate simulated 'mock surveys' to help understand both theory and error analysis. Accuracy and sampling errors are reduced by simulating as large a volume as possible with high resolution. The combined requirements of large volumes and high resolution necessitates the use of billions of mass elements in the simulation, which in turn requires massively parallel computing.

Observations of the CMB and supernova distance surveys [3] indicate that the evolution of structure in the Universe is dominated by two competing phenomena, the repulsion of the vacuum energy of universe Einstein's 'Cosmological Constant' and an unseen, massive component, 'Dark Matter'. The cosmological constant acts globally and hence the growth of structure on cosmological scales is dominated by the evolution of gravitational perturbations. Collapse of these perturbations proceeds rapidly, with cosmic expansion acting as a drag term. The resulting collapsed objects, such as galaxies, are many thousands of times denser than their surroundings. Modeling such large density contrasts, and the interactions that occur when structures merge to form larger ones, requires the use of Lagrangian 'particle' descriptions. Hydrodynamics can be included in particle-based simulations by using Smoothed Particle Hydrodynamics (SPH,[4]).

Particle-based solvers of interest in cosmology can be broadly divided into mesh-based solvers such as particle-particle, particle-mesh (P^3M, [5]) and "Tree" methods which rely an approximation method to evaluate the force for distant particles [6]. The adaptive P^3M algorithm [8] is an advancement of the P^3M algorithm designed to cope with highly inhomogeneous particle distributions. Special purpose hardware such as GRAPE [7] has rendered the direct PP method competitive in small simulations (less than 16 million particles), but it remains unlikely that it will ever be used for larger simulations. For conducting larger scale simulations the P^3M algorithm has proven very popular, with the first billion particles simulations being conducted by the Virgo Consortium in 1998 [9].

The design of our code has been heavily influenced by our research on the publically available serial [10] and earlier parallel versions of the adaptive P^3M code. We first developed a parallel implementation [11] on the Cray T3D using the CRAFT API which greatly aided development by providing a global address space. Shortly after, we developed a highly efficient implementation of the code in OpenMP which we currently use for a large body of our research [12]. On distributed memory systems the dynamic nature of the data movement in the algorithm necessitates high performance message passing to be efficient. Initially we chose to use Cray SHMEM for message passing [13] but we have since converted to the more portable remote memory access facilities provided by MPI-2[14].

The layout of this paper is as follows: we first review the physical system being studied and the AP^{3}M algorithm. This is followed by a discussion of our parallelization scheme and performance figures. Finally we comment upon the status of MPI-2 RMA support and conclude with a brief summary.

2 The Adaptive P^{3}M Algorithm

Given a set of initial conditions, which are usually constrained by observational data (*e.g.* the MAXIMA data-set) we must solve the following gravito-hydrodynamic equations,

1. the continuity equation,

$$\frac{d\rho}{dt} + \rho\nabla.\mathbf{v} = 0, \tag{1}$$

2. the Euler equation (equation of motion),

$$\frac{d\mathbf{v}}{dt} = -\frac{1}{\rho}\nabla P - \nabla\phi, \tag{2}$$

3. the Poisson equation,

$$\nabla^2\phi = 4\pi G\rho, \tag{3}$$

4. the internal energy equation,

$$\frac{du}{dt} = -\frac{P}{\rho}\nabla.\mathbf{v}, \tag{4}$$

with the dynamical system being closed by the equation of state $P = P(\rho, s)$. Dissipation, viscosity and thermal conductivity are usually ignored (*i.e.* an ideal fluid) with the only source entropy coming from an artificial viscosity.

The purpose of the adaptive P^{3}M algorithm is to solve Poisson's equation. Euler's equation and the energy equation are solved using SPH. The continuity equation is recovered immediately by using a particle based method.

The starting point of the P^{3}M algorithm is the idea that the gravitational force can be separated into short and long range components. The long-range component can be efficiently calculated by a Fourier-based solver and the short-range component can be calculated by performing a direct sum over particles within a given short-range radius. The long-range component is usually termed the 'PM force', for Particle-Mesh, while the short-range force is termed the 'PP force', for Particle-Particle.

Calculating the gravitational force on a mesh requires solving Poisson's equation. To do this a mesh representation of the particle masses must first be made, which is done using interpolation kernels (often called 'assignment functions'). We use a 27-point quadratic function, the 'Triangular Shaped Cloud', which strongly suppresses aliasing of frequencies from above the Nyquist frequency. The gravitational potential can be found from the density mesh simply by conducting a Fourier convolution with the Green's function[1] $1/k^2$. Once the potential has been recovered the gravitational force can be found by numerically differencing the mesh, and we use a 10-pt stencil. Finally, the acceleration on a particle is determined by interpolating from the force mesh using the inverse procedure to the initial mass assignment. The number of operations for this algorithm is αN+βL^{3}log L where N is the number of particles, L is the size of the (cubic) mesh and α and β are constants.

The PP force component used in the P^{3}M algorithm only needs to be calculated out to a small radius (typically 2.2 potential mesh cells). Thus the P^{3}M algorithm has an operation count that scales as αN+βL^{3}log L +$\gamma\sum$N$^2_{pp}$, where γ is a constant and N$^2_{pp}$ corresponds to the number of particles in the short range force calculation within a specified region. The summation is performed over all the PP regions, which are identified using a chaining mesh of size close to the short range cutoff. However, P^{3}M suffers the drawback that as clustering of matter develops more particles contribute to the N$^2_{pp}$ term, producing a drastic slowdown in solution time for a given number of particles. It is possible to see slowdowns of the order of 100-fold.

Adaptive P^{3}M remedies the slow-down under clustering of P^{3}M by isolating regions where the N$^2_{pp}$ term dominates and solving for the short range force in these regions, termed 'refinements', using FFT methods on a sub-mesh, supplemented by less expensive short-range calculations. This process is a repeat of the P^{3}M algorithm except that the FFT is now calculated with isolated boundary conditions. At the expense of a little additional bookkeeping, this method dramatically circumvents the clustering slowdown. The operation count is now,α N + β L^3 log L + $\sum_j^R$(α_j N$_j$ + β_j L$_j^3$ log L + $\gamma_j \sum N^2_{jpp}$), where R is the number of refinements. The α_j and γ_j are all expected to be very similar to the α and γ of the main solver, while the β_j are approximately four times larger than β due to the isolated Fourier transform. Dependent upon clustering, AP^{3}M is as much as 10 times, or more, faster than P^{3}M.

The basis of the SPH method is the smoothing kernel, $W(\Delta r, h)$ which depends on a local smoothing scale, h, and the radial separation, Δr. The concept of the smoothing scale comes from the following discreteness approximation;

$$< A(\mathbf{r}) >= \int d^3\mathbf{r}' A(\mathbf{r}')W(\mathbf{r}-\mathbf{r}', h)$$
$$\rightarrow \sum_j m_j \frac{A(\mathbf{r}_j)}{\rho(\mathbf{r}_j)} W(\mathbf{r}-\mathbf{r}_j, h), \tag{5}$$

where m_j is the mass of a neighbour particle and ρ the density. In the limit $h \rightarrow 0$, $W(\mathbf{r}-\mathbf{r}', h) \rightarrow \delta(\mathbf{r}-\mathbf{r}')$. Thus the smoothing kernel can be viewed as a mechanism to interpolate continuous fields between discrete points. The smoothing kernel also has the property that, by using integration by parts, all derivatives of fields can be calculated using derivatives of the smoothing kernel. Therefore, terms

[1] More complex Green's functions are used to remove noise from the interpolation process, but the procedure is the same.

in the equation of motion can be calculated by summing over products of fields and kernel derivatives without having to do explicit local differencing. A number of detailed reviews [15,16] of the SPH method are available.

Shock capturing is facilitated by using an artificial viscosity term in the Euler equation. We also apply 'shear-correction' [17] to prevent spurious angular momentum transfer by the artificial viscosity. Written in terms of sums of neighbouring particles the Euler equation and energy equations we use are;

$$\frac{d\mathbf{v}_i}{dt} = -\sum_j^N m_j \left(\frac{P_i}{\rho_i^2} + \frac{\Pi_{ij}}{2}\right) \nabla_i \overline{W}(\Delta\mathbf{r}_{ij}, h_i, h_j)$$

$$+\sum_j^N m_j \left(\frac{P_j}{\rho_j^2} + \frac{\Pi_{ji}}{2}\right) \nabla_j \overline{W}(\Delta\mathbf{r}_{ij}, h_j, h_i), \quad (6)$$

and,

$$\frac{du_i}{dt} = \sum_j^N m_j \left(\frac{P_i}{\rho_i^2} + \frac{\Pi_{ij}}{2}\right) \Delta\mathbf{v}_{ij}.\nabla_i \overline{W}(\Delta\mathbf{r}_{ij}, h_i, h_j). \quad (7)$$

where $\Delta\mathbf{X}_{ij} = \mathbf{X}_i - \mathbf{X}_j$, the bar denotes arithmetic averaging of a quantity and Π_{ij} is the artificial viscosity described in [18].

Finding solutions to the Euler and energy equations is comparatively straightforward. It is first necessary to create a list of neighbours for each particle. The contribution to the local density of each particle from neighbours is then evaluated using the smoothing kernel. Because we write the equation of motion in a form that does not depend on the density of neighbouring particles we do not need to calculate *all* particle densities first. Instead we store the list of neighbours during the density calculation and then reuse this list to calculate the kernel derivatives used in the Euler and energy equations.

The (greatly simplified) solution cycle of one time-step may be summarized as follows: (1) Place refinements within top level mesh, (2) Accumulate all (low cost) PP forces, (3) Assign mass to the density mesh, (4) Calculate forces via Fourier convolution, (5) Apply mesh force and accelerate particles, (6) Repeat 1-5 on the sub-meshes, (7) Calculate densities, hydrodynamic forces and energy changes for gas particles. Note that the procedure of placing meshes is hierarchical in that a further sub-mesh may be placed inside a sub-mesh. This procedure can continue to an arbitrary depth but, typically, speed-up only occurs to a depth of six levels.

3 Parallel Implementation

As can be seen from the solution cycle AP^{3}M is a sophisticated multi-part algorithm. Load balance strategies adopted in one part of the algorithm are not guaranteed to work in another. Thus we have had to use a combination of static and dynamic load balancing approaches. Our static load balancing tactic is the same as that discussed in [13], although, for completeness, we review this approach in the following paragraphs.

Both the PM and PP algorithms require a particle-in-cell bookkeeping method. A linked or ordered list may be used, or particle indices can be reordered to be contiguous within chaining cells (which optimizes data locality). We use particle reordering and have observed up to a two-fold performance improvement for clustered particle distributions [12] versus using a linked list. Note that these clustered regions are potentially millions of times denser than their surroundings. Naturally, such dense regions can lead to potentially huge load imbalances because processors store particles by geographic regions. Recursive orthogonal bisection is commonly used in treecodes to domain decompose particles to avoid this issue. However, bookkeeping becomes complex and some regions can develop obscure geometries (*e.g.* very long thin boxes) and strenuous communication patterns.

The solution adopted in our P^{3}M code is to use a 2-d block cyclic decomposition of columns of chaining cells over processors. We arrived at this distribution primarily since it represents a good balance between the desire to minimize memory overheads (determined by the surface area of any stored region) while at the same time providing a comparatively small quantum of work, thereby enabling good load balance. Load balance is ultimately a function of how many columns are assigned to a given processor, and good load balance requires a reasonably large number of blocks. Our decomposition also has the benefit of enabling a fixed communication pattern for ghost particles that can be optimized during code development. Four barriers are used in the computation corresponding to transfers of the left,right,top, and bottom ghost cell regions. Full details of the communication pattern are given in [13].

The PM calculation is more complex. Although particles are administered using the 2-d decomposition of chaining cells, the Fourier convolution is best calculated using a slab decomposition. To address this issue we first interpolate the particles on to a density mesh that is distributed in the same 2-d fashion as the particles. We then perform a 2-d to 1-d domain decomposition transformation of the density mesh. Once complete, the Fourier convolution is calculated in planes and then we perform the inverse 1-d to 2-d decomposition to ensure that all particles can interpolate forces from a local copy the potential mesh. The domain decomposition transformations are extremely fast on the T3E (less than 2% of the time of the solution cycle).

Our recent work has focused on adding adaptivity. Early on during development it was decided that one sided communication (via MPI-2) was necessary for refinements so that data could be retrieved without interrupting the calculation on the host PE. Without one sided communication it is necessary to use either polling or a multi-threaded implementation to check for incoming requests at regular intervals. Because placement of the sub-meshes is adaptive no fixed communication strategy can be adopted, and hence we were forced to use the `MPI_WIN_LOCK` primitives in

MPI-2. This primitive allows fine grained locking of individual PEs to enable asynchronous communication.

To implement the solution for a sub-mesh, which uses an isolated FFT, it was necessary to implement a new convolution routine. To aid code reuse we wrote a routine that can compute both periodic and isolated convolutions. This process was comparatively straightforward since we had previously built the full 3-d FFT from a series of 1-d FFTs. To ensure fast execution of the FFT we use the FFTW [19] computational kernel. We have also added a parallelized Green's function routine since each sub-mesh requires a different Green's function (the base mesh function can be saved).

Perhaps the most significant intellectual challenge in developing the parallel code has been the task of determining optimal refinement placement. This is a difficult global optimization problem since it is possible that regions that are spatially close may be more optimally calculated via a larger mesh that covers both of them. However, the problem is at least well posed; we need to determine the set of refinements that minimize the cost function for the entire mesh. Thus we must consider the cost of the PP work in each cell versus placing it into a refinement while, at the same time, considering the effect on local cells which may or may not be placed in refinements. The algorithm we use in the serial code proved to be implicitly serial and hence a new algorithm had to be developed. The steps in our new sub-mesh placing algorithm are as follows: (1) For each chaining cell evaluate the cost of doing PP work, (2) Identify all cells above a maximum work threshold - these are cells that ideally should be placed in sub-meshes and are called 'target' cells, (3) 'Flood fill' regions that have been flagged into cuboidal shapes, (4) Sub divide any regions which are (a) too long or (b) contain too few target cells (5) Ensure boundary regions around sub-meshes are correctly clipped. Self-tuning of cost parameters on different platforms could potentially aid performance in this section of code and is being considered.

Because the placement of sub-meshes is hierarchical, at some point mesh boundaries must be defined by coordinates that do not map to chaining cell boundaries. One must then test whether remote particles lie inside or outside a refinement boundary. To avoid rounding errors we use a global integer coordinate system and map refinement boundaries and particle positions on to this grid when testing for location.

Once the sub-meshes on the top level mesh have been placed, calculation of the solutions for the refinements proceeds using a task-farm controlled by a master PE. The master PE carries a list of all outstanding refinements which is updated by slave PEs which calculate the placement of new refinements during the calculation of any refinement they have been given. As refinements are calculated they are erased from the master list so that memory is not wasted on calculations which have already been performed. Each slave may place up to 200 new refinements and the master PE can carry a maximum of 1000 refinements at any particular time, although both these limits can be changed given available memory resources.

To ensure good load balance we divide up the placed sub-meshes into the following categories: (1) Refinements large enough to be calculated across the entire machine, (2) Refinements too large to be calculated on a single processor, but are sufficiently small to be calculated on a 'sub-machine' with n processors (where n< machine size), (3) Refinements that can be calculated on one PE. The calculation order is as follows: first calculate all refinements requiring the whole machine, then decompose machine into a combination of sub-machines and single processors. Calculate a combination of sub-machine refinements and single processor refinements. When all sub-machine refinements are completed further decompose sub-machines into single processors and calculate all remaining single processor refinements. We also ensure that refinements are calculated in the order of work load. Therefore as the calculation progresses load balance is likely to be assured since the work quanta are getting progressively smaller as the end of the calculation is approached.

In the serial code and OpenMP versions we have an explicit barrier between levels of refinements. For example all sub-meshes placed within the top level mesh are calculated before proceeding to sub-meshes placed within the sub-meshes. The situation arose because refinement placement must be performed before calculating a sub-mesh however, preventing race conditions means waiting until the sub-mesh calculation has been performed before proceeding to calculate the sub-mesh placed within the sub-mesh. In the MPI code we only return the new refinement details once the sub-mesh has been calculated, therefore calculation of the new refinements may proceed once the master PE has received any new refinements.

The communication involved in calculating a refinement is as follows: the machine/sub-machine master PE, or individual PE receives the geographic location of the refinement and the number of particles from the global communicator master PE. The remote particle data is then retrieved by a series of `MPI_GET` operations within an access window defined by `MPI_WIN_LOCK` and `MPI_WIN_UNLOCK`. For small refinements all the data may be contained on one PE, while for larger refinements a number of messages may be required. The master PE in the *local* communicator is responsible both retrieving and redistributing the data within the sub-machine. Once the data has been distributed the calculation proceeds in precisely the same fashion as for the main mesh (no optimizations for refinements calculated on one PE have been included). Once the calculation cycle is complete the particle forces are then accumulated back to PEs from whence they came. The local master PE is again responsible for this operation and the `MPI_ACCUMULATE` operation is used within another `MPI_WIN_LOCK(UNLOCK)` access epoch.

Once the AP^3M algorithm was complete we decided to implement SPH in a separate module. In both the serial and OpenMP versions of the code the SPH and AP^3M solvers

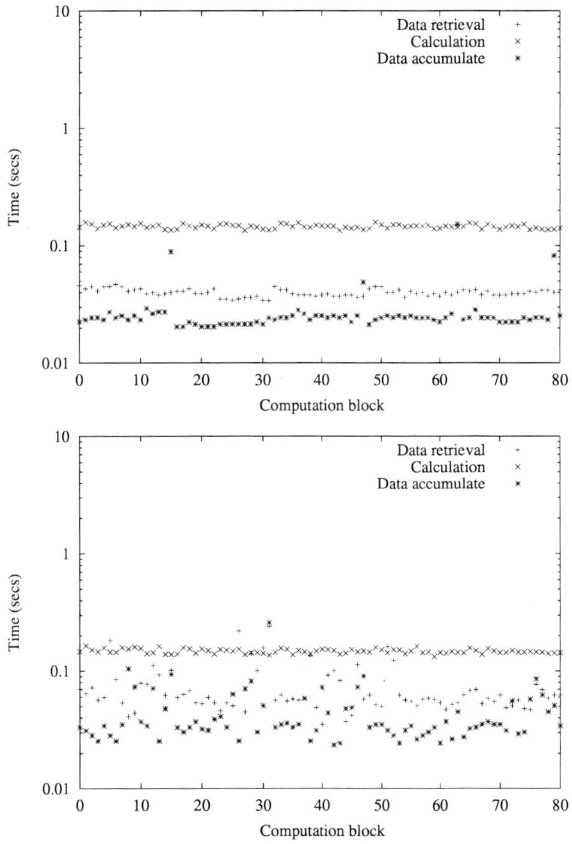

Figure 1. Comparison of MPI-2 performance for fully loaded versus half loaded SMP nodes. The top graph was run using only 2 cpus out of 4 in each SMP node, while the bottom graph was run using all 4 cpus in each SMP node. Both runs used a total of 16 processors. When the SMP nodes are fully loaded communication times become highly inconsistent and large fluctuations in execution time result. Although the messaging fluctuations appear innocuous in the fully loaded run, parallel efficiency is strongly impacted by the slowest PE.

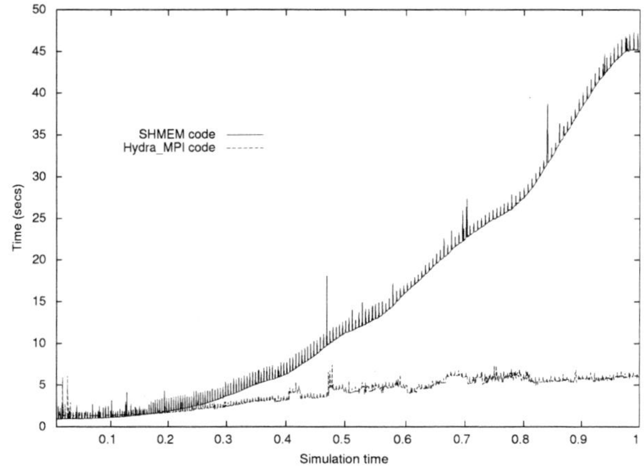

Figure 2. Comparison of solution cycle time for P^3M (SHMEM) compared to AP^3M (HYDRA-MPI). Each simulation used 16 PE's on a Cray T3E-900 and 2×10^5 particles. Spikes on both plots are associated with I/O overheads for checkpointing.

are intertwined, with the SPH solver borrowing the list mechanism from the gravity solver. This is a highly efficient way of doing things since the SPH code can reuse the neighbour list calculated for the AP^3M solver. However, it limits the maximum neighbour search radius of the SPH to be one chaining cell which is insufficient for a number of cosmological simulations and it also icreases code complexity. Hence we separated the two solvers.

Because SPH is approximately an order N algorithm we can rely upon the block cyclic distribution of particles for load balance. Each PE must calculate the SPH for each column of chaining cells after first retrieving all the of the ghost particles. We retrieve two layers of chaining cells for the ghost particles which would be expensive memory-wise if we used the same calculation pattern as the PP part of the code. However, instead we pay a small communication latency to trade-off memory use, and the overhead is still significantly smaller than the calculation load. In figure 1 we plot the calculation and communication overheads for a number of columns in the initial configuration of a simulation. This plot also shows overheads associated with MPI-2 communication threads.

At all stages during the development we have paid great attention to correctness checking. Unfortunately the complexity of the algorithm can make this difficult. For example, the distribution of optimal refinements is different for the serial versus parallel codes, and force errors will be subtly different between the two codes. However, because the refinements are calculated to preserve a given force accuracy both codes return forces with errors within a given RMS bound and hence both sets of forces are acceptable. Therefore, to establish correctness we have compared forces on a particle-by-particle basis to the full P^3M solution. All tests show the MPI code reproduces errors in agreement with the RMS limits for a variety of different particle configurations.

4 Parallel Performance

Performance details for the non-adaptive parts of the MPI-2 code are the same as the Cray SHMEM code [13]. To test the adaptive parts of the algorithm we have conducted two simulations, one examining the performance of the raw gravity solver, and the other the performance of the combined AP^3M+SPH solver. The speed of the adaptive gravity solver for a simulation with 2×10^5 particles is compared to the unadaptive algorithm in figure 2. Under clustering the adaptive algorithm slows only by a factor of around 6, while the unadaptive algorithm slows by a factor of almost 50. Improving the placement of refinements could probably speed the adaptive algorithm up further, the serial code slows only by a factor of around 3 on a similar particle distribution. Refinement placing in the parallel code is not yet fully optimized.

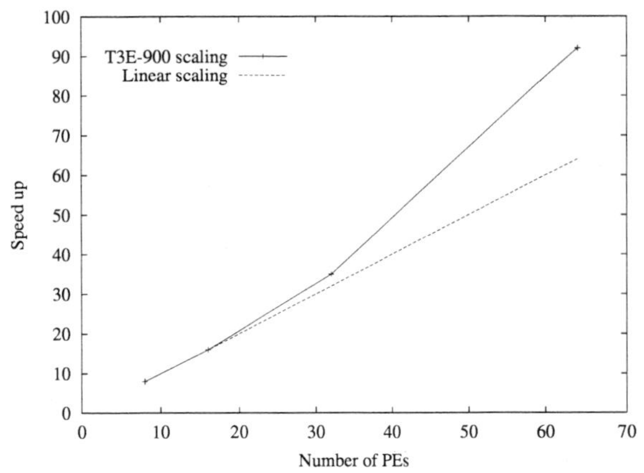

Figure 3. Parallel scaling for the initial configuration of the Santa Barbara cluster simulation (2×64^3 particles, half dark matter, half gas) on the T3E-900. Results are super-linear due to the reduced messaging thread overhead as the amount of data per PE is reduced.

To test the full algorithm we ran the 'Santa Barbara' galaxy cluster simulation [20]. Parallel speed up figures for the beginning of the simulation are shown in figure 3. The scaling is super-linear because the overhead of threads used in MPI-2 RMA becomes smaller as the amount of data per PE is reduced (a PE deals with fewer messages). Under clustering the speed of the code slows down by around a factor of 6 on 8 PEs, we have not yet tested on higher numbers of PEs. It should be borne in mind that the number of particles per PE is expected to be in the region of 2-3$\times 10^5$ in full production runs, while our figures show close to this number distributed across a large number of PEs. We expect excellent parallel scaling due to the large work quantum in production runs. In terms of the number of particle updates per second (PUPS), we achieve a maximum speed of around 15,000 PUPS/PE for gravity and around 6,000 PUPS/PE for the SPH on the T3E-900. Results on the SC cluster at McMaster are 70,000 PUPS/PE for gravity, and 30,000 PUPS/PE for SPH. These numbers are reduced by clustering in the particle distribution.

5 MPI-2 RMA implementations

Our decision to use MPI-2 was strongly motivated by the nature of the AP^{3}M algorithm. The need to load and unload data to remote processors, that may be involved in a calculation at that time, necessitates one-sided communication or a multi-threaded implementation to work effectively. For simplicity we chose to embark on the one-sided route. As adaptive mesh algorithms become more popular we believe that other researchers will be faced with similar dilemmas.

This design decision has created significant problems: at the time of writing we have only worked on 1 platform that has a fully compliant and *stable* version of MPI-2, namely the Cray T3E (although both Fujitsu and IBM claim to have fully compliant MPI-2 libraries). Neither is there a publically available version of MPI-2, although progress on MPICH-2 [21] is moving forward. On our SC cluster we have been able to use Compaq's 'Alaska MPI' distribution. However, as of time of writing (March 2003) a fully stable version of 'Alaska MPI' has only just been released, and unfortunately it remains an unsupported product. We are working with Compaq/HP to address this issue.

Implementing MPI-2 efficiently entails hidden costs. Because it is impossible to map non-simply connected regions to contiguous memory addresses our remote memory requests are non-contiguous[2]. Implementing this operation is difficult since a stencil of the required memory addresses must be passed to a thread on the target processor which then retrieves and packs the required addresses before sending the message back to the origin processor. Also, because any particular particle may receive contributions to its force update from a number of other remote particles we use the `MPI_ACCUMULATE` operation extensively. This operation is used in a mode equivalent to performing a remote addition on the target processor. However, implementation of this operation again requires a remote thread that consumes memory and CPU time. Figure 1 gives a clear representation of these overheads.

It is interesting to note that similar problems relating to copy overheads and TCP/IP stacks are appearing in high performance networking. The latest high performance Gigabit ethernet cards have 'TCP off-load engines' (TOEs) to remove TCP kernel overheads from the CPU. The overheads associated with copying memory (which is a slow operation due to limitations of memory bandwidth) have lead researchers to examine 'zero copy' implementations of MPI as well as remote direct memory access (RDMA) over TCP/IP. It is our belief that the best way of ensuring high performance for *all* the RMA operations possible within MPI-2 is to provide some kind of hardware RMA off-load engine. Given the growth of TOEs and that current high performance networking cards, *e.g.* the Quadrics Elan3 card, contain a programmable co-processor, hardware assistance appears to be more than a possibility.

6 Summary and Discussion

We have described the design and implementation of an MPI-2 version of the AP^{3}M+SPH algorithm: HYDRA-MPI. The code has been executed in a non-adaptive form on a number of different architectures: Cray T3E, Compaq SC, Sun E3500 SMP, SGI Origin 2000 and Beowulf systems. At present only platforms supporting the MPI-2 `MPI_WIN_LOCK` RMA functionality can run the full adaptive algorithm. This limits the number of architectures that we can currently utilize due to the slow adoption of MPI-2.

The non-adaptive code is known to scale well to hundreds of processors. The adaptive code is as yet untested

[2] Of course non-contiguous regions of memory can be broken into a series of contiguous regions, but maximal network bandwidth is not usually achieved with small messages.

on large problems, although for small problems we observe excellent, in some cases super-linear, scaling. The MPI code contains improvements that were observed to speed up both the serial and parallel OpenMP codes.

Over the coming months we plan to test the code on both the (US) Terascale and NERSC facilities. Unfortunately, at present, there are no large scale facilities in Canada with the MPI-2 support necessary to run our code. Once we gain experience of working with the code in an MPP environment we plan to embark on an aggressive simulation program. Our near-term goal is to conduct simulations with 10^{10} particles. This calculation will require close to 10^{18} Flops, or about 10 days on a *sustained* Teraflop class facility. Detailed analysis and visualization of the multi-Terabyte data-set that will result will present a whole new set of challenges.

This project has greatly benefitted from the input of J-C Desplat, Adrian Jenkins, Tom MacFarland, Peter Thomas, Frazer Pearce and Richard Warren of HP. RJT is supported by the Canadian Computational Cosmology Consortium. HMPC acknowledges the support NSERC and the CIAR.

References

1. MAXIMA Collaboration http://cosmology.berkeley.edu/group/cmb/
2. DEEP2 Galaxy Survey http://deep.berkeley.edu/ ~marc/deep/
3. Supernova Cosmology Project http://www-supernova.lbl.gov/
4. Gingold R. A. & Monaghan J. J. Monthly Notices of the Royal Astronomical Society, 181, 375 (1977).
5. Hockney R. W. & Eastwood J. W. Computer Simulation Using Particles, McGraw-Hill (1988).
6. Barnes J. & Hut P. Nature 324, 446 (1986).
7. Sugimoto D. *et al.* Nature 345, 33 (1990).
8. Couchman H. M. P., Astrophysical Journal, 368, L23 (1991).
9. Evrard A. *et al.*, Astrophysical Journal, 573, 7 (2002).
10. The HYDRA Consortium http://coho.mcmaster.ca/hydra
11. Pearce F. R. & Couchman H. M. P. New Astronomy, 2, 411 (1997).
12. Thacker R. J. PhD Thesis, University of Alberta, (1999).
13. MacFarland T., Couchman H. M. P., Pearce F. R. & Pichlmeier J., New Astronomy, 3, 687 (1998).
14. Official documentation of the MPI standard http://www.mpi-forum.org/docs/docs.html
15. Monaghan J. J. Annual Review of Astronomy and Astrophysics, 30, 543 (1992).
16. Steinmetz M. Monthly Notices of the Royal Astronomical Society, 278, 1005 (1996).
17. Balsara D., Journal of Computational Physics, 121, 357 (1995).
18. Thacker R. J., Tittley E. R., Pearce F. R., Couchman H. M. P. & Thomas P. A., Monthly Notices of the Royal Astronomical Society, 319, 619 (2000).
19. FFTW subroutine library http://www.fftw.org
20. Frenk C. S. *et al.*, Astrophysical Journal, 525, 554 (1999).
21. MPICH-2 status http://www-unix.mcs.anl.gov/ ~gropp/projects/parallel/MPICH/mpich2/

High Performance Computing In Astrophysics: Parallel Gasdynamics And Gasoline

James Wadsley[a]

[a]Physics and Astronomy & SHARCNET, McMaster University, Ontario, Canada
wadsley@mcmaster.ca

High Performance Computing is steadily increasing in importance for theoretical and observational astronomy. Largely through CFI, Canadian astrophysicists have unprecedented access to near world-class facilities. We review the contributions of computational astrophysics as a leading-edge player in the development of highly parallel applications and scalable algorithms with a particular focus on self-gravitating gasdynamical simulations. We present Gasoline, our portable parallel tree code for gasdynamical simulations. We review current applications in theoretical astrophysics and chart the future development of the field in the direction of increasing physical complexity and larger dynamic ranges in time and space.

L'importance du calcul de haute performance en astronomie d'observation et en astronomie théorique croît constamment. En bonne partie grâce à la FCI, les astrophysiciens canadiens ont un accès sans précédent à une infrastructure de calcul de classe mondiale. Nous présentons une revue de la contribution de l'astrophysique numérique au développement d'applications et d'algorithmes parallèles, en insistant sur les simulations de gaz gravitationnels. Nous présentons Gasoline, *notre code portable parallèle de dynamique gravitationnelle des gaz. Nous décrivons des applications courantes à l'astrophysique théorique et dressons un plan du développement futur de ce domaine vers une complexité physique croissante et des échelles de temps et d'espace plus vastes.*

Introduction

Astronomy and astrophysics are very computer intensive. With the widespread adoption of the CCD camera, even traditional observational astronomy has become dependent on computer image processing. New wide-area surveys will involve enormous data rates. For example, the upcoming Atacama Large Millimeter Array[1] will require routine processing of three-dimensional imaging datasets arriving at rates of 1 TB per day. The Cosmic Microwave Background (CMB) has embedded fluctuations that ultimately lead to all structure in the present universe. High Performance Computing is essential to manipulate CMB data coming from new satellite experiments such as PLANCK[3], where a full analysis would require 10^{24} FLOP.

Theoretical astrophysics has always been at the forefront of technology, with N-body simulations predating the use of digital computers, such the use of light bulbs and light intensity measurements as an analog of gravity for manual simulations of a many-body self-gravitating system [2]. Astrophysical objects including planets, individual stars, interstellar clouds, star clusters, galaxies, accretion disks, clusters of galaxies through to large scale structure have all the been the subject of numerical investigations. The most challenging extreme is probably the evolution of space time itself in computational general relativistic simulations of colliding neutron stars and black holes. Since the advent of digital computers, improvements in storage and processing power have dramatically increased the scale of achievable simulations. This, in turn, has driven remarkable progress in algorithm development. Increasing problem sizes have forced simulators who were once content with $\mathcal{O}(N^2)$ algorithms to pursue more complex $\mathcal{O}(N)$ algorithms and adaptivity in space and time.

In this paper we begin by tracing past progress in computational astrophysics with a particular focus on self-gravitating systems (N-body) and the inclusion of hydrodynamics. Historically, many codes began as pure N-body solvers and later had gasdynamics and other physics added. The Gasoline parallel gasdynamics code discussed here evolved from the Pkdgrav N-body code. We describe aspects of hydrodynamics in astrophysical systems to motivate Smoothed Particle Hydrodynamics as our choice of method. We describe the current implementation in Gasoline in the context of parallel gravity plus gasdynamics codes generally. A more detailed technical discussion of the implementation is available elsewhere[33,42]. We explore how the need to perform higher resolution studies and to include additional physics is driving the development of algorithms. We give specific examples of how Gasoline is being adapted to future needs. We present examples of state-of-the-art simulations performed with Gasoline.

1 Simulating Self-Gravity

Gravity is the key driving force in most astrophysical systems. With assumptions of axisymmetry or perturbative approaches an impressive amount of progress has been made with analytical methods, particularly in the areas of solar system dynamics, stability of disks, stellar dynamics and quasi-linear aspects of the growth of large scale structure in the universe. In many systems of interest, however, non-linear interactions play a vital role. This ultimately requires the use of self-gravitating N-body simulations. Even in the apparently regular solar system numerical simulations have revealed the fundamentally chaotic nature of orbits and the long-term stability of the solar system is no longer taken for granted[5].

Fundamentally, solving gravity means solving Poisson's equation for the gravitational potential, ϕ, given a mass density, ρ: $\nabla^2\phi = 4\pi G\rho$ where G is the Newtonian gravitational constant. In a simulations with discrete bodies it is common to start from the explicit expression for the acceleration, $a_i = \nabla\phi$ on a given body in terms of the sum of the influence of all other bodies, $a_i = \sum_{i \neq j} GM_j/(r_i - r_j)^2$ where the r_i and M_i are the position and masses of the bodies respectively. In practical work it is essential to soften the gravitational force on some scale $r < \epsilon$ to avoid problems with the integration and to minimize two-body scattering as each simulated body represents many bodies in an effectively collisionless system.

Early N-body work such as studies of relatively small stellar systems were approached using a direct summation of the forces on each body due to every other body in the system[4]. This direct $\mathcal{O}(N^2)$ approach is impractical for large numbers of bodies, N, but has enjoyed a revival due to high throughput special purpose hardware such as GRAPE[6]. The GRAPE hardware performs the mutual force calculation for sets of bodies entirely in hardware and remains competitive with other methods on more standard floating hardware up to $N \sim 100,000$.

A popular alternative scheme is the Particle-Mesh (PM) method which has long been used in electrostatics and plasma physics. The adoption of PM was strongly related to the realization of the existence of $\mathcal{O}(N\,log\,N)$ Fast Fourier Transform (FFT) in the 1960's. The FFT is used to solve for the gravitational potential from the density distribution interpolated onto a regular mesh. In astrophysics sub-mesh resolution is often desired in which case the force can be corrected with local direct sums as in the Particle-Particle Particle-Mesh (P^3M) method. PM is popular in stellar disk dynamics and P^3M has seen widespread adoption in Cosmology[7]. PM is similar to Multigrid[13] and other iterative schemes. However, working in Fourier space is not only more efficient, but it also allows force error control through optimization of the Green's Function and smoothing. Fourier Methods are widely recognized as ideal for large, fairly homogeneous, periodic simulations. Multigrid has some advantages in parallel due to the local nature of the iterations. The Particle-Particle correction can get expensive when particles cluster in a few cells. Both Multigrid[8,9] and P^3M[10] can adapt to address this via a hierachy of submeshes. With this approach the slow down due to heavy mass clustering tends towards a fixed multiple of the unclustered run speed.

In applications such as galactic dynamics where high resolution in phase space is desirable and particle noise is problematic, the smoothed gravitational potentials provided by an expansion in modes is useful. PM does this with Fourier modes however a more elegant approach is the Self-Consistent Field method[11,12] (SCF). Using a basis set closely matched to the evolving system dramatically reduces the number of modes to be modeled however the system must remain close to axi-symmetric and similar to the basis. SCF parallelizes well and is also used to generate initial conditions such as individual galaxies within merging simulations.

A current popular choice is to use tree algorithms which are inherently $\mathcal{O}(NlogN)$. This approach recognises that details of the local mass distribution become less important for accurate gravity with increasing distance. Thus the remote mass distribution can be expanded in multipoles on the different size scales set by a tree-node hierachy. The appropriate scale to use is set by the *opening angle* subtended by the tree-node bounds relative to the point where the force is being calculated. The original Barnes-Hut[14] method employed oct-trees but this is not essential[15]. The tree approach can adapt to any topology and thus the speed of the method is somewhat insensitive to the degree of clustering. Once a tree is built it can also be re-used as an efficient search method for other physics such as particle based hydrodynamics.

A particularly useful property of tree-codes is the ability to efficiently calculate forces for a subset of the bodies. This is critical if there is a large range of time-scales and multiple independent timesteps are employed. At the cost of force calculations no longer being synchronized among the particles substantial gains in time-to-solution may be realized. Multiple timesteps are particularly important for current astrophysical applications where the interest and thus resolution tends to be focused on small regions within large simulated environments such as individual galaxies, stars or planets. Dynamical times can become very short for small numbers of particles. P^3M codes are faster for full force calculations but are difficult to adapt to calculate a subset of the forces

In order to treat periodic boundaries it is necessary to effectively infinitely replicate the simulation volume which may be approximated with an Ewald summation[16]. An efficient alternative which is seeing increasing use is to use trees in place of the direct Particle-Particle correction to a Particle-Mesh code, often called Tree-PM[17–19].

The Fast Multipole Method (FMM) recognizes that the applied force as well as the mass distribution may be expanded in multipoles. This leads to a force calculation step that is $\mathcal{O}(N)$ as each tree node interacts with a similar number of nodes independent of N. Building the tree is still $\mathcal{O}(NlogN)$ but this is a small cost for simulations up to $N \sim 10^7$[22]. The Greengard-Rohklin[20] method used spherical harmonic expansions where the desired accuracy is achieved solely by changing the order of the expansions. For the majority of astrophysical applications the allowable force accuracies make it much more efficient to use fixed order cartesian expansions and an opening angle criterion similar to standard tree codes[21,22]. This approach has the nice property of explicitly conserving momentum (as do PM and P^3M codes). The prefactor to cartesian FMM is quite small so that it can outperform tree codes even for small N[22]. It is a significantly more complex algorithm to implement, particularly in parallel. One key obstacle to its widespread adoption is the fact that the speed benefit over a tree-code is much reduced when small subsets of the particles are having forces calculated (i.e. for multiple timesteps).

1.1 Pkdgrav

Pkdgrav is a state-of-the art parallel tree-code designed by Joachim Stadel[23] and coded with Thomas Quinn. The code was designed to very portable, using a compact machine dependent library (MDL) to encapsulate the architecture-dependent communication aspects. Ports exists for specialized shared memory (e.g. T3E), SMP (threads) and MPI (many architectures). MDL uses a scalable on-request system to acquire remote particle and tree-node data and maintains a local cache for efficiency. The overall design is modular and additional physics such as collisions between bodies (with Derek Richardson) and gasdynamics (with James Wadsley to create the Gasoline code) have been incorporated easily. Pkdgrav has been applied to a large range of astrophysical problems ranging from solar system formation to the evolution of large scale structure in the universe.

Some key features of Pkdgrav are 1) a binary tree for both domain decomposition and gravity calculations; 2) multipole expansions to hexadecapole order; 3) local caching for parallel gravity; and 4) Multiple timesteps. These features combine to make the code exceptionally flexible in handling large dynamic ranges in space and time.

In parallel the simulation volume is decomposed through recursive splits so that each processor ends up with a comparable workload and a box-shaped domain. The splitting procedure does not place any restrictions on the number of processors. It is efficient for relatively homogeneous simulations, even if the local level of clustering is high. In each processor domain a local binary tree is formed by recursive binary splits of the largest axis and the bounds are continuously shrunk to exactly enclose the particles. Thus the code adapts to flat two-dimensional topologies such as disks and the tree depth is controlled.

Hexadecapole (4th order) expansions of the mass distribution result in higher accuracy for a given value of the opening angle and thus less node interactions for a set level of accuracy than more typical quadrupole tree-codes. In parallel this reduces the communication overheads.

Multiple timesteps have been implemented using nested hierachy of time step *rungs* where each substep is performed with a Kick-Drift-Kick (KDK) operation[24]. This scheme would be symplectic in the absence of particles changing rungs. With KDK force calculations are synchronized across many rungs and the integration is more accurate than the similar Drift-Kick-Drift scheme. Multiple timesteps and the standard tree-code approximation to the forces prevent explicit momentum conservation however the conservativeness of the timestep criteria are more important for accurate integrations.

2 Computational Fluid dynamics in Astrophysics

Astrophysical systems are in predominantly at very low particle densities and experience wide-ranging temperature variations. Most of the material is in a highly compressible gaseous phase. In general this means that a perfect gas is an excellent approximation. Direct physical processes such as shear viscosity and diffusion can usually be neglected. High-energy processes and the action of gravity tend to create large velocities so that flows are both turbulent and supersonic: strong shocks and very high Mach numbers are common. Radiative cooling processes can be important, however the timescales can often be much longer or shorter than dynamical timescales. In the latter case isothermal gas is often assumed for simplicity. In many areas of computational astrophysics, particularly cosmology, gravity tends to be the dominant force driving the evolution of the system. Visible matter, often in the form of radiating gas, provides the essential link to observations. Radiative transfer is always present but may not significantly affect the energy and thus pressure of the gas during the simulation. Table 1 lists areas commonly explored with self-gravitating gas simulations and indicates the importance of physical processes to recover the basic observed properties. To match observations in detail involves more physics than is often practical. For example, a detailed model of solar system formation would include dust grains and full radiative transfer. Recent advances in computer power and algorithms are bringing real-time radiative transfer within reach of simulators[25].

Table 1 is also a guide to the range of physical scales present in representative simulations in astrophysics. The dynamical timescale for gas scales as $\mathrm{density}^{-1/3}\,\mathrm{temperature}^{-1/2}$ and for gravity it scales as $\mathrm{density}^{-1/2}$. For adiabatic temperature variations the gas dynamical time scales as $\mathrm{density}^{-2/3}$. With gas cooling (or the isothermal assumption) simulations can achieve very high gas densities. These two factors mean that gas sets the shortest dynamical timescales and that gas simulations are much more demanding (many more steps to completion) than corresponding gravity only simulations.

2.1 Methods

Fluid dynamical methods can be broadly classified into Eulerian or Lagrangian methods. Eulerian methods use a fixed computational mesh through which the fluid flows via explicit advection terms. Regular meshes provide for cleaner analysis and thus high order methods such as PPM[26] and TVD schemes[27,28] have been developed. The inner loops of mesh methods can often be pipelined for high performance. Lagrangian methods follow the evolution of fluid parcels via the full or comoving derivatives. This requires a deforming mesh or a mesh-less method such as Smoothed Particle Hydrodynamics[29] (SPH). Data management is more complex in these methods however advection is handled implicitly and the resolution elements naturally adapt to follow density contrasts.

Large variations in physical length scales in astrophysics have limited the usefulness of Eulerian grid codes. Adaptive Mesh Refinement[8,30] (AMR) overcomes this at the cost of data management overheads and increased code complexity. In the cosmological context there is the added complication of dark matter, which must be modelled with particles. There is more dark matter than gas in the universe so it dominates the gravitational potential. Perturbations present on all scales in the dark matter guide the formation of gaseous structures including galaxies and the first stars. A fundamental limit to AMR in computational cosmology is matching the AMR resolution to the underlying dark matter resolution. Particle based hydrodynamics (e.g. SPH) is well matched to this constraint. A useful feature of Lagrangian simulations is that bulk flows (which can be highly supersonic in the simulation frame) do not limit the timesteps. Particle methods are well suited to rapidly rotating systems such as astrophysical disks where arbitrarily many rotation periods may have to be simulated (e.g. SPH explicitly conserves angular momentum). A key concern for all methods is correct angular momentum transport.

2.2 Smoothed Particle Hydrodynamics

Smoothed Particle Hydrodynamics is a mesh-less particle method. It has been applied to astrophysical problems since it was first conceived[31,32]. It relies on a spatially second-order smoothing interpolation procedure over nearby neighbours to determine fluid forces on each particle. The SPH pairwise forces may be symmetrized resulting in exact energy, momentum and angular momentum conservation to the accuracy of the integration scheme. There are several effective schemes for converting the Navier-Stokes fluid flow equations to SPH interpolation formulas. SPH can be formulated in terms of energy or entropy integration[34]. We implemented the standard asymmetric energy form in Gasoline[42,33]. SPH velocities (and often pressure) are needed for the SPH force calculation. This tends to favour second order predictor-corrector time-integration schemes. The timesteps are limited by the Courant condition and often an acceleration based limiter. Ongoing issues with SPH include: the effects of artificial viscosity for shock capturing on angular momentum transport; and energy integration, particularly in strong cooling regimes.

3 Parallel SPH-Gravity codes

The components of parallel SPH plus Gravity codes tends to be as follows: a spatial domain decomposition; a softened gravity solver tuned for a force accuracy of around 1%; a wide variety of SPH formulations making detailed code comparisons difficult; implicit radiative cooling on a per-particle basis; and second order time-integration with multiple-time steps where practical.

Codes established in the literature can be separated on the basis of the gravity method into mesh (P^3M) codes (e.g. HYDRA[35,36], P^3MSPH[37]) and Tree-like codes (e.g. TreeSPH[38,39], GADGET[40], Hashed-Tree[21], GRAPESPH[41] and Gasoline). The key trade-off in this separation is the raw speed of the gravity solution versus the ease with which multi-stepping can be applied. Tree based codes are significantly slower on bulk gravity calculations: timesteps involving most of the particles tend to be entirely dominated by the gravity calculation. Any method with individual particle gravity force calculations such as GRAPE, direct summation or tree-codes may use multiple timesteps and make gravity solution costs much smaller for reduced numbers of active particles. For P^3M codes the FFT is a large fixed cost and it is harder to realize benefits from multiple-timesteps.

Typical applications such as those shown in table 1 tend to have a distribution of timesteps with the bulk of the simulation on larger timesteps and a long tail going to the smallest timesteps (Gasoline simulations have had a range of 2^{18} in timesteps). This situation is ideal for multiple-timesteps. Maximizing the throughput from multiple timesteps requires that operations scale as the number of active particles, N_{active}. A typical gravity tree-walk dominates code time in single-stepping but scales as $\mathcal{O}(N_{active} logN)$ and becomes less important when N_{active} is small. Tree-building from scratch is $\mathcal{O}(NlogN)$. Historically tree building has been a relatively small cost (roughly 1% of the gravity calculation time for single stepping with Gasoline) however as the range of simulated dynamical time expands new developments must consider tree-repair operations that partly reconstruct the tree at $\mathcal{O}(N_{active} logN)$ cost or extrapolate from old tree node data. With re-use of old trees overlapping node boundaries will result in slightly more expensive tree operations. For gravity, care must also be taken when dealing with old multipole moment expansions so that the accuracy of the time integration is not compromised. Tree repair is a successful feature of some current codes[40].

An additional cost in parallel is the domain decomposition. A popular and obvious choice is large rectangular domains or straightforward aggregates of rectangular domains. A more complex alternative is the partitioning of a space filling curve that threads a full oct-tree of the particles[21]. The common principle is always to divide up the work evenly to achieve load balance. The constraint is to have enough memory to hold all the assigned particles. Work load balance usually implies evenly distributed active particles however spatial partitions can result in very uneven distributions of the inactive particles. A domain decomposition that moves away from localized or simply connected domains to attempt to be better balanced for a wider range of time-step rungs will incur larger communication overheads during the force calculations. This idea is yet to be explored in depth for astrophysical particle codes. The FLASH[8] parallel AMR code makes no attempt to keep domains connected. The associated cost is a multiplication of the simulation time and the parallel scaling is otherwise unaffected. Full domain decompositions are a significant cost due to the large communication requirements. For tree codes the cost is much smaller than solving gravity if N_{active} is a significant fraction of N. A common practice is to re-use old decompositions for small N_{active} however this tends to create load imbalance.

The increasing availability of cheap SMP systems makes the idea of domains per node instead of per processor appealing. This allows any problem with the domain decompositon and load balancing to be postponed to higher processor numbers. An idea related to per-node domains is per-processor caching of remote data so that multiple processes can amortize the overhead of the original communication.

SPH is an entirely local operation so, in principle, it is well adapted to multiple timesteps and parallel processing. The non-local data aspects can be addressed through a cache that reports back to the original particle owner (combiner cache) or one-sided force evaluations which may require some duplication of effort but a single communication of data per particle.

In a multistepping SPH calculation as N_{active} decreases, the number of inactive neighbours tends to increase so that the work involved in the SPH calculation decreases more slowly than $\mathcal{O}(N_{active})$. The limiting case is that every neighbour is inactive. Tree-searching operations scale as $\mathcal{O}(N_{active} log N)$ and are thus well suited for this regime. The original SPH formulation calls for repeated operations on neighbours for a single force calculation. In practice, most SPH quantities can be predicted or extrapolated so that only one neighbour interaction is absolutely required per step[35]. Following this route has marginal impacts on accuracy but no systematic problems have been reported and the cost of the SPH calculation can be reduced by a large factor.

3.1 Gasoline: Current status and Future developments

Gasoline is the result of the addition of gas dynamics to pkdgrav using the SPH method. It is a robust code and performs well on comprehensive sets of test problems[33,42]. Gasoline has been applied to a wide range of problems in astrophysics and some recent examples are shown in section 3.2. Its efficient modular parallel design, finely tuned algorithms and the resulting ability to deal efficiently with large dynamic ranges in space and time make Gasoline one of the highest performing codes used in astrophysics.

Gasoline, like Pkdgrav, achieves a big part of its throughput (faster time to solution) through multiple timesteps. Large portions of the code scale in proportion to N_{active} to facilitate this, including the gravity walk and the SPH. In parallel there are some extra costs associated with caching that are discussed below. As the dynamic range in time of our target simulations increases the cost of the $\mathcal{O}(N, log, N)$ tree-build is becoming an issue. Current development ideas focus on repairing the trees as discussed above.

Gasoline relies upon efficient tree-based search operations to identify particle neighbours for SPH and a combiner cache. Each particle interacts with the nearest N_s particles to itself (gather neighbours) plus any particle for which it numbers among that particle's nearest N_s (scatter neighbours). With multiple timesteps the scatter neighbours may not be actively calculating a new acceleration and therefore we perform an inverse k-th nearest neighbour search explicitly using interaction distances stored on tree-nodes to avoid the $\mathcal{O}(N)$ work of an SPH force evaluation over all particles.

It is standard practice to implicitly integrate the energy equations so as to avoid limiting the dynamical timesteps to stable cooling integration timescales. With multiple timesteps we need intermediate values of the pressures for neighbour particles. We do this by interpolating after taking a large implicit (predictor) step. A side-effect of the multistepping is the exact conservation properties of SPH are lost however our timesteps are sufficiently conservative that there are no significant differences between multistepping and single-stepping runs. This makes the integration costs scale as $\mathcal{O}(N_{active})$

In parallel the MDL layer hides the latency of fetching off-processor particle information using a cache. For large numbers of active particles the cost of filling the cache is hidden. For small numbers the early cache misses dominate and prevent the work decreasing in proportion to N_{active}. Techniques such as bulk cache refreshes based on previous fetching histories or re-use of old cached data will be used to address this.

For homogeneous simulations Gasoline scales very well in parallel. For example, a single gravity step on 96 nodes of the McMaster AlphaServer (Idra) scales with 80% efficiency from a single node step for a large cosmological volume. The issue of scaling for less homogeneous simulations (such as renormalized galaxy formation simulations) relates mainly to load balancing in the face of multiple timesteps. The issue is not whether a good decomposition can be found for $N_{active} << N$, but that the cost of doing so is large compared to the rest of the work required. The significant load imbalance related to re-using an old decomposition may not result in a large change to the *overall* work balance once all costs in the code scale as N_{active} *if* N_{active} is sufficiently small for these cases. This problem is the subject of active research and development by the code authors.

3.2 Gasoline Applications

Gasoline has recently been used to provide new insight into clusters of galaxies, galaxy formation, gas-giant planet formation and large scale structure.

Galaxy clusters contain hot gas with temperatures of up to $10^8 K$ which emits X-rays. Gasoline simulations[43] have demonstrated that shock-heating during infall is insufficient to explain the temperature profiles implied by X-ray observations as shown in figure 1.

Galaxy formation is a particularly challenging subject for numerical work. Gasoline has been used to generate state-of-the-art realization of disk galaxies (see figure 2) with properties approaching those of observed galaxies[45].

Some commonly held theories of gas-giant planet formation relied on slow forming rocky cores as a seed for forming planets such as Jupiter. Gasoline simulations[44] shown in figure 3 have demonstrated that self-gravitating gaseous disks around new stars can form gas-giants on timescales of hundreds of years.

Cosmic Microwave Background (CMB) experiments are increasing in sensitivity and angular resolution. In this regime the small perturbations to the temperature of the CMB via the Sunyaev-Zeldovich effect due to gas in and around clusters of galaxies are critically important if the primordial CMB signal is to be recovered. We have simulated these effects with the largest cosmological SPH simulation to date[46] (270 million particles). A slice of the simulation is shown in figure 4.

Common themes in these simulations are large dynamic ranges in space and time. This is the cutting edge for gasdynamical simulations of self-gravitating astrophysical systems. The challenge to simulators is to adapt techniques developed only recently for large scale homogeneous simulations to this challenging new regime.

References

1. Atacama Large Millimeter Array : `http://www.alma.nrao.edu/`
2. Homberg, Erik 1947, *Astrophysical Journal*, 94, 385
3. PLANCK surveyor satellite `http://astro.estec.esa.nl-/SA-general/Projects/Planck/`
4. Aarseth, S., Lecar, M. 1975, ARAA, 13, 1
5. Sussman, G.J. and Wisdom, J. 1992, Science, vol. 257, 56
6. Hut, P. and Makino, J. 1999, Science,283, 501
7. Efstathiou, G., Davis, M., Frenk, C.S., White, S.D.M. 1985, ApJS, 57, 241
8. FLASH AMR Code, ASCI, `http://flash.uchicago.edu`
9. Kravtsov, A.V., Klypin, A.A. and Khokhlov, A.M.J. 1997, ApJS, 111, 73
10. Couchman, H.M.P. 1991, ApJ, 368, 23
11. Hernquist, L. and Ostriker, J. 1992, ApJ, 386, 375
12. Weinberg, M., 1999, Astron. J., 117, 629
13. Press, W.H., Teukolsky, S.A., Vetterling W.T., Flannery, B.P. 1995, Numerical Recipes in C, Cambridge University Press
14. Barnes, J., and Hut, P. 1986, *Nature*, 324:446
15. Jernigan, J.G. and Porter, D.H. 1989, ApJS, 71, 871
16. Hernquist, L., Bouchet, F., and Suto, Y. 1991, ApJS, **75**, 231–240.
17. Wadsley, J.W., 1998, Ph.D. Thesis, University of Toronto
18. Bode, P., Ostriker, J.P., Xu G., 2000 ApJS, 128, 561
19. Bagla, J.S., 1999, preprint astro-ph/9710043.
20. Greengard, L. and Rokhlin, V. 1987, J. Comput. Phys., 73, 325
21. Salmon, J. and Warren, M. 1994, J. Comput. Phys., 111, 136
22. Dehnen, W. 2000, ApJ, 536, 39
23. Stadel, J. 2001, Ph.D. Thesis, University of Washington
24. Quinn, T., Katz, N., Stadel, J., and Lake, G. 1997, preprint, astro-ph/9710043.
25. Razoumov, A, Norman, M., Abel, T., Scott, D. 2002, ApJ, 572, 695
26. Woodward, P. & Collela, P. 1984, J. Comput. Phys, 54, 115
27. Harten, A., Enquist, B., Osher, S. and Charkravarthy, S., 1987, J. Comput. Phys., 71, 231-303
28. Kurganov, A. and Tadmor, E, 2000, J. Comput. Phys., 160, 241
29. Monaghan, J.J. 1992, ARAA, 30, 543
30. Bryan, G. & Norman, M. 1997, Proc. 12th Kingston Conference, Halifax, Oct. 1996 (PASP), 363
31. Gingold, R.A. & Monaghan, J.J. 1977, MNRAS, 181, 375
32. Lucy, L. 1977, AJ, 82, 1013
33. Stadel, J., Wadsley, J. and Richardson, D.C. 2000, HPCS 2000, Kluwer Academic Publishers
34. Springel, V. and Hernquist, L. 2001, preprint astro-ph/0111016
35. Couchman, H. M. P., Thomas, P. A., Pearce, F. R. 1995, ApJ, 452, 797
36. Thacker *et al*, “Hydra MPI”, *in preparation*
37. Evrard, A. 1988, MNRAS, 235, 911
38. Hernquist, L. & Katz, N. 1989, ApJS, 70, 419
39. Dave, R., Dubinski, J., Hernquist, L. 1997, New Astronomy, 2, 277
40. Springel, V., Yoshida, N., White, S. D. M. 2001, New Astronomy, 6, 79
41. Steinmetz, M. 1996, MNRAS, 278, 1005
42. Wadsley, J., Stadel, J. and Quinn, T., *in preparation*
43. Borgani, S., Governato, F., Wadsley, J., Menci, N., Tozzi, P., Quinn, T., Stadel, J., Lake, G. 2002, MNRAS, 336, 409
44. Mayer, L., Quinn, T., Wadsley, J, Stadel, J. 2002, Science, 298, 1756
45. Governato, F., Mayer, L., Wadsley, J., Gardner, J.P., Willman, B., Hayashi, E., Quinn, T., Stadel, J., Lake, G. 2002, preprint astro-ph/0207044
46. Contaldi, *et al*, Proc. XVIII IAP Colloquium ‘On the nature of dark energy’, Paris, 1-5 July 2002, astro-ph/0210303

Application	Gas	Density Range, (cm^{-3})	Temperature Range (K)	Additional physics
Cosmological Large Scale structure	Tracer	$10^{-7} - 10^{-1}$	$1000 - 10^8$	-
Clusters of Galaxies	Secondary	$10^{-7} - 1$	$1000 - 10^8$	-
Galaxy Formation	Primary	$10^{-7} - 100$	$100 - 10^7$	Radiative Cooling, Star Formation
Interstellar Medium	Primary	$10^{-2} - 10^5$	$10 - 10^6$	Magnetic fields?
Accretion disks	Primary	$10^5 - 10^{13}$	$100 - 10^6$	Magnetic fields
Planet Formation	Primary	$10^5 - 10^{18}$	$10 - 10^4$	Aggregating Solids?

Table 1
Gas Applications and minimum physics requirements. The density and temperatures ranges present in representative high-resolution simulation are listed.

Figure 1. A qualitative look at the effect of extra heating on X-ray clusters. Entropy maps are shown for the same Virgo cluster analogue at the current epoch, within a box of 12.5 Mpc (41 million light years) where the nature of the extra-heating was varied for each simulation. Left panel: gravitational heating only; central panel: Supernova feedback with unity (high) efficiency; right panel: entropy floor $S_{fl} = 50$ keV cm^2 imposed at early times ($z = 3$). Brighter regions indicate gas with lower entropy. The associated extremes of temperature are around $10^8 K$.

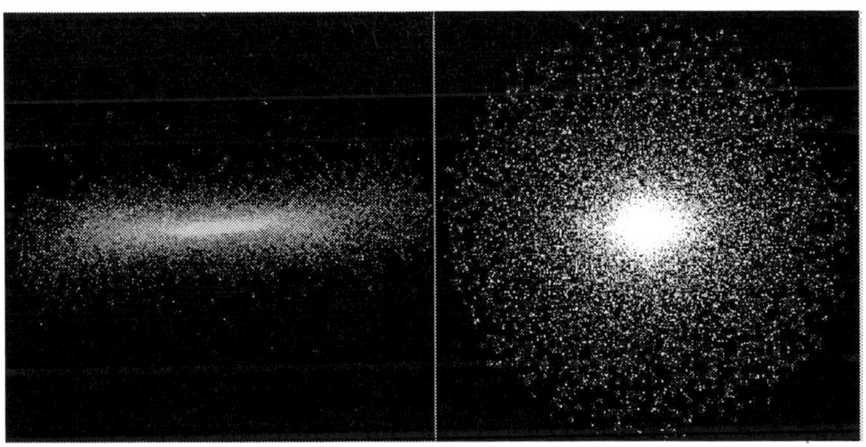

Figure 2. A spiral disk galaxy of comparable size to the Milky Way seen edge on at the current epoch. The left panel shows the younger stars that form the galactic disk and the right panel shows the old or spheroid component. The galaxy was formed from random initial conditions assuming the current preferred Lambda-CDM cosmological model.

Figure 3. Formation of gas-giant planets in a self-gravitating gaseous disk 300 years after the start of the simulation. The bright points are large Jupiter-like planets. The initial condition was a million particle 0.1 solar mass disk extending from 4 to 20 A.U. with a $r^{-3/2}$ surface density profile. The gas was evolved isothermally from an initial temperature profile set by a standard radiative transfer model for disks around very young stars.

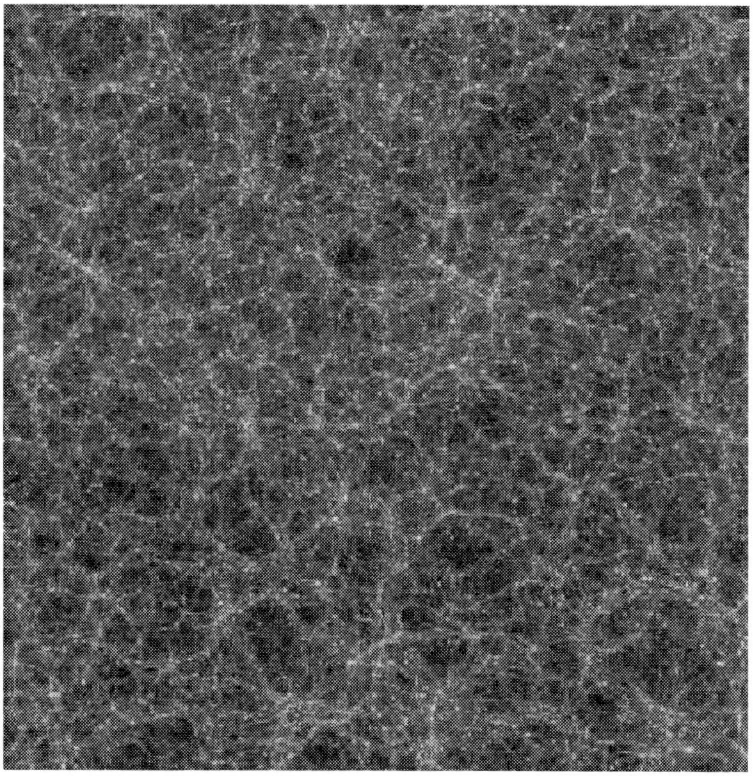

Figure 4. The gas distribution in the Sunyaev-Zeldovich simulation unrolled as a 290 million lightyear thick periodically extended 2.9 x 2.6 billion light year sheet. The bright filaments are dotted with bright points representing hot gas in cluster of galaxies that distort the primary signal present in the Cosmic Microwave Background. The volume of the 2×512^3 simulation is $(400Mpc)^3$ comoving and the initial perturbation spectrum was taken from a currently preferred Λ-CDM cosmological model.

Molecular dynamics study of ablation of solids under femtosecond laser pulses

Danny Perez and Laurent J. Lewis [a]

[a]Département de physique et Groupe de recherche en physique et technologie des couches minces (GCM), Université de Montréal, C. P. 6128 Succursale Centre-Ville, Montréal (Québec) H3C 3J7, Canada

We study the mechanisms of ablation of solids under femtosecond laser pulses using a two-dimensional molecular-dynamics model. By using a novel method to obtain the thermodynamic relaxation path of different sections of the target in the phase diagram, it is shown that four mechanisms can account for ablation for fluences (energy injected per unit surface) under the threshold for plasma formation: (i) spallation resulting from the loss of stability of the solid target following the passage of a tensile pressure wave; (ii) phase explosion resulting from important homogeneous nucleation of gas bubbles inside a superheated, metastable liquid; (iii) fragmentation of a highly strained supercritical fluid; and (iv) complete vaporization of the surface layers of the target. As many as three of these mechanisms can be active at the same time, inducing ablation of material at different depths under the surface of the sample. The occurrence of these mechanisms is linked to the characteristics of the thermodynamic relaxation path followed by the material after the absorption of the laser pulse.

Nous étudions les mécanismes d'ablation des solides par des impulsions laser femtosecondes en utilisant un modèle de dynamique moléculaire bidimensionnel. En utilisant une nouvelle méthode d'obtention du chemin de relaxation thermodynamique de différentes sections de la cible dans le diagramme de phase, on montre que quatre mécanismes peuvent expliquer l'ablation pour des fluences (énergie injectée par unité de surface) sous le seuil de formation de plasma : (i) spallation résultant de l'instabilité de la cible solide après le passage d'une onde de pression tensile; (ii) explosion de phase résultant de la nucléation de bulles de gaz au sein d'un solide surchauffé; (iii) fragmentation d'un fluide surcritique fortement contraint; et (iv) évaporation complète de la couche de surface de la cible. Jusqu'à trois de ces mécanismes peuvent être actifs en même temps, causant une ablation à des profondeurs différentes sous la surface. L'existence d ces mécanismes est liée aux caractéristiques du chemin de relaxation thermodynamique suivi par le matériau après l'absorption de l'impulsion laser.

1 Introduction

When a laser is shined on a solid target, material can be ejected following the intense heating caused by the light absorption. This process — laser ablation — plays an incresingly important role in many different technological applications. These include thin film growth, micromachining and chemical analysis, to name only a few. In the last decade, it was made clear that very short pulses (lasting pico or femtoseconds) can offer numerous advantages over longer ones (high yield and limited thermal damages to the target, for example).

To be efficient, these applications require a precise control of the properties of both the ablated material (yield, stoichiometry, size distribution and temperature of clusters) when used in thin-film growth or chemical analysis, and of the remaining sample (ablation depth, crater profile, extent of the thermal and mechanical damages) when used in a micro-machining setting. However, the basic mechanisms leading to ablation are still subject to debate, largely because theoretical modeling is difficult. Indeed, absorption of a large quantity of energy on such short timescale induces many different processes. On a microscopic scale, these include: dielectric breakdown in transparent solids, [1] change of optical and electronic properties, [2] nonthermal melting of covalent materials, [3] and semiconductor-to-metal transitions. [4] On a mesoscopic scale, the pressure wave generation, [5–7] the thermodynamical evolution of the expanding matter, [8,9] and the identification of the collective ejection processes [8,10–17] must all be understood in order to provide a complete picture of the phenomenon. Clearly, a complete microscopic description of the ablation process is out of reach of present models.

However, for fluences below the threshold for plasma formation, experiments show that ablation occurs hundreds of picoseconds after the absorption of the pulse [18]. This time is longer than the time required for the equilibrium between electronic and atomic degrees of freedom to establish. Hence, the details of the complex non-thermal processes which occur shortly after the absorption of the pulse are not expected to play a crucial role in the material removal. Ablation should thus be dominated by the thermodynamics or by processes occurring on a mesoscopic scale. Taking advantage of this simplifying factor, we identify the relevant ablation mechanisms for low fluences. We show that ablation involves four different processes — spallation, homogeneous nucleation, fragmentation and vaporization — which sometimes occur simultaneously at different positions under the surface of the target. A complete account of this study can be found in Refs. [17] and [19].

2 Computational Methods

2.1 Model

We study the ablation process using molecular dynamics in two dimensions. This type of simulations consists in integrating the equation of motion of the atoms in the system [20]. This integration is here carried out using the velocity-Verlet algorithm, which proceeds in two steps: first, updated positions and mid-step velocities are obtained from

$$x_i(t+\delta t) = x_i(t) + \delta t v_i(t) + \frac{1}{2}\delta t^2 a_i(t) \qquad (1)$$

and

$$v_i(t + \frac{1}{2}\delta t) = v_i(t) + \frac{1}{2}\delta t a_i(t). \qquad (2)$$

At this point, the forces (and hence the accelerations) at time $t+\delta t$ are obtained using the updated positions. Finally, the velocities are adjusted using

$$v_i(t + \delta t) = v_i(t + \frac{1}{2}\delta t) + \frac{1}{2}\delta t a_i(t + \delta t). \qquad (3)$$

The forces are deduced from an *a priori* specified interatomic potential, in our case a simple Lennard-Jones potential adjusted so as to vanish at the cutoff distance r_c:

$$\begin{aligned} \phi_{\mathrm{LJ}}(r) = \;& 4\epsilon[(\sigma/r)^{12} - (\sigma/r)^6 & r \leq r_c \\ & -(\sigma/r_c)^{12} + (\sigma/r_c)^6] & \\ \phi_{\mathrm{LJ}}(r) = \;& 0 & r > r_c \end{aligned}$$

with ϵ (typically a few eV) and σ (a few angströms) the usual energy and length scales, respectively. In the following, all results are reported in reduced units, i.e., ϵ/k_B for temperature and $\tau = (m\sigma^2/\epsilon)^{1/2}$ for time (m is the atomic mass).

The usual optimization procedures were implemented in our code. First, to shorten the time required for the force calculation, a neighbor list is kept for every atom. However, since the state of the system changes strongly during a simulation, these lists have to be updated periodically. This is carried out using the cells and linked-list method [20]. With these optimizations, the computational load is proportional to the number of atoms in the system.

Simulation were carried out using samples consisting of 800 atomic layers in the y direction and 500 layers in the x direction, for a total of 400 000 atoms initially forming a triangular lattice thermalized at low temperature.

In order to simulate the ablation process, other components were added to the MD code; they are schematically presented in Fig. 1. We model the laser pulse (incident in the y direction) as an ensemble of discrete photons of energy 4.5ϵ. The pulse has a Gaussian temporal profile with a width at half maximum of $\Delta t = 0.5\tau$ ($\sim$ 100 fs) and a constant spatial profile. The depth at which the photons are absorbed in the target is chosen randomly so that the absorption profile follows a Beer-Lambert law ($I = I_0 e^{-\alpha y}$) where $\alpha = 0.002\sigma^{-1}$ is the absorption coefficient. During absorption, the photon energy is transfered to a "carrier". Here, a carrier is a particle which follows a Drude dynamics, i.e., the dynamics is governed by successive collisions occurring on average every 0.005τ. Evolution of the carrier gas proceeds in a Monte Carlo fashion. At each collision between a carrier and an atom, the former is allowed to emit a small quantity of energy (0.07ϵ) that is converted into heat. This mimics the emission of phonons during the relaxation of the hot carrier gas.

The important pressure waves produced following the rapid heating of the surface region of the sample are absorbed using special boundary conditions at the bottom of the sample [21]. Periodic boundary conditions are used in the x direction.

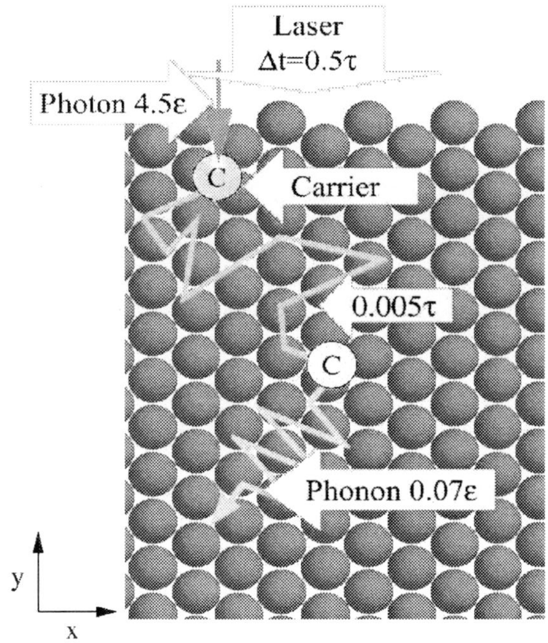

Figure 1. Schematic representation of the model system. See text for details.

With this model, a typical ablation simulation involves integrating the equation of motion over 120 000 time-steps ($600\tau \simeq 120$ ps). This take about 10 days on a single SGI R12000 CPU.

2.2 Calculation of local thermodynamic properties

The analysis which follows relies heavily on local, phase-specific thermodynamic properties of small subsections of the system. Specifically, we are interested in following the thermodynamic evolution of groups of atoms that have absorbed similar quantities of energy. We are also interested in the time evolution of the morphology of the material. Here we describe the method used to obtain this information.

First, the sample is separated into four-atomic-layer-thick "slices" perpendicular to the incident pulse. This grouping is preserved during the whole simulation. To minimize the effect of mixing between adjacent slices, only the N atoms lying within one standard deviation of the mean y position of atoms in the slice are used to compute the local thermodynamic quantities ρ, T and P as a function of time. The temperature and pressure are obtained using

$$T = \frac{1}{2N}\sum_{i=1}^{N}(v_i - v_{cm})^2 \qquad (4)$$

and

$$P = A^{-1}(\mathcal{W} + NT), \qquad (5)$$

where v_{cm} is the center-of-mass velocity of the slice, $\mathcal{W}$ the virial sum and A the area occupied by the slice. This

Figure 2. Phase-specific density calculation. White: condensed bulk atoms; dark gray: condensed surface atoms; light gray: isolated atoms.

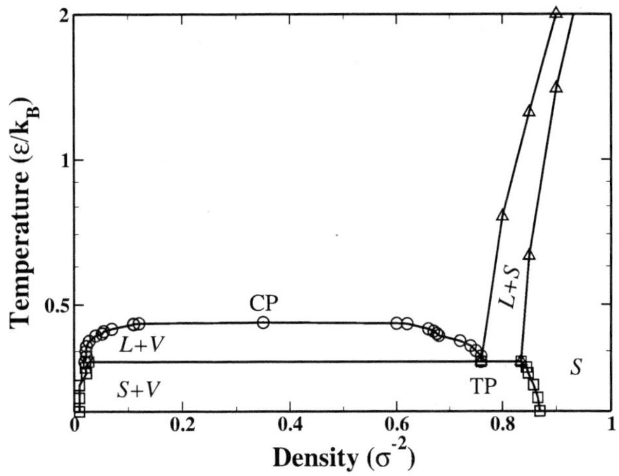

Figure 3. Phase diagram of the 2D truncated and shifted Lennard-Jones potential in the $\rho - T$ plane. Circles: binodal line (liquid-vapor coexistence); squares: solid-vapor coexistence line; triangles: solid-liquid coexistence line. The solid line is drawn to guide the eye. The italic letters refer the the phases in each regions (*S,L,V*: solid, liquid and vapor respectively). **CP**: critical point, **TP**: triple point.

last quantity (also required to obtain the density) is most difficult to obtain reliably. To circumvent this difficulty, we use a tessellation of space into Voronoi polygons centered around atomic positions. The area occupied by the slice is then taken as the sum of the area of the Voronoi polygons of atoms in this slice. This process is illustrated in Fig. 2. The thermodynamic trajectory obtained this way is refered to as *average*.

To couple thermodynamic and structural informations about a given slice, two other *phase-specific* trajectories were also defined: a *condensed* and a *gas* branch. In order to do this, clustered and isolated atoms are first identified using the Hoshen-Kopelman algorithm [22] with a clustering radius chosen so that the critical point density separates the gas and condensed phases. The condensed atoms are then separated into two subgroups: bulk (fully-coordinated) and surface (under-coordinated). The area occupied by the condensed phase is defined as the total number of condensed atoms times the mean area of the Voronoi atoms in the bulk subgroup (see Fig. 2). The difference between the total area of the slice and the area occupied by the condensed phase is attributed to the gas phase. The thermodynamic quantities are finally obtained using Eqs. 4 and 5 by averaging over the appropriate subgroup of atoms.

With this method, the onset of void formation is signaled by a split between the average and condensed branches. Further, the ratio of the densities on the different branches is an indication of the porosity and of the gas content of this part of the target.

2.3 Phase diagram

The method just described is not useful unless the phase diagram of the model system is known. For this purpose we used Monte Carlo simulations in the Gibbs ensemble [23] to complete a previously published section of the phase diagram [24]. The results are shown in Fig. 3. Properties of specific regions of this phase diagram will be discussed later on, as required by the discussion.

3 Results

3.1 Visual analysis

We first discuss the global reaction of the system after the absorption of the pulse in a qualitative manner by presenting snapshots of the simulation at different moments during the ablation process. The evolution of the system at low fluence ($F = 1.2F_{\text{th}}$, where F_{th} is the threshold fluence for ablation) is exhibited in Fig. 4. Here, the laser pulse is fired during the first 2τ of the simulation. In spite the important heating occurring during the relaxation of the carrier gas, the target does not react appreciably until $t = 5\tau$. At this point, a very important pressure wave generated by the isochoric heating is emitted and expansion of the target begins. Aside from the ejection of a few monomers, it can be seen that it takes about 100τ for voids to form in the surface region. By $t = 200\tau$, it is apparent that the pores are filled with gas. These bubbles then continue to grow and coalesce until ablation is induced. In this case, two regions are easily distinguished: the non-ablated solid-region and the porous region, labeled I and II respectively.

Figure 5 shows that the situation becomes more complex as the fluence is increased to $F = 2.8F_{\text{th}}$. Expansion and emission of monomers is now much more intense than at lower fluence. By $t = 100\tau$, a few voids begin to appear

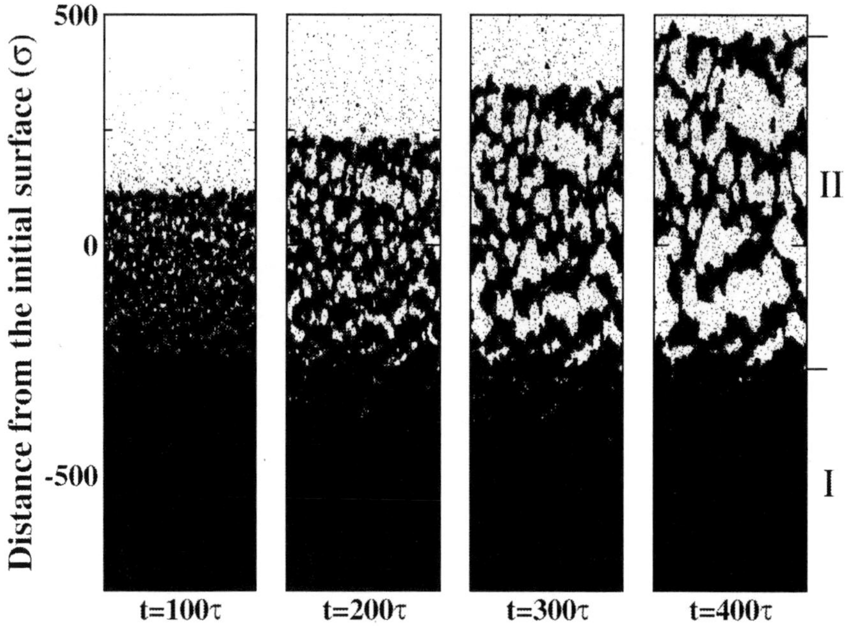

Figure 4. Snapshots of a simulation with $F = 900\epsilon/\sigma = 1.2\,F_{\mathrm{th}}$ and $\alpha = 0.002\sigma^{-1}$. Roman numerals identify different regions of the target (see text).

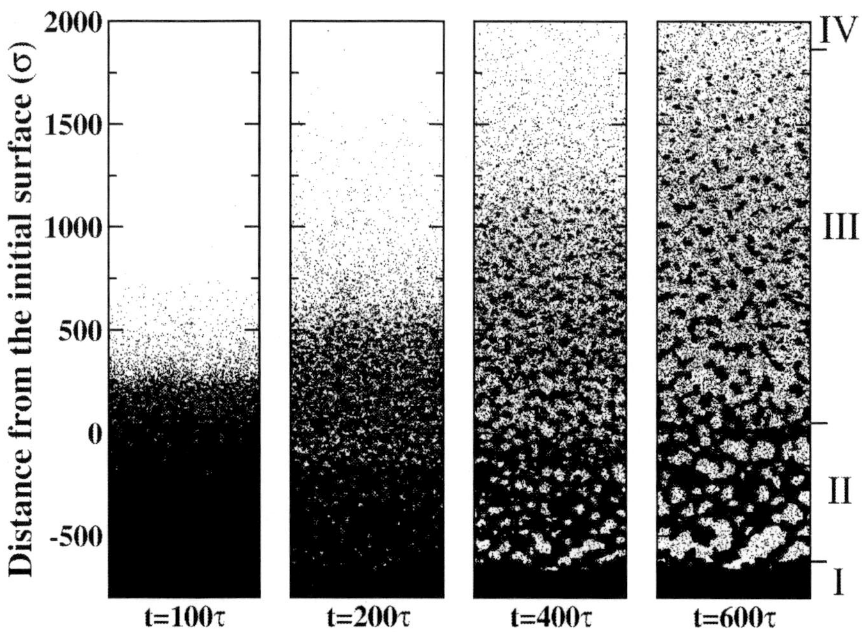

Figure 5. Snapshots of a simulation with $F = 2100\epsilon/\sigma = 2.8\,F_{\mathrm{th}}$ and $\alpha = 0.002\sigma^{-1}$. Roman numerals identify different regions of the target. Region IV is the gaseous region (out of the range of the last snapshot).

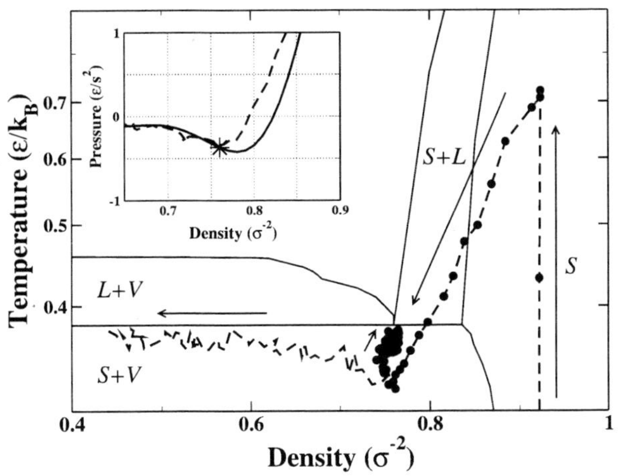

Figure 6. Typical thermodynamic evolution for regions of the target where spallation occurs. Dashed line: average branch; filled circles: condensed branch. Arrows indicate the flow of time. Inset: average trajectory in the $\rho - P$ plane (dashed line) and $T = 0.36$ isotherm (solid line). The star indicates the point of fracture.

close to the surface. In the following 300τ, the surface region is totally decomposed into small liquid clusters. Evaporation from the surface of these hot clusters quickly fill the surroundings with gas. At $t = 400\tau$, gas-filled pores begin to form deeper into the target. The morphology of this region quickly becomes very similar to that of region II in Fig. 4. In this case, four different regions can thus be identified inside the sample: a non-ablated solid region I, a porous region II, a cluster-filled region III and a purely gaseous region IV. The strongly-varying morphologies of these regions suggests that different ablation mechanisms may be effective as a function of depth, and hence as a function of locally absorbed energy. (Recall that the energy locally absorbed decreases exponentially with depth). By following the thermodynamic evolution of the material in every one of these regions, it will now be shown that this is indeed the case.

3.2 Mechanisms of ablation

3.2.1 Spallation

While not apparent in Figs. 4 and 5, ablation can occur from the solid phase (region I) in specific conditions, namely when strong tensile pressure waves are running through the system. If ablation occurs following mechanical fracture caused by the passage of such wave, one speaks of spallation. This mechanism was already observed in experiments of ablation on gels [14] and biological tissues [7]. Simulations of ablation of organic solids in the stress-confinement regime have also been interpreted in terms of a spallation-like process [15]. We now show that it could also be important in more cohesive solids.

Indeed, Fig. 6 shows a typical thermodynamic trajectory for a region of the target in which spallation occurs. First, it can be seen that the laser pulse initially heats the lattice up to a very high, supercritical, temperature; notice that the heating occurs at constant density for such short pulses. Expansion then quickly sets in and the temperature decreases below the triple point. At this moment, the system enters the solid-vapor coexistence region. Upon entrance in this region, a tensile wave (negative pressure wave) reaches this part of the sample (see inset of Fig. 6) and further stretches the material. The split between the average and condensed branches indicates that failure occurred during the passage of this wave, around $\rho \simeq 0.76\sigma^{-2}$. The average density then continues to decrease (the voids are growing) until ablation finally occurs. The inset shows that fracture occurred because the system was pushed into a mechanically unstable state by the passage of the pressure wave. Indeed, mechanical stability requires a positive isothermal compressibility, i.e., a positive slope of the isotherm in the $\rho - P$ plane of the phase diagram. It can be seen that this condition was violated just before signs of fracture were observed in this slice. Spallation is thus indeed responsible for ablation in this case.

3.2.2 Homogeneous nucleation

When the energy injected in the system increases, relaxation eventually proceeds above the triple point, i.e., the system melts during its expansion. If the maximum temperature is not too high, the thermodynamic evolution of the material can bring the system into the liquid-vapor coexistence region. This corresponds to region II in Figs. 4 and 5.

In this region, the free-energy of the gas phase becomes lower than that in the liquid phase, i.e., the homogeneous liquid is no longer the most stable configuration. For long enough waiting times or a high enough degree of metastability, gas bubbles are expected to form inside the metastable liquid by a process called *homogeneous nucleation*. For high nucleation rates, the liquid can rapidly decompose into an equilibrium mixture of liquid droplets and monomers; in this case one speaks of *phase explosion*. This process is widely considered to be a common ablation process in the ultrashort pulse regime [8,10–12,25–27]. However, a clear evidence of its occurrence still lacks.

We now show that our simulations provide a direct confirmation of the relevance of homogeneous nucleation to the description of ablation. Fig. 7 presents the evolution of the system when the liquid-vapor coexistence region is entered. This figure shows that the onset of bubble nucleation (marked by the split between the average and condensed branches) occurred shortly *after* the entrance in the liquid-vapor metastable region. Further, the trajectories show clear signs of phase separation: i) the density of the liquid phase stays constant during the entire process and ii) the gas phase also stays at constant density, precisely on the liquid-vapor equilibrium line. Our simulations thus provide clear evidence that homogeneous nucleation is indeed responsible for ablation at moderate energy.

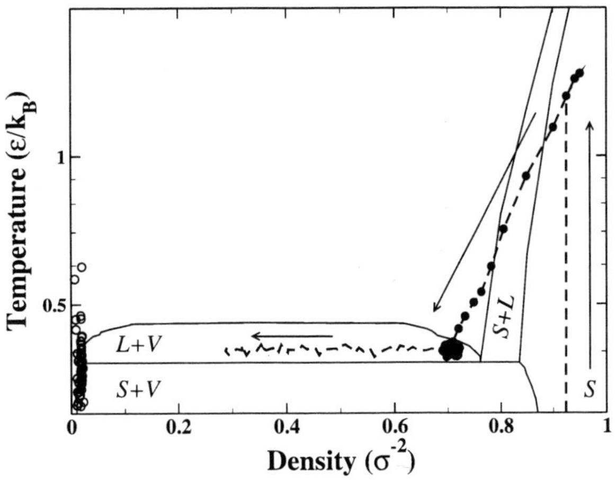

Figure 7. Typical thermodynamic evolution for regions of the target where homogeneous nucleation occurs. Dashed line: average branch; filled circles: condensed branch; empty circles: gas branch.

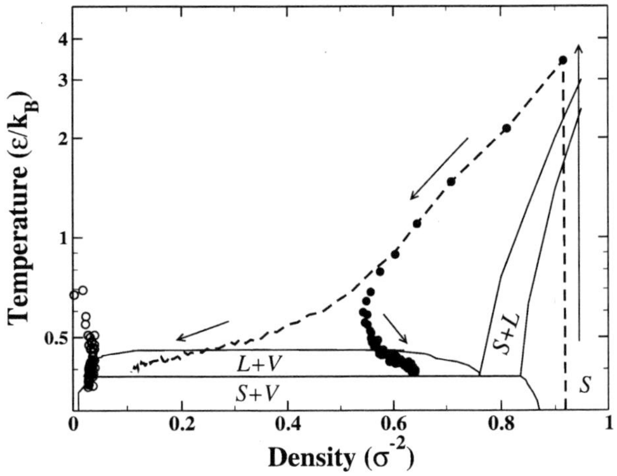

Figure 8. Typical thermodynamic evolution for regions of the target where fragmentation occurs. See Fig. 7 for the definition of symbols and lines.

3.2.3 Fragmentation

As the energy continues to increase, relaxation at some point becomes supercritical, i.e., proceeds above the critical point. In this situation, homogeneous nucleation is no longer possible. This is the case for the material found in region III in Fig. 5.

A typical thermodynamic trajectory in this regime is shown in Fig. 8. The figure confirms that the void formation leading to ablation occurred *outside* of the liquid-vapor metastable region, so that homogeneous nucleation cannot be held responsible for ablation. Indeed, the split between the average and condensed branches occurs at a temperature exceeding the critical temperature. However, by comparing the different snapshots of Fig. 5, we see that expansion in region III proceeds at a very high rates compared to that in region II. This is a hint that ablation might have a mechanical origin in this case. Indeed, separation of supercritical fluids subject to important strain rates into small clusters has been observed before in numerous situations: computer simulation of two and three-dimensional Lennard-Jones systems under homogeneous expansion [28] and of rapid heating of liquid drops [29,30], experiments on the free-jet expansion of liquids [31,32], etc. This process is called fragmentation.

In this context, the size of the clusters formed during the expansion should decrease with increasing strain rate. This is verified in Fig. 9 where the mean cluster mass is plotted against the local strain rate at their formation depth. Further, the apparent power-law dependence between these two quantities can be explained by a simple model due to Ashurst and Holian [28]. This model states that fragmentation results from the conversion of some of the internal stress stored in the expanding target into surface energy of clusters. For uniaxial expansion in two dimensions, this model predicts that the mean cluster mass should be given by:

$$M = 4\zeta\rho(r_0\gamma)^{2/3}\eta^{-4/3} \qquad (6)$$

where ζ is a geometric factor of the order of unity, η is the strain rate, r_0 is the equilibrium bond length, and γ is the surface energy per unit mass. The same power-law dependence is predicted by the energy-minimization model of Grady [33,28] and thus constitutes a strong signature of fragmentation.

The prediction of the model is also plotted in Fig. 9 for comparison. One can see that the strain rate dependence is very well accounted for using this simple model. This thus confirms that fragmentation is responsible for ablation at high energy.

3.2.4 Vaporization

Finally, if the energy injected by the laser is high enough, the surface layers of the target are completely atomized (cf. part IV of Fig. 5). Figure 10 shows the evolution of the material in this region. We see that the condensed and average branches split at a very early time and that the average and gas branches merge soon after inside the vapor region of the phase diagram, showing that the slice as a whole is behaving like a gas. The trajectory thus simply illustrates a vaporization process occuring when the energy injected by the laser pulse is comparable to the cohesive energy of the material.

4 Conclusion

By using molecular-dynamics simulation on a two-dimensional Lennard-Jones system we showed that low-fluence laser ablation in the ultrashort-pulse regime involves four different mechanisms: spallation, homogeneous nucleation, fragmentation and vaporization. The dif-

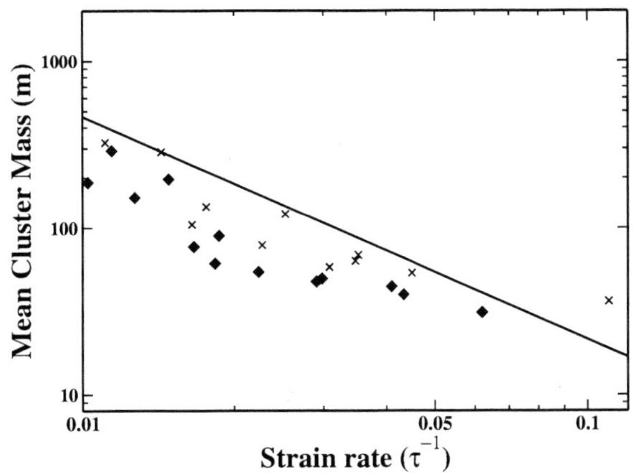

Figure 9. Mean cluster mass versus local strain rate for for $\alpha = 0.01\sigma^{-1}$. Crosses: $F = 750\epsilon/\sigma$; diamonds: $F = 900\epsilon/\sigma$. The solid line is Eq. 6.

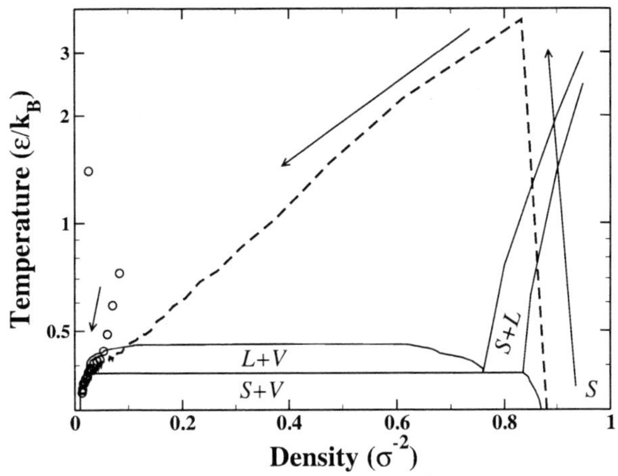

Figure 10. Typical thermodynamic evolution for regions of the target where vaporization occurs. See Fig. 7 for the definition of symbols and lines.

ferent mechanisms are effective in different ranges of energy, and hence can occur simultaneously at different positions inside the target. One of these mechanisms — fragmentation — is proposed for the first time in the context of laser ablation.

Acknowledgments

We thank Patrick Lorazo, Ralf Meyer and Michel Meunier for numerous enlightening discussions. This work has been supported by grants from the Canadian *Natural Sciences and Engineering Research Council* (NSERC) and Québec's *Fonds québécois de la recherche sur la nature et les technologies* (FQRNT). We are indebted to the *Réseau québécois de calcul de haute performance* (RQCHP) for generous allocations of computer resources.

References

1. A. Kaiser, B. Rethfeld, M. Vicanek, and G. Simon. Microscopic processes in dielectrics under irradiation by subpicosecond laser pulses. *Physical Review B*, 61:11 437, 2000.
2. J.S. Graves and R.E. Allen. Response of gaas to fast intense laser pulses. *Physical Review B*, 58:13 627, 1998.
3. K. Sokolowski-Tinten, J. Bialkowski, M. Boing, A. Cavalleri, and D. von der Linde. Thermal and nonthermal melting of gallium arsenide after femtosecond laser excitation. *Physical Review B*, 58:11 805, 1998.
4. J.P. Callan, A.M.-T. Kim, C.A.D. Roeser, and E. Mazur. Universal dynamics during and after ultrafast laser-induced semiconductor-to-metal transitions. *Physical Review B*, 64:073201, 2001.
5. J. C. Bushnell and D. J. McCloskey. Thermoelastic stress production in solids. *J. Appl. Phys.*, 39:5541, 1968.
6. J. I. Etcheverry and M. Mesaros. Molecular dynamics simulation of the production of acoustic waves by pulsed laser irradiation. *Physical Review B*, 60:9430, 1999.
7. I. Itzkan, D. Albagli, M.L. Dark, L.T. Perelman, C. von Rosenberg, and M.S. Fields. The thermoelastic basis of short pulsed laser ablation of biological tissues. *Proc. Natl. Acad. Sci. USA*, 92:1960, 1995.
8. K. Sokolowski-Tinten, J. Bialkowski, A. Cavalleri, D. von der Linde, A. Oparin, J. Meyer ter Vehn, and S.I. Anisimov. Transient states of matter during short pulse laser ablation. *Phys. Rev. Lett.*, 81:224, 1998.
9. V.V. Zhakhovskii, K. Nishiara, S.I. Anisimov, and N.A. Inogamov. Molecular-dynamics simulations of rarefaction waves in media that can undergo phase transitions. *JETP Letters*, 71:167, 2000.
10. R. Kelly and A. Miotello. Comments on explosive mechanisms of laser sputtering. *Applied Surface Science*, 96-98:205–215, 1996.
11. A. Miotello and R. Kelly. Critical assessment of thermal models for laser sputtering at high fluences. *Applied Physics Letters*, 67:3535, 1995.
12. A. Miotello and R. Kelly. Laser-indiced phase explosion: new physical problems when a condensed phase approaches the thermodynamic critical temperature. *Applied Physics A*, 69:S69–S73, 1999.
13. B. N. Chichkov, C. Momma, S. Nolte, F. von Alvensleben, and A. Tünnermann. Femtosecond, picosecond and nanosecond laser ablation of solids. *Appl. Phys. A*, 63:109, 1996.
14. G. Paltaud and H. Schmidt-Kloiber. Microcavity dynamics during laser-induced spallation of liquids and gels. *Applied Physics A*, 62:303, 1996.
15. L. V. Zhigilei and B. J. Garrison. Microscopic mechanisms of laser ablation of organic solids in the thermal and stress confinement irradiation regimes. *J. Appl. Phys*, 88:1281, 2000.
16. F. Vidal, T.W. Johnston, S. Laville, O. Barthélemy, M. Chaker, B. Le Drogoff, J. Margot, and M. Sabsabi. Critical-point phase separation in laser ablation of conductors. *Phys. Rev. Lett.*, 86:2573, 2001.
17. D. Perez and L. J. Lewis. Ablation of solids under femtosecond laser pulses. *Physical Review Letters*, 89:255504, 2002.
18. D. von der Linde, K. Sokolowski-Tinten, and J. Bialkowski.

Laser-solid interaction in the femtosecond time regime. *Applied Surface Science*, 109:1, 1997.
19. D. Perez and L. J. Lewis. Molecular-dynamics study of ablation of solids under femtosecond laser pulses. *Physical Review B, in press*, 2003.
20. M.P. Allen and D.J. Tildesley. *Computer Simulation of Liquids*. Oxford Science Publications, Oxford, 1987.
21. L. V. Zhigilei and B. J. Garrison. Pressure waves in microscopic simulations of laser ablation. *Mat. Res. Soc. Symp. Proc.*, 538:491, 1999.
22. J. Hoshen and R. Kopelman. Percolation and cluster distribution. i. cluster multiple labelling technique and critical concentration algorithm. *Physical Review B*, 14:3438, 1976.
23. A. Z. Panagiotopoulos. Direct determination of phase coexistence properties of fluids by monte carlo simulation in a new ensemble. *Molecular Physics*, 61:813, 1998.
24. B. Smit and D. Frenkel. Vapor-liquid equilibria of the two-dimensional lennard-jones fluid(s). *J. Chem. Phys.*, 94:5663, 1991.
25. J.H. Yoo, S.H. Jeong, X.L. Mao, R. Grief, and R.E. Russo. Evidence for phase-explosion and generation of large particles during high power nanosecond laser ablation of silicon. *Applied Physics Letters*, 76:783, 1999.
26. J.H. Yoo, S.H. Jeong, R. Grief, and R.E. Russo. Explosive change in crater properties during high power nanosecond laser ablation of silicon. *Journal of Applied Physics*, 88:1638, 2000.
27. N.M. Bulgakova and A.V. Bulgakov. Pulsed laser ablation of solids: transition from normal vaporization to phase explosion. *Applied Physics A*, 73:199, 2000.
28. Wm. T. Ashurst and B. L. Holian. Droplet formation by rapid expansion of a liquid. *Phys. Rev. E*, 59:6742, 1999.
29. J. A. Blink and W. G. Hoover. Fragmentation of suddenly heated liquids. *Phys. Rev. A*, 32:1027, 1985.
30. A. Strachan and C. O. Dorso. Caloric curve in fragmentation. *Phys. Rev. C.*, 58:R632, 1998.
31. E. L. Knuth and U. Henne. Average size and size distribution of large droplets produced in a free-jet expansion of a liquid. *Journal of Chemical Physics*, 110:2664–2668, 1999.
32. Wm. T. Ashurst and B. L. Holian. Droplet size dependance upon volume expansion rate. *Journal of Chemical Physics*, 111:2842–2843, 1999.
33. D. E. Grady. Local inertial effects in dynamic fragmentation. *J. Appl. Phys.*, 51:322, 1981.

Molecular Dynamics Simulations of Polymers in Micro–environments

M. Kenward, F. Tessier, Y. Tatek, Y. Gratton, S. Guillouzic, and G. W. Slater[a]

[a]Department of Physics, University of Ottawa, 150 Louis Pasteur, Ottawa, ON, K1N 6N5, gslater@science.uottawa.ca

We provide an overview of ongoing work using large scale Molecular Dynamics (MD) simulations to study systems comprising macromolecules and explicit fluid in various contexts relevant to emerging bioanalytical microdevices and single molecule manipulation techniques. In particular, we discuss the application of MD simulations to polymer translocation through a nanopore, electroosmotic flow control in small capillaries, polymer stretching, and polymer collisions with obstacles. We also present more fundamental applications of MD to the study of molecular-scale friction coefficients and planar perturbations in a fluid. The simultaneous increase in available computational resources and decrease in relevant system dimensions offers unprecedented opportunities to perform realistic simulations to refine our knowledge of these issues and guide future developments in this field.

Nous présentons un panorama de nos travaux basés sur la dynamique moléculaire (DM) à grande échelle appliquée à des systèmes comportant des macromolécules et des fluides dans divers contextes reliés aux dispositifs bioanalytiques en émergence ou aux techniques de manipulation de molécules individuelles. En particulier, nous discutons de l'application de la DM au déplacement d'un polymère à travers un nanopore, au contrôle d'écoulement électro-osmotique dans les capillaires, à l'étirement des polymères et aux collisions des polymères avec des obstacles. Nous présentons aussi des applications plus fondamentales de la DM à l'étude des coefficients de frottement à l'échelle moléculaire et aux perturbations planaires dans un fluide. L'augmentation de la puissance de calcul, combinée à la diminution de la taille des systèmes d'intérêt, nous permet d'effectuer des simulations réalistes et ainsi de raffiner notre compréhension du domaine et de guider les développements futurs.

1 Introduction

With the development of micro- and even nanofluidic devices, more robust modeling is required in order to understand observed behaviour in these systems. Many of the physical mechanisms involved have no macroscopic analogue and are ill understood. For example, there is a major effort to design and utilize microelectromechanical systems (MEMS) in a variety of situations ranging from diagnostic tools to smart materials, and in order to effectively do so we need to understand the dynamics of the components which constitute these devices. Of particular interest to our group are systems which incorporate polymeric materials, at either the micro- or nanoscale. In this paper we combine computer simulations and theoretical methods to examine the behaviour of polymers and other macromolecules in a number of model systems.

Large scale computer simulations which aim to explore mesoscale systems (with upwards of millions of particles), have become an invaluable research tool. Simulation methodologies including Monte Carlo [1,2], continuum models such as Navier-Stokes [3], coarse grained and atomistic Molecular Dynamics [4,5] and Brownian Dynamics are the most prevalent form of simulation for these types of systems. The simulation method used depends on a balance between the:

1. Required level of detail (e.g., length scales).
2. Time scales associated with observed behaviour.
3. Available computational resources.
4. Effort required for a timely implementation.

Figure 1 illustrates the level of detail and computational time of each method. For the particular systems we are examining, coarse grained Molecular Dynamics provides the most useful length and time scales, along with the preservation of hydrodynamics and the molecular properties of the system.

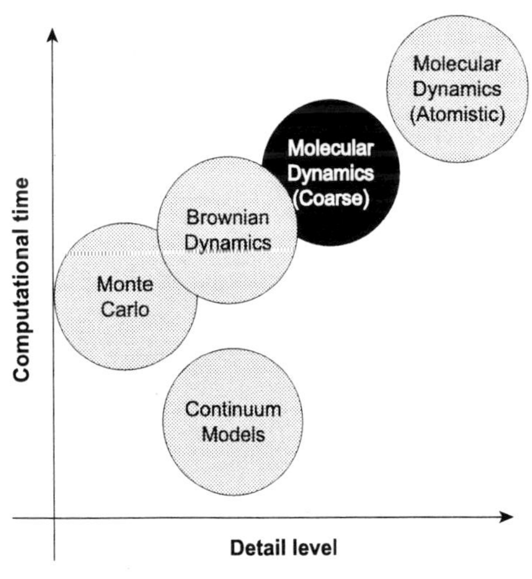

Figure 1. *Schematic illustration of several methods of simulation in terms of their relative computational time and level of detail.*

1.1 Molecular Dynamics: A brief overview

Since the aim of this paper is to illustrate the application of MD simulations to a variety of systems and not to provide a detailed description of Molecular Dynamics, we only give a brief overview and list appropriate references for the interested reader. In short, from the perspective of a physicist, MD is the solution of the set of classical equations of motion for a fully interacting collection of objects (atoms for example) [6,5], i.e., the solution of the N-body equations of motion for a system.

Since in general this solution cannot be obtained analytically, we must resort to numerical solutions. This amounts to discretizing the equations of motion using an appropriate finite difference scheme. In particular we utilize a second order method (in time), referred to as the Velocity Verlet algorithm [5]. This method is both relatively straightforward to implement and also allows relatively large time steps δt. Moreover the Velocity Verlet algorithm is amenable to parallelization [6].

The systems we examine contain one or several of the following components: polymers, solvent, walls, charged species and external forces. One important addition to our simulations is the explicit inclusion of solvent and hence hydrodynamics. Although hydrodynamics is usually discussed in the guise of Navier-Stokes equations, its existence is really a molecular property of the system. Moreover it plays a crucial role in many phenomena at the microscopic and nanoscopic level, which may fall beyond the reach of a continuum description of fluid dynamics.

1.2 Model Fluid and Polymers

In this model we represent a single fluid particle as a soft sphere of radius $\sigma/2$ which interacts with other fluid particles via the Lennard-Jones potential given by

$$V_{\mathrm{LJ}}(r) = \begin{cases} 4\epsilon\left(\left(\frac{\sigma}{r}\right)^{12} - \left(\frac{\sigma}{r}\right)^{6}\right) + \epsilon, & r \leq r_{\mathrm{c}} \\ 0, & r \geq r_{\mathrm{c}} \end{cases}$$

We further simplify by choosing $r_{\mathrm{c}} = 2^{1/6}\sigma$ and we therefore have a fluid with purely repulsive interactions. All distances are expressed in terms of σ, masses in terms of m, times in terms of $\tau = \sqrt{m\sigma^2/\epsilon}$ and velocities in terms of $v = \sqrt{\epsilon/m}$. For all of the simulations presented here we work in the micro-canonical ensemble at fixed reduced temperature $T^* = 1$, reduced density $\rho^* = 0.85$ and a time step of $\delta t = 0.005\tau$ unless otherwise specified.

A schematic illustration of a Lennard-Jones fluid particle and the first layer of solvent around it is shown in Figure 2 b). To illustrate the fluid like structure, Figure 3 shows the radial distribution function of a pure Lennard-Jones fluid. This radial distribution function is characteristic of a fluid local packing with peaks at $r \approx \sigma, 2\sigma, 3\sigma \ldots$

In order to model the polymers, we utilize a coarse grained approximation which replaces the real physical polymers with beads, representing one or many chemical units, and springs which represent the bonds between neighbouring units along a chain. The interactions between non-bonded beads along the chain are given by the Lennard-Jones potential whereas the bonded interactions are modeled via the Finitely Extensible Non-Linear Elastic (FENE) potential,

$$V_{\mathrm{FENE}}(r) = -\frac{k}{2}R_0^2 \ln\left(1 - \frac{r^2}{R_0^2}\right) \tag{1}$$

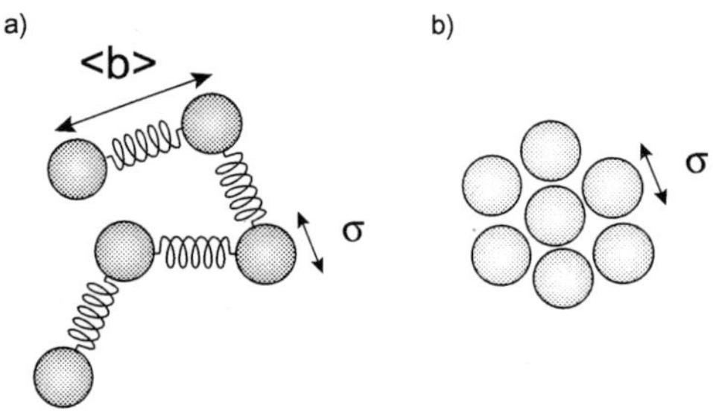

Figure 2. *Illustration of a) model polymers composed of Lennard Jones beads connected via FENE springs where $\langle b \rangle$ denotes the average bond length and σ the diameter of a bead b) model Lennard-Jones fluid particles with first layer of solvent.*

where R_0 is an upper bound on the bond distance and k is essentially a "spring constant" [5]. For more detailed descriptions and implementation details, the reader can consult references [6,7,5,8,9].

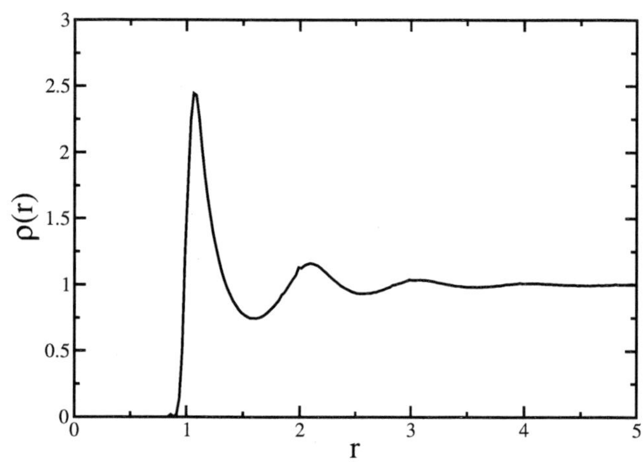

Figure 3. *Radial distribution function $\rho(r)$ for a pure Lennard-Jones fluid obtained from the MD simulations. Characteristic peaks are evident at $r \approx \sigma, 2\sigma, 3\sigma, \ldots$ corresponding to the first, second, third ... solvent layers.*

Since our long term goal for these simulations is to examine mesoscopic and macroscopic systems with $> 10^6$ particles, we require the use of High Performance Computing resources such as those available via HPCVL (**www.hpcvl.org**). Parallelization of Molecular Dynamics simulations with short range interactions is typically done using either; so-called atom-, force-, and spatial-decomposition algorithms [10]. As such our next step will be the parallelization of the simulations using one of the above algorithms, in order to begin examining much larger systems.

1.3 Visualization Tools

Visualizing the results from a simulation provides not only an inherently useful debugging tool but also a physically intuitive way to examine a system and its properties. In this vein, we have developed some generic tools for the visualization of results from the Molecular Dynamics simulations. In particular we have written graphical interfaces, in **OpenGL**, which allow us to visualize our results in both real-time and post simulation modes. Snapshots from this Molecular Dynamics viewer are shown in Figure 4. Though there are similar tools openly available, our viewer has the advantage of being tailored for our specific project. Furthermore we can easily add, modify, and adapt this viewer for a number of distinct projects in our group.

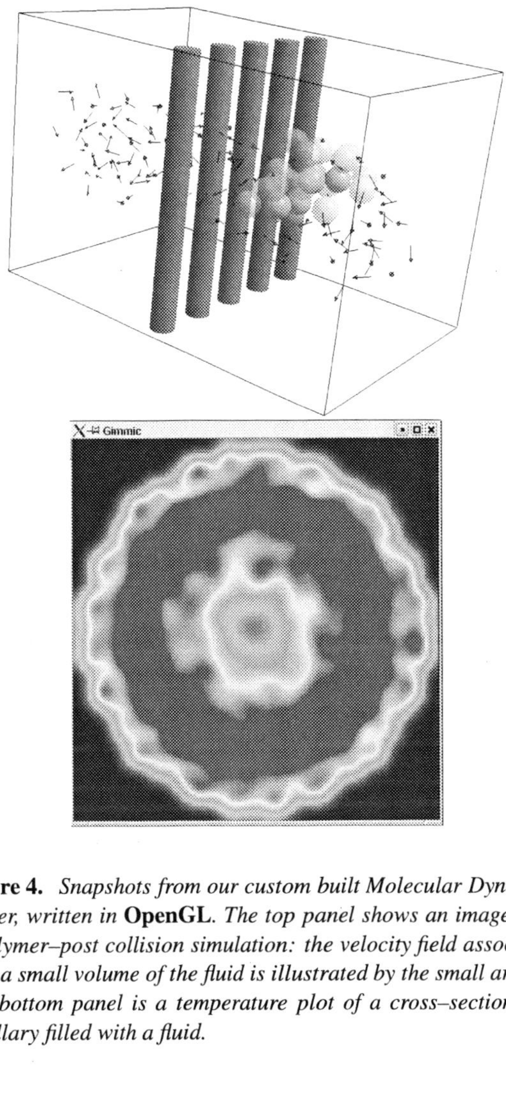

Figure 4. *Snapshots from our custom built Molecular Dynamics viewer, written in* **OpenGL**. *The top panel shows an image from a polymer–post collision simulation: the velocity field associated with a small volume of the fluid is illustrated by the small arrows. The bottom panel is a temperature plot of a cross–section of a capillary filled with a fluid.*

2 Molecular Dynamics: Applications and Examples

2.1 Polymer Translocation in Nanopores

The sequencing of the human genome has become one of the crowning achievements of human-kind. This information has the potential to lead to both better understanding and treatment of human diseases. Though the scientific community has managed to sequence a generic version of the genomic text, the ultimate goal is to sequence individual genomes in a short period of time (a few hours) which could allow for the diagnosis and prevention of diseases.

One promising sequencing method is the use of the translocation of single-stranded DNA molecules through a nanopore in a membrane or a solid surface [11–13]. As the polymer either diffuses or is pulled through the opening, the individual bases of the DNA strand can ideally be read, providing a tool for sequencing. This proposed method could potentially sequence the entire genome in minutes. In order to better understand the relevant physics, we have carried out MD simulations of polymer translocation. A schematic illustration of polymer diffusing through a nanopore is given in Figure 5.

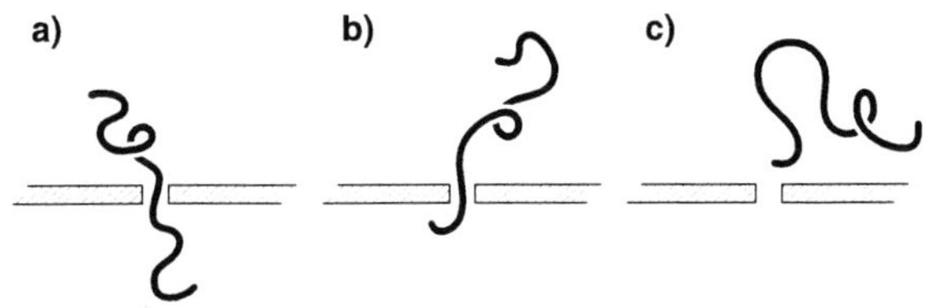

Figure 5. *Schematic illustration of a model polymer diffusing through a nanopore. a) The polymer is centered in the nanopore. b) The polymer begins to diffuse away from the pore. c) Eventually the polymer escapes.*

Our simulations consist of placing a polymer in a single void in a monolayer [111] face-centered cubic structure. We first let the polymer relax while fixing its center bead in the pore. After this relaxation period, we release the polymer and observe its behaviour, until it escapes.

A recent theory of Chuang *et. al.* [14] predicts the scaling behaviour of the mean end-to-end translocation time τ_{trans} of a polymer through a nanopore. In 3D, with no external force and no hydrodynamics, it scales as $\tau_{\text{trans}} \propto N^{2.2}$ while with hydrodynamics it scales as $\tau_{\text{trans}} \propto N^{1.8}$ (where N is the number of monomers in the chain). Chuang *et. al.* [14] also predict that the variance of the translocation coordinate s scales as $\langle \Delta s^2 \rangle \propto t^{1.12}$ when hydrodynamic interactions are present and $\langle \Delta s^2 \rangle \propto t^{0.92}$ when they are not (where the translocation coordinate is the length of the polymer on a given side of the pore).

From the MD simulations we obtain

$$\langle \Delta s^2 \rangle \propto t^{0.918 \pm 0.016} \tag{2}$$

and

$$\tau_{\text{trans}} \propto N^{\beta} \quad \text{with} \quad \beta \geq 2.27 \pm 0.04 \tag{3}$$

for the variance of the translocation coordinate and the mean escape times respectively. Although these results are preliminary, they agree nicely with the predictions of Chuang *et. al.* for translocation in the presence of excluded volume but with no hydrodynamic interactions. This seems to be reasonable since the presence of the wall is expected to screen hydrodynamic interactions to some extent [15].

2.2 Friction coefficients of Rigid Rods

A classic problem from fluid dynamics is determining the friction coefficient of an object. The so-called slender body theory of Batchelor [16] provides well known results for friction coefficients of arbitrarily shaped objects. These results are obtained from the solution of Navier-Stokes equations for low Reynolds number flow subject to appropriate boundary conditions and typically for macroscopic objects. Though these results are known to be accurate for macroscopic systems, when the objects under consideration are on the same scale as the fluid particles, these results do not necessarily remain valid.

We use MD simulations to explore fluid behaviour and microscopic fluid dynamics of objects on the same scale as the fluid. We have carried out simulations which directly determine the friction coefficient of rigid rods composed of spheres. Further to this we can illustrate as the size of the object is decreased to the scale of the fluid particles, the friction coefficient does indeed reduce to that of a single solvent particle. Here we present the case for all particle sizes from the fluid scale to an object composed of 60 fluid size particles. Similar work has been done experimentally for chains of spheres composed of magnetically induced linear chains of super-paramagnetic particles, where the friction coefficient is measured during sedimentation [3,17], though the sphere size is much larger than the size of the fluid particles.

Slender body theory predicts friction coefficients ξ for rigid rods, moving either parallel $||$ or perpendicular $\perp$ to a field, of the form

$$\xi_{||}(L) = \frac{C\pi\eta L}{\ln(L/2b) + \gamma_{||}}, \quad \xi_{\perp}(L) = \frac{2C\pi\eta L}{\ln(L/2b) + \gamma_{\perp}} \tag{4}$$

where $C, \gamma_{\perp}$ and $\gamma_{||}$ are constants and η is the viscosity. The crucial thing to note is that this theory predicts the following relationship

$$\frac{\xi_{\perp}(L)}{\xi_{||}(L)} \approx 2 \tag{5}$$

Indeed, from the simulations we can recover this asymptotic behaviour and the crossover from microscopic to this large scale friction. Figure 6 illustrates the friction coefficients as a function of chain length and the ratio $\xi_{\perp}(L)/\xi_{||}(L)$. This illustrates that MD can be used to examine fluid dynamics starting from a non-continuum based description of the fluid. As we begin to examine larger systems, with on the order of millions of particles we can further examine the crossover from microscopic single particle fluid dynamics to mesoscopic and ideally macroscopic fluid behaviour.

2.3 Polymer–Obstacles Collisions

Another field where the use of computer simulations may reap many benefits is that of separation science, i.e., the separation of DNA, or other polymers by mass, charge or shape. Typically polydisperse solutions of polymers are separated using either gel or capillary electrophoresis [18–20]. A better understanding of the dynamics of polymers in microenvironments can lead to both optimized and novel methods of separating DNA. One such method is the use

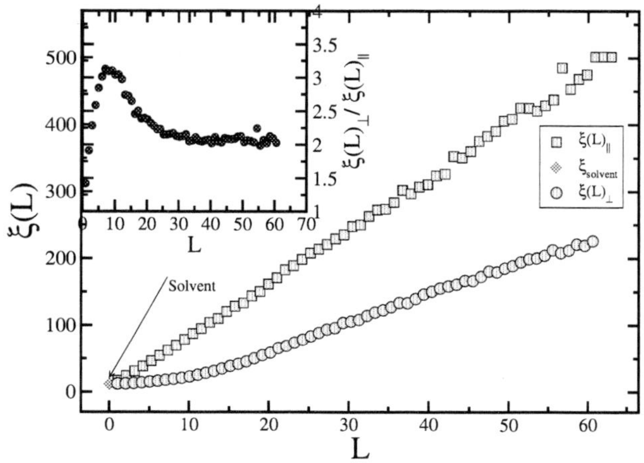

Figure 6. *Friction coefficients for a chain of spheres moving perpendicular $\xi_{\perp}(L)$ and parallel $\xi_{||}(L)$ to an applied field. Inset figure is the ratio of $\xi_{\perp}(L)$ to $\xi_{||}(L)$ as a function of L. Clearly the ratio tends asymptotically to a value of 2, as predicted by slender-body theory.*

of self-assembled arrays of paramagnetic obstacles created by the application of a magnetic field to a suspension of super paramagnetic particles confined between layers of glass [21]. This results in the formation of small quasi-regular arrays of posts (or obstacles) which can serve as a sieve to separate polymer. Such as system has been designed, built and used effectively to separate double-stranded DNA by Doyle *et. al.* [21].

In such a system, the polymers migrate under the presence of an external electric field. They consequently collide with posts, are deformed and form pulley like structures. The release time of the polymer is dictated by its length and a competition between the opposing arms of the pulley like conformation which results. One of the long standing questions is to what degree does the presence of hydrodynamics dictate the release time of the polymer [22,23].

We have carried out extensive MD simulations which examine this process. Figure 7 shows a snapshot from one of the simulations, illustrating a collision and release of a polymer. Using these simulations we can effectively carry out an autopsy of the collision dynamics of a single polymer chain with a post. Figure 8 shows the position of center of mass of a single polymer chain as it undergoes a collision with a post in the MD simulation. From this we can generate a good qualitative model of the behaviour of a polymer during collision. The polymer moves through the solvent with constant velocity v_0, until the center of mass is within about R_g of the post, it is then deformed by the presence of the post and later becomes trapped. There is a competition between the two arms of the resultant pulley like structure which forms, the longer arm winning. This results in the eventual release of the polymer. At this point, it accelerates and returns to a random walk conformation and eventually reaches constant velocity v_0 again.

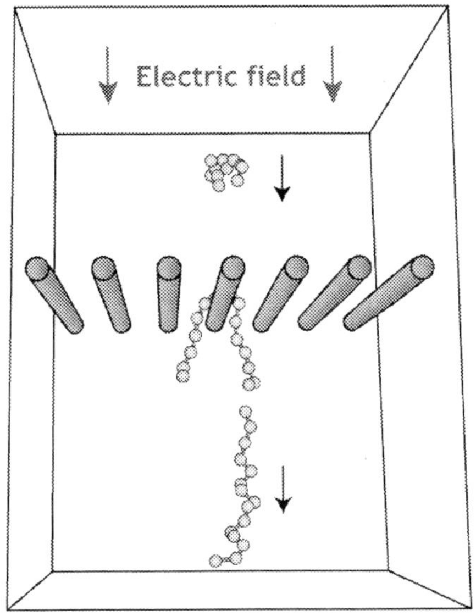

Figure 7. *Illustration of a polymer post collision sequence from the MD simulations.*

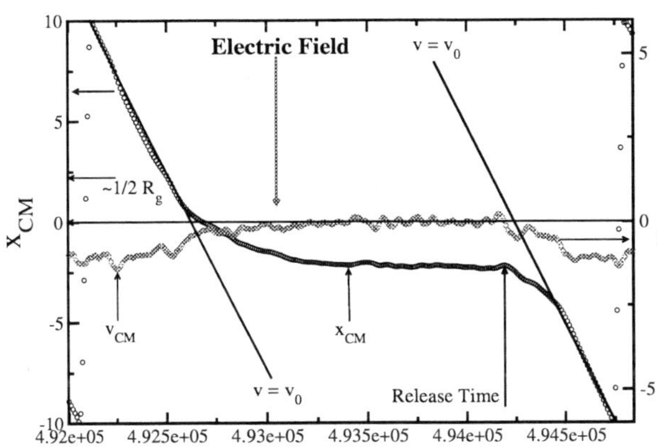

Figure 8. *Instantaneous position x_{CM} and velocity of the center of mass v_{CM} of a polymer before, during and after a collision with a post.*

2.4 MD simulations of Electroosmotic Flow

Electroosmotic flow (EOF) refers to a fluid flow induced by an external electric field applied along a solid surface, and occurs when a space charge builds up in the fluid near the surface [24]. This interfacial charge may arise for different reasons, a common one being the dissociation of chemical groups from the solid and the ensuing accumulation of counterions or ions from the solution in an electrical double-layer (EDL) near the surface [25]. When an external electric field is applied parallel to the surface, this layer of mobile charges is set in motion and eventually drags the bulk of the fluid by viscosity into a flow with a flat profile (a so-called *plug flow*, see Figure 9). Hence EOF serves as a very efficient fluid transport mechanism in small capillaries [26]. Calculations based on mean-field arguments have been used time and again to characterize the EOF in various geometries, including channels with rectangular cross-section, cylindrical capillaries and narrow slits, in steady-state, transient, and oscillating regimes [27,28,26,29–31].

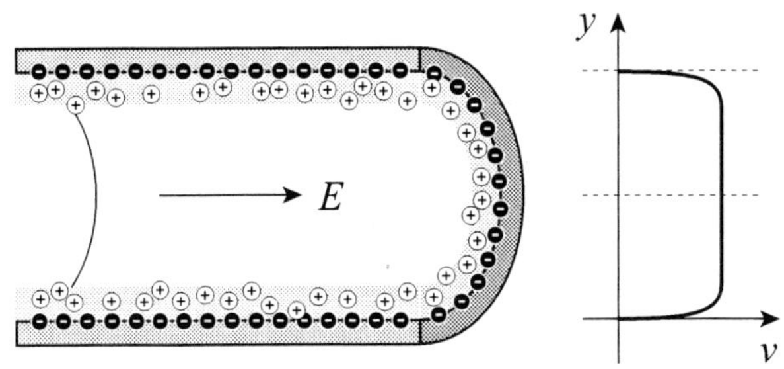

Figure 9. *Schematic representation of EOF generation inside a cylindrical capillary. Bound charges on the wall surface induce a net charge layer in the fluid. Upon the application of an external field, this mobile layer is set in motion, and eventually drags the whole fluid into a plug flow with a flat profile, depicted schematically on the right.*

The typical approach to treat this problem analytically or numerically is to consider on one hand the Poisson equation for the electrostatic potential $\phi(\mathbf{r})$ at position $\mathbf{r}$ in the system, and on the other hand the Boltzmann distribution for the density of mobile ions in the solution in terms of the valence z_k and the bulk concentration n_{ko} of each of the N ionic species [24]. These two expressions together yield the well-known Poisson-Boltzmann (PB) equation for $\phi(\mathbf{r})$ in a polyelectrolyte solution at thermal equilibrium:

$$\nabla^2\phi(\mathbf{r}) = -\frac{e}{4\pi\varepsilon_o\varepsilon}\sum_{k=1}^{N} z_k n_{ko}\, e^{-ez_k\phi(\mathbf{r})/k_B T}, \qquad (6)$$

where ε_o and ε are the permittivity of the vacuum and the relative permittivity of the fluid, e is the elementary charge, and $k_B T$ is a measure of the mean thermal energy. With appropriate boundary conditions, we can solve equation (6) numerically for any geometry, and by substituting the results in a finite difference Navier-Stokes equation solver we can obtain the flow field induced by the EOF, in both transient and steady-state regimes. Analytical work is also possible, albeit with a linearized version of equation (6) and for simple geometries only.

Despite all the knowledge gained in this way over the last thirty years, revisiting EOF with Molecular Dynamics simulations is interesting and important for two main reasons. First, as modern analytical chemistry devices shrink to the micrometer and even to the nanometer scale, the validity of the continuum picture of hydrodynamics itself becomes questionable. In particular, the correct representation of the velocity field near the fluid-solid interface (e.g. *slip* vs. *no-slip* boundary condition) becomes critical in devices so small that the *bulk* of the fluid lies, in fact, near a solid surface. Secondly, we want to study surface modification using polymer molecules grafted or adsorbed on the capillary wall. Such polymer coatings are of great industrial interest, especially for the control of EOF in bioanalytical microdevices [32]. However the complexity of the system is such that we cannot hope to describe it accurately within a model based on equation (6). Molecular Dynamics simulation, a firmly established and robust method to study fluids, electrolytes, macromolecules, etc., stands as a natural choice for a realistic investigation of EOF.

Studying EOF requires that we add charged species in our simulations. Long-range electrostatic forces generally pose problems because of interactions between ions in different periodic images, although robust schemes based on Ewald summations have been developed [33–35]. However, our narrow capillary here is essentially one-dimensional on large length scales and we can include electrostatics directly, provided that the periodic box is long enough. We moderate Joule heating inside the system by controlling the temperature of the wall. The first object of our investigation is the distribution of ions which we will compare with that predicted by equation (6), as we vary the capillary diameter and the ionic strength of the buffer solution. Further on, we will add an external electric field and study the transient and steady state EOF flows. Assuming we reproduce EOF correctly, we can then include grafted or adsorbed polymer chains on the wall to gain a sound understanding of their effect on EOF.

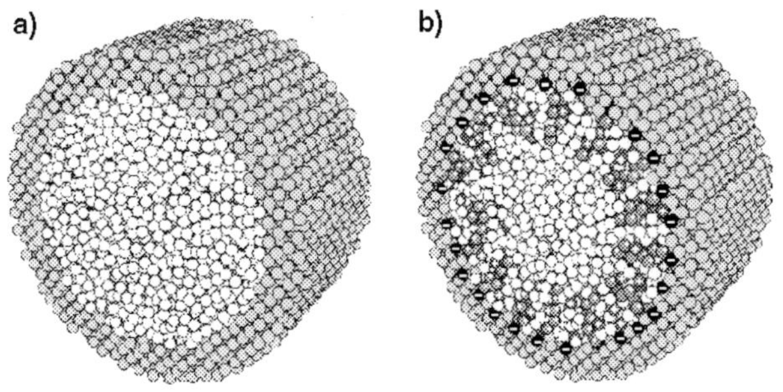

Figure 10. *a) A snapshot from an MD simulation of a short section of a capillary filled with fluid. b) A mock-up of the simulation of* EOF *control using polymer coatings we are setting out to perform, complete with polymer chains, ions on the capillary walls and counterions in solution.*

2.5 Stretching Single Polymers

Understanding the properties of single linear chains in good solvent is important to better describing single chains in microenvironments. With the development of techniques such as optical tweezers and single molecule fluorescence spectroscopy it is now possible to experimentally manipulate and observe single polymer chains. This technology enables us to stretch a DNA molecule and measure forces on the order of femtonewtons! One of the most useful analytical tools for examining polymers is the scaling theory developed by de Gennes [36]. In essence, this theory utilizes the fact that all properties in the system can be related to some universal scale (for example a length scale) such as the mean squared end-to-end distance $\langle h^2 \rangle$.

This section presents a brief overview of two simple models: the Freely Jointed Chain (FJC) and the Rouse model applied to the stretching of a single polymer [36–38]. At first glance, a polymer looks like a random walk (RW) where every monomer is subjected to Brownian motion caused by the surrounding solvent. From this observation, a simplistic model can describe the polymer as a series of links of fixed length b (the Kuhn length) which allow all possible orientations. In RW theory, it is a well known fact that for a chain of N links, the mean squared end-to-end distance $\langle h^2 \rangle$ is

$$\langle h^2 \rangle = Nb^2 \tag{7}$$

The Rouse model consists of a series of beads connected by springs [37]. Compared with the FJC model, the Rouse model re-groups $n < N$ links to form a spring. These Gaussian springs have an elastic constant of $K_n = 3k_BT/nb^2$ and a mean squared end-to-end distance $\langle b_n^2 \rangle = nb^2$. The n links in a spring produce $M = N/n$ springs connecting $M+1$ beads. The Rouse chain conserves $\langle h^2 \rangle$:

$$\langle h^2 \rangle = M \langle b_n^2 \rangle = Mnb^2 = Nb^2 \tag{8}$$

One caveat in the Rouse model is the spring constant: it does not accurately model the finite extensibility of a real chain. A polymer will always have a maximum extension after which it will break. We need a more realistic spring constant which ensures finite extension of the chain while keeping the mean value fixed. One possibility is to use the Finitely-Extensible Nonlinear Elastic (FENE) model. It is important to note that these models do not take into account either the presence of a solvent (hydrodynamic effects) or excluded volume interactions.

There are two ways to describe polymer stretching: the stress and the strain ensemble. In the stress ensemble, an external force is applied to the ends of the chain. The strength of this force is fixed to $\pm f$ but the ends are able to move freely. One can then calculate the mean end-to-end distance $\langle h(F) \rangle$. It is given by [39]

$$\frac{\langle h(F) \rangle}{h_{\max}} \approx \coth(F) - \frac{1}{F} \tag{9}$$

For $F \gg 1$,

$$\frac{\langle h(F) \rangle}{h_{\max}} \simeq 1 - \frac{1}{F} \tag{10}$$

where $F = fb/k_BT$ is the scaled force. Note that for $F \gg 1$, $\langle h \rangle$ tends to $h_{\max} = Nb$. A polymer in the strain ensemble has it ends fixed in space and the force felt by the ends F(h) is measured. We do not discuss the strain ensemble here.

To understand the stretching of real chains, one must incorporate excluded volume interactions, i.e., those interactions which prohibit any two monomers from occupying the same volume of space. Excluded volume interactions tend to swell the polymer compared to the FJC model. Inclusion of excluded volume in theoretical calculations is highly non-trivial. The MD simulations implicitly include all of the aforementioned effects and allow us to analyze chain stretching with excluded volume and hydrodynamics.

The stretching of single polymer chains is classified by four distinct regimes. Figure 11 illustrates these four regimes along with the associated scaling relationships for the mean squared end-to-end distance. We have successfully used Molecular Dynamics simulations to investigate and recover known force extension relationships of single isolated polymers in the strong stretching regime of the stress ensemble, i.e., Figure 11 c). We have also determined the difference between the stress and strain ensembles along with examining the relaxation of a polymer following the removal of the forces $\pm F$. In the latter case, hydrodynamics leads to highly nontrivial effects.

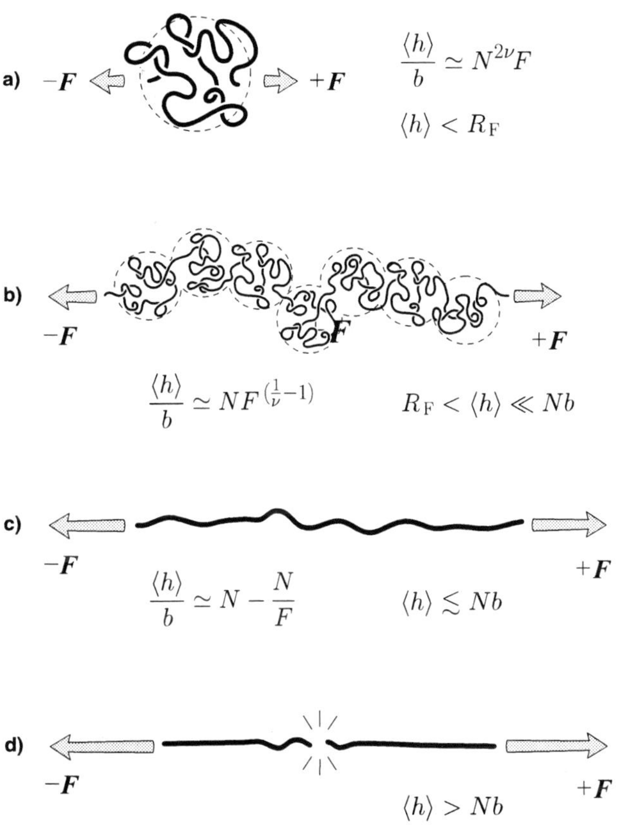

Figure 11. *Illustration of the four stretching regimes. a) The entropy of the polymer is able to keep both ends inside the Flory radius R_F. The forces applied to the polymer are too small to substantially deform it. This regime acts like an entropic spring and $\langle h^2\rangle/b$ scales as $N^{6/5}$ compared to N^1 for the FJC. b) The second regime is referred to as the Pincus regime. It corresponds to a stronger force which stretches the polymer beyond R_F. The polymer can then be treated as a series of "blobs"; the inside of the blobs is considered as a real chain while blobs are almost perfectly aligned. This regime predicts $\langle h\rangle \simeq F^{2/3}$ in 3 dimensions, but $\langle h\rangle \simeq N^1$ like the FJC model. c) In this regime the polymer is stretched to nearly full extension. We can treat it as an ideal chain since it is highly improbable that non-consecutive beads will interact with one another. d) The last regime occurs when one goes beyond an end-to-end distance of Nb. At this extension a polymer would be inclined to break into two subchains.*

2.6 Planar Perturbation in a Lennard-Jones Fluid

The present study is intended to examine a planar perturbation taking place in a Lennard-Jones fluid in terms of velocity, diffusion and absorption. There are several dissipation mechanisms like viscosity, heat conduction and relaxation taking place in a fluid. They are responsible for the amplitude reduction of sound waves. This phenomenon is different from the attenuation which takes place in a spherical wave field for example, which is a pure geometrical effect. As a result no energy is actually lost; instead it is spread over a larger area.

In our simulations a planar perturbation is propagated along the x-axis. Two different ways have been employed to simulate a planar perturbation. The first technique consists in displacing a plane of particles perpendicular to the x-axis by 0.3σ. The thickness of the plane is also 0.3σ. The second way is by giving an impulse to particles belonging to a plane of the same width. The first technique leads to an increase of both the kinetic and potential energy whereas the second produces an increase only in the kinetic energy. In both cases there will be a slight increase in the temperature of the system.

We have calculated the displacement amplitudes of fluid particles at different distances in the x direction from the perturbation source. To do so we have averaged the displacement amplitudes over all the atoms in planes of width 0.3σ along the x direction. Figure 12 shows the displacement amplitude profiles for each plane. The curves present a quasi-symmetrical bell-shaped distribution with a decreasing maximum as x increases. The width of the distribution increases as the perturbation moves away from the source. This indicates that the perturbation diffuses along its trajectory. The diffusing tail becomes more and more pronounced when one is far from the source. As noted earlier, the diffusion is due to the dissipation taking place in the fluid. At a microscopic level the dissipation can be interpreted as a slow redistribution of the perturbation energy among all the particles.

Although the planes are equally spaced, the maxima in Figure 12 are not, leading to an apparent non-constant velocity of the perturbation. That is why we cannot compute the perturbation velocity by a simple peak to peak distance measurement. These distributions can be fitted with the well known Gaussian distribution

$$\langle \Delta x(D,x,v,t)\rangle \sim \frac{1}{\sqrt{Dt}} \exp\left(-\frac{(x-vt)^2}{4Dt}\right) \qquad (11)$$

where D is the diffusion coefficient of the plane and v its velocity. From Eqn. (11) we can derive the arrival time of the maximum amplitude

$$t_{\max}(x) = \frac{D}{2v^2}\left[2\sqrt{\frac{1}{4}+x^2\frac{v^2}{D^2}}-1\right] \qquad (12)$$

We can approximate relation (12) for two extreme values of x. When $x \gg D/2v$, $t_{max}(x)$ can be expressed by $t_{max} \sim x/v$, and the peak is moving with the same velocity as the perturbation. Near the source, i.e., at $x \simeq 0$,

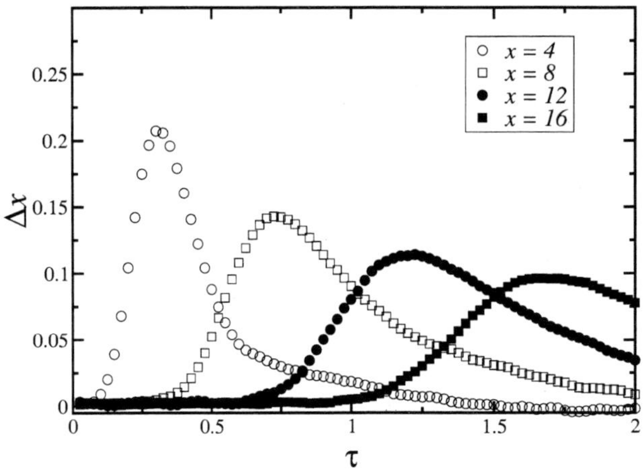

Figure 12. *Displacement amplitudes Δx of the perturbation at various positions from the source as a function of time τ. This simulations is carried out in a cube with $L = 41.8$ and reduced temperature $T^* = 1.1$.*

$t_{max} \sim x^2/2D$ and the peak movement is dominated by diffusion. We are currently looking at the measurement of fluid viscosity, the solvent diffusivity and the speed of sound using this novel approach. Our next step is to examine the effects of walls and polymers on this propagation phenomenon.

3 Conclusions and Remarks

With this survey of current projects, we have both illustrated the versatility of the Molecular Dynamics method to examine a wide variety of phenomena related to polymers in microenvironments and the scope of the research which our group is undertaking. We have hopefully illustrated the use of MD simulations in this regard.

4 Acknowledgements

The authors would like to thank the Natural Sciences and Engineering Research Council of Canada (NSERC) for a Research Grant to GWS. MK and SG also thank NSERC for a postgraduate scholarship and a postdoctoral fellowship respectively. MK, YG and FT thank the University of Ottawa for scholarships. YT would like to thank Materials Manufacturing Ontario (MMO-EMK) for funding. We would also like to acknowledge computational resources provided by the High Performance Computing Virtual Laboratory (HPCVL) and C3.ca.

References

1. R. G. Larson. Monte carlo simulation of amphiphilic systems in two and three dimensions. *J. Chem. Phys.*, 89(9):1642–1650, 1988.
2. R. G. Larson, L. Scriven, and H. T. Davis. Monte carlo simulation of model amphiphile–oil–water systems. *J. Chem. Phys.*, 83(5):2411–2420, 1985.
3. K. Zahn, R. Lenke, and G. Menke. Friction coefficient of rod-like chains of spheres at very low reynolds numbers. i. experiment. *J. Phys. II France*, 4:555–560, 1994.
4. K. Kremer and G. Grest. Molecular dynamics simulation for polymers in the presence of a heat bath. *Physical Review A*, 33(5):3628–3631, 1986.
5. K. Kremer, G. S. Grest, and I. Carmesan. Crossover from rouse to reptation dynamics: A molecular dynamics simulation. *Phys. Rev. Letters*, 61(5):566–569, 1988.
6. D. C. Rapaport. *The Art of Molecular Dynamics Simulation.* Cambridge University Press, 1995.
7. D. C. Rapaport. Molecular dynamics study of a polymer chain in solution. *J. Chem. Phys.*, 71(5):3299–3303, 1979.
8. K. Kremer and G. S. Grest. Dynamics of entagled linear polymer melts: A molecular dynamics simulation. *J. Chem. Phys*, 92(8):5057–5086, 1990.
9. M. P. Allen and D. J. Tildesley. *Computer Simulations of Liquids*. Oxford Science Publications, Oxford, 4th edition, 1987.
10. S. J. Plimpton and B. A. Hendrickson. *Parallel Computing in Computational Chemistry*, chapter Parallel Molecular Dynamics Algorithms for Simulation of Molecular Systems, pages 114–132. American Chemical Society, Symposium Series 592, 1995.
11. M. Muthukumar. Translocation of a confined polymer through a hole. *Physical Review E*, 86(14):3188–3191, 2001.
12. M. Muthukumar. Polymer translocation through a hole. *Macromolecules*, 111(22):10371–10374, 1999.
13. J. K. Kasianowicz, E. Brandin, D. Branton, and D. W. Deamer. Characterization of individual polynucleotide molcules using a membrance channel. *Proc. Natl. Acad. Sci. USA*, 93:13770–13773, 1996.
14. Jeffrey Chuang, Yacov Kantor, and Mehran Kardar. Anomalous dynamics of translocation. *Physical Review E*, 65:011802, 2001.
15. O. B. Bakajin, T. A. J. Duke, C. F. Chou, S. S. Chan, R. H. Austin, and E. C. Cox. Electrohydrodynamic stretching of dna in confined environments. *Phys. Rev. Letters*, 80(12):2737–2740, 1998.
16. G. K. Batchelor. Slender-body theory for particles of abitrary cross section in stokes flow. *J. Fluid Mech.*, 44(3):307–312, 1970.
17. A. Meunier. Friction coefficient of rod-like chains of spheres at very low reynolds numbers. ii. numerical simulations. *J. Phys. II France*, 4:561–565, 1994.
18. A. E. Barron, H. W. Harvey, and D. S. Soane. A transient entanglement coupling mechanism for dna separation by capillary electrophoresis in ultradilute polymer solutions. *Electrophoresis*, 15:597–615, 1994.
19. B. Braun, H. W. Blanch, and J. M. Prausnitz. Capillary electrophoresis of dna restriction fragments: Effect of polymer properties. *Electrophoresis*, 18:1994–1997, 1997.
20. F. Han, B. H. Huynh, Y. Ma, and B. Lin. High–efficiency dna separation by capillary electrophoresis in a polymer solution with ultralow viscosity. *Anal. Chem*, 71(13):2385–2389, 1999.
21. P. S. Doyle, J. Bibette, A. Bancaud, and J. Viovy. Self–assembled magnetic matrices for dna separation chips. *Science*, 295(22):2828–2831, 2002.
22. P. André, D. Long, and A. Ajdari. Polyelectrolyte/post collisions during electrophoresis: Influence of hydrodynamics. *Eur. Phys. J. B*, 4(1):307–312, 1998.
23. E. M. Sevick and D. R. M. Williams. Long lived states in electrophoresis: Collision of a polymer chain with two or

more obstacles. *Euro. Phys. Letters*, 56(4):529–535, 2001.

24. W. B. Russel, D. A. Saville, and W. R. Schowalter. *Colloidal Dispersions*. Cambridge University Press, 1989.
25. S. Griffin and R. E. Majors. Fused-silica capillary – the story behind the technology. *Lc Gc N. Am.*, 20:928–938, 2002.
26. J. P. Gleeson. Electroosmotic flows with random zeta potential. *J. Colloid Interface Sci.*, 249:217–226, 2002.
27. C. L. Rice and R. Whitehead. Elektrokinetic flow in a narrow capillary. *J. Chem. Phys.*, 69:4017–4024, 1965.
28. A. T. Conlisk, J. McFerran, Z. Zheng, and D. Hansford. Mass transfer and flow in electrically charged micro- and nanochannels. *Anal. Chem.*, 74:2139–2150, 2002.
29. P. Dutta and A. Beskok. Analytical solution of time periodic electroosmotic flows: Analogies to stokes' second problem. *Anal. Chem.*, 73:5097–5102, 2001.
30. P. Dutta and A. Beskok. Analytical solution of combined eloectoossmotic/pressure driven flows in two-dimensional straight channels: Finite debye layer effects. *Anal. Chem.*, 73:1979–1986, 2001.
31. S. Z. Qian and H. H. Bau. A chaotic electroosmotic stirrer. *Anal. Chem.*, 74:3616–3625, 2002.
32. E. A. S. Doherty, R. J. Meagher, M. N. Albarghouthi, and A. E. Barron. Microchannel wall coatings for protein separations by capillary and chip electrophoresis. *Electrophoresis*, 24:34–54, 2003.
33. M. Deserno and C. Holm. How to mesh up ewald sums. i. a theoretical and numerical comparison of various particle mesh routines. *J. Chem. Phys.*, 109:7678–7693, 1998.
34. M. Deserno and C. Holm. How to mesh up ewald sums. ii. an accurate error estimate for the particle-particle-particle-mesh algorithm. *J. Chem. Phys.*, 109:7694–7701, 1998.
35. C. Sagui and T. A. Darden. Molecular dynamics simulations of biomolecules: Long-range electrostatic effects. *Annu. Rev. Biophys. Biomolec. Struct.*, 28:155–179, 1999.
36. P.-G. de Gennes. *Scaling Concepts in Polymer Physics*. Cornel University Press, Ithaca, 1979.
37. M. Doi and S. F. Edwards. *The Theory of Polymer Dynamics*. Oxford Science Publications, New York, 1986.
38. I. Teraoka. *Polymer Solution: An Introduction to Physical Properties*. John Wiley & Sons, Inc., New York, 2002.
39. G. W. Slater, S. J. Hubert, and G. I. Nixon. Construction of approximate entropic forces for finitely extensible nonlinear elastic (fene) polymers. *Macromolecular Theory and Simulation*, 3:695–704, 1994.

Ab initio study of the electronic and structural properties of $CsSnI_3$ perovskite

Jean-François Chabot, Michel Côté, Jean-François Brière [a]

[a] Département de physique et Groupe de recherche en physique et technologie des couches minces (GCM), Université de Montréal, C. P. 6128 Succursale Centre-ville, Montréal (Québec) H3C 3J7, Canada,
email: michel.cote@umontreal.ca

The $CsSnI_3$ crystal belongs to an interesting class of semiconducting perovskite which is currently used in thin-film field-effect transistor made of organics-inorganics hybrid compounds. The benefit of using hybrid compounds resides in their ability to combine the advantage of these two classes of compounds: the high mobility of inorganic materials and the ease of processing of organic materials. In spite of the growing attention of this new material, very little is known about the electronic and structural properties of the inorganic part of this compounds. The $CsSnI_3$ is known to adopt 3 crystalline phases depending on the temperature: cubic (α-phase, $T_\alpha > 426K$), tetragonal (β-phase, $351K < T_\beta \leq 426K$) and orthorhombic (γ-phase, $T_\gamma \leq 351K$). We have calculated the electronic properties for these 3 phases within the frame work of density functional theory where a generalized gradient approximation was used to represent the exchange and correlation energy of the electrons. The calculations of the band structures show an increase of the band gap as the symmetry of the structure is reduced from the α to γ phases. All the calculations were carry out using the Abinit code and details of these calculations will be presented.

Le cristal de $CsSnI_3$ appartient à une classe intéressante de pérovskites semiconducteurs présentement utilisée dans les transistors à effet de champ basés sur des couches minces de composés hybrides organiques-inorganiques. L'avantage de ces composés hybrides tient à ce qu'ils combinent les qualités de ces deux classes de composés : la forte mobilité des inorganiques et la simplicité du procédé associée aux organiques. En dépit de l'attention croissante que l'on porte à ces matériaux, très peu de choses sont connues quant à la structure électronique de la partie inorganique. On sait que le $CsSnI_3$ adopte trois structures cristallines selon la température : cubique (phase α, $T_\alpha > 426K$), tétragonale (phase β, $351K < T_\beta \leq 426K$) et orthorhombique (phase γ, $T_\gamma \leq 351K$). Nous avons calculé la structure électronique pour ces trois phases dans le cadre de la théorie de la fonctionnelle de densité, où une approximation du gradient généralisée a été utilisée pour tenir compte des termes d'échange et de corrélation. Les calculs montrent une augmentation de la bande interdite quand la symétrie de la structure est réduite de la phase α à la phase γ. Tous les calculs ont été effectués avec le code Abinit *et les détails en sont présentés.*

1 Introduction

The family of perovskite crystals (ABX_3) is an interesting class of material which exhibit a vast range of physical properties (superconductivity, magnetoresistance, ferroelectric, ...)[1]. A new application for the perovskite is found in hybrid organics-inorganics material which was recently used in thin-film field-effect transistors [2] [3]. This hybrid compound is made of a layered perovskite which is attached by organic molecules on each side as showed in figure 1. This hybrid compound has the potential to combine the high mobility of inorganic crystal and the ease of processing of the organic compound. However, as reported by Kagan *et al.* [2], the measured mobility of the hybrid compound $(C_6H_5C_2H_4NH_3)_2SnI_4$ was found to be 0.6 $cm^2V^{-1}s^{-1}$ which should be compared with the 3D hybrid cubic perovskite $CH_3NH_3SnI_3$ mobility of 50 $cm^2V^{-1}s^{-1}$, i.e. the layered structure has a mobility 100 times lower. As a first step in order to understand the low mobility in the layered hybrid compound, we will study the electronic and structural properties of perovskite $CsSnI_3$. We choose $CsSnI_3$ instead of $CH_3NH_3SnI_4$ for the following reasons:

- Both belong to the same class of semiconducting perovskite halides [4]. This mean that their electronic and structural behaviors should be quite similar.
- The role of the cation Cs^{+1} and $(CH_3NH_3)^{+1}$ is essentially in donating their electron to the system.
- The Cs has only one valence electron compared to 15 for the CH_3NH_3.
- Only one atom need to be treated for the Cs instead of 3 different atoms for the CH_3NH_3. Furthermore, the molecule CH_3NH_3 decreases the symmetry of the crystal which would complicate the interpretation of our calculations.

In doing so, we will make the *ab initio* calculations much faster and simpler to analyse.

The perovskite structure ABX_3 (in our case A=Cs, B=Sn and X=I) is composed of two cations (A and B) and one anion (X). In the cubic structure the cation A is placed at the 8 corners of the cube and the cation B is placed at the center surrounded by 6 anions X at the face centers of the cube forming a regular octahedron around the cation B (see figure 2).

The purpose of this discussion will be to describe the *ab initio* calculations, to compare experimental and theoretical data, to compute and analyse the electronic band structures for the 3 structural phases of $CsSnI_3$, and to investigate the phase transition between the α and the β phases using the phonon band structure.

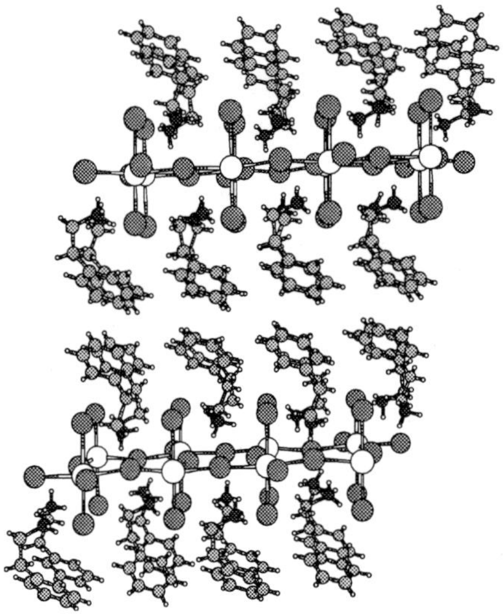

Figure 1. Organic-inorganic hybrid $(C_6H_5C_2H_4NH_3)_2SnI_4$ molecule

2 Computational Method

The results were obtained with the help of an *ab initio* method based on density functional theory (DFT) [5] [6] [7]. We use the Abinit code (www.abinit.org) [8] for all the calculations. Only the valence electrons are included explicitly and the effects of the core electrons are integrated in the pseudopotentials employed. The electronic wavefunctions are described by a plane wave basis set up to an energy cutoff of 30 Hartree and dense k-point grids were used to garanty convergence to better than 0.5 mHa/atom (for the α-phase: 8x8x8, β-phase: 6x6x6, and for γ-phase: 4x4x4, all shifted). Non-linear core correction was included for the alkaline atom. The exchange-correlation (xc) functional GGA (Generalized Gradient approximation) of Perdew-Burke-Ernzerhof was employed[9]. Response function calculations were also performed to get the phonon band structure.

The DFT is a method based on *ab initio* calculation initially proposed by Hohenberg, Kohn and Sham [10] [11] (1964-1965) which has the advantage to not rely on any experimental parameter. The idea of this method is to replace the interacting electronic system by a fictitious non-interacting electronic system which gives the same electronic density as the interacting system. The xc potential affecting the non-interacting electronic system can be obtained from the xc energy which is only a functional of the electronic density. However, no exact functional exists but many approximative functionals have been developed (LDA(local density approximation), GGA, ...).

The Kohn-Sham equations start in writing the Schrödinger's equation in the following form:

$$\left(-\frac{\hbar^2}{2m}\nabla^2 + V_{ion}(r) + V_H(r) + V_{xc}(r)\right)\Psi_j(r) = \varepsilon_j\Psi_j(r) \quad (1)$$

such that

$$n(r) = \sum_{j=occupied\ states} \Psi_j^*(r)\Psi_j(r). \quad (2)$$

Here $V_{ion}(r)$ is the ionic potential, $V_H(r)$ is the Hartree potential and $V_{xc}(r)$ is the xc potential obtained using some approximate functional. The last 2 potentials can be calculated knowing the density as shown in the following equations:

$$V_H(r) = e^2 \int \frac{n(r')}{\mid r - r' \mid} dr', \quad (3)$$

$$V_{xc}(r) = \frac{\delta E_{xc}[n(r)]}{\delta n(r)}, \quad (4)$$

where the form of $E_{xc}[n(r)]$ would depend on the chosen functional. For a given density $n(r)$ (call it the initial density $n_i(r)$), we first calculate V_H and V_{xc} and then find the eigenstates in solving the Schrödinger's equation (eq. 1). From the eigenstates $\Psi_j(r)$, the density $n(r)$ (call it the final density $n_f(r)$) is calculated using equation 2. Then, we pose $n_{i+1}(r) = n_f(r)$ and iterate the procedure until the initial and the final density converge to a common value, a procedure to assure self-consistency in the problem. This method gives in general results in excellent agreement with the experimental data such as lattice parameters, band structure, atomization energies, etc... However, the energy gaps from the band structures calculated with the DFT using the xc functional GGA or LDA are known to underestimate the experimental band gap but the result can be used to predict trends within a single family of compound.

3 Calculations

3.1 α, β and γ structures of the CsSnI3

The perovskite $CsSnI_3$ is known to exist in 3 different phases depending on the temperature [12]. At high temperature ($T > 426K$), the $CsSnI_3$ adopts a cubic structure (α-phase) as presented in the previous section (see figure 2). With decreasing temperature ($T < 426K$) the cubic structure change to a tetragonal structure (β-phase)(see figure 3). This structure is characterized by the rotation of the octahedra composed of iodine atoms about the center tin atom in a manner that each octahedron in the xy-plan rotates in opposite directions as we will show in subsection 3.3. Decreasing the temperature further ($T < 351K$), the tetragonal structure changes to an orthorhombic structure (γ-phase)(see figure 4). In this structure the rigidity of the octahedra is not conserved and the relative position of the cesiums atoms are distorted.

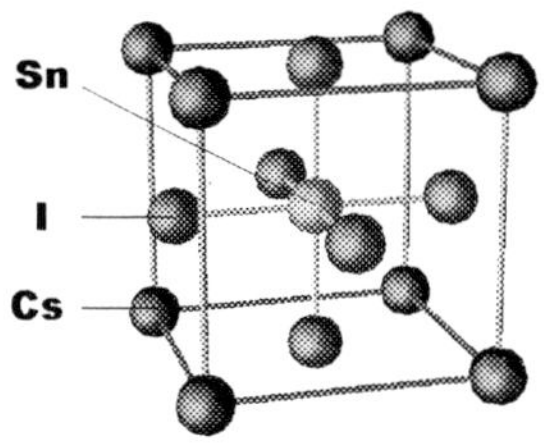

Figure 2. α-phase of the $CsSnI_3$

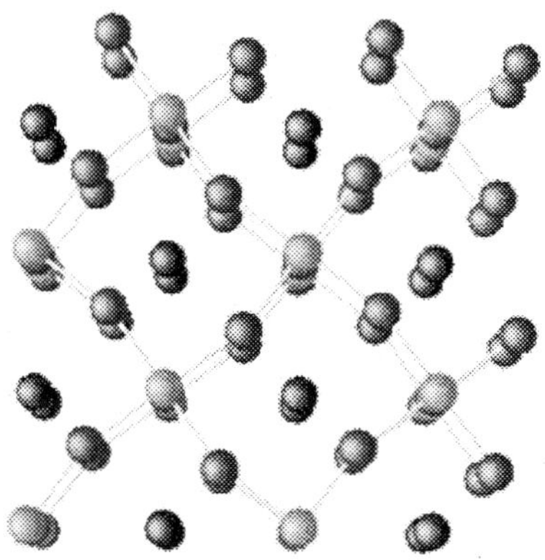

Figure 3. β-phase of the $CsSnI_3$

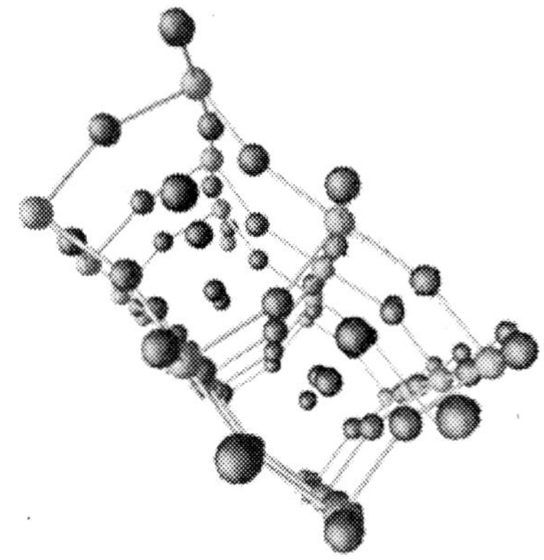

Figure 4. γ-phase of the $CsSnI_3$

Table 1
Experimental data [12] versus theoretical data of the lattice parameters and volume of the $CsSnI_3$ structures.

	lattice (exp.) (Å)	V_{exp} (Å^3/mol)	V_{th} (Å^3/mol)
α	a = 6.219	241	245 (+1.8%)
β	a = 8.772 c = 6.261	241	243 (+0.8%)
γ	a = 8.688 b = 8.643 c = 12.378	232	242 (+4.1%)

The figure 5 shows the calculations of the energies (Hartree / basic block of $CsSnI_3$) with respect to the volume for the 3 phases of the perovskite $CsSnI_3$. The γ-phase is represented by the lower curve, i.e. the curve with the smallest energies for a given volume. Since our calculations does not include any thermal motion of the atoms, corresponding essentially to a zero temperature limit, this result shows that the γ-phase is the most stable structure. The α-phase's curve (with the higher energies) and the β-phase's curve (with intermediate energies) represent structure which are stable for $T \neq 0$ where $T_\alpha > T_\beta$. This corresponds to the experimental observations from Yamada *et al.* [12].The volumes that minimize the energies of each phase are presented in table 1.

For the α-phase, all the atom positions are determined by the symmetry of the structure. The β and γ phases have a certain number of internal degrees of freedom which we can evaluate by a structural optimization for a given volume. The experimental atomic coordinations for these 2 phases are presented in table 2. For the β-phase, the c/a ratio is plotted in figure 6 and the internal parameters are plotted in figure 7. For the γ-phase, the c/a and a/b ratios are plotted in figure 8 and the internal parameters are plotted in figure 9. From these figures, the errors on the lattice parameters and the internal parameters are quite acceptable.

Table 2
Atomic coordinates of the β (with space group P4/mbm) and γ (Pnam) phases of the $CsSnI_3$.

	Atom	Position[1]	x	y	z
β	Cs	2d(mmm)	0	0.5	0
	Sn	2b(4/m)	0	0	0.5
	I(1)	2a(4/m)	0	0	0
	I(2)	4h(mm)	I_x	I_y	0.5
γ	Cs	4c(m)	Cs-x	Cs-y	0.25
	Sn	4b($\bar{1}$)	0.5	0	0
	I(1)	4c(m)	I(1)-x	I(1)-y	0.25
	I(2)	8d(1)	I(2)-x	I(2)-y	I(2)-z

From the curves of each phase we have performed the calculation of the bulk modulus ($B = -\frac{1}{V}\frac{\partial^2 E}{\partial V^2}$). The 3 bulk modulus are quite similar ($\sim$ 8 GPa) which was expected since the structures are nevertheless quite similar. No experimental data on the bulk modulus are available to

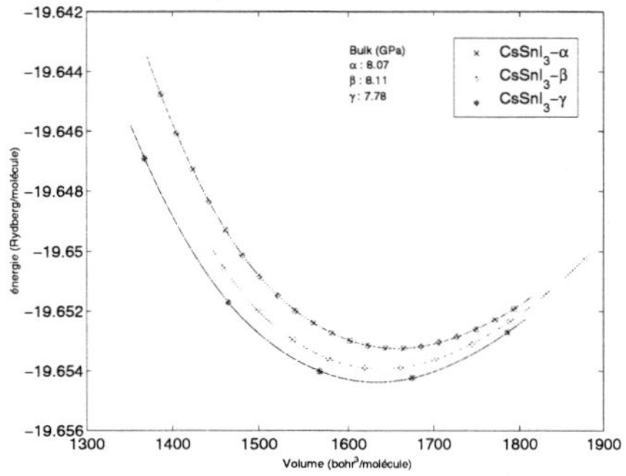

Figure 5. Energy vs Volume of the $CsSnI_3$ structures

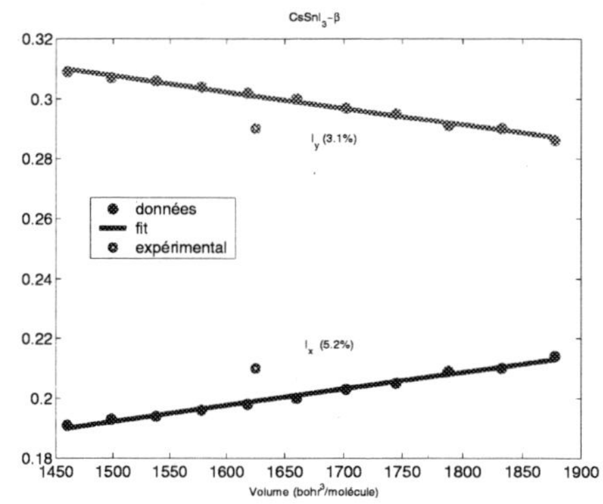

Figure 7. internal parameters of the $CsSnI_3$-β

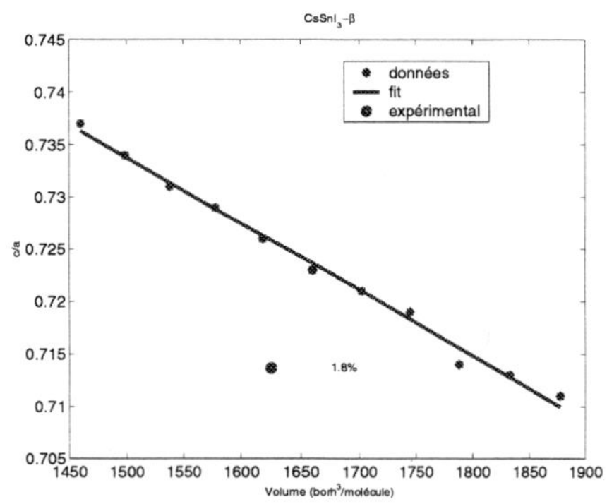

Figure 6. ratio c/a of the $CsSnI_3$-β

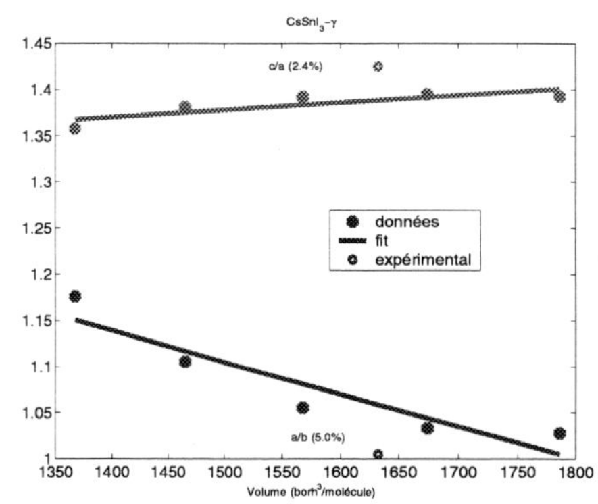

Figure 8. ratio a/b and c/a of the $CsSnI_3$-γ

make a comparison.

3.2 Band Structure

The band structure for the relaxed α-phase is shown in figure 10. The α-phase behaves like a semiconductor with a small gap ($E_{gap} = 0.434eV$) located at **R** ($\frac{1}{2}\frac{1}{2}\frac{1}{2}$) in the Brillouin zone. The conduction bands at that point are three fold degenerated whereas the valence band is a singlet. As we decrease the volume, the band gap decreases as showed in figure 14. For a certain volume the structure become metallic (see figure 11) and we observe, still at **R** point, that the last valence band joins with the two first conduction bands to form a triplet. The third conduction band now becomes a singlet. To explain this behavior, we have to know first that group theory of cubic system implies that the bands cannot be degenerated more than 3 times. This is why the triplet and the singlet cannot mix. For the semiconductor structure, when we look at the **R** $\rightarrow$ Γ direction, the symmetry group is smaller and the triplet split in a doublet and a singlet. Near the **R** point, the valence band singlet and the conduction band singlet have the same symmetry, and group theory postulate that such band cannot mix. Then, when we decrease the volume, the last valence and the first conduction band join each other, the two singlet repulse each other and the doublet becomes mixed with the singlet of the valence band showing a metallic form. The band structures for the relaxed structure of the β-phase and the γ-phase are showed in figure 12 and 13 respectively. We find a gap of 0.641 eV for the β-phase and 0.885 eV for the γ-phase. So we can observe that when we decrease the symmetry of the $CsSnI_3$, the gap becomes larger.

We have also calculated the gap of each structure with respect to the volume (figure 14). In general, for a given volume, the α-phase has the smallest gap and the γ-phase has the largest gap. The α-phase and the β-phase become metallic for a certain volume, which is not the case for the γ-phase.

3.3 Phonon band structure

The phonon band structure is shown in figure 15. Negative frequencies are used to represent imaginary frequencies. Such frequency are present at **M** ($\frac{1}{2}\frac{1}{2}0$) and **R** points and these correspond to instabilities in the α-phase as expected from the known phase transitions. We know that at T = 0K the β-phase and γ-phase are preferred to the α-phase, so we expect the α structure to be unstable. We have visualized the displacement vector at **M** and **R** points to distinguish which mode corresponds to the phase transi-

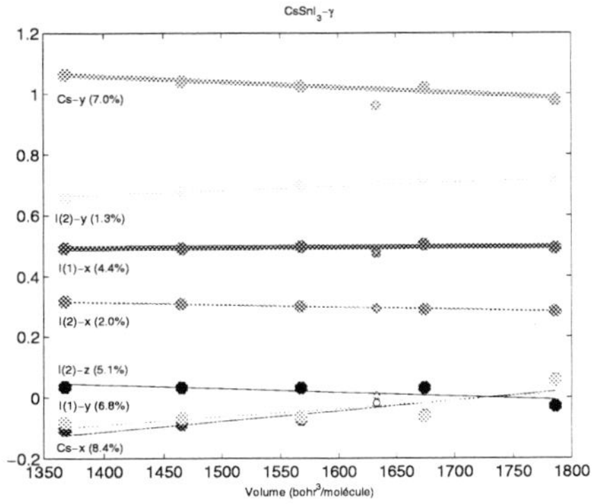

Figure 9. internal parameters of the $CsSnI_3$-γ

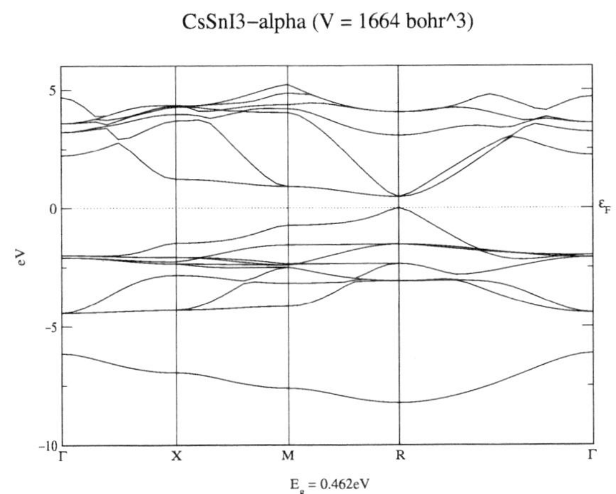

Figure 10. Bands structure of the $CsSnI_3$-α

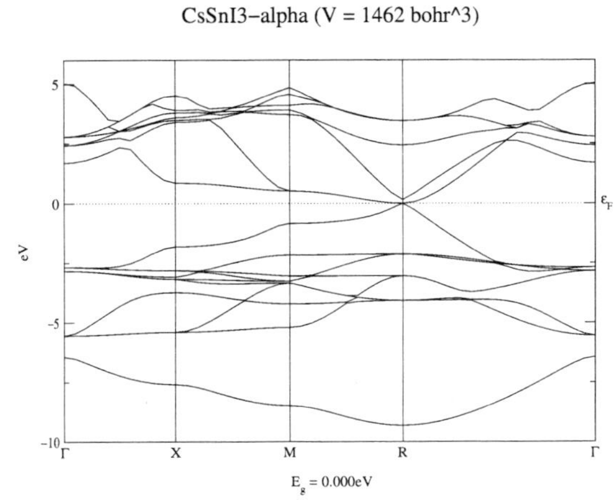

Figure 11. Bands structure of the $CsSnI_3$-α

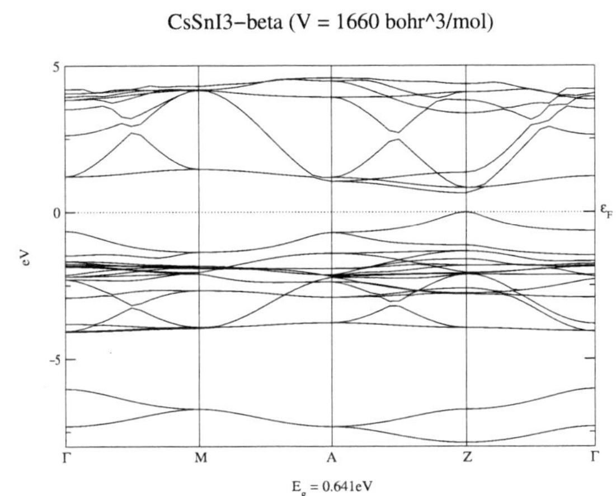

Figure 12. Bands structure of the $CsSnI_3$-β

tion to the β-phase.

In visualizing the displacement vector at M point we found that this corresponds to the transition to the β-phase. It looks like a rotation around the z-axis centered on the Sn atom which affects the iodine on the xy-plane. But for a given Sn, its nearest neighbors must rotate inversely because of the relative phase between the periodic cells given by the Bloch functions at **M** point. We can see this rotation in figure 16. Note that the β-phase preserve the rigidity of the octahedra formed by the iodines around the Sn atoms.

Now the visualization of the 3 displacement vectors at **R** point correspond exactly to the same vectors than at **M** point, but this time the rotation is about the 3 axes x, y and z. On a simple cubic first Brillouin Zone, there is 12 **M** points, but they are not all equivalent. There is 3 groups of 4 equivalent **M** points which each corresponds to rotation about one axis. Then the **R** point doesn't seem to correspond to the γ-phase transition because the γ structure can't be explained by using only the rotation about the Sn atom. Furthermore, the γ-phase doesn't respect the rigidity of the octahedra. The only way to explain the transition from the β-phase to the γ-phase is to plot the phonon band structure of the β structure and check the displacement vectors at the instable point.

4 Conclusion

We have showed in this article that the DFT calculations give good prediction on the lattice parameters of the $CsSnI_3$ and we can also predict the phase transition from the α-phase to the β-phase in computing the phonon band structure. The main purpose of this paper was to determine the electronic properties for the 3 structures of the $Cain_3$. We found that for high symmetric structure (α-phase) the band gap is smaller than the β-phase which is also smaller than the γ-phase.

Acknowledgments

This work has been supported by grants from the Natural Sciences and Engineering Research Council of Canada

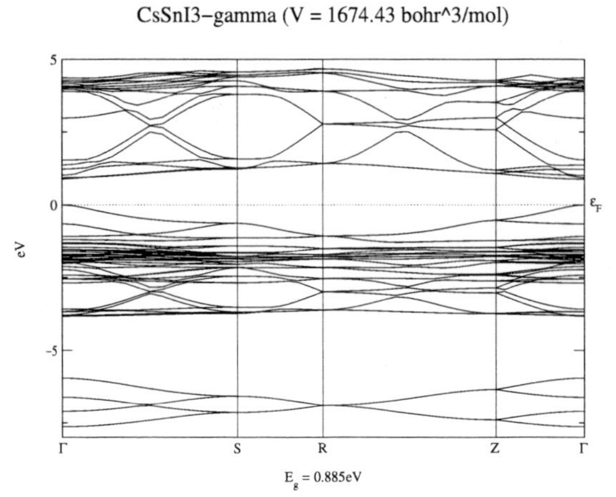

Figure 13. Bands structure of the $CsSnI_3$-γ

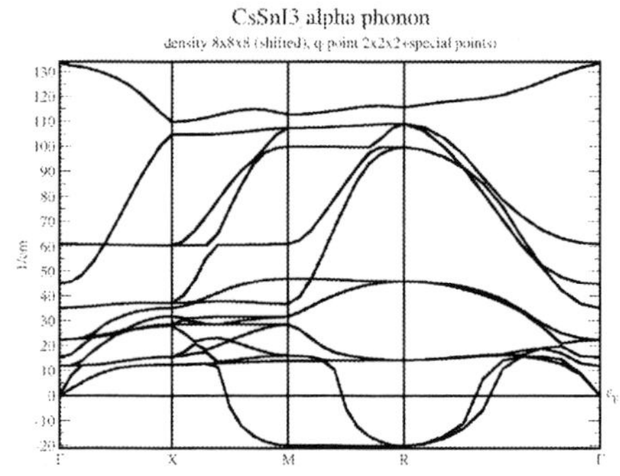

Figure 15. Phonon bands structure of the $CsSnI_3$-α

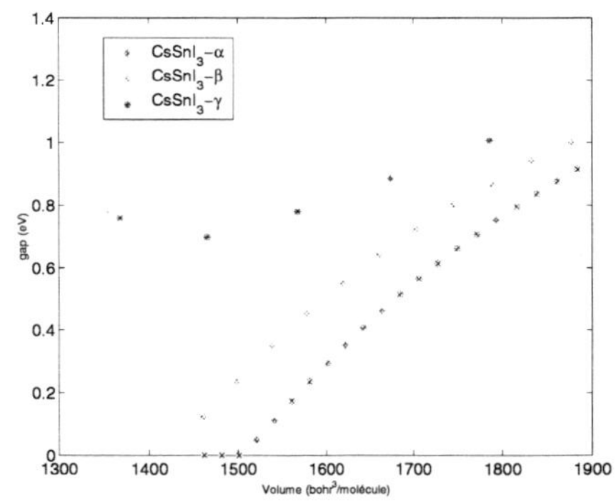

Figure 14. Bands structure of the $CsSnI_3$-γ

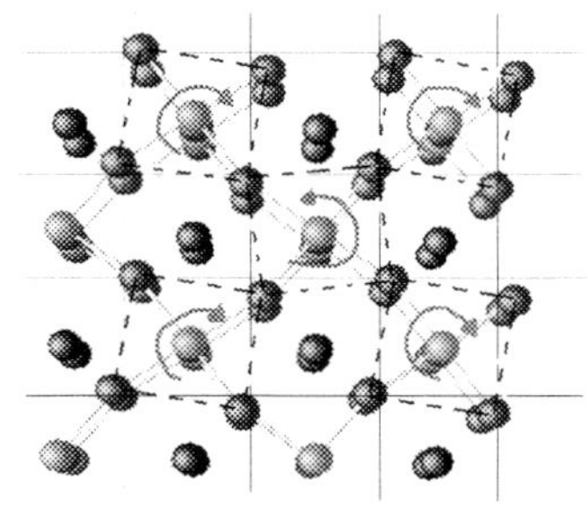

Figure 16. Rotation of the tin's atoms for the β-phase

(NSERC) and the Fonds québécois de la recherche sur la nature et les technologies (FQRNT). The computational resources were provided by the Réseau québécois de calcul de haute performance (RQCHP).

References

1. N. Mathur and P. Littlewood. Mesoscopic texture in manganites. *Physics Today, p.25*, January 2003.
2. C. R. Kagan, D. B. Mitzi, and C. D. Dimitrakopoulos. Organic-inorganic hybrid materials as semiconducting channels in thin-film field effect transistors. *Science, 286, 945*, 1999.
3. H. Klauk. Molecular electrics on the cheap. *Physics World, 13, 1, 18*, 2000.
4. D. B. Mitzi, C. A. Feild, Z. Schlesinger, and R.B. Laibowitz. Transport, optical, and magnetic properties of the conducting halide perovskite $ch_3nh_3sni_3$. *Journal of Solid State Chemistry, 114, 159*, 1995.
5. N. Argaman and G. Makov. Density functional theory: An introduction. *Am. J. Phys., Vol. 68, No. 1, p.69*, January 2000.
6. H. L. Neal. Density functional theory of one-dimensional two particles systems. *Am. J. Phys., Vol. 66, No. 6, p.512*, June 1998.
7. A. Schindlmayr. Universality of the hohenberg-kohn functional. *Am. J. Phys., Vol. 67, No. 10, p.933*, October 1999.
8. X. Gonze, J.-M. Beuken, R. Caracas, F. Detraux, M. Fuchs, G.-M. Rignanese, L. Sindic, M. Verstraete, G. Zerah, F. Jollet, M. Torrent, A. Roy, M. Mikami, Ph. Ghosez, J.-Y. Raty, and D.C. Allan. First-principles computation of material properties : the abinit software project. *Computational Materials Science 25, 478-492*, 2002.
9. Burke Perdew and Ernzerhof. Generalized gradient approximation made simple. *Phys. Rev. Lett. 77, 3865*, 1996.
10. P. Hohenberg and W. Kohn. Inhomogeneous electron gas. *Phys. Rev. 136, B864*, 1964.
11. W. Kohn and L. J. Sham. Structural phase transitions of the polymorphs of $cssni_3$ by means of rietveld analysis of the x-ray diffraction. *Phys. Rev. 140, A1133*, 1965.
12. K. Yamada, S. Funabiki, H. Horimoto, T. Matsui, T. Okuda, and S. Ichiba. Structural phase transitions of the polymorphs of $cssni_3$ by means of rietveld analysis of the x-ray diffraction. *Chemistry Letters, p.801*, 1991.

A Cluster Method for Spectral Properties of Correlated Electrons

David Sénéchal[a]

[a]Département de physique, Université de Sherbroke, Québec, Canada
David.Senechal@USherbrooke.CA

Some technical aspects of Cluster Perturbation Theory (CPT) are presented. CPT is an approximation scheme for calculating the one-particle Green function of the Hubbard model of interacting electrons on a lattice. It proceeds by (i) dividing the lattice into identical clusters and calculating the Green function by exact diagonalization on a given cluster (ii) extending this Green function to the whole lattice by using Dyson's equation. The exact diagonalization technique for the Hubbard model is explained in some detail. Embedding the cluster in the full lattice is then discussed, and two alternate emdedding schemes are briefly described.

Quelques aspects techniques de la théorie des perturbations inter-amas (CPT) sont présentés. La CPT est une méthode approximative pour le calcul de la fonction de Green à une particule du modèle de Hubbard, qui décrit des électrons en interaction sur un réseau cristallin. Elle procède par (i) dallage du réseau en amas identiques et calcul de la fonction de Green par diagonalisation exacte sur un amas (ii) extension de ce résultat au réseau entier via l'équation de Dyson. La méthode de diagonalisation exacte du modèle de Hubbard est expliquée en détail. L'insertion de l'amas dans le réseau est aussi discutée, et deux méthode d'insertion alternatives sont décrites.

1 Introduction

1.1 Context

The quantum theory of electrons in solids is a complicated many-body problem. Even if we accept that core electrons are well localized within atoms, solving the Schrödinger equation for the outer electrons of every atom in a crystal is impossible and practical approximation schemes must be developed. The most common starting point is the independent-electron approximation : each electron is moving in the average potential created by all the others (including the exchange potential), but they are otherwise independent. In principle, the best approximate solution within this scheme is obtained by solving the Hartree-Fock equations. In practice, one uses even simpler approximations, such as the local density approximation (LDA) of Density Functional Theory (DFT, for a review, see [1]). Calculating the band structure of solids within that approximation has become an almost standard procedure, and very efficient programs are available for this task.

However, the very notion of band structure is approximate. It merely provides a basis of states in terms of which the two-body interaction between electrons is, in some sense, minimal. Basic semiconductor Physics is based largely on this picture. So is our understanding of ordinary metals, provided the residual interactions are taken into account in a perturbative way. The Landau theory of Fermi liquids aims precisely at preserving the physical picture of independent electrons while taking into account the main effects of residual electron-electron interactions [2]. However, in a large class of materials – called strongly correlated – those residual interactions are too strong and the picture of independent electrons breaks down completely (see, e.g., [3]). Such are the high-temperature superconductors, organic conductors, colossal magneto-resistance materials, and so on. Strongly correlated materials are typically very anisotropic (quasi two-dimensional or quasi one-dimensional), because in low dimensions quantum or thermal fluctuations suppress the onset of broken symmetry phases that would otherwise replace the high-temperature metallic phase. The latter evolves instead towards a quantum state poorly described in terms of one-electron states.

1.2 The Hubbard model

The most basic model commonly used to study the behavior of electrons with strong residual interactions in the Hubbard model [4]. It is usually expressed in the Wannier basis and assumes that the residual electrostatic repulsion between electrons is purely local, i.e., felt only between electrons states located on the same atom (or lattice site). The Hamiltonian reads

$$H = -\sum_{i,j,\sigma} t_{ij} c_{i\sigma}^\dagger c_{j\sigma} + U \sum_i n_{i\uparrow} n_{i\downarrow} \tag{1}$$

where $c_{j\sigma}$ annihilates an electron of spin σ ($\uparrow$ or $\downarrow$) in a Wannier state centered on site j of the lattice and $n_{j\sigma} = c_{j\sigma}^\dagger c_{j\sigma}$ is the number of electrons in that state. U is the strength of on-site electrostatic repulsion and t_{ij} is the probability amplitude for an electron to hop from site j to site i. If $U = 0$, this model reduces to the tight-binding description of a band of independent electrons, the dispersion relation being

$$\varepsilon(\mathbf{k}) = \frac{1}{N} \sum_{i,j} t_{ij} \mathrm{e}^{i\mathbf{k}\cdot(\mathbf{r}_i - \mathbf{r}_j)} \tag{2}$$

where N is the number of lattice sites ($N \to \infty$) and $\mathbf{r}_i$ the position of site i. On the other hand, when U is large compared to t_{ij}, the strong repulsion suppresses states with more than one electron per site, and this favors an insulating state, at least when the system contains one electron per site on average (density $n = 1$). Thus, the degree of correlations can be tuned by varying the ratio U/t_{ij}.

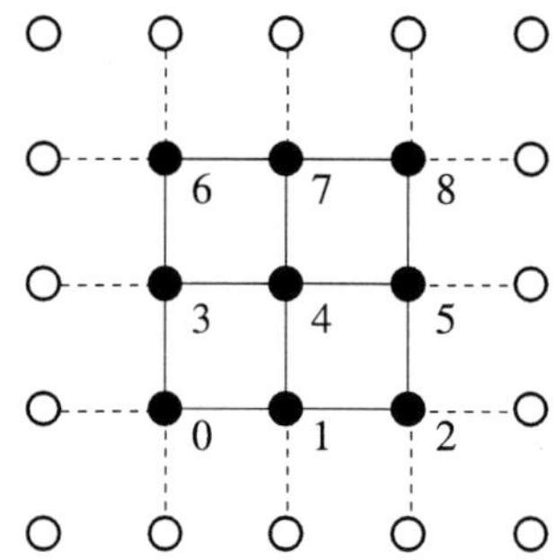

Figure 1. An example of 9-site cluster on a square lattice. The numbering of sites used in practice is illustrated. Full lines indicate intra-cluster hoppings, and dashed-line inter-cluster hoppings.

1.3 Cluster Perturbation Theory

In this paper we will explain in some detail the numerical aspects of an approximate method for calculating the one-particle properties of the Hubbard model. This method, called Cluster Perturbation Theory (or CPT [5,6]) is based on the exact diagonalization of the Hubbard model on a small cluster of sites (typically a dozen), and on a particular way to extend the results of a cluster to the full infinite lattice. We will restrict the discussion to some methodological aspects that are not covered in detail in [5,6].

The quantity we wish to calculate is the one-particle Green function $G(\mathbf{k}, z)$, defined as

$$\begin{aligned} G(\mathbf{k}, z) &= G_e(\mathbf{k}, z) + G_h(\mathbf{k}, z) \\ G_e(\mathbf{k}, z) &= \langle\Omega|c(\mathbf{k})\frac{1}{z - H + E_0}c^\dagger(\mathbf{k})|\Omega\rangle \\ G_h(\mathbf{k}, z) &= \langle\Omega|c^\dagger(\mathbf{k})\frac{1}{z + H - E_0}c(\mathbf{k})|\Omega\rangle \end{aligned} \tag{3}$$

where $c(\mathbf{k})$ and $c^\dagger(\mathbf{k})$ respectively annihilate and create an electron of wavevector $\mathbf{k}$ (the spin index of these operators is suppressed). E_0 is the ground-state energy. From the Green function many other quantities can be derived, such as the spectral function

$$A(\mathbf{k}, \omega) = -2 \lim_{\eta \to 0^+} \operatorname{Im} G(\mathbf{k}, \omega + i\eta) \tag{4}$$

which is the probability for an electron of momentum $\hbar\mathbf{k}$ to have an energy $\hbar\omega$. The negative-frequency part of this function (coming from G_h) is experimentally accessible by angle-resolved photoemission spectroscopy (ARPES).

Cluster perturbation theory proceeds by first tiling the infinite lattice into identical clusters of L sites ($L \leq 16$; see for instance, Fig. 1. The hopping amplitude of the Hubbard model can then be labelled as t_{ab}^{mn}, where the subscripts refer to sites within a cluster, and the superscripts to clusters. The terms with $m = n$, together with the local interaction of the Hubbard model, define a model local to a given cluster, that can be solved numerically by a suitable exact diagonalization technique, as described in the next section. 'Solved' here means that the real-space Green function

$$\begin{aligned} G_{ab}^{(c)}(z) &= G_{ab,e}^{(c)}(z) + G_{ab,h}^{(c)}(z) \\ G_{ab,e}^{(c)}(z) &= \langle\Omega|c_a\frac{1}{z - H + E_0}c_b^\dagger|\Omega\rangle \\ G_{ab,h}^{(c)}(z) &= \langle\Omega|c_b^\dagger\frac{1}{z + H - E_0}c_a|\Omega\rangle \qquad (5) \end{aligned} \tag{6}$$

is calculated. The superscript (c) stands for 'cluster' : this Green function describes the motion of electrons on a small cluster only.

The hopping terms with $m \neq n$, that connect different clusters, are treated approximately: We write

$$t_{ab}^{mn} = t_{ab}^{(c)}\delta_{mn} + V_{ab}^{mn} \tag{7}$$

where $t_{ab}^{(c)}$ is the hopping amplitude within a cluster, which is accounted for exactly, and V_{ab}^{mn} the remainder, corresponding to inter-cluster hopping. In terms of matrices with indices (a, m) and (b, n), our approximation consists in taking the full Green function to be

$$\hat{G}^{-1} = \hat{G}^{(c)-1} - \hat{V} \tag{8}$$

This can be viewed as the lowest order approximation in a formal perturbation expansion in powers of $|V|/U$, where $|V|$ stands for the typical size of an inter-cluster hopping amplitude [6]. It can also be viewed, more heuristically, as an approximation where the full self-energy $\hat{\Sigma}$ of the model is replaced by the cluster self-energy [7]. Recall that the self-energy is defined by Dyson's equation

$$\hat{G}^{-1} = \hat{G}_0^{-1} - \hat{\Sigma} \tag{9}$$

where $\hat{G}_0$ is the noninteracting Green function ($U = 0$):

$$\hat{G}_0^{-1} = \omega - \hat{t} = \omega - \hat{t}^{(c)} - \hat{V} \tag{10}$$

Applying Dyson's equation to the exact, cluster Green function gives

$$\hat{G}^{(c)-1} = \omega - \hat{t}^{(c)} - \hat{\Sigma}^{(c)} \tag{11}$$

and Eq. (8) may then be written as

$$\hat{G}^{-1} = \hat{G}_0^{-1} - \hat{\Sigma}^{(c)} \tag{12}$$

Eq. (8), or its equivalent form (12), is the basic equations of Cluster Perturbation Theory.

2 Exact Diagonalization

The numerically intensive part of the problem, at least as far as memory is concerned, is the exact diagonalization, i.e. the calculation of $G_{ab}^{(c)}$. We will describe the method used in some detail, even though it is fairly straightforward, because the nuts and bolts, at least applied to the Hubbard model, are not necessarily easy to find in the literature.

2.1 Coding of the states

The first step in the exact diagonalization procedure is to define a coding scheme for the quantum basis states. A basis state may be specified by the occupation number $n_{a\sigma}$ ($= 0$ or 1) of electrons spin σ at the site a ($a = 1, \ldots, L$). Thus the string of $n_{a\sigma}$'s forms the binary representation of a 32-bit unsigned integer (if $L \leq 16$) and represents the state

$$(c_{1\uparrow}^\dagger)^{n_{1\uparrow}} \cdots (c_{L\uparrow}^\dagger)^{n_{L\uparrow}} (c_{1\downarrow}^\dagger)^{n_{1\downarrow}} \cdots (c_{L\downarrow}^\dagger)^{n_{L\downarrow}} |0\rangle \qquad (13)$$

where the order in which the creation operators are applied is a matter of convention, but important.

There are 2^{2L} such states, but not all are relevant, since the Hamiltonian of the Hubbard model is block-diagonal : the number of electrons of a given spin ($N_\uparrow$ and $N_\downarrow$) are conserved quantities, which commute with the Hamiltonian H. The exact diagonalization is to be performed in a sector (i.e. a subspace) of the total Hilbert space with fixed values of $N_\uparrow$ and $N_\downarrow$. The number of states with these fixed values, i.e. the dimension of the relevant sector, is

$$d = \left(\frac{L!}{N_\uparrow!(L-N_\uparrow)!}\right)\left(\frac{L!}{N_\downarrow!(L-N_\downarrow)!}\right) \qquad (14)$$

Note that the ground state $|\Omega\rangle$ of the Hamiltonian generally belongs to the sector $N_\uparrow = N_\downarrow$. The density $n = (N_\uparrow + N_\downarrow)/L$ is fixed in a given calculation; it can only take a limited number of values (although the use of "superclusters" gives us more flexibility in this matter [6]).

Since the number of states is less than 2^{2L}, one needs a lookup table that gives the index of a given state from its binary representation $(n_{1\uparrow} \cdots n_{L\downarrow})$. This table can be deleted as soon as the Hamiltonian matrix has been built, before allocating the Lanczös vectors.

The next step is to construct the Hamiltonian matrix in the chosen sector. The particular structure of the Hubbard model Hamiltonian brings a considerable simplification. Indeed, the Hilbert space is the tensor product of a space of 'up' electrons with a space of 'down' electrons ($\mathcal{H} = \mathcal{H}_\uparrow \otimes \mathcal{H}_\downarrow$), of dimension $d = d_\uparrow d_\downarrow$. The Hamiltonian has the form

$$H = K_\uparrow \otimes 1 + 1 \otimes K_\downarrow + V_{\text{int.}} \qquad (15)$$

where $K_\uparrow$ only acts on the up electrons and $K_\downarrow$ on the down electrons, and where the Coulomb repulsion term $V_{\text{int.}}$ (the second term of (1)) is diagonal in the basis chosen. Thus storing the Hamiltonian in memory is not a problem : the diagonal $V_{\text{int.}}$ is stored (an array of size d), and the kinetic energy K_σ (a matrix having a small fraction of d_σ^2 elements) is stored in sparse form. Constructing this matrix, formally expressed as

$$K = \sum_{a,b} t_{ab} c_a^\dagger c_b \,, \qquad (16)$$

needs some care with the signs. Basically, two states $|\psi\rangle$ and $|\psi'\rangle$ are connected with this matrix if their binary representations $(n_1, n_2, \ldots, n_L)$ (see Eq. (13)) differ at two positions i and j. The matrix element is then $(-1)^{M_{ab}} t_{ab}$, where M_{ab} is the number of occupied sites between a and b, i.e., assuming $a < b$,

$$M_{ab} = \sum_{c=a+1}^{b-1} n_c \qquad (17)$$

For instance, the two states (10010110) and (10011100) with $L = 8$ are connected with the matrix element $+t_{46}$, where the sites are numbered from 0 to $L-1$.

2.2 The Lanczös algorithm

Next, one must apply the exact diagonalization method per se, using the Lanczös algorithm. Calculating the Green function (5) requires a two-step procedure.

2.2.1 *First step: the ground state*

In the first step, the ground state $|\Omega\rangle$ is obtained from two consecutive sequences of Lanczös iterations : the first sequence to find the tridiagonal representation of the Hamiltonian, and the second one to find the ground state itself. The sequence of states built during the Lanczös procedure obey a two-step recursion relation:

$$|\phi_{n+1}\rangle = H|\phi_n\rangle - a_n|\phi_n\rangle - b_n^2|\phi_{n-1}\rangle \qquad (18)$$

where

$$a_n = \frac{\langle\phi_n|H|\phi_n\rangle}{\langle\phi_n|\phi_n\rangle} \qquad b_n^2 = \frac{\langle\phi_n|\phi_n\rangle}{\langle\phi_{n-1}|\phi_{n-1}\rangle} \qquad (19)$$

and we set the initial conditions $b_0 = 0$, $|\phi_{-1}\rangle = 0$. At any given step, only three state vectors are kept in memory (ϕ_{n+1}, ϕ_n and ϕ_{n-1}). In the basis of normalized states $|n\rangle = |\phi_n\rangle/\sqrt{\langle\phi_n|\phi_n\rangle}$, the Hamiltonian has the tridiagonal form

$$H = \begin{pmatrix} a_0 & b_1 & 0 & 0 & \cdots & 0 \\ b_1 & a_2 & b_2 & 0 & \cdots & 0 \\ 0 & b_2 & a_3 & b_3 & \cdots & 0 \\ \vdots & \vdots & \vdots & \vdots & \ddots & \vdots \\ 0 & 0 & 0 & 0 & \cdots & a_N \end{pmatrix} \qquad (20)$$

The initial state $|\phi_0\rangle$ is chosen at random. The iteration sequence terminates when either (i) the lowest eigenvalue of the tridiagonal Hamiltonian converges, (ii) b_n^2 is smaller than a chosen value (e.g. 10^{-14} in double-precision arithmetic) or (iii) the number of iterations has reached a preset maximum (typically a few hundreds). The ground state energy E_0 and the ground state $|\Omega\rangle$ are very well approximated by the lowest eigenvalue and the corresponding eigenvector of that matrix, which are obtained by standard methods. This provides us with the ground state $|\Omega\rangle$ in the reduced basis $\{\phi_n\}$. But we need the ground state in the original basis, and this requires retracing the Lanczös iterations a second time – for the $|\phi_n\rangle$ are not stored in memory – and constructing the ground state progressively at each iteration from the known coefficients $\langle\Omega|\phi_n\rangle$.

2.2.2 *Second step: the Green function*

Once the ground state is known, the second step of the procedure consists in calculating the Green function (5). Because the Hubbard model conserves spin, we need only to consider the creation and annihilation of up-spin electrons. Consider first the case $a = b$ in $G^{(c)}_{aa,e}$. One first calculates the state $|\phi\rangle = c_a^\dagger|\Omega\rangle$, and then

$$G^{(c)}_{aa,e} = \langle\phi|\frac{1}{z - H + E_0}|\phi\rangle \qquad (21)$$

This expression is again calculated using the Lanczös algorithm. A Lanczös sequence is calculated from the initial, normalized state $|\phi_0\rangle = |\phi\rangle/b_0$ where $b_0^2 = \langle\phi|\phi\rangle$. This sequence generates a tridiagonal representation of H, albeit in a different Hilbert space sector : that with $N_\uparrow + 1$ up-spin electrons and $N_\downarrow$ down-spin electrons. Once the preset maximum number of Lanczös steps, or a minimum value of b_n, has been reached, the tridiagonal representation (20) may then be used to calculate (21). This amounts to the matrix element $b_0^2[(z - H + E_0)^{-1}]_{00}$ (the first element of the inverse of a tridiagonal matrix), which has a simple continued fraction form :

$$G^{(c)}_{aa,e} = \cfrac{b_0^2}{z - a_0 - \cfrac{b_1^2}{z - a_1 - \cfrac{b_2^2}{z - a_2 - \cdots}}} \qquad (22)$$

Thus, evaluating the Green function, once the arrays $\{a_n\}$ and $\{b_n\}$ have been found, reduces to the calculation of a finite continued fraction.

Consider next the case $a \neq b$. The continued fraction representation applies only to the case where the same state $|\phi\rangle$ appears on the two sides of (21). If $a \neq b$, this is no longer the case, but we may use the following trick : we define the combinations

$$G^{\pm}_{ab,e}(z) = \langle\Omega|(c_a \pm c_b)\frac{1}{z - H + E_0}(c_a \pm c_b)^\dagger|\Omega\rangle \qquad (23)$$

Using the symmetry $G_{ab,e}(z) = G_{ba,e}(z)$, this leads to

$$G_{ab,e}(z) = \frac{1}{4}(G^{+}_{ab,e}(z) - G^{-}_{ab,e}(z)) \qquad (24)$$

where $G^{\pm}_{ab,e}$ can be calculated in the same way as $G_{aa,e}$, i.e., with a simple continued fraction. We proceed likewise for $G^{\pm}_{ab,h}(z)$.

2.3 Cluster symmetries

One does not need to perform the second Lanczös step for each pair (a, b) of sites on the cluster, since some pairs are related by symmetries of the cluster, such as reflections and rotations. For instance, in a one-dimensional cluster of length L, a reflection with respect to the cluster's center sends site a ($a = 0, 1, \ldots, L - 1$) to site $L - a - 1$. The cluster Hamiltonian is invariant under such a reflection, and so $G^{(c)}_{a,b} = G^{(c)}_{L-a-1,L-b-1}$. The number of Lanczös sequences to perform, instead of being L^2, reduces to $L(L + 1)/2$. On a two-dimensional, rectangular cluster, reflections about the center along the x and y directions, and their combination, reduces the number of sequences by a factor of 4 in the limit of a large cluster, but in practice, for a 3×4 cluster, from $12^2 = 144$ to 48. On a square cluster, the symmetry is even higher since rotations of $\pi/2$ generate an additional set of transformations that can further reduce the number of pairs, by a factor 8 in the limit of large square clusters, but in practice from $16^2 = 256$ to 55 for a 4×4 cluster, the largest one practically available.

Using these symmetries not only saves times because of the economy in Lanczös sequences, but also later in the calculation, when the cluster Green function is calculated from the continued fraction representation $\{a_n, b_n\}$. That calculation is performed only for pairs of sites (a, b) unrelated by symmetry.

The symmetry of the cluster could also be used to reduce the size of the Hilbert space considered in the Lanczös procedure. Indeed, the Hamiltonian would be block-diagonal in a new basis of eigenfunctions of these symmetry operations. However, this has not been implemented by us, basically because the complexity of the coding involved and the development time needed would, in our opinion, offset the benefits.

2.4 Memory requirements

The memory needed to perform the exact diagonalization comes mainly from storing the diagonal part of the Hamiltonian matrix and three Lanczös vectors, which means $4d$ double precision floating point numbers. For a half-filled, 12 site cluster, $d = 853,776$ and this is modest 26 MB. Had we needed to store the full kinetic energy operator K instead of its tensor product factors, this would have been multiplied by roughly four. But the growth of the Hilbert space is exponential as a function of system size. The same procedure with a half-filled 16 site cluster would require slightly over 5.0 GB of memory. Computing time also explodes, since the Lanczös procedure scales like $d \ln d$ and the number of Lanczös sequences needed for calculating the Green function scales like L^2.

Once the Lanczös sequences are over, one needs to keep in memory the tridiagonal representations $\{a_n, b_n\}$ for each nonequivalent pair (a, b), which takes negligible memory. The calculation then proceeds to the next phase, described in the following section.

3 Embedding the cluster in the lattice

3.1 Restoring translation invariance

Let us go back the basic formulas 8 or 12 of Cluster Perturbation Theory. The indices m, n labelling different clusters can be replaced by wavevector indices in the description of inter-cluster quantities, through a Fourier transform. For instance, the inter-cluster hoppings may be arranged in a $L \times L$ matrix $V_{ab}(\mathbf{K})$, where $\mathbf{K}$ is a wavevector in the Brillouin zone of the lattice of clusters (the so-called superlattice) :

$$V_{ab}(\mathbf{K}) = \sum_n t^{0,n}_{a,b} \mathrm{e}^{i\mathbf{K}\cdot\mathbf{r}_n} \tag{25}$$

where $\mathbf{r}_n$ is the position of the cluster labelled n with respect to the position of the "base" cluster. We then write Eq. 8 as

$$\hat{G}^{-1}(\mathbf{K},\omega) = \hat{G}^{(c)-1}(\omega) - \hat{V}(\mathbf{K}) \tag{26}$$

where frequency dependence has been explicitly restored, to stress that the matrix $V(\mathbf{K})$ is frequency independent.

Since inter-cluster hoppings V^{mn}_{ab} are treated differently from intra-cluster hoppings ($t^{(c)}_{ab}$), the full translation symmetry of the lattice is broken, and must be restored in some way. The procedure we adopt, explained in Ref. [6], is to perform a residual Fourier transform in order to obtain a fully momentum dependent Green function:

$$G_{\mathrm{CPT}}(\mathbf{k},\omega) = \frac{1}{L}\sum_{a,b=1}^{L} G_{ab}(\mathbf{k},\omega)\mathrm{e}^{-i\mathbf{k}\cdot(\mathbf{r}_a-\mathbf{r}_b)} \tag{27}$$

where $\mathbf{r}_a$ is the position of site a within the cluster. We have replaced the wavevector $\mathbf{K}$, belonging to the reduced Brillouin zone (the Brillouin zone of the superlattice), by the wavevector of interest $\mathbf{k}$ belonging to the full Brillouin zone. The difference $\mathbf{q} = \mathbf{K} - \mathbf{k}$ belongs to the reciprocal superlattice, and so $V_{ab}(\mathbf{K}) = V_{ab}(\mathbf{k})$ since $\mathrm{e}^{i\mathbf{q}\cdot\mathbf{r}_n} = 1$.

To summarize, evaluating the Green function for a given wavevector $\mathbf{k}$ and complex frequency $\omega \to z$ proceeds according to the following steps:

1. For that value of z, the cluster Green function $G^{(c)}_{ab}$ is calculated from the continued fraction representation (22) – whose coefficients were stored in memory – for all pairs (a,b) of sites that are not related by a symmetry of the cluster.

2. For that value of $\mathbf{k}$, one forms the matrix $V_{ab}(\mathbf{k})$ following Eq. (25) and calculates the matrix

$$G_{a,b}(\mathbf{k},z) = \left(\frac{\hat{G}^{(c)}(z)}{1-\hat{V}(\mathbf{k})\hat{G}^{(c)}(z)}\right)_{a,b} \tag{28}$$

which implies two multiplications and one inversion of a complex-valued matrix of dimension L.

3. One perform the residual Fourier transform (27)

The merits and limitations of this method have been commented on in Ref. [6] and we will avoid repeating what was done in that paper. However, let us stress the most important points, by comparing the spectral function $A(k,\omega)$ obtained by this method to what is obtained by an ordinary exact diagonalization and to the known exact solution in a very special case: that of the one-dimensional Hubbard model with nearest-neighbor hopping t in the $U \to \infty$ limit. In that case, the exact solution is known [8] and can be used to assert the effectiveness of the method we propose. One sees from Fig. 2 the main benefits of CPT :

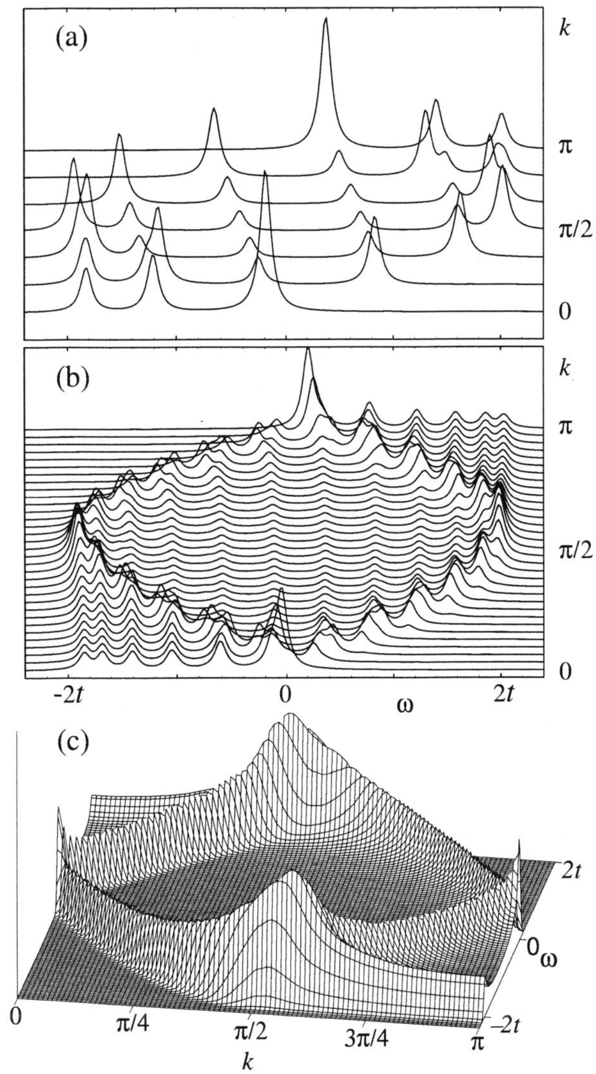

Figure 2. The spectral function of the $U \to \infty$ limit of the one-dimensional Hubbard model, as calculated from (a) an exact diagonalization of the Hubbard model with $U/t = 100$ on a periodic 12-site cluster; (b) the same, but with CPT, on a 12-site cluster with open boundary conditions; (c) the exact solution, taken from [8]; beware: the axes are oriented differently. In (a) and (b) a finite width η (see Eq. (4)) has been given to peaks that would otherwise be Dirac δ-functions.

1. The number of wavevectors is as large as one wishes. the exact diagonalization yields only $L/2+1 = 7$ wavevectors from $k = 0$ to $k = \pi$, in contrast to CPT, for which 32 wavevectors are displayed.

2. The number of poles of the Green function (i.e., peaks in the spectral function) is larger in CPT than in an exact diagonalization, even though both methods proceed through almost identical Lanczös se-

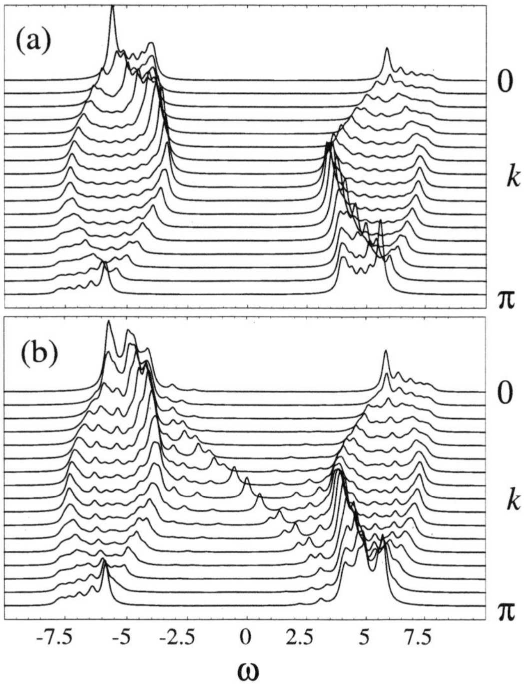

Figure 3. The spectral function of the one-dimensional Hubbard model at $U = 10t$ and $n = 1$ (half-filling), as calculated from (a) the CPT procedure of Sect. 3.1 and (b) from a Fourier transform of the cluster self-energy. One notices in the latter the appearance of spectral weight within the Mott gap.

quences with the same number of steps, and therefore the same number of floors in the continued fraction representation (22). The difference is that the CPT Green function formula (28), like Dyson's equation, rearranges these poles and the corresponding residues to something closer to the thermodynamic limit.

Moreover, the method falls back on the exact result in the $U \to 0$ limit, as well as on the trivial atomic limit in the $t_{ij}/U \to 0$ limit. One thus expects it to be applicable in between, in the intermediate coupling regime ($t_{ij} \sim U$).

3.2 Alternative I : Fourier transform of the self-energy

One possible alternative to the procedure described above would be to restore the translation symmetry by taking the Fourier transform of the self-energy rather than that of the CPT Green function. Explicitly, this amounts to calculating

$$\Sigma(\mathbf{k},\omega) = \frac{1}{L}\sum_{a,b=1}^{L} \Sigma_{ab}^{(c)}(\omega) e^{-i\mathbf{k}\cdot(\mathbf{r}_a - \mathbf{r}_b)} \tag{29}$$

where $\hat{\Sigma}^{(c)}$ is defined in Eq. (11), and then to write the full Green function from Dyson's equation:

$$G(\mathbf{k},\omega) = \frac{1}{\omega - \varepsilon(\mathbf{k}) - \Sigma(\mathbf{k},\omega)} \tag{30}$$

While it is difficult to dismiss this procedure from the start, an explicit calculation shows that it fails (Fig. 3) to reproduce a key feature of the known properties of the one-dimensional Hubbard model : the appearance of a Mott gap for all values of U. Indeed, it is known from the exact solution of the Hubbard model [9] that a gap opens in the spectrum as soon as the interaction U is turned on. This is also the behavior observed in CPT. By contrast, Fourier transforming the cluster self-energy leads to a Mott transition at $U/t = \infty$ instead of $U/t = 0$. Notice, however, that this approach, like CPT, is exact in the two limiting cases $U/t = 0$ and $U/t \to \infty$.

3.3 Alternative II : Minimal self-consistence

CPT is not a self-consistent procedure. This means that the CPT Green function $G_{CPT}(\mathbf{k},\omega)$, when Fourier transformed to calculate the local Green function $G_{ab}^{CPT}(\omega)$, does not yield the cluster Green function $G_{ab}^{(c)}(\omega)$ calculated by exact diagonalization. This is no surprise, since $G_{ab}^{(c)}(\omega)$ feels the effects of the cluster boundary, while $G_{ab}^{CPT}(\omega)$ is translation invariant.

One possible variation of the CPT method would be to make it self-consistent at that level : the local Green function $G_{ab}^{CPT}(\omega)$ calculated from $G_{CPT}(\mathbf{k},\omega)$ would be used to obtain a new CPT Green function through Eq. (28) and then Eq. (27), thus closing the self-consistent loop, which would be iterated until convergence. When doing so, it turns out that the self-consistent solution obtained is identical to what would be found by applying the CPT procedure to a cluster with periodic boundary conditions. Using periodic boundary conditions is possible in CPT provided the hopping terms that need to be added to the cluster to make it periodic are also subtracted in V_{ab}^{mn}, as described in [6]. In other words, the periodic-cluster version of CPT is self-consistent in its spatial dependence. Unfortunately, it is also further from the exact solution than the open-cluster version, as explicitly illustrated in [6]. Thus, it appears that self-consistence is not necessarily a virtue.

4 Relation to other cluster approaches and Outlook

In Cluster Perturbation Theory, a cluster is embedded in its environment by Dyson's equation only. There are other methods currently or recently developed that simulate the cluster's environment, i.e., the rest of the lattice, by a bath of fermionic levels chosen in a self-consistent way. These are the Dynamical Cluster Approximation (DCA) [10] and the Cellular Dynamical Mean Field Theory (CDMFT) [11]. They are both offshoots of Dynamical Mean Field Theory (DMFT), in which a "cluster" of one site is embedded in a self-consistent bath (for a review and additional references, see [12]). Common to DCA and CDMFT is the need to couple the Hubbard model defined on a cluster with an Anderson impurity model (the bath). The whole system (bath + cluster) is then solved, for instance by Quantum Monte

Carlo or exact diagonalization, which implies in the latter case that the physical size of the cluster has to be small (e.g. 4 to 6 sites) to leave space for the bath. The DCA and CDMFT differ in that the former is a momentum-space technique using periodic boundary conditions on the cluster, whereas the latter is a real-space technique using open boundary conditions. CPT does not use a bath, and thus can handle bigger clusters. But it is not self-consistent as the DCA and CDMFT are.

Cluster Perturbation Theory has limitations : In its present state, it cannot handle more than the one-particle Green function, i.e., susceptibilities cannot be calculated. Long-range order is also unaccessible, because of the small cluster sizes involved and the absence of self-consistence.

This being said, CPT passes the test very well when compared to the available exact results in one dimension. It is also capable of accounting for the experimentally observed disappearance of the Fermi surface in high-T_c superconductors [13]. A finite-temperature version of CPT is under development, and already gives interesting results on a 2×2 cluster. Future development will also include treating an ordered state self-consistently. Eventually, it is hoped that some mutual enrichment, if not convergence, will occur between the various cluster techniques for strongly correlated electron systems.

Acknowledgments

Stimulating discussions with A.M. Tremblay, G. Kotliar, M. Jarrell, S. Kancharla, D. Plouffe and X. Barnabé-Thériault are gratefully acknowledged. Calculations were performed on Beowulf clusters whose components were bought thanks to grants from NSERC and CFI. I am grateful to the members of the Centre de Calcul Scientifique (CCS) of the Université de Sherbrooke, who designed and assembled the clusters, in particular to M. Barrette, M. Bozzo-Rey, B. des Ligneris, C. Gauthier, J.-P. Turcotte, P. Vachon and A. Veilleux. Finally, this work is financially supported by NSERC (Canada) and FQRNT (Québec).

References

1. W. Kohn. *Rev. Mod. Phys.*, 71:1253, 1999.
2. A.A. Abrikosov, L.P. Gorkov, and I.E. Dzyaloshinski. Dover, New York, 1963.
3. A.-M. S. Tremblay, C. Bourbonnais, and D. Sénéchal. *Physics in Canada*, 2000.
4. J. Hubbard. *Proc. Royal. Soc. London*, 276:238, 1963.
5. D. Sénéchal, D. Pérez, and M. Pioro-Ladrière. *Phys. Rev. Lett.*, 84:522, 2000.
6. David Sénéchal, Danny Perez, and Dany Plouffe. *Phys. Rev. B*, 66:075129, 2002.
7. Claudius Gros and Roser Valenti. *Annalen der Physik*, 3:460, 1994.
8. J. Favand, S. Haas, K. Penc, F. Mila, and E. Dagotto. *Phys. Rev. B*, 55:R4859, 1997.
9. E.H. Lieb and F.Y. Wu. *Phys. Rev. Lett.*, 20:1445, 1968.
10. Th. Maier, M. Jarrel, Th. Pruschke, and J. Keller. *Eur. Phys. J. B*, 13:613, 2000.
11. C.J. Bolech, S.S. Kancharla, and G. Kotliar. *cond-mat/0206166*, 2002.
12. A. Georges, G. Kotliar, W. Krauth, and M.J. Rozenberg. *Rev. Mod. Phys.*, 68:13, 1996.
13. D. Sénéchal and A.-M. S. Tremblay. *in preparation*, 2003.

What is the Hamiltonian for parent high-temperature superconductors?

Alexis Gagné-LeBrun[a] and A.-M.S. Tremblay[a, b]

[a]Département de physique and Centre de recherche sur les propriétés électroniques de matériaux avancés, Université de Sherbrooke, Sherbrooke Québec, Canada, J1K 2R1

[b]Institut canadien de recherches avancées

Previous studies of the half-filled Hubbard model suggest that high-energy spin excitations in the high-temperture superconductor parent compound La_2CuO_4 are well described when the interaction strength is in the weak to intermediate-coupling regime. Using the same methodology as a previous Quantum Monte Carlo study, it is shown in this paper that even weaker coupling is necessary to obtain agreement with experiment when realistic second-neighbor hopping is included. The value of the interaction strength obtained is too small to explain the Hubbard gap at half-filling, suggesting either that the single-mode approximation used in this work is inappropriate to describe high-energy spin excitations or that a more complicated Hamiltonian including either three bands or direct ferromagnetic Heisenberg exchange is necessary to describe the Physics.

Des études antérieures du modèle de Hubbard à demi rempli suggèrent que les excitations de spin à haute énergie du matériau La_2CuO_4 sont bien décrites quand la force de l'interaction est dans le régime de couplage faible à intermédiaire. Utilisant la même méthodologie qu'une étude antérieure basée sur le Monte-Carlo quantique, il est démontré ici qu'un couplage encore plus faible est nécessaire pour obtenir l'accord avec l'expérience lorsqu'un saut au deuxième voisin réaliste est inclus dans l'hamiltonien. La valeur de l'interaction ainsi obtenue est trop faible pour expliquer le gap de Hubbard à demi rempli. Ceci suggère soit que l'approximation à un mode utilisée dans ce travail n'est pas valable pour décrire les excitations de spin à haute énergie, ou qu'un hamiltonien plus compliqué, incluant trois bandes ou un échange ferromagnétique direct de type Heisenberg, est nécessaire pour décrire la physique.

1 Introduction

Electronic properties of a large fraction of solids can be predicted using band theory in its modern form, namely density functional theory combined with the so-called GW approach [1]. However, the understanding of materials with d and f electrons is most often beyond the capabilities of this approach. High temperature superconductors belong to this category. This is especially striking for the parent compounds, namely the undoped, non-superconducting versions of the high-temperature superconductors. Band theory predicts that they have a half-filled band and hence should be good metals, but experiment shows that they are antiferromagnetic insulators at low temperature, and that they remain insulators above their antiferromagnetic transition temperature. They are so-called Mott insulators. First-principle approaches combining density-functional theory and many-body theory are being developed right now [2] but still the most common approach in d and f electron systems is to work with phenomenological Hamiltonians that include band structure information in the form of hopping amplitudes that reproduce the calculated band structure, and residual interaction terms that have to be treated by many-body approaches. Experience indicates that at least the ratios of the hopping parameters obtained from band structure calculations are reliable. The value of the interaction strength and the absolute scale of hopping parameters can be better obtained by comparing the results of calculations with experiment.

For high-temperature superconductors, the Hamiltonian that is most commonly used is the two-dimensional Hubbard model on a square lattice with both first and second-neighbor hopping. It reads,

$$\begin{aligned} H &= -t\sum_{\langle \mathbf{i},\mathbf{j}\rangle,\sigma}(c^\dagger_{\mathbf{i},\sigma}c_{\mathbf{j},\sigma}+c^\dagger_{\mathbf{j},\sigma}c_{\mathbf{i},\sigma}) \\ &\quad -t'\sum_{\langle\langle \mathbf{i},\mathbf{j}\rangle\rangle,\sigma}(c^\dagger_{\mathbf{i},\sigma}c_{\mathbf{j},\sigma}+c^\dagger_{\mathbf{j},\sigma}c_{\mathbf{i},\sigma})+U\sum_{\mathbf{i}}n_{\mathbf{i},\uparrow}n_{\mathbf{i},\downarrow} \end{aligned} \quad (1)$$

where $c^\dagger_{\mathbf{i},\sigma}(c_{\mathbf{i},\sigma})$ creates (annihilates) an electron of spin σ on site $\mathbf{i}$, $n_{\mathbf{i},\sigma}$ is the number of electrons of spin σ on site $\mathbf{i}$, t is the hopping amplitude over all nearest-neighbor bonds $\langle\mathbf{i},\mathbf{j}\rangle$, t' is the hopping amplitude over all next-nearest-neighbor bonds $\langle\langle\mathbf{i},\mathbf{j}\rangle\rangle$ and U is the on-site repulsion parameter. We work in units where hopping t, Boltzmann's constant k_B and Planck's constant $\hbar$ are all unity. Band structure calculations [3] reveal that a third neighbor hopping should also be included. Detailed comparisons with photoemission experiments [4][5][6], for example, confirm this result. Unless very detailed fits with experiment are required however, the third neighbor hopping can be neglected since it is generally smaller than the other two terms. Neglect of second-neighbor hopping t' however leads to qualitatively wrong results for the shape of the Fermi surface of both hole- and electron-doped high temperature superconductors. Also, $t' = 0$ would not lead to good fits to experimental photoemission or optical [7] data at half-filling.

In the present paper, we study the spin excitations of the above Hamiltonian in the insulating parent compound. This is motivated by recent neutron scattering experiments [8] on La_2CuO_4 that have, for the first time, allowed high resolution study of the high-energy dispersion of spin excitations (or magnons). These are sensitive to details of the Hamiltonian, unlike the long-wavelength low-energy modes. By comparing the results of experiments with those of the effective spin Hamiltonian found in the large U limit of the above Hamiltonian, [9][10][11] the authors of Ref. [8] concluded that t' leads to effects that can be neglected since they are smaller than the ring-exchange contributions that are the first corrections to simple near-neighbor exchange. Given the nearest-neighbor exchange $J = 4t^2/U - 24t^4/U^3$, the ring-exchange $J_c = 80t^4/U^3$ and the second and third neighbor exhanges $J' = J'' = 4t^4/U^3$ (the latter are subdominant), they were able to find both U and t. At $10K$ for example, they found $t = 0.30 \pm 0.02eV, U = 2.2 \pm 0.4eV$. Unfortunately, this value of $U = 7.3t \pm 1.8t$ is at the limit of validity of the expansion in powers of $8t/U$ (where $W = 8t$ is the bandwidth). In addition, these authors [8] used only the leading order spin-wave analysis on the biquadratic part of the ring exchange Hamiltonian to obtain the theoretical predictions that they compare with experiment. It has been argued [12] that to the same order in (t/U), biquadratic and bilinear terms are in just the right ratio that linear spin wave analysis leads to a flat dispersion on the zone boundary, just like the Heisenberg model at the same level of approximation. Dispersion at high-frequency should be a purely quantum effect (higher order in $1/S$) when both biquadratic and bilinear terms are taken into account. So, Katanin and Kampf [13] found it appropriate to perform more sophisticated self-consistent spin-wave theory and they found a J that is a few percent larger than in Ref. [8], but their J_c is considerably smaller, namely about half the value found in Ref. [8]. If we use the same expression [9][10] as that used in Ref. [8] , $J_c/J = 20\,(t/U)^2\left(1 - 6\,(t/U)^2\right)^{-1}$, the ratio $J_c/J = 0.24$ found by Katanin and Kampf [13] leads to $U = 9.5t$ that is more consistent with previous estimates, $U = 10t$, from photoemission [6]. It is noteworthy that the W/U expansion should be better justified for this value. Again, in this limit, the effect of t' would manifest itself through the second-neighbor hopping exchange integral, but its contribution should be more important since the ring-exchange term is smaller.

A lingering possibility is that the W/U expansion does not converge very well [11] and that, instead of effective spin models, one should really compare the full Hubbard Hamiltonian with experiments. This is what Sengupta, Scalettar and Singh [12] achieved by comparing Quantum Monte Carlo calculations with the experimental results of Ref. [8]. Using in addition the so-called single-mode approximation (SMA), they found that the frequency at $(\pi/2, \pi/2)$ is smaller by 12% than the frequency at the $(\pi, 0)$ wave-vector when $U/t = 6$ on an 8×8 lattice [12]. This corresponds well to the experimental value found in Ref. [8]. The value $U/t = 6$ found in that work confirmed an earlier independent result of Peres and Araujo[14] obtained using the Random Phase Approximation (RPA) for the Hubbard model. However, $U = 6t$ certainly corresponds to a regime where the W/U expansion breaks down so that it does not make sense to talk about direct and ring exchanges. Then, one cannot invoque the ring exchange contribution to neglect the second-neighbor hopping t'. In addition, the estimate $U = 6t$ is lower than that obtained by most other workers and is on the lower side of the critical value estimated necessary to obtain a finite-temperature Mott gap at half-filling [15][16].

The question of the effect of t' on the high-frequency spin excitations of the Hubbard model at half-filling is thus important. One would hope that comparison with experiment would lead us to a higher value of U, in better agreement with other estimates and more consistent with the large value of U necessary to obtain a Mott insulator at half-filling. Two studies based on the RPA have appeared for this problem.[17][18] The present paper addresses the same question using quantum Monte Carlo simulations.

In the following, the amplitude of the next-nearest neighbor hopping has been chosen such that as many wave vectors as possible cross the Fermi surface. For an 8×8 lattice, the optimal value is $t' = -0.35$ [19]. This is larger than $t' = -0.17$ obtained from band structure calculations [20][3] for La_2CuO_4 but comparable to values found in other high-temperature superconductors such as $YBa_2Cu_3O_7$ and $Bi_2Sr_2CaCu_2O_8$. Since our purpose is to answer whether in the presence of t' the value of U should be larger or smaller to obtain agreement with experiment, we find it preferable to work with a value of t' that is sufficiently large to clearly show the trend.

In the next section, we discuss several methodological aspects of this problem. First we describe details of the Quantum Monte Carlo calculations and then the single-mode approximation. We then present the results and conclude.

2 Methodological aspects

2.1 Quantum Monte Carlo simulations

In the context of this conference on high-performance computing, we find it appropriate to mention some technical details on the Quantum Monte Carlo simulations. We want to obtain thermal averages of operators in the grand-canonical ensemble. Direct calculation of the partition function $\mathrm{Tr}\left[e^{-\beta(H-\mu N)}\right]$ with $\beta = 1/T$ and μ the chemical potential, is basically impossible even on an 8×8 lattice. In that case, taking into account the fact that each site can be either empty, doubly occupied, or singly occupied with spin up or down, there are $4^{8\times8} = 3.4 \times 10^{38}$ possible states. Monte Carlo methods with importance sampling are a method of choice in the case of statistical problems with huge state spaces. In the case of classical mechanics, it is quite simple to compute how $e^{-\beta(H-\mu N)}$ is modified when it is applied on two states that differ by a local change. That is all that is needed to perform Monte Carlo simulations. In the quantum case, the exponential of $\beta\,(H - \mu N)$ can be computed only if H can be diagonalized, which is the problem we are faced with from the very beginning: H has a kinetic part K and a potential part V that are diagonal respectively in momentum and in coordinate space. The basis where $K + V$ is diagonal is unkown. To address this difficulty, the problem is first made to look more classical by using the so-called Trotter decomposition, $e^{-\beta(H-\mu N)} = e^{-\Delta\tau(H-\mu N)}e^{-\Delta\tau(H-\mu N)}\ldots e^{-\Delta\tau(H-\mu N)}$ with the number of exponentials, or number of "time slices" N_τ given by $N_\tau = \beta/\Delta\tau$. In the limit $\Delta\tau \to 0$ one can write $e^{-\Delta\tau(H-\mu N)} = e^{-\Delta\tau K}e^{-\Delta\tau(V-\mu N)} + O\left(\Delta\tau^2\right)$ which means progress since we know the basis where either exponential is diagonal. However, the change of basis necessary to move from one operator to the next is still a formidable task for a many-body problem like the one we consider now, where the motion of electrons is not independent. To go around this, one performs a so-called Hubbard-Stratonovich transformation on $e^{-\Delta\tau(V-\mu N)}$. More specifically, one can use an identity [21] that is easily proven by recalling that $n_{\mathrm{i},\uparrow}$ and $n_{\mathrm{i},\downarrow}$ can take only the values 1 and 0 :

$$e^{-\Delta\tau U\left(n_{\mathrm{i},\uparrow}-\frac{1}{2}\right)\left(n_{\mathrm{i},\downarrow}-\frac{1}{2}\right)} = e^{-\Delta\tau U/4}\frac{1}{2}\sum_{x_i=\pm 1} e^{\lambda x_i\left(n_{\mathrm{i},\uparrow}-n_{\mathrm{i},\downarrow}\right)} \tag{2}$$

where $\cosh(\lambda) = e^{\Delta\tau U/2}$. There is now one Hubbard-Stratonovich variable x_i per site in space-time, in other words on a $L \times L$ lattice there are $2^{L^2 N_\tau}$ possible values for the set of Hubbard-Stratonovich variables. At first it looks as if we have complicated the problem by increasing the number of variables to be traced over. However, at the end it is only the trace over Hubbard-Stratonovich variables that is finally sampled by Monte Carlo methods because the use of the above identity allows us to transform the problem into one where the electrons are independent but move in a space and time dependent potential (coming from the Hubbard-Stratonovich variables). This means that the quantum mechanical trace over fermions can now be performed exactly in algebraic time for any given configuration of the Hubbard-Stratonovich variables. The trace over fermions, however, is a determinant that can be either positive or negative, which means that to apply importance sampling, one must take the absolute value of the determinant and move the sign to the observable. That leads to the so-called sign problem: There are cases where the sign changes so often from one configuration to the next that importance sampling becomes exponentially inefficient. There are many other technical difficulties one must address, in particular the question of numerical stability at low temperature [22]. The reader is refered to a recent review [23] and to the original literature on this so-called Determinant Quantum Monte Carlo Method [24]. A review in French is also available [25].

For the simulations presented in this paper, we typically use 1.25×10^5 measurements, each measurement being performed after a full update of all the Hubbard-Stratonovich variables of the space-time lattice. The measurements are grouped in blocks of 250 measurements for estimation of the statistical error. The value of $\Delta\tau$ is $1/10$. We checked that, given the statistical uncertainties, larger $\Delta\tau = 1/8$ would not have changed our results. This is discussed further in the next section. The numerical stabilization at low temperature is performed by Gram-Schmidt decomposition every five time slices [22]. Also, averaging over independent simulations that each have their warmup cycles reduces ergodicity problems.

There are different possible estimators, namely $\langle S_z S_z\rangle$ and $\langle S_+S_-\rangle + \langle S_-S_+\rangle$, for the spin-spin correlation functions that we will need. We checked that $\langle S_z S_z\rangle$ had smaller statistical error at the temperatures of interest, so that is what we used. Since we do not have particle-hole symmetry, the average sign is different from unity and in addition the chemical potential corresponding to half-filling must be found by iteration. For example, at $\beta = 3$, $U = 6$ the average sign is 0.724 and the value $\mu = -.27995$ gives a filling of $0.99967\pm\ 0.4 \times 10^{-4}$. For such high temperature and high-energy properties, size 8×8 should be enough. A 6×6 lattice gives results for intermediate values of the wave vectors that are consistent interpolations between the wave vectors of the 8×8 lattice [12]. Further discussion of size effects is given in the section on results below.

The program is written in Fortran 90 with allocatable memory. It is compiled with the Intel Fortran Compiler, which is free for academia and performed faster than others we have tested. For an 8×8 lattice at these high temperatures, $\beta = 3$, the program typically takes $6.6\ MB$ of memory and 44 hours of computation time for 1.25×10^5 measurements and 1×10^4 warmups on a pentium IV processor running at $2.5GHz$. Computation time scales roughly like $\left(L^2\right)^3 N_\tau$. For example, 10^5 measurements and 2×10^4 warmups on a 12×12 system at the same temperature take 480 hours and $33\ MB$. Typically, 10 jobs with a thousand warmups and tens of thousands of measurements each are sent on the nodes of a Beowulf cluster and the results are averaged to obtain of order 10^5 measurements. In this way, one run at fixed U and temperature for an 8×8 system takes roughly a day for example on a cluster of $667MHz$ pentium III machines.

2.2 Single-mode approximation

Ideally, one should compute the imaginary part of the frequency and wave vector dependent spin susceptibility, which is accessible through neutron scattering. But this means that one should perform analytical continuation of the Quantum Monte Carlo calculations since these are performed in imaginary-time. This is usually achieved by using the so-called Maximum Entropy method [26]. For the problem at hand, in agreement with the authors of Ref. [12], we were unable to obtain reliable data using this approach. We thus followed the procedure of Ref. [12] and obtained the dispersion relation of the spin excitations from the so-called single-mode approximation (SMA)

$$\omega(\mathbf{q}) = 2S(\mathbf{q})/\chi(\mathbf{q}) \tag{3}$$

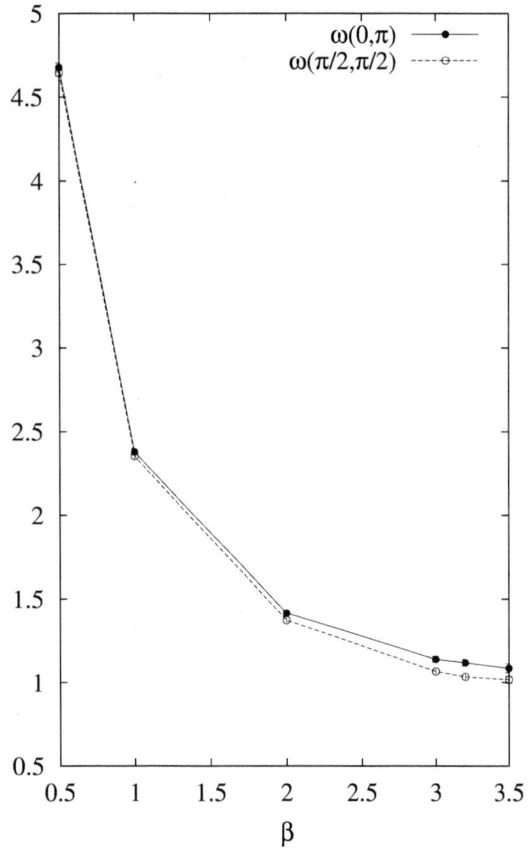

Figure 1. Frequency as a function of temperature for two wave vectors at $U = 6$ on an 8×8 lattice. The continuous line represents the energy at wave-vector $(0, \pi)$, and the dash-line the energy at wave-vector $(\pi/2, \pi/2)$. We observe that at low temperature (high β), the dispersion converges. Error bars are smaller than the symbols.

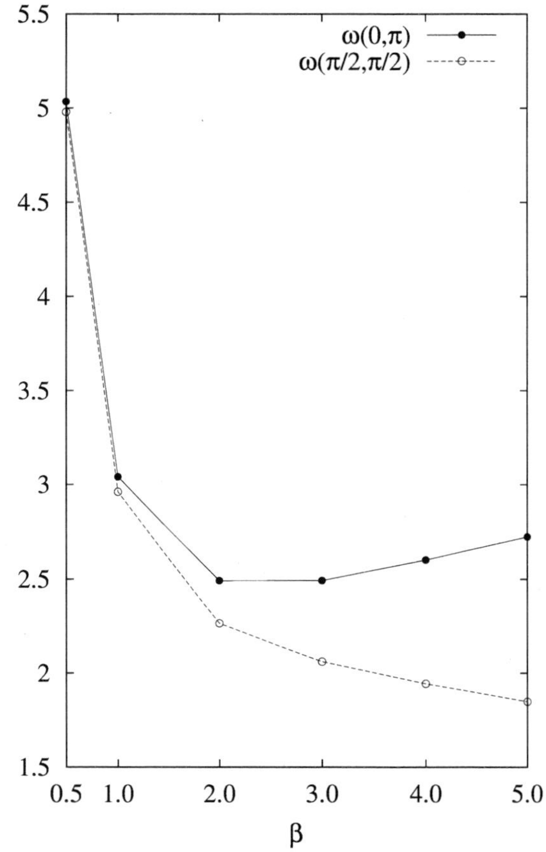

Figure 2. Frequency as a function of temperature for two wave vectors at $U = 0$ on an 8×8 lattice. This $U = 0$ case illustrates that when the SMA does not work, there is a strong temperature dependence. The symbols have the same meaning as in the previous figure.

where $S(\mathbf{q})$ is the spin structure factor and $\chi(\mathbf{q})$ is the zero-frequency spin susceptibility obtained simply from integration over imaginary time. This result becomes exact in the limit where the imaginary part of the spin susceptibility is peaked at only one frequency for any given wave vector. Indeed, using the fluctuation-dissipation theorem,

$$S(\mathbf{q}) = \int \frac{d\omega}{2\pi} \frac{2}{1 - e^{-\beta\omega}} \chi''(\mathbf{q},\omega) \tag{4}$$

and the spectral representation

$$\chi(\mathbf{q}) = \int \frac{d\omega}{\pi} \frac{\chi''(\mathbf{q},\omega)}{\omega}, \tag{5}$$

if the odd function $\chi''(\omega)$ is proportional to $\delta(\omega - \omega(\mathbf{q})) - \delta(\omega + \omega(\mathbf{q}))$ then the result Eq.(3) follows when $1 \gg e^{-\beta\omega(\mathbf{q})}$. As we shall see shortly, we work with $\beta = 3$ and $\omega(\mathbf{q}) \sim 1$ so the inequality is satisfied. It is known [27] however, that for $t' = 0$ and large U there is a broad multimagnon continuum above the single magnon mode. We expect an analogous continuum with finite t'. Sengupta *et al.* [12], based on the work of Ref. [27], argue that while the magnitude of the frequency found from the SMA is affected by the high frequency multimagnon continuum (the SMA in that case gives and upper bound for $\omega(\mathbf{q})$), nevertheless the overall shape of the dispersion relation is not affected by the continuum. Since we shall be using only information on ratio of frequencies, it is argued that this should be a sufficiently accurate approach.

We are interested in high-frequency modes hence the simulations, as in Ref. [12], can be performed at relatively high temperature. To prove this, Fig. (1) shows the value of the high-frequency modes at $(\pi, 0)$ and $(\pi/2, \pi/2)$ estimated from the SMA as a function of inverse temperature β for $U = 6$ and $t' = -0.35$. Although the estimated mode frequencies appear weakly temperature dependent at $\beta = 3$, their differences for $\beta = 3.0$, 3.2 and 3.5 are, respectively, 6.8%, 8.1% and 6.7%. There is no systematic drift in this difference. The fluctuation of about 13% seen between these last three numbers should be considered as coming from the error bars of the Quantum Monte Carlo.

With $t' = 0$ [12], the temperature dependence is weaker

beyond $\beta = 3$. The sign problem prevents us from doing simulations at $\beta = 4$, so we choose the same temperature as in Ref. [12], namely $\beta = 3$. Fig. (2) contrasts the same calculation in the case where the SMA does not work, namely at $U = 0$. Clearly, there is a strong temperature dependence, even at low temperature. In addition, a plot of the dispersion relation in the $U = 0$ case (not shown) reveals that the mode at (π, π) is not soft. The softening of the (π, π) point observed when $U = 6$ in Fig. (3) signals that antiferromagnetism is setting in. We checked that at $t' = 0$ we recover all the results of Ref. [12]

3 Results

3.1 No second-neighbor hopping

We first performed additional tests for dependence on size, temperature and impaginary time discretization. Size dependence was checked further by performing the simulations at $U = 6t$, $\beta = 3$ for a 12×12 lattice, which corresponds to the size where systematic convergence to the thermodynamic limit was better than about 3% percent in the work on the Heisenberg model of Ref.[27]. The values of $\omega(\pi, 0), \omega(\pi/2, \pi/2)$ that we found are identical to those for the 8×8 lattice to within the 0.5% statistical accuracy. Close to 10^6 samples were used for these tests. We also tried to check for size dependence at lower temperature on larger lattices, but results on 10^5 samples for $\beta = 5$ on a 12×12 lattice, for example, only give about 20% statistical accuracy, which is not enough. Simulations with better statistical accuracy for these parameters are prohibitive. Finally, as a further check of the systematic error introduced by the Trotter decomposition, we checked that for the 8×8 lattice, $\Delta\tau = 1/8$ and $\Delta\tau = 1/10$ give identical results for $\omega(\pi, 0), \omega(\pi/2, \pi/2)$ within 0.5% statistical accuracy.

Given that the work of Katanin and Kampf [13] suggests the value $U = 10t$ for a good fit to experiment, we performed simulations on 8×8 systems at $\beta = 3$. A large number of Monte Carlo samples (10^6) is needed. We found that the dispersion between $\omega(\pi, 0)$ and $\omega(\pi/2, \pi/2)$ is flat to the 1.5% statistical accuracy. Not surprisingly, this interpolates between the results found in Ref. [12] for $U = 8t$ and for the Heisenberg model, which corresponds to the very large U limit. This disagreement with the results of Katanin and Kampf [13] may come from the fact that the SMA is not valid or from the fact that the self-consistent $1/S$ expansion is not justified in the presence of ring exchange.[28] Indeed, in that approach, the ring exchange contribution, which should be a correction to the direct exchange term, is in fact larger than direct exchange term by a factor S^2.

3.2 Finite second-neighbor hopping

We plot on Fig. (3) the magnon dispersion relation obtained for an 8×8 system at $U = 6$, $\beta = 3$ when $t' = 0$ and when $t' = -0.35$. In the latter case, the Quantum Monte Carlo error bars are much larger because of the sign problem. Let us focus on the dispersion on the line going between $(\pi/2, \pi/2)$ and $(\pi, 0)$. For this value of U, the case $t' = 0$ that was studied in Ref. [12] leads to $1 - \omega(\pi, 0)/\omega(\pi/2, \pi/2) = -12\%$ that corresponds to the experimental value of Ref. [8]. With $t' = -0.35$ the absolute value of this ratio is smaller.

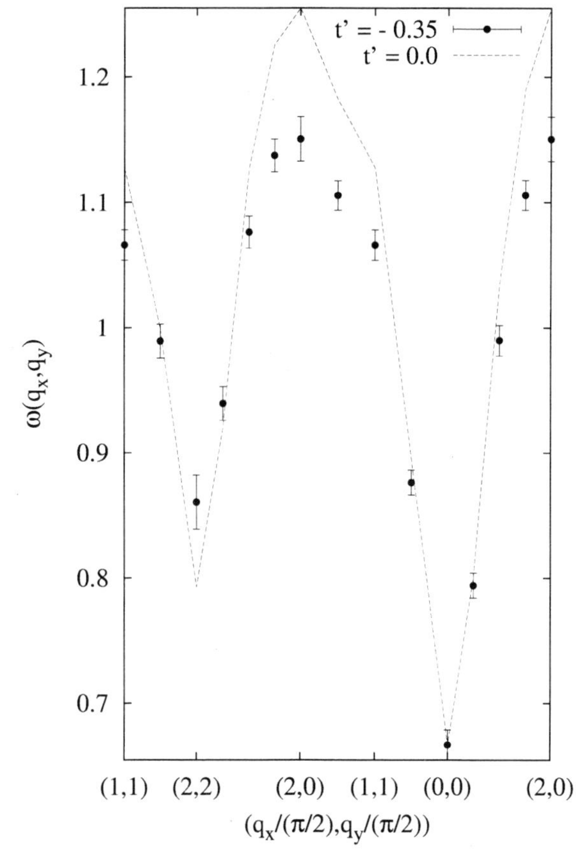

Figure 3. Energy dispersion relation in the SMA as a function of wave vector for $\beta = 3.0$ and $U = 6.0$ for an 8×8 lattice. The coordinates on the horizontal axis must be multiplied by $\pi/2$. The line corresponds to the case $t' = 0.0$, and the points correspond to the case $t' = -0.35$. Error bars represent the statistical Quantum Monte Carlo errors.

To fit the experimental value of the dispersion, we need a smaller value of U/t as demonstrated in Fig. 4 where we plot the dispersion relation along the $(0, \pi)$ to $(\pi/2, \pi/2)$ to $(\pi, 0)$ line. The data is normalized for each U such that, $\omega(\pi, 0) = 1$. Clearly, the dispersion increases with decreasing U and reaches the experimental value around $U = 5.0t \pm 0.5t$.

4 Discussion and conclusions

Previous QMC simulations [12] have suggested, in agreement with RPA calculations, [14][17] that the dispersion of high-frequency spin-wave excitations in the parent high-temperature superconductor La_2CuO_4 can be explained with the Hubbard model at $U = 6t$. We have

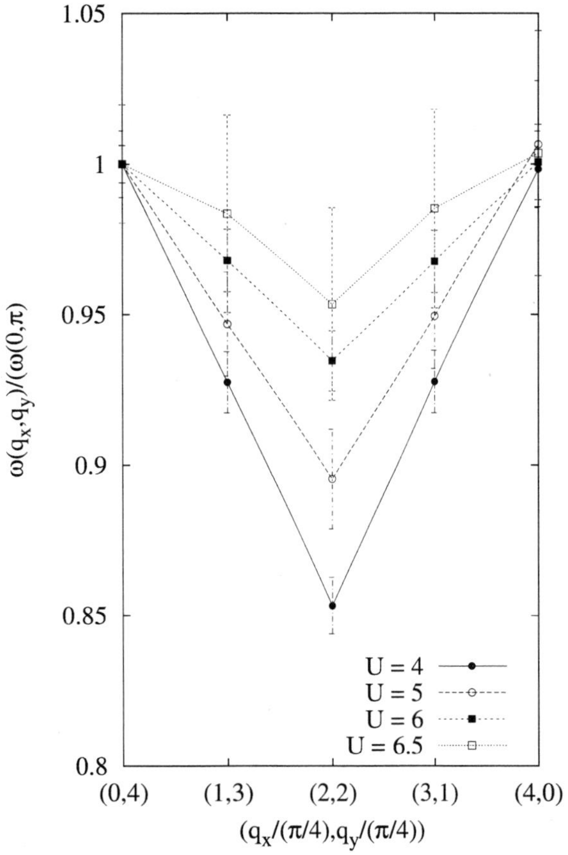

Figure 4. Energy dispersion relation along the $(0,\pi)$ to $(\pi/2,\pi/2)$ to $(\pi,0)$ line for $\beta = 3.0$ and $t' = -0.35$. The coordinates on the horizontal axis must be multiplied by $\pi/4$. Each line correspond to a fixed value of U. The dispersion increases with smaller U. Error bars represent the statistical quantum Monte Carlo error.

shown here that the addition of second-neighbor hopping $t' = -0.35t$ leads to an even smaller value of the interaction strength, namely $U = 5t \pm 0.5t$. This lowering of U is in agreement with RPA calculations [17][18] and is what would have been expected if we had been at strong coupling. Indeed, it is known that second-neighbor ferromagnetic exchange ($J_2 < 0$) can explain the experimental dispersion [8] but second-neighbor hopping in a Hubbard model leads to an antiferromagnetic second-neighbor exchange ($J_2 > 0$). This has to be compensated by a smaller U since lowering U tends to increase the dispersion in that weak coupling range of U values.

However, U of order $6t$ is too small to explain the Mott gap at half-filling. Comparisons of photoemission experiments with the results of exact diagonalization for example suggests $U = 10t$ [6].

One possibility is that the SMA is not accurate and that finite size effects are important so that the agreement with RPA calculations is fortuitous. Indeed, in the Heisenberg limit it is known [12] that the dispersion obtained with the QMC+SMA approach leads to a $(\pi/2,\pi/2)$ mode that is only 2% higher than the $(\pi,0)$ mode while more sophisticated calculations [27] suggest that this number should be 5% on an 8×8 system and 10% in the thermodynamic limit. The SMA in particular can be questioned since there is a multimagnon continuum at high frequency [27] that is different for the two wave vectors of interest. We however did several tests that did not invalidate the SMA nor suggested large size effects.

If the SMA is valid and size effects are not important, then the effective Hamiltonian obtained from the Hubbard model at $U = 10t$ is not sufficient to describe spin excitations. It is conceivable that direct ferromagnetic exchange between next-nearest neighbors J_2 has to be included explicitly in the effective Hamiltonian [8] but ab initio calculations [29] suggest antiferromagnetic J_2. Comparisons of exact diagonalizations with phonon assisted multimagnon infrared scattering also suggest antiferromagnetic J_2.[30] However, the convergence of the strong coupling expansion for mapping the three-band model onto an effective spin Hamiltonian is not so clear. In particular the sign of J_2 is ambiguous.[11] Another possibility is that in mapping the three-band model to a single-band model, the ring-exchange and direct-exchange contributions are not in the same proportion as those predicted from the simple one-band Hubbard model. [31] In other words, the mapping from a three-band model to a single-band model most probably leads to effective Hamiltonians in the spin and single-particle sectors whose relation is different from that expected from the simple Hubbard model.

A.-M.S.T. would like to thank B. Kyung, D. Sénéchal and Y.B. Kim for useful suggestions, and especially M. Gingras for pointing out Ref.[12] and for numerous discussions on this subject. We are grateful to S. Allen, H. Touchette and D. Poulin for major contributions to the codes used for this project. Calculations were performed on home made Beowulf clusters whose components were bought thanks to grants from the Natural Sciences and Engineering Research Council of Canada (NSERC) and from the Canadian Foundation for Innovation (FCI). We are grateful to the Sherbrooke Centre de Calcul Scientifique (CCS) team that designed and assembled the clusters, in particular to M. Barrette, M. Bozzo-Rey, B. des Ligneris, M. Lutfy, C. Gauthier, J.-P. Turcotte, P. Vachon and A. Veilleux. This work was partially supported by the Natural Sciences and Engineering Research Council of Canada (NSERC), by the Fonds pour la Formation de Chercheurs et l'Aide à la Recherche (FCAR) from the Québec government, by the Canadian Institute for Advanced Research and by the Tier I Canada Research Chair program (A.-M.S.T).

References

1. G. Onida, L. Reining, and A. Rubio, Rev. Mod. Phys. **74**, 601 (2002).
2. S. Biermann, Aryasetiawan, and A. Georges, Phys. Rev. Lett. **90**, 086402 (2003).

3. E. Pavarini, I. Dasgupta, T. Saha-Dasgupta, O. Jepsen, and O. K. Andersen, Phys. Rev. Lett. **87,** 047003/1-4 (2001).
4. T. Tohyama and S. Maekawa, Phys. Rev. B **49**, 3596 (1994).
5. R. J. Gooding, K. J. E. Vos, and P. W. Leung, Phys. Rev. B **50**, 12866 (1994).
6. C. Kim, P. J. White, Z.-X. Shen, T. Tohyama, Y. Shibata, S. Maekawa, B. O. Wells, Y. J. Kim, R. J. Birgeneau, and M. A. Kastner, Phys. Rev. Lett. **80**, 4245 (1998).
7. H.-B. Schüttler and A. J. Fedro, Phys. Rev. B **45**, 7588 (1992).
8. R. Coldea, S. M. Hayden, G. Aeppli, T. G. Perring, C. D. Frost, T. E. Mason, S.-W. Cheong, and Z. Fisk, Phys. Rev. Lett., **86**, 5377 (2001).
9. M. Takahashi, J. Phys. C **10**, 1289 (1977).
10. A.H. MacDonald, S.M. Girvin, and D. Yoshioka, Phys. Rev. B **41**, 2565 (1990).
11. E. Müller-Hartmann and A. Reischl, Eur. Phys. J. B 28, 173 (2002).
12. Pinaki Sengupta, Richard T. Scalettar, and Rajiv R. P. Singh, Phys. Rev. B, **66**, 144420 (2002).
13. A. A. Katanin, and A. P. Kampf, Phys. Rev. B **66**, 100403 (2002).
14. N. M. R. Peres and M. A. N. Araujo, Phys. Rev B **65**, 132404 (2002).
15. M. Vekic, and S.R. White, Phys. Rev. B **47**, 1160 (1993).
16. A. Georges, G. Kotliar, W. Krauth, and M. J. Rozenberg, Rev. Mod. Phys. **68**, 13 (1996).
17. Avinash Singh annd Pallab Goswami, Phys. Rev. B **66**, 092402 (2002).
18. N. M. R. Peres, M. A. N. Araujo, Phys. Stat. Sol. **236**, 523 (2003).
19. Alain F. Veilleux, Anne-Marie Daré, Liang Chen, Y.M.Vilk, and A.-M.S. Tremblay, Phys. Rev. B **52**, 16 255 - 16 263 (1995).
20. W.E. Pickett, Rev. Mod. Phys. **61**, 433 (1989); M.S. Hybertsen, E.B. Setchel, M, Shluter, and D.R. Jennison, Phys. Rev. B **41**, 11 068 (1990).
21. J. E. Hirsh, Phys. Rev. B **31**, 4403 (1985).
22. S. R. White, D.J. Scalapino, and R. L. Sugar, E. Y. Loh, Jr., J. E. Gubernatis, and R. T. Scalettar, Phys. Rev. B **40**, 506 (1989).
23. Raimundo R. dos Santos, Braz. J. Phys. **33**, 36 (2003).
24. R. Blankenbecler, D.J. Scalapino, and R.L. Sugar, Phys. Rev. D **24**, 2278 (1981).
25. A.-M.S. Tremblay, *Méthode Monte Carlo pour les électrons sur réseau* in "Simulations numériques en physique", p.529, Eds. L. Lewis, J. Lopez, G. Slater and A.-M.S. Tremblay (CRPS internal report) (1993). http://www.physique.usherb.ca/tremblay/cours/Ecole306.pdf. See also, H. Touchette and D. Poulin, http://www.physique.usherb.ca/tremblay/david/rapport.pdf.
26. R. K. Bryan, Eur. Biophys. J. **18**, 165 (1990); M. Jarrell and J. E. Gubernatis, Phys. Rep. **269**, 133 (1996).
27. A. W. Sandvik and R. R. P. Singh, Phys. Rev. Lett. **86**, 528 (2001).
28. Yong Baek Kim, private communication.
29. Carmen J. Calzado and Jean-Paul Malrieu, Phys. Rev. B **63**, 214520 (2001)
30. J. Lorenzana, J. Eroles, and S. Sorella, Phys. Rev. Lett. **83**, 5122 (1999).
31. M. Roger and J. M. Delrieu, Phys. Rev. B **39**, 2299 (1989).

Exact diagonalization and Quantum Monte Carlo studies of quantum dots

A.D. Güçlü and Hong Guo[a]

[a]Center for the Physics of Materials and Department of Physics, McGill University, Montreal, PQ, Canada H3A 2T8

We report exact diagonalization and diffusion quantum Monte Carlo calculations of quantum dots (QDs) in which energetics due to electron-electron interactions, magnetic field, and geometrical factors compete and induce interesting ground state configurations. The geometrical effects are generated by different confining potentials such as parabolic shaped, ring shaped, and disordered potentials. The addition spectra, spin configurations and Hund's rules are investigated for QDs containing up to 13 strongly interacting electrons. In addition to the familiar Coulomb and spin blockades, a new transport blockade is predicted when the electrons are spatially localized in different potential minima. While the transition energy between spin states is found to be affected by the disorder, closed shell Hund's rule is maintained for the disorder strength considered here.

Nous avons effectué des calculs de diagonalisation exacte et de Monte-Carlo quantique sur des points quantiques (QD) dans lesquels le bilan énergétique impliquant les interactions électron-électron, le champ magnétique et des facteurs géométriques sont en compétition et produisent des états fondamentaux intéressants. Les effets géométriques sont déterminés par la forme du potentiel de confinement (parabolique ou en anneau) et du potentiel de désordre. Les spectres d'addition, les configurations de spin et les règles de Hund sont étudiés pour des points quantiques comportant jusqu'à 13 électrons en forte interaction. En plus du blocage de Coulomb et de spin, un nouveau blocage de transport est prédit lorsque les électrons sont localisés dans l'espace sur des minimums différents du potentiel. Alors que l'énergie de transition entre les états de spin est affectée par le désordre, la règle de Hund sur les couches fermées est encore valable pour les degrés de désordre considérés ici.

1 Introduction

Quantum dots (QD) has attracted much attention experimentally and theoretically as they provide a high level of control for electron dynamics and correlation[1–5]. QD's are also called artificial atoms because they have many properties similar to an atom. For instance it is now possible to experimentally determine the atomic-like properties of QD's such as the addition energy, shell structure and spin configurations. Due to the experimental accessibility, QD systems will continue to provide a crucial testing ground for many important concepts of mesoscopic and nanoscopic physics. On the theoretical side, the most accurate treatment of QD's is based on exact diagonalization of the QD Hamiltonian[6–12]. Since computational cost grows exponentially with the electron number N, exact diagonalization is so far limited to highly symmetric QD systems with small number of electrons ($N < 7$). Indeed, conservation of total angular momentum and total spin makes possible to reduce the many-body Hamiltonian of a circular QD system into smaller matrices which can be calculated by parallel computation techniques. Typical size of matrices needed to reach the convergence of a 5 electrons system is about 30000×30000. Larger systems require approximations such as tight-binding[13,14] models. For a qualitative understanding of some properties of QD's, mean-field approximations such as Hartree-Fock[15–24] and density functional theory[25–31] may be used. It is however recognized that in strongly correlated systems, these mean-field approximations can give substantial errors in energy and many-body wave function. A more accurate alternative is quantum Monte Carlo (QMC) methods[32–48] which treat correlation effects exactly while keeping the amount of computation to rise as $\sim O(N^3)$. QMC can be used to study QD systems which do not have a particular spatial symmetry. Indeed, problems lacking spatial symmetry make exact diagonalization calculation powerless if not impossible. Unlike the exact diagonalization technique, QMC method does not require a lot of memory since there is no need of matrix conversion. Computation time is the most important factor in QMC simulations, and this method is well suited for parallel computation techniques.

Experimental investigations[49–53] have provided clear indications that the confining potential landscape can play an essential role to the many-body states of the QD. Several theoretical analysis have been reported in order to elucidate geometrical effects coming from random disorder[13,14, 17,20,21,30,31], chaotic dots[18,23], QD molecules[12,19, 32], non-circular dots[28,29], impurities[34,35], and ring shaped dots[58–61]. Despite the many contributions so far, electron correlation and ground state properties of disordered QD systems remain an active subject of study.

It is the purpose of this paper to report our investigation of geometrical factors in QD's under an external uniform magnetic field. Using an exact diagonalization technique in a continuous potential landscape, with up to five confined electrons. An exact calculation on the energetics of interaction, magnetic field, and geometry is very valuable for elucidating many-body phenomena in QDs. In particular, this model allows us to observe and understand electron charging properties and transport characteristics of QDs under the influence of wave function localization and charge blockade effects.

In order to study the effects of symmetry breaking random disorder we use a diffusion QMC (DQMC) numerical procedure. To the best of our knowledge, QMC analysis of QD's containing impurities have been limited to 2 electrons[34,35], and we are not aware of any previous exact calculations on energetics and spin configurations of completely disordered QD's up to $N = 13$. Moreover, our DQMC data allows us to probe the physics of clean QD's under external magnetic field with larger number of electrons than studied before. We focus on investigating the competing energetics of electron-electron interaction, magnetic field, and disorder.

2 Model and Method

We consider cylindrically symmetric QDs with a parabolic confinement potential to which we add a distortion potential, and an uniform magnetic field B in the z direction. In the effective mass approximation, single particle Hamiltonian of this system is

$$\begin{aligned} H_0 &= \frac{1}{2m^*}\left(\mathbf{p} - \frac{e}{c}\mathbf{A}(\mathbf{r})\right)^2 + \frac{1}{2}m^*\omega_0^2\mathbf{r}^2 \\ &+ g^*\mu_B Bs + V_d(\mathbf{r}), \end{aligned} \quad (1)$$

where m^* is the effective mass of electron, $\mathbf{A}$ is the vector potential, ω_0 is the parameter characterizing the parabolic part of the confinement potential of the QD, g^* is the effective Landé factor. The parabolic confining potential is distorted by a function $V_p(\mathbf{r})$. The solutions to the parabolic part of the confinement potential are the well known Fock-Darwin states, which will be used as basis set through this work.

2.1 Exact Diagonalization

When the function $V_d(\mathbf{r})$ is a radial barrier potential creating two distinct potential regions (a ring region and a core region), the system remains cylindrically symmetric. The total angular momentum is then conserved and an exact diagonalization technique is suitable to study electronic properties of such system. To calculate the many-body states of the interacting electrons, we start from the second-quantized form of the isolated QD Hamiltonian,

$$H_{QD} = \sum_i \epsilon_i c_i^\dagger c_i + \frac{1}{2}\sum_{ijkl} V_{ijkl} c_i^\dagger c_j^\dagger c_l c_k, \quad (2)$$

where ϵ_i is the *single* electron energy level corresponding to the single-particle state labeled by quantum indices (n_i, m_i, σ_i). c ($c^\dagger$) is the annihilation (creation) operator and V_{ijkl} are the Coulomb interaction matrix elements given by

$$\begin{aligned} V_{ijkl} &= \frac{e^2}{\epsilon}\int dx_1 dx_2 \\ &\times \ \psi_i^*(x_1)\psi_j^*(x_2)\frac{1}{|\mathbf{r}_1 - \mathbf{r}_2|}\psi_k(x_1)\psi_l(x_2), \end{aligned} \quad (3)$$

where the integration includes the summation over spin states. Here, ψ_i are the eigenstates of the single-electron Hamiltonian (which includes $V_d(r)$). We note that, if one is interested in a distortion-free QD with the z-direction neglected, V_{ijkl} do not depend on B apart from a rescaling factor. In our case, however, numerical calculations of the V_{ijkl} must be performed for every value of magnetic field, which is a computationally intensive process. We calculated twenty one points between $B = 0$ and 9 tesla. Exact diagonalization of the many-body Hamiltonian is performed up to $N = 5$ electrons. In addition to the total spin in z-direction S_z, total angular momentum M is a good quantum number due to the cylindrical symmetry of the QD. Therefore, the many-body Hamiltonian can be separated into subspaces with different (M,S_z) configurations. The ground state and lowest excited states are calculated by diagonalizing each subspace using the standard Lanczos procedure for larger matrices.

2.2 Diffusion quantum Monte Carlo

In order to study completely disordered systems, we now consider the distortion function $V_d(\mathbf{r})$ to be a sum of Gaussian profiles with randomly chosen position, width and strength. Since the total angular momentum M is no longer conserved for this system, exact diagonalization becomes powerless. Thus, we consider the many-body Hamiltonian in real space, $H_{QD} = \sum H_0 + H_I$ where H_I is the Coulomb interaction between electrons, and we apply a diffusion quantum Monte Carlo technique. The accuracy of DQMC depends largely on the quality of trial wave functions. Several different trial functions have been used in the literature, including solutions by local density approximation[40], single- or multiple-configuration states of non-interacting electrons[33], optimized with Jastrow factors. Our DQMC method uses unrestricted Hartree-Fock (UHF) solutions as trial states. Since spatial symmetry is broken by disorder, it is unclear *a priori* how to make assumptions on the form of trial wave function. We expect UHF solutions to be a good starting point as we have checked (see below) by comparing DQMC solutions using UHF trial states with exact diagonalization in a disorder-free QD: a very good agreement is found.

The presence of impurities in the Hamiltonian H adds a new degree of complexity to DQMC, because UHF solutions become complex numbers even at zero magnetic field. Since QMC methods can only deal with positive real numbers, a fixed-phase approximation[46,33], which is a generalization of the fixed-node approximation[48], must be used. In the fixed phase approximation, the exact solution of the many-body problem is assumed to have the same phase as the trial wave function. This approximation was introduced[46] to deal with the 2D electron gas and later applied to clean QD's[33], in the presence of a magnetic field. The application of the fixed-phase approximation to disordered QD is technically similar and we refer interested readers to these two references[46,33].

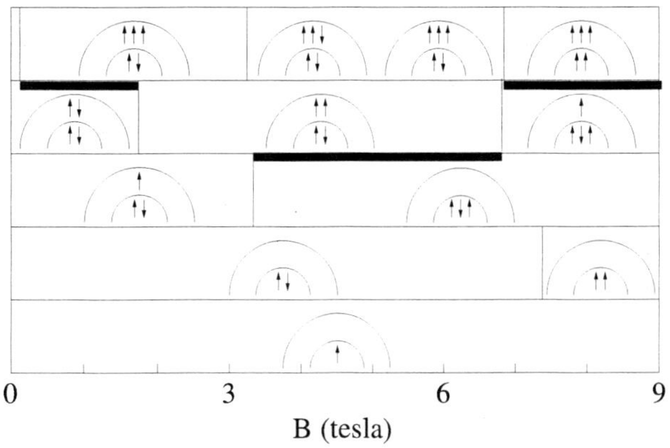

Figure 1. Many-body ground states up to 5 electrons as a function of B, for a strongly distorted QD. The QD is schematized by an inner disc representing the core region and an outer ring representing the peripheral potential minimum. Thick lines represent blockaded regions during a transport measurement. The arrows indicate spin configuration of the electrons. For simplicity, only those states with equivalent localization-spin configuration representing more than 95% contributions to the exact ground state for $B < 3$ tesla, and more than 99.9% contributions for $B > 3$ tesla, are shown. For this QD, the transition from $N = 3$ to $N = 4$ between $B \approx 3.8$ tesla to 7.3 tesla, and the transition from $N = 4$ to $N = 5$ between $B \approx 7.3$ tesla to 9 tesla are geometrically blockaded.

3 Results and Discussion

3.1 Ring-shaped QD

The exact diagonalization of the ring-shaped QD produces the many-body ground state configurations schematically shown in Fig. 1, as a function of magnetic field B. In order to make the interpretation easier, only those states which have different spin and spatial configuration are shown. Configurations in Fig. 1 represent the most relevant Slater determinants which contribute to the ground state in the corresponding ranges of field. The QD is symbolized with two semi-circles, the inner circle represents the core region (central potential minimum), and the outer circle represents the peripheral region (outer potential minimum). The arrows indicate spin states of the electrons occupying the regions. The thick black lines represents forbidden transitions between a $(N-1)$-electron QD and a N-electron QD. For instance, for the 5-electron QD, in the region between $B = 0-2$ tesla, the spin blockade occurs, *i.e.* the ground state transition from the 4-electron QD to the 5-electron QD involves changing the total spin of the QD by more than $1/2$, which has zero probability.

Most interesting, however, is the finding that there is another forbidden transition going from the 3-electron QD to the 4-electron QD in the field range $B \approx 3.2 - 6.8$ tesla. This is *not* due to spin blockade because the total spin is changed by only $1/2$. Our investigation indicates that this a new blockade regime that is induced by the fact that electrons can be localized in the two potential minima. Therefore, to add one electron to the 3-electron QD, the $3 \rightarrow 4$ transition requires the addition of a new electron plus a redistribution of one core electron to the peripheral region. The transition probability of such a process is proportional to that given by the spectral function $\Delta(N) \sim \sum_i |\langle N|c_i^\dagger|N-1\rangle|^2$ which turns out to be practically zero. To understand why is this, we denote the 4-electron QD wave function as $|c, c, , p, p>$ indicating that there are two core electrons (c) and two peripheral electrons (p), and the 3-electron QD wave function after one more electron is added as $|c, c, c, X\rangle$, which indicates the three original core electrons and the newly added electron in region X where $X = c$ or $X = p$. Therefore the spectral function is $\Delta = \sum_i |\langle c, c, p, p|a_i^\dagger|c, c, c\rangle|^2 \sim |\langle c, c, p, p|c, c, c, X\rangle|^2$. This transition probability is extremely small because mixing between Slater states with different localization configuration is extremely small (smaller than 0.1%) due to the spatial separation of the single particle states that make up the many-body Slater determinants. Such a *geometry induced blockade* is near 100% complete: it would greatly reduce the tunneling current when it occurs.

Another interesting result is how the spatial separation of electrons correlate with the orbital and spin degrees of freedom. Returning to Fig. 1, for 2-electron wave functions, our calculations show that the only effect of potential distortion is to push the singlet-to-triplet transition to near 7 tesla from ~ 3 tesla when there is no distortion. A large field is needed for our distorted dot because of the larger energy gap between core states which makes the change of an electron from $m = 0$ to $m = 1$ more difficult. For three electrons the effect is more striking: the peripheral and core regions are in competition for the third electron. At low field, the third electron (keeping in mind that we are using single electron language in these discussions) has two possibilities: it may reside in the core region and occupy the next single particle state, or it may reside in the peripheral region. For our QD, it turns out that the ground state is for the third electron to reside in the peripheral region at low B, because of the large energy gap between the core states at low B so that the third electron rather enters the peripheral region even though that region is a higher potential minimum. Another reason is that a reduction of total Coulomb interaction occurs when the third electron goes into the outer region of the QD. As B increases, the energy gap between the core states decreases, and as a result, an abrupt *redistribution* of an electron into the core region occurs at $B \sim 3.8$ tesla. For the 4-electron QD at $B < 2$ tesla, there are two electrons in the core and two in the peripheral region with total spin minimized. At ~ 2 tesla, the outer electrons become spin polarized. Then, at ~ 7 tesla, a transition between the two local potential minima occurs by which an outer electron redistributes into the core region. For the 5-electron QD, the localization configuration does not change in the magnetic field range studied here, *e.g.* there are two electrons in the core and three in the peripheral regions all the way to $B = 9$ tesla.

In Fig. 2 we plot the addition spectra as function of B.

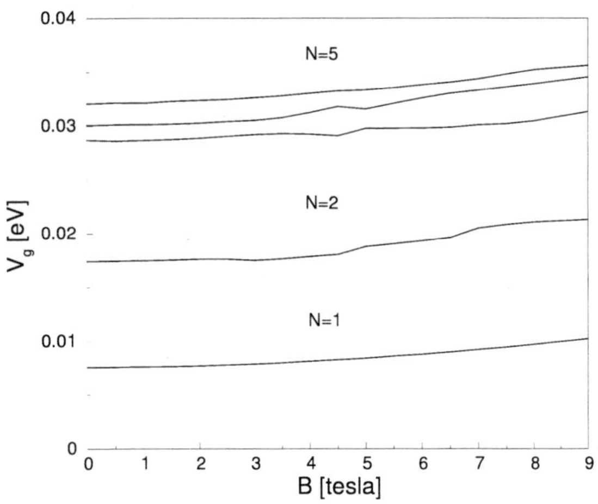

Figure 2. The addition spectra (chemical potential) of a strongly distorted QD as a function of B. The charging energy is substantially reduced after $N = 3$ due to spatial localization of electrons.

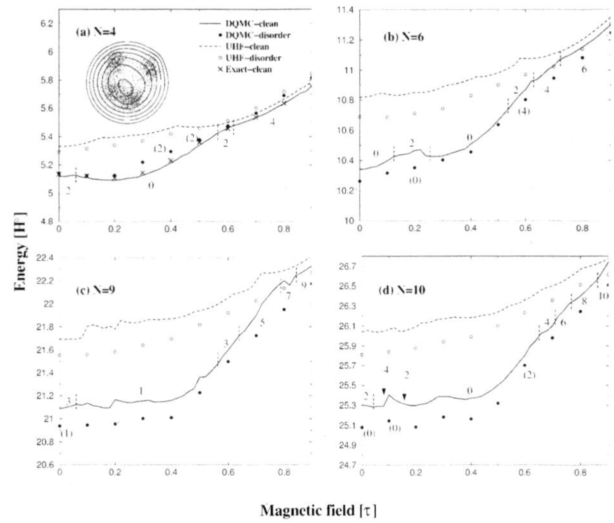

Figure 3. Many-body ground state energy as a function of magnetic field for (a) 4 electrons, (b) 6 electrons, (c) 9 electrons, and (d) 10 electrons. DQMC results are shown by solid lines (clean QD) and filled circles (disordered QD); UHF results are shown by dashed lines (clean QD) and open circles (disordered QD). For 4 electrons QD, exact results are also shown. The inset represents the confining potential of the first disordered QD (see Fig. 1) and walker positions for $B = 0.9\ \tau$ and $N = 4$.

The first 3 electrons enter the QD with an addition energy between $8 - 10$ meV. However, the next electrons have addition energies which are decreased considerably. There are several reasons for this behavior. First, interaction between electrons sitting in different potential minima is much weaker, only about 2 meV (with essentially no exchange energy due to weak wave function overlap). The direct Coulomb energy between peripheral states is low, ~ 3 meV, because they lie on large orbitals; whereas the attractive exchange energy between the nearest peripheral states can be as high as 1.5 meV due to their substantial overlap. In addition, as mentioned earlier, the energy difference between the lowest peripheral states are smaller than 0.1meV. As a result, the overall addition energy for 4 and 5 electrons is about $1 - 3$ meV.

3.2 Disordered QD

In Fig. 3 we present ground state energies obtained by UHF and DQMC for $N = 4, 6, 9$, and 10 electrons for a given disorder configuration. In these calculations we use effective atomic units determined by taking into account the effective mass and dielectric constant of GaAs. This gives an effective Bohr radius $a_0^* = 9.793$ nm and an effective Hartree $\mathrm{H}^* = 11.86$ meV. For magnetic field, we use the unit defined by $\tau = (m^*/m_0\kappa)^2(\epsilon_0/2\mu_B)$ T which gives 6.862 T for the material parameters considered here. Here DQMC results are represented by solid lines for clean QD and filled circles for disordered QD; UHF results are represented by dashed lines for clean QD and open circles for disordered QD. For comparison, we also include results of exactly diagonalizing the many-body Hamiltonian H for $N = 4$ electrons in a disorder-free QD. The vertical dashed lines represent spin transitions as obtained by DQMC for clean QD, and total spin in the z-direction ($2 \times S_z$) are also indicated as integers in different magnetic field ranges separated by the vertical dashed lines. The numerical numbers in parenthesis are spins for states of disordered QD, and are indicated only if they differ from the clean QD results. The shaded area in the confining potential indicate the random walker positions in our DQMC simulation at $B = 0.9\ \tau$ and $N = 4$.

First, we consider results for clean-QD's. We have verified that results from exact diagonalization and DQMC agree very well, as shown in Fig. 3(a) for a clean QD with $N = 4$ electrons. The DQMC results are actually *lower* by $\sim 0.03\ \mathrm{H}^*$ in the low-field region, indicating a slightly better convergence of the DQMC results. The exact diagonalization produced a slightly higher energy in the range of B-field presumably due to the limited number of Landau levels used in our analysis[55], but the agreement between DQMC and exact diagonalization is very satisfactory. In the maximum density droplet[57,44] (MDD) region, *i.e.* $B > 0.6\ \tau$, results from DQMC and exact diagonalization become indistinguishable[56]. The essentially perfect agreement in the MDD region is not surprising since the MDD state has a very small correlation energy and is well approximated by a single Slater determinant. This is also the reason that UHF results are rather close to the DQMC/exact results in the MDD state, see Fig. 3(a). However, for lower magnetic fields it is well known that the HF method does not give accurate energies and correct spin states[10], as clearly seen in Fig. 3 for up to ten electrons. Our DQMC results for 6 electrons in a clean QD (solid line of Fig. 3(b)) agree well with a previous variational QMC calculations[32]: our results give the same spin transition sequences of $0 \rightarrow 2 \rightarrow 0 \rightarrow 2 \rightarrow 4 \rightarrow 6$ with an increasing magnetic field. For $N = 9$ and $N = 10$ clean-QD's, spin transition sequences are found to be $3 \rightarrow 1 \rightarrow 3 \rightarrow 5 \rightarrow 7 \rightarrow 9$ and $0 \rightarrow 2 \rightarrow 0 \rightarrow 4 \rightarrow 0 \rightarrow 2 \rightarrow 0 \rightarrow 4 \rightarrow 6 \rightarrow 8 \rightarrow 10$ as seen in the Fig. 3(c) and (d), respectively. The spin states which appear for very small magnetic field windows are shown by arrows in Fig. 3(d).

Next, we discuss the disorder effects shown in Fig. 3. The most striking result is the deformation caused by disorder in energy as a function of magnetic field. For instance, the energy difference between clean QD and disordered QD for $N = 6$ is about 0.1 H* at $B = 0.2\ \tau$, while it is about 0.02 H* at $B = 0.3\ \tau$, as shown in Fig. 3(b). Due to these differences, the structures in the $E = E(B)$ curve, which are caused by different spin or momentum transitions, are drastically reduced for disordered QD. Such an effect is also observed for other electron numbers, and can make experimental observation of many-body transitions difficult. Analyzing the spin transitions, we find that disorder can strongly affect the total spin. For instance, in a 4-electron QD, $0 \rightarrow 2$ transition occurs at much smaller B (see Fig. 3(a)), and in the 10-electron QD, $S_z = 2$ state appears at $B = 0.6\ \tau$, while no such a state exists in the corresponding clean QD.

In atomic physics, Hund's rule determines whether a spin-down or a spin-up electron is added in order to fill the shells sequentially. For closed shells, *i.e.* at atomic numbers (magic numbers) 2, 10, 18,..., total spin must be zero. For any other atomic numbers, total spin in the open shell must be maximized. Due to the cylindrical symmetry, the magic numbers for the QD system we are studying are 2, 6, 12,... Experimentally, magic numbers as well as the half-shell electron numbers (4, 9,...) can be observed since they are responsible for maxima in addition energies in QD's[53,54]. The stability of Hund's rule against elliptical deformation[28], random disorder[31] and non-parabolicity of the confinement potential[54] were tested by density functional theories[28,31,54].

In Fig. 3, we show addition energy up to 13 electrons at zero magnetic field, calculated for a clean QD (the lowest line) and 8 different disorder configurations following the order presented in Fig. 1 (2nd line and up). It is clear that closed shell structures are not affected by disorder at least for the disorder strengths we have used, giving a higher peak at magic numbers $N = 2, 6$ and 12 corresponding to closed shells. On the other hand, although the half-shell peak at $N = 4$ is not affected by disorder, the half-shell peak at $N = 9$ is found to be less robust against disorder. Our calculations show that for the eight disordered QD's we investigated, the 9−th peak is an energy minimum in four of them; in addition, statistical noise in the DQMC calculation prevented us from reaching conclusive results for another three QD's. Finally, we note that a very clear dip at $N = 11$ is observed in all our results.

In Fig. 4, the numbers on the lowest spectrum represents $2 \times S_z$ for different N. For disordered QD's, S_z is plotted only if it differs from the clean QD case. According to Hund's rule, the total spin must be maximized in the outer shell. Moreover, it is believed that, in disordered QD's, high-spin states are suppressed due to a lifting of degeneracy [31]. We note that since we are using single Slater determinants, only z component of the total spin can be resolved, and so in the following, we limit our discussions to S_z. Without disorder, our DQMC results are in perfect agreement with Hund's rule. When disorder is added, we found that Hund's rule is especially stable for closed shells as well as for the second open shell ($N = 3, 4, 5$). For the third open shell ($N = 7 - 11$), Fig. 4 shows that there are some deviations in S_z from that of the clean QD, especially for $N = 10$ where $S_z = 0$ was found in five out of the eight disordered QD's, different from the $S_z = 2$ for the clean QD. A higher probability of $S = 0$ state for $N = 10$ was also found in density functional calculations[31]. These results also show that maximal spin alignment does not guarantee a peak at half-shell filling in agreement with density functional calculations[54] as seen, for instance, in the disorder configuration number two. Other deviations from the clean QD case are observed for the third shell of disordered QD number one; spin is minimized for $N = 7$, 8, and 9 QD's.

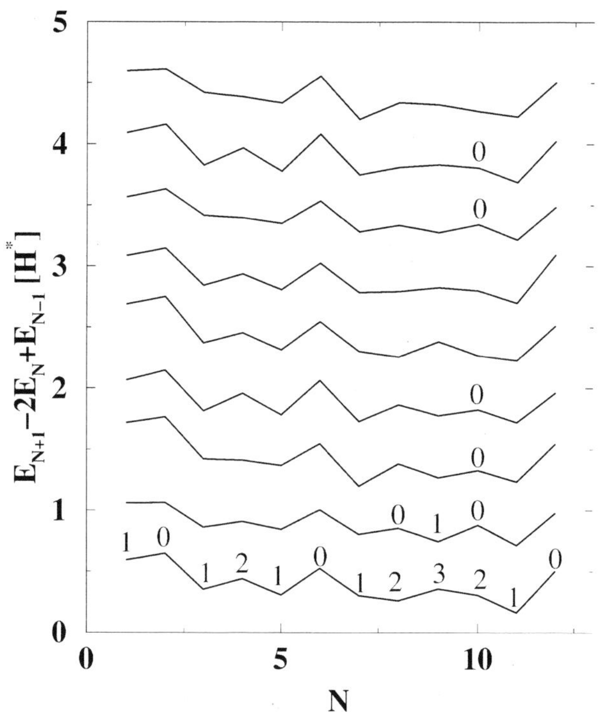

Figure 4. Addition energy at $B = 0$ up to 13 electrons for clean QD (the lowest line) and 8 different disorder configuration following the order represented in Fig. 1 (2nd line and up). The numbers represent $2 \times S_z$, and they are shown for disordered QD's only if they differ from the clean QD results.

4 Conclusion

To summarize, We have investigated the competing energetics of electron-electron interaction, magnetic field, and geometrical factors, in quantum dots with up to thirteen electrons, using exact numerical techniques such as exact diagonalization and DQMC. The ring-shaped potential landscape provides a competition of various contributions to the total energy by spatially separating electrons. Such effects have interesting implications for tunneling current in the Coulomb blockade regime, at least for cases involving a small number of strongly interacting electrons as we have studied. By localizing in different potential minima, the total ground state energy is minimized. However, due to the energetics competition, adding an electron to the QD may involve a charge redistribution between the two potential minima. We found that this redistribution occurs abruptly as the magnetic field is increased. A most interesting outcome of the redistribution is a new blockade phenomenon which is caused by a drastic reduction of the spectral weight for the transition from a $(N-1)$-electron QD to a N-electron QD due to the spatial localization of the electrons. The geometric blockade leads to a drastic reduction of the tunneling current which should be measurable experimentally.

DQMC is shown to give excellent total energy and spin configuration for clean-QD's as compared with exact diagonalization, and is very powerful for investigating disordered QD's which do not possess any spatial symmetry. The lack of spatial symmetry makes an exact calculation very difficult if not impossible for $N > 7$, even for modern computers. Compared with the UHF technique, DQMC gives superior advantages in total energy accuracy, especially for low magnetic field before the transition to maximum density droplet states. Disorder is found to have very significant effects to the total energy of QD. In particular, the energetic transition (the kinks in energy) between many-body states is made much less clear due to disorder, and the required magnetic field to induce such transitions may be rather different than that of clean-QD, this may have important implications to interpreting tunneling spectroscopy data. We found that Hund's rule for closed shell is robust against even strong disorder, but less so for open shells. For the lower shells, the spin states are largely unaffected by disorder, but for higher shells (larger number of electrons N) this may change due to disorder.

Acknowledgments

We gratefully acknowledge financial support from Natural Science and Engineering Research Council of Canada, le Fonds pour la Formation de Chercheurs et l'Aide à la Recherche de la Province de Québec, and NanoQuebec. We gratefully acknowledge Prof. J.S. Wang for helping us in developing the DQMC code, and we thank Dr. Pawel Hawrylak for several useful discussions on spin configurations and Hund's rule of quantum dots.

References

1. See, for example, articles in *Mesoscopic Electron Transport*, edited by L.L. Sohn, L.P. Kouwenhoven and G. Schön, (Kluwer, Series E 345, 1997).
2. R.C. Ashoori, Nature (London) **379**, 413 (1996).
3. R.C. Ashoori, H.L. Stormer, J.S. Weiner, L.N. Pfeiffer, S. J. Pearton, K.W. Baldwin, and K.W. West, Phys. Rev. Lett. **68**, 3088 (1992).
4. R.C. Ashoori, H.L. Stormer, J.S. Weiner, L.N. Pfeiffer, K.W. Baldwin, and K.W. West, Phys. Rev. Lett. **71**, 613 (1993).
5. L. P. Kouwenhoven, T. H. Oosterkamp, M. W. S. Danoesastro, M. Eto, D. G. Austing, T. Honda, and S. Tarucha, Science **278**, 1788 (1997).
6. P.A. Maksym, and T. Chakraborty, Phys. Rev. Lett. **65**, 108 (1990).
7. U. Merkt, J. Huser, and M. Wagner, Phys. Rev. B **43**, 7320 (1991).
8. N.F. Johnson, and M.C. Payne, Phys. Rev. B **45**, 3819 (1992).
9. S.R.Eric Yang, A.H. MacDonald, and M.D. Johnson, Phys. Rev. Lett. **71**, 3194 (1993).
10. J.J. Palacios, L. Martin-Moreno, G. Chiappe, E. Louis, C. Tejedor, Phys. Rev. B **50**, 5760 (1994);
11. A. Wojs, and P. Hawrylak, Phys. Rev. B **56**, 13227 (1997).
12. J.J. Palacios, P. Hawrylak, Physical Rev. B **51**, 1769 (1995).
13. R. Berkovits, Phys. Rev. Lett. **81**, 2128 (1998).
14. C.M. Canali, Phys. Rev. Lett. **84**, 3934 (2000).
15. M. Fujito, A. Natori, and H. Yasunaga, Phys. Rev. B **53**, 9952 (1996).
16. H.-M. Muller, and S.E. Koonin, Phys. Rev. B **54**, 14532 (1996).
17. H. Tamura, and M. Ueda, Phys. Rev. Lett. **79**, 1345 (1997).
18. K.-H. Ahn, K. Richter, and In-Ho Lee, Phys. Rev. Lett. **83**, 4144 (1999).
19. C. Yannouleas, and U. Landman, Phys. Rev. Lett. **82**, 5325 (1999).
20. A. Cohen, K. Richter, and R. Berkovits, Phys. Rev. B **60**, 2536 (1999).
21. S. Levit, and D. Orgad. Phys. Rev. B **60**, 5549 (1999).
22. M.-C. Cha, and S.-R. Eric Yang, Phys. Rev. B **61**, 1720 (2000).
23. D. Ullmo, and H.U. Baranger, Phys. Rev. B **64**, 245324 (2001).
24. B. Reusch, W. Hausler, and H. Grabert **63**, 113313 (2001).
25. M. Koskinen, and M. Manninen, and S. M. Reimann, Phys. Rev. Lett. **79**, 1389 (1997).
26. S. M. Reimann, M. Koskinen, J. Helgesson, P.E. Lindelof, and M. Manninen, Phys. Rev. B **58**, 8111 (1998).
27. O. Steffens, U. Rossler, and M. Suhrke, Europhys. Lett. **42**, 529 (1998).
28. K. Hirose, and N. S. Wingreen, Phys. Rev. B **59**, 4604 (1999).
29. C. A. Ullrich, and G. Vignale, Phys. Rev. B **61**, 2729 (2000).
30. K. Hirose, F. Zhou, and N. S. Wingreen, Phys. Rev. B **63**, 075301 (2001).
31. K. Hirose, and N. S. Wingreen, Phys. Rev. B **65**, 193305 (2002).
32. H. Saarikoski, E. Rasanen, S. Siljamake, A. Harju, M. J. Puska, and R. M. Nieminen, Eur. Phys. J. B **26**, 241 (2002).
33. F. Bolton, Phys. Rev. B **54**, 4780 (1996).
34. Y. Wan, G. Ortiz, and P. Phillips, Phys. Rev. B **55**, 5313 (1997).
35. E. Lee, A. Puzder, M. Y. Chou, T. Uzer, and D. Farrelly, Phys.

Rev. B **57**, 12281 (1998).

36. A. Harju, V. A. Sverdlov, and R. M. Nieminen, Europhys. Lett. **41**, 407 (1998).
37. A. Harju, V. A. Sverdlov, R. M. Nieminen, and V. Halonen, Phys. Rev. B **59**, 5622 (1999).
38. A. Harju, S. Siljamaki, and R. M. Nieminen, Phys. Rev. B **60**, 1807 (1999).
39. R. Egger, W. Hausler, C. H. Mak, and H. Grabert, Phys. Rev. Lett. **82**, 3320 (1999).
40. F. Pederiva, C. J. Umrigar, and E. Lipparini, Phys. Rev. B **62**, 8120 (2000).
41. S.-R. Eric Yang, M.-C. Cha, and J. H. Han, Phys. Rev. B **62**, 8171 (2000).
42. J. Harting, O. Mulken, and P. Borrmann, Phys. Rev. B **62**, 10207 (2000).
43. L. Coletti, F. Pederiva, E. Lipparini, and C. J. Umrigar. Eur. Phys. J. B **27**, 385 (2002).
44. S. Siljamaki, A. Harju, R. M. Nieminen, V. A. Sverdlov, and P. Hyvonen, Phys. Rev. B **65**, 121306 (2002).
45. K. S. Liu, M. H. Kalos, and G. V. Chester, Phys. Rev. A **10**, 303 (1974).
46. G. Ortiz, D. M. Ceperley, and R. M. Martin, Phys. Rev. Lett. **71**, 2777 (1993).
47. C. J. Umrigar, M. P. Nightingale, and K. J. Runge, J. Chem. Phys. **99**, 2865 (1993).
48. W. M. C. Foulkes, L. Mitas, R. J. Needs, and G. Rajagopal, Rev. Mod. Phys. **73**, 33 (2001).
49. N.B.Zhitenev, R.C. Ashoori, L.N. Pfeiffer, and K.W. West, Phys. Rev. Lett. **79**, 2308 (1997).
50. M. Brodsky, N.B. Zhitenev, R.C. Ashoori, L.N. Pfeiffer, and K.W. West, Phys. Rev. Lett. **85**, 2356 (2000).
51. L.P. Rokhinson, L.J. Guo, S.Y. Chou, and D.C. Tsui , Phys. Rev. B **63**, 035321 (2001).
52. S. Luscher, T. Heinzel, K. Ensslin, W. Wegscheider, and M. Bichler, Phys. Rev. Lett. **86**, 2118 (2001).
53. S. Tarucha, D. G. Austing, and T. Honda, R. J. van der Hage, and L. P. Kouwenhoven, Phys. Rev. Lett. **77**, 3613 (1996).
54. P. Matagne, J. P. Leburton, D. G. Austing, and S. Tarucha, Phys. Rev. B **65**, 85325 (2002).
55. In our exact diagonalization calculation, we have used three Landau levels for $B < 5\ \tau$, and two Landau levels for $B > 5\ \tau$, to obtain numerical convergence of the results.
56. The statistical noise of our DQMC results vary between 0.003 and 0.01 H*, depending on values of electron number N, the magnetic field B, and the total spin S_z. The statistical noise at the MDD region is about 0.003 H*.
57. T.H. Oosterkamp, J.W. Janssen, L.P. Kouwenhoven, D.G. Austing, T. Honda, and S. Tarucha, Phys. Rev. Lett. **82**, 2931 (1999).
58. T. Chakraborty, and P. Pietilainen, Phys. Rev. B **50**, 8460 (1994).
59. K. Varga, P. Navratil, J. Usukura, and Y. Suzuki, Phys. Rev. B **63**, 205308 (2001).
60. A. Emperador, M. Barranco, E. Lipparini, M. Pi, and L. Serra, Phys. Rev. B **59** 15301 (1999).
61. A. D. Guclu, Q. F. Sun, H. Guo, and R. Harris, Phys. Rev. B. **66**, 195327 (2002).
62. V. Fock, Z. Phys. **47**, 446 (1928); C.G. Darwin, Proc. Cambridge Philos. Soc. **27**, 86 (1930).

NEGF-DFT: a first principles formalism for modeling molecular electronics

Nikolai Sergueev and Hong Guo [a]

[a]Center for the Physics of Materials and Department of Physics, McGill University, Montreal, PQ, Canada H3A 2T8

By carrying out density functional theory (DFT) analysis within the Keldysh non-equilibrium Green's function (NEGF) framework, we have investigated quantum transport properties of an $\mathrm{Au}-\mathrm{C}_{60}-\mathrm{Au}$ molecular junction. In this paper we briefly review the NEGF-DFT formalism and present our data.

En procédant à un calcul de théorie de la densité fonctionnelle (DFT) dans le formalisme de Keldysh de la fonction de Green hors d'équilibre (NEGF), nous étudions les propriétés de transport quantique d'une jonction moléculaire $\mathrm{Au}-\mathrm{C}_{60}-\mathrm{Au}$. *Nous présentons ici une brève revue du formalisme, ainsi que nos résultats.*

1 Introduction

Using molecules as functional units for electronic device application[1] is an interesting perspective and a possible goal of nano-electronics. Work in this field has clearly demonstrated that many of the important molecular device characteristics relate specifically to a strong coupling between the *atomic* and the *electronic* degrees of freedom. However, from a theoretical point of view, the accurate prediction of the properties of atomic and molecular scale devices – including the true I-V curves with as few adjustable parameters as possible – still represents a formidable challenge, despite the advances and wide-spread application of large scale density functional theory (DFT) based *ab initio* modeling over the last two decades.

Recall that most of the previous DFT-based *ab initio* condensed matter simulations[2,3] solve only two kinds of problems: (i) finite systems such as isolated molecules, as in quantum chemistry; (ii) periodic systems consisting of supercells, as in solid state physics. However, a molecular electronic device is neither finite nor periodic: it typically has open boundaries which are connected to long and different electrodes extending to electron reservoirs far away, where the external bias potentials are applied. In other words, calculations of finite or periodic systems do not have the correct boundary conditions for quantum transport. Therefore, new formalisms for electronic analysis are required to carry out first principles transport modeling for molecular electronics.

In this work, we breifly outline a formalism that combines DFT with the Keldysh non-equilibrium Green's functions (NEGF) so that nonequilibrium quantum transport properties can be predicted from atomistic approach without any phenomenological parameters[4,5]. We then apply our NEGF-DFT approach to investigate a C_{60} molecular junction connected to Au electrodes. The rest of the paper is organised as follows. In Sec.2 we present the NEGF-DFT formalism. In Sec. 3 we present the transport properties of the Au-C_{60}-Au tunnel junction. Sec. 4 is reserved for a short summary and outlook of future work.

2 NEGF-DFT Formalism

The simplest model of a molecular device is schematically shown in Fig.1 where a C_{60} molecule is contacted by two semi-infinite Au electrodes which extend to $z = \pm\infty$ where bias voltage is applied. To calculate the electronic states of such a device, two problems should be solved. First, the infinitely large problem—due to the electrodes, must be reduced to that manageble on a computer, *i.e.* one has to solve a open boundary problem. Second, one has to construct charge density when there is a bias voltage across the molecule—a non-equilibrium problem. From the computational point of view, it is convenient to divide our system into three parts: a scattering region with some portion of electrodes and two metal electrodes extending to $z = \pm\infty$, as shown by the vertical lines in Fig.1.

To reduce the infinitely large problem to that defined inside the scattering region (see Fig.1), we notice that the effective Kohn-Sham (KS) potential $V_{eff}[\rho(\mathbf{r})]$, where charge distribution is $\rho(\mathbf{r})$, deep inside a solid surface (the lead) is very close to the corresponding bulk KS potential. This fact makes the boudary conditions to be written in the following form[4]

$$V_{eff}(\mathbf{r}) = \begin{cases} V_{l,eff}(\mathbf{r}) = V_{l,bulk}(\mathbf{r}) & Z < Z_l \\ V_{c,eff}(\mathbf{r}) & Z_l < Z < Z_r \\ V_{r,eff}(\mathbf{r}) = V_{r,bulk}(\mathbf{r}) & Z > Z_r \ , \end{cases} \tag{1}$$

where the planes $Z = Z_{l(r)}$ are the left (right) limits of the scattering region (See Fig.1). In practice, within DFT where we only need to match the Hartree potential $V_H[\rho(\mathbf{r})]$ at the boundaries, this can be accomplished by solving the Poisson equation in a 3D real space grid. Once $V_H[\rho(\mathbf{r})]$ is matched, we can show that $V_{r,eff}(\mathbf{r})$ will also be matched within DFT. The 3D real space Poisson solver also allows us to deal with any gate potentials as they provide additional boundary conditions for the electrostatics. Furthermore, once $V_{r,eff}(\mathbf{r})$ is matched across the boundaries, the charge density $\rho(\mathbf{r})$ will automatically match at the boundaries. The lower panel of Fig.1 shows the charge density: although the densities in the leads and in the scattering region are calculated by separate calculations, they match perfectly across the boundaries.

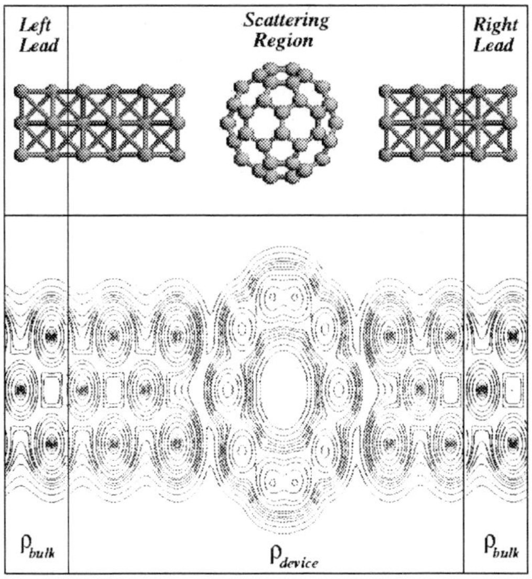

Figure 1. Schematic plot of the Au-C_{60}-Au molecular tunnel junction. The Au electrode consist of repeated unit cells extending to $z = \pm\infty$, and its surface is oriented along the (100) direction. The lower panel shows the calculated charge density at equilibrium where perfect matching is obtained across the boundaries between the leads and the central scattering region.

The above "screening approximation"[4] allows us to reduce the infinitely large problem to one defined inside the scattering region. In this approximation, we neglected any influence the scattering region may give to the leads, but if the portion of the leads included inside the scattering region is long enough, such an approximation is well controlled. On the other hand, the semi-infinite leads will contribute to the scattering region. That contribution is included through the self-energies in the Green's function of the scattering region.

In order to calculate charge density away from equilibrium (due to bias voltage), we apply NEGF[6]. The density matrix is calculated from NEGF $\mathbf{G}^<(E)$, as

$$\rho = -\frac{i}{2\pi}\int dE\mathbf{G}^<(E) \text{ , where} \quad (2)$$

$$\mathbf{G}^< = \mathbf{G}^R\mathbf{\Sigma}^<[f_l, f_r]\mathbf{G}^A \text{ ,} \quad (3)$$

where $\mathbf{G}^{R(A)}$ is the retarded (advanced) Green's function. $\mathbf{G}^<$ is defined through the Keldysh equation[6]. The lesser self-energy $\mathbf{\Sigma}^<[f_l, f_r]$ within DFT can be evaluated by:

$$\mathbf{\Sigma}^<[f_l, f_r] = -2iIm[f_l\mathbf{\Sigma}_l^R - f_r\mathbf{\Sigma}_r^R] \text{ ,} \quad (4)$$

where $\mathbf{\Sigma}_{l(r)}^R$ is the retarded self-energy of the left (right) electrode and they can be calculated for the semi-infinite leads by an iterative technique[4]. $f_{l(r)}$ are the corresponding Fermi distribution functions. Note that $\mathbf{\Sigma}^<[f_l, f_r]$ is not a Fermi distribution: a fact reflecting the non-equilibrium nature of the problem.

In our numerical procedure, we use a LCAO *s,p,d* atomic basis set[3] to expand the wavefunction and to define the Hamiltonian matrix. The atomic core is defined by standard norm conserving nonlocal pseudopotential[7]. We evaluate $\mathbf{G}^{R(A)}$ by direct matrix inversion, and construct $\rho(\mathbf{r})$ by numerical evaluation of Eq.(3) aided by a contour integration trick. Once $\rho(\mathbf{r})$ is obtained, we evaluate the KS potential and iterate the above procedure untill numerical convergence.

Because we construct $\rho(\mathbf{r})$ by NEGF which takes care of the non-equilibrium statistics, and we calculate the Hartree potential by directly solving the 3D Poission equation that includes all external fields as electrostatic boundary conditions, our NEGF-DFT formalism is able to solve charge transport problems in addition to the conventional electronic structure calculations.

3 The Au-C_{60}-Au Molecular Tunnel Junction

In this section we report our analysis on the transport properties of an Au-C_{60}-Au molecular tunnel junction calculated using our NEGF-DFT electronic package as discussed above. The device structure is shown in the upper panel of Fig.1. So far a considerable amount of theoretical and experimental effort has been devoted to investigate transport properties of C_{60} and other fullerene molecules[8–10]. The device we present consists of fullerene molecule C_{60} fixed in between two gold electrodes with an Au-C_{60} distance of 3.3a.u.(1a.u.= 0.529Å.). Each electrode consists of repeated unit cells with nine Au atoms in the (100) direction and extended to infinity. The entire calculation is performed on a Pentium-IV processor with 512 Mb of RAM. A typical solution of KS equation for this device requires a few hours of runtime.

The current-voltage (I-V) characteristics is calculated by

$$I = \frac{2e^2}{h}\int T(E, V_b)[f_l(E) - f_r(E)]dE \text{ ,} \quad (5)$$

where $T(E, V_b)$ is the transmission coefficient at energy E and bias voltage V_b. The Fermi distribution functions $f_{l(r)}(E)$ limit the integration to a small energy range eV_b at the Fermi level of the electrodes. Transmission coefficient $T(E, V_b)$ is calculated using Green's function[11] which we have already obtained during the NEGF-DFT self-consistent iterations,

$$T(E, V_b) = tr[\mathbf{\Gamma}_l\mathbf{G}_c^R\mathbf{\Gamma}_l\mathbf{G}_c^A] \text{ .} \quad (6)$$

The function $\mathbf{\Gamma}_\lambda$ describes the line-width resulting from the coupling of the scattering region to the lead λ and is evaluated in terms of corresponding self-energies $\mathbf{\Sigma}_\lambda$ as

$$\mathbf{\Gamma}_\lambda = i[\mathbf{\Sigma}_\lambda - \mathbf{\Sigma}_\lambda^\dagger], \ (\lambda = l, r). \quad (7)$$

The retarded Green's function of the scattering region, $\mathbf{G}_c^R$, in Eq.(6) is given as

$$\mathbf{G}_c(E) = [E\mathbf{I} - \mathbf{H}_c - \mathbf{\Sigma}]^{-1} \text{ ,} \quad (8)$$

where $\mathbf{H}_c$ is the Hamiltonian of the scattering region and $\mathbf{\Sigma} = \mathbf{\Sigma}_l + \mathbf{\Sigma}_r$ is the total self-energy.

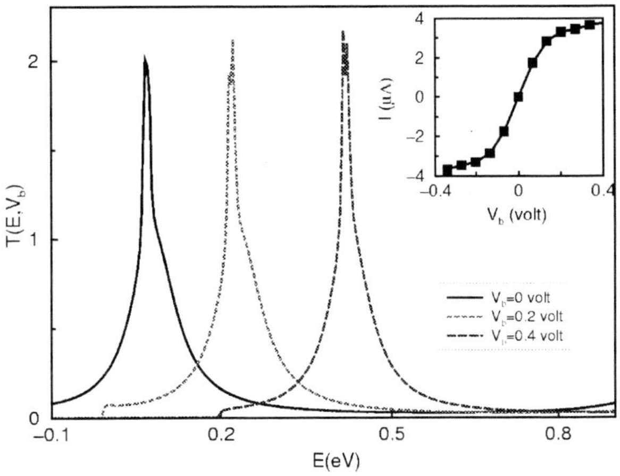

Figure 2. Transmission coefficient $T(E, V_b)$ versus electron energy E for three bias voltages V_b. The sharp transmission peak, which results from a resonance of the fullerene+contacts Hamiltonian, dominates the conductance as well as the current-triggered dynamics. The inset shows the calculated I-V curve from which metallic behavior is evident.

The transmission coefficient obtained from Eq.(6) is presented on Fig.2 as a function of the electron energy E for three different bias voltages at zero gate potential. The sharp peak in $T(E, V_b)$ is the result of a resonance transmission through the LUMO of the C_{60}. At zero bias, this resonance lies just above the Fermi level of the leads (Fermi level is $E_F = 0$ in Fig.2). As a bias voltage is applied, the peak position shifts to higher energies. If the system is absolutely symmetric, we would expect the same voltage drop at the two electrode-molecule junctions. In our system, the atomic structure of C_{60} facing the two electrodes are not the same thereby breaking the left-right symmetry. We therefore observe an asymmetrical voltage drop at the two contacts. Consequently the transmission peak position shifts by about ~ 0.15 eV when V_b is increased by 0.2V, *i.e.*, the voltage drops more on one side than on the other side of the C_{60}. We also calculated the I-V curve from Eq.(5) for this device, shown in the inset of Fig.2. Similar metallic behavior has been reported before[8] for Al contacted C_{60} device. The interesting physics is that despite the large HOMO-LUMO gap of C_{60} (~ 1.8eV), here we predict a metallic transport characteristics of the Au-C_{60}-Au device. The reason is that when a C_{60} molecule is bonded to metallic leads, there is a strong charge transfer from the leads to the C_{60} cage, thereby partially filling the original empty LUMO. In other words, charge transfer from leads to C_{60} aligns the LUMO to the Fermi energy of the leads, which gives a large conductance and hence a metallic I-V curve.

4 Summary

We have shown that the NEGF-DFT formalism is a powerful technique for modeling charge transport properties of molecular electronic devices. The novelty of this technique is in constructing electron charge density via nonequilibrium Green's functions and the very effective screening approximation. Since the entire algorithm is based on evaluating Green's function, the technique is intrinsically O(N): this is because atoms far away from each other do not have overlap and the Hamiltonian matrix is therefore block-diagonal. This has tremendous computational advantage which we demonstrated by calculating the nonlinear I-V curve of the Au-C_{60}-Au molecular tunnel junction.

Acknowledgments

We gratefully acknowledge financial support from Natural Science and Engineering Research Council of Canada, le Fonds pour la Formation de Chercheurs et l'Aide à la Recherche de la Province du Québec, and NanoQuebec. We gratefully acknowledge Prof. Jeremy Taylor and Dr. Brian Larade for their contributions throughout the work presented here.

References

1. A. Aviram and M. A. Ratner, *Chem. Phys. Lett.* **29** (1974) 277.
2. M. C. Payne, M. P. Teter, D. C. Allan, T. A. Arias and J. D. Joannopoulos, *Rev. Mod. Phys.* **64** (1992) 1045.
3. P. Ordejón, E. Artacho, and J. M. Soler, *Phys. Rev. B* **53** (1996) R104441.
4. J. Taylor, H. Guo and J. Wang, *Phys. Rev. B* **63** (2001) 245407.
5. M. Brandbyge, J.-L. Mozos, P. Ordejón, J. Taylor, and K. Stokbro, *Phys. Rev. B* **65** (2002) 165401.
6. H. Haug and A.-P. Jauho, *Quantum Kinetics in Transport and Optics of Semi-conductors*, Springer-Verlag, New York (1998).
7. G. B. Bachelet, D. R. Hamann, and M. Schlüter, *Phys. Rev. B* **26** (1982) 4199.
8. J. Taylor, H. Guo, and J. Wang, *Phys. Rev. B* **63** (2001) R121104.
9. H. Park, J. Park, A. K. L. Lim, E. H. Anderson, A. P. Alivisatos, and P. L. McEuen, *Nature* **407** (2000) 57.
10. S. Alavi and T. Seideman, *J. Chem. Phys.* **115** (2001) 1882.
11. S. Datta, *Electronic Transport in Mesoscopic Systems*, Cambridge University Press (1997).

A Singularity-Free Method for the Time-Dependent Schrödinger Equation for Nonlinear Molecules

A.D.Bandrauk[a,*], Hui-Zhong Lu[a]

[a]Labo. de Chimie Théorique, Faculté des Sciences, Université de Sherbrooke, Sherbrooke, PQ ,Canada J1K 2R1
{ andre.bandrauk, huizhong.lu}@usherbrooke.ca
* Canada Research Chair in Computational Chemistry and Photonics

We present a new method for the numerical solution of the Schrödinger equation using cylindrical/polar coordinates systems. For cylindrical coordinates systems, after use of a split-operator method which separates the z direction propagation and the (x, y) plane propagation, we approximate the wave function in each (x, y) section by a Fourier series $(\sum c_m(\rho)e^{im\phi})$ which offers an exponential convergence in the ϕ direction and is naturally applicable for polar coordinates system. The coefficients $(c_m(\rho))$ are then calculated by Finite Difference Method (FDM) in the ρ direction. We adopt the Crank-Nicholson method for the temporal propagation. The final linear system consists of a set of independent one-dimensional (ρ) linear systems and the matrix for every one-dimensional linear systems is sparse, so the whole linear system may be very efficiently solved. The most important advantage of the new method is that it is unitary at all steps and is analytically convergent every where even near the $\rho = 0$ origin, in contrast to most other numerical method based on cylindrical/polar coordinates systems which are not unitary and introduce a numerical singularity at $\rho = 0$. We also speculate on its generalization to the general case of dimension > 3 and the necessary computation power.

Nous présentons une nouvelles méthode de solution de l'équation de Schrödinger en coordonnées cylindriques ou polaires. En coordonnées cylindriques, après l'utilisation d'une opération qui sépare les propagations dans la direction z et dans le plan, nous appliquons une approximation de la fonction d'onde dans chaque section (x, y) *par une série de Fourier* $(\sum c_m(\rho)e^{im\phi})$ *qui offre l'avantage d'une convergence exponentielle dans la direction* ϕ *et qui s'applique naturellement en coordonnées sphériques. Les coefficients* $(c_m(\rho))$ *sont ensuite calculés par la méthode des différences finies dans la direction* ρ*. Nous adoptons la méthode de Crank-Nicholson pour la propagation temporelle. Le système linéaire final est un ensemble de systèmes linéaires unidimensionnels (en* ρ*) et la matrice associée est creuse, donc le tout peut être résolue de manière efficace. Le principal avantage de la méthode est qu'elle est unitaire à chaque étape et converge analytiquement partout, même près de l'origine (*$\rho = 0$*), contrairement à la plupart des autres méthodes numériques basées sur les coordonnées cylindriques ou sphériques, qui ne sont pas unitaires et qui introduisent une singularité numérique à* $\rho = 0$*. Nous discutons de sa généralisation possible au cas de dimension* > 3 *et de la puissance de calcul requise.*

1 Introduction

Because of efficiency, in many cases we use cylindrical coordinates for the numerical solution of the 3-D Time Dependent Schrödinger Equation, TDSE, for molecules exposed parallel to a intense laser pulse: H_2^+ [1–4], H_2 [5]. Generally, we use the split-operator method or the ADI method which separate the propagation in the different directions. This process reduces a lot of computing time and is very precise [6]. After splitting, we must propagate the wave function in each section plane in the polar coordinate. Polar coordinates have also been used in 2-D simulations of molecular alignment [3]. But in the polar coordinate system, one encounters often the (unitarity,precision) problem in the ρ direction when one uses Finite Difference Methods (FDM) and the difficulty of very expensive algorithms in CPU-time when one uses a development based on special functions such as Bessel function [1].

Because of its simplicity,the FDM is the most used in the ρ direction [1–4]. In order to avoid the boundary condition problem — there is no natural physical boundary condition at $\rho = 0$, one usually adopts the following nonlinear (stretching) transformation:

$$\rho = T(\tilde{\rho}), \qquad (1)$$

$$\tilde{\psi}(\tilde{\rho}) = \sqrt{T'T}\psi(\rho), \qquad (2)$$

$$i\frac{\partial\tilde{\psi}}{\partial t} = -\frac{1}{2}\left[\frac{1}{T'^2}\frac{\partial^2}{\partial\tilde{\rho}^2} - 2\frac{T''}{T'^3}\frac{\partial}{\partial\tilde{\rho}}\right]\tilde{\psi} + \left[\frac{5}{4}\frac{T''^2}{T'^4} - \frac{1}{2}\frac{T'''}{T'^3} + \frac{1}{4T^2} + V\right]\tilde{\psi}, \qquad (3)$$

$$\tilde{\psi}(0) = 0, \qquad \tilde{\psi}(\tilde{\rho}_{max}) = 0, \qquad (4)$$

The equation is restricted in the ρ direction after the use of the split-operator or ADI method in the polar coordinate (ρ, ϕ). Two problems (unitarity,convergence) occur as:
First:, when we discretize the differential operators in (3) with standart central difference schemes we find immediately the problem of unitarity: if $\rho/\tilde{\rho}$ is not constant, the resulting propagation matrix will not be symetrical, so the final discrete propagator is not unitary. This is just what occurs with transformations like $\rho = \tilde{\rho}^{3/2}$ (Kono and Kawata): $1/T' = 2/[3\sqrt{\tilde{\rho}}]$ shows that the coefficients of the second order derivative (kinetic energy) change very quickly near the origin so the propagation matrix is far from being symetrical near $\tilde{\rho} = 0$.
Second:, there is a problem of convergence which is very little discussed. It is well known that the convergence of

the FDM is based on the relation :

$$\tilde{\psi}(\tilde{\rho}+h) = \sum_{i=0}^{n} \frac{h^i}{n!}\frac{d^i\tilde{\psi}}{d\tilde{\rho}^i}(\tilde{\rho}) + \frac{h^n}{(n+1)!}\int_{\tilde{\rho}}^{\tilde{\rho}+h} \frac{d^{i+1}\tilde{\psi}(x)}{d\tilde{\rho}^{i+1}}dx, \quad (5)$$

where the coefficient of the remaining term (integration) must be limited to obtain convergence. Now, after the transformation above we have $\rho = \tilde{\rho} \Longrightarrow \tilde{\psi}(\tilde{\rho}) = \sqrt{\tilde{\rho}}\psi(\tilde{\rho})$, $\rho = \tilde{\rho}^{3/2} \Longrightarrow \tilde{\psi}(\tilde{\rho}) = \sqrt{3/2}\tilde{\rho}\psi(\tilde{\rho}^{3/2})$. When $\psi(\rho)$ is an analytical function, we can make the development:

$$\begin{aligned}\frac{\partial^{i+1}\tilde{\psi}}{\partial\tilde{\rho}^{i+1}} &= \frac{\partial^{i+1}}{\partial\tilde{\rho}^{i+1}}\left[\sqrt{\tilde{\rho}}\psi(\tilde{\rho})\right] \\ &= \frac{\partial^{i+1}}{\partial\tilde{\rho}^{i+1}}\sum_{k=0}^{\infty} c_k\tilde{\rho}^{k+1/2} \\ &= \sum_{k=0}^{\infty} d_k\tilde{\rho}^{(2k-2i-1)/2} \text{ for } \rho=\tilde{\rho}, \quad (6)\end{aligned}$$

or

$$\begin{aligned}\frac{\partial^{i+1}\tilde{\psi}}{\partial\tilde{\rho}^{i+1}} &= \frac{\partial^{i+1}}{\partial\tilde{\rho}^{i+1}}\left[\sqrt{3/2}\tilde{\rho}\psi(\tilde{\rho}^{3/2})\right] \\ &= \frac{\partial^{i+1}}{\partial\tilde{\rho}^{i+1}}\sum_{k=0}^{\infty} c_k\tilde{\rho}^{1+3k/2} \\ &= \sum_{k=0}^{\infty} e_k\tilde{\rho}^{(3k-2i)/2} \text{ for } \rho=\tilde{\rho}^{3/2}. \quad (7)\end{aligned}$$

The two preceding equations show directly that with transformed wave function the integration term in (5) will not be finite (bounded) near $\tilde{\rho}=0$ for general cases. We also conclude that if $c_k = 0$ for all k odd, equation (7) gives an analytical function so the equality (5) upon which the FDM's convergence is based is satisfied. This means that when $\psi(\rho)$ is an even function (*i.e* $\psi(\rho) = \psi(-\rho)$) the transformation $\rho = \tilde{\rho}^{3/2}$ will offer a convergent numerical scheme which is the special case of 2-D (ρ, ϕ) section non-passing by protons for 3-D H_2^+ exposed to a linearly polarize laser pulse which is parallel to the axis of the molecule [4] .

It is worth to note that when the wave function is independent of ϕ (eg. – molecule and laser parallel), some previous numerical methods (TaoZuo) have continued the function to the $\rho < 0$ area by symmetry thus avoiding the boundary condition problem at $\rho = 0$. Even without the preceding singular transformation, the original differential operator $\frac{\partial^2}{\partial\rho^2} + \frac{1}{\rho}\frac{\partial}{\partial\rho}$ is not in self-adjoint form, so the discrete propagator is still non-unitary. Another weakness of this method of propagation is that it is not available for wave functions which are dependent on ϕ as is the case for the one-electron H_2^+ in a perpendicular laser field or for the two-electrons H_2 exposed to a general laser pulse.

The consequence of the above two problems is that the non-unitarity may make the numerical method unstable and the non-analytic behaviour of the transformed wavefunction near the origin make the method very poor in precision. For the continuation to $\rho < 0$ method (TaoZuo), we have found that: for H_2^+ parallel to a linear laser pulse, after preparation of the initial condition by an imaginary time step method, and coming back to real time with zero laser intensity, the population diminishes to 95% because of the non-unitarity of the discretized operator.

To overcome the preceding difficulties of FDM in the ρ direction, our idea is to first write the operator $\frac{\partial^2}{\partial\rho^2} + \frac{1}{\rho}\frac{\partial}{\partial\rho}$ in self-adjoint form — $\frac{1}{\rho}\frac{\partial}{\partial\rho}\rho\frac{\partial}{\partial\rho}$ which help us to obtain a unitary discrete operator (for detail, see next section). To avoid the problem of boundary conditions at $\rho = 0$, we propagate the wave function in the whole plane without separating ρ and ϕ so we do not use the above wave function transformations which cause problems of convergence.

We must emphasise that the separation $(1 + c\frac{\partial^2}{\partial\rho^2} + c\frac{1}{\rho}\frac{\partial}{\partial\rho})(1 + c\frac{1}{\rho^2}\frac{\partial^2}{\partial\phi^2}) = 1 + c(\frac{\partial^2}{\partial x^2} + \frac{\partial^2}{\partial y^2}) + c^2(\frac{\partial^2}{\partial\rho^2} + c\frac{\partial}{\partial\rho}/\rho)(\frac{\partial^2}{\partial\phi^2}/\rho^2)$ results that the error term (3rd term of this equality) is very difficult to be limited in numerical simulation and this is just the error term appearing in the split-operator method which separates ρ and ϕ direction propagation. We will demonstrate the advantage of our choice to propagate the wave function in the whole plane without separating ρ and ϕ.

2 The numerical method

As explained in the preceding section, after using the splitting method in 3-D which separates the z-coordinate, the main numerical difficulty comes from the free propagation of the wave function in the remaining 2-D plane in polar coordinates (ρ, ϕ).

For details for the splitting method we refer to [6], and we concentrate here on studing the approximation of the free propagation equation in 2-D:

$$i\frac{\partial F}{\partial t} = -\alpha\left[\frac{\partial^2}{\partial\rho^2} + \frac{1}{\rho}\frac{\partial}{\partial\rho} + \frac{1}{\rho^2}\frac{\partial^2}{\partial\phi^2}\right]F. \quad (8)$$

We adopt the Crank-Nicholson method for the temporal approximation of (8):

$$\begin{aligned}&\left\{1 - i\frac{\delta t}{2}\alpha\left[\frac{1}{\rho}\frac{\partial}{\partial\rho}\rho\frac{\partial}{\partial\rho} + \frac{1}{\rho^2}\frac{\partial^2}{\partial\phi^2}\right]\right\}F(\rho,\phi,t_{l+1}) \\ =& \left\{1 + i\frac{\delta t}{2}\alpha\left[\frac{1}{\rho}\frac{\partial}{\partial\rho}\rho\frac{\partial}{\partial\rho} + \frac{1}{\rho^2}\frac{\partial^2}{\partial\phi^2}\right]\right\}F(\rho,\phi,t_l). \quad (9)\end{aligned}$$

For the spatial approximation of (9), we use the truncated Fourier series,

$$\begin{aligned}&F(\rho,\phi,t_l) \\ =& \frac{1}{N}\sum_{n=0}^{N-1} c_n^l(\rho)e^{in\phi} \quad (10) \\ =& \frac{1}{N}\left[\sum_{n=0}^{N/2-1} c_n^l(\rho)e^{in\phi} + \sum_{n=N/2}^{N-1} c_n^l(\rho)e^{i(n-N)\phi}\right],\end{aligned}$$

where $\{c_n(\rho)\}$ is the unknown set of functions on ρ. The preceding formula shows that for fixed ρ, $\{c_n^l(\rho)\}_{n=0}^{N-1}$ is just the discrete Fourier coefficients of $F(\rho, \phi, t_l)$ as a function of ϕ. So we have:

$$\begin{aligned} c_n^l(\rho) &= \sum_{m=0}^{N-1} F(\rho, \frac{m}{N}2\pi, t_l)e^{-in2\pi m/N} \\ &\qquad \text{for n=0,N-1,} \qquad (11) \\ &\equiv \sum_{m=0}^{N-1} F(\rho, \frac{m}{N}2\pi, t_l)e^{-i(n-N)2\pi m/N} \\ &\qquad \text{for n=N/2,N-1.} \end{aligned}$$

For a regular function F, we can demonstrate that $c_{n\neq0}(\rho = 0)$ should be zero by developping the function in the series:

$$F(\rho, \phi) = \sum_{i,j} a_{i,j}x^i y^j. \qquad (12)$$

At $\rho = 0$, only the $a_{0,0}$ term of the series contributes to the integration in (11), but for $n \neq 0$ we have $\int a_{0,0}e^{in\phi}d\phi = 0$. It should be noted that the $c_{n\neq0}(\rho = 0) = 0$ condition insures also that the function in the series (10) is well defined at the origin ($\rho = 0$). To study the coefficient $c_0(\rho)$, we first rewrite it from (11) as:

$$\begin{aligned} c_0(\rho) &= \sum_{m=0}^{N-1} F(\rho, \frac{m}{N}2\pi) = \frac{N}{2\pi}\int_0^{2\pi} F(\rho,\phi)d\phi \\ &= \frac{N}{2\pi}\sum a_{j,k}\int_0^{2\pi} x^j y^k d\phi. \qquad (13) \end{aligned}$$

For $j + k$ even, the integral $\int_0^{2\pi} x^j y^k d\phi$ will be zero because of the anti-symmetry. So we have :

$$c_0(\rho) = \frac{N}{2\pi}\sum_{j+k\in 2\aleph} a_{j,k}\int_0^{2\pi} x^j y^k d\phi = \sum_m b_{2m}\rho^{2m}. \qquad (14)$$

More precisely, for regular function F, we have:

$$\begin{aligned} c_{2n}(\rho) &= \sum_{2m\geq 2n} a_{2m}\rho^{2m} \\ &\qquad \text{for } 0 \leq 2n < N/2, \\ c_{2n+1}(\rho) &= \sum_{2m+1\geq 2n+1} a_{2m+1m}\rho^{2m+1} \\ &\qquad \text{for } 0 \leq 2n+1 < N/2, \\ c_{2n}(\rho) &= \sum_{2m\geq(N-2n)} a_{2m}\rho^{2m} \qquad (15) \\ &\qquad \text{for } N/2 \leq 2n \leq N-1, \\ c_{2n+1}(\rho) &= \sum_{2m+1\geq(N-2n-1)} a_{2m+1m}\rho^{2m+1} \\ &\qquad \text{for } N/2 \leq 2n+1 \leq N-1. \end{aligned}$$

This permits us to use higher order finite difference schemes as accurate as necessary.

Now using (10) in (9), we get:

$$\begin{aligned} &\sum_{n=0}^{N/2-1}\left[1 - i\frac{\delta t}{2}\alpha D_{\rho,n}\right]c_n^{l+1}e^{in\phi} \\ &+ \sum_{n=N/2}^{N-1}\left[1 - i\frac{\delta t}{2}\alpha D_{\rho,n}\right]c_n^{l+1}e^{i(n-N)\phi} \\ &= \sum_{n=0}^{N/2-1}\left[1 - i\frac{\delta t}{2}\alpha D_{\rho,n}\right]c_n^{l}e^{in\phi} \\ &+ \sum_{n=N/2}^{N-1}\left[1 - i\frac{\delta t}{2}\alpha D_{\rho,n}\right]c_n^{l}e^{i(n-N)\phi}, \qquad (16) \end{aligned}$$

with the differential operator:

$$\begin{aligned} D\rho, n &= \frac{1}{\rho}\frac{\partial}{\partial\rho}\rho\frac{\partial}{\partial\rho} - \frac{n^2}{\rho^2} \text{ for } 0 \leq n < N/2 \qquad (17) \\ &= \frac{1}{\rho}\frac{\partial}{\partial\rho}\rho\frac{\partial}{\partial\rho} - \frac{(n-N)^2}{\rho^2} \text{ for } N/2 \leq n < N. \end{aligned}$$

So we get the following set of ODE's for $c_n^{l+1}(\rho)$:

$$\left[1 - i\frac{\delta t}{2}\alpha D_{\rho,n}\right]c_0^{l+1} = \left[1 + i\frac{\delta t}{2}\alpha D_{\rho,n}\right]c_0^{l} \qquad (18)$$

for $0 \leq n < N$.

We adopt the following second order FDM to approximate $c_n(\rho)$ of (18) at a set of grid points — $\{\rho_m, m \geq 0\}$ with $\rho_0 = 0$:

$$\begin{aligned} \frac{1}{\rho}\frac{\partial}{\partial\rho}\rho\frac{\partial}{\partial\rho}c_n(\rho_m) &= \rho_{m+1/2}c_n(\rho_{m+1})/\rho_m h^2 \qquad (19) \\ &- (\rho_{m+1/2} + \rho_{m-1/2})c_n(\rho_m)/\rho_m h^2 \\ &+ \rho_{m-1/2}c_n(\rho_{m-1})/\rho_m h^2 + \mathcal{O}(h^2) \end{aligned}$$

where h is the uniform spatial step. We need to fix the boundary condition here:

1. at $\rho = \rho_{max}$, we use the zero Dirichlet condition as usual;
2. at $\rho = 0 = \rho_0$:
   for $c_{n\neq0}$, we have demonstrated in the preceding section that $c_{n\neq0}(\rho = 0) = 0$;
   for c_0, we have no explicit boundary condition, but we can use

   $$\frac{1}{\rho}\frac{\partial}{\partial\rho}\rho\frac{\partial}{\partial\rho}c_0(\rho = 0) = 4\frac{c_0(h) - c_0(0)}{h^2} + \mathcal{O}(h^2) \qquad (20)$$

   which can easily be shown by using (14).

Finally, it is not difficult to show that the resulting propagation matrix is *always symetric* with respect to the discrete L_2 scalar product: $< F, G >= \frac{\pi\rho_1^2}{4}F(\rho = 0)G^*(\rho = 0) + \sum_{n=0...N-1,m=1..M}\frac{2\pi}{N}hF(\rho_m,\phi_n)G^*(\rho_m,\phi_n)$. The important consequence is that the propagator will be always unitary.

3 Numerical results

First, we have implemented four numerical methods to compare their convergence and unitarity when applied to the 2-D Schrödinger equation in polar coordinates:

1. The splitting method with FFT in xy – Cartesian coordinate (denoted SPLIT-xFFT-yFFT);

2. The splitting method with FFT in ϕ and FD in ρ – polar coordinate (denoted SPLIT-ρDF-ϕFFT-1) where the wave function is transformed by (2) with $\bar{\rho} = \rho$. In this transformation, the first derivative is eliminated but a new singular potential, $1/4T^2 = 1/4\rho^2$ is added (equation (3));

3. The splitting method with FFT in ϕ and FD in ρ – polar coordinate (denoted SPLIT-ρDF-ϕFFT-2) where the wave function is transformed by (2) with $\rho = \bar{\rho}^{3/2}$. In this transformation, in adition to the singular potential added, the transformed wavefunction becomes a singular function at origin;

4. The present method without splitting of ρ and ϕ (denoted GLOBAL-ρDF-ϕFFT).

3.1 Unitarity of the 3 methods in polar coordinate

In order to test the unitarity, we have initialized the wave function with $\psi(k*h, \phi) = (k*h)*(-1)^k*(1+e^{i\phi}+e^{i\phi*N/2})$ which is very singular but every unitary discrete propagator should conserve it's norm. The discrete propagators are obtained with the three methods in polar coordinates for H_3^{++} in 2-D and a laser pulse of intensity $I = 10^{14}W/cm^2$ and $\lambda = 800nm$. In Fig 1, we compare the evolution of the total population without absorber near boundaries for all three methods: SPLIT-ρDF-ϕFFT-1,SPLIT-ρDF-ϕFFT-2,GLOBAL-ρDF-ϕFFT. We can't distinguish the curves for SPLIT-ρDF-ϕFFT-1 and GLOBAL-ρDF-ϕFFT, but we see a clear fluctuation for the result of SPLIT-ρDF-ϕFFT-2 which demonstrates the non-unitarity of this method of transformation.

3.2 Problem of numerical sigularity

To illustrate the precision of the three different methods in polar coordinates, we have solved numerically the 2-D Schrödinger equation for H_3^{++} exposed to a linearly polarized (in x axis direction) laser field: intensity $I = 10^{14}W/cm^2$, wavelength $\lambda = 800nm$. The 3 protons' position are shown in Fig 2 with $R = 6$, $\theta = 60^o$ and $\alpha = 0^o$. It's well known that the convergence on the phase of the wave function is much more difficult to obtain than it's absolute value [6] .

Here, the converged solution has been obtained by SPLIT-xFFT-yFFT and we show the numerical results for the 3 methods in polar coordinates for the real (R) and imaginary (Im) parts in Fig 4 for $t = 1$ and 5 cycles. We see that the two methods of nonlinear transformation ($\rho = \tilde{\rho}$ and $\rho = \tilde{\rho}^{3/2}$) have introduced numerical sigularities at the

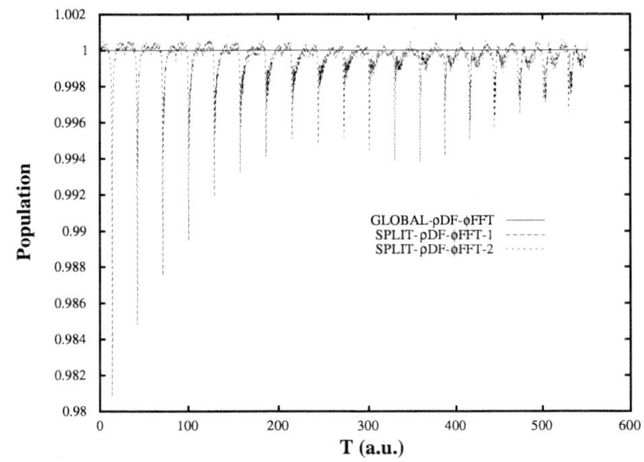

Figure 1. Evolution of the total population for 3 methods in polar coordinates

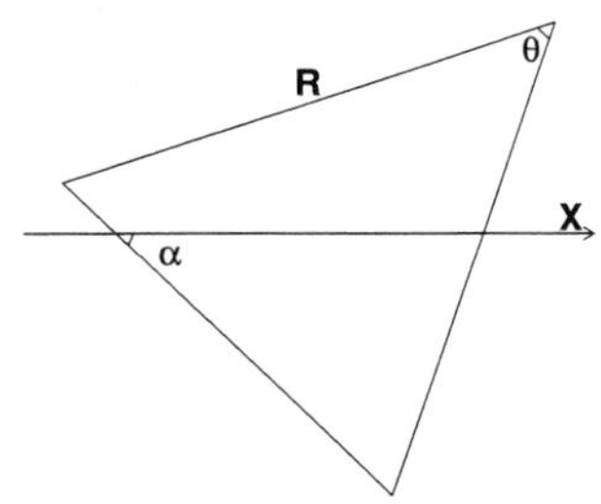

Figure 2. The protons' position for H_3^{++}

origin. In contrast, the present method does not introduce any numerical singularity at $\rho = 0$ and gives very good convergence. It's to be noted that all three methods in polar coordinates have used the same number of discretization points in each direction (ρ,ϕ). As illustration, we show also the population contour for $t = 5$ cycles in Fig 5 for all four methods which confirm again that the SPLIT-ρDF-ϕFFT-1 method has not yet converged to the exact solution. The SPLIT-ρDF-ϕFFT-2 method performs well away from the singularity.

3.3 New numerical results with circularly polarized laser field

Finally, we show some numerical results for H_3^{++} with different configurations exposed to a circularly polarized laser field: intensity $I = 2 \times 10^{14}W/cm^2$, wavelength $\lambda = 800nm$. We have calculated the ionization for different combination of R and θ: $(R, \theta) = (4+0.25*k, j*7.5^o)$ for $0 \leq k \leq 24$ et $1 \leq j \leq 24$. In Fig 3, we show the contour of the ionized population as function of (R, θ) at $t = 10$ cycles. In Fig 6, we show the population contour for some special configuration at $t = 10$ cycles where the ionization is maximum.

4 Conclusion

We have developped a new numerical method for the numerical solution of the Time-Dependent Schrödinger Equation in polar (2-D) / cylindrical (3-D) coordinates. Our numerical results have demonstrated the advantage of the present method compared to other methods in these coordinates: unitarity of the discrete propagator, and no numerical singularity. This method will be extended to solve the problem of two electron interaction in H_3^+ with a laser field in 2-D: we first map the processors on a 2-D Cartesian grid, then the data will be distributed through the 2-D grid along the (ρ_1, ρ_2) direction; with this distribution the FFT transformation will be local in each processor and the solution of the 1-D discrete linear system obtained with splittin method in (ρ_1, ρ_2) or the 2-D discrete system without splitting will be worked out in parallel. Later, this method can be easily extended to H_3^+ with nuclear R variable – leading to a 5 variable $(R, \rho_1, \theta_1, \rho_2, \theta_2)$ problem.

References

1. S. Chelkowski, T. Zuo, A.D. Bandrauk, "Ionization Rates of H_+^2 in an Intense Laser Field by Numerical Integration of the Time-dependent Schrödinger Equation", Phys. Rev. **A46**, R5342 (1992).
2. T. Zuo, A.D. Bandrauk, M. Ivanov, P.B. Corkum, "Control of High-order Harmonic Generation in Strong Laser Fields", Phys. Rev. **A51**, 3991 (1995).
3. C. Dion, "Simulation Numérique de l'Isomérisation de HCN en Champ Laser Intense", (Mémoire de maîtrise en sciences, 1995).
4. H. Kono, A. Kita, Y. Ohtsuki, Y. Fujimura, "An Efficient Quantum Mechanical Method for the Electronic Dynamics of the Three-dimensional Hydrogen Atom Interacting with a Linearly Polarized Strong Laser Pulse", J. Comp. Phys. **130**, 148 (1997).
5. K. Harumiya, H. Kono, Y. Fujimura, I. Kawata, A.D. Bandrauk, "Intense Laser-field Ionization of H_2 Enhanced by Two-electron Dynamics" Phys. Rev. **A66**, 043403 (2002).
6. A.D. Bandrauk, H. Shen, "Exponential Split Operator Methods for Solving Coupled Time-dependent Schrodinger Equations", J. Chem. Phys. **99**, 1185 (1993).

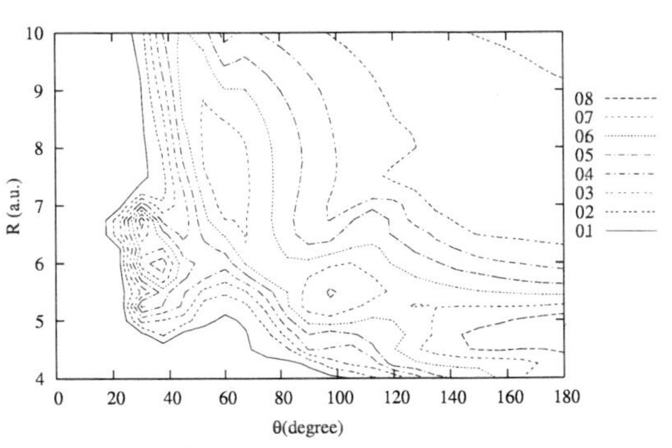

Figure 3. Ionization of H_3^{++} exposed to circularly polarized laser filed in different (R, θ) configuration

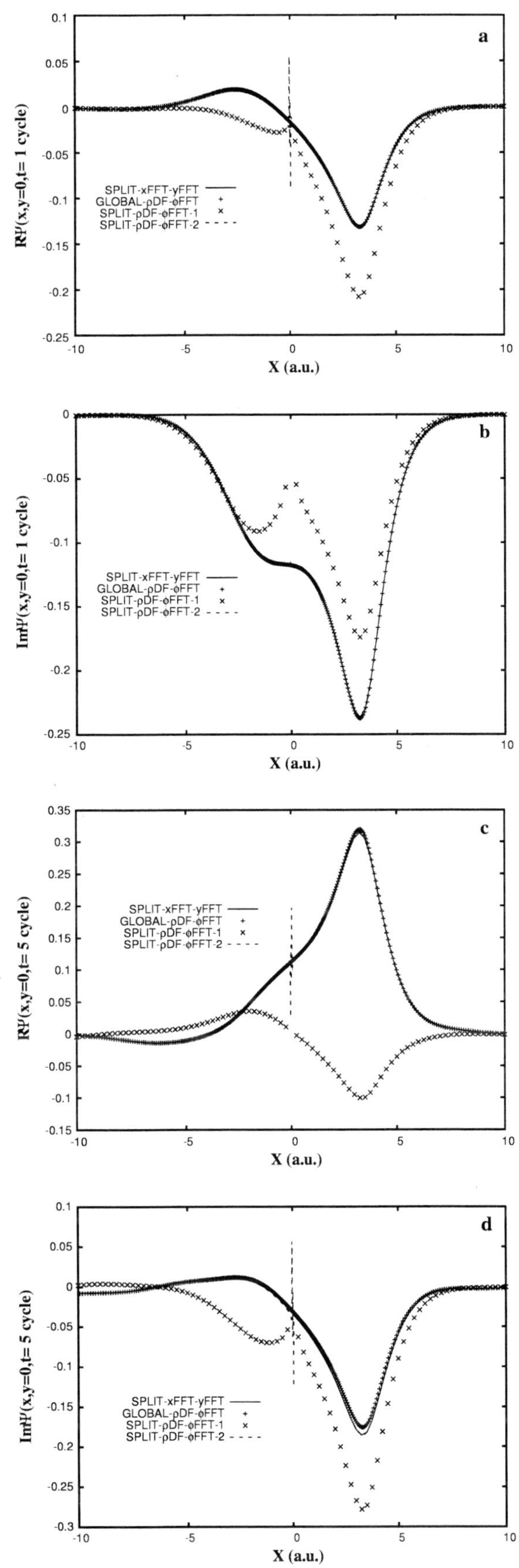

Figure 4. Numerical singularity

Figure 5. Population iso-line contour: a — SPLIT-xFFT-yFFT, b — GLOBAL-ρDF-ϕFFT, c — SPLIT-ρDF-ϕFFT-1, d — SPLIT-ρDF-ϕFFT-2

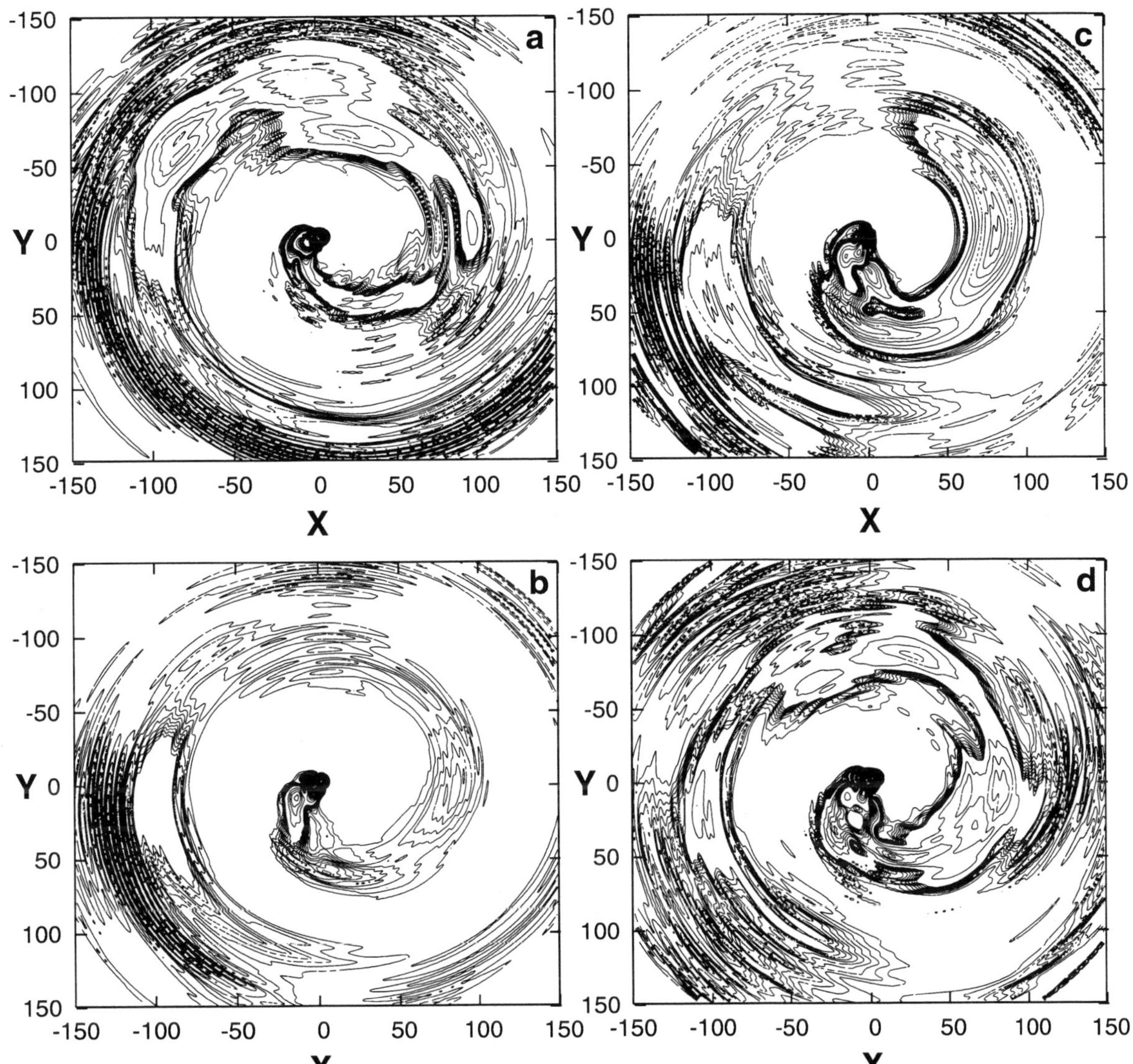

Figure 6. Population iso-line contour of H_3^{++} exposed to circularly polarized laser filed, at $t = 10$ cycles for the configurations: a — $R = 5.5a.u.,\theta = 97.5^o$; b — $R = 6a.u.,\theta = 37.5^o$; c — $R = 6.75a.u.,\ \theta = 30^o$; d — $R = 7.75a.u.,\theta = 60^o$.

Molecular modeling used as a Probe of Interactions to study the polymeric glass transition

Armand Soldera[a]

[a]Département de Chimie, Université de Sherbrooke, Sherbrooke (Québec), J1K 2R1

Poly(methyl methacrylate), PMMA, exhibits different glass transition temperatures, T_gs, according to the configuration of its chain. Consequently, molecular modeling offers an ideal tool to understand from molecular interactions the reasons that give rise to such a difference, and as a matter of fact, to better understand the tricky problem of glass transition. However, an intimately link has to be completed with experience, theory, and actual computing resources, to give an accurate interpretation. Differences between the two configurations were then observed from variation of the non-bond energy, intra-diad angle and the local dynamics. More specifically, a different coupling is observed between the side-chain and the backbone. All these differences tend to explain the reason for a variation in T_gs.

Le poly(méthyle méthacrylate), PMMA, offre la particularité de présenter une température de transition vitreuse, Tg, différente selon la tacticté de sa chaîne. De ce fait, la modélisation moléculaire est un outil de choix pour tenter de comprendre à partir des seules interactions moléculaires, les raisons d'une telle différence, et de ce fait, de mieux appréhender le délicat problème de la transition vitreuse. Toutefois, une utilisation concertée de la modélisation moléculaire avec les résultats expérimentaux, théoriques, et les ressources informatiques, est nécessaire afin de donner une interprétation cohérente du phénomène. Des différences entre les deux configurations du PMMA ont ainsi pu être constatées dans les termes d'énergie intermoléculaire, dans l'angle intra-diade et au sein de la dynamique locale. Plus spécifiquement, une coopérativité différente est constatée entre la chaîne latérale et le squelette. Toutes ces différences contribuent à une meilleure compréhension de la variation de Tg.

Molecular modeling is playing an increasing role in a laboratory since it grants insight into the factors that give rise to specific properties, and thus it both helps to the understanding of molecular phenomena, and guides the synthesis of new compounds with enhanced properties. Actually, it could highlight microscopic behavior that experimental techniques could not deal with. However, accuracy of the simulation obviously stems from appropriate models and computer resources. If they are suitably employed, they could shed light on tricky problems in polymer science, such as the glass transition.

The glass transition temperature, T_g, is of great importance in polymer applications since it splits apart two domains of different mechanical behaviors. Below T_g, the material exhibits high Young's modulus, and above T_g, it displays elastic properties. Different theories, free volume[1], kinetics[2] and thermodynamics[3], try to explain such a transition. With the help of molecular modeling, microscopic behavior could be revealed. However, this procedure has to follow a methodology based on perpetual interaction with experimental and theoretical results.

Poly(methyl methacrylate), PMMA, whose repeat unit is displayed in figure 1, presents a specific regard on the understanding of the glass transition: according to the alternation of its side-chain (C(O)OCH3), a different Tg is obtained. Consequently, this variation might be interpreted in terms of changes in molecular characteristics that can be investigated by molecular modeling.

Initial Parameters

Due to the great number of atoms in polymers, empirical methods, molecular mechanics and dynamics, are usually employed. They are based on the use of a force field4. A force field expresses the interaction between atoms considering the electronic interactions in average. A sum of analytical functions tend to represent these interactions, they are actual mathematical translations of specific interactions: for instance the stretching energy term is usually represented by an harmonic function, or a Morse function, etc ... Depending on the quality of the force field, numerous terms can be added such as the cross terms, yielding to a greater transferability between compounds, and to a better accuracy of the results. Nevertheless, it involves an increase in the computational time. Moreover, each function presents adjustable parameters. They stem from the fit of the function to experimental data or theoretical curves. Since one atom can be surrounded by different electronic environment, numerous fitting parameters can exist for one atom. Consequently, greater is the number of these descriptors for one atom, better is the transferability. The force field used in the glass transition study is pcff from Accelrys: it exhibits a great transferability and was specifically designed to represent interactions among polymers. Its mathematical form is presented in the appendix.

Once the force field is selected the simulation of the amorphous phase of a polymer has to be undertaken. Due to the great number of atoms, the configurational space cannot be covered: the ergodic hypothesis is not satisfied. Nevertheless, statistical rules exist to compute physical properties that are in agreement with experimental data5. The problem lies in the fact that simulations are carried out on a low number of chains. Consequently, the region of the configurational space has to be properly selected. This can actually be done by, firstly, performing a generation procedure based on the Self-Avoiding-Walk6; secondly, building a cubic cell whose volume is in agreement with the knowledge of the density and the mass of the polymer; thirdly, imposing the periodic limit conditions7; lastly, optimizing the cell containing the polymer. A number of 20-30 initial configurations is usually necessary to represent the phase space of a polymer.

Molecular Modeling Techniques

Molecular dynamics integrates the equation of motion to give a movement to the atoms, and thus to get a trajectory that can be latter handled. The customary integration algorithm is the Verlet-leapfrog algorithm since it is simplectic (reversible in time), stable, and requires a high integration step, in order of 1 fs. This integration is performed on the microcanonic ensemble to conserve the energy. To use such equation in another ensemble, such as NPT (number of atoms, temperature and pressure are kept constant), algorithms have to be used. To control the temperature, the Nose-Hoover algorithm was used[8,9], and to control the pressure, it was the Parrinello-Rahman algorithm[10].

Two kinds of software were employed: Discover_3© from Accelrys, and DL_POLY[11].

T_g Determination

Using the NPT ensemble at one temperature and one pressure, the energy and the volume vary until equilibrium is reached. Since the volume is directly related to the density, ρ, the inverse of the specific volume, a graph with the specific volume versus the temperature can be obtained. Such a technique is analogous to the experimental dilatometry[12]. This procedure was applied to PMMA[13] with a time duration for a molecular dynamics simulation of 100 ps for each specific volume value. From a simulated dilatometry experiment[13], the difference between the two Tgs is 55 °C, which is in good agreement with the experimental one, 69 °C. Consequently, further analysis can be carried out. Specific programs have been developed to correctly picture the physical properties. Moreover, configurations at different temperatures have been selected and submitted to simulation of 1 ns. As a result, the averages are more accurate, and the precision in longer times of the time autocorrelation functions is increased.

Results and Discussion

Local molecular motions constitute the basic process of many physical phenomena such as the glass transition. To establish the link between chemical structure and the local dynamics, molecular dynamics simulation fits perfectly. However, relevant parameters have to be extracted from trajectories. These parameters are the differences in energy[13], in geometrical factor[14], and in time correlation[15].

Differences in energy

A difference in the non-bond energy was observed. The major contribution comes from s-PMMA (syndiotactic PMMA where the side-chains alternate along the backbone chain) which exhibits the highest T_g. This result is in accordance with the free volume theory since higher interactions between neighboring chains give a higher T_g: greater are the interchain interactions, greater is the thermal energy brought to the system for the phenomenon to occur, hence greater is the T_g. A difference was also observed in the bending angle energy, which was due to a difference in the intra-diad bending angle, θ' (figure 1).

Difference in the intra-diad bending angle

i-PMMA (isotactic PMMA where the side-chains are in the same side along the backbone chain) which exhibits the lowest T_g, presents an intra-diad angle 1 deg. higher than in the case of s-PMMA. Such a difference is due to a greater interaction between the side-chains. As a result, a greater mobility of those side-chains was observed[14].

1. Computation of the correlation times[15]

The normalized autocorrelation bond vector function of the vector **u**, $\langle \mathbf{u}(t)\cdot\mathbf{u}(0)\rangle$, gives insight into the local dynamics of the motion associated with the bond vector, **u**. It directly stems from a molecular dynamics trajectory. It could then allow the computation of the second Legendre polynomial term:

$$P_2(t)=\frac{1}{2}\left[3\left\langle\left(\mathbf{u}(t)\cdot\mathbf{u}(0)\right)^2\right\rangle-1\right]$$

Actually $P_2(t)$ expresses the decorrelation of the bond vector **u**. It thus yields to a correlation time. Since the motion of the bond vector is not isotropic, the decorrelation cannot be fitted with a simple exponential. The usual fitted function is a stretching exponential function, or a Kolrausch-Williams-Watt (KWW) function,

$$\phi(t)=\exp\left[-(t/\tau)^{\beta_{\mathrm{KWW}}}\right].$$

The use of this stretching function directly yields to the correlation time since it substitutes $P_2(t)$ in the integral from 0 to infinity. Consequently, the correlation time is:

$$\tau_c=\frac{\tau}{\beta_{\mathrm{KWW}}}\Gamma\left(\frac{1}{\beta_{\mathrm{KWW}}}\right)$$

τ and β_{KWW} are adjustable parameters. The physical significance of β_{KWW} will be outlined in the discussion part. This procedure was carried out at different temperatures, and thus correlation times can be obtained for the two PMMA configurations and for different bond vectors. They are then fitted using the VFT equation:

$$\tau_c(T)=A\exp\left(\frac{B}{T-T_o}\right)$$

T_o is the temperature at which the configurational entropy vanishes. B can be related to the apparent activation energy. It is not a real activation energy since the equation does not represent an Arrhenius behavior. It has to be pointed out that the Williams-Landel-Ferry (WLF) equation is similar to the VFT equation. The apparent activation energy is then $2.303RC_1^g C_2^g$ [16].

The two bond vectors used to compute correlation time are displayed in figure 1. $\vec{u}_{CH}$ represents the local motion associated with the backbone, and $\vec{u}_{CO}$ actually displays three motions: the librational motion (eliminated by the use of the stretching function), the motion due to the side-chain, and the motion due to the backbone. The two latter motions cannot be easily separated. Nevertheless, their computation allows to determine the coupling that could exist between the side-chain and the backbone. Actually, this cooperativity is described by the stretching function exponent, β_{KWW} [17]. A near unity exponent describes a "strong liquid" (Arrhenius behavior). As it departs from unity, the polymers become more and more fragile (non-arrhenian behavior of the relaxation time)[18]. The knowledge of this exponent is thus a key to exploring the coupling behavior of the motion it refers to.

In figure 2, are presented the behavior of β_{KWW} associated with $\vec{u}_{CH}$, with respect to the inverse of the relative temperature, for both PMMA configurations. No significant difference is observed. Actually this is reflected in the value of the apparent activation energy B in the VFT equation: 11.8 kJ.mol-1 for s-PMMA, and 12.5 kJ.mol-1 for i-PMMA[15]. Consequently, at a relative temperature above T_g, both backbone dynamics are similar. The difference stays in the absolute temperature since the T_g of i-PMMA is lower than the T_g of s-PMMA.

Figure 3 shows the difference in the β_{KWW} behavior associated with $\vec{u}_{CO}$ for the two configurations with respect to the inverse of the relative temperature. Actually, the apparent activation energies, B in the VFT equation, are different according to the chain configuration: 11.5 kJ.mol-1 for s-PMMA, and 5 kJ.mol-1 for i-PMMA[15]. Consequently, at a temperature higher than Tg, the two configurations exhibit different behavior. To accurately compare the two polymers, backbone and side-chains have to be very mobile. In this case, the two correlation times are comparable. At high temperatures, the two correlation times overlapped. Consequently, the Kolrausch coefficient, β_{KWW}, really unveils the coupling between the backbone and the side-chain. As β_{KWW} of i-PMMA is lower than β_{KWW} of s-PMMA, a greater cooperativity between the side-chain and the backbone exists in i-PMMA. Such a correlation affects most the mobility of the backbone and consequently, decreases the Tg according to the free volume theory. It has to be pointed out that intramolecular coupling between the side-chain and the backbone motions have been observed experimentally by Kuebler et al, by comparing PMMA with PEMA (an ethyl group is substituted to the methyl group of the side-chain). The distinction between the two PMMA configurations was not investigated. Molecular modeling is thus complementary to experimental data, and due to the good agreement, it can be used to probe the differences between specific polymers.

In conclusion, the variation of the T_g between the two PMMA configurations stems from a different behavior of the side-chain. A greater mobility of the side-chain in i-PMMA, in accordance with a greater intra-diad angle, involves a greater mobility of the backbone due to the coupling between the two chains. This behavior results in a T_g lower for i-PMMA since the backbone chain is more mobile. A concerted use of computer resources, models, experimental data and theories, enabled to better understand the difference in the glass transition temperatures between the two PMMA configurations. However, investigations have to be pursued to fit our results with the mode coupling theory, to the particular thermal behavior of PMMA confined in thin film, …

Acknowledgment

Financial support of this work from Université de Sherbrooke is gratefully acknowledged.

Appendix

Potential Energy Expression

$$
\begin{aligned}
V = & \sum_b \left[K_2(b-b_0)^2 + K_3(b-b_0)^3 + K_4(b-b_0)^4 \right] + \sum_\theta \left[H_2(\theta-\theta_0)^2 + H_3(\theta-\theta_0)^3 + H_4(\theta-\theta_0)^4 \right] \\
& + \sum_\phi \left[V_1\left[1-\cos(\phi-\phi_1^0)\right] + V_2\left[1-\cos(2\phi-\phi_2^0)\right] + V_3\left[1-\cos(3\phi-\phi_3^0)\right]\right] + \sum_\chi K_\chi \chi^2 \\
& + \sum_b \sum_{b'} F_{bb'}(b-b_0)(b'-b'_0) + \sum_\theta \sum_{\theta'} F_{\theta\theta'}(\theta-\theta_0)(\theta'-\theta'_0) + \sum_b \sum_\theta F_{b\theta}(b-b_0)(\theta-\theta_0) \\
& + \sum_b \sum_\phi (b-b_0)\left[V_1\cos\phi + V_2\cos 2\phi + V_3\cos 3\phi\right] + \sum_{b'} \sum_\phi (b'-b'_0)\left[V_1\cos\phi + V_2\cos 2\phi + V_3\cos 3\phi\right] \\
& + \sum_\theta \sum_\phi (\theta-\theta_0)\left[V_1\cos\phi + V_2\cos 2\phi + V_3\cos 3\phi\right] + \sum_\phi \sum_\theta \sum_{\theta'} K_{\phi\theta\theta'} \cos\phi(\theta-\theta_0)(\theta'-\theta'_0) \\
& + \sum_{i>j} \frac{q_i q_j}{\varepsilon r_{ij}} + \sum_{i>j} \left[\frac{A_{ij}}{r_{ij}^9} - \frac{B_{ij}}{r_{ij}^6} \right]
\end{aligned}
$$

References

(1) Rigby, D.; Roe, R.-J. *Macromolecules* **1990**, *23*, 5312-5319.

(2) Doi, M.; Edwards, S. F. *Theory of Polymer Dynamics*; Clarendon Press: Oxford, 1986.

(3) Gibbs, J. H.; DiMarzio, S. F. *J. Chem. Phys.* **1958**, *28*, 373.

(4) Burkert, U.; Allinger, N. L. *Molecular Mechanics*; ACS: Washington, 1982; Vol. 177.

(5) Flory, P. J. *Statistical Mechanics of Chain Molecules*; Hanser Publishers: New York, 1989.

(6) Theodorou, D. N.; Suter, U. W. *Macromolecules* **1985**, *18*, 1467-1478.

(7) Allen, M. P.; Tildesley, D. J. *Computer Simulation of Liquids*; Clarendon Press: Oxford, 1987.

(8) Nosé, S. *J. Chem. Phys.* **1984**, *81*, 511.

(9) Hoover, W. G. *Phys. Rev. A* **1985**, *31*, 1695.

(10) Parrinello, M.; Rahman, A. *J. Appl. Phys.* **1981**, *52*, 7182.

(11) DL_POLYis a package of molecular simulation routines written by W.Smith and T.R.Forester, copyright for the Central Laboratory of the Research Councils, Daresbury Laboratory at Daresbury, Nr. Warrington (1996).

(12) Rigby, D.; Roe, R. J. *J. Chem. Phys.* **1987**, *87(12)*, 7285-7292.

(13) Soldera, A. *Macromol. Symp.* **1998**, *133*, 21-32.

(14) Soldera, A. *Polymer* **2002**, *43*, 4269-4275.

(15) Soldera, A.; Grohens, Y. *Macromolecules* **2002**, *35*, 722-726.

(16) Ferry, J. D. *Viscoelastic Properties of Polymers*: New York, 1970.

(17) Ngai, K. L. *J. Chem. Phys.* **1998**, *109*, 6982-6985.

(18) Ediger, M. D.; Angell, C. A.; Nagel, S. R. *J. Phys. Chem.* **1996**, *100*, 13200-13212.

Figures

Figure 1: PMMA repeat unit with the two vectors, $\vec{u}_{CH}$ and $\vec{u}_{CO}$, which reveal the backbone and side-chain/backbone local dynamics, respectively

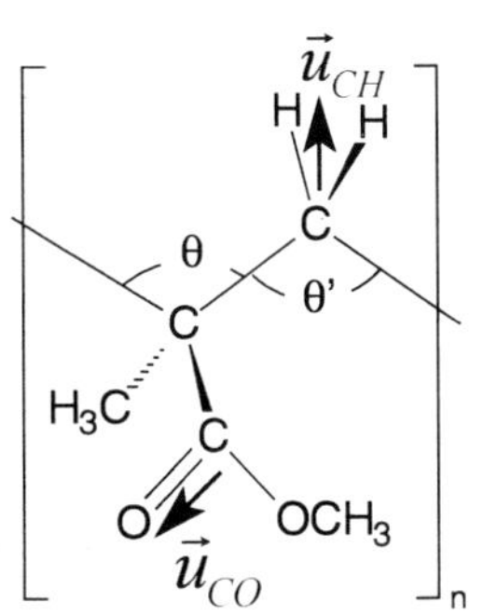

Figure 2: KWW exponent, *n*, of the i-PMMA (θ), and s-PMMA (ρ) C-H bond vector orientation, with respect to the Tg/T ratio.

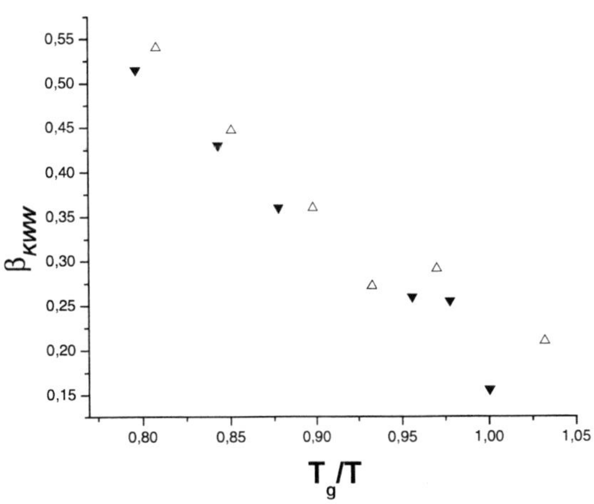

Figure 3: KWW exponent, *n*, of the i-PMMA (θ), and s-PMMA (ρ) C=O bond vector orientation, with respect to the Tg/T ratio.

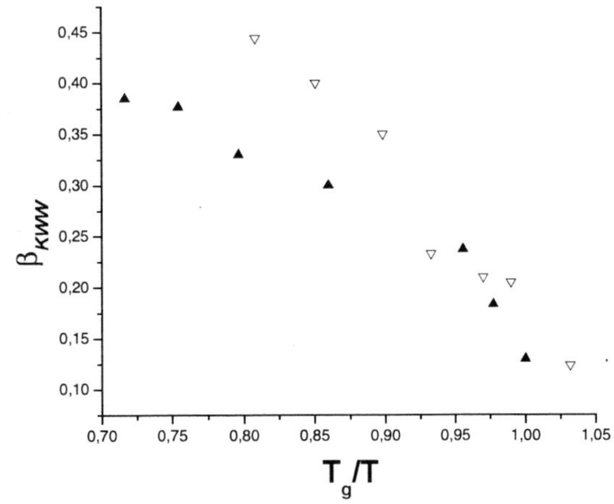

Using simply contracted basis functions with the Lanczos algorithm to calculate vibrational spectra

Xiao-Gang Wang and Tucker Carrington Jr.[a]

[a]Département de chimie, Université de Montréal

We demonstrate that the combination of simply contracted basis functions and the Lanczos algorithm yields an extremely efficient method for computing vibrational energy levels. In this paper we discuss the ideas, and present some results for CH_4. The basis functions we use are products of eigenfunctions of reduced-dimension Hamiltonians obtained by freezing coordinates at equilibrium.

Nous montrons qu'en combinant une base de fonctions simplement contractées et l'algorithme de Lanczös, on obtient une méthode très efficace pour le calcul des niveaux vibratoires. Dans ce travail, nous présentons cette méthode ainsi que certains résutlats pour la molécule de CH_4. Les fonctions de base utilisées sont des produits de fonctions propres de hamiltoniens de dimension réduite obtenus en gelant certaines coordonnées à l'équilibre.

1 Introduction

The development of good methods for calculating vibrational and ro-vibrational spectra of small molecules is a longstanding goal of theoretical chemistry. [1–7]. If one uses a simple product basis the size of the matrix for which one must calculate eigenvalues and eigenvectors is n^f, where n represents the number of basis functions in each degree of freedom and f is the number of degrees of freedom. For a triatomic molecule, with only three vibrational degrees of freedom, it is now straightforward to calculate vibrational levels. For a four-atom molecule the product-basis matrix is so large that it cannot be stored in memory. It is nevertheless possible to calculate vibrational spectra of molecules with four atoms by using one of two established strategies. (1) one uses contracted basis functions obtained by diagonalising reduced dimension Hamiltonians and the usual diagonalization method. [8,4,9]; (2) one use simple product basis functions and an iterative eigensolver (usually the Lanczos[10] or the filter diagonalization method). [11–24]

The two strategies are successful for different reasons. The success of the contracted-direct strategy is due to the small size of the contracted basis used to compute the spectrum. The success of the product-iterative strategy is due to two factors. First it obviates the need to store the Hamiltonian matrix. Second, the product basis makes it possible to evaluate matrix-vector products, and hence to compute eigenvalues, efficiently.

It is enticing to consider the possibility of using contracted basis functions with an iterative eigensolver: it might be possible to exploit *both* the smallness of the contracted basis and the efficiency of the iterative eigensolver.[16,25–27] The basis functions used in most previous attempts to combine a contacted basis and an iterative method are adiabatic contracted functions. [16,25,26] The contracted functions we use, denoted "simply contracted functions" in Ref [16], are eigenfunctions of reduced dimension Hamiltonians obtained by fixing the values of some coordinates. [28]

2 Bend stretch contraction scheme

As vibrational coordinates we use, for an N atom molecule, the lengths of $N-1$ vectors, $N-2$ planar angles, and $N-3$ dihedral angles. [29] The kinetic energy operator (KEO) in these coordinates is surprisingly simple. We use "orthogonal" vectors so that there is no momentum coupling between stretch and bend coordinates.[30–32]

The reduced-dimension Hamiltonian for the bend contraction is,

$$H^{(b)} = T_{ben}(\theta, r_e) + V(\theta, r_e). \qquad (1)$$

Its wavefunctions are denoted by

$$X_b(\theta) = \sum_l C_{lb} f_l(\theta) \qquad (2)$$

and the energies by E_b. The f_l are primitive FBR (finite basis representation) bend basis functions[33] and the number of retained bend wavefunctions is denoted by n_b. Similarly, the reduced-dimension Hamiltonian for the stretch contraction is,

$$H^{(s)} = T_{str}(r) + V(\theta_e, r). \qquad (3)$$

and its wavefunctions are denoted by,

$$Y_s(r) = \sum_\alpha D_{\alpha s} g_\alpha(r) \qquad (4)$$

and the energies by E_s. The g_α are primitive DVR (discrete variable representation) [33] stretch basis functions and the number of retained stretch wavefunctions is denoted by n_s. θ_e and r_e represent equilibrium values of all the bend coordinates and all the stretch coordinates.

The final basis is a product of the retained stretch and bend eigenfunctions

$$|bs\rangle = |X_b\rangle |Y_s\rangle \qquad (5)$$

Of course, only the eigenvectors of the reduced-dimension Hamiltonian matrices whose eigenvalues are below a given cutoff energy are retained.

2.1 Matrix-vector products with a simply contracted basis

To facilitate evaluation of matrix-vector products we write the full Hamiltonian

$$H = H^{(b)} + H^{(s)} + \Delta T + \Delta V \quad (6)$$

Matrix-vector products for ΔV are the most difficult. A matrix element of ΔV in the product contracted basis is,

$$\begin{aligned} \langle b's'|\Delta V(\theta,r)|bs\rangle &= \sum_{\substack{l'l \\ \alpha}} C_{l'b'}C_{lb}D_{\alpha s'}D_{\alpha s}\langle l'\alpha|\Delta V(\theta,r)|l\alpha\rangle \\ &= \sum_{\substack{l'l \\ \alpha\beta}} C_{l'b'}C_{lb}D_{\alpha s'}D_{\alpha s}T_{l'\beta}T_{l\beta}\Delta V_{\beta\alpha}\ , \quad (7) \end{aligned}$$

where

$$\begin{aligned} T_{l\beta} &= \sqrt{w_\beta} f_l(\theta_\beta) \\ \Delta V_{\beta\alpha} &= \Delta V(\theta_\beta, r_\alpha)\ . \quad (8) \end{aligned}$$

(θ_β, w_β) are quadrature points and weights for the angles. Note that if there is more than one bend coordinate l and β are composite indices and if there is more than one stretch coordinate α is a composite index. It is sometimes advantageous to rewrite Eq. (7) as

$$\langle b's'|\Delta V(\theta,r)|bs\rangle = \sum_{\alpha\beta} \tilde{C}_{\beta'b'}\tilde{C}_{\beta b}D_{\alpha s'}D_{\alpha s}\Delta V_{\beta\alpha}\ , \quad (9)$$

where

$$\tilde{C}_{\beta b} = \sum_l C_{lb}T_{l\beta}\ . \quad (10)$$

In the standard approach, the ΔV matrix-vector product is evaluated as

$$\begin{aligned} u'_{b's'} &= \sum_{bs}\langle b's'|\Delta V(\theta,r)|bs\rangle u_{bs} \\ &= \sum_\alpha D_{\alpha s'}\sum_\beta \tilde{C}_{\beta b'}\Delta V_{\beta\alpha}\sum_s D_{\alpha s}\sum_b \tilde{C}_{\beta b}u_{bs} \quad (11) \end{aligned}$$

The matrix-vector product can be done more efficiently by introducing an $\mathbf{F}$ matrix defined by,

$$F_{b'b,\alpha} = \sum_\beta \tilde{C}_{\beta b'}\tilde{C}_{\beta b}\Delta V_{\beta\alpha}\ . \quad (12)$$

in terms of which,

$$\langle b's'|\Delta V(\theta,r)|bs\rangle = \sum_\alpha F_{b'b,\alpha}D_{\alpha s'}D_{\alpha s}\ . \quad (13)$$

To use our method one calculates and stores all the $F_{b'b,\alpha}$. One then does the ΔV matrix-vector product in three steps. The CPU cost of the matrix-vector product is $n_\alpha(n_b^2 + 2n_b n_s)$. Assuming $n_b > n_s$ the CPU cost scales as $n_\alpha n_b^2$. The cost is much less than the cost of a product-basis matrix-vector product.

Of course this comparison is not really fair, to estimate the total CPU cost of the calculation, one needs to also include the cost of calculating $\mathbf{F}$. The $\mathbf{F}$ matrix is computed prior to and not during the Lanczos recursion. The calculation of $\mathbf{F}$ can be trivially parallelized as one can allocate the stretch DVR (α) points to different computers or processors and allow each to calculate a block of $\mathbf{F}$ for the allocated α points. Because $\mathbf{C}$, and $\tilde{\mathbf{C}}$ are discarded *before* matrix-vector products are evaluated, one can use an extremely large bend basis to converge the contracted bend functions without increasing the memory cost of the calculation (the CPU cost of the calculation of $\mathbf{F}$ does increase moderately). In contrast if one uses the standard approach (Eq. (11)) increasing the size of the bending basis increases both the CPU and the memory cost dramatically.

3 Application to CH_4

For CH_4 the product-iterative method is not feasible. A contracted-iterative calculation is possible.

3.1 Symmetry-adapted basis and Hamiltonian matrix

We use 4+1 Radau vectors[34] and their associated polyspherical coordinates. The bend KEO is written in terms of angular momentum operators and parity-adapted primitive basis functions are used. We use parity adapted basis functions that are linear combinations of the product functions,

$$|l_1 l_2 m_2 l_3 m_3\rangle = \Theta_{l_1}^{m_1}(\theta_1)Y_{l_2}^{m_2}(\theta_2,\phi_2)Y_{l_3}^{m_3}(\theta_3,\phi_3)\ . \quad (14)$$

Potential matrix elements in the parity-adapted basis are evaluated by Gauss quadrature. [35] We use Legendre weights and points for the polar angles and the trapezoid rule for the azimuthal angles. See Ref. [36]. Although the parity-adapted basis functions are not products of functions of a single variable we have been able to evaluate matrix-vector products efficiently. [36]. As primitive stretch basis functions we use PODVR functions computed from a sinc DVR. [33]

3.2 Results

We use the T8 potential surface of Schwenke described in Ref. [37]. It is an accurate *ab initio* global surface.

The bend energy and wavefunctions are obtained by using a parity-adapted FBR basis with $l_{max} = m_{max} = 25$. We use a potential ceiling value of 20000 cm^{-1}. We retain the bend levels up to $(n_2, n_4) = (4, 1)$, all of which are below 7670 cm^{-1}. There are 133 A levels and 113 B levels. The bend wavefunctions are compacted with a cutoff energy equal to the potential ceiling value. We have checked to make sure that this compaction cutoff energy is appropriate.

The stretch energies and wavefunctions are obtained from a product of 10 PODVR basis functions for each stretch coordinate, these in turn are built from a sinc DVR basis in the range $[1.2a_0, 7.0a_0]$. We discard all the PODVR points whose potential energy is above 30000 cm^{-1}. This reduces the stretch basis size from 10000 to 5049. We retain all the stretch levels up to 20000 cm^{-1}. There are 161 A levels and 99 B levels.

The size of the final product basis of bend and stretch wavefunctions is 63960; there are 32600 A symmetry functions and 31360 B symmetry functions. In the final Lanczos calculation a potential ceiling value of 30000 cm^{-1} is used.

Some of our levels are reported in Table I. We show three groups of levels. The first group contains all the levels up to the (00)(30) band where the notation is defined as $(n_1 n_3)(n_2 n_4)$. The second group contains the $v = n_1 + n_3 = 2$ stretch overtone. The third group contains the highest five levels reported by Schwenke.[37]. Our levels are better converged than those of Schwenke.

Acknowledgments

We are grateful to David Schwenke for providing his potential energy surface. Some of the calculations were done on a computer of the Réseau Québécois de Calcul de Haute Performance. This work has been supported by the Natural Sciences and Engineering Research Council of Canada.

References

1. Spectrochim. Acta Part A **58**, (2002). A special issue on *First Principles Rovibrational Spectroscopy*.
2. T. Carrington, Jr., in *Encyclopedia of Computational Chemistry*, edited by P. von Ragué Schleyer (Wiley, New York, 1998), Vol. 5.
3. E. L. Sibert, Int. Rev. in Phys. Chem. **9**, 1 (1990).
4. Z. Bačić and J. C. Light, Annu. Rev. Phys. Chem. **40**, 469 (1989).
5. S. Carter and N. C. Handy, Comp. Phys. Rep. **5**, 115 (1986).
6. J. Tennyson, Comp. Phys. Rep. **4**, 1 (1986).
7. G. D. Carney, L. L. Sprandel and C. W. Kern, Adv. Chem. Phys. **37**, 305 (1978).
8. S. Carter and N. C. Handy, Comput. Phys. Com. **51**, 49 (1988).
9. J. R. Henderson and J. Tennyson, Chem. Phys. Lett. **173**, 133 (1990).
10. G. H. Golub and C. F. Van Loan, *Matrix Computations* (Johns Hopkins University Press, Baltimore, 1989).
11. H. Koeppel, W. Domcke, and L. S. Cederbaum, Adv. Chem. Phys. **57**, 59 (1984).
12. C. Iung and C. Leforestier, J. Chem. Phys. **90**, 3198 (1989).
13. R. E. Wyatt, Adv. Chem. Phys. **73**, 231 (1989).
14. A. McNichols and T. Carrington, Jr., Chem. Phys. Lett. **202**, 464 (1993).
15. M. J. Bramley and T. Carrington, Jr., J. Chem. Phys. **99**, 8519 (1993).
16. M. J. Bramley and T. Carrington, Jr, J. Chem. Phys. **101**, 8494 (1994).
17. N. R. Wall and D. Neuhauser, J. Chem. Phys. **102**, 8011 (1995).
18. T. P. Grozdanov, V. A. Mandelshtam, and H. S. Taylor, J. Chem. Phys. **103**, 7990 (1995).
19. V. A. Mandelshtam and H. S. Taylor, J. Chem. Phys. **102**, 7390 (1995).
20. V. A. Mandelshtam and H. S. Taylor, J. Chem. Phys. **106**, 5085 (1997).
21. H.-G. Yu and S. C. Smith, Ber. Bunsenges. Phys. Chem. **101**, 400 (1997).
22. R. Chen and H. Guo, J. Chem. Phys. **108**, 6068 (1998).
23. S.-W. Huang and T. Carrington, Jr., J. Chem. Phys. **112**, 8765 (2000).
24. B. Poirier and T. Carrington, Jr., J. Chem. Phys. **114**, 9254 (2001).
25. X. T. Wu and E. F. Hayes, J. Chem. Phys. **107**, 2705 (1997).
26. R. A. Friesner, J.A. Bentley, M. Menou, and C. Leforestier, J. Chem. Phys. **99**, 324 (1993).
27. A. Viel and C. Leforestier, J. Chem. Phys. **112**, 1212 (2000).
28. X.-G. Wang and T. Carrington, Jr, J. Chem. Phys. **117**, 6923 (2002).
29. X. Chapuisat and C. Iung, Phys. Rev. A **45**, 6217 (1992).
30. X. Chapuisat, A. Belfhal, and A. Nauts, J. Molec. Spectrosc. **149**, 274 (1991).
31. F. Gatti, C. Iung, M. Menou, Y. Justum, A. Nauts, and X. Chapuisat, J. Chem. Phys. **108**, 8804 (1998).
32. M. Mladenović, J. Chem. Phys. **112**, 1070 (2000).
33. J. C. Light and T. Carrington Jr., Adv. Chem. Phys. **114**, 263 (2000).
34. F. T. Smith, Phys. Rev. Lett. **45**, 1157 (1980).
35. Press, W. H.; Teukolsky, S. A.; Vetterling, W. T.; Flannery, B. P. *Numerical Recipes in Fortran, Second Edition;* Cambridge University Press: Cambridge, 1992.
36. X.-G. Wang and T. Carrington, Jr., J. Chem. Phys. (submitted).
37. D. W. Schwenke and H. Partridge, Spectrochim. Acta Part A **57**, 887 (2001).
38. E. Venuti, L. Halonen, and R. G. Della Valle J. Chem. Phys. **110**, 7339 (1999).

Table 1
Vibrational wavenumbers of methane(in cm^{-1}).

$(n_1n_3)(n_2n_4)$	sym	This work	Schwenke	Col. 4 – Col. 3	exp.[b]
(00)(00)	1 A1	9688.94	9691.56	2.62	
(00)(01)	1 F2	1311.39	1311.76	0.37	1310.76
(00)(10)	1 E	1532.84	1533.26	0.42	1533.33
(00)(02)	2 A1	2589.11	2589.92	0.81	2587.04
(00)(02)	2 F2	2615.56	2616.30	0.74	2614.26
(00)(02)	2 E	2626.61	2627.40	0.79	2624.62
(00)(11)	3 F2	2830.78	2831.77	0.99	2830.32
(00)(11)	1 F1	2846.16	2847.04	0.88	2846.08
(10)(00)	3 A1	2912.95	2913.77	0.82	2916.48
(01)(00)	4 F2	3012.82	3014.20	1.38	3019.49
(00)(20)	4 A1	3062.68	3063.74	1.06	3063.65
(00)(20)	3 E	3064.20	3065.27	1.07	3065.14
(00)(03)	5 F2	3873.78	3878.34	4.56	3870.49
(00)(03)	5 A1	3911.30	3917.83	6.53	3909.18
(00)(03)	2 F1	3923.10	3929.98	6.88	3920.50
(00)(03)	6 F2	3934.34	3940.95	6.61	3930.92
(00)(12)	4 E	4103.41	4109.08	5.67	4105.15
(00)(12)	3 F1	4130.22	4136.63	6.41	4128.57
(00)(12)	6 A1	4134.71	4140.19	5.48	4132.99
(00)(12)	7 F2	4143.78	4150.21	6.43	4142.86
(00)(12)	5 E	4152.66	4159.19	6.53	4151.22
(00)(12)	1 A2	4163.26	4169.73	6.47	4161.87
(10)(01)	8 F2	4220.74	4222.23	1.49	4223.46
(01)(01)	9 F2	4313.10	4315.90	2.80	4319.21
(01)(01)	6 E	4316.46	4318.93	2.47	4322.15
(01)(01)	4 F1	4316.71	4319.61	2.90	4322.58
(01)(01)	7 A1	4317.30	4320.23	2.93	4322.72
(00)(21)	10 F2	4348.96	4355.27	6.31	4348.77
(00)(21)	5 F1	4363.59	4369.53	5.94	4363.31
(00)(21)	11 F2	4378.60	4384.32	5.72	4379.10
(10)(10)	7 E	4431.10	4432.60	1.50	4446.41
(01)(10)	6 F1	4530.19	4538.85	8.66	4537.57[b]
(01)(10)	13 F2	4536.64	N/A		4543.76[b]
(00)(30)	8 E	4591.44	4596.10	4.66	4592.03
(00)(30)	2 A2	4594.46	4599.15	4.69	4595.32
(00)(30)	8 A1	4594.73	4599.45	4.72	4595.56
(20)(00)	15 A1	5780.78	5783.20	2.42	5790.25
(11)(00)	27 F2	5852.46	5856.91	4.45	
(02)(00)	18 A1	5959.44	5962.76	3.32	5968.09
(02)(00)	30 F2	5991.96	5996.29	4.33	6004.69
(02)(00)	20 E	6030.30	6034.60	4.30	6043.87
(00)(05)	33 F2	6401.71	6428.34	26.63	
(00)(05)	20 A1	6429.52	6461.34	31.82	
(00)(05)	34 F2	6474.02	6778.67	304.65	
(00)(05)	35 F2	6529.48	6824.36	294.88	
(00)(14)	5 A2	6702.66	6906.35	203.69	

[a] From Ref. [38]. [b] There are typos in these two levels in Ref. [37].

First-Principles Excited-State Molecular Dynamics Simulations: Application to Cluster Photochemistry

Qadir K. Timerghazin[a] and Gilles H. Peslherbe[a]

[a]Centre for Research in Molecular Modeling and Department of Chemistry & Biochemistry, Concordia University, Montréal, Québec, Canada, H3G 1M8

Computer simulations of the real time-evolution of complex chemical systems in their electronically excited states, resulting for example from photoexcitation, represent many challenges for modern computational chemistry. In this contribution, we discuss the application of first-principles molecular dynamics simulations of the excited state dynamics of clusters made up of a halide ion and a number of solvent (water) molecules. The number of difficulties encountered in such simulations is outlined, and preliminary results are reported and discussed in connection with available experimental data. A brief outlook for the future development of the current research is also given in light of recent progress in high-performance computing.

La simulation sur ordinateur de la dynamique de systèmes chimiques complexes et de leur états électroniques excités, résultant par exemple d'une photoexcitation, présente un défi de taille pour la chimie numérique moderne. Dans ce travail, nous décrivons une simulation de dynamique moléculaire des états excités d'amas comportant un ion halogène entouré d'un certain nombre de molécules de solvant (eau). On décrit les difficultés généralement rencontrées dans de telles simulations, et on discute de résultats préliminaires en relation avec les données expérimentales disponibles. Une brève perspective des développements futurs pressentis est donnée, à la lumière des progrès récents dans le domaine du calcul de haute performance.

Introduction

The end of the twentieth century has been marked by scientific breakthroughs of paramount importance for chemistry, physics, biology and many other disciplines. Progress in technological and conceptual tools has made it possible to study chemical reactions with unprecedented time resolution. Femtochemistry [1-3], a new field pioneered by the group of A. Zewail, 1999 Nobel Prize winner, allows to explore the ultrafast dynamics of chemical reactions on the timescale of atomic vibrations, *i.e.* on the femtosecond timescale (1 fs = 10^{-15} s). With ultrafast spectroscopic techniques even such ephemeral species as transitions states of chemical reactions can be probed [4]. If the initial developments of femtochemistry mainly dealt with very simple systems composed of a few atoms, femtochemistry is now expanding into studies of increasingly complex systems, such as macromolecules, molecular clusters and condensed phases. These systems can also be studied now with comparable precision, and on the same timescale, with computer simulations, thanks to recent advances in computational chemistry methods and progress in high-performance computing. Molecular dynamics studies are actually necessary for the interpretation of increasingly complex and convoluted experimental results. In this respect, realistic molecular dynamics simulations, based on potential energy surfaces calculated by first-principles quantum chemical methods are very important, especially for investigating systems evolving in their electronically excited states, following for example photoexcitation.

Of particular interest to us are clusters, *i.e.* agglomerates of two or more molecules bound to each other by intermolecular forces. The properties of clusters can be considered to be intermediate between the gas and condensed phases [5], and for instance, cluster studies are critical for understanding fundamental processes such as solvation in chemical, biochemical, and photochemical reactions. In the field of cluster research, halide-water clusters seem to be particularly important, due to the prevalence of dissolved halide salts in the Earth biosphere, hydrosphere and atmosphere [6]. While the structural and energetic properties of $X^-(H_2O)_n$ clusters (X = F, Cl, Br, I) has been a subject of long-standing interest, very little experimental data had been reported of their photochemical properties till recently. One of the fascinating features of anions dissolved in water, especially halides, is the possibility to photochemically transfer an electron from the ion into the bulk solvent, where it will be stabilized by the field of polar solvent molecules, giving rise to so-called charge-transfer-to-solvent (CTTS) excited states, which can eventually lead to the solvated electron. In 1996, M. Jonhson and co-workers [7] were able to experimentally observe cluster analogs of the bulk CTTS states in clusters of iodide with one to four water molecules. It was found that subsequent relaxation of the excited cluster may lead to the ejection of the neutral iodine atom and formation of a dipole-bound water cluster anion $(H_2O)_n^-$.

Shortly after, D. Neumark and co-workers [8] applied state-of-the-art femtosecond photoelectron spectroscopy techniques to study the relaxation dynamics of photoexcited $I^-(H_2O)_n$ clusters (n= 4–6) on a timescale of 2 ps following photon absorption (Fig. 1). This work revealed interesting dynamical characteristics of the excited electron in clusters of different sizes by measuring the evolution of the electron binding energy throughout the relaxation process. For the smallest cluster investigated $I^-(H_2O)_4$, the electron binding energy was found to remain constant throughout the measurement time window, and the population of photoexcited clusters decayed exponentially because of the spontaneous ejection of the dipole-bound electron from the vibrationally excited water cluster. On the other hand, clusters with five and six water molecules exhibited much more interesting dynamics: an induction period of *ca.* 500 fs was observed, during which the electron binding energy is constant. The electron binding energy then increases by *ca.* 0.3 eV, suggesting that the cluster undergoes some kind of reorganization which leads to the stabilization of the excited electron. Only after this increase of electron binding energy does the population of excited clusters start decaying until the end of observation time (2 ps or 2000 fs). In order to rationalize their observations, Neumark and co-workers put forward the hypothesis [8,9] that the rise in electron binding energy after the first 500 fs is due to a reorganization of the water molecules in $I^-(H_2O)_5$ and $I^-(H_2O)_6$ clusters. This suggests that the four water molecules in $I^-(H_2O)_4$ are not able to rearrange and efficiently stabilize the excess electron transferred from iodide, while five and six water molecules are known to bind an excess electron in a number of cluster configurations. Therefore, in the 500 fs following photoexcitation, the water molecules in $I^-(H_2O)_5$ and $I^-(H_2O)_6$ clusters are assumed to gain configurations which can support the excess electron much more efficiently than in the initial cluster configuration. This model is based solely on the consideration of solvent dynamics, neglecting the possible role of the neutral iodine atom formed by photoexcitation, and is hereafter referred as the "solvent-driven" relaxation dynamics model.

Recently, Chen and Sheu [10,11] performed a quantum-chemical study in which they propose an alternative interpretation for the femtosecond experiments of Neumark and co-workers: in this model, the stabilization of the excited electron is rationalized by the ejection of the neutral iodine atom from the water cluster. Quantum-chemical calculations show that the presence of the neutral iodine atom can considerably destabilize the excited electron in excited $I^-(H_2O)_n$ clusters, and thus as the iodine atom leaves the water cluster, the electron binding energy must significantly increase. According to this "iodine-driven" model of relaxation dynamics, a cluster with four water molecules undergoes iodine atom ejection on a very fast timescale, *i.e.* less than 100 fs, and only the dynamics of the free $(H_2O)_4^-$ cluster can be monitored. On the other hand, iodine leaves photoexcited clusters with 5 and 6 water molecules more slowly, giving rise to the experimentally observed induction period. The main problem with the latter model is that it is based on static quantum-chemical calculations, which have the water cluster moiety frozen in the geometry of the cluster before photoexcitation.

At this stage, none of the models proposed so far to interpret femtosecond experiments, treats the relaxation of

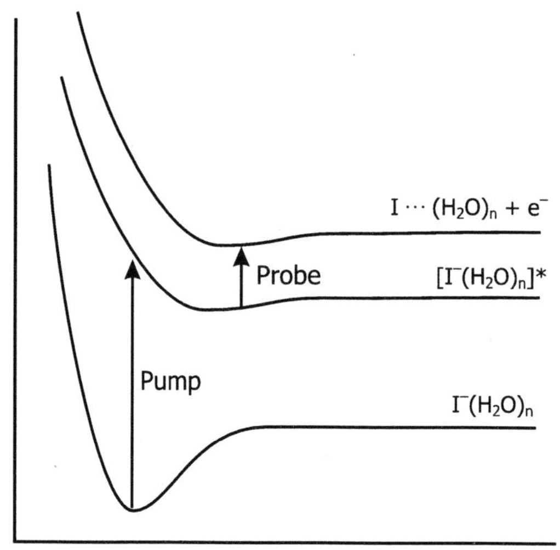

Fig. 1. Schematic representation of femtosecond photoelectron spectroscopy experiments by Neumark and co-workers [8]. The pump laser pulse excites the iodide-water cluster $I^-(H_2O)_n$, and the probe pulse monitors the evolution of the excited state $[I^-(H_2O)_n]^*$ via ejection of the loosely bound excited electron.

iodide-water clusters as a whole, neglecting either the role of the iodine atom or that of solvent reorganization. First-principles molecular dynamics simulations [12] appear to be a method of choice for investigating the time-evolution of photoexcited halide-water clusters. In this approach, the energy and its gradient are calculated "on the fly" during the propagation of the atomic equations of motion by first-principles, or *ab initio*, methods. One should emphasize that the proper theoretical treatment of such complex systems poses several computational chemistry challenges. First, the electronic structure of the ground and excited states must be treated explicitly by high-level quantum chemical methods. This is especially important in the case of dipole-bound excited states of halide-water clusters, where the excited electron spatial distribution is extremely diffuse, which dictates the use of very large, specific, one-electron basis sets augmented by many diffuse basis functions [13]. Further, in order to propagate trajectories on the potential energy surface, both the potential energy and the energy gradient, *i.e.* the forces governing the motion of atoms, must be readily available for the excited states of interest. All these factors make first-principles molecular dynamics simulations of photoexcited iodide-solvent clusters particularly complex and computer-intensive, especially in comparison to routine, conventional static *ab initio* ground-state electronic structure calculations, and dictate the use of advanced software and hardware.

We have recently engaged into *ab initio* excited-state dynamics simulations of the relaxation process of halide-solvent clusters. In the present article we report preliminary results of the $I^-(H_2O)_3$ relaxation dynamics, based on a few trajectories. In spite of its small size, this cluster possesses the crown-like structure characteristic of $I^-(H_2O)_n$ clusters with $n \leq 6$, and it can thus serve as a good model to gain an insight into complex excited-state relaxation processes in the larger clusters. We will also conclude by an outlook of the impact of high-performance computing on future research, *i.e.* the extension of the current simulations to larger clusters, which will require a large number of trajectories to allow a thorough connection with experiment.

Computational Details

Ground and excited state electronic structure calculations were carried out using the state-averaged (SA) Complete Active Space Self-Consistent Field (CASSCF) formalism [14,15], with the active space consisting of two *p*-orbitals of the iodine atom – which are doubly occupied in the ground state – and the lowest unoccupied orbital – which accommodates the excited electron upon photoexcitation. The basis set used in this work is based on the standard 6-31+G(d,p) basis set by Pople and co-workers [16], which was used in its original form for hydrogen and oxygen atoms. For iodine, we used the LANL2DZ effective core potential (ECP) basis set by Hay and Wadt [17-19], augmented by *d*-polarization functions with the optimized exponents of Check *et al.* [20]. Further, a special set of uncontracted Gaussian basis functions, with diffuse exponents, was added to allow for a proper description of the dipole-bound excited electron. In contrast to static quantum chemical calculations of dipole-bound cluster anions $(H_2O)_n^-$ or dipole-bound $[I^-(H_2O)_n]^*$ excited states, the *ab initio* molecular dynamics simulations demand an even more diffuse basis set, which can describe the excited electron along the whole trajectory, where the cluster structure can change dramatically during the relaxation process. In order to construct a diffuse basis set, flexible enough for dynamical calculations, we added a number of diffuse *sp*-shells centered on the iodine atom, with exponents α_{sp}= 3.0800×10^{-2}, 4.4000×10^{-3}, and 6.2857×10^{-4}. We also centered two *sp*-shells with exponents α_{sp}= 3.6000×10^{-2}, 5.1429×10^{-3} and one *s*-shell with exponent α_s=7.3469×10^{-4} on each of the three "dangling" hydrogen atoms, *i.e.* those that are not involved in water-water hydrogen bonding in the cluster (*cf.* Fig. 2). All quantum-chemical calculations were performed with the MOLPRO suite of *ab initio* programs by H.-J. Werner and P. J. Knowles [21].

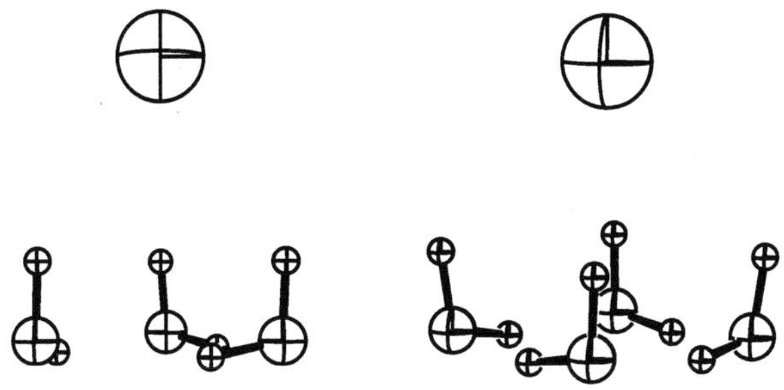

$I^-(H_2O)_3$ $I^-(H_2O)_4$

Fig. 2. Equilibrium structures of $I^-(H_2O)_3$ and $I^-(H_2O)_4$ clusters [22]

The classical equations of motion were propagated for all atoms with the standard constant-energy velocity Verlet algorithm [12], with energy and gradient calculated at each time step by the quantum-chemical procedure described above. A time-step of 0.3 fs was used, and the trajectories were propagated for up to 900 fs. Calculations were performed on an AlphaServer ES40 and on a local cluster based on dual-CPU Intel Xeon processors.

Results and Discussion

It is now well established [22,23] that small to medium size iodide-water clusters tend to have so-called surface structures, where the iodide ion tends to sit at the surface of the hydrogen-bonded water network. The smallest clusters have crown-like structures like those shown for $I^-(H_2O)_3$ and $I^-(H_2O)_4$ clusters in Fig. 2 [22]. These structures are governed by a combination of the interaction of the negatively charged I^- with the dipole moment of the entire water network, and the hydrogen-bonding interactions of the "dangling" hydrogen atoms with the iodide ion. We chose $I^-(H_2O)_3$ as an initial, representative, yet computationally feasible, model for excited state dynamics studies of $I^-(H_2O)_n$ clusters. Even though there are no explicit experimental data on the relaxation dynamics for this cluster size, it can be used as a model to gain some insight into general features of the excited state time-evolution of $I^-(H_2O)_n$ species.

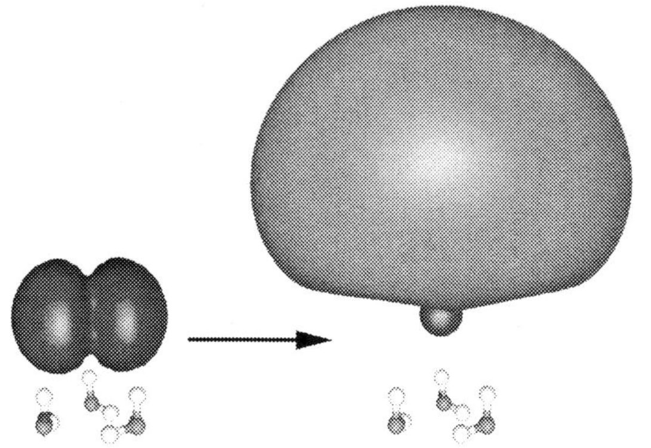

Fig. 3. Electronic density difference between the $I^-(H_2O)_3$ ground and excited states. The negative density difference isosurface is plotted on the left side, and basically shows one of the *p* orbitals of iodide from where the electron is transferred upon photoexcitation. The positive difference isosurface is plotted on the right side, and shows the diffuse orbital that accommodates the excited electron [24].

The nature of the photoexcitation process in iodide-solvent clusters has been studied in great detail for water and acetonitrile clusters [25,24]. It has been shown that, upon photoexcitation, an electron from I^- is transferred to a very diffuse molecular orbital (*cf.* Fig. 3), where it is supported by the stabilizing interaction with the dipole moment of the solvent network. Further, the excited electron distribution in the excited state of iodide-solvent clusters in the Frank-Condon region has been found to be very similar to the electronic structure of the corresponding dipole-bound solvent cluster anions. The only significant difference between excited $[I^-(S)_n]^*$ and $(S)_n^-$, where S represents water or acetonitrile solvent molecules, is the presence of the neutral iodine atom which destabilizes the excited electron. Moreover, the ion-dipole interactions, which kept the ion and solvent molecules together in the ground state, no longer exist in the excited state. Thus, profound structural changes are expected as the system starts relaxing after photoexcitation.

According to our simulations, the "dangling" hydrogen atoms which formed hydrogen bonds with iodide in the ground state, start moving away from the iodine atom, and in less than 50 fs the structure of the water cluster becomes almost flat (Fig. 4, 48 fs), which is accompanied by a drop in potential energy of the whole system (*cf.* Fig. 5). But because of the kinetic energy acquired, hydrogen atoms keep moving, until the water cluster moiety reaches an "inverted crown" structure (Fig. 4, 96 fs). The latter structure is higher in energy than the "flat" structure, and the hydrogen atoms thus continue their oscillatory motion. In general, the relaxation process involves rapid oscillatory motion of the water molecules which results in abrupt oscillations in the system potential and kinetic energies (*cf.* Fig. 6). After the first oscillation, the synchronicity of the water motion appears to be disrupted (Fig 4, 186 fs) as energy is transferred to other cluster vibrational modes and the oxygen atoms and the hydrogen atoms which are involved in the water-water hydrogen bonding start gaining additional kinetic energy (*cf.* Fig. 6). The water network undergoes deformations during the trajectory, and water-water hydrogen bonds break and form back and forth a few times. Meanwhile, the heavy iodine atom is slowly leaving the water cluster: the distance between iodine and the centre of mass of the $(H_2O)_3$ moiety reaches 6.3 Å in less than 900 fs (Fig. 4, 822 fs), while it is only 3.44 Å in the initial Frank-Condon geometry. The fraction of kinetic energy of the heavy iodine atom in the total kinetic energy of the system is not surprisingly very small, with a maximum at 200 fs, and it then slightly decreases, probably due to weak inductive and/or dispersion attractive interactions between the iodine atom and the $(H_2O)_3^-$ cluster (*cf.* Fig. 6). The kinetic energy is thus mainly partitioned into the rotational and vibrational degrees of freedom of water molecules, as evident from Fig. 6.

The main features of the relaxation of photoexcited iodide-water clusters that emerge from this preliminary study are the oscillatory motion of water molecules and the slow recoil motion of the neutral iodine atom. Rapid changes in the relative orientation of the water molecules that result from the interconversion of "crown" and "inverted crown" structures cause rapid changes in the total dipole moment of the $(H_2O)_n$ moiety, and thus, the binding

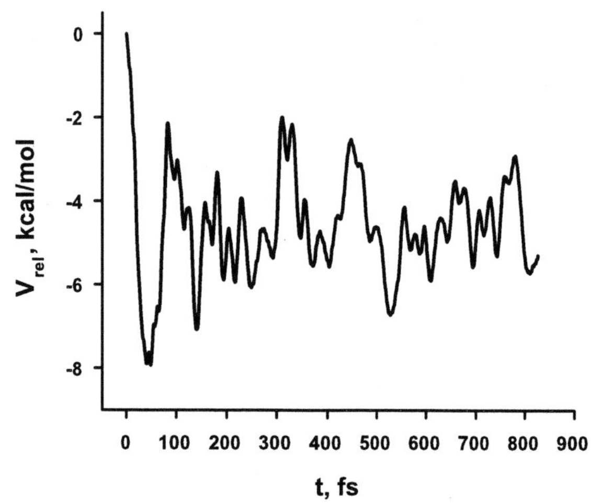

Fig. 5. Time-evolution of the potential energy for the photoexcited $I^-(H_2O)_3$ cluster

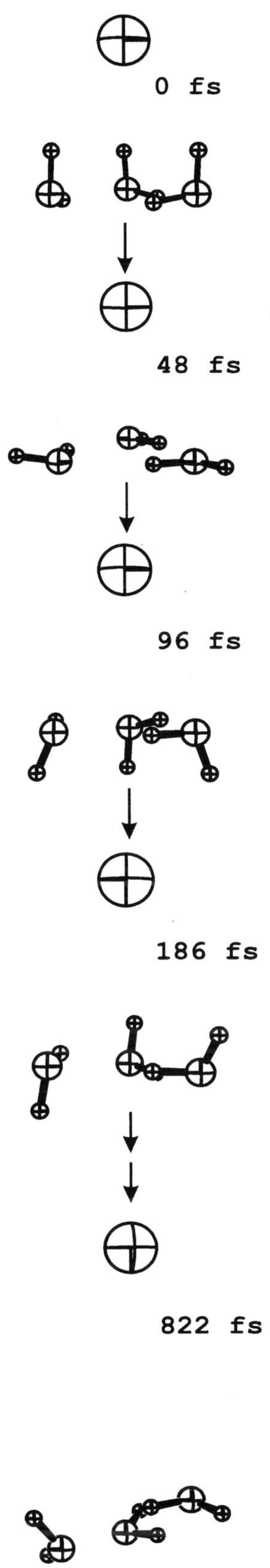

Fig. 4. Snapshots of selected configurations along a typical trajectory of photoexcited $I^-(H_2O)_3$ relaxation.

energy of the excited electron must also undergo oscillatory changes along a given trajectory. However, in the femtosecond experiments of Neumark and co-workers [8], the measured electron binding energy is changing quite smoothly. This may be explained by the fact that at finite experimental temperatures, ground-state $I^-(H_2O)_n$ clusters exist in various configurations and isomers. The observed experimental signal is an average over the whole *ensemble* of possible initial cluster structures, which may lead to observed smooth changes in ensemble-averaged electron binding energies. A large number of trajectories, starting with many different initial cluster configurations, will thus be needed to make a thorough connection with experiment. However, the present simulations, which include only a few trajectories, already suggest that the relaxation of photoexcited $I^-(H_2O)_n$ clusters is a complex process, where both the role of iodine and solvent motion must be included in order to fully rationalize experimental observations [8].

Concluding Remarks and Outlook

The excited-state dynamics of iodide-solvent clusters represents a challenging, yet very important and fascinating problem in modern chemical physics, and a thorough understanding of $I^-(H_2O)_n$ photoexcitation is not possible without supplementing experimental results with computer simulations. For such a complex system, realistic molecular dynamics simulations must be performed using a reliable potential energy surface, based on high-level quantum-chemical calculations. The preliminary results reported here, suggest that the relaxation of excited $[I^-(H_2O)_n]^*$ clusters is characterized by rapid rotational motion of water molecules, which somewhat supports the "solvent-driven" model of relaxation dynamics. On the other hand, the role of iodine motion may also be critical in determining the time-evolution of the electron binding energy following photoexcitation, which is consistent with the "iodine-driven" model of cluster relaxation dynamics. To thoroughly elucidate the relaxation mechanism of photoexcited $I^-(H_2O)_n$ clusters, more extensive *ab initio* molecular dynamics simulations, which take into consideration various possible initial cluster geometries, combined with accurate calculations of the electron binding energies along trajectories, will be necessary.

Ab initio excited-state molecular dynamics simulations are still very taxing at this point. For instance, propagating a single trajectory for 900 fs for the $I^-(H_2O)_3$ cluster on an AlphaServer ES40 (667 MHz, SPECfp2000 rating 500 [26]) takes 25 days. However, progress in computer hardware will make it possible to perform more extensive simulations in the near future. While it would take *ca.* 17

months to propagate 20 trajectories on the ES40 platform, the computing time decreases to *ca.* 10 months with Intel Xeon-based machines (2.4 MHz, SPECfp2000 rating 803 [26]), and a cluster of 20 Xeon computers will allow to perform the whole simulation is less than 16 days, by simply distributing trajectories to each computer node.

Finally, the quantum-chemical calculations needed at every step of the trajectories typically scale as N^3–N^4, where N is the number of basis functions. If a proper treatment can be achieved for $I^-(H_2O)_3$ with a basis set containing 134 functions, the number of basis functions required for a similar level of accuracy for $I^-(H_2O)_5$ and $I^-(H_2O)_6$, for which detailed experimental data is available, increases to 255 and 301, respectively. This represents an increase in computing time by a factor of *ca.* 10 and 20 respectively. As a result, a detailed investigation of $I^-(H_2O)_6$ relaxation dynamics, involving as many as 100 trajectories, may be performed in 10 months on a distributed cluster of 100 Xeon processors.

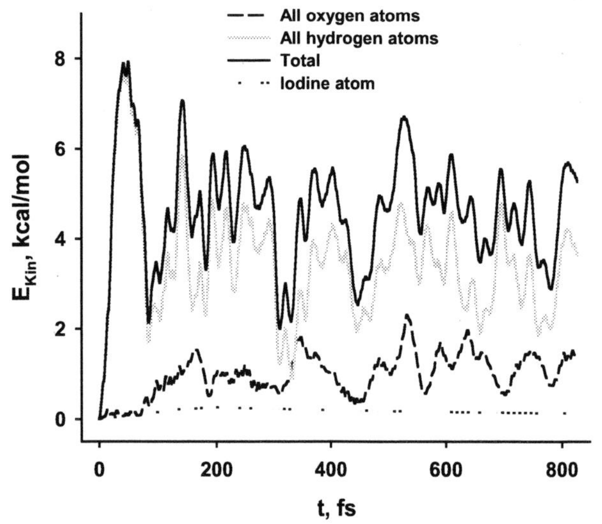

Fig. 6. Time-evolution of the kinetic energy for the photoexcited $I^-(H_2O)_3$ cluster: total kinetic energy, kinetic energy of the iodine atom and kinetic energy of all oxygen and all hydrogen atoms.

References

1. Zewail, A. H. *Prix Nobel* **2000**, 110-203.
2. Zewail, A. H. *Angew. Chem. Int. Ed.* **2000,** *39*, 2586-2631.
3. Zewail, A. H. *J. Phys. Chem. A* **2000,** *104*, 5660-5694.
4. Polanyi, J. C.; Zewail, A. H. *Acc. Chem. Res.* **1995,** *28*, 119-32.
5. Castleman, A. W., Jr.; Bowen, K. H., Jr. *J. Phys. Chem.* **1996,** *100*, 12911-12944.
6. Niedner-Schatteburg, G.; Bondybey, V. E. *Chem. Rev.* **2000,** *100*, 4059-4086.
7. Serxner, D.; Dessent, C. E., H.; Johnson, M. A. *J. Chem. Phys.* **1996,** *105*, 7231-7234.
8. Lehr, L.; Zanni, M. T.; Frischkorn, C.; Weinkauf, R.; Neumark, D. M. *Science* **1999,** *284*, 635-638.
9. Davis, A. V.; Zanni, M. T.; Weinkauf, R.; Neumark, D. M. *Chem. Phys. Lett.* **2002,** *353*, 455-458.
10. Chen, H.-Y.; Sheu, W.-S. *Chem. Phys. Lett.* **2001,** *335*, 475-480.
11. Chen, H.-Y.; Sheu, W.-S. *Chem. Phys. Lett.* **2002,** *353*, 459-462.
12. Bolton, K.; Hase, W. L.; Peslherbe, G. H. Direct Dynamics Simulations of Reactive Systems. In *Multidimensional Molecular Dynamics Methods;* Thompson, D. L. Ed.; World Scientific Publishing Co., 1998.
13. Gutowski, M.; Jordan, K. D.; Skurski, P. *J. Phys. Chem. A* **1998,** *102*, 2624-2633.
14. Knowles, P. J.; Werner, H. J. *Chem. Phys. Lett.* **1985,** *115*, 259-67.
15. Werner, H. J.; Knowles, P. J. *J. Chem. Phys.* **1985,** *82*, 5053-63.
16. Hehre, W. J.; Radom, L.; Schleyer, P. v. R.; Pople, J. A. *Ab Initio Molecular Orbital Theory*; John Wiley and Sons: New York et al., 1985.
17. Hay, P. J.; Wadt, W. R. *J. Chem. Phys.* **1985,** *82*, 270-83.
18. Wadt, W. R.; Hay, P. J. *J. Chem. Phys.* **1985,** *82*, 284-98.
19. Hay, P. J.; Wadt, W. R. *J. Chem. Phys.* **1985,** *82*, 299-310.
20. Check, C. E.; Faust, T. O.; Bailey, J. M.; Wright, B. J.; Gilbert, T. M.; Sunderlin, L. S. *J. Phys. Chem. A* **2001,** *105*, 8111-8116.
21. MOLPRO is a package of ab initio programs written by H.-J. Werner and P. J. Knowles, version 2002.3, with contributions from R. D. Amos, A. Bernhardsson, A. Berning, P. Celani, D. L. Cooper, M. J. O. Deegan, A. J. Dobbyn, F. Eckert, C. Hampel, G. Hetzer, T. Korona, R. Lindh, A. W. Lloyd, S. J. McNicholas, F. R. Manby, W. Meyer, M. E. Mura, A. Nicklass, P. Palmieri, R. Pitzer, G. Rauhut, M. Schütz, H. Stoll, A. J. Stone, R. Tarroni, and T. Thorsteinsson.
22. Combariza, J. E.; Kestner, N. R.; Jortner, J. *J. Chem. Phys.* **1994,** *100*, 2865-70.
23. Koch, D. M.; Peslherbe, G. H. *Chem. Phys. Lett.* **2002,** *359*, 381-389.
24. Timerghazin, Q. K.; Peslherbe, G. H. *Chem. Phys. Lett.* **2002,** *354*, 31-37.
25. Chen, H.-Y.; Sheu, W.-S. *J. Am. Chem. Soc.* **2000,** *122*, 7534-7542.
26. SPECfp2000, by Standard Performance Evaluation Corporation, available at http://www.spec.org/.

Large Scale Molecular Dynamics Simulations of Lipid-Drug Interactions

Justin L. MacCallum, Parag Mukhopadhyay, Huaqiang Luo, D. Peter Tieleman*

Department of Biological Sciences, University of Calgary, 2500 University Dr. NW, Calgary, Alberta T2N 1N4
http://moose.bio.ucalgary.ca

* *tieleman@ucalgary.ca*

Molecular dynamics is a powerful computational technique for studying biochemical systems at the atomic resolution. We will present the results of several recent studies in our laboratory that apply molecular dynamics to the distribution and behaviour of small molecules within lipid bilayer environments similar to the membrane surrounding all cells. Specifically, we have studied the distribution of hexane, halothane, and PCP within a lipid bilayer, and the orientation and dynamics of PCP and tryptophan within the bilayer. The results are in good agreement with experiment and yield valuable insight into these systems. We also overview the computational requirements of molecular dynamics and schemes for overcoming the inherently serial nature of molecular dynamics simulations.

La dynamique moléculaire est une technique de calcul numérique efficace pour l'étude des systèmes biochimiques à l'échelle atomique. Nous présentons ici les résultats de plusieurs études récentes, effectuées dans notre laboratoire, où nous avons appliqué la dynamique moléculaire au comportement et à la distribution de petites molécules dans des environnements à deux couches lipides, semblables à la membrane entourant les cellules. Plus précisément, nous avons étudié la distribution de l'hexane, de l'halothane et du PCP dans un environnement à deux couches lipides, ainsi que l'orientation et la dynamique du PCP et du tryptophan dans cet environnement. Les résultats sont en accord avec l'expérience, et mènent à une meilleure compréhension de ces systèmes. Nous exposons également les besoins de la dynamique moléculaire, en termes de puissance de calcul, ainsi que les solutions possibles pour passer outre la nature série des simulations de dynamique moléculaire.

Introduction

Biomolecular simulation has made major progress in recent years. Thanks to powerful computers and improved algorithms many new problems have come within range of atomistic simulations. One such problem is the distribution of small molecules in biological membranes such as the lipid bilayer membrane surrounding all cells. The interactions of small molecules and membranes are of significant importance in a number of areas of research:

- The distribution of small molecules such as water, oxygen and nitrogen is the main determinant of passive transport of these molecules into and out of cells.
- Bioavailability of drugs depends largely on their solubility in cell membranes. Prediction or calculation of this property would be a great advantage in drug design and screening.
- Biopollutants such as pentachlorophenol, a wood preservative, or polyaromatic hydrocarbons accumulate in cell membranes. Changes in cell membrane composition in microorganisms are a primary defense against this, which we could understand in detail if the properties that determined the distribution and solubility of these molecules were known.
- The mechanism of general anesthesia may involve the distribution of the anesthetic in the membrane, but this distribution is currently not well characterized.
- The membrane environment is inhomogeneous, with large gradients in density, available free volume, and polarity on a length scale of *ca.* 3 nm. It is of great basic physical chemistry interest to understand the partitioning of small molecules in such environments, with important implications for a better understanding of hydrophobic and other solvent effects, protein folding, and analytical separation methods such as reverse-phase chromatography.

We are using large-scale computer simulations to calculate the distribution and behavior of several small molecules inside model membranes. Such simulations provide not only the distribution and behavior of solutes in the membrane environment, but also insight into the physiochemical features of the lipid bilayer and the solute that lead to the observed behavior.

We will present an overview of the results from several recent studies in our laboratory. Specifically, we will present the free energy profile and its enthalpy and entropy contributions for hexane in a DOPC bilayer. We have also determined the free energy profile for the local anesthetic halothane in a DOPC bilayer. Additionally we will show the distribution of the wood preservative pentachlorophenol (PCP) in a lipid bilayer, and its effects on the bilayer. Finally, we will present results on the orientational dynamics of a tryptophan analogue at its preferred location in the lipid bilayer. First, we will begin with a brief overview of the theory of classical molecular dynamics simulation followed by a brief review of the available literature on the interactions of small molecules with lipid bilayers.

Theory of MD Simulations

Molecular dynamics simulations have become a widely used tool to study complex biomolecular systems. The basic method is straightforward. An empirical potential function is used to describe the interactions between atoms in a model of the system of interest. From this potential function forces on individual atoms are derived, which are then used to integrate equations of motion for all atoms in the system at once. A typical potential function commonly used in MD simulations includes the following terms:

$$V(\mathbf{r}^N) = \sum_{bonds} \frac{k_i}{2}(l_i - l_{i,0})^2 + \sum_{angles} \frac{k_i}{2}(\theta_i - \theta_{i,0})^2 + \sum_{torsions} \frac{V_n}{2}(1 + \cos(n\omega - \gamma)) + \sum_{i=1}^{N} \sum_{j=i+1}^{N} \left(4\varepsilon_{ij}\left[\left(\frac{\sigma_{ij}}{r_{ij}}\right)^{12} - \left(\frac{\sigma_{ij}}{r_{ij}}\right)^{6}\right] + \frac{q_i q_j}{4\pi\varepsilon_0 r_{ij}} \right). \qquad (1)$$

Bonds and angles are modeled by simple harmonic functions, dihedral rotations (rotations around a central bond) are modeled as a cosine function, and non-bonded interactions are approximated by the Lennard-Jones and Coulomb interaction functions for Van der Waals and electrostatic interactions respectively. The constants k_i are harmonic force constants, l_i, is the current, $l_{i,0}$ the reference bond length, θ_i the current, $\theta_{i,0}$ the reference angle, V_n, n and γ describe dihedral angles, ε and σ are Lennard-Jones parameters (a different pair for each combination of two different atom types), q_i and q_j are the partial atomic charges, and r_{ij} is the distance between two atoms. All parameters are empirical and are fit to reproduce the experimental properties of model compounds. Using this potential function the forces (derivative of the potential with respect to position) on all atoms in the system of interest are calculated and used to solve classical equations of motions to generate a trajectory of all atoms in time. This trajectory is the primary result of the simulation, from which specific details of the system can be analyzed. This is an exciting idea, because atoms can be followed as they move in real time, on a timescale currently limited to *ca.* 100 ns, although longer simulations have also been reported. In principle, any properties that depend on coordinates, velocities or forces can be calculated, given sufficient simulation time. The main limitations of molecular dynamics simulations are in the maximum system size and simulation length – which depend mostly on the available computer time, and the accuracy of the empirical potential function that describes the interactions between atoms.

Simulations of Lipid-Small Molecule Interactions

There have been several studies in the past that used computer simulations to study small molecules in lipid bilayers. Much of the older literature has been reviewed in ref. 1. We will just highlight a few studies here to give an idea of the rapidly increasing possibilities. One of the first and still one of the most thorough papers is the study of Marrink and Berendsen on the distribution and permeation of water in a phospholipid membrane[2]. This was followed by further studies on other small molecules such as oxygen and ammonia[3]. Stouch and coworkers have done MD simulations of benzene and some drug analogues in DPPC bilayers[4,5]. More recently, Mezei used Monte Carlo simulations to calculate the distribution of a series of small molecules[6]. Several recent studies[7-9] from Koubi *et al* have examined the distribution of halothane, which is a potent anaesthetic, and structurally related molecules that surprisingly have no anaesthetic effect at all. Xiang and Anderson have calculated[10] the functional group contribution to the free energy of transport of various derivatives of p-toluic acid from water to the ordered region of the lipid chains. Using the umbrella sampling method, Grossfield and Woolf have calculated[11] the distribution of tryptophan within a POPC bilayer. Pohorille *et al* have calculated the distribution and interactions of small molecules[12,13] and anaesthetics[14,15] at water-membrane and water-hexane interfaces.

Calculating the Distribution of Small Molecules

There are two different paths to calculate the distribution of small molecules in a lipid bilayer. In the first, equilibrium simulations directly provide the average distribution from a histogram of positions of the small molecules as a function of depth in the bilayer. Although this is a straightforward method, it fails even for a simple hydrophobic molecule like hexane because the likelihood of finding hexane in the least favorable part of the bilayer in a direct simulation is too small to give statistically significant data. Nonetheless, these less likely regions critically determine permeation rates and other important properties. Additionally it is very hard to parallelize these simulations because extensive and frequent communication is required between processors. Thus unless expensive shared memory machines or expensive high speed interconnects are used, one is limited to running on only a few processors.

A second method of calculating the distribution of small molecules in a lipid bilayer is known as umbrella sampling. In umbrella sampling, a series of independent simulations, often referred to as windows, are performed in which the small molecule is restrained at different depths in the bilayer by means of a biasing (umbrella) potential. The distribution of the molecule in the presence of this biasing potential is obtained from each window. By combining the results from many windows together spanning the lipid bilayer, the bias can be removed and the full potential of mean force (PMF, $G(z)$, directly related to the distribution through Equation 2) can be reconstructed using the weighted histogram analysis method (WHAM)[16]. Umbrella sampling offers an additional advantage in that each individual window is completely independent of the others and thus the windows can be simulated in an embarrassingly parallel manner.

$$\rho(z) = \exp(-G(z)/RT) \quad (2)$$

The WHAM method combines all of the available data to produce a statistically optimal PMF. Additional data can later be added to difficult regions, for example where the PMF is changing rapidly. Thus the combination of umbrella sampling and WHAM allows the computational effort to be focused on the most difficult parts of the problem.

Methods

All simulations were carried out using the GROMACS 3 software package[17,18]. All simulations were performed in a realistic, fully hydrated lipid bilayer containing 64 or 128 lipids (Figure 1). For the hexane, halothane, and tryptophan systems 64 dioleoyl-phosphatidylcholine (DOPC) lipids were used, and for the PCP simulations 128 palmytoyloleoylphosphatidylcholine

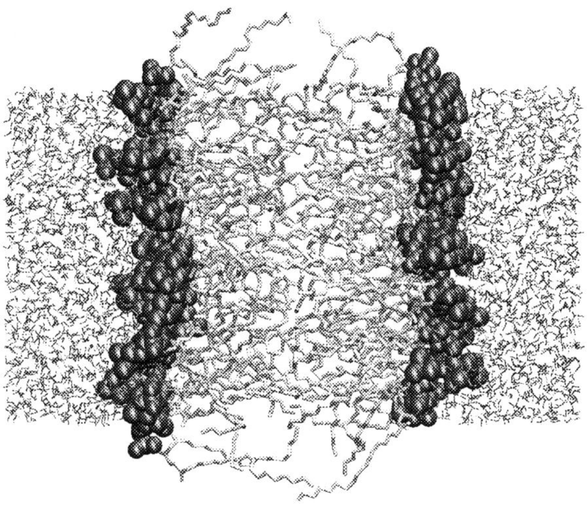

Figure 1. Snapshot of a DOPC bilayer system. Water is shown as thin grey lines. The lipids are shown as grey tubes for the tails and dark spheres for the head groups. This system contains 64 lipids (32 per leaflet) and 2807 water molecules. The z-axis of the coordinate system runs parallel to the bilayer normal – left to right in this figure.

(POPC) or 128 palmytoyloleoylphosphatidylethanolamine (POPE) were used. The lipid parameters are the same as ref. 19 and have been extensively used in the past. In all simulations the temperature was held constant using the weak-coupling algorithm. In the PCP and tryptophan simulations the pressure was coupled using the weak-coupling algorithm. A time step of 2 fs was used except for the halothane simulations where a time step of 5 fs was used.

Hexane was modeled using standard OPLS united atom parameters[20,21], while tryptophan was modeled using GROMOS96 parameters[22]. Halothane was modeled using the parameters of Scharf and Laasonen[23]. For PCP, the charges were derived from quantum calculations using the Hartree-Fock method and the 6-31G* basis set. The

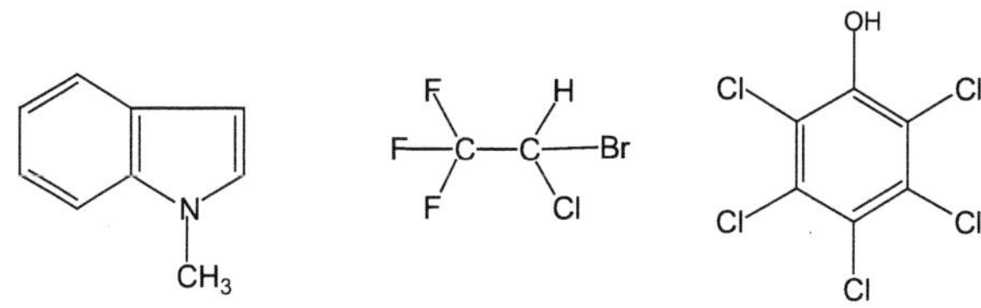

Figure 2. Chemical formulas for a methylindole – a tryptophan analogue (left), halothane – a general anaesthetic (middle) and PCP – an environmental pollutant (right).

Lennard-Jones parameters were taken from the OPLS all-atom[24] force field and the bonded parameters were taken from the GROMOS96[22] force field. The chemical formulas of halothane, PCP, and tryptophan are shown in Figure 2.

Hexane

The distribution of hexane in a DOPC bilayer was obtained using the combination of umbrella sampling and WHAM. Two hexane molecules were placed in the bilayer, one per leaflet. The molecules were restrained to 25 different z coordinates within each leaflet and simulated for 20 ns. Using one molecule of hexane per leaflet allows an estimation of the statistical error because given sufficient sampling both leaflets should yield the same result. The simulations were performed at a fixed area to avoid having to sample over slow fluctuations in the area per lipid. These simulations were carried out at three different temperatures (283, 298, and 323 K) in order to decompose the PMF into enthalpic and entropic contributions. In total these simulations represent 1.5 μs of simulation time. These simulations were performed on our local cluster, and each simulation required approximately 37 days of CPU time on a single Pentium III 1GHz processor, for a total computer time of approximately 8 years.

For comparison, the distribution of hexane was also obtained directly, using a 50 ns simulation of 32 hexane molecules in a 64 lipid DOPC bilayer. This calculation was carried out on 4 Pentium III 1GHz processors in parallel using Myrinet (Myricom, Arcadia, CA) high speed interconnects. This simulation was completed in approximately 30 days.

Halothane

The distribution of halothane in a DOPC bilayer was also calculated using the combination of umbrella sampling and WHAM. This calculation was performed as part of the CISS2 project[31]. Briefly, the Trellis software package[25] was used to aggregate many high-performance computing sites in Canada into a single metacomputer. The computational requirement was that each simulation should complete in approximately 24 hours or less. To fulfill this requirement, the umbrella sampling was decomposed differently than it was for hexane. For these simulations, 37 different z coordinates spaced at 0.1 nm intervals were used. For each z coordinate, 20 independent simulations of 2 ns each were constructed by using a random lipid configuration taken from a previous 100 ns simulation and a random orientation and lateral position of the halothane molecule. As with hexane, these calculations were carried out at three different temperatures (283, 298, 323 K) to determine the enthalpic and entropic contributions to the PMF. In total these simulations represent 4.4 μs of simulation time. They were run on a wide variety of systems, many of which are faster than our local cluster. This fact, combined with the use of a 5 fs time step allowed these calculations to be completed within two weeks, using roughly 10 years of computer time in total.

PCP

MD simulations of PCP in POPC and POPE phospholipid bilayers were carried out. The PCP-POPC system consisted of 16 PCP, 128 POPC and 2460 water molecules, and the PCP-POPE system consisted of 16 PCP, 128 POPC and 6032 water molecules. Two independent simulations for each of the lipid bilayers were carried out in which PCP was randomly placed inside (Figure 3 – lower) or outside (Figure 3 – upper) the phospholipid bilayer in the starting configuration. In all there were four independent simulations of the PCP-phospholipid bilayer systems. All simulations were carried out at 298 K.

For the PCP-POPC system a 40ns simulation for each of the two starting configurations (Figure 3) was carried out, while for the PCP-POPE system a 30ns simulation for each of the two starting configurations was carried out. The PCP simulations were performed in parallel on 2 Pentium III 1GHz processors and required approximately 180 days of computer time total for all four simulations.

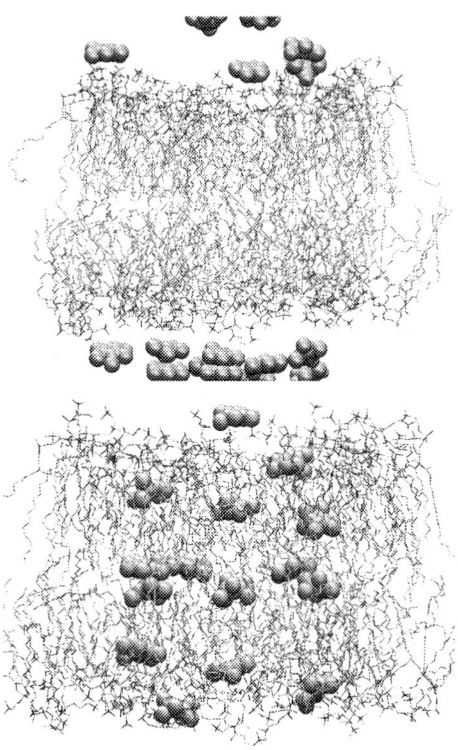

Figure 3. Starting configuration of PCP simulations. For both POPC and POPE 16 PCP molecules were placed either inside (lower) or outside (upper) of the lipid bilayer. PCP is shown as grey spheres. Lipid molecules are shown as grey lines. Water is omitted for clarity. The *z*-axis runs vertically in these figures.

Tryptophan

Tryptophan was restrained to its preferred location[11] within a 64 lipid DPPC bilayer using a harmonic restraint on the *z* coordinate. Ten different simulations with different starting orientations of the molecules were performed. Each simulation was between 1 and 10 ns long and required several days to several weeks of computer time on a single Pentium III 1GHz.

Results

Hexane

For comparison the results obtained using umbrella sampling and direct simulation are shown in Figure 4. The difference between leaflets is small for both the umbrella sampling and direct cases, which would normally be a good indicator that the simulations are converged. However, while it is clear that the two profiles have the same overall shape, there is a significant difference in the free energies obtained. In particular, the free simulation displays a difference in free energy between bulk water (*ca.* 3.5 nm) and the bilayer center (0 nm) that is roughly half as large as from umbrella sampling. Additionally, the barrier at *ca.* 2 nm is higher in the free case than from umbrella sampling. As a test, thermodynamic integration calculations (which are an independent way to determine free energy changes) were performed to determine the free energy of transferring a hexane from water to the bilayer center. These calculations yielded a value of –26 kJ/mol (data not shown), which is consistent with the umbrella sampling results, but not the free simulations. The poor results from the free simulation are due to a lack of sampling. The simulations simply are not long enough for a particle to move from the water phase into the membrane and *vice versa*. Thus the final result will depend strongly on the initial arrangement of hexane molecules within the bilayer. In this case, some of the hexane molecules were placed in the water phase at the start and were trapped there for some time – leading to a free energy that is much too favourable relative to the bilayer center.

The free energy profile displays a clear minimum in the center of the bilayer, with a slight barrier in the head group region. The PMF is flat beyond about 2.7 nm, indicating that this is bulk water.

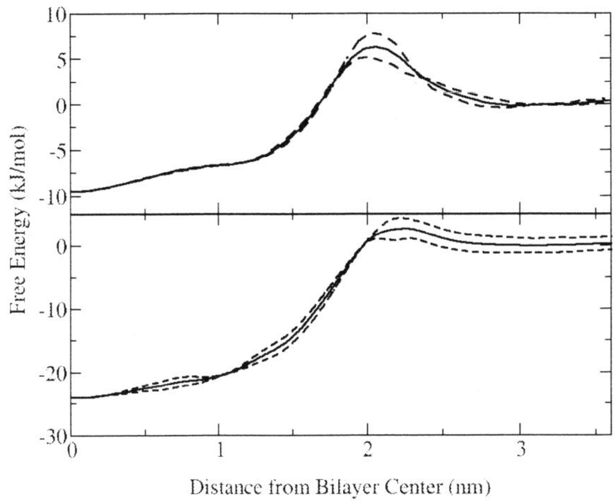

Figure 4. Comparison of direct (upper) and umbrella sampling (lower) results for hexane in a DOPC bilayer at 298 K. The results from each leaflet are shown as a dashed line. The average is shown as a solid line.

The umbrella sampling calculations were carried out at three different temperatures. If the three PMF curves are aligned so that hexane in bulk water corresponds to zero in each case, we can calculate the enthalpic and entropic contributions to the PMF using Equation 3.

$$-T\Delta S = T\frac{\Delta G(T+\Delta T)-\Delta G(T-\Delta T)}{2\Delta T} \qquad (3)$$

$$\Delta H = \Delta G + T\Delta S$$

The results of this decomposition are shown in Figure 5. The hexane is driven into the bilayer interior by entropy with a very small enthalpy change – consistent with the hydrophobic effect. We find that partitioning into the upper region of the acyl chains, near the carbonyl group is driven by enthalpy but opposed by entropy. At around the position of the phosphate and choline groups, partitioning is favoured by enthalpy, but more strongly opposed by entropy.

The distribution of hexane is consistent with previous neutron diffraction studies[26] that determined that hexane is confined almost exclusively to the center of low-hydration egg-PC bilayers. The results are also consistent with the work of De Vido *et al*[27] which indicate that solutes will be driven more towards the center of the bilayer at higher temperatures because of the unfavourable entropy of partitioning into the upper chain region.

Halothane

The free energy profile of halothane partitioning in a DOPC bilayer is shown in Figure 6. The profile displays a local minimum within the phosphate and choline groups at around 2.25 nm from the bilayer center, and a global minimum just inside the carbonyl groups at about 1.5 nm. The presence of a local minimum at the interface is consistent with other recent simulations[14, 15, 28] that propose that anaesthetics, while being hydrophobic,

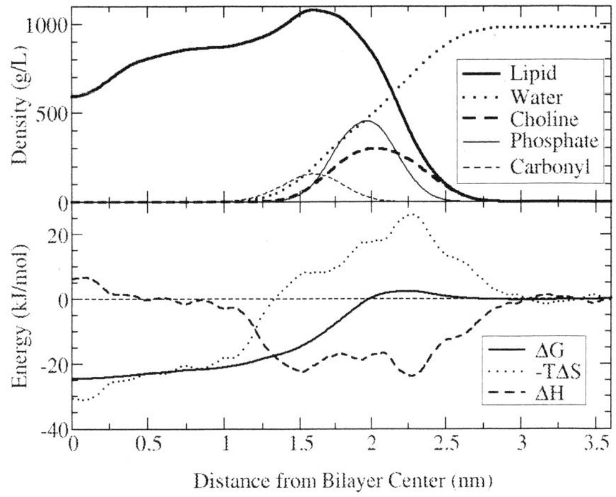

Figure 5. Free energy and enthalpy/entropy decomposition of hexane partitioning in a DOPC bilayer. The lower panel displays the free energy (ΔG), and its entropic (-TΔS), and enthalpic (ΔH) components. The upper panel displays the distribution of various chemical groups to serve as a roadmap.

partition to the water-bilayer interface. Simulations were carried out at three different temperatures, however the analysis of the enthalpy/entropy decomposition is still underway and will be reported in a future publication.

Pentachlorophenol

The two different starting configurations (Figure 3) converge to give a similar area per lipid after 20ns of simulation. The last 20ns was thus used for analyses of the trajectory.

Figure 7 shows the distribution of PCP in a POPC bilayer. PCP tends to occupy a similar position in both POPC and POPE bilayers (data not shown). The density of PCP shows significant overlap with the carbonyl group and the carbon-carbon double bonds. Thus PCP tends to occupy regions between the carbonyl groups and the carbon-carbon double bonds of the alkyl chains in the

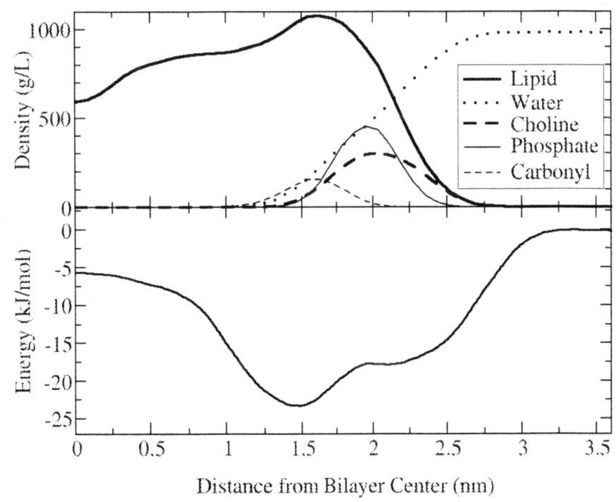

Figure 6. Free energy of partitioning halothane in a DOPC bilayer. The lower panel shows the PMF of halothane in a DOPC bilayer at 298 K, while the upper panel shows the distribution of various functional groups within the bilayer.

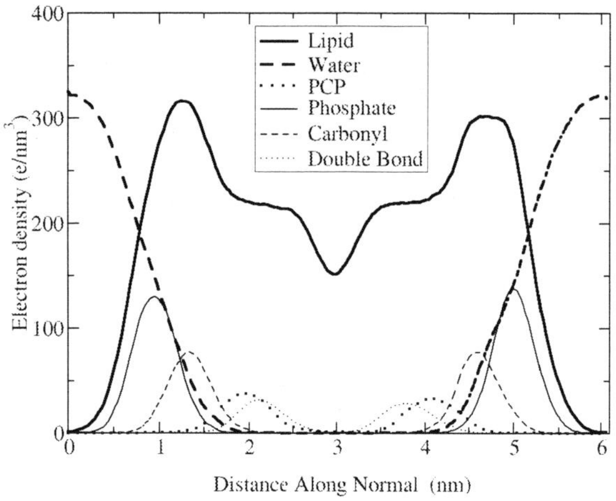

Figure 7. Electron density profile along the POPC bilayer normal, z, averaged over the last 20ns of the trajectory. The results for the POPE bilayer are very similar.

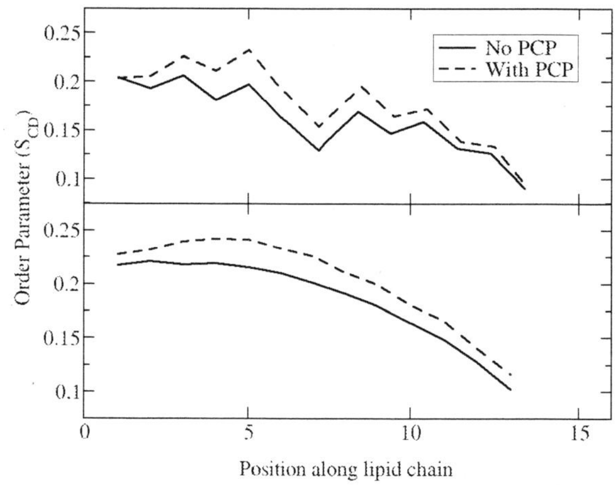

Figure 8. Average deuterium acyl chain segment order parameters (S_{CD}) with PCP in POPC bilayer (dashed line) compared with S_{CD} for the pure POPC bilayer (solid line). The upper panel shows the result for the unsaturated chain. The lower panel shows the result for the saturated chain.

phospholipid bilayer, which is referred as the soft polymer region of the lipid bilayer[1,2]. PCP is thus similar to halothane in its interfacial location.

Figure 8 compares the average deuterium alkyl chain segment order parameter (S_{CD}) of POPC in the L_α phase bilayer with and without PCP. Order parameters are a measure of the spatial restriction of the motion of a C-H bond vector and are measurable by ^{2}H NMR. PCP increases the molecular order parameter of POPC in the bilayer for both the saturated and unsaturated chain. The fraction of dihedral angles in trans conformation along the alkyl chains of POPC in the pure lipid bilayer is comparable to that of the lipid bilayer with PCP (data not shown). Thus PCP decreases the "fluidity" of the phospholipid bilayer by making the bilayer more rigid. Similar results were obtained for the PCP-POPE system.

Changes in the cell membrane composition in microorganisms are one of the defence mechanisms to reduce the toxicity of the biopollutants on the organism[9]. In order to understand the effect of PCP on the lipid composition of PCP degrading microorganisms, it is important to understand how changes in lipid composition of a phospholipid bilayer influence the distribution of PCP in the bilayer. We carried out MD simulations of the distribution of PCP in POPC and POPE to address the above question.

Similar distributions of PCP were obtained in both POPC and POPE bilayers. PCP showed a strong preference to occupy the soft polymer region of the lipid bilayer, as obtained from two different starting structures (Figure 3) by the end of two 40ns simulations, indicating that the average position was well converged. Analyses of the orientation of PCP in these bilayers show that they align parallel to the alkyl chains of the lipid thereby maximizing the Van der Waal's interaction with the alkyl chains to have optimum packing in the highly dense soft polymer region of the bilayer. PCP increased the rigidity of the phospholipid bilayer as shown by the increase in the order parameters of the alkyl chain segments.

The simulation results thus show that the distribution and the effect of PCP on the bilayer structure is unaffected by changing the head group functionality of the phospholipid between choline and ethanolamine. In both of these lipids, the presence of PCP decreases the fluidity. This concurs with the experimental observation that in certain PCP degrading microorganisms, the percentage of POPE and POPC phospholipid in the cell membrane remains unchanged while the percentage of cardiolipin increases in response to the toxic effect of PCP[30].

Tryptophan

The orientational dynamics of the tryptophan analogue methylindole (Trp) were studied by restraining the tryptophan to its equilibrium position within the bilayer[11]. The work represents, to our knowledge, the first

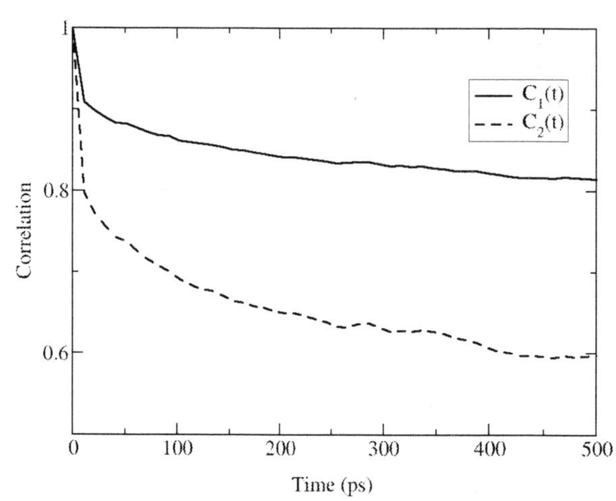

Figure 9. Orientational time-correlation functions, C_1 and C_2, of the vector normal to the plane of Trp in DPPC lipid bilayer.

MD simulation on the orientational dynamic properties of the aromatic protein residues in lipid bilayer systems. These systems attracted significant attention recently due to the findings that the aromatic residues, Trp in particular, tend to stay near the membrane-water interface region, instead of the interior region of the bilayer that would be expected based on the hydrophobic effect. Previous MD studies[11] confirmed Trp's preference for the lipid-water interface region, but the simulation was based on stochastic dynamics and the results were limited to equilibrium and static properties only.

We consider the 1st and 2nd order orientational time-correlation functions,

$$C_1(t) = \langle P_1(\mathrm{I}(t) \bullet \mathrm{I}(0)) \rangle \quad (4)$$

$$C_2(t) = \langle P_2(\mathrm{I}(t) \bullet \mathrm{I}(0)) \rangle \quad (5)$$

where **I**(t) is the unit vector of the normal direction of the aromatic ring of Trp, and P_1 and P_2 are the 1st and 2nd Legendre polynomials, respectively. The orientational time-correlation functions show how well a molecule "remembers" its initial orientation and are well measurable by NMR and other spectroscopy experiments. It is well known that the dynamic properties of non-isotropic molecules, especially their long-time limit, are dominated by the orientational contribution in liquid-like condensed phase. The long-time dynamic behaviour, and its orientational contribution in particular, of the present system is thus of special interest because of the non-isotropic conformation of the molecules involved. Note that here not only the Trp molecule itself is plane-like and thus non-isotropic, the lipids are also long and highly ordered, thus providing a highly non-isotropic background.

The orientational time-correlation functions of Trp in its equilibrium position in the lipid interface region were calculated and shown in Figures 9 and 10. In Figure 10, we also show the Trp centre of mass velocity auto-correlation (VAC) and compared it with the orientational time correlation functions in the short-time range. The most interesting feature of the figures is the remarkable long-time tail as well as the sharp initial decay of the orientational correlation functions. The similar time scales of the VAC and the short-time initial decay of the orientational correlation functions indicate that the short-time dynamics is governed by short-ranged direct intermolecular collisions. On the other hand, the decoupling of the time scales of the correlations of the translational and orientational motions confirmed that long-time dynamics is dominated by the orientational contribution. To estimate the two-tier time scale of the orientational dynamics quantitatively, we fitted the correlation functions by a simple bi-exponential function. The parameters of the fitted functions are given in Table 1. Clearly, the translational correlation and the initial decay of the orientational correlation are both within a time scale of *ca.* 10 ps, while the long-time orientational correlation is in the order of 1-10 ns, a remarkably long time scale in molecular dynamics.

Note that Figure 9 does not show the full-length time decay of the orientational time-correlation functions. Unfortunately this is due to the above-mentioned long time scale and the corresponding extremely high computation cost. In fact, to calculate a time-correlation function, several thousand independent time trajectories are needed for meaningful statistics. For a time-correlation function of decay time τ, this means several thousand separate MD runs of length τ, or a single MD run with time length of several τ for an equivalent statistics. Since 100ns is about the upper limit of the MD run length of with the typical computer power currently available, the 1-10 ns orientational dynamics considered in present work is an extremely difficult task.

Table 1. Relaxation times and pre-exponential factors of the bi-exponential fit of the orientational time correlation functions, C_1 and C_2, of Trp in DPPC lipid bilayer. The function fit is:

$$f(t) = a_1 \exp(-t/\tau_1) + a_2 \exp(-t/\tau_2).$$

	$C_1(t)$	$C_2(t)$
a_1	0.14	0.31
a_2	0.86	0.69
τ_1 (ps)	3.8	7.2
τ_2 (ps)	9.4×10^3	4.5×10^3

Outlook

For all four systems studied here, the simulations yield insight into why the small molecule behave the way they do and provide a "picture" that helps to interpret experimental results.

With increasing computer power, faster networking technology, increasingly sophisticated algorithms, and techniques such as umbrella sampling – molecular simulations stand to make increasingly important contributions to our understanding of biological (and other) membranes.

Acknowledgements

DPT is a Scholar of the Alberta Heritage Foundation for Medical Research. Work described in this paper has been supported by the Natural Sciences and Engineering Research Council (Canada), the Protein Engineering Network of Centres of Excellence, and a University of Calgary Research Grant. JLM and DPT would like to thank Paul Lu and the CISS2 team, as well as all of the C3 sites that participated in the CISS2 experiment.

References

(1) Tieleman, D. P.; Marrink, S. J.; Berendsen, H. J. C. Biochim. Biophys. Acta-Rev. Biomembr. **1997**, 1331, 235-270.
(2) Marrink, S. J.; Berendsen, H. J. C. J. Phys. Chem. **1994**, 98, 4155-4168.

(3) Marrink, S. J.; Berendsen, H. J. C. J. Phys. Chem. **1996**, 100, 16729-16738.
(4) Bassolino-Klimas, D.; Alper, H. E.; Stouch, T. R. J. Am. Chem. Soc. **1995**, 117, 4118-4129.
(5) Alper, H. E.; Stouch, T. R. J. Phys. Chem. **1995**, 99, 5724-5731.
(6) Jedlovszky, P.; Mezei, M. J. Am. Chem. Soc. **2000**, 122, 5125-5131.
(7) Koubi, L.; Tarek, M.; Bandyopadhyay, S.; Klein, M. L.; Scharf, D. Anesthesiology **2002**, 97, 848-855.
(8) Koubi, L.; Tarek, M.; Bandyopadhyay, S.; Klein, M. L.; Scharf, D. Biophys. J. **2001**, 81, 3339-3345.
(9) Koubi, L.; Tarek, M.; Klein, M. L.; Scharf, D. Biophys. J. **2000**, 78, 800-811.
(10) Xiang, T. X.; Anderson, B. D. Biophys. J. **2002**, 82, 2052-2066.
(11) Grossfield, A.; Woolf, T. B. Langmuir **2002**, 18, 198-210.
(12) Pohorille, A.; New, M. H.; Schweighofer, K.; Wilson, M. A. In Membrane Permeability, 1999; Vol. 48, pp 49-76.
(13) Pohorille, A.; Wilson, M. A. J. Chem. Phys. **1996**, 104, 3760-3773.
(14) Pohorille, A.; Wilson, M. A.; New, M. H.; Chipot, C. Toxicol. Lett. **1998**, 101, 421-430.
(15) Pohorille, A.; Cieplak, P.; Wilson, M. A. Chem. Phys. **1996**, 204, 337-345.
(16) Kumar, S.; Bouzida, D.; Swendsen, R. H.; Kollman, P. A.; Rosenberg, J. M. J. Comp. Chem. **1992**, 13, 1011-1021.
(17) Lindahl, E.; Hess, B.; van der Spoel, D. J. Mol. Modelling **2001**, 7, 306-317.
(18) Berendsen, H. J. C.; van der Spoel, D.; van Drunen, R. Comp. Phys. Comm. **1995**, 91, 43-56.
(19) Tieleman, D. P.; Bentz, J. Biophys. J. **2002**, 83, 1501-1510.
(20) Jorgensen, W. L.; Madura, J. D.; Swenson, C. J. J. Am. Chem. Soc. **1984**, 106, 6638.
(21) Jorgensen, W. L. J. Phys. Chem. **1986**, 87, 5304.
(22) Van Gunsteren, W. F.; Billeter, S. R.; Eising, A. A.; Hunenberger, P. H.; Kruger, P.; Mark, A. E.; Scott, W. R. P.; Tironi, I. G. Biomolecular Simulation: The GROMOS96 manual and user guide; Hochschulverlag AG and ETH Zurich: Zurich, Switzerland, 1996.
(23) Scharf, D.; Laasonen, K. Chem. Phys. Lett. **1996**, 258, 276-282.
(24) Jorgensen, W. L.; Maxwell, D. S.; TiradoRives, J. J. Am. Chem. Soc. **1996**, 118, 11225-11236.
(25) Pinchak, C.; Lu, P.; Goldenberg, M. In 8th Workshop on Job Scheduling Strategies for Parallel Processing: Edinburgh, Scotland, 2002; pp 85-105.
(26) White, S. H.; King, G. I.; Cain, J. E. Nature **1981**, 290, 161-163.
(27) DeVido, D. R.; Dorsey, J. G.; Chan, H. S.; Dill, K. A. J. Phys. Chem. B **1998**, 102, 7272-7279.
(28) Chipot, C.; Wilson, M. A.; Pohorille, A. J. Phys. Chem. B **1997**, 101, 782-791.
(29) Sikkema, J.; Debont, J. A. M.; Poolman, B. Microbiol. Rev. **1995**, 59, 201-222.
(30) Lohmeier-Vogel, E. M.; Leung, K. T.; Lee, H.; Trevors, J. T.; Vogel, H. J. Appl. Environ. Microbiol. **2001**, 67, 3549-3556
(31) Pinchak, C.; Lu, P.; Schaeffer, J.; Goldenberg, M.; In 17th Annual International Symposium on High Performance Computing Systems and Applications (HPCS), **2003**, Sherbrooke, Quebec, Canada.

Delayed Propagation of Derivatives in a Two-dimensional Aircraft Design Optimization Problem

H. Martin Bücker, Arno Rasch, Emil Slusanschi, Christian H. Bischof [a]

[a]Institute for Scientific Computing, Aachen University, 52056 Aachen, Germany
{buecker, rasch, slusanschi, bischof}@sc.rwth-aachen.de

In computational fluid dynamics (CFD), the use of high-performance computers is often indispensable, simply to manage the high request for computation time and storage. We consider a particular two-dimensional aircraft design problem and report on the use of automatic differentiation (AD) to obtain accurate derivatives rather than approximations based on numerical differentiation. More precisely, we apply the AD system ADIFOR to the large-scale CFD solver TFS and quantify the computational savings of a technique starting the derivative computations in a delayed manner over a black box AD approach.

En dynamique des fluides (CFD), l'utilisation d'ordinateurs performants est souvent indispensable, en raison des besoins énormes en temps de calcul et en stockage de données. Nous considérons un problème de conception d'avion en deux dimension. Nous utilisons une technique de différentiation automatique (AD) pour obtenir des dérivées précises, plutt que des approximations basées sur des dérivées numériques. Plus précisément, nous appliquons le système de AD appelée ADIFOR au programme de CFD TFS et quantifions les gains en temps de calcul d'une technique initiant les calculs de dérivées d'un manière progressive, en comparaison d'une approche AD de type "boîte noire".

1 Introduction

High-performance numerical simulations are among the indispensable tools used in the design and analysis of flight vehicles. We consider a particular computational fluid dynamics (CFD) simulation with the long-term aim to create an airfoil with the highest possible lift-over-drag ratio. A crucial preprocessing step of this design optimization problem consists in efficiently evaluating the derivatives of the lift-over-drag ratio with respect to some given geometric parameters characterizing the geometry of the underlying airfoil. Here, efficiency of the derivative computation is of major importance because the evaluation of the objective function includes the solution of the Navier-Stokes equations, representing a hard computational problem on its own. Therefore, one has to be careful when adding further computational work by the evaluation of derivatives.

In a previous work [1], we used a technique called automatic differentiation (AD), whose basics are summarized in Sect. 2, to obtain derivatives for a two-dimensional airfoil design optimization problem and demonstrated the advantages of the AD approach over a numerical approach in terms of accuracy and reliability. In this note, we extend our previous work [1] sketched in Sect. 3 by delaying the derivative computations resulting in a significant increase of the efficiency of the black box AD approach. The new approach is detailed in Sect. 4.

2 Automatic differentiation

When a function is given in the form of a computer code, automatic differentiation (AD) may be used to generate another computer program capable of evaluating the function *and* its derivatives. The basic idea of AD is to treat a computer program as the composition of a large sequence of elementary functions and intrinsics whose derivatives are known. Then, these derivatives are accumulated using the chain rule. From a computer science point of view, AD represents a program transformation not preserving the semantics of a given program. There are AD tools mechanically transforming computer codes by augmenting a given computer program with statements for the computation of derivatives.

When using an AD tool a user has to specify the output variables whose derivatives are sought, called *dependent* variables, and the input variables with respect to which one is differentiating, called *independent* variables. More details on AD are given in [2–6]. The AD technology is not only applicable to small computer codes but also scales to large programs of several hundred thousand lines of code.

Automatic differentiation is not to be confused with symbolic differentiation implemented in computer algebra packages like Maple. In contrast to symbolic differentiation, AD is applicable to large computer codes with loops, conditional branches, and subroutine calls. AD generates a program for evaluating derivatives rather than a mathematical formula. Yet the results obtained by an AD-generated code are accurate up to machine precision due to the absence of any numerical approximation scheme such as divided differencing.

3 Differentiating the TFS Program

In the present work, we mainly use the automatic differentiation system ADIFOR [7] to obtain derivatives in an aerodynamic application. The underlying computer simulations is carried out with the CFD solver TFS, developed at the Aerodynamics Institute, Aachen University. The TFS program [8,9] is capable of solving the Navier–Stokes equations of a compressible ideal gas in two or three space dimensions with a finite volume formulation. The spatial discretization of the convective terms follows a variant of the advective upstream splitting method (AUSM+) proposed by Liou [10,11]. The viscous stresses are centrally discretized to second-order accuracy. The implicit method employed in this work uses a relaxation-type linear solver whereas the explicit method relies on a multigrid scheme. The TFS code consists of about $25,000$ lines of Fortran 77 source code. Applying ADIFOR to TFS results in an AD-augmented program referred to as TFS.AD hereafter. The size of the automatically generated AD-code, TFS.AD, depends on the choice of the derivatives being computed. Typically, TFS.AD together with the original code consists of about $45,000$ lines of Fortran code.

After the successful application of ADIFOR to TFS, running TFS.AD results in accurate derivatives of the flow field with respect to various flow parameters, like the angle of attack, the Mach number, or the pressure; see the previous work [12,13] for details. In a more recent study [1], we are interested in the derivatives with respect to some geometric shape parameters. In this particular two-dimensional aircraft design optimization problem, the function to be differentiated consists of a sequence of three programs: The first program written in MATLAB generates an airfoil from given eight scalar geometric shape parameters $\xi_1, \xi_2, \dots, \xi_8$; a Fortran 77 program is used in a second step to generate a grid around the airfoil; finally, the solver TFS is used to compute the flow field around the airfoil.

In [1], we use ADIFOR as well as ADiMat [14], a recent AD tool for MATLAB programs, to get derivatives of the entire sequence of programs in a black box fashion. AD is shown to reliably compute accurate derivatives whereas numerical differentiation based on divided differencing turns out to be inadequate. The reason for the latter is that, in this particular problem, it is extremely hard, if not impossible, to determine a step size for divided differencing so that the derivative values are meaningful. Compared to the original simulation program, the storage of the AD-generated program increases by a factor of 8.3, while the execution time increases by a factor of 16.5. Recall that eight scalar derivatives are computed and, thus, the approach reported in [1] is feasible to get accurate derivatives, but expensive in terms of execution time. In the following section, we show how to improve the efficiency of the black box AD approach.

4 Delaying the derivative propagation

When optimizing the geometry of an airfoil, and implicitly solving the two-dimensional Navier-Stokes equations, the efficiency of the derivative computation is crucial for the overall efficiency of the solution of the design optimization problem. For small problems in two-dimensions, the black box AD approach described in the previous section is sufficient. However, when more complex and realistic problems in three dimensions are considered, the computation of accurate derivatives should be more efficient.

The black box AD approach in [1] is to compute, from the very beginning, the original function, the lift-over-drag ratio, together with the derivatives with respect to the geometric parameters $\xi_1, \xi_2, \dots, \xi_8$. The efficiency can be improved by delaying the derivative computations. That is, the original code TFS is started to compute the lift-over-drag ratio and, after a suitable number of iteration steps, TFS is stopped to continue the computation with TFS.AD, where the parts of the code associated to the original simulation are started using the data from the last iteration of the TFS run. Thus, the iteration of the original function is computed as in the original simulation while the iteration of the derivatives is started not until the original function is already converged to a certain precision. The theory behind that approach is outlined in [2] and is also applied in [15–19].

We consider the following steady state flow problem. The grid consists of four blocks totaling $17,428$ points. The transonic flow conditions are described by a Mach number of 0.74 and a Reynolds number of $2.4 \cdot 10^6$. The angle of attack is set to 1.5593 degrees, because a lift coefficient $c_L = 0.5$ is desired for the initial geometry of the airfoil. On the airfoil, a no slip condition and an adiabatic wall is assumed, the flow variables on the far field boundary are computed with one-dimensional linearized characteristics. Throughout the following the iteration steps of the implicit method used to compute the flow field are called "(local) time steps". All the computations are performed in double precision. The stopping criterion of the original simulation for the lift-over-drag ratio is as follows. The changes in the values of the lift and drag coefficients, c_L and c_D, respectively, are checked every 100 time steps. The simulation is considered to be converged if both of these changes are smaller than 10^{-4}. Using this stopping criterion, the original simulation converges after 1700 time steps. Notice that the values of c_L and c_D continue to vary in the range of 10^{-5}, but the engineers consider the precision to be sufficient.

The convergence history of a subset of the derivative computations is depicted in Figure 1. The figure shows, on a logarithmic scale, the derivatives $\partial c_D / \partial \xi_1$. Recall that these quantities are among the crucial ingredients for the derivatives of c_L / c_D with respect to $\xi_1, \xi_2, \dots, \xi_8$. The derivatives of the lift-over-drag ratio with respect to the geometric parameters are checked for convergence every 100 time steps and are considered to be converged if there is no change larger than 10^{-2} from one time step to the next. It is worth noting that all these derivatives computed with the approaches described in the following, were consistent with each other, meaning that they were the same within the given limit of 10^{-2}. The only difference is the time taken to compute these derivatives.

Let k denote the number of time steps the original TFS is run before switching to TFS.AD to start the derivative computations. Then, in Figure 1, the convergence history of the derivative of the drag coefficient with respect to the first geometry parameter, $\partial c_D / \partial \xi_1$, is given for three different

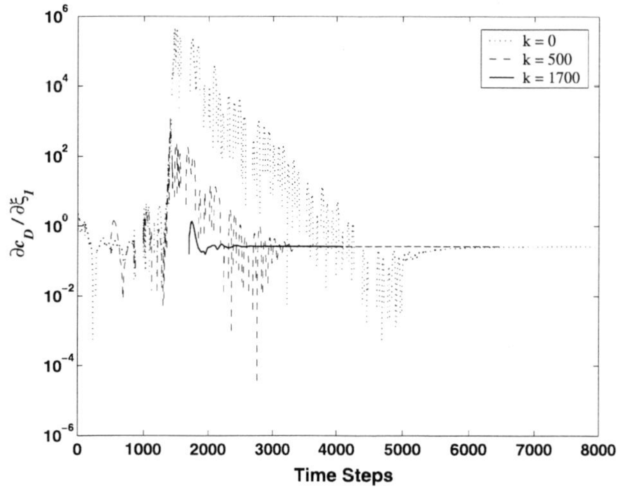

Figure 1. Convergence history when starting the derivative computations after $k = 0$, $k = 500$ and $k = 1700$ time steps.

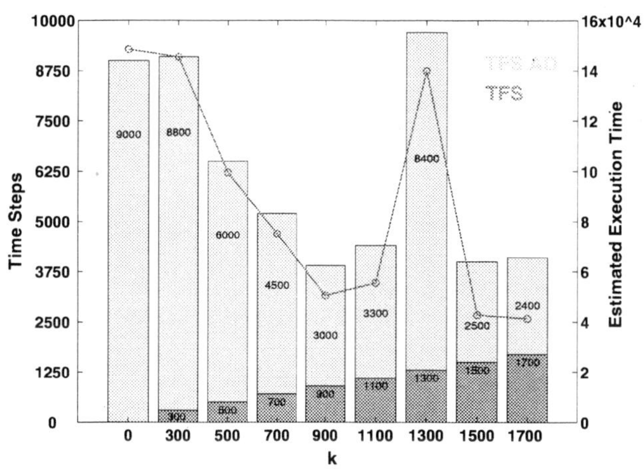

Figure 2. Performance of the approach delaying the derivative computations by k time steps.

values of k. The first curve, $k = 0$, describes the behavior of the derivative that is computed from the beginning together with the original function, i.e., a black-box-like AD approach. The second curve represents the delayed computation of the derivatives after the original function has already iterated for $k = 500$ time steps and has a precision of about 10^{-2}. Finally the third curve, depicts the delay of $k = 1700$ time steps, where the original function has converged to 10^{-4}. The figure demonstrates the strong influence of the parameter k on the convergence behavior of $\partial c_D / \partial \xi_1$. All curves converge to the same value but the convergence tends to be increased when increasing the delay of starting the derivative computations.

In order to better understand the degree of the improvement in efficiency that the delayed employment of the AD-enhanced code provides, a series of experiments is conducted in which the computation of derivatives is started after k time steps of the original function. Figure 2 represents the corresponding results. At the bottom of each column, the number of time steps representing the computation of the original function without any derivatives is presented as a TFS bar, labeled with the respective number of time steps. Above each TFS bar, there is a TFS.AD bar, representing the number of time steps that are performed by the AD-augmented code, in order to satisfy the convergence criterion. For example, the first experiment illustrated by the leftmost column represents the computation of the derivatives from the beginning, together with the original function, i.e., $k = 0$. The rightmost experiment is composed of $k = 1700$ time steps of TFS and then another 2400 time steps of TFS.AD.

As the figure shows, the number of time steps required for the computation of the desired derivatives decreases as the number of initial original TFS time steps increases, with the exception of the experiment where $k = 1300$. Recall that the execution time of a single time step of TFS.AD is approximately 16.5 times that of a single time step of TFS. Therefore, the optimal efficiency is obtained with a minimal number of TFS.AD time steps. An estimate of the execution time of the approach starting the derivative computation after k TFS time steps is given by $k + 16.5 \cdot \ell$, where ℓ is the number of TFS.AD time steps. This estimated execution time, given in the corresponding number of TFS time steps, is depicted in the right of Figure 2 showing that the best combination is obtained in the last experiment corresponding to $k = 1700$, with the smallest overall execution time of $41,300$.

The use of the delayed computation of derivatives startsing from a "converged" original function, results in a significant increase in efficiency with respect to the execution time and in this way accelerates the optimization process that makes use of the derivatives. Here an important issue is the convergence behavior of the original function. If the function is too far away from convergence then a large increase of the number of time-consuming time steps of the AD-enhanced program may occur as in the experiment with $k = 1300$ as shown in Figure 2. Therfore, it is important to run the original simulation until it is properly converged.

5 Concluding remarks

Automatic differentiation turns out to be a crucial ingredient to efficiently solving a particular aircraft design optimization problem. For the problem at hand, automatic differentiation reliably computes accurate derivative values whereas numerical differentiation is inadequate because of the difficulties involved in finding an appropriate step size. Note that this technique is not only applicable to fairly small codes but scales to large programs like the computational fluid dynamics solver TFS consisting of about $25,000$ lines of Fortran 77.

For the computation of accurate derivatives, a black box

application of automatic differentiation is shown to be feasible. However, the efficiency of a black box approach can be significantly improved by delaying the derivative computations. More precisely, the original simulation is run for a certain number of time steps before switching to the derivative computations. That is, the derivative-enhanced code is started with the values from the last iteration of the original code. Thus, the original function is computed as without any modifications while the time-consuming derivative computations are only started when the function is converged. In this way, the derivative computations are likely to converge faster than in a black box approach of automatic differentiation.

6 Acknowledgments

The authors would like to thank Jakob Risch for his notable contribution during the initial phase of this project and Andre Vehreschild for providing the ADiMat tool. We would also like to thank the Aerodynamics Institute, Aachen University, for making available the source code of the flow solver TFS. In particular, Matthias Meinke and Ehab Fares deserve special recognition. This research is partially supported by the Deutsche Forschungsgemeinschaft (DFG) within SFB 401 "Modulation of flow and fluid–structure interaction at airplane wings," Aachen University, Germany.

References

1. C. H. Bischof, H. M. Bücker, B. Lang, A. Rasch, and E. Slusanschi. Efficient and accurate derivatives for a software process chain in airfoil shape optimization. *Future Generation Computer Systems*, 2002. To appear.
2. A. Griewank. *Evaluating Derivatives: Principles and Techniques of Algorithmic Differentiation*. SIAM, Philadelphia, 2000.
3. L. B. Rall. *Automatic Differentiation: Techniques and Applications*, volume 120 of *Lecture Notes in Computer Science*. Springer-Verlag, Berlin, 1981.
4. George Corliss, Christèle Faure, Andreas Griewank, Laurent Hascoët, and Uwe Naumann, editors. *Automatic Differentiation of Algorithms: From Simulation to Optimization*. Springer, New York, 2002.
5. A. Griewank and G. Corliss. *Automatic Differentiation of Algorithms*. SIAM, Philadelphia, 1991.
6. M. Berz, C. Bischof, G. Corliss, and A. Griewank. *Computational Differentiation: Techniques, Applications, and Tools*. SIAM, Philadelphia, 1996.
7. C. Bischof, A. Carle, P. Khademi, and A. Mauer. ADIFOR 2.0: Automatic differentiation of Fortran 77 programs. *IEEE Computational Science & Engineering*, 3(3):18–32, 1996.
8. E. Fares, M. Meinke, and W. Schröder. Numerical simulation of the interaction of flap side-edge vortices and engine jets. In *Proceedings of the 22nd International Congress of Aeronautical Sciences, Harrogate, UK, August 27–September 1, 2000*, ICAS 0212, 2000.
9. E. Fares, M. Meinke, and W. Schröder. Numerical simulation of the interaction of wingtip vortices and engine jets in the near field. In *Proceedings of the 38th Aerospace Sciences Meeting and Exhibit, Reno, NV, USA, January 10–13, 2000*, AIAA Paper 2000–2222, 2000.
10. M. S. Liou and Ch. J. Steffen. A new flux splitting scheme. *Journal of Computational Physics*, 107:23–39, 1993.
11. M. S. Liou. A sequel to AUSM: AUSM^{+}. *Journal of Computational Physics*, 129:164–182, 1996.
12. H. M. Bücker, B. Lang, A. Rasch, and C. H. Bischof. Sensitivity Analysis of an Airfoil Simulation Using Automatic Differentiation. In M. H. Hamza, editor, *Proceedings of the IASTED International Conference on Modelling, Identification, and Control, Innsbruck, Austria, February 18–21, 2002*, pages 73–76, Anaheim, CA, USA, 2002. ACTA Press.
13. H. M. Bücker, B. Lang, A. Rasch, and C. H. Bischof. Computation of Sensitivity Information for Aircraft Design by Automatic Differentiation. In P. M. A. Sloot, C. J. K. Tan, J. J. Dongarra, and A. G. Hoekstra, editors, *Computational Science – ICCS 2002, Proceedings of the International Conference on Computational Science, Amsterdam, The Netherlands, April 21–24, 2002. Part II*, volume 2330 of *Lecture Notes in Computer Science*, pages 1069–1076, Berlin, 2002. Springer.
14. C. H. Bischof, H. M. Bücker, B. Lang, A. Rasch, and A. Vehreschild. Combining source transformation and operator overloading techniques to compute derivatives for MATLAB programs. In *Proceedings of the Second IEEE International Workshop on Source Code Analysis and Manipulation (SCAM 2002)*, pages 65–72, Los Alamitos, CA, USA, 2002. IEEE Computer Society.
15. B. Mohammadi and O. Pironneau. *Applied Shape Optimization for Fluids*. Oxford University Press, Oxford, 2001.
16. A. Carle, L. L. Green, C. H. Bischof, and P. A. Newman. Applications of automatic differentiation in CFD. In *Proceedings of the 25th AIAA Fluid Dynamics Conference, Colorado Springs, CO, USA, June 20–23, 1994*, AIAA Paper 94–2197, 1994.
17. L. L. Green, P. A. Newman, and K. J. Haigler. Sensitivity derivatives for advanced CFD algorithm and viscous modeling parameters via automatic differentiation. *Journal of Computational Physics*, 125(2):313–324, 1996.
18. Shaun A. Forth and Trevor P. Evans. Aerofoil optimisation via AD of a multigrid cell-vertex Euler flow solver. In Corliss et al. [4], chapter 17, pages 153–160.
19. A. Carle, M. Fagan, and L. L. Green. Preliminary results from the application of automated adjoint code generation to CFL3D. In *Proceedings of the 7th AIAA/USAF/NASA/ISSMO Symposium on Multidisciplinary Analysis and Optimization, St. Louis, MO, USA, September 2–4, 1998*, AIAA Paper 98–4807, 1998.

An Efficient Parallel Strategy for the Simulation of Particle Sedimentation

S. Fourmanoit[a], F. Bertrand[b] and R. Roy[a]
{Sylvain.Fourmanoit,Francois.Bertrand,Robert.Roy}@PolyMtl.CA

[a]Dept. of Computer Engineering, École Polytechnique de Montréal – P.O Box 6079, Stn. CV, Montréal, QC, Canada H3C 3A7

[b]Dept. of Chemical Engineering, École Polytechnique de Montréal – P.O Box 6079, Stn. CV, Montréal, QC, Canada H3C 3A7

Many packages have emerged over the years to provide efficient implementations of a large spectrum of numerical methods, from linear algebra to complex finite element solvers. In this paper, we will show how carefully selected open source packages can be used as toolboxes to prototype in just a few days efficient parallel simulation strategies for the sedimentation of a large number of particles.

De nombreux outils logiciels ont déjà vu le jour pour permettre l'implémentation efficace d'un large éventail de méthodes numériques, depuis l'algèbre linéaire jusqu'aux solveurs complexes à éléments finis. Dans cet article, nous montrerons comment la selection judicieuse d'outils logiciels à code source libre permet, en quelques jours seulement, la production de simulations parallèles efficaces pour le calcul de la sédimentation d'un grand nombre de particules.

Introduction

Multiphase flows are very common in fluid mechanics applications. However, due to their complex nature, large scale simulation of such flows is still an area of active research in CFD. As a result, many commercial and non-commercial pieces of software of high quality have been produced, so much that it is generally easy to find a fair to very good open source implementation of any method older than two years referenced in the literature.

Consequently, the problem a researcher is facing nowadays is usually not to program from scratch a good code that fits specific needs, but to find a way to combine stable and well-tested independent pieces of code in order to exploit their strengths without running into their known limitations and weaknesses. Of course, the main reason for integrating open source pieces of code is economical.

In this paper, we are interested in simulating the behavior of a large number (typically from 10K to 1 million) analytically-shaped (ellipsoidal) solid particles immersed in a viscous, Newtonian fluid at $\mathrm{Re} \leq 20$. The numerical strategy will be based on an immersed boundary technique developed by Fogelson and Peskin [1], the characteristics of which lead to an easy parallelization. After briefly presenting this technique, we will explain how a simulation strategy based upon it can be prototyped very easily using freely available code. Finally, simulation results will be shown to illustrate the accuracy and efficiency of the proposed method.

1 Immersed Boundary Method

The technique that was used to simulate the sedimentation of a large number of solid rigid particles immersed in a continuous phase will now be described.

1.1 Fluid behavior

The Navier-Stokes equations describe the motion of a Newtonian fluid:

$$\rho\frac{\partial \mathbf{v}}{\partial t} + \rho(\mathbf{v}\cdot\nabla)\mathbf{v} = -\nabla p + \eta\nabla^2\mathbf{v} + \mathbf{f}\ , \qquad (1)$$

where ρ and η are respectively the fluid density and viscosity, and where $\mathbf{v}$ and p are the velocity and pressure fields. $\mathbf{f}$ stands for the body force and accounts in this work for the buoyant force and a force inherent to the immersed boundary technique, as will be described later.

We will also suppose that the fluid is incompressible ($\nabla\cdot\mathbf{v} = 0$). It should be noted that incompressibility is not required for the overall simulation strategy, but is only a simplifying hypothesis.

A MAC based (*staggered marker and cell*) second order finite difference method in space [2] is used to discretize equation (1). The incompressibility constraint is accounted for using a fractional step method:

$$\begin{aligned}\rho\frac{\mathbf{v}^* - \mathbf{v}^\mathbf{n}}{\Delta t} &= -\rho(\mathbf{v}^\mathbf{n}\cdot\nabla)\mathbf{v}^\mathbf{n} + \eta\nabla^2\mathbf{v}^\mathbf{n} + \mathbf{f}^\mathbf{n}\ , &(2)\\ \rho\frac{\mathbf{v}^{\mathbf{n+1}} - \mathbf{v}^*}{\Delta t} &= -\nabla p^{n+1}\ , &(3)\end{aligned}$$

where n represents the time iteration. If we apply the divergence operator on this last equation, we get, since $\nabla\cdot\mathbf{v}^{\mathbf{n+1}} = 0$:

$$\nabla^2 p^{n+1} = \frac{\rho}{\Delta t}\nabla\cdot\mathbf{v}^*\ . \qquad (4)$$

This step can then be viewed as a projection of the velocity field onto a divergence-free subspace. Of course, initial and boundary conditions must be imposed for mathematical well-posedness. For the sedimentation problem, two sets of boundary conditions for the velocity where considered:

- no slip boundary conditions everywhere;
- periodic boundary conditions everywhere.

Moreover, the Neumann conditions for equation (4), which are obtained by projecting (3) onto $\hat{n}$, the normal unit vector, are

$$\frac{\rho}{\Delta t}(v_\perp^{n+1} - v_\perp^*) = -(\hat{n} \cdot \nabla)p^{n+1} , \tag{5}$$

and can be shown to vanish. To summarize, the computation of a time iteration consists in the following steps:

1. Given $\mathbf{v^n}$, solve explicit equation (2) for $\mathbf{v}^*$.
2. Given $\mathbf{v}^*$, solve Poisson problem (4) for p^{n+1} with boundary conditions (5). In this work, this problem is solved using a multigrid solver.
3. Given p^{n+1}, solve explicit equation (3) for $\mathbf{v^{n+1}}$.

We want to emphasize here that, in the case of the sedimentation problem, one must solve at each time iteration a Poisson equation on a structured Cartesian 3D mesh, a task that can be done efficiently in parallel. Finally, since (2) and (3) are explicit schemes, the step-size must satisfy a CFL stability criterion.

1.2 Fluid-particle interactions

In this work, the sedimentation of solid particles is modeled through what is referred to as the immersed boundary method. In a nutshell, the advantage of this method lies in the fact that it relies on one single mesh for the entire simulation. The particles and their position in the suspending fluid are rather taken into account by means of a space- and time-dependent force term in equation (1). Another possibility would have been to resort to the fictitious domain method as proposed by Glowinski et al. [3] and used by one of the authors of this work to simulate fluid flow in complex mixing systems [4].

The whole idea is to express the coupling between the solid and the liquid. To realize this, we define n_i nodes (also called control points) that discretize particle i in a frame of reference with the particle center of gravity as the origin. The position of these control points can be expressed as:

$$\mathbf{x_{ij}^r} = \mathbf{x_i(t)} + \mathbf{O_i(t)} \cdot \mathbf{r_{ij}^r} , \tag{6}$$

where $\mathbf{x_i(t)}$ is the position of the center of gravity of particle i, $\mathbf{O_i(t)}$ an orientation matrix and $\mathbf{r_{ij}^r}$ the position of control point j in the (local) frame of reference of the particle.

For each control point discretizing a particle, a corresponding marker $\mathbf{x_{ij}^m}$ can be defined to take into account the relative fluid motion:

$$\dot{\mathbf{x}}_{\mathbf{ij}}^{\mathbf{m}} = \mathbf{v}(\mathbf{x_{ij}^m}) . \tag{7}$$

It is then possible to calculate the distance $\xi_{\mathrm{ij}} = \mathbf{x_{ij}^m} - \mathbf{x_{ij}^r}$ between control point j of particle i and its associated fluid marker. One way to compel the control point to stick to the fluid marker is to introduce into equation (1) the following Hookean force:

$$\mathbf{f_{ij}} = (-k\,\xi_{\mathrm{ij}} - 2\gamma\,\dot{\xi}_{\mathrm{ij}})\,\delta(\mathbf{x} - \mathbf{x_{ij}^m}) , \tag{8}$$

where k is the Hooke's coefficient, γ the damping constant and δ the Dirac distribution. With this explicit technique, k has to be large enough so that $\max \|\xi_{\mathrm{ij}}\| \ll h$ at all times. Similarly, γ has to be negligible compared to other energy dissipation sources in the system. Following (8), $\mathbf{f} = \sum_{i,j} \mathbf{f}_{ij}$ is then added to the body force of equation (1).

Values for k and γ in the immersed boundary method must be determined. It can be showed [1] that suitable values for k must satisfy:

$$k \propto \frac{M}{n_i(\Delta t)^2} , \tag{9}$$

where M is related to the mass of the largest particle in the system. As for γ, our tests in 3D showed that setting $\gamma = 0$ does not affect significantly the results.

1.3 Particle behavior

Following Newton's third law of motion, the driving forces $\mathbf{f_{ij}}$ introduced to enforce a quasi-rigid fluid motion also apply on the particles but in the opposite direction:

$$\mathbf{F_{ij}} = k\,\xi_{\mathrm{ij}} + 2\gamma\,\dot{\xi}_{\mathrm{ij}} . \tag{10}$$

The corresponding torque, τ_{ij}, on particle i is given by

$$\tau_{\mathrm{ij}} = (\mathbf{x_{ij}^r} - \mathbf{x_i}) \wedge \mathbf{F_{ij}} . \tag{11}$$

Moreover the buoyant force reads as

$$\mathbf{F_i^g} = (\rho - \rho_p)\,V_i\,\mathbf{g} , \tag{12}$$

where V_i stands for the volume of particle i.

In this work, it is assumed that particles do not collide, which in the case of the free and even hindered settling of particles can be justified by the relative importance of the lubrification forces between neighboring particles. Of course, in the case of the consolidation of settling particles on a flat surface, for instance, the situation would be different; one would then have to model particle collision using, for example, the discrete element method (DEM). In our proposed strategy, particles collisions are prevented by introducing for two neighboring particles i and k a repulsive force $\mathbf{F_{ik}^p}$ of module inversely proportional to the distance

1. **Prediction** Obtain the positions of the particles and that of their associated markers based on previously computed values.

2. **Force calculation** Compute the $\mathbf{f}_{ij}$ corresponding to the new positions of the particles and markers.

3. **Navier-Stokes solution** Solve equation (1) using a MAC grid and a multigrid solver, as explained in subsection 1.1.

4. **Correction** From the velocity computed in step 3, get new positions of the particles and markers and go back to 2 if needed.

Figure 1. Overall Simulation strategy

between these two particles. Finally, the Brownian effects are neglected, which is a reasonable hypothesis if, for instance, the particles are not too small.

The total force $\mathbf{F}_i$ and total torque τ_i on particle i are given by

$$\mathbf{F}_i = \mathbf{F}_i^g + \sum_k \mathbf{F}_{ik}^p + \sum_j \mathbf{F}_{ij} \,, \quad (13)$$

$$\tau_i = \sum_j \tau_{ij} \,. \quad (14)$$

Finally, a predictor/corrector scheme is used to integrate

$$\begin{cases} \ddot{\mathbf{r}}_i = \mathbf{F}_i / M_i \\ \ddot{\mathbf{O}}_i = \tau_i / I_i \end{cases} \quad (15)$$

and obtain the position and orientation of particle i over time.The simulation strategy is summarized on figure 1.

2 Implementation strategy

From an algorithmic point of view, the immersed boundary technique described above is a good candidate for parallelization. A closer look at this method also shows that only a few statically-sized data structures are required to implement it:

- **Particles data structures**
  For analytically-described particles, the position of the control points will be inferred from their centers of gravity and orientation, so that only the markers have to be stored explicitly.

- **Fluid data structures**
  Two velocity fields are needed, since the computation of $\mathbf{v}^*$ requires $\mathbf{v}^n$, and that of $\mathbf{v}^{n+1}$ requires $\mathbf{v}^*$.

Other quantities such as $\mathbf{f}$, for instance, are computed on the fly.

For a given particle concentration (also called solids content), the size of the particles and fluid data structures varies linearly with the number of grid nodes. Overall, the memory needed to store the data structures related to the particles is much less that that for the fluid data structures. Algorithmically speaking, the prediction, force collocation and correction steps of the overall strategy (Fig.1) are $\mathcal{O}(n)$ (n being the number of particles). Consequently, step 3 is the most consuming both in terms of computational time and storage.

2.1 Parallel multigrid solver

As explained in subsection 1.1, fluid flow is predicted by solving at each time step a Poisson problem. Fortunately, well-designed octree-like domain decompositions can be used in conjunction with multigrid solvers [5]. A 2D quadtree-like multilevel decomposition is given in Fig.2 as an illustration of this partitioning technique.

We recall that a multigrid solver (see [6] for instance) is an iterative solver that combines solutions obtained with other iterative methods (Jacobi in this work) using overlapping grids of different mesh sizes so that long-range perturbations propagate with high speed. Multigrid exhibits a convergence rate that is independent of the number of unknowns in the discretized system, and is optimal in the sense that the number of operations required varies linearly with it.

The domain partitioning scheme in Fig.2 was extended in 3D. The multigrid solver comes from `http://www.mgnet.org/`. Since all the nodes of a mesh also belong to the finer ones, inter-domain communication is required. To avoid sending many small messages between processes (latency would then be the bottleneck), it is more efficient that each process store not only the data for its corresponding sub-grid, but also a small portion of data, the so-called ghost layers, from its neighbors. To fit the specific nature of our domain partitioning scheme, we designed a multilevel ghost layer that is sent asynchronously to the relevant neighbors at each step of the multigrid method. This layer contains not only the connected nodes on the finest grid, but those on coarser grids as well (see Fig.3).

This multilevel technique combined with this domain partitioning scheme yields impressive parallel characteristics:

- **Predictable behavior**
  - **Static memory use** The exact size of the problem is always known before the simulation begins.
  - **Almost perfect load balancing** Processes have similar loads; small differences can only result from a non-uniform particle distribution.

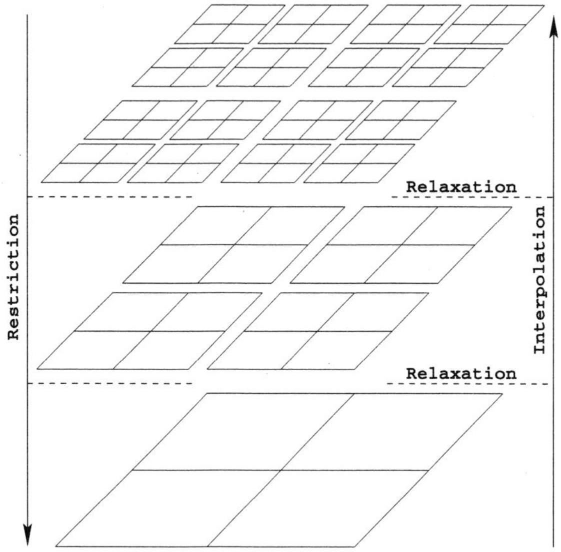

Figure 2. Parallel Multilevel domain decomposition of a square

- **Coarse granularity** Reduced amount of communication. The MAC grid associated to a given process never changes, and data at different grid resolutions overlap or belong to the multilevel ghost layer. As a result, the algorithms can be implemented efficiently on loosely-coupled parallel machines like Beowulf clusters or massively parallel architectures.

- **Good scalability** The overall solution strategy including the immersed boundary technique and the multigrid solver has a time complexity that is a linear function of the problem size. It has been shown [5] that the scalability of the solver layout (i.e. $\lim_{p\to\infty} T(n,1)/T(pn,p)$, where $T(n,p)$ is the time to solve a system of n unknowns on p processors) is $\mathcal{O}(1)$, including communications, provided that some simple constraints are respected regarding domain partitioning. Further experimentations with our prototype will be needed to assert this.

2.2 Other aspects

Two other pieces of code were needed to implement our solution strategy: Gear's predictor/corrector method from Numerical recipes (`http://www.nr.com/`), and a driver written in Objective ML (`http://caml.inria.fr/`) to initiate and pilot the simulations. This driver binds all the pieces of code while storing the particles data, the fluid data being of course kept inside the multigrid solver program (see Fig.4).

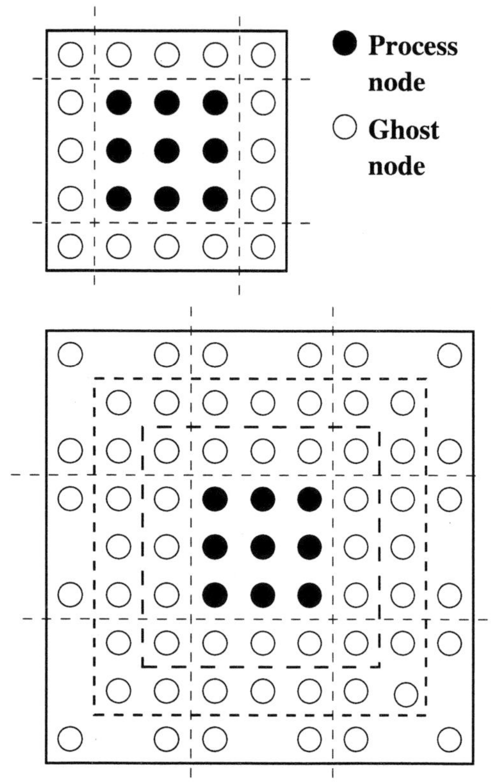

Figure 3. Normal and multilevel ghost layers on a 2D domain

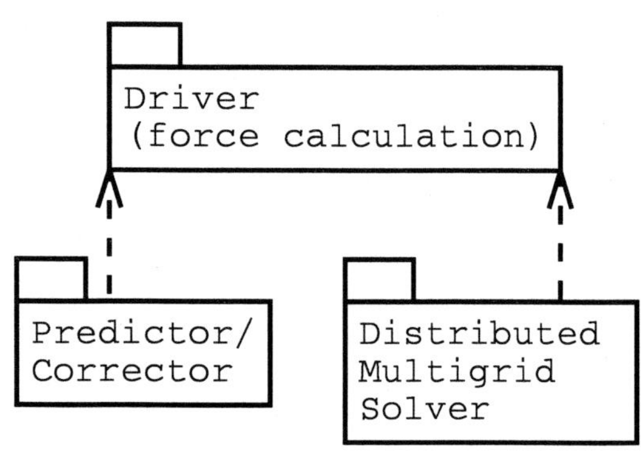

Figure 4. Software packages

3 Numerical results

The terminal velocity of spherical particles settling in a viscous Newtonian fluid with respect to their concentration ϕ is well described by an empirical law called the Richardson and Zaki correlation [7]. It stipulates that the terminal velocity varies as $v_s = v_0(1-\phi)^n$, where v_0 is the terminal velocity of a single particle and $n \in [5,6]$ an index that depends on the Reynolds number. In our simulations, particles radius, a, was chosen such that

$$Re = \frac{2}{9}\frac{a^3}{\eta^2}\rho(\rho_p - \rho)g \approx 0.1 \,. \qquad (16)$$

The computational domain consists of a cube of size $12a \times 12a \times 12a$, This geometry was discretized using a grid size $h = a/2$. We recall that, with the immersed boundary method, the particles are not meshed as such, but are rather taken into account through a series of control points. In this work, $4\pi a^2/h = 8\pi a$ control points were used and located along the surface of the particles. The mean terminal velocity was computed as:

$$v_s = \frac{1}{N}\sum_{i=1}^{N} \mathbf{v}_i \cdot \hat{z} \,, \qquad (17)$$

where $\hat{z}$ is a unit vector pointing in the settling direction. The values of v_s versus ϕ (see Fig.5) agree very well with the correlation of Richardson and Zaki. The slight underestimation of v_s at large concentration values is not really significant. In fact, we observed that it disappears almost completely if the exponent n, a very sensible parameter in the correlation, is slightly modified.

4 Conclusion

The objective of this work was to show how open source packages can be harnessed to prototype and test out a solution strategy for the simulation of the sedimentation of a large number of particles. The whole software process required about two weeks for programming and led to an efficient parallel implementation of the immersed boundary method that proved to be very flexible and accurate.

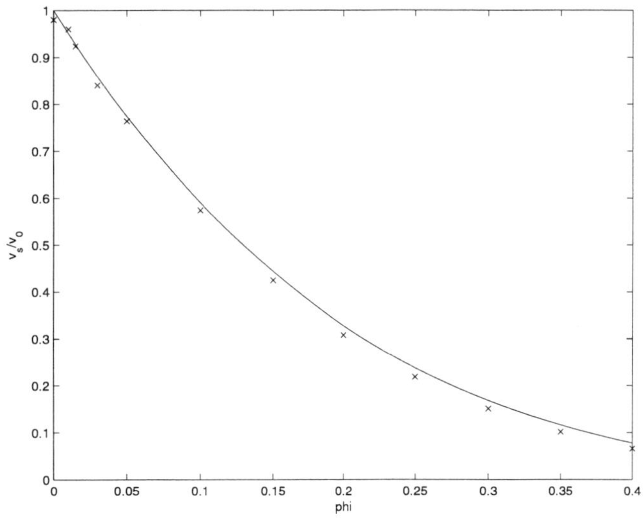

Figure 5. Comparison with the Richardson and Zaki correlation

References

1. A. L. Fogelson and C. S. Peskin. A fast numerical method for solving the three-dimensional Stokes equations in the presence of suspended particles. *Journal of Computational Physics*, pages 50–69, 1988.
2. S. Popinet and S. Zaleski. A front-tracking algorithm for accurate representation of surface tension. *International Journal for Numerical Methods in Fluids*, pages 775–793, 1999.
3. R. Glowinski, T. W. Pan, T. I. Hesla, D. D. Joseph, and J. Periaux. A fictitious domain method with distributed Lagrange multipliers for the numerical simulation of particulate flow. In *Domain Decomposition Methods*, volume 10, pages 121–137, Providence, RI, 1998.
4. P. A. Tanguy F. Bertrand and F. Thibault. A 3D fictitious domain method for incompressible fluid flow problems. *International Journal for Numerical Methods in Fluids*, pages 719–736, 1997.
5. R. D. Falgout and J. E. Jones. Multigrid on massively parallel architectures. In *Multigrid Methods VI*, volume 14, pages 101–107, Berlin, 2000.
6. P. Wesseling. *An Introduction to Multigrid Methods*. Wiley, New York, 1991.
7. E. Guyon, J. P. Hulin, and L. Petit. *Hydrodynamique physique*. CNRS Editions, Paris, 1994.

Parallel Computing Techniques for Metal Plasticity Applications

K. Inal[a], K.W. Neale[a] & P.D. Wu[b]

[a]Faculty of Engineering, University of Sherbrooke, Sherbrooke, Quebec, Canada.
[b]Alcan International Limited, Kingston R&D Centre, Kingston, Ontario, Canada.

Parallel computing algorithms for the finite element method have been developed to simulate multiscale large deformation plasticity problems. Due to the nature of these problems and the computational methods involved, different parallel computing techniques must be employed for the Taylor-type crystal plasticity (TFE) and the so-called "finite element per single crystal" (FESC) models. For the FESC model, the global stiffness matrix is formed in parallel and a parallel solver employing a number of Krylov iterative methods is used to solve the systems of equations. For the TFE model, a data parallel implementation technique is employed. This technique provides a large reduction in the storage required on a single processor and thus allows for an effective solution of computationally demanding crystal plasticity problems. The efficiency and the performance of the parallel finite element models that have been developed are investigated by comparing simulations performed on an IBM POWER3 SP parallel supercomputer.

Nous avons développé des algorithmes parallèles pour la méthode des éléments finis dans le but de simuler des problèmes de grandes déformations plastiques. En raison de la nature des problèmes étudiés et des méthodes de calcul employées, des schémas de parallélisation différents doivent être utilisés pour la plasticité cristalline de type Taylor (TFE) et pour les modèles à un élément par monoscristal (FESC). Dans le modèle FESC, la matrice de rigidité gloable est construite en parallèle et un code parallèle utilisant des méthodes itératives de Krylov est utilisé pour résoudre le système d'équations. Dans le modèle TFE, une méthode de parallélisation des données est utilisée plutôt. Celle-ci permet de réduire la mémoire requise sur chaque processeur et permet ainsi la résolution efficace de problèmes cristallins très exigeants. L'efficacité et la performance de ces deux algorithmes sont étudiées en comparant des simulations exécutées sur un superordinateur parallèle IBM SP3.

1 Introduction

Metal forming has, for a long time, been an important processing operation. In many manufacturing areas such as the automotive, aerospace, packaging and electronic industries, the optimization of metal processes has become a key factor to reduce product development time and final cost. In general, metal forming involves large strains due to stretching, drawing, bending or various combinations of these basic deformation modes. From the view point of mechanics, the analysis of metal working involves nonlinearities in geometry, material and contact. In an effort to better understand metal forming processes, various research works have been carried out using diverse technologies involving experimental, analytical and computational methods.

Essentially two classes of models have been developed for numerical simulations of metal forming operations: phenomenological (macroscopic) models and polycrystal (microscopic) models. Metal forming can be modelled accurately based on crystal plasticity theories where the initial texture and its evolution, as well as the anisotropy induced by the evolution of microstructure and microscopic properties, are accounted for [1, 2, 3, 4, 5].

The mathematical modelling of material behaviour is a very effective way of reducing time and costs involved in optimizing manufacturing processes. Indeed, numerous complex forming operations have been simulated using numerical methods in order to predict critical parameters. Among these methods, the finite element method (FEM), has been widely applied to the study of metal forming because of its flexibility, accuracy and efficiency. Considering the rapid advancement of computer capabilities, the finite element method has become a powerful tool in modelling metal forming operations.

Up to the 1980's, most applications involving the finite element method have been based on phenomenological constitutive models since microscopic models involve significantly more demanding computations. However the introduction of parallel computers has rendered metal forming modelling based on crystal plasticity feasible since they offer more computational power and storage than serial computer architectures. With proper parallelization techniques, realistic applications based on crystal plasticity can be performed on parallel computers such as the IBM SP3. Beaudoin et al. [6] presented a data parallel formulation for the analysis of polycrystalline solids where parallel computing algorithms were considered for both crystal equations and the iterative solution procedure. Later on, Sorensen and Andersen [7] developed a parallel finite element method suitable for the analysis of 3D quasi-static crystal plasticity problems. This method was based on substructuring of the original mesh into a number of substructures which were treated as isolated finite element models related via the interface conditions. Their method showed a good speedup with increasing number of processors.

In this paper, parallel computing algorithms for both the finite element method and crystal plasticity theory have been developed to simulate the plastic deformation of polycrystalline solids. First the parallel computing algorithms that have been developed for the Taylor-type crystal plasticity (TFE) and the so-called finite element per single crystal (FESC) models are described respectively. Then the efficiency of the parallel computing algorithms that we have developed are discussed by comparing simulations performed on the parallel computer IBM RS/6000 POWER3 (WinterHawk2) SP.

2 Parallel Computing Algorithms for Finite Element Analysis Based on Crystal Plasticity

In this section parallel computing algorithms developed for the TFE and the FESC models will be described. Due to the nature of these problems and the computational methods involved, different parallel computing techniques had to be developed. For the TFE model, parallelization focuses on the crystal aggregate, while for the FESC model, the finite element domain is divided into subdomains.

2.1 Constitutive Model

A rigorous framework for the kinematics of the finite plastic deformation of a crystal has been firmly established for some time. This basic formulation has been incorporated into a rate-dependent description of crystal plasticity constitutive relations. For details of this formulation we refer to [8].

2.2 Parallel Computing Algorithms for the TFE Model

For polycrystalline simulations based on the Taylor hypothesis (TFE), the microstructural calculations for the stress and crystal reorientations are essentially independent. At a material point representing a polycrystal of N grains, the deformation in each grain is taken to be identical to the macroscopic deformation of the continuum. Furthermore, the macroscopic values of all quantities, such as stresses, stress-rates and elastic moduli, are obtained by averaging their respective values over the total number of grains at the particular material point.

In general, Taylor-type polycrystal models are ideally suited for the parallelization of the computational procedures. Especially, when CPU time is considered, the simulations fall in the category of "embarrassingly parallel" (e.g., Sorensen [7], Inal [9]) applications, and they provide significant computational improvements. However, such "embarrassingly parallel" applications are strictly feasible only if the total program size fits within a single processor of the parallel computer. This is not always the case for simulations with TFE models since they involve extremely demanding computational resources due to the amount of information at the grain level that must be tracked.

The parallel algorithms employed in the TFE model are designed to distribute data on the microscopic level (crystal data) over the processors of the IBM SP3 parallel computer. By this method, the global size of the simulation is distributed between the processors of the parallel computer. To illustrate this, consider a simulation with a total number N of crystals (Fig.1). The basic idea in the finite element formulation is that each material point is representing a polycrystal comprised of N crystals and the constitutive response is given through the Taylor polycrystal model (Fig. 1a). The global crystal data is distributed between the processors (Fig. 1b) such that each processor runs a part of the global program for $B = N / A$ crystals where A is the total number of processors used in the simulation. (Note that the processors read only the crystal data to which they are assigned and all arrays containing microscopic quantities have the maximum size of B instead of N.) Thus all processors compute microscopic arrays (for the set of crystals that they have assigned) independently. However, to compute the global stiffness matrix, the macroscopic values of stresses, stress rates and the moduli are required (eqn. 1). These values are obtained by collective communication between the processors using the Message Passing Interface (MPI) Library. Note that,

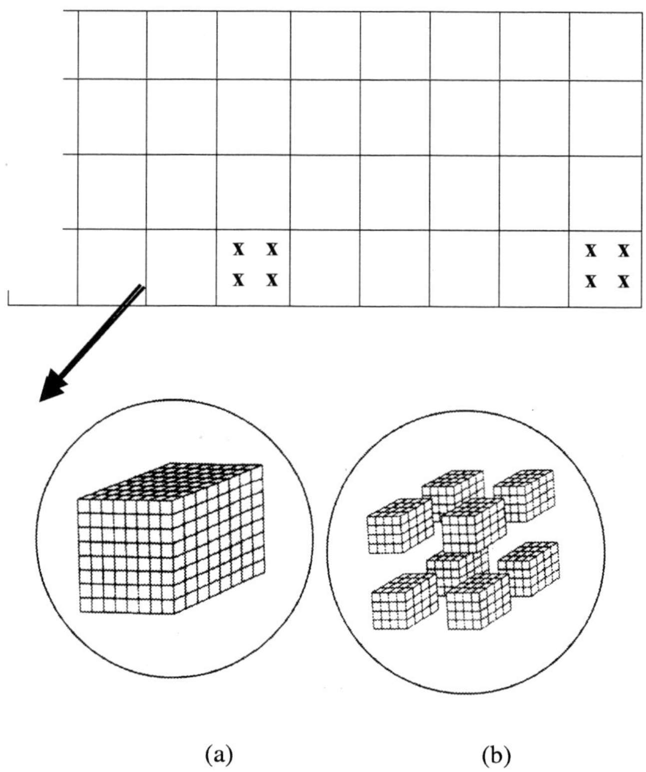

Figure 1 (a) Polycrystal aggregate comprised of N crystals; (b) the distribution of this polycrystal aggregate between processors

that, after this communication, although macroscopic values of stresses, stress rates and the moduli are computed, microscopic values of these tensors are still stored since the microscopic quantities are updated each increment. As a result, each processor has its own microscopic data; however, all of the processors have the same macroscopic data. We should mention that the total number of crystals should be distributed as evenly as possible between the processors. Otherwise the large difference in the number of crystals per processor adversely affects the CPU time per processor, and in such cases blocking commands are required during communication between processors. To avoid this the parallel algorithms developed here distribute the crystals as evenly as possible among the available processors.

The size of any array storing microscopic quantities is equal to M, where M is equal to the product of the number of elements times number of integration points times number of crystals times number of slip systems. For the simulation presented above, the mesh consists of 1792 elements with 4 integration points per element. The initial texture is represented by 400 discrete orientations in Euler space, and with 12 active slip systems per crystal M becomes

$$M = 1972 \text{ x } 4 \text{ x } 400 \text{ x } 12$$
$$M = 34406400$$

Table 1 compares the CPU times for the above problem obtained from simulations with various number of processors. Note that we start comparing results with 16 processors, since this is the minimum number of processors required to provide enough memory for our global data. It can be seen that the parallelization employed in the TFE model provides an excellent speed-up with values very close to the theoretical maximum achievable speed-up by parallel computing.

No. of processors	CPU time (s)	Speed-up factor
16	169,200	1
24	113,557	1.49
32	85,454	1.98
56	48,760	3.47

Table 1. CPU time and speed-ups as a function of the number of processors

2.3 Parallel Computing for the FESC Model

The FESC model utilizes finite element methodologies to discretize the crystals of an aggregate using one or more elements for every crystal. In this model, a polycrystalline aggregate is treated as a continuum where both compatibility and equilibrium among the individual grains are automatically satisfied.

Parallel computing algorithms developed for the FESC model are completely different than the algorithms developed for the TFE model since, due to the basic assumptions of modelling, they require significantly less memory. For the FESC model, parallel computing algorithms focus on the finite element mesh and the solution procedure.

In general, the global finite element equations can be written in the form

$$[\mathbf{K}]\{\dot{\mathbf{u}}\} = \{\dot{\mathbf{F}}\} \tag{1}$$

where $[\mathbf{K}]$ is the global stiffness matrix, $\{\dot{\mathbf{u}}\}$ is the vector containing the unknown incremental nodal displacements and $\{\dot{\mathbf{F}}\}$ is the vector of applied incremental nodal forces. Note that, due to the nature of finite elements, $[\mathbf{K}]$ is a n x n sparse matrix where n is the total number of degrees of freedom within the system. To reduce storage requirements, the "skyline" storage strategy is adopted since this has the effect of reducing the number of zero terms that would be stored in a vector due to bandwidth variability using conventional methods.

A parallel solver employing a number of Krylov iterative methods is used to solve the systems of equations. The parallel solution process is carried out in two steps:

- The global stiffness matrix is formed in parallel. To illustrate this, consider a simulation with the finite element mesh comprised of 16 elements (Fig. 2a). This finite element mesh is divided into 2 subdomains with 8 elements (Fig.2b) and each subdomain is assigned to a single processor. Once input is read globally, each processor starts to compute the elemental stiffness matrix for the elements in their subdomain. All vector elements are explicitly stored on the processor and are defined by a set of indices referred to as the processor's "main set". The "main set" is further divided into two subsets: "internal" and "border". A component corresponding to an index in the "internal set" performs all computations using only information on the current processor. The "border set" defines elements that would require values from other processors in order to compute correct global values (line A-A' in Fig. 2b). Thus, a component corresponding to an index in the "border set" is computed by point-to- point communication using the MPI Library between the processors that share information. Note that, if the finite element mesh is distributed evenly between the processors, blocking commands are not necessary during these point-to-point communications. However, if one of the subdomains is a contact surface, it is obvious that special attention must be paid to the point-to-point communications between the processors.

- The iterative parallel solver employed in our code was specifically designed to solve the linear systems of equations $Ax = b$ where A is a sparse matrix. However, it has already been mentioned that the global stiffness matrix was stored in 2 vectors: A (contains the non zero terms in the upper diagonal) and C (contains the non zero terms in the lower diagonal). Thus, from these 2 vectors the global stiffness matrix must be reconstructed. This is performed by creating pointers and an integer vector which holds information regarding the position of the diagonal terms and the non zero terms to be stored up to each diagonal term. Note that the global stiffness matrix in never constructed completely; using pointers, it is constructed block by block on the processors. Once the equations are solved, updating of all quantities is performed in parallel without any communication.

To assess the efficiency of the parallel computing algorithms that have been developed for the FESC model, plane strain tension of a commercial aluminum alloy was simulated with 8000 elements. Figure 3 presents the speed-up curve for a simulation where the total number of equations $n = 8181$. It can be seen that a maximum speed-up of 2.8 (saturation value) was obtained with 8 processors; when more than 8 processors are employed, the speed-up starts to decrease. These results are expected since the communications performed during the parallel iterative solution process involving a sparse matrix are much more costly (in terms of CPU) in comparison to solutions involving a triangular or a diagonal matrix. However, it should be noted that the performance of parallel computing will noticeably increase when the number of the equations to be solved is increased.

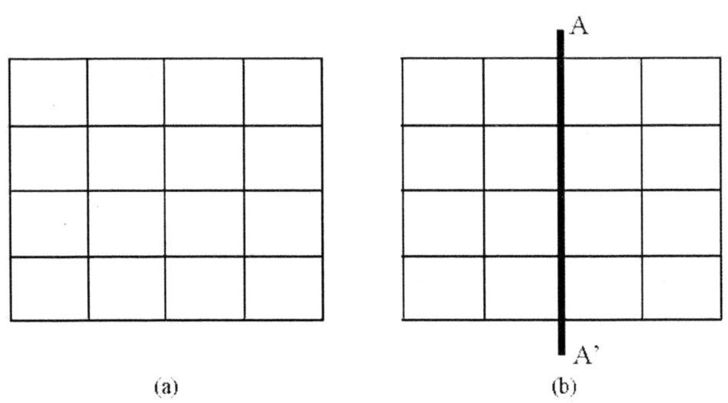

Figure 2 Domain decomposition for the finite element mesh

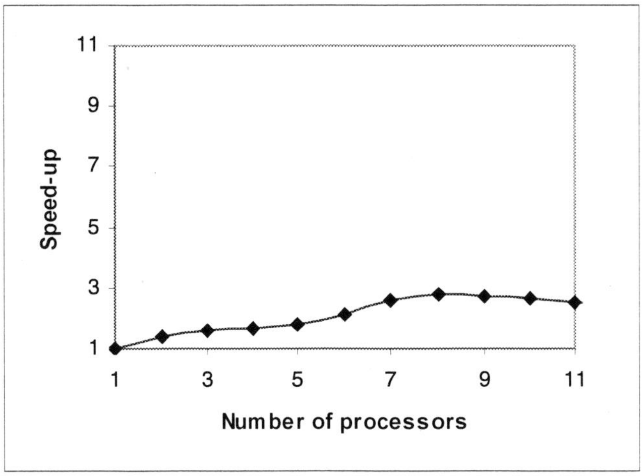

Figure 3 Speed-up as a function of the number of processors

3 Conclusion

In this paper, parallel computing algorithms that have been developed for both the finite element method and crystal plasticity theory to simulate plastic deformation of polycrystalline solids were discussed. The combination of polycrystal plasticity theory and modern parallel processing provides a powerful tool for the analysis of plastic deformation for a large class of engineering materials.

The TFE model demands significant amounts of memory and CPU time due to the amount of information at the grain level that must be tracked. Thus parallel computing algorithms were developed to distribute the global polycrystal aggregate into smaller aggregates between the processors. With this technique, the total capacity of all processors combined can be employed for the numerical simulations.

The FESC model requires significantly smaller memory compared to the TFE model. Thus parallel computing algorithms were developed to improve CPU time where the global stiffness matrix was computed in parallel (employing "skyline" storage), and the global systems of equations were then solved in parallel using an iterative solver. The efficiency of this type of parallelization depends directly on the total number of degrees of freedoms for the finite element system of equations. As the total number of equations to be solved increases, the performance of parallel computing will improve.

References

[1] Inal, K., Wu, P.D. & Neale, K.W., Simulation of earing in textured aluminium sheets. International Journal of Plasticity, **16**, pp. 635-648, 2000.

[2] Inal, K., Wu, P.D. & Neale, K.W., Instability and localized deformation in polycrystalline solids under plane strain tension. *International Journal of Solids and Structures*, **39**, pp. 983-1002, 2002.

[3] Inal, K., Wu, P.D. & Neale, K.W., Large strain behaviour of aluminum sheets subjected to in-plane simple shear. *Modelling and Simulation in Materials Science and Engineering,* **10**, pp. 237-252, 2002.

[4] Inal, K., Wu, P.D. & Neale, K.W., Finite element analysis of localized deformation in fcc polycrystals under plane stress tension. *International Journal of Solids and Structures*, (in press).

[5] Wu, P.D., Inal, K., Neale, K.W., Kenny, L.D., Jain, M. & MacEwen, S.R., Large Strain Behaviour of Very Thin Aluminium Sheets Under Planar Simple Shear. *Journal de Physique IV*, **11**, pp. 229-236, 2001.

[6] Beaudoin, A.J., Mathur, K.K., Dawson, P.R. & Johnson, G.C., Three-dimensional deformation process simulation with explicit use of polycrystal plasticity models. *International Journal of Plasticity*, **9**, pp. 833-860, 1993.

[7] Sorensen, N.J. & Andersen, B.S., A parallel finite element method for the analysis of crystalline solids. DCAMM Report, The Technical University of Denmark, 1995.

[8] Asaro, R.J. & Needleman, A., Texture development and strain hardening in rate dependent polycrystals. *Acta Metallurgica*, **33**, pp. 923-953, 1995.

[9] Inal, K., Modélisation numérique de l'aluminium à grandes déformations plastiques: applications au calcul parallèle," *M.A.Sc. Thesis*, Department of Civil Engineering, University of Sherbrooke, Sherbrooke, Québec, Canada, 1998.

Part II : Systems
Partie II : systèmes

HPCx: A New Resource For UK Computational Science

Mike Ashworth[a,1], Ian J. Bush[a], Martyn F. Guest[a,2], Martin Plummer[a], Andrew G. Sunderland[a], Stephen Booth[b], David S. Henty[b], Lorna Smith[b] and Kevin Stratford[b]

[a]Computational Science and Engineering Department, CLRC Daresbury Laboratory, Daresbury, Warrington, Cheshire, WA4 4AD, UK
[b]Edinburgh Parallel Computing Centre, University of Edinburgh, JCMB, The King's Buildings, Mayfield Road, Edinburgh, EH9 3JZ, UK

[1] *m.ashworth@dl.ac.uk*

[2] *m.f.guest@dl.ac.uk*

We introduce HPCx - the UK's new National HPC Service - which aims to deliver a world-class service for capability computing to the UK scientific community. HPCx is targeting an environment that will both result in world-leading science and address the challenges involved in scaling existing codes to the capability levels required. Close working relationships with scientific consortia and user groups throughout the research process will be a central feature of the service. A significant number of key user applications have already been ported to the system. We present initial benchmark results from this process and discuss the optimisation of the codes and the performance levels achieved. We find a range of performance with some algorithms scaling far better than others.

Nous introduisons ici HPCx, le nouveau Service national de CHP de la Grande-Bretagne. Ce service vise à fournir un service CHP de classe mondiale à la communauté scientifique de Grande-Bretagne. HPCx vise à fournir un environnement qui permettra la production de recherche scientifique de pointe, et s'attaquera aux défis que pose la mise à l'échelle des codes existants pour atteindre la puissance requise. Le travail étroit avec les regroupements scientifiques et les utilisateurs occupera une place prépondérante dans le processus de recherche de cet organisme. Un nombre significatif d'applications-clées ont déjà été adaptées. Nous présentons ici les premiers tests effectués, et discutons de l'optimisation des codes et des divers niveaux de performance obtenus. Nous observons une plage de performance où certains algorithmes démontrent une croissance d'échelle nettement supérieure à celle des autres.

1. Introduction

HPCx is the name of the UK's new National High Performance Computing Service. It is a large IBM p690 cluster whose configuration is specifically designed for high-availability capability computing[1]. The Engineering and Physical Sciences Research Council (EPSRC) is overseeing the project, on behalf of the UK scientific community. HPCx is a joint venture between the Daresbury Laboratory of the Central Laboratory for the Research Councils (CLRC) and Edinburgh Parallel Computing Centre (EPCC) at the University of Edinburgh. IBM (UK) Ltd has been chosen as the hardware supplier for the six-year duration of the project.

2. The HPCx Project

The British Government, through EPSRC, has funded the project to approximately £53M (~USD 85M). The scope of the project is to operate and support the principal academic and research high performance computing service for the UK. The principal objective is to provide a capability computing service to run key scientific applications that can only be run on the very highest performing computing platforms.

The project is a collaboration between three partners: CLRC Daresbury Laboratory, Edinburgh Parallel Computing Centre (EPCC) and IBM. HPCx, formally known as UoE HPCx Limited, is a wholly-owned subsidiary of the University of Edinburgh. It is under contract to EPSRC to provide HPC services and it sub-contracts appropriate packages to the consortium partners. The partnership combines two of Europe's leading academic HPC, e-Science and technology transfer centres, with significant experience in operating and supporting national grand challenge and capability services on novel architectures.

CLRC Daresbury Laboratory has been an HPC service provider to the UK academic community for over 25 years - the first Cray 1 in Europe was delivered there in 1978. CLRC's Computational Science and Engineering Department is the UK's premier research, development and support centre for leading-edge academic science and engineering simulation codes. CLRC also provides distributed computing support for COTS processor and network technologies, evaluating scalability and performance [1]. CLRC also hosts the UK Grid Support Centre.

EPCC, located at the University of Edinburgh, was established in 1991 as the University's interdisciplinary focus for high-performance computing and its commercial exploitation. EPCC has hosted specialised

[1] Jobs which use a significant fraction of the total resource.

HPC services for the UK's QCD community since 1989. The 5Tflop/s QCDOC system is due to be installed in 2003, in a project with Columbia, IBM and Brookhaven National Laboratory. From 1994 until 2002, EPCC operated and supported UK national services on Cray T3D and T3E systems.

Within HPCx, CLRC and EPCC both provide "Added Value" services (primarily scientific support, code optimisation, and code development) and operations and system support services. The physical accommodation is provided at CLRC's Daresbury Laboratory. IBM is the technology partner, providing the hardware, system software and appropriate maintenance and support services. They offer world-leading and competitively priced HPC technology, an aggressive road map over the next 6 years and significant resources for science support.

HPCx is a six-year project and the technology will be provided in three phases, with defined performance levels at year 0, year 2 and year 4. The performance targets for the three phases are defined in terms of Linpack Rmax performance. The targets for the three phases are approximately 3 Tflop/s, 6 Tflop/s and 12 Tflop/s, roughly following Moore's Law. Online and offline storage will increase proportionately, with 50, 100 and 200 TB in the three phases. There is a flexible approach to the technology refreshes in phases 2 and 3, and future upgrades are likely to feature the "Federation" switch and POWER5-based architectures.

The focus is on maximising the delivery of capability computing; the service is not intended to be used as a task farm or for multiple modest-sized throughput jobs. There is a comprehensive support service providing porting, optimisation, training and new applications outreach. The service has a 7 x 24 operating regime with high RAS requirements.

3. The HPCx Phase 1 System

Delivery of the Phase 1 system commenced on 4th October 2002. The full user service opened officially on 9th December 2002, although many users had benefited from up to a month's early access prior to this date. The system comprises 40 Regatta-H SMP compute nodes connected by the "Colony" SP Switch2.

Each shared memory node has 32 1.3GHz POWER4 processors and 32 GB memory giving the system an aggregate memory of 1.28 TB. The POWER4 processor has dual floating point units each of which, through the fused multiply-add instruction, is capable of delivering two results per clock cycle. This gives each processor a peak performance of 5.2 Gflop/s and the whole system a peak of some 6.6 Tflop/s.

In order to increase connectivity to the switch and improve communications throughput, each compute node is configured as four 8-way logical partitions (LPARs). The "Colony" SP Switch2 allows each LPAR to have two connections (PCI adapters) into the switch fabric (dual plane), providing approximately 20 usec latency and 350 MBytes/sec bandwidth. Two additional 16 processor nodes are provided as I/O systems. The system runs AIX version 5, with GPFS for file system support (18TB EXP500) and HSM for backup and archive to tape storage (35TB LTO tape library).

4. Towards Capability Computing

Perhaps the key challenge for the HPCx service is to deliver on the capability aspirations of the UK community across a broad spectrum of disciplines. We outline in sections 5-10 below initial progress towards this goal by illustrating the current levels of delivered performance from a number of codes across a variety of disciplines, including materials science, molecular simulation, atomic and molecular physics, molecular electronic structure, computational engineering and environmental science.

Considering a total of 10 application codes, we compare performance on the IBM SP/Regatta-H with that found on a number of platforms from other vendors. These include the Cray T3E/1200E ("Turing") and the SGI Origin 3800/R12k-400 system ("Green"), both operated by CSAR at the University of Manchester, UK, and the SGI O3800/R14k-500 system ("Teras") at SARA, Amsterdam. Also included is the Compaq AlphaServer ES45/1000, the TCS-1 system at Pittsburgh Supercomputing Centre, PSC.

5. Materials Science

5.1. CRYSTAL, AIMPRO and CASTEP

CRYSTAL [2] permits the calculation of wave-functions and properties of crystalline systems, using a periodic Hartree-Fock or density functional Kohn-Sham Hamiltonian and various hybrid approximations. The wavefunctions are expanded in atom centred Gaussian type orbitals (GTOs) providing a highly efficient and numerically precise solution with no shape approximation to the density or potential. The code is developed within a long standing collaboration between the Theoretical Chemistry Group at the University of Torino, Italy, and the Computational Materials Science Group at Daresbury Laboratory, and is widely distributed internationally. Details of the code and its applications can be found on the CRYSTAL web pages [2,3].

Recent enhancements to the parallel distributed data version of the code, MPP CRYSTAL, include the incorporation of a somewhat faster, and more numerically stable version of the parallel Jacobi diagonalizer [4]. Further, since it can diagonalize not only real symmetric but also Hermitian matrices, the ScaLAPACK library routines are no longer required. This is advantageous because the latter routines both scale poorly and also, dependent upon the eigenvalue spectrum, may require unacceptably large amounts of replicated memory.

The rationalization of the memory management within the code has continued. All large arrays are now dynamically allocated, and further general purpose Fortran 90 modules are available for more complex data structures, such as linked lists. On MPP systems disk access is often an expensive process, and so as far as is possible this is now avoided. Data is either recalculated or, for distributed objects, stored in memory, the latter being possible because of the memory capacity typically found on these machines.

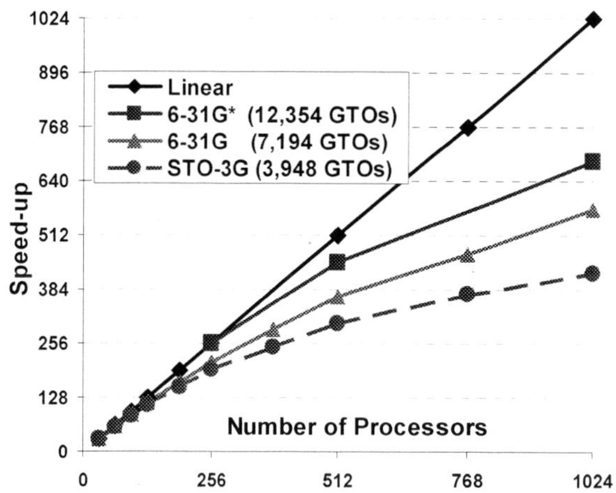

Figure 1. Scalabiliy of CRYSTAL-2000 in Calculations on Crystalline Crambin.

Timings on the IBM SP/Regatta-H and Origin 3800/R12k-400 of CRYSTAL 2000 for a benchmark calculation on crystalline crambin [5] with 1284 atoms per cell are reported in Table 1. These calculations were performed in basis sets of increasing quality, with reported times for the STO-3G (3,948 GTOs) and 6-31G (7,194 GTOs) basis sets referring to 3 cycles of the iterative SCF process, and the times for the 6-31G** basis (12,354 GTOs) being for a single SCF iteration. The corresponding speedups on the IBM SP/Regatta-H shown in Figure 1 reveal excellent scalability that is enhanced with improvements in the basis set.

AIMPRO (Ab Initio Modelling PROgram) was written by Patrick Briddon et al. at Newcastle University [6]. It can be used to study both molecules and 3D periodic systems using a Gaussian basis set.

The AIMPRO benchmark models a carbon impurity in a silicon lattice; 216 atoms are present in total (1 carbon, 215 silicon) and four k points are used, with a total of 5180 basis functions. The major operation to be performed in the calculation is a diagonalization of size the number of basis functions in the benchmark.

Table 1. Time in Wall Clock Seconds for CRYSTAL calculations of Crystalline Crambin on the IBM SP/Regatta-H and SGI Origin 3800/R12k-400 for Three Different Basis Sets.

CPUs	SGI Origin 3800 / R12k-400	IBM SP / Regatta-H
STO-3G Basis (3,948 GTOs)		
32	6559	3238
64	3400	1762
96	2327	1183
128	1810	921
192	1289	682
256	1038	531
384	772	416
512		343
768		278
1024		245
6-31G Basis (7,194 GTOs)		
32	23457	11970
64	12130	6333
96	8240	4248
128	6251	3305
192	4437	2317
256	3496	1801
384	2449	1321
512		1043
768		817
1024		668
6-31G* Basis (12,354 GTOs)		
256		1924
512		1099
1024		716

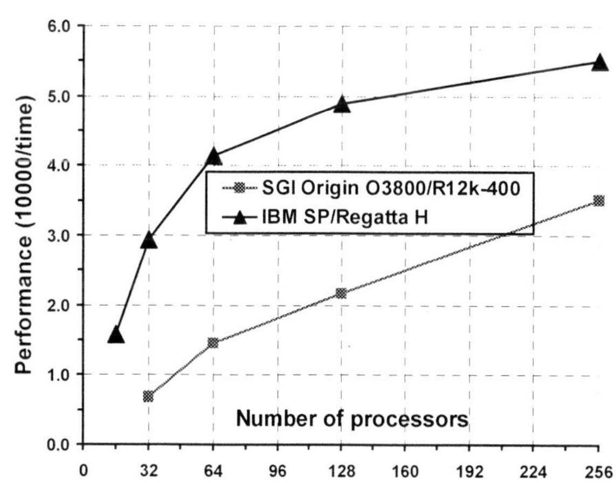

Figure 2. The AIMPRO Benchmark

Performance figures on the IBM/SP Regatta-H (HPCx) and SGI Origin 3800/R12k-400 are shown in Figure 2. These suggest that the IBM / SGI Origin performance ratio of 4.3 up to 64 processors falls beyond this CPU count, to 2.3 on 128 and only 1.6 on 256 processors.

The major performance-related problem with AIMPRO is the diagonalizations it has to perform. These are conducted at present using the ScaLAPACK routine PDSYEVX. This routine uses the QR method which, while well suited for AIMPRO in that only a subset of the eigenvalues need be calculated, does not scale well to high processor count.

CASTEP [7] is an *ab initio* computational materials code using the plane-wave pseudopotential method. It has been developed by the UKCP Consortium and is distributed commercially by Accelrys Plc. In common with many plane-wave based codes, CASTEP uses 3-dimensional FFTs to transform between real-space and wave-space. In order to perform the FFTs efficiently on each processor, there is a data transformation step using the MPI collective, MPI_Alltoallv. Given the latency dependency of this collective, it is clear that this step will be critically dependent on interconnect, and will not scale as well on, for example, the IBM SP as on the Cray T3E/1200E. Where a case has more than 1 k-point it is important to use "kG" parallelization to minimize the number of processors involved in calls to MPI_Alltoallv; the fewer the number of k-points, the greater the number of processors involved (finally leading to "G" parallelization).

The first CASTEP benchmark reported is an 8 k-point total energy calculation of a 33-atom slab of TiN, using the Vanderbilt ultrasoft pseudo-potential. Employing "kG" parallelisation, the benchmark involves a total of 88,000 plane waves (ca. 11,000 per k-point) and a 3D FFT grid size of 108x36x36. Convergence was achieved in 30 SCF cycles using the Pulay density mixing minimiser scheme. In this case, the "kG" parallelization divides the processors into 8 groups, each dealing with one k-point. The 3D FFTs are then distributed over processors within a group rather than across all processors so that ideally 8 independent 3D FFTs may be performed simultaneously. Timings are reported (Table 2) on the Cray T3E/1200E, Compaq AlphaServer SC ES45/1000, IBM SP/Regatta-H and SGI Origin 3800/R14k-500. A second benchmark involved applying a dense Monkhorst Pack (MP) mesh to the 8 k-point test case above, leading to 32 k-points. We label these two benchmarks as "1x1x1-8"and "1x1x1-32" respectively.

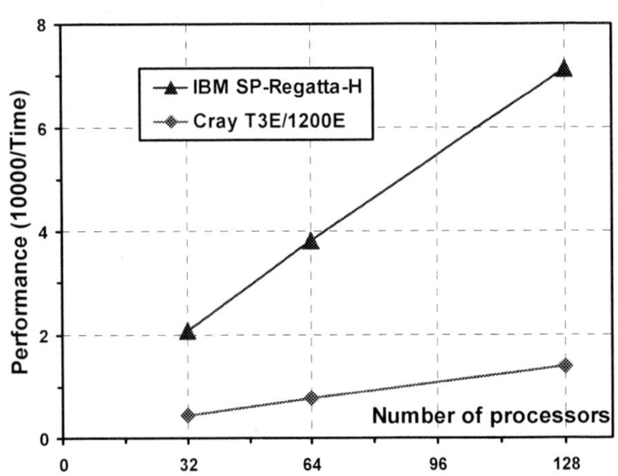

Table 2. Time in Wall Clock Seconds for the 8k and 32-kpoint CASTEP TiN Benchmark Calculations.

CPUs	Cray T3E/ 1200E	SGI O3800 R14k-500	Compaq AlphaServer ES45/1000	IBM SP / Regatta-H Cheetah
TiN, 1x1x1, 8 k-points				
32	6038	2287	1312	1149
64	3109	1096	800	610
128	1712	536	560	577†
TiN, 1x1x1, 32 k-points				
32	22561			4816
64	13033			2621
128	7244			1403

† 404secs currently on the HPCx system

Figure 3. CASTEP TiN Benchmark, 32 k-points (1x1x1-32)

The performance of CASTEP varies greatly with the size of the problem and the number of k-points. With few k-points and large numbers of processors MPI_Alltoallv dominates, so that the overall performance on the IBM SP scales far less effectively than on the Cray T3E/1200E. For the 1x1x1-8 case, respectable IBM / Cray T3E performance ratios of around 5.6 (32 processors) and 5.0 (64 processors) appear to fall rapidly beyond this CPU count, to only 3.0 on 128 processors (1x1x1-8, Table 2). In contrast, the performance of the 32 k-point case remains respectable with ratios of around 4.7, 4.9 and 5.1 on 32, 64 and 128 processors respectively (Figure 3, 1x1x1-32). The 128 processor run takes around 1,403 seconds on the IBM SP/Regatta-H. Large numbers of k-points are typical for calculations of metals.

Two potential developments are being undertaken to look at improving the current CASTEP performance. It is possible to call MPI_Alltoallv for several FFTs at once, thus reducing the number of message passing calls. Initial investigation suggests that while this does improve matters, it is only a major improvement for G parallelism, at least for the test cases. Secondly, use may be made of the additional memory available on the IBM SP to avoid some of the FFTs. In the program a number of these are repeated, the reason being memory constraints on older machines, and so on more modern machines this may be avoided. Initial investigations show a similar improvement as above for kG and G parallelization. Recent improvements in the communications have led to the 128-processor 1x1x1-8 time reducing from 577 to 404 secs.

What is clear from the above benchmarks is the limited scalability likely to arise on the HPCx system in any application that involves global communication routines (CASTEP), or a dependency on linear algebra routines with extensive communication requirements (AIMPRO). This comes as little surprise given the known limitations of the present Colony-based interconnect.

6. Molecular Simulation

6.1. DL_POLY and NAMD

DL_POLY [8] is a general-purpose molecular dynamics simulation package designed to cater for a wide range of possible scientific applications and computer platforms, especially parallel hardware. Two graphical user interfaces are available, one based on the CERIUS^2 Visualiser from Accelrys and the other on the Java programming language.

DL_POLY supports a wide range of application areas, including [9] ionic solids, solutions, metals, zeolites, surfaces and interfaces, complex systems (e.g. liquid crystals), minerals, bio-systems, and those in spectroscopy. Comprehensive benchmarking of the replicated data (RD) version (Version 2.11) of DL_POLY [10,11] clearly reveals the limitations inherent in the RD strategy, with restrictions in the size of system amenable to study, and limited scalability on current high-end platforms. These limitations apply not only to systems possessing complex molecular topologies and constraint bonds, but also to systems requiring simple atomic descriptions, systems that historically exhibited excellent scaling on the Cray T3E/1200E. Significant enhancements to the codes capabilities have arisen from the recent release of the distributed data (or domain decomposition) version (DL_POLY 3), developments that have been accelerated in light of the arrival of the HPCx system.

Evaluation of the Coulomb potential and forces in DL_POLY is performed using the smooth particle mesh Ewald (SPME) algorithm [12]. As in all Ewald [13] methods, this splits the calculation into two parts, one performed in real space and one in Fourier space. The former only requires evaluation of short ranged functions, which fits in well with the domain decomposition used by DL_POLY 3, and so scales well with increasing processor count. However the Fourier component requires 3 dimensional FFTs to be performed. These are global operations and so a different strategy is required if good scaling is to be achieved.

The original implementation involved replicating the whole FFT grid on all processors and performing the FFTs in serial after which each processor could evaluate the appropriate terms for the atoms that it held. This method clearly has a number of well known drawbacks.

While both open source 3D parallel FFTs (such as FFTW [14]) and proprietary routines (such as Cray's PCCFFT) are available, neither adequately address all the issues. The problem is that they impose a data distribution, typically planes of points, that is incompatible with DL_POLY's spatial domain decomposition, so while a complete replication of the data is not required, it is still necessary to perform extensive data redistribution which will limit the scaling of the method.

To address these limitations, a parallel 3D FFT has been written [15] which maps directly onto DL_POLY's data distribution; this involved parallelizing the individual 1D FFTs in an efficient manner. While the method will be slower than the proprietary routines for small processor counts, at large numbers it is attractive, since (a) while moving more data in total, the method requires much fewer messages, so that in the latency dominated regime it should perform better, and (b) global operations, such as the *all to all* operations used in both FFTW and PCCFFT, are totally avoided. More generally the method is extremely flexible, allowing a much more general data distribution than those of other FFTs, and as such should be useful in other codes which do not map directly onto a "by planes" distribution.

In the present section we present recent results obtained on the IBM SP/Regatta-H, Compaq AlphaServer ES45/1000 and SGI Origin 3800/R14k-500, results which highlight the drastic improvements in both system size and performance made possible through these developments. The four benchmarks reported in Table 3 include two Coulombic-based simulations of NaCl, one with 27,000 ions, the second with 216,000 ions. Both simulations involve use of the Particle Mesh Ewald Scheme, with the associated FFT treated by the algorithm outlined above [15] in which the traditional all-to-all communications are replaced by the scheme that relies on column-wise communications only. The reported timings are for 500 time steps in the smaller calculation, and 200 time steps in the larger simulation.

The other two benchmarks are macromolecular simulations based on Gramicidin-A; the first includes a total of 99,120 atoms and 100 time steps. The second, much larger simulation, is for a system of eight Gramicidin-A species (792,960 atoms), with the timings reported for just 50 time steps. In terms of time to solution, we see that the AlphaServer SC outperforms the Origin 3800 at all processor counts in all four benchmarks; both 256 CPU runs for the larger NaCl and Gramicidin-A simulations suggest factors of 1.3-1.4.

These results show a marked improvement in performance compared to the replicated data version of the code, with the gratifying characteristic of enhanced scalability with increasing size of simulation, both in the ionic and macromolecular simulations. Considering the NaCl simulations, we find speedups of 139 and 122 respectively on 256 processors of the Origin 3800 and AlphaServer SC in the 27,000-ion simulation. These figures increase to 172 and 171 respectively in the larger simulation featuring 216,000 ions. While the total times to solution on the IBM SP are broadly in line with the AlphaServer SC, the scalability remains inferior.

For these systems the FFT routine remains the poorest scaling; the time required to exchange scales poorly on the IBM SP with increased processor count. Doubling the number of processors roughly halves the amount of data a processor has to send, so one would expect the time to roughly halve. In practice this is not the case, and

Table 4: Elapsed Time per time step (seconds) for the NAMD ApoA-I Benchmark on the IBM SP/Regatta H and Compaq AlphaServer SC ES45/1000.

Number of processors	Compaq Alphaserver SC ES45/1000	IBM SP/Regatta-H
1	7.86	7.97
2		4.47
4		2.19
8		1.11
16		0.580
32		0.305
64		0.163
128	0.0715	0.0985
256	0.0403	0.0664
512	0.0239	0.0424
1024	0.0176	0.0252

Table 3. Time in Wall Clock Seconds for four DL_POLY 3 benchmark Calculations on the Compaq AlphaServer SC ES45/1000, IBM SP/Regatta-H and SGI Origin 3800.

CPUs	SGI Origin 3800 / R14k-500	Compaq Alpha ES45 / 1000	IBM SP / Regatta-H
NaCl ; 27,000 ions, 500 time steps			
16	313	183	160
32	168	103	97
64	92	57	61
128	53	37	42
256	36	24	
NaCl; 216,000 ions, 200 time steps			
16	764	576	455
32	387	326	234
64	201	168	128
128	116	91	78
256	71	54	48
512			41
Gramicidin A; 99,120 atoms, 100 time steps			
16	282	173	166
32	167	109	107
64	100	75	74
Gramicidin A; 792,960 atoms, 50 time steps			
32	661	370	349
64	273	186	189
128	140	109	114
256	97	68	77
512			56

at certain processor counts the time dramatically increases. This can be traced to the message passing occurring via the switch rather than through shared memory. For example, for the x direction, which never has to use the switch in the present case, the scaling is reasonable, while for the z direction, which has to use the switch for the first time at 16 processors, there is a major spike in the timings.

A more compelling improvement with system size is found in the macromolecular Gramicidin-A simulations. Again the SPME algorithm is used for evaluation of the Coulomb field, but in these simulations there is the extra complication of constraints on the atoms' motions, which reflects chemical bonds in the system. The shake algorithm is used to evaluate the constraints, and this is again potentially a global operation and so, as for the FFT, good scaling is difficult to achieve. In the distributed data implementation, both SHAKE and short-range forces require only nearest neighbour communications, suggesting that communications should scale linearly with the number of nodes, in marked contrast to the replicated data implementation. This is borne out in practice. In the larger simulation (with 792,960 atoms) we find speedups of 218 and 175 on 256 processors of the Origin 3800 and AlphaServer SC respectively. This level of scalability represents a significant advance over that exhibited by both DL_POLY 2 and CHARMM [10].

NAMD is the parallel, object-oriented molecular dynamics program designed for high performance simulations of large biomolecular systems [16]. NAMD employs the prioritized message-driven execution capabilities of the Charm++/Converse parallel runtime system, allowing excellent parallel scaling on both massively parallel supercomputers and commodity-based workstation clusters. An initial implementation of the code on HPCx was carried out by Rik Kufrin (NCSA), and Table 4 shows the elapsed time per time step for the standard NAMD ApoA-I benchmark [17], a system comprising 92,442 atoms, with 12Å cutoff and PME every 4 time steps, periodic. Also shown are the timings from the optimised version of the code running on PSC's AlphaServer SC ES45/1000. These show that the AlphaServer marginally outperforms the IBM SP on a single CPU, and with a speed-up of 447 on 1024 processors, exhibits superior scalability compared to the IBM SP (a corresponding speed-up of 316). This is to be expected in light of the superior interconnect associated with the AlphaServer. We would expect these scalability figures to improve with larger simulations in light of performance attributes demonstrated on the TCS-1 system at Pittsburgh (e.g. a speedup of 778 on 1024 CPUs in a 327K particle simulation of F_1-ATPase).

7. Atomic & Molecular Physics

7.1. H2MOL and PFARM

H2MOL [18] is a code from the Multiphoton and Electron Collision Consortium (CCP2) written by Ken Taylor & Daniel Dundas, Queens University Belfast. It solves the time-dependent Schrödinger equation to produce estimates of energy distributions for laser-driven dissociative ionization of the H_2 molecule. A cylindrical computational grid is defined with ϕ, ρ and Z co-ordinates, with the Z domain distributed amongst an array of processors arranged logically in a triangular grid (to take advantage of symmetry). A feature of the way this code has been written is that it specifies as constant the number of grid points **per processor** in the z-direction. Thus with increasing numbers of processors it is working with an increasingly refined mesh i.e., for this benchmark, perfect scaling would be represented by a flat timing profile across the different processor counts.

The results of Table 5 refer to a problem definition with ϕ points = 11, ρ points = 30 and Z points = 11 (per processor). This is the maximum problem size that the restricted memory on the Cray-T3E/1200E (256 MByte) can accommodate.

The IBM SP / Cray T3E performance ratio starts at around 3 on 6 processors and reduces to just above 2.5 on 231 processors. For calculations involving low numbers of processors, performance is ESSL / LIBSCI intensive (highly optimized ZGEMM, ZAXPY, ZDOT routines) and corresponds to around a third of peak for both IBM and Cray machines. Therefore the best relative performance to be expected on low processor counts reflects the peak ratios of the two machines i.e. 5.2 Gflops (IBM SP) / 1.2 Gflops (Cray T3E) = 4.3. By 120 processors (8 tasks on 15 nodes) there is no more than a factor of two performance gain from the IBM SP. At 231 processors, with partially occupied nodes (7 tasks on each of 33 nodes), the performance ratio has improved to around 2.5. Table 5 demonstrates that the timings on large processor counts of HPCx are fairly flat, representing reasonable scaling. Runs undertaken with fully occupied L-PAR'd nodes (*) are slower than those with at least one free task per node.

Table 5: To p es (seconds) for the fixed-point H2MOL Benchmark (ϕ points = 11, ρ points = 30 and Z points = 11 (per processor)).

Number of processors	Cray T3E/1200E	IBM SP / Regatta-H	(Tasks,T) X (Nodes,N)
6	5650	2098	6T x 1N
15	5935	2343	5T x 3N
28	6155		
45	6396		
66	6622	2660	6T x 11N
91	7123		
120	7198	3353	8T x 15N*
		2550	6T x 20N
231	7742	3004	7T x 33N
325		3071	5T x 65N
435	†	3269	5T x 87N
496	†	3952*	8T x 62N*

† Memory Exceeded

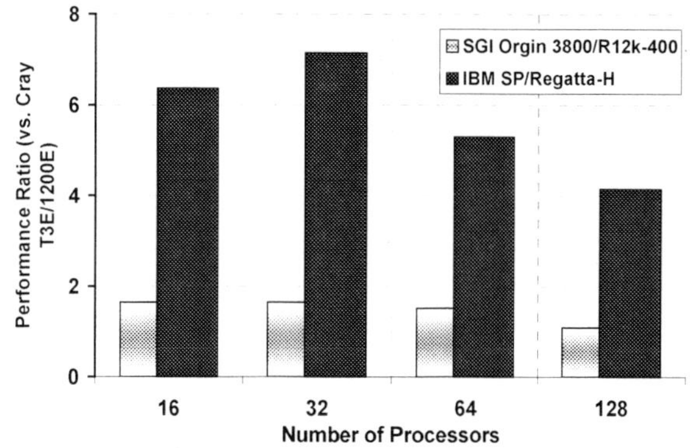

Figure 5. The PFARM Benchmark

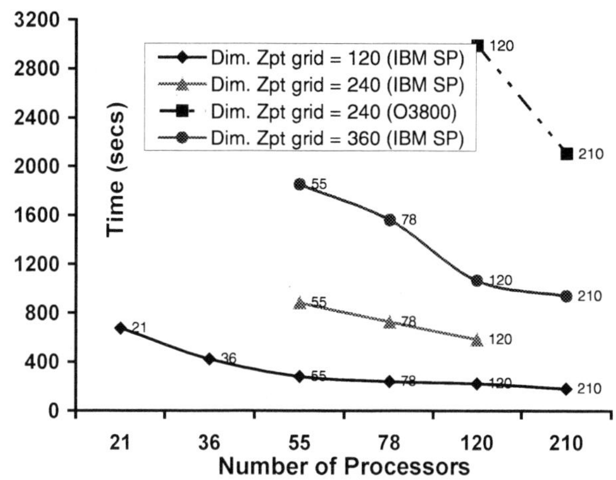

Figure 4. The H2MOL Benchmark with Fixed Problem Size

Fixing a global number of Z points, rather than a local number of Z points, allows the scaling of the code to be examined more clearly. The results of Figure 4 involve the ϕ and ρ parameters being set as above, with the total (global) number of Z points remaining fixed for different sized processor arrays. Hence, each run is now computing an identical problem. In the graph below, the number of timesteps has been reduced to increase throughput (this has no impact on scaling).

Evidently, the scalability improves as the problem size increases. Currently, users of the code are investigating problems with over 400 Z points on the SGI Origin 3800 at CSAR.

PFARM: In recent years new high performance codes and techniques have been developed to extend the successful R-matrix formalism to treat applications such as the description of the edge region in Tokamak plasmas (fusion power research) and for the interpretation of astrophysical spectra. The parallel R-matrix program PFARM has been optimised to treat open d-shell atoms and ions as well as intermediate energy scattering problems [19]. Several new facilities have been incorporated into PFARM to improve its efficiency for these calculations. In electron-ion scattering calculations it is necessary to perform separate computations at a very large number of scattering energies in order to compute the thermally averaged collision strengths required in applications. The program splits this energy mesh into a fine region (below all target thresholds) and coarse region (above all target thresholds). By treating each region separately, optimisations specific to each can be made. The parallel calculation has been designed to take advantage of the near-optimal performance of serial BLAS 3 routines; this operation is the computational rate-determining step. Therefore the effect of factors such as matrix dimension, matrix transposes and symmetry have been studied closely, and data is now arranged to maximise the BLAS 3 performance [19]. The major outstanding efficiency issues now relate to the required matrix diagonalisations (using the PeIGS parallel eigensolver [20]) and to load balancing. To address the latter problem, automated load balancing that adapts to each specific application has been developed. A computational model of the parallel calculation has been constructed that describes the relative speed of each component of the functional decomposition. Factors such as physical properties, hardware, relative BLAS/LAPACK performance and channel-splitting are all included in the model. The model is incorporated into a controlling Perl script that can predict dynamically an optimum configuration of processors for a particular physical problem. For each computation, processor configurations and the associated timing data is saved in order to refine the model for future runs.

The code has been ported to the IBM SP/Regatta-H and SGI Origin. Figure 5 shows the performance of the IBM SP and Origin 3800/R12k-400 relative to the Cray T3E/1200E for a typical Ni^{3+} scattering problem. This figure suggests that the IBM SP outperforms the SGI Origin 3800 and Cray T3E/1200E by factors of 3.8 and 4.2 on 128 processors.

8. Molecular Electronic Structure

8.1. GAMESS-UK

GAMESS-UK [21] represents a typical established electronic structure code, comprising some 800K lines of Fortran that permits a wide range of computational methodology to be applied to molecular systems. Improving the scalability of the parallel code has been addressed in part by adopting a number of the tools developed by the High Performance Computational Chemistry (HPCC) group from the Environmental Molecular Sciences Laboratory at PNNL, in Richland, Washington. These include the Global Array (GA) toolkit [22] that provides an efficient and portable "shared-memory" programming interface for distributed-memory computers, and the scalable, fully parallel eigensolver, PeIGS whose numerical properties satisfy the needs of the chemistry applications [20].

The main source of parallelism in the DFT module is the computation of the one- and two-electron integrals together with the exchange correlation contributions, and their summation into the Fock matrix. The computation of these quantities is allocated dynamically using a shared global counter. With the capabilities afforded by the GA tools [22], some distribution of the linear algebra becomes trivial. As an example, the SCF convergence acceleration algorithm (DIIS - direct inversion in the iterative subspace) is distributed using GA storage for all matrices, and parallel matrix multiply and dot-product functions. This not only reduces the time to perform the step, but the use of distributed memory storage (instead of disk) reduces the need for I/O during the SCF process. Diagonalisation of the resulting Fock matrix is now based on the PeIGS module from NWChem [23].

Table 6. Time in Wall Clock Seconds for Four GAMESS-UK Benchmark Calculations on the Compaq AlphaServer SC ES45/1000, IBM SP/Regatta-H and SGI Origin 3800/R14k-500.

CPUs	SGI Origin 3800 / R14k-500	Compaq Alpha ES45 / 1000	IBM SP / Regatte-H
Cyclosporin (1000 GTOs) DFT/B3LYP 6-31G			
32	1191	713	666
64	704	424	424
128	481	310	322
Cyclosporin (1855 GTOs) DFT/B3LYP 6-31G**			
32	4731	2504	2614
64	2838	1584	1681
128	1867	1100	1281
Valinomycin (882 GTOs) DFT/HCTH			
32	2306	1301	1329
64	1228	705	749
128	734	415	493
$(C_6H_4(CF_3))_2$ SCF 2nd Derivatives			
16	1490		860
32	803	501	621
64	494	360	371
128		246	213

Substantial modifications were required to enable the SCF 2nd derivatives [24] to be computed in parallel. The conventional integral transformation step has been omitted, with the SCF step performed in direct fashion and the MO integrals, generated by re-computation of the AO integrals, and stored in the global memory of the parallel machine. The GA tools manage this storage and subsequent access. The basic principle by which the subsequent steps are parallelised involves each node computing a contribution to the current term from MO integrals resident on that node. For some steps, however, more substantial changes to the algorithms are required. The coupled Hartree-Fock (CPHF) step and construction of perturbed Fock matrices are again parallelised according to the distribution of the MO integrals. The most costly step in the serial 2nd derivative algorithm is the computation of the 2nd derivative two-electron integrals. This step is trivially parallelised through a similar approach to that adopted in the direct SCF scheme - using dynamic load balancing based on a shared global counter. In contrast to the serial code, the construction of the perturbed Fock matrices dominates the parallel computation. It seems almost certain that these matrices would be more efficiently computed in the AO basis, rather than from the MO integrals as in the current implementation, thus enabling more effective use of sparsity when dealing with systems comprising more than 25 atoms.

The performance of the DFT and SCF 2nd Derivative modules on the SGI O3800/R14k-500, Compaq AlphaServer SC ES45/1000 and IBM SP/Regatta-H are shown in Table 6. Note that the DFT calculations did not exploit CD fitting, but evaluated the coulomb matrix explicitly. Considering the DFT results, modest speedups of 81, 73 and 65 are obtained on 128 processors of the Origin 3800, AlphaServer SC and IBM SP respectively for the larger cyclosporin calculation. Somewhat better scalability is found in the Valinomycin DFT calculation where a greater proportion of time is spent in integral evaluation arising from the more extended basis sets [25]; speedups of 101, 100 and 86 respectively are obtained on 128 processors of the Origin, AlphaServer and IBM SP. The enhanced performance of the SCF 2nd Derivative module on the IBM SP/Regatta H arises from the decreased dependency on latency exhibited by the current implementation compared to the DFT module. Thus the timings of Table 6 suggest that the SP is outperforming the AlphaServer SC on 128 processors.

The less than impressive scalability of both GAMESS-UK (and also NWChem) on the IBM SP arises to some extent from the dependency of both codes on a Global Array implementation that is based on IBM's LAPI communication library [26]. The current implementation of LAPI on POWER4-based architectures is far from optimal, with the measured latencies and bandwidths significantly inferior to those measured on corresponding POWER3-based systems. We are currently working with PNNL and IBM's LAPI team to further understand and address these shortcomings.

9. Computationn Engineering

9.1. PCHAN

Fluid flows encountered in real applications are invariably turbulent. There is, therefore, an ever-increasing need to understand turbulence and, more importantly, to be able to model turbulent flows with improved predictive capabilities. As computing technology continues to improve, it is becoming more feasible to solve the governing equations of motion – the Navier-Stokes equations – from first principles. The direct solution of the equations of motion for a fluid, however, remain a formidable task and simulations are only possible for flows with small to modest Reynolds numbers. Within the UK, the Turbulence Consortium (UKTC) has been at the forefront of simulating turbulent flows by direct numerical simulation (DNS). UKTC has developed a parallel version of a code to solve problems associated with shock/boundary-layer interaction. The code (SBLI) was originally developed for the Cray T3E and is a sophisticated DNS code that incorporates a number of advanced features: namely high-order central differencing; a shock-preserving advection scheme from the total variation diminishing (TVD) family; entropy splitting of the Euler terms and the stable boundary scheme [27]. The code has been written using standard

Figure 6. PCHAN T3 Benchmark

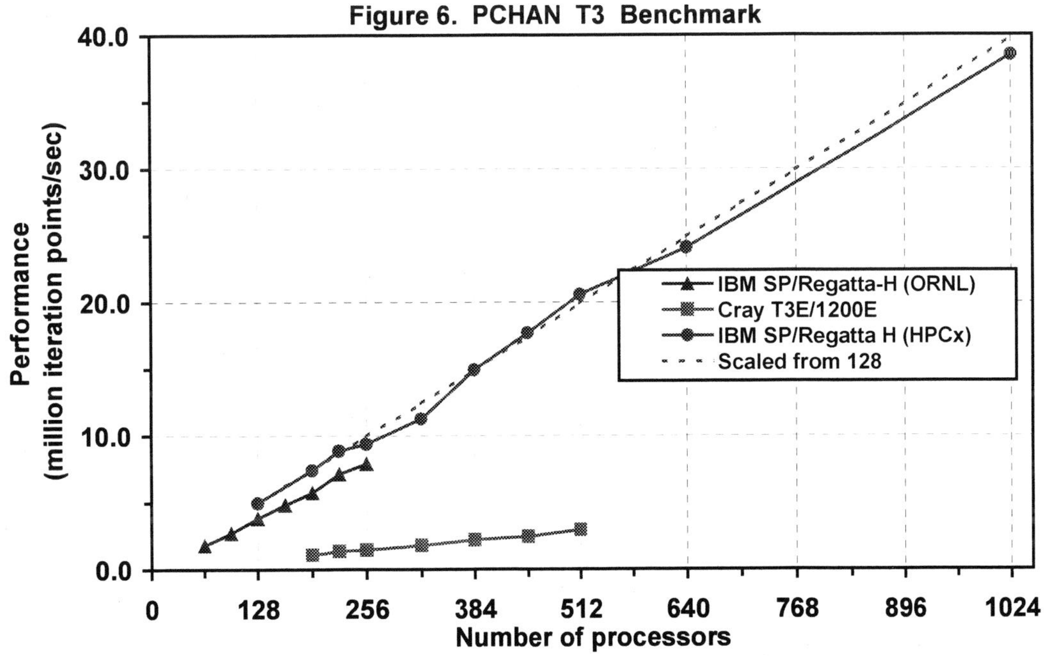

Fortran 90 code together with MPI in order to be efficient, scalable and portable across a wide range of high-performance platforms.

The PCHAN benchmark is a simple turbulent channel flow benchmark using the SBLI code. Performance with the T3 Grid Benchmark data case (360x360x360) shows close to ideal scaling on both the Cray T3E/1200E and on the IBM SP/Regatta-H systems, for which we have data from both the Cheetah system (at ORNL) and from the HPCx system. Where benchmark runs allow direct processor-for-processor comparison between the IBM and Cray systems (192-512 processors), the performance ratio is fairly constant at around 6.2 to 7.2. e.g., the 512 CPU T3 Benchmark required 227 elapsed seconds, with the HPCx system outperforming the Cray T3E/1200E (1,575 seconds) by a factor of 6.94. Figure 6 shows performance results from the T3E and the two IBM systems. The HPCx runs incorporate code optimisations, which account for a 20%-30% improvement; these were not present in the Cheetah implementation.

The most important communications structure within PCHAN is a halo-exchange between adjacent computational sub-domains. Providing the problem size is large enough to give a small surface area to volume ratio for each sub-domain, the communications costs are small relative to computation and do not constitute a bottleneck. Code optimisation for the POWER4 cache architecture has shown to be highly beneficial in increasing the performance.

10. Environmental Science

10.1. POLCOMS

The Proudman Oceanographic Laboratory Coastal Ocean Modeling System (POLCOMS) has been developed to tackle multi-disciplinary studies in coastal/shelf environments [28]. The central core is a sophisticated 3-dimensional hydrodynamic model that provides realistic physical forcing to interact with, and transport, environmental parameters.

The hydrodynamic model is a 4-dimensional finite difference model based on a latitude-longitude Arakawa B-grid in the horizontal and S-coordinates in the vertical. Conservative monotonic PPM advection routines are used to ensure strong frontal gradients. Vertical mixing is through turbulence closure (Mellor-Yamada level 2.5).

In order to study the coastal marine ecosystem, the POLCOMS model has been coupled with the European Seas Regional Ecosystem Model (ERSEM) [29]. Studies have been carried out, with and without the ecosystem sub-model, using a shelf-wide grid at 12km resolution. This results in a grid size of approx. 200 x 200 x 34. In order to improve simulation of marine processes, we need accurate representation of eddies, fronts and other regions of steep gradients. The next generation of models will need to cover the shelf region at approximately 1km resolution.

In order to assess the suitability of the POLCOMS hydrodynamic code for scaling to these ultra-high

Figure 7. Performance of the POLCOMS Hydrodynamics code as a Function of Grid Size

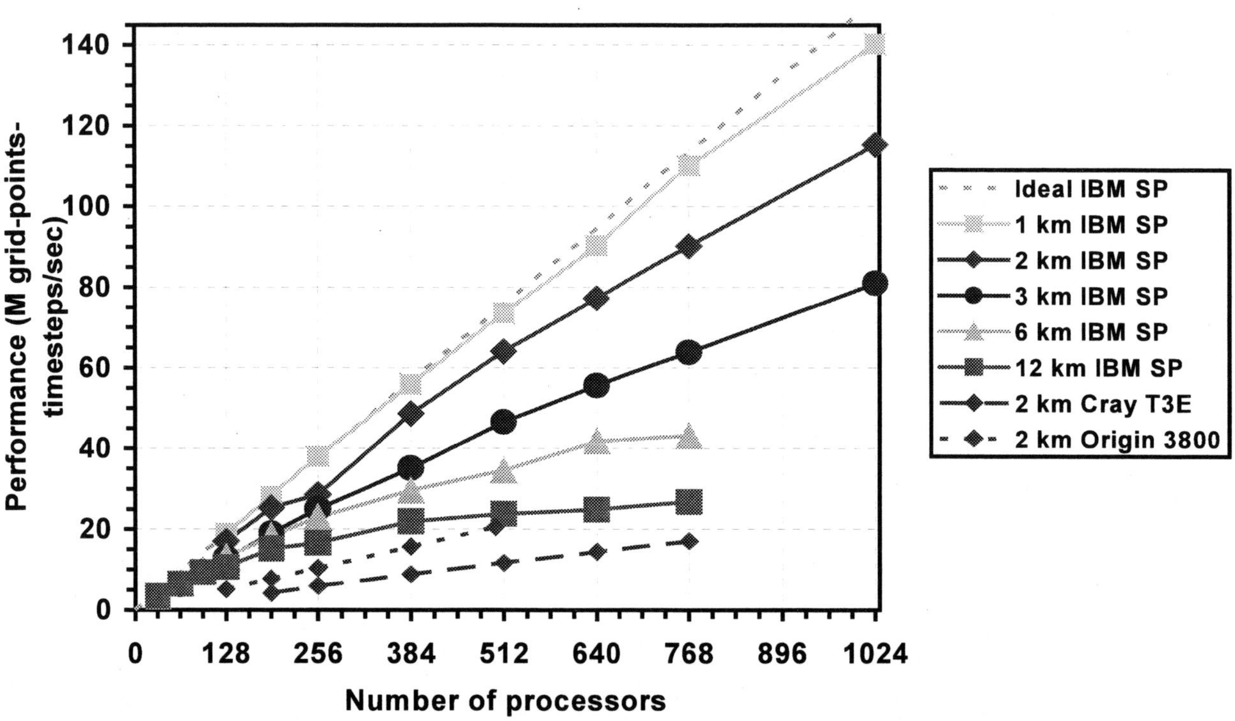

resolutions we have designed a set of benchmarks which runs (without the ecosystem model) at grid sizes representative of resolutions from the current 12km down to 1km. The resolutions (and horizontal grid dimension) chosen are 12km (200), 6km (400), 3km (800), 2km (1200) and 1km (2400). The number of vertical levels was fixed at 34. In order to keep benchmark run times manageable, the runs were kept short (100 timesteps) and the initialisation and finishing times were subtracted from the total run time. So as to compare properly runs with different grid sizes, performance is reported in Figure 7 as the amount of work (gridpoints × timesteps) divided by the time. Runs using up to 1024 processors of the HPCx system are shown compared to the Cray T3E-1200E and Origin 3800/R12k-400 systems operated by CSAR at the University of Manchester, UK.

We find, as expected, that, as the grid size increases, the ratio of communication to computation in the code improves and so does the scalability. At 2km resolution the code is scaling almost linearly on all three systems with the HPCx system delivering approx. 5.5 times the performance of the Cray T3E and 3.1 times the Origin 3800.

11. Summary

We have introduced HPCx, the UK's new National HPC Service which aims to deliver a world-class service for capability computing to the UK scientific community. HPCx is targeting an environment that will both result in world-leading science and address the challenges involved in scaling existing codes to the capability levels required.

A significant number of key user applications have already been ported to the system. The initial benchmark results from this process and the performance levels achieved have highlighted a wide range of performance, with some algorithms scaling far better than others. What is clear is that the current limitations, arising in the main from inadequacies associated with the Colony switch, demand a major focus on algorithm development designed to remove existing dependencies on collective, global operations. Where this has been addressed e.g., CRYSTAL, PCHAN and POLCOMS, we find excellent levels of scalability and performance.

12. References

[1] *Computational Chemistry Applications: Performance on High-End and Commodity-class Computers* M. F. Guest and P. Sherwood. Proceedings of HPCS 2002, Moncton, Canada, 2002

[2] See www.cse.dl.ac.uk/Activity/CRYSTAL, www.chimifm.unito.it/teorica/crystal

[3] *Ab Initio* Modelling in Solid State Chemistry, European Summerschool, MSSC2002, 8-13 Sept. 2002, Torino, Italy http://www.chimifm.unito.it/teorica/mssc2002.

[4] http://www.cse.clrc.ac.uk/arc/bfg.shtml

[5] The structure of Crambin is derived from XRD data at 0.52 Å. This crystal structure contains 1284 atoms.

[6] AIMPRO, S. Öberg, J. Goss, R. Jones, and P.R. Briddon.

[7] *Iterative Minimization Techniques for Ab Initio Total Energy Calculations: Molecular Dynamics and Conjugate Gradients*, M. C. Payne, M. P. Teter, D. C. Allan, T. A. Arias, J. D. Joannopoulos, Rev. Mod. Phys. **64** (1992) 1045.

[8] *DL_POLY: A general purpose parallel molecular dynamics simulation package*, W Smith and T R Forester, J. Molec. Graphics **14** (1996) 136.

[9] DL_POLY: *Applications to Molecular Simulation*, W Smith, C Yong and M Rodger, Molecular Simulation **28** (2002) 385.

[10] *Application Performance on High-end and Commodity-class Computers*, M.F. Guest, http://www.ukhec.ac.uk/publications

[11] W. Smith, http://www.dl.ac.uk/TCSC/Software/DL_POLY/main.html

[12] Darden et al., J. Chem.Phys. **103** (1995) 19.

[13] P.P. Ewald, Ann. Physik. **64** (1921) 253.

[14] Frigo and Johnson, ICASSP Conference Proceedings (1998).

[15] http://www.cse.clrc.ac.uk/arc/fft.shtml

[16] *NAMD2: Greater scalability for parallel molecular dynamics*, L. Kalé, R. Skeel, M. Bhandarkar, R. Brunner, A. Gursoy, N. Krawetz, J. Phillips, A. Shinozaki, K. Varadarajan, and K. Schulten. J. Comp. Phys., **151** (1999) 283-312.

[17] http://www.ks.uiuc.edu/Research/namd/performance.html

[18] Dundas D, Meharg K, McCann J F and Taylor K T, to be published

[19] *A parallel R-matrix program PRMAT for electron-atom and electron-ion scattering calculations*, A.G. Sunderland, C.J. Noble, V.M. Burke and P.G. Burke, Comput. Phys. Commun., **145** (2002) 311.

[20] *Parallel inverse iteration with reorthogonalization*, G. Fann and R.J. Littlefield in: *Sixth SIAM Conference on Parallel Processing for Scientific Computing (SIAM)*, (1993) pp.409-413.

[21] GAMESS-UK is a package of ab initio programs written by M.F. Guest, J.H. van Lenthe, J. Kendrick, K. Schoeffel and P. Sherwood, with contributions from R.D. Amos, R.J. Buenker, M. Dupuis, N.C. Handy, I.H. Hillier, P.J. Knowles, V. Bonacic-Koutecky, W. von Niessen, R.J. Harrison, A.P. Rendell, V.R. Saunders, and

A.J. Stone. The package is derived from the original GAMESS code due to M. Dupuis, D. Spangler and J. Wendoloski, NRCC Software Catalog, Vol. 1, Program No. QG01 (GAMESS), 1980.

[22] *A non-uniform memory access programming model for high-performance computers*, J. Nieplocha, R.J. Harrison, and R.J. Littlefield, 1996, Global Arrays: *J. Supercomputing* **10** (1996) pp.197-220.

[23] M.F. Guest, E. Apra, D.E. Bernholdt, H.A. Fruechtl, R.J. Harrison, R.A. Kendall, R.A. Kutteh, X. Long, J.B. Nicholas, J.A. Nichols, H.L. Taylor, A.T. Wong, G.I. Fann, R.J. Littlefield and J. Nieplocha, *Future Generation Computer Systems* 12 (1996) pp. 273-289.

[24] *A Parallel Second-Order Møller Plesset Gradient*, G. D. Fletcher, A. P. Rendell and P. Sherwood. *Molecular Physics.* **91** (1997) 431.

[25] N. Godbout, D. R. Salahub, J. Andzelm and E. Wimmer, Can. J. Chem. **70**, (1992) 560.

[26] *Performance and Experience with LAPI – a New High-Performance Communication Library for the IBM RS/6000 SP*, G. Shah , J. Nieplocha , J. Mirza, C. Kim, R.J. Harrison, R.K. Govindaraju, K. Gildea, P. DiNicola, C. Bender, Supercomputing 2002.

[27] *Direct Numerical Simulation of Shock/Boundary Layer Interaction*, N. D. Sandham, M. Ashworth and D. R. Emerson, http://www.cse.clrc.ac.uk/ceg/sbli.shtml

[28] *Coupled Marine Ecosystem Modelling on High-Performance Computers*, M. Ashworth, R. Proctor, J.T. Holt, J.I. Allen, and J.C. Blackford in Developments in Teracomputing, eds. W. Zwieflhofer and N. Kreitz, 2001, pp. 150-163, (World Scientific).

[29] *A highly spatially resolved ecosystem model for the North West European Continental Shelf*, J.I. Allen, J.C. Blackford, J.T. Holt, R. Proctor, M. Ashworth and J. Siddorn, SARSIA **86** (2001) pp. 423-440.

Acknowledgements

The success of the early stages of the HPCx project and of the implementation of the application benchmarks owes considerably to the efforts of many people. Among those without whom this work would not have been possible are Richard Blake, Paul Durham, Paul Sherwood, Bill Smith and Nic Harrison from CLRC, Mike Brown, Alan Simpson and Arthur Trew from EPCC, and Luigi Brochard and colleagues from IBM.

We are grateful to CSAR, ORNL, PSC and SARA for access to machines.

McKenzie: A Teraflops Linux Beowulf Cluster for Computational Astrophysics

John Dubinski [a,1], Robin Humble[a], Chris Loken[a], Ue-Li Pen[a] and Peter Martin[a]

[a] Department of Astronomy and Astrophysics and Canadian Institute for Theoretical Astrophysics, Mclennan Labs, 60 St. George St., University of Toronto, Toronto, ON M5S 3H8

[1] *dubinski@astro.utoronto.ca*

We describe a new 512-CPU Linux Beowulf cluster built at Toronto dedicated to problems in computational astrophysics. The cluster incorporates a new network topology based on inexpensive, 24-port gigabit switches and exploitation of a second gigabit port on each server. This topology provides network performance competitive with more expensive networking configurations. Our speed rating is 1.11 Teraflops on 512 CPUs according to the HPL Linpack benchmark on the Top 500 Supercomputers list. We also describe some preliminary results from our first simulations on this new machine.

Nous décrivons ici une nouvelle grappe 512 processeurs, de type Beowulf, conçue à Toronto et dédiée à la résolution de problèmes numériques en astrophysique. La grappe prend avantage d'une nouvelle topologie réseau basée sur l'utilisation de commutateurs gigabit de 24 ports peu dispendieux, ainsi que sur l'usage d'un deuxième port gigabit pour chacun des serveurs.B Cette topologie réseau permet d'atteindre une performance comparable à celle de configurations réseau plus dispendieuses. La puissance mesurée est de 1.11 Teraflops sur 512 processeurs selon le test HPL Linpack cité sur la liste Top 500 des plus puissants superordinateurs. Nous montrons également quelques résultats préliminaires provenant de nospremières simulations sur cette nouvelle grappe.

Overview

The Olympic motto "Citius, altius, fortius" ("Swifter, higher, stronger") succinctly describes the direction of 21st century supercomputing - swifter processors, higher resolution and stronger algorithms. In computational astrophysics, the need for all of these qualities is even greater than most supercomputing applications. While the bulk of the physics of the formation of the planets, stars, galaxies and the large-scale structure in the universe are now well understood and in many cases the initial conditions are well posed, the challenge of computing the formation of objects and structures in the universe is difficult. The standard methods of computational fluid dynamics (including magnetohydrodynamics) and gravitational N-body simulation are stressed by the huge dynamic range in physical quantities - density, pressure, temperature - that exist in nature. Ever-finer computational meshes and greater numbers of N-body particles are needed to capture the physics of the formation of things in the universe correctly.

The steady growth of computational speed and capacity through Moore's law has played a large role in improving the quality and reality of simulation results. However, the development of parallel algorithms has allowed researchers to leap ahead another factor of up to 1000 or more by harnessing the computational power of symmetric multi-processor (SMP) supercomputers or clusters of networked computers running Linux commonly called Beowulf clusters.

In recent years, the relative low cost of commodity servers running the Linux operating system and more importantly switches and network interface cards has led to the growth in performance and competitiveness of Beowulf clusters versus SMPs. The recent list of the Top 500 fastest supercomputers (www.top500.org) reveals that 55 out of the top 100 are clusters rather than SMPs or vectorized supercomputers. The price of commodity gigabit networking using familiar copper ethernet has dropped dramatically this past year and for many applications is competing directly with low-latency but higher-priced networking options such as Quadrics and Myrinet.

The spirit of building a Beowulf cluster is to get the most bang for the buck in terms of gigaflops per dollar. Most high performance Beowulfs now use low-latency networking with costs several times the cost of current commodity gigabit networking. Large-scale 200+ port gigabit switches are a slightly cheaper option but still eat significantly into the cost of a cluster. Networking costs alone can be more than half the cost. We describe here a new cheaper option that uses off-the-shelf 24-port commodity gigabit switches in a 256- node/512 CPU cluster. We see below that this configuration performs well with a HPL LINPACK benchmark of 1.11 Tflops placing it in the top 50 computers (rank 41) according to the Top 500 list of November 2002 and currently number one in Canada by this same measure. The key to achieving this high performance is new innovation in the networking topology involving both a stack of commodity 24-port gigabit SMC switches and the configuration of each Linux server as a network router through a second gigabit network port. Our economical networking strategy competes directly with both large-scale 200+ port switches and low-latency networking at a fraction of the cost. The ability to optimize the Linux kernel's various functions is also critical to getting the best performance.

Cluster Hardware Specifications

In this section, we describe the design and hardware

specifications of the cluster. The hardware was assembled and installed by Mynix Technologies, Montreal, PQ at the University of Toronto. The CITA Beowulf Cluster dubbed McKenzie is comprised of 268 dual Xeon 2.4 Ghz rack-mounted format Linux servers (536 processors in total) distributed over 7 racks (Figure 1). All the nodes are 1U format (1.75" high) with the exception of two 2U format head nodes. The hardware specifications for each server are given in Table 1. From the total of 268 nodes, 256 nodes are dedicated to parallel, message passing supercomputing, 8 nodes for code development and smaller scale applications, 2 spare nodes also running to act as hot replacements in case of hardware failures on the compute nodes and 2 head nodes. The main head node "bob" contains the home disk space as well as the root space images and Linux kernels for the compute slave nodes. All slave nodes boot through the network from bob using PXElinux allowing easy kernel upgrades and maintenance for the cluster nodes. A secondary master node "doug" mirrors bob's root and home directories on a daily basis and acts a backup in case of a bob crash. This allows quick recovery and continued operation if bob fails.

Motherboard, CPUs and Memory

Each server is based on the Intel Westville motherboard that fits into a 1U chassis and runs dual Xeon 2.4 Ghz processors and 4 memory slots. We currently are running with 1 GB RAM per node though we could expand to 2 GB. There are also 2 integrated gigabit network ports both of which we exploit in our networking topology. There is also one PCI slot that is unused.

Disks

Each server contains two 80 GB IDE hard drives each of which is divided into 3 partitions - 2 small 2 GB partitions to hold the root filesystem and the swap space and one large partition for scratch disk space. The root filesystem is installed on the first disk and swap on the second. Two empty partitions are reserved for possible new future Linux installations. The large partitions are joined with the Linux software RAID0 providing about 150GB of scratch disk space per node. This space is intended for checkpointing data but also future applications designed for out-of-core memory usage. The total available scratch space is about 46 TB.

The Westville board includes a Promise hardware raid controller. We discovered that detection of this controller in the BIOS made network booting impossible so we disabled the hardware raid configuration in the BIOS. We did examine the performance of the onboard raid controller using a patched Redhat installation provided by Intel. The RAID performance was similar if not slightly worse than Linux software RAID. The NFS performance of the Intel patched distribution was poor. This patch only worked for one specific kernel so we decided to go with Linux software raid to allow us the flexibility of kernel tuning for networking, disk and other performance issues. Network booting is also a necessity for installation and operation of a cluster our size so the Promise raid controller was seen as a major pain rather than a benefit. In the end, we are forced to boot the compute nodes with PXE or a boot CDROM and the head nodes themselves can only be booted with a boot CDROM. We hope these BIOS issues are resolved soon.

We also have attached a 3 TB RAID box on the head node to act as a centralized repository for simulation data.

The head nodes bob and doug were configured with 20 GB root partitions plus a spare 20 GB partition used for mirroring. Bob is used to install and monitor nodes on the cluster as well as acting as the cluster entry point and repository of centralized home disk space for users. Bob's root partition is mirrored daily on doug's spare partition and vice versa. Essential system files and the home filesystem are also mirrored from bob to doug daily. If bob crashes, doug can quickly take over cluster operation through a quick reboot of the mirrored partition and some minor system reconfiguration.

Cooling

Cooling is important for a densely packed 1U rack-mounted configuration. Each chassis contains 3 high-powered fans that draw air in through openings in the front and the sides of the chassis. Hot air is blow out the back. Our racks are located in a central machine room with large air-conditioning capacity. Floor tiles in the front and back of the machine are grilled to maximize cool airflow. We carefully monitor the temperature of each node using onboard sensors through the Linux kernel using the Ganglia toolkit. Generally, we find the cooling is adequate though we have identified a few hot nodes running near 70 deg. C and have taken action to cool them down. The mean node temperature when the machine is fully loaded is 50 deg. C that is within specs for the motherboard.

Power

We have allocated about 350 W of power per node according to the motherboard specifications. At full operation, the cluster requires about 90 kW of power.

Switches and Cables

The cluster is networked using 19 SMC Tiger 24-port configurable gigabit switches. Seventeen switches are used for the main 256-node cluster network while the development cluster is connected to its own switch and the 19th switch is reserved as a spare and connected to the running spare nodes. We defer the discussion of the network topology to the section below.

Rack Configuration

The nodes and switches are mounted on 7 racks as shown in Figure 1. The racks are 44U high with 128 compute nodes mounted on the first 3 and last 3 racks. The central rack is reserved for the head nodes, development nodes and spares as well as the stack of switches. The switches are mounted on the back of the racks to simplify the cabling. The interface is a special 1U monitor and keyboard which slide in and out of the rack.

TABLE 1. Mynix PowerRACK-HX Parts List

Nodes: 256 compute nodes + 8 development nodes + 2 head nodes + 2 spares = 268 total
Chassis: Chenbro RM11802 1U format (1.75" high)

Motherboard:	Intel Westville SE7500WV2
CPUS:	Dual Xeon 2.4GHz processors E7500 chipset/512KB L2 cache, 400 MHz system bus
Memory:	1 Gbyte DDR-200 RAM
Disk Drives:	2X80 Gbyte Seagate IDE drives
Networking:	Dual Intel Pro/1000XT gigabit ethernet Ports
Switches:	19 SMC Tiger SMC8624T 24-port managed gigabit switches 1U format

The head nodes are the same except that they have 2GB RAM and an extra 200GB hard drive housed in a 2U chassis (Chenbro RM21400).

Additional storage (beyond the disks on the individual nodes) is provided by a 3TB Arena RAID array. This unit has 16x200GB drives and is SCSI-attached to a master node.

Summary: In total, we have 46TB of distributed disk storage, 270GB RAM, 2km of cat6 network cables, 60m of Velcro to bundle cables together, and 40m of labeling tape to label the ends of all cables.

Figure 1. Mynix Technology Inc. PowerRACK-HX

Installation

Work on the cluster began a couple of weeks prior to delivery of the main hardware. We received some test nodes from Mynix, tested Linux kernel configurations and developed the installation procedure. Mynix delivered and installed the bulk of the hardware within 2 days and the machine was cabled and the Linux operating system was installed on each node by a small team of local experts in CITA and astronomy over the next few days.

The cluster was installed using OSCAR 2.0, an open source package designed for efficient Linux cluster installation[2]. We first installed a complete Redhat 7.3 distribution on the head node bob (a requirement for OSCAR) and ran the installation script. Building an oscar image was straightforward and node configuration and installation using PXElinux worked smoothly (after debugging the raid controller/netbooting BIOS conflict) in tests on single nodes but installing a cluster of our large size proved to be problematic.

It is important to know the identity of each node for maintenance as well as our networking topology. The only broadcast identifier is the MAC address unique to each network interface. Oscar does provide a MAC collection facility by listening on thc nctwork for DHCP requests. Unfortunately, the servers take a few minutes to reach the network booting stage in the BIOS and so simple interactive collection of MAC addresses and node installation one by one using the OSCAR MAC tool would have required more than 24 continuous hours of tedious work with human error playing a major factor.

We came up with a simple fast solution for installing and collecting MACs. We configured the dhcp server on the head node to assign IP numbers randomly to incoming requests to run the oscar PXElinux installation initrd ramdisk. In this way, large blocks of 10-20 nodes could be powered up simultaneously, netbooted and then oscar-installed through the head node. We tried larger number of power-ons but found that in practice that overloaded the head node so 10-20 was the practical limit. We signalled the completion of an installation by executing a script to initiate some hard drive activity and light up the red indicator light on the front of the node (Node shutdown + power down would have been preferable but did not work with our motherboard). In this way, the whole cluster was installed in a few hours with random IP number assignment.

At this stage, each node was fully installed and functional but the relation between the MAC/IP address and it's position on the racks was unknown. To determine each node's MAC address, we set up a simple network running through the second gigabit port and used it as a probe with a laptop point-to-point connection to determine the MAC addresses of the first port. MACs collected in this way took only a couple of hours. Once the table of MAC addresses and node positions on the rack were assembled a master /etc/dhcpd.conf file could be reset in some oscar database files using available scripts in the oscar packager. Nodes were then rebooted and assigned a sequential rather than a random IP number making easy identification on the racks.

We also double-checked this procedure by using the configurable SMC switch tools that report the probed MAC addresses on each switch port. This allowed us quickly to find a few misprobed nodes and establish the node identities on the racks unambiguously.

Networking

When considering options for networking the cluster, we discovered to our dismay that it can be very expensive. We decided against the proprietary low-latency networking options but learned that large-scale 200+ port switches were also very expensive and while cheaper than low-latency options would still consume a significant fraction of our budget. On the other hand, 24-port gigabit switches were very affordable and performed reasonably well according to specs so we considered networking schemes that could take advantage of this inexpensive hardware.

Fat-tree networks that link switches together through a hierarchy are a straightforward configuration that provide connectivity but relatively low cross-sectional bandwith. Each node comes with a second gigabit port, however, which could be exploited in some way through point to point connections with other machines. With this in mind we came up with the following scheme. Switches (or pairs of trunked switches) can be thought of as separate tightly coupled networks of a few dozen nodes. These nodes can be assigned to vertices in some more complex network topology. How can you connect these vertices to form a high-bandwidth global network linking all the compute nodes? After loading a switch with compute nodes there are few ports left to link to other vertices. However, each compute node provides a single connection through its second port that can in principle be connected to a compute node on an adjacent network vertex. If we enable routing capability in each compute node, network traffic can be relayed through the second port to other nodes. This was the strategy we employed in setting up a high-bandwidth global network.

The Fat-Tree Maintenance Network

Before setting up our high performance global network, we first set up a simple fat-tree that we treat as a robust but lower-performance maintenance network. This network was used to install the cluster originally. In our configuration, we trunk pairs of switches together making network vertices containing 48 ports with a total of 8 vertices using 16 switches. We first connect 32 compute nodes to each vertex. For 6 vertices, we run a 4-port trunk to a 17th master switch filling it to capacity. The fat-tree networking is completed by connecting the last two vertices with 4-port trunks to 2 vertices trunked to the master switch. The head nodes bob and doug, plus the development and spare nodes are all plugged into this network as well allowing direct communication between all available nodes.

This fat-tree network configuration is robust and provides connectivity to all the 256 nodes and is adequate for maintenance, installation and embarassingly parallel applications. However, the cross-sectional bandwidth is not at all ideal for heavy duty MPI applications. We now describe how we use this fat-tree network to bootstrap to our high-bandwidth network which runs predominantly through point to point connections between the second network ports of all machines.

The Cross-Diagonally Connected Cube Network

The network vertices described above can be thought of as independent networks that we can connect to each other according to some topology. The use of a master switch to build a fat tree is one such topology but it has fairly low cross-sectional bandwidth. How can we use the second port on each compute node to connect these vertices to increase the network bandwidth and minimize network hops to reduce latency? There are many possibilities but we finally settled on a cubic network topology with a twist (see Figure 2.)

In our chosen topology, the 8 network vertices are arranged on the corners of a cube. Communication between vertices can occur along the edges of the cube but we also connect opposite corners through diagonals that cross through the cube centroid. We call this topology a Cross-Diagonal Connected Cube (CDCC) (although we're sure it has its own name in the computer science literature). Each vertex then has 4 outgoing lines of communication to its adjacent corners and opposite along the diagonal.

The CDCC topology requires hard-wired routing tables between nodes as described below. We have 32 gigabit lines on each vertex provided by the second network port on each compute node and 4 vertex connections. We therefore assign 8-gigabit lines to each vertex connection. These lines connect 8 compute nodes on one vertex to another 8 on a neighbouring vertex through direct port to port connections with a straight-thru cable. In this way, there is an 8-gigabit pipeline connecting each vertex which must be shared between 32 compute nodes. Also, the 4-port trunks connecting pairs of switches are 4-gigabit pipelines relaying traffic for 16 compute nodes per switch.

In this way, the CDCC topology with 256 nodes approximately represents a fully-switched network running at 250 Mbit, although it may be slightly better since nodes on the same switch are fully-switched at 1 Gbit. When constructing the routing tables, the maximum number of network hops to get from one node to another is 4 so latency can be greater than a fully-switched system as well. The performance of this configuration is about half the 500 Mbit performance that is expected for large gigabit switches that typically connect 16 ports to an 8-gigabit backplane internally. Latency is also about 4 times greater. However, the total cost for the 17 required 24-port switches plus cabling is currently about 20% the cost of a large switch. We show below that our cluster provides competitive benchmark speeds for similar clusters with better networking and performs well for our applications.

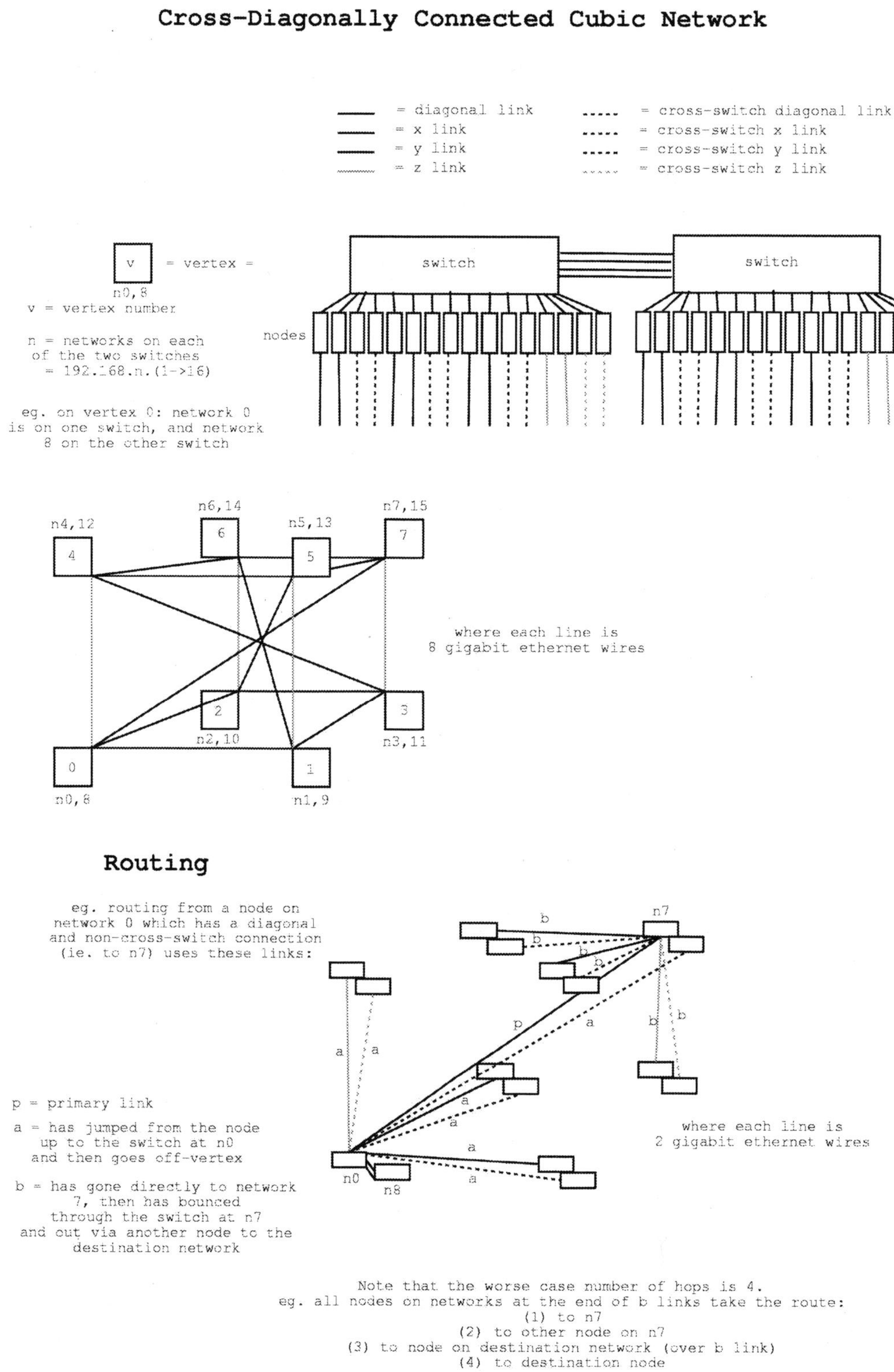

Figure 2. Cross-Diagonally Connected Cubic Networking Topology, Cabling and Routing Scheme

Cabling

The task of cabling the cluster also proved to be formidable but we came up with some ways to minimize confusion and tangling. Connections from the first ethernet port to the switches is straightforward if the switches are centralized to one location at the centre of the rack array in a stack. Network cables are run over and under the cluster in small bundles and colour coded by rack number and then plugged into their appropriate ports in the central stack of switches. Although tedious, this stage of the cabling took a small team of people including Peter Martin's sons and their girlfriends about two days to complete. We point out that the same cabling effort is required even for more expensive multi-port switches so there is no significant overhead in manual labour.

In the second stage, it was necessary to wire the CDCC network using the point to point connections through the second network port on each node. Wiring these connections could potentially lead to a tangled mess of cables if the nodes are ordered sequentially according to their vertex numbers. A simple solution to this wiring problem is to re-order the nodes on the racks in pairs that are to be connected to one another. In this way, only a short 1 foot length of cable is required and wiring can be done quickly. The logic of the connectivity of the CDCC network was used to create the correct ordered list of nodes on the rack for this arrangement as well as a wiring diagram for the connecting cables to the right switches in the fat-tree diagram. The only extra level of complexity for doing things this way in comparison to 200+ port monster switches is the node ordering and the need to make sure each cable is connected to the correct port in the switch stack. In practice, we have re-wired the network a couple of times to test the performance of different topologies and it generally only takes a few hours to do.

Routing

Another essential (and complex) part of getting the CDCC network to perform was the configuration of the routing tables for each Linux server. Network packets relayed through each server on this server have to know where to go according to our defined network topology.

A nice part of our design is that we have a back-up maintenance network (the fat-tree) that we can always use to gain access to each node in case of routing problems or broken links in the CDCC network. This allowed us to experiment extensively with the scripts for generating the routing tables of the CDCC and led to an optimized system. Our strategy is to generate purely static routing tables on each server with a simple script at startup. Each of these scripts contains routing commands to establish about 50 static routes to individual nodes and sub-networks (vertices) in the CDCC network. We find this system works very well in practice and can be taken up and down quickly if necessary.

Our arrangement is also very fault-tolerant in case of node failures or broken links. If one or more nodes fails in the system, it will create holes in the CDCC network but as a contingency we can route around the broken nodes simply by using the fat-tree network. We have written a simple network repair script that pings all neighbours on the CDCC - if a node fails to answer we attempt to establish a direct route to it through the fat-tree - if that fails the node is assumed to be dead. In this way, we can continue to run jobs on the cluster even when main compute nodes go down. Either the hot spares, or development nodes can fill in while we replace the failed nodes.

Figure 2. shows some final details of our routing scheme that are worth pointing out. It turned out that the network performance of the trunks was not as good as we expected. We therefore modified our routing scheme to avoid using the trunks as much as possible. Network traffic from one node to another on different vertices used cross links that avoid the trunks. The only network traffic going through the trunks is between the nodes on bonded pairs of switches.

Benchmarks

We ran the High-performance Linpack Benchmark (HPL), a portable implementation for Distributed-Memory Computers to measure the speed of our cluster and compare with others on the Top 500 list [1]. This code uses the Message Passing Interface (MPI) libraries. The actual benchmark involves the inversion of the largest matrix that can be stored on your cluster. In our case, the matrix size was 160000 X 160000 elements. We compiled the code using the Intel C compiler icc version 7.0 and linked to the Intel MKL math libraries and Kazushige Goto's optimized BLAS libraries [3]. We used the LAM version 6.6b1 for the as the MPI library. The HPL output from our fastest benchmark is shown in Table 2. We achieved a speed of 1.11 Teraflops about 45% the peak speed of 2.46 Teraflops. This ratio of real to peak speed is comparable to many of the machines quoted on the November 2002 Top 500 list including similar sized clusters running with proprietary networking such as Myrinet. Our ranking on the list would currently be number 41 making us the fastest quoted supercomputer in Canada. Of course, it remains to be seen how we will rank on the next list released in a few months since these trends tend to evolve very quickly!

Table 2. HPL logfile output for our 512 processor benchmark. The measured speed is 1113 Gflops or 1.11 Teraflops.

```
============================================================
T/V            N      NB   P   Q    Time          Gflops
----------------------------------------------------------------------------
W01R2L4     160000  200   8   64   2452.90       1.113e+03
----------------------------------------------------------------------------
||Ax-b||_oo / ( eps * ||A||_1  * N        ) =     0.0043290 ...... PASSED
||Ax-b||_oo / ( eps * ||A||_1  * ||x||_1  ) =     0.0023799 ...... PASSED
||Ax-b||_oo / ( eps * ||A||_oo * ||x||_oo ) =     0.0004091 ...... PASSED
```

SCIENCE

At the time of writing this paper, we have just begun some scientific production runs using the cluster. These include a simulation of the collision of two galaxies each containing central supermassive blackholes and magnetohydrodynamic (MHD) simulations of the accretion of gas onto blackhole.

The galaxy collision is a pure N-body simulation using more than 300 million particles integrated for about 10000 timesteps representing a physical time of several billion years. The goal is learn about the process of the formation of central blackhole binaries and their effect on the internal structure of galaxies. Figure 3. is a snapshot from the simulation showing the galaxies shortly after collision. While the current results are still preliminary, the ability to run simulations at this spatial and time resolution will be revolutionary in helping our understanding of the dynamics and evolution of galaxies.

Figure 3. A snapshot of the collision of two spiral galaxies using 307.2 million particles computed on the CITA Beowulf Cluster McKenzie

References

[1] Top 500 Supercomputers website, http://www.top500.org
[2] The OSCAR cluster installation package, http://oscar.sourceforge.net
[3] Kazushige Goto's Optimized BLAS Library, http://www.cs.utexas.edu/users/flame/goto/

Performance Evaluation of a Speculative Network Processor

Jürgen Foag, Maresa Praxenthaler, Thomas Wild [a]

[a] Institute for Integrated Circuits, Technical University of Munich, 80290 Munich, Bavaria, Germany
{Juergen.Foag, Maresa.Praxenthaler, Thomas.Wild}@ei.tum.de

Beside high bandwidth, real-time networking applications mainly require short end-to-end latencies. Up to now, network processors are focused in particular on application flexibility and throughput, but generally neglect fundamental new approaches concerning processing delay reduction. This paper describes the implementation and the evaluation of the parallel speculative packet processing architecture and of a reference architecture We show that a latency reduction of up to 26.3 percent can be obtained by the speculative approach in comparison to traditional implementations.

Au delà d'une forte bande passante, les applications réseau en temps réel demandent de basses latences. Jusqu'à maintenant, les processeurs réseau sont dédiés en particulier à la flexibilité des applications et au débit, mais négligent généralement la réduction du temps de traitement. Cet article expose l'implémentation et l'évaluation d'une architecture parallele de traitement spéculatif de paquets, par rapport à une architecture de référence. Nous montrons que cette approche spéculative peut mener jusqu'à 26.3% de réduction de la latence par rapport à des implémentations traditionnelles.

1 Introduction

Distributed high performance computing systems possess a strong dependency on the performance of the underlying network infrastructure. By increasing network throughput, the performance bottleneck is shifting from the bandwidth of transmission media to the processing capacity of hosts and transmit systems like routers [1]. The performance of these devices is significantly affected by their architecture [2]. High-speed networking consists not only of the quest for high bandwidth. In the same way, low latency as well as the ability to cope with high bandwidth-x-delay product paths is required [3].

Recently, *network processors (NP)* have been introduced to cope with throughput requirements of OC-48 (2.5 Gbit/s) and higher. They normally comprise multiple micro-programmable RISC processor cores, each realizing a simultaneous multithreading architecture [4]. By means of an efficient software implementation of message-parallelized protocol processing, high performance on NPs can be achieved. In addition, some NP provide dedicated hardware blocks to accelerate calculation intensive networking functionalities.

While these properties made a throughput increase possible, optimization of packet processing delay on a NP was rather uncared. To make real-time applications possible, the delay problems are bypassed: For instance, *content delivery networking (CDN)* shifts centralized real-time application content through the network closer to the user to distributed content engines [5]. Consequently, essential drawback is a high administration effort for the distributed system components.

A new concept called *speculative packet processing* was presented in [6]. Therein, the benefits were demonstrated by an abstract concept verification. Now in this paper, the ongoing work is presented, which describes the system implementation and presents the results of the performance evaluation. The principal contribution is the demonstration of the benefits of the new concept for packet processing based on a real networking simulation environment.

The remainder of this paper is organized as follows. Section 2 gives a short overview to previous work done in packet processing optimization and parallelization. The concept already presented and the architecture model are briefly summarized in section 3. Section 4 describes the performance evaluation of the speculative system and discusses the results. Finally, the conclusion and future work is discussed in section 5.

2 Related Work: Protocol Processing Methodologies

To cope with increasing transmission rates for high-speed networking, extensive research of protocol processing methodologies has been done or is still done [7] [8] et al. Principally, the results can be classified into suitable *protocol specifications* and appropriate *protocol implementations* [9]. The most common methodologies are:

Parallel Protocol Processing:

To allow parallel protocol processing, parallelization uses replications to perform the work of a single processing unit. In [10], various process architecture models are summarized. They fall into three general categories: *horizontal* (layer parallelism, functional parallelism), *vertical* (connection parallelism, message parallelism) and *hybrid*. Although each process architecture has different structural characteristics, it is generally possible to implement the same protocol functionality [11].

Pipelining:

Pipelining is an implementation technique whereby multiple instructions are overlapped in execution [12]. To achieve a performance gain by processing packets in parallel, protocol layer tasks can be assigned to different pipeline stages. Packet data enter into the pipeline, progress through the connected stages and exit the pipeline. Thus, processing latency corresponds to the sum of individual pipeline stage delays.

Multithreading:

The majority of network processors use multithreading (MT) as execution concept. Originally, MT was introduced in the domain of microprocessors with the target of an increased number of instructions per cycle. It is enabled through the capability of context switches between threads to obtain an efficient load of CPU resources. Examples for the different kinds of MT are coarse-grained MT [13], fine-grained MT [14] and simultaneous MT [15].

Jacobsons' header prediction and Woodsides' protocol bypass:

As in [16], Jacobson header prediction supports unidirectional data transfer (TCP) by handling two common cases:

1. If TCP is sending data, the next expected segment for this connection is an ACK for outstanding data.
2. If TCP is receiving data, the next expected segment for this connection is the next in-sequence data segment.

In [17], Woodside presents a generalization of Jacobson's Header Prediction using a protocol bypass on sender and on receiver side. For frequent receipts of packets with identical protocol control information, the usual implementation of the protocol stack is bypassed via a fast path.

Summary:

Dominating factors on packet processing time for simple data manipulation functions, such as checksumming, and field value incrementation are the primary memory access times, i.e. time to write and read. Consequently, performance will most likely be limited by the capacity of the shared bus and the memory system [1]. This is intensified by the fact that access latency of memory systems using DRAMs is decreasing at a slower speed than CPU clock rates are increasing [18]. Parallel processing is focused on increasing protocol processing performance in terms of system bandwidth [19]. However, processing latency of individual packets stays unaffected. While pipelining increases the packet throughput, the complete latency which is the sum of the individual stage processing latencies keeps unchanged [20]. Multithreading is an effective technique when multiple threads share a system. But, single-thread performance is not improved [21]. Fig. 1 shows exemplarily two threads T_1 and T_2 which are processed multithreaded or speculatively, respectively. Each comprises the packet processing tasks of one data packet.

The latency of a packet in case of multithreading support is the sum of processing delay of the context in the processor units (PU), memory (MEM) access times and arbitra-

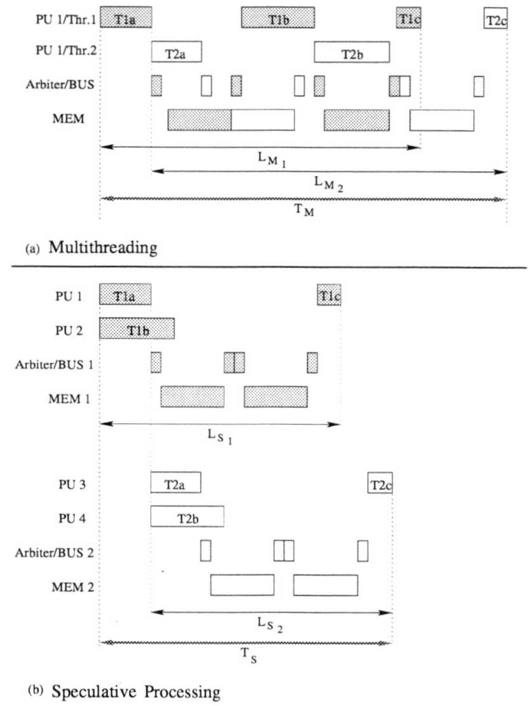

Figure 1. Multithreading and Parallel Processing

tion times of shared resources. It is obvious that processing latency of the second packet in case of multithreading support L_{M_2} is less than in case of starting it not until termination of the previous one.

However, a decrease of packet processing delay, i.e. the time interval between thread processing start T_{1_a} and end T_{1_c} in conjunction with memory requests, is only achieved if shared resources between multiple packet contexts are avoided.

In case of speculative processing (b), the complete thread that refers to one packet is subdivided into several. Arbitration for the memory bus as well as MEM is shared between them. By duplication of shared resources, i.e. MEM1 and MEM2, the access bottleneck between contexts of different packets can be eliminated. Thus, latencies T_{S_1} and T_{S_2} are significantly reduced in comparison to their multithreading counterparts.

Weaknesses of protocol bypass and TCP header prediction are constraints which are inherent to the methodology. The applied prediction is based upon control and state transition information of connection-oriented TCP traffic, e.g. connection establishment and termination. The state information of a packet is merely kept in network end systems, but not in transmit nodes [22]. Furthermore, prediction of connectionless traffic, which is used commonly used for real-time applications, i.e. UDP, is not supported [23].

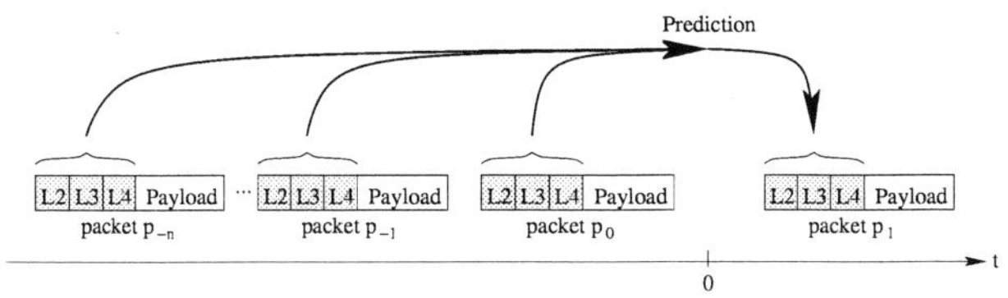

Figure 2. Protocol Stack Prediction Scheme

3 Protocol Processing Methodology & Architecture

The concept is based on two components: *Protocol Stack Prediction* and *Speculative Packet Processing*. Using both, this packet processing concept serves to overcome processing latency limitations which result from network layer hierarchies.

Protocol Stack Prediction:

The decision how to handle and forward a packet is done upon the information which is contained in the packet header. The header of the data-link layer, the network layer and the transport layer is hierarchically arranged. I.e. the type of a higher layer of the ISO/OSI reference model of communication is derived from the header of the lower layer [24]. To circumvent a serial extraction, *protocol stack prediction* predicts the protocol stack of the next packet. The scheme is depicted in Fig. 2.

The prediction is based on the history of packets received earlier. It should be noted, that the prediction *not* only delivers protocol layer types of a packet. In a store-and-forward architecture, this information could be gathered quickly from the packet but would not influence significantly processing delay. Furthermore, additional information which is required for control point processing is implicitly provided by the prediction. For instance, costly processing for checksum verification of layer 2 has to be done in front of processing of layer 3 as in Fig. 3.

Speculative Data Packet Processing:

Based on the prediction results, execution of protocol stack processes is done as described above. In this context, a process means a functional task of packet header field analysis or manipulation. Examples are value verification, checksum calculation or address compare. Their execution order depends on associated protocols, supported applications (e.g. Differentiated Services or Multiprotocol Label Switching) as well as on requirements of the networking environment (access, core or edge). In Fig. 4, the flow of speculative data packet processing is illustrated.

Tasks T_{Li_j} of one protocol layer i are grouped to a *thread*. The order of processing is indicated by an increasing value of j. Threads for protocol layer 2, 3 and 4 are started simultaneously. The determination of the protocol layer type of layer 3 is done by execution of a so-called

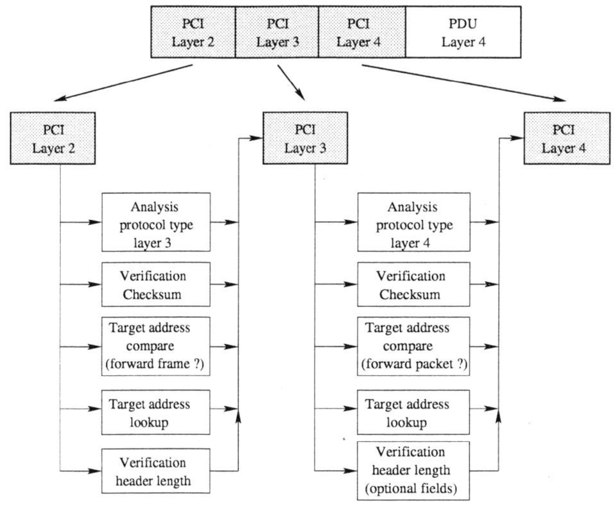

Figure 3. Protocol Stack Prediction

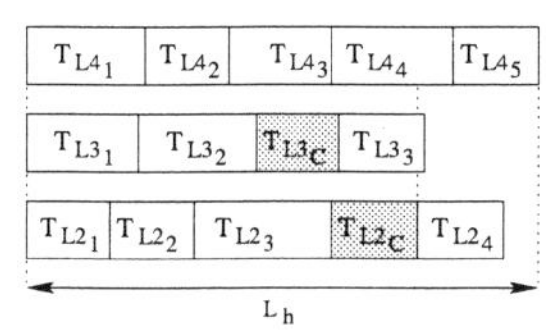

Figure 4. Speculative Packet Processing

checktask T_{L2_C} which is highlighted in grey. For layer 4, the checktask is T_{L3_C}. By finishing checktask processing, the data dependency for the next higher protocol layer is resolved (see dashed line). Two cases can occur: a prediction hit or a misprediction. The first case, which is illustrated in the figure above, delivers a correct assumption of the higher layer type. Consequently, execution of tasks for the upper layer has been made on correct input data and the results can be kept. Tasks which are simultaneously processed can be proceeded. Remaining tasks can be executed in the following. The complete processing time is called hit latency L_h. Else, in case of a misprediction for layer 3, which results from analysis of T_{L2_C}, a second prediction is requested. It provides the layer type of layer 4 based on knowledge of layer 2 and 3. Dependent on its output, either a prediction hit for layer 4 follows the latency L_{mh}, Figure 5, or a misprediction L_{mm} (not shown). Both latencies possess a larger value than L_h.

Summarized, the mean processing latency for a sample of N packets is

$$\overline{L} = \frac{1}{N}\left[N_h L_h + N_{mh} L_{mh} + N_{mm} L_{mm}\right] \quad (1)$$

with the number of packets N_h for case hit, N_{mh} for case layer three miss / layer four hit and N_{mm} for case layer three miss / layer four miss. Goal of the concept is to

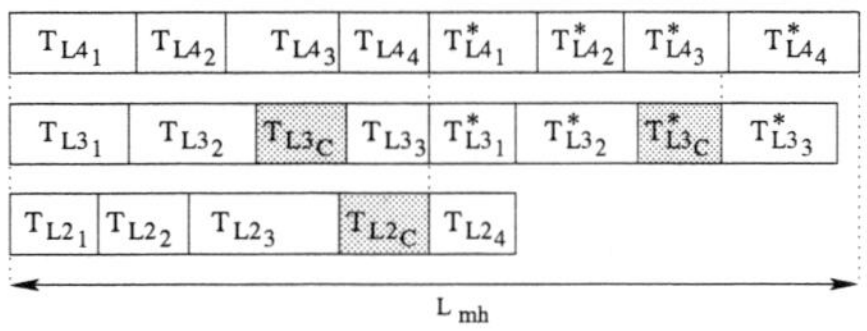

Figure 5. Speculative Packet Processing: Case Layer 2 miss/ Layer 3 hit

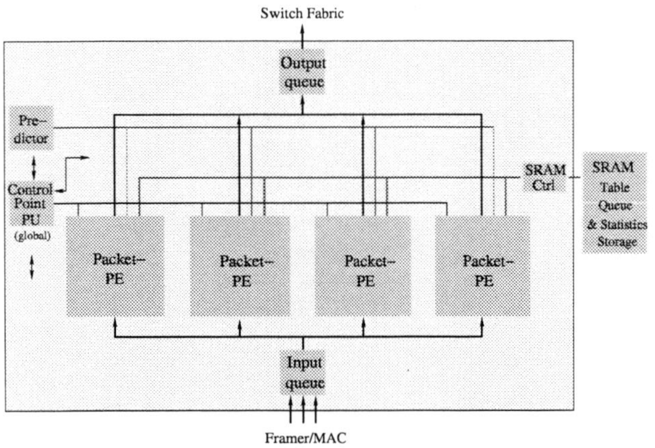

Figure 6. System architecture

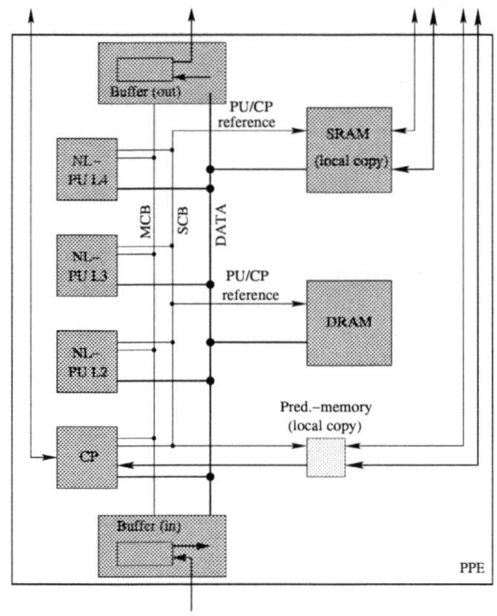

Figure 7. PPE architecture

achieve a value for $\overline{L_N}$ which is less than in case of traditional processing.

Architecture

In Fig. 6, the hybrid system architecture is depicted. It implements per-packet parallelism with one received packet per packet processing element (PPE). The predictor unit delivers the value that stands for the protocol-stack characteristic. The global control-point processing unit (PU) maintains the system procedure.

In detail, one of the four PPE from above is illustrated in Fig. 7. The received packet data is stored in DRAM. Based on predicted header boundaries, the headers of layer 2, 3 and 4 are stored in the general purpose registers of the assigned network-processing units (NW-PU). One NW-PU completely processes the layer packet header. The local prediction memory disposes of a small table which contains the prediction values.

4 Performance Evaluation

To evaluate the proposed processing concept within a real networking environment, the system implementation is done in SystemC [25]. As reference model, an additional implementation is done which follows the pseudo-parallel processing methodology. This method disposes of identical parallel processing resources. Only difference is the lack of a prediction unit and the fact, that processing of upper protocol layers is started immediately after resolution of their types. Thus, the protocol stack differs from another only in the predictive process steps. The system is stimulated at its ingress by actual network traffic which is composed as listed below (T: *Traffic*; GE: *Gigabit E.*):

T	Protocol Stack
1	95% TCP/IP4/GE 5% UDP/IP4/GE
2	50% TCP/IP4/GE 50% UDP/IP4/GE
3	50% TCP/IP4/GE 50% UDP/IP6/GE
4	50% TCP/IP4/GE 50% UDP/IP6/PoS
5	80% TCP/IP4/GE 20% UDP/IP4/GE
6	100% TCP/IP4/GE

While T_1 corresponds to real protocol distributions [26], remaining traffic serve only for performance studies under worst case conditions.

Fig. 8 shows the mean latency per PPE and per packet. For traffic 1, the number of processing cycles for the speculative is 858 versus 1107 in the pseudo parallel case. The least difference occurs for traffic 4 with 1160 versus 1239 cycles. For actual network processor cycles of 400 MHz, the difference of 249 cycles concludes to a latency reduction of 0.6225 μs. Along the networking path, at each Internet service provider ingress, time consuming diffserv functionalities have to be done, e.g. packet classification and policing. Thus, multiple times the reduction can be achieved. Considering real-time applications and additional queuing delays along the network path, the putative small latency reduction of one network processor cannot be neglected.

Thus, the latency reduction r within a PPE for traffic 1 is 26.3 % as in Fig. 9. In case of a worse prediction hit rate, which is achieved for traffic 4, r is 6.3 %. However, it is nevertheless positive.

Considering a network processor cycle of 400 MHz and

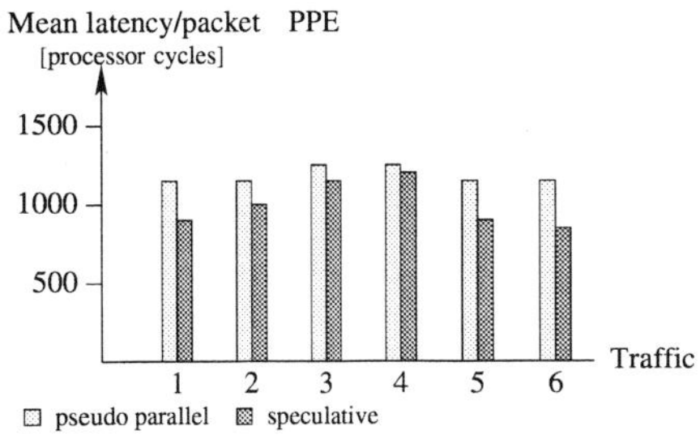

Figure 8. PPE Latency

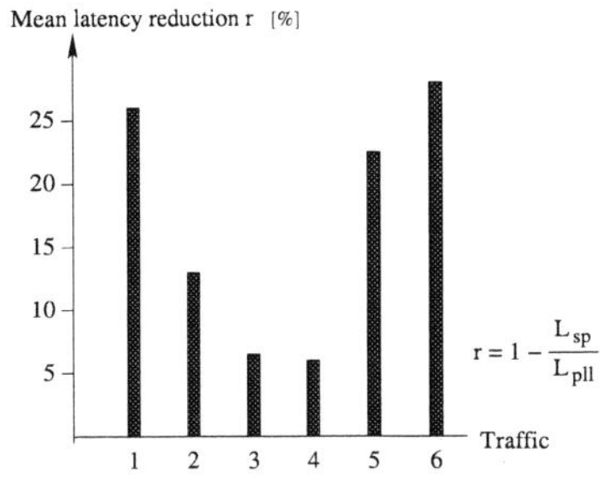

Figure 9. Latency Reduction

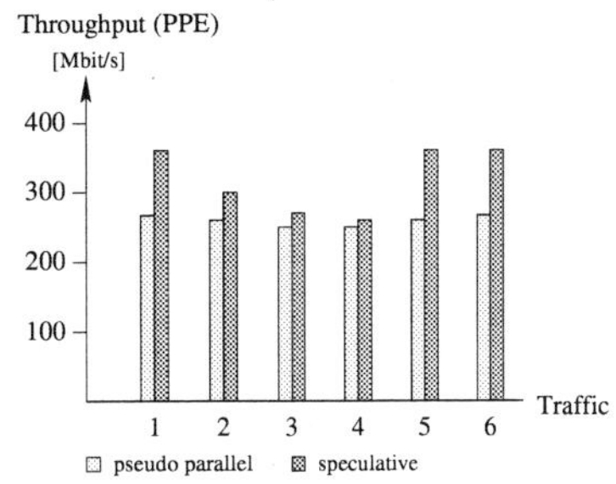

Figure 10. Throughput

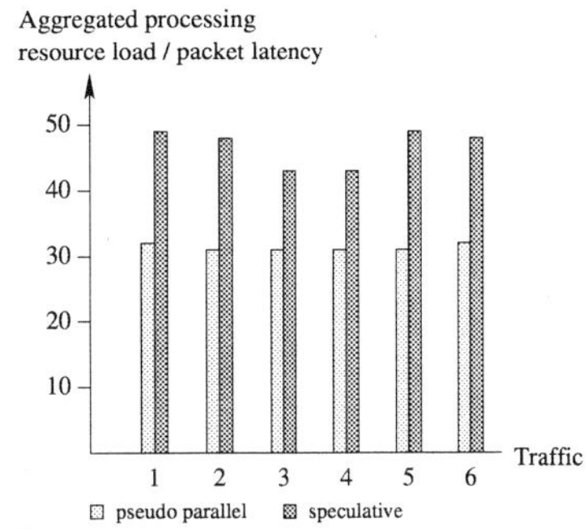

Figure 11. Aggregated Processing Resource Load

simulation packets of 96 bytes length, the throughput for traffic 1 of one speculative PPE is 358 Mbit/s. In case of pseudo-parallel processing, 278 Mbit/s is obtained.

Fig. 11 shows the aggregated processing resource load. It is the sum of busy times of the layer-PU 2, 3 and 4 compared to three times the simulation duration. The load of the speculative system is about 12 to 18 percent higher than the reference model load. This results from blocked shared memory requests due to concurrent access trials. Furthermore, for traffic 1 to 5, occurring mispredictions require additional layer processing. Despite of a worse prediction hit rate in case of traffic 3 and 4, the value of the relative system load is less due to a larger amount of processing cycles.

Fig. 12 shows the layer-processor load separated into layer-PU 2, 3 and 4. In particular, costly diffserv functionalities comprise classification, policing and accounting. These tasks are processed by the layer-4 processor. In case of mispredictions, the load is 77 percent, while 44 percent load is used in case of pseudo-parallel processing.

Reasons for the significant increase of system load can be derived from Fig. 13. Due to concurrent trials to accesses shared resources, the shared bus arbiter of the speculative system is busy between 74 and 82 percents of the packet processing time. In the reference model, only 4 percents of concurrent arbitration is present. This results from the fact, that request of shared resources is more relaxed. Utilization of the shared bus is about 19 to 27 percents which results from occurring mispredictions. For pseudo-parallel processing, it is only 7 percent.

5 Conclusions

We have presented simulation results, stimulated by real network traffic, which demonstrate the benefit of the proposed speculative processing concept. Processing delay can be reduced up to 26.3 percent without drawbacks on system throughput. Further work will concentrate on other prediction algorithms as well as on optimized egress scheduling algorithms.

References

1. M. Bjoerkman, P. Gunningberg, *Locking Effects in Multiprocessor Implementations of Protocols* ACM Sigcomm 93, Sep. 1993.
2. D.D. Clark, *Modularity and Efficiency in Protocol Implementation* NIC RFC 817, 1982.
3. J.P.G. Sterbenz, *Protocols for High-Speed Networks: A Brief Retrospective Survey of High-Speed Networking Research* IFIP/IEEE Workshop on Protocols for High Speed Networks, May 2002.
4. S. Lakshmanamurthy, K. Liu, Y. Pun, L. Huston, U. Naik, *Network Processor Performance Analysis Methodology* Intel Technical Journal, Vol. 6, Aug. 2002.
5. T. Vaseeharan, M. Maheswaran, *Towards a Novel Architecture for Wide-Area Data Caching and Replication* Interna-

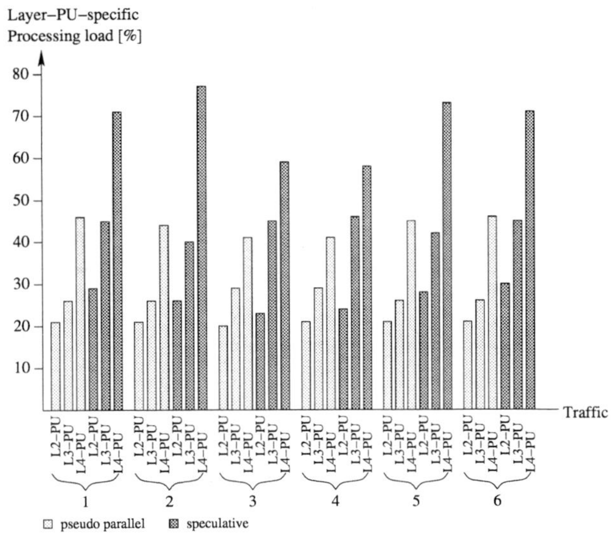

Figure 12. Individual Processing Resource Load

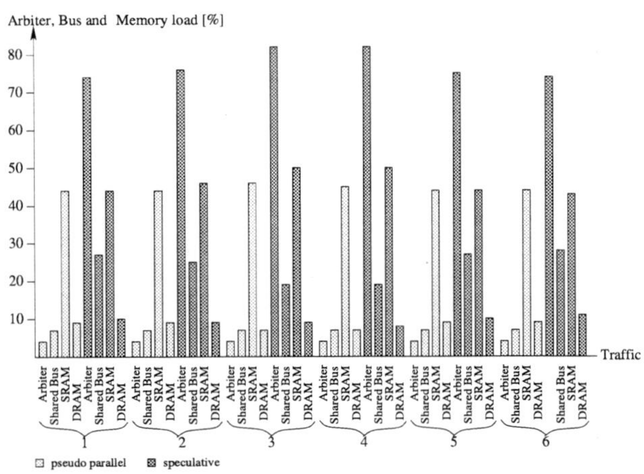

Figure 13. Arbitration- / Bus- and Memory-Load

tional Conference on Internet Computing, Las Vegas, Jun. 2000.

6. J. Foag, N. Pazos, T. Wild, W. Brunnbauer, *Self-adaptive Parallel Processing Architecture for High-Speed Networking* Proc. 16th Annual International Symposium on High Performance Computing Systems and Applications, Jun., 2002.
7. D. Clark, *Protocol Design and Performance* Proc. IEEE INFOCOM'95, Boston, Apr. 1995.
8. M. Zitterbart, B. Stiller, A. Tantawy, *A Model for Flexible High-Performance Communication Subsystems* IEEE Journal on Selected Areas in Communications 11, May 1993.
9. M. Heddes, E. Ruetsche, *A Survey of Parallelism in Communication Subsystems* IBM Zurich Research Laboratory, Res. Rep. RZ 2570, 1994.
10. D.C. Schmidt, T. Suda, *The Performance of Alternative Threading Architectures for Parallel Communication Subsystems* Submitted to Journal of Parallel and Distributed Processing, 1996.
11. D.C. Schmidt, T. Suda, *Adaptive: A Framework for Experimenting with High-Performance Transport System Process Architectures* International Conference on Computer Communication Networks, San Diego, Jun. 1993.
12. J. Hennessy, D. Patterson, *Computer Architecture, A Quantitative Approach* 2nd Edition, Morgan Kaufmann Publishers, Inc., San Francisco, 1996.
13. S. Storino, A. Aipperspach, J. Borkenhagen, S. Levenstein, *A commercial multithreaded RISC processor* International Solid State Circuits Conference, Feb. 1998.
14. R. Alverson, D. Callahan, D. Cummings, B. Koblenz, A. Poerterfield, B. Smith, *The Tera computer system* International Conference on Supercomputing, Jun. 1990.
15. D. Tullsen, S. Eggers, H. Levy, *Simultaneous Multithreading: Maximizing On-Chip Parallelism* Proc. of 22nd Annual International Symposium on Computer Architecture, Santa Kargherita Ligure, Jun. 1995.
16. V. Jacobson, *Congestion Avoidance and Control* ACM Computer Communication Review, Oct. 1988.
17. C.M. Woodside, K. Ravinadran, R.G. Franks, *The Protocol Bypass Concept for High Speed OSI Data Transfer* IFIP Workshop on Protocols for High Speed Networks, Nov. 1990.
18. D. Patterson, J. Hennessy, *Computer Organization and Design: The Hardware/Software Interface* Morgan Kaufmann Publishers, 1994.
19. D. Schmidt, T. Suda, *Measuring the Perfomance of Parallel Message-based Process Architectures* IEEE INFOCOM, Boston, Apr. 1995.
20. M. Kaiserswerth, *The Parallel Protocol Engine* IEEE/ACM Transactions on Networking, 1993.
21. S. Wallace, B. Clader, D. Tullsen, *Threaded Multiple Path Execution* 25th International Symposium on Computer Architecture, Jun. 1998.
22. K. Ravindran, G. Singh, C. Woodside, *Architectural Concepts in Implementation of End-system Protocols for High Performance Communications* IEEE International Conference on Network Protocols, Oct. 1996.
23. W. R. Stevens, *TCP/IP Illustrated, Volume 1* Addison-Wesley, Logman Inc., 1999.
24. *ISO 7498. Information Processing Systems - Open Systems Interconnection - Basic Reference Model* International Standard, ISO, 1984.
25. *http://www.systemc.org*
26. K. Claffy, G. Miller, K. Thompson, *The nature of the beast: recent traffic measurements from an Internet backbone* Proc. of INET 98.

Traffic Prediction Algorithm for Speculative Network Processors

Jürgen Foag, Thomas Wild [a]

[a] Institute for Integrated Circuits, Technical. University of Munich, 80290 Munich, Bavaria, Germany
{Juergen.Foag, Thomas.Wild}@ei.tum.de

To support real-time applications, for instance Voice-over-IP, network infrastructure has to provide high bandwidth as well as short end-to-end latency. To cope with both, network processors (NP) are selected. Current NP support transmission rates of OC-48. However, due to sequential packet layer processing, processing delay is not optimized. To solve this problem, speculative packet processing is applied, which requires accurate traffic prediction. In this article, we present a flexible dynamic protocol stack prediction algorithm which is well-suited for accurate traffic prediction and simulations show that it can sustain traffic bursts as well as transitions to changed traffic characteristics.

Afin d'assurer le support d'applications en temps-réel, comme par exemple la téléphonie IP,les infrastructures réseau doivent fournir à la fois une forte bande-passante, de même qu'une latence minimale. Les processeurs réseau (NP) sont utilisés afin de gérer ces deux nécessités. Les processeurs réseau actuels supportent les taux de transmission OC-48 mais le délai de traitement n'est pas optimisé, notamment à cause du traitement séquenciel de la couche paquet. Afin de résoudre ce probléme, un traitement spéculatif au niveau des paquets est appliqué.Ceci recquiert une prévision précise du traffic. Nous présentons dans cet article un algorithme dynamique prédictif adapté aux prévisions précises de trafic. Les simulations montrent qu'il est capable de prendre en compte à la fois les pics de trafic, mais aussi les changements de caractéristiques du trafic.

1 Introduction

Distributed high performance computing systems possess a strong dependency on the performance of the underlying network infrastructure. By increasing network throughput, the performance bottleneck is shifting from the bandwidth of transmission media to the processing capacity of hosts and transmit systems like routers [1]. The performance of these devices is significantly affected by their architecture [2]. High-speed networking consists not only of the quest for high bandwidth. In the same way, low latency as well as the ability to cope with high bandwidth-x-delay product paths is required [3].

Recently, *network processors (NP)* have been introduced to cope with throughput requirements of OC-48 (2.5 Gbit/s) and higher. They normally comprise multiple micro-programmable RISC processor cores, each realizing a simultaneous multithreading architecture [4]. By means of an efficient software implementation of message-parallelized protocol processing, high performance on NPs can be achieved. In addition, some NP provide dedicated hardware blocks to accelerate calculation intensive networking functionalities.

While these properties made a throughput increase possible, optimization of packet processing delay on a NP was rather uncared. To make real-time applications possible, the delay problems are bypassed: For instance, *content delivery networking (CDN)* shifts centralized real-time application content through the network closer to the user to distributed content engines [5]. Consequently, essential drawback is a high administration effort for the distributed system components.

In [6], as a new concept speculative packet processing was introduced. To evaluate it, an abstract concept verification was done, which illustrated the benefits. The concept comprises two components: *protocol stack prediction* and *speculative data processing*. The latter exploits speculative resolution of network layer dependencies inherent to the packet. To obtain a significant decrease of processing latency, the former has to provide a high prediction accuracy. In [7], the system implementation, which is realized in SystemC , is shown together with results of the associated performance evaluation.

The main contribution of the ongoing work, which is presented within this article, is the presentation of the dynamic prediction algorithm. It is capable of fast self-adaptation to modified traffic characteristics, for example for changes during daytime. With randomized generated traffic, which complies with current traffic distributions, the algorithm is evaluated and showed high accuracy. In addition, the architecture of the prediction instance is explained to insert it in the speculative packet processing device.

The remainder of this paper is organized as follows. Section 2 gives an overview to previous work done in network traffic characterization. The concept, the proposed architecture model and the performance evaluation are summarized in section 3. Section 4 presents the prediction algorithm and discusses the results. Finally, the conclusion and the future work is given in section 5.

2 Related Work

Network simulation and characterization of communication networks targets on obtaining network traffic knowledge to dimension more efficiently network and network devices [9] et al. Thus, Internet traffic prediction is a trial to obtain an a priori knowledge of the behavior of future data sent through communication networks [10].

2.1 Characteristics

Extensive research has been done to understand the nature of network traffic. One result was the observation of *self-similarity* in various Internet traffic measurements [11]. The expression self-similarity is used for processes which show scale-independent invariant correlational structure. In other word, appearance is unchanged regardless of the scale at which it is viewed. Self-similarity is closely associated with *heavy-tailed distributions*. The expression heavy-tailed results from extremely large values with non-negligible probability [12]. Such distributions decline via a power law with small exponent (less than 2). As a consequence, when $\alpha < 2$, the random variable shows infinite variance. Self-similar processes can show *long-range dependence*. A process with long-range dependence is defined by an autocorrelation function of $s_{xx} \sim x^{-\beta}, x \to \infty, 0 < \beta < 1$. Some essential observations concerning traffic characteristics are listed in the following. However, their reasons are still not entirely determined. Due to [13], burst sizes of FTP transfers and Telnet inter-arrival times follow a heavy-tail distribution. Examinations in [14] show that transmission and idle times of Ethernet traffic between source and destination pairs are heavy-tailed.

2.2 Statistics

To understand the behavior of routing in the Internet, a multitude of measurements have been done [15] [16] et al. In 1997, simulation results were obtained from the MCI backbone [17]: On IP protocols, TCP is the dominant layer 4 protocol of 90 percent of the packets. UDP has second highest level at about 5 to 10 percent. Other protocols make up an almost negligible percentage. More recent results can be taken from the IP Monitoring system of the Sprint Tier-1 IP backbone network. It is deployed at a Point-of-Presence (POP). Summarized, some essential results are the following [18], [19]:

- Local traffic distribution: two of the used POPs, which are located in the east and west, respectively, are dominant and receive about $\frac{2}{3}$ of the complete traffic. This can be explained by a higher population and the termination of international trunks.

- Time of day behavior of large, medium and small POPs: While small POP remain fairly stable during the time of day, medium POPs show a long slow small decline. The most, large POPs decrease rapidly up to 60 percent.

- Elephants-and-mice phenomena: Streams which are aggregation of packets lead to a distribution of a few very high-volume streams (elephants) and many low-volume traffic streams (mice).

- Impact of new applications: On some simulation links, over 60 percent of traffic is generated by applications such as distributed file sharing and streaming media.

- Traffic breakdown by protocols: Over 90 percent of traffic is TCP traffic, even on the links with a significant percentage of streaming media. This can be explained by the use of firewalls which are commonly configured for preference of TCP than UDP for streaming media.

The monitored protocol breakdown of [20] showed a traffic distribution of approximatively 82 - 90 percent of TCP, 8 - 16 percent UDP and 1 - 3 percent ICMP.

3 Protocol Stack Processing

The packet processing concept is based on two components: *Protocol Stack Prediction* and *Speculative Packet Processing*. Objective is to overcome processing latency limitations which result from network layer hierarchies.

Protocol Stack Prediction:

The decision how to handle and forward a packet is done upon the information which is contained in the packet header. The header of the data-link layer, the network layer and the transport layer is hierarchically arranged. I.e. the type of a higher layer of the ISO/OSI reference model of communication is derived from the header of the lower layer. To circumvent a serial extraction, *protocol stack prediction* predicts the protocol stack of the next packet. The scheme is depicted in Fig. 1.

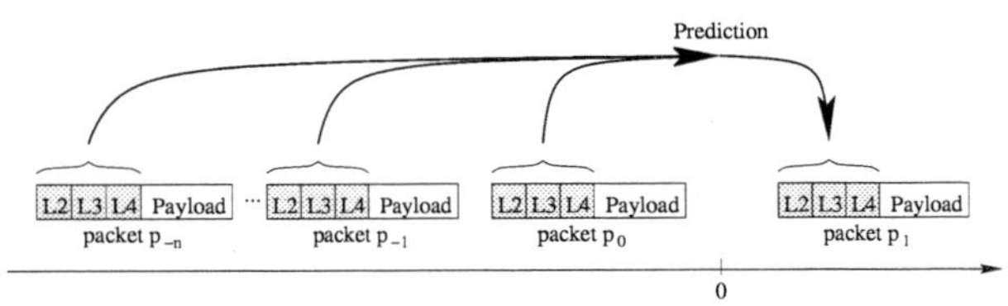

Figure 1. Protocol Stack Prediction Scheme

The prediction is based on the history of packets received earlier. It should be noted, that the prediction *not* only delivers protocol layer types of a packet. In a store-and-forward architecture, this information could be gathered quickly from the packet but would not influence significantly processing delay. Furthermore, additional information which is required for control point processing is implicitly provided by the prediction. For instance, costly processing for checksum verification of layer 2 has to be done in front of processing of layer 3 as in Fig. 2.

Starting from the prediction result, packet processing is started speculatively. I.e. the inherent data dependency is temporarily resolved and processing of layer 2, 3 and 4 is

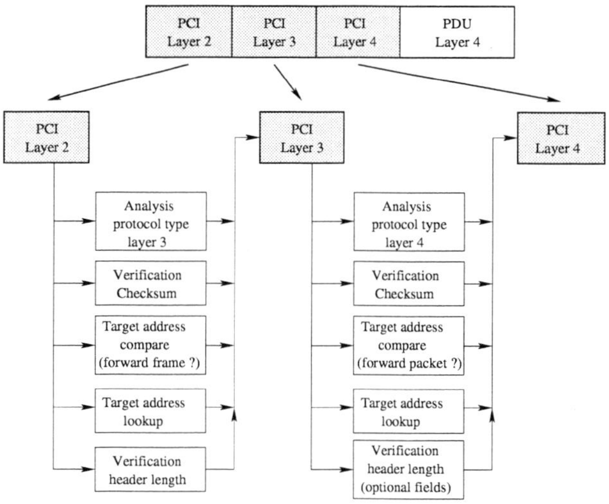

Figure 2. Protocol Stack Prediction

started simultaneously. If tasks which concern the identification of the upper layer protocol type are terminated, the prediction is verified. In case of correctness, processing results can be kept. Else, i.e. in case of misprediction, results have to be dropped and task processing has to be restarted. Further details can be taken from [7].

Through the use of both components, mean latency can be reduced. Thus, it is less than the sum of individual processing delays of network layer 2, 3 and, if differentiated services is supported, layer 4. Prerequisite is an accurate prediction.

4 Protocol Stack Prediction

4.1 Dynamic Algorithm

Static predictor algorithms take advantage of statistical invariance of considered processes. For this purpose, a traffic profile has to be generated before start of operation.

In section 2, traffic statistics were presented that show variable behavior. Reasons are changes of traffic during a day or week, asymmetric traffic volumes, local aspects of operation and other. Thus, a dynamic algorithm seems to be well-suited to achieve better prediction accuracies [18]. However, considering the fact that routers or switches represent aggregation points, and having self-similarity in mind, modeling a prediction algorithm based on stochastic event sequences, i.e. Markov chains, seems no to be precise. Alternatively, an algorithm is proposed that exploits majority of occurring process events.

To distinguish between different protocol stacks which are supported by the system, a stack identifier (SID) is defined. It contains an unique data pattern for each stack. Output of prediction is the SID of the packet which is expected to be received next.

The prediction algorithm is depicted in Figure 3.

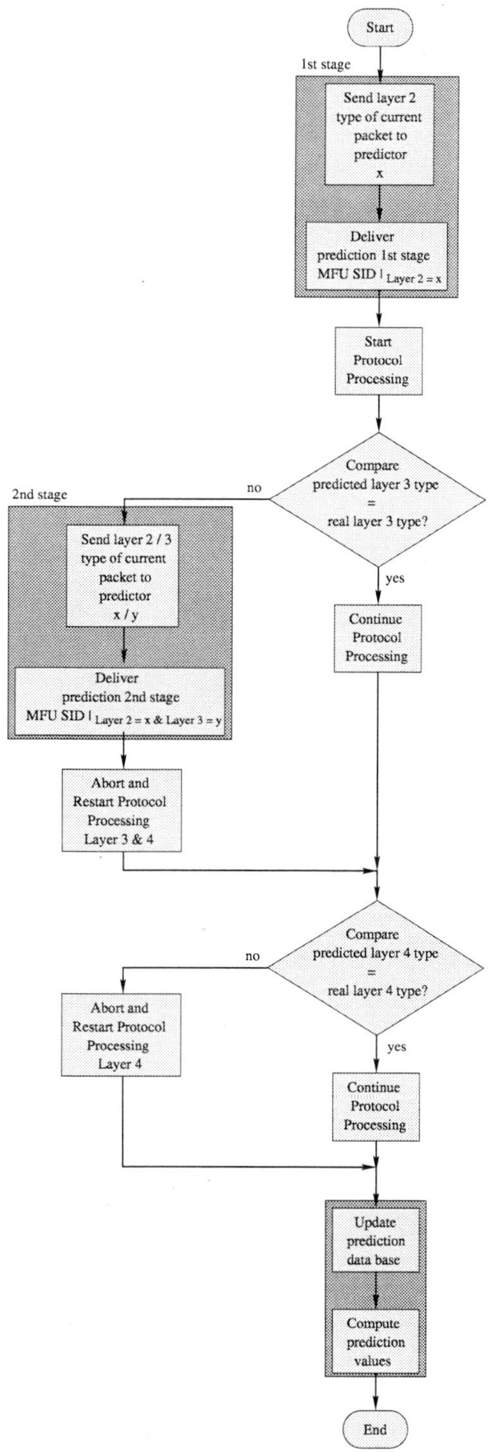

Figure 3. Dynamic prediction algorithm

Protocol stack prediction comprises protocol layer 3 and 4. At first, when a packet arrives, the type of protocol layer two is indicated by the precedent data-link layer device. Based on this knowledge, a first prediction value is requested. In the following, packet processing is started. When the type of layer three is derived through analysis of the upper layer type field which is part of layer two, the prediction is verified. In case of correctness, no further prediction is required. Else, a second prediction concerning the type of layer four has to be requested. The request considers then the available type of layer three. Thus, multiple MFU values are provided. They differ for the first prediction stage in the type of layer two and for the second stage in the types of layer two and three.

After analysis of each packet, the prediction values are updated to make a dynamic behavior possible. The SID of the current packet is transferred to the prediction data base. Therein, the frequency of each SID is recorded through summation of receive events. The prediction algorithm takes this packet history information as input to calculate the prediction values. The computation of the prediction values, i.e. the SIDs, follows the policy of *most frequently used (MFU)* [22]. Output is a value that identifies the protocol stack which occurred most frequently in the past. As an extension of the policy, an additional weight factor is appended during prediction computation to each SID [23]. Objective is to prioritize delay sensitive traffic in case of equal stack frequencies.

The flow of computation is illustrated in Figure 4.

When a new SID is transferred to the data base, the associated entry is updated. Depending on the type of protocol layer 2, the MFU values of the referring path have to be recalculated. In the example, two types for layer 2 (Packet-over-SONET (POS), Gigabit-Ethernet (G-E)) and layer 3 (IP version 4, IP version 6) are used. In case of control protocols, e.g. ICMP, protocol processing is done by the separate control plane.

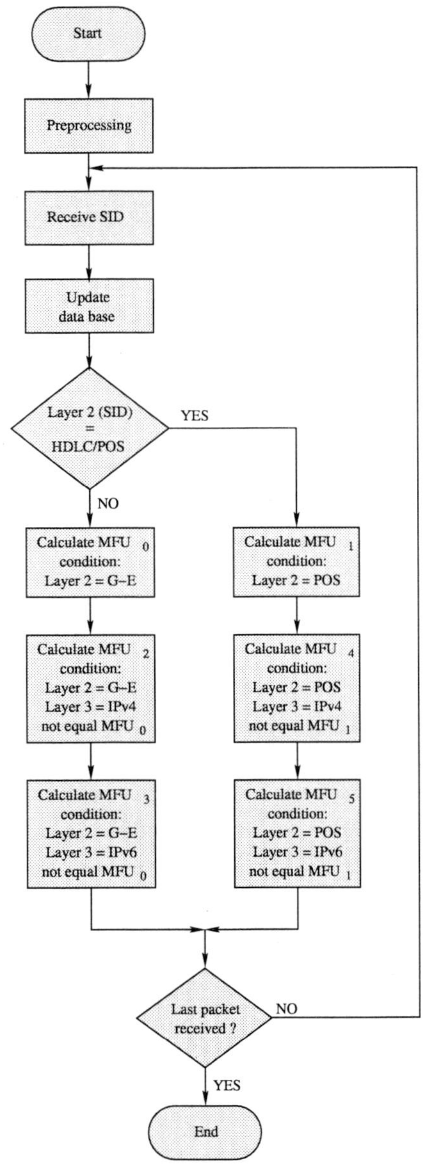

Figure 4. MFU computation flow

4.2 Architecture

The progress of protocol layer analysis of a current packet is kept in the Protocol-Stack Status Word (PSSW). To request a prediction value, the PSSW is used to address the prediction values. The format of the PSSW is shown in Fig. 5.

Two flag fields are used to indicate if the type of protocol layer 2 and 3 is already determined. A defined numerical value that characterizes the types of layer 2, 3 and 4 is stored in the corresponding type fields.

The prediction values are stored in a decode history table (DHT) as shown in Fig. 6 [24].

The lines of the DHT correspond to MFU_i with $i \in \{1, ..., 6\}$. The DHT returns the predicted SID stack to proceed packet processing.

Layer4 type	Layer4 flag	Layer3 type	Layer3 flag	Layer2 type

Figure 5. Protocol-stack status word (PSSW)

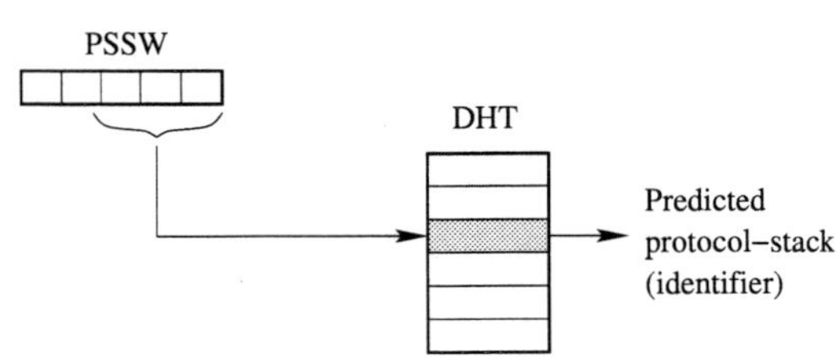

Figure 6. Prediction table lookup

4.3 Simulation and Discussion

To evaluate the algorithm, various packet protocol breakdowns were generated. Having a software implementation in mind, deterministic test traffic was used to obtain the number of processing cycles necessary for MFU entry update. With regard to the most essential metric of sorting algorithms, the number of compare instructions has been extracted. Based on a SUN-RISC instruction set, it serves for consolidation of the proposed algorithm. By use of a random generator, prediction accuracy as well as the self-adaption on transitions of traffic characteristics have been measured.

The prediction accuracy for various test traffic and identical weight factors is shown in Figure 7.

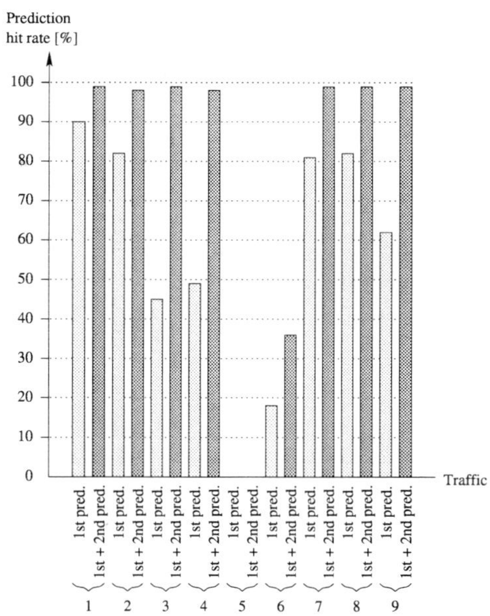

Figure 7. Prediction accuracy

Traffic 1 [21] and 2 [18], shown by curly brackets, show hit rates for the first prediction level of 90 % and 82 %, respectively. For both, 90 % and 89 % can be achieved. Other simulation traffic differ in equal protocol breakdown distribution, contain bursts and traffic transitions. For instance, traffic 4 generates 4 different packets 25 % each. Traffic 5, which is generated of a periodical sequence of 8 different packets, is used as unrealistic worst case scenario. Thereby, a regular replacement of the entries in the DHT takes place.

As mentioned above, modified prediction weight factors allow prioritization of certain traffic. Traffic 6 is composed of equal packet distribution for TCP and UDP, IPv4 and IPv6 as well as POS and G-E. Through a weight factor of 4 for UDP traffic versus default weights of 1, the misprediction rate can be reduced from 64 % to 28.8 %.

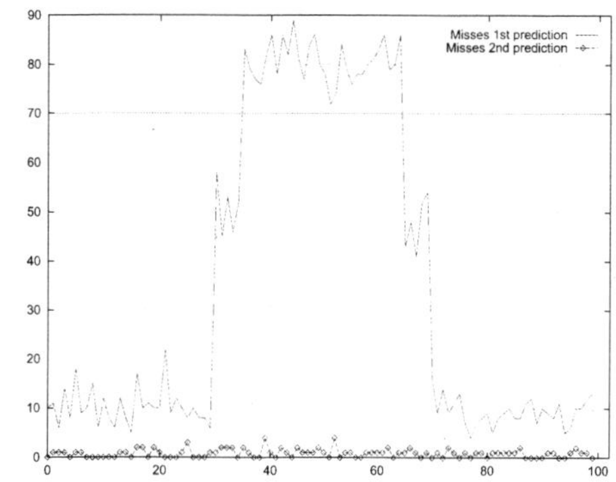

Figure 8. Number of mispredictions (traffic R8)

In Figure 8, the prediction convergence of random traffic R8 is presented.

The unit of the x-axis corresponds to 100 packets. R8 is composed of five ranges of different packet distributions. The distribution of the first 3000 packets is: 90 % TCP; 9 % UDP; 1 % ICMP. Two bursts of 500 packet each follow with 50 % TCP; 49 % UDP; 1 % ICMP. Between, the distribution shifts to 19 % TCP; 80 % UDP for 3000 packets. For the last 3000 packets, the distribution is equal to the beginning.

While the misprediction rate is about 10 for the first and last period, the hit rate of the first prediction stage for the meantime is worse at about 80 percent. However, it should be noted, that the misprediction rate of the second stage remains constant at about 1 %. An additional reset facility of the data pool that detects longer periods of continuous occurring mispredictions would compensate the misconduct of the first stage.

4.4 Implementation costs

The additional effort which has to spent for speculative packet processing is a prediction data base and the DHT. To obtain a fast memory access, both might be realized as small part of an embedded SRAM. Today, a 4k bit SRAM requires an access delay of about 2.8 ns and has an area of about 0.44 mm^2 [25].

The calculation effort for data base update and computation of prediction values has been determined based on a software implementation on a RISC architecture. For traffic 1, mean number of processing cycles is 324.

As in [7], mean processing delay of a packet is 858 cycles. Thus, considering a realization within a RISC core, dynamic prediction update can be done at line-speed for each packet.

Furthermore, the portion of compare instructions necessary for prediction value computation has be measured. Traditional sorting algorithms such as heap sort, bubble sort or quicksort require between $ln(N) \cdot N$ and N^2 compare instructions for N sorting elements [26]. In case of N = 16 supported protocol stacks and six MFU values to calculate, only 26.9 compare instructions were necessary.

5 Conclusions

We have presented a dynamic protocol stack prediction algorithm that delivers high accuracy. Its appropriateness for use in speculative network processors has been demonstrated. Due to a small amount of processing cycles required for DHT computation, prediction update at line-speed is feasible. Further work will concentrate on system output queuing algorithms for limitation of delay jitter in case of misprediction.

References

1. M. Bjoerkman, P. Gunningberg, *Locking Effects in Multiprocessor Implementations of Protocols* ACM Sigcomm, Sep. 1993.
2. D.D. Clark, *Modularity and Efficiency in Protocol Implementation* NIC RFC 817, 1982.
3. J.P.G. Sterbenz, *Protocols for High-Speed Networks: A Brief Retrospective Survey of High-Speed Networking Research* Workshop on Protocols for High Speed Networks, May 2002.
4. S. Lakshmanamurthy, K. Liu, Y. Pun, L. Huston, U. Naik, *Network Processor Performance Analysis Methodology* Intel Technical Journal, Vol. 6, Aug. 2002.
5. T. Vaseeharan, M. Maheswaran, *Towards a Novel Architecture for Wide-Area Data Caching and Replication* Intl. Conference on Internet Computing, Las Vegas, Jun. 2000.
6. J. Foag, N. Pazos, T. Wild, W. Brunnbauer, *Self-adaptive Parallel Processing Architecture for High-Speed Networking* Proc. Int'l. Symposium on High Performance Computing Systems and Applications, Moncton, Jun. 2002.
7. J. Foag, M. Praxenthaler, T. Wild, *Performance Evaluation of a Speculative Network Processor* Proc. Int'l. Symposium on High Performance Computing Systems and Applications, Sherbrooke, May 2003.
8. *http://www.systemc.org*
9. L. Trajkovic, A. Neidhardt, *Traffic characterization and time scales for designing efficient network control policies* Invited paper, Proc. NOLTA'97, Hawaii, Dec. 1997.
10. L. Trajkovic, A. Neidhardt, *Internet traffic prediction* Centre for Systems Science, Simon Fraser University, Vol. 12, Issue 1, Mar. 2000.
11. M.E. Crovella, A. Bestavros, *Self-similarity in world wide web traffic: Evidence and possible causes* IEEE/ACM Transactions on Networking, vol. 6, pp. 835-846, Dec. 1997.
12. L. Guo, M. Crovella, I. Matta, *TCP Congestion Control and Heavy Tails* Technical Report BU-CS-2000-017, Boston University, Computer Science Department, Jul. 2000.
13. V. Paxson, S. Floyd, *Wide-Area Traffic: The Failure of Poisson Modeling* IEEE Transactions on Networking, Jun. 1995.
14. W. Willinger, M. Taqqu, R. Sherman, D. Wilson, *Self-Similarity Through High-Variability: Statistical Analysis of Ethernet LAN Traffic at the Source Level* IEEE/ACM Transactions on Networking, Feb. 1997.
15. V. Paxson, *End-to-End Routing Behavior in the Internet* IEEE/ACM Transactions on Networking, Oct. 1997.
16. k. Claffy, *Internet Measurement and Data Analysis: Topology, Workload, Performance and Routing Statistics* NAE Workshop, 1999.
17. K. Thompson, G. Miller, R. Wilder, *Wide-Area Internet Traffic Patterns and Characteristics* IEEE Network, 11(6), Nov. 1997.
18. C. Fraleigh, S. Moon, C. Diot, B. Lyles, F. Tobagi, *Packet-Level Traffic Measurement from a Tier-1 IP Backbone* Submitted for publication, Sept. 2002.
19. S. Bhattacharyya, C. Diot, J. Jetcheva, N. Taft, *Pop-Level and Access-Link-Level Traffic Dynamics in a Tier-1 POP* ACM Sigcomm Internet Measurement Workshop IMW 2001, San Francisco, Nov. 2001.
20. *http://ipmon.sprintlabs.com* date: 17th march 2002.
21. K. Claffy, G. Miller, K. Thompson, *The nature of the beast: recent traffic measurements from an Internet backbone* Proc. of INET 98.
22. J. Smith, *A Study of Branch Prediction Strategies* Proc. 8th Intern. Symposium of Computer Architecture, May 1981.
23. M. Doshi, U. Pandit, R. Kumbharathi, W. Zhu, J. Tan, *XML-based Data Manipulation* Class CSE 812, Advanced Operating System, University of Illinois at Urbana-Champaign, 2001.
24. J. Pino, B. Singh, D. Culler, *Performance Evaluation of One and Two-Level Dynamic Branch Prediction Schemes over Comparable Hardware Costs* Technical Report, UCB/ERL M94/45, Jun. 1994.
25. T. Sherwood, *Embedded Memories* CSE 291E / EE260C, University of California at San Diego, 2002.
26. R. Sedgewick, *Algorithms* 2nd edition, Addison Wesley, Reading, MA, 1992.

The Impact of Hyper-Threading on Communication Performance in HPC Clusters

Tau Leng[a], Rizwan Ali, Celebioglu, Onur, Jenwei Hsieh, Victor Mashayekhi, Reza Rooholamini

[a]Dell Computer Corp.
RR5-3 One Dell Way, Round Rock, TX 78682

The effects of Intel Hyper-Threading® (HT) technology on a system's performance vary according to the characteristics of the application running on the system and the configuration of the system. HPC clusters introduce additional hardware variables, such as the interconnection that can affect the performance of MPI applications. In this paper, we study the effect of HT on MPI-based applications by varying two hardware components: Processor cache sizes and interconnect networks. What we have found out is that larger cache sizes leads to better performance when HT is enabled, in particular for the cache-friendly applications. For instance, enabling HT in a cluster made up of Xeon MP based machines improves performance, but in a cluster of Xeon DP based machines degrades performance. For interconnect communication, enabling HT in a cluster interconnected with a low latency, high-bandwidth interconnect like Quadrics, may not improve performance in the case that the CPU resources are highly utilized. On the other hand, in a cluster interconnected with slower speed, higher latency interconnects like Gigabit Ethernet, enabling HT improves performance via claiming the underutilized resources, which were caused by the inefficient communication.

Les effets sur les performances du système Hyper-Threading® (HT) d'Intel varient en fonction des caractéristiques des applications et de la configuration du système d'exploitation. Les grappes de CHP introduisent des variables matérielles additionnelles, comme l'interconnection entre les noeuds qui peut affecter la performance des application MPI. Dans cet article, nous étudions les effets du HT sur les applications MPI en faisant varier deux paramètres matériels: La dimension de la mémoire cache et le type d'interconnection. Nous avons observé que l'utilisation du HT améliore la performance lorsque la dimension de la ménoire cache est grande, en particulier pour les applications profitant déjà de la mémoire cache. Par exemple, l'utilisation du HT sur une grappe de Xeon MP améliore les performances, tandis que sur une grappe de Xeon DP l'utilisation du HT diminue les performances. En ce qui concerne l'interconnection, l'utilisation du HT sur une grappe utilisant un réseau à basse latence et grande bande passante comme Quadrics, ne devrait pas augmenter les performances dans le cas où le processeur est pleinement utilisé. En contre partie, sur une grappe utilisant un réseau à plus haute latence et plus faible bande passante comme Gigbit Ethernet, l'utilisation du HT améliore les performances en profitant du temps de processeur non utilisé, causé par la communication inefficace.

1. Introduction

Intel's Hyper-Threading (HT) technology makes a single physical processor appear as two logical processors. The physical processor resources are shared and the architectural state is duplicated for the two logical processors [1]. The premise is that this duplication allows a single physical processor to execute instructions from different threads in parallel rather than in serial, and therefore, could lead to better processor utilization and overall performance. However, sharing the system resources, such as caches or memory bus by the additional logical processors might create negative impact on the performance. Particularly, in a HPC cluster environment, additional hardware variables introduced, that create more parameters of determining whether HT will help or hinder the performance. For example, the communication capability between processes within a compute node or among the nodes in the cluster will influence the overall performance, when running the parallel applications.

1.1 Level of Parallelism

Two levels of parallelism have been addressed in the modern computer processor design to improve performance. Instruction-level-parallelism (ILP) refers to techniques of increasing the number of instructions executed each clock cycle. Although it is possible that the multiple execution units in a processor can execute multiple instructions at the same time, the dependencies that exist among the instructions makes it a challenge to finding enough instructions to execute simultaneously. Several mechanisms have been implemented to increase ILP. For example, "out-of-order execution" is a technique of evaluating a set of instructions and sending them for execution in parallel, regardless of their original order defined by the program, and yet preserving the dependencies among the instructions.

Thread-Level Parallelism (TLP), on the other hand, enables a processor or multiprocessor system to concurrently run multiple threads from an application or from multiple, independent programs. SMT, or Simultaneous Multi-Threading technology, upon which HT is based, permits a processor to exploit both ILP and TLP. Multiple threads can run on an SMT processor, and the processor will dynamically allocate resources between the threads, enabling a processor to adapt to the varying requirements of the workload. Intel's HT implements SMT in such a way that each logical processor maintains a separate architectural state, which consists of general-purpose, control, machine state, and advanced programmable interrupt controller (APIC) registers [1]. The chip real estate required for the architectural states is negligible compared to the total die size. Thus, threads or separate programs using separate architectural states must

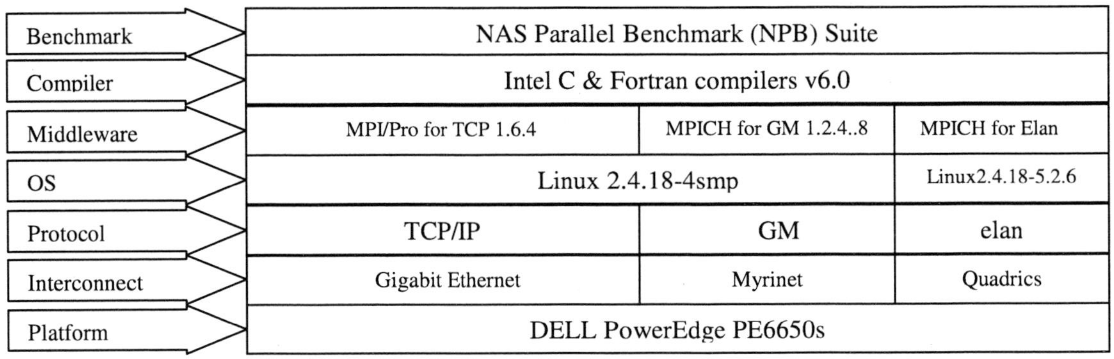

Figure 1. Architectural stack of the test environment. NPB benchmark is compiled with Intel C and FORTRAN compilers. The Linux is RedHat 7.3 distribution with kernel version 2.4.18-4smp and 2.4.18-elan.

share most of the physical processor resources, such as trace cache, L2-L3 unified caches, translation look aside buffer, execution units, branch history table, branch target buffer, control logic, and busses. This simultaneous sharing of resources between two threads creates a potential for performance degradation.

1.2 Multithreading and Message-passing Applications

In general, processors enabled with HT technology can improve the performance of applications with high degree of parallelism. Previous studies have shown that the HT technology improves multi-threaded applications' performance by a range of 10 to 30 percent depending on the characteristics of the applications [2]. These studies also suggest that the potential gain is only obtained if the application is multi-threaded by any means of parallelization techniques. A multithreaded program is capable of creating multiple processes, or threads, at a time without having to have multiple copies of the program running in the computer.

In our area of interest, high performance computing (HPC) clusters, applications are commonly implemented by using standard message-passing interface, such as MPI or PVM. Applications developed by a message-passing programming model usually employ a mechanism, *"mpirun"* for example, to spawn multiple processes and map them to processors in the systems. Parallelism is achieved through the message-passing interface among the processes to coordinate the parallel tasks. Unlike the multithreaded programs in which the values of application variables are shared by all the threads, a message-passing application runs as a collection of autonomous processes, each with its own local memory. For most of the case, the number of processes spawned is equal to the number of processors in the cluster, to obtain the optimal performance. Therefore, this type of applications could also benefit from HT technology in the sense that the number of processes spawned is doubled, which makes the parallel tasks potentially execute faster. Applying HT and doubling the processes that simultaneously run on the cluster will increase the utilization rate of the processors' execution resources. Consequently, the performance may be improved. On the other hand, overheads might be introduced in the following ways:

- The logical processes of the same physical processor may compete for accesses to the caches, and thus could generate more cache-miss situations
- More processes running on the same compute node may create additional memory contention, when the processes are accessing the memory bus or communicating through the shared memory at the same time
- More processes on each node increase the communication traffic (message passing) within and between nodes, which could oversubscribe the communication capacity of the shared memory, the I/O bus or the interconnect networking, and thus create performance bottlenecks

Whether the performance benefits of HT – better resource utilization – can nullify these overhead conditions, primarily depends on the application's characteristics [10].

In this paper, we focused on the communication performance of the cluster affected by HT, and discussed the adaptability of the technology to HPC clusters when using various interconnects. In the next section, we introduce the cluster interconnects used in our study and how they effect the overall cluster performance. Section 3 explains the configurations and the tools for our experiments including the benchmark programs. Section 4 shows the benchmark results along with the performance analysis. The causes of performance gain or degradation in applying HT in the cluster with different interconnects are discussed. Section 5 is the conclusion.

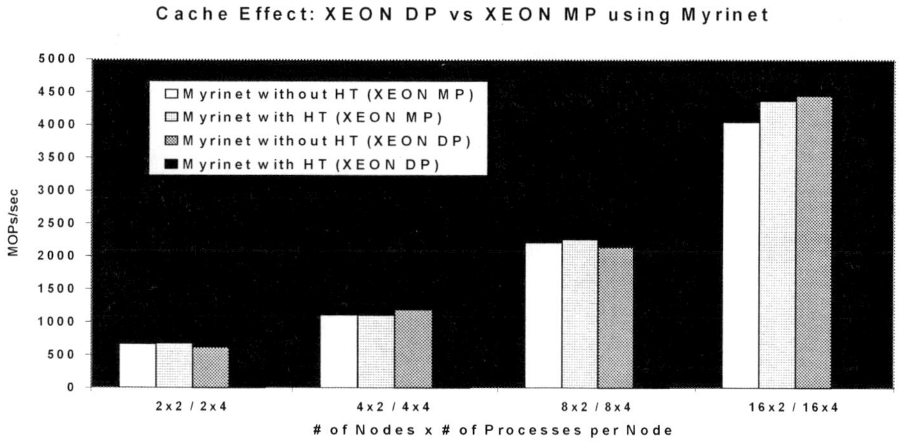

Figure 2. The FT (Class B) benchmark results of Hyper-Threading enabled and disabled on a Xeon MP and a Xeon DP cluster using Myrinet as the interconnect. The Large L3 Cache on Xeon MP helps FT's performance.

2. The Interconnects

The interconnect that networks the individual compute nodes converts a group of computers into a single system, an HPC cluster, which is capable of executing parallel jobs. The performance of the interconnect is an important factor which effects the cluster performance significantly when the applications running on the cluster are communication centric. When Hyper-Threading is applied, the cluster performance may be decreased because the communication links might not be able to accommodate more communications among the (doubled number of) processes. Conversely, if the communication links are capable of handling the increased communication traffics, the cluster performance might benefit from HT. In our study, we used three interconnects, Gigabit Ethernet, Myrinet, and Quadrics respectively to understand the performance impact on each cluster when HT is enabled versus disabled.

Ethernet is the most popular networking configuration today. However, due to its inefficiency, the conventional TCP/IP protocol is not necessarily suitable for a dedicated system area network, like a HPC cluster interconnect, to accomplish communication intensive jobs. Nevertheless, familiarity and the cost factor make Fast Ethernet and Gigabit Ethernet the more popular and cost-effective choices for many applications.

Myrinet and Quadrics are two of the leading cluster interconnects technologies for HPC clusters. Both provide low latency, high bandwidth, and end-to-end communication between two nodes in the cluster. Myrinet [3] is a connection-less interconnect which leverages packet switching technologies from experimental Massively Parallel Processors (MPP) networks. Myrinet uses an efficient communication mechanism called the Glenn's Message (GM) message-passing system. This system gives a user process direct access to the network interface, avoiding immediate copies of data and bypassing the operating system (OS) networking stack in a protected fashion. Quadrics [9] uses a similar technique to efficiently transfer messages between the communicating nodes. The Quadrics elan network interface provides efficient and protected access to a global virtual memory via remote DMA operations.

The following table summarizes the specifications of the three interconnects we used for our experiments.

Interconnect	Gigabit Ethernet	Myrinet – 2000	Quadrics
Network Interface Card	Broadcom 5701 64-bit 66Mhz PCI	Myrinet-2000 64-bit 66Mhz PCI	Elan III 64-bit 66Mhz PCI
Network Switch	Gigabit Ethernet Switch	Myrinet-2000 32 port switch	Quadrics QM S16 16-port switch
Link speed	1 Gbps	2 Gbps	2.72 Gbps
Topology	Non-blocking	Clos network	Fat Tree
Protocol	TCP/IP	GM	Elan

3. Experimental Environment

Our testing environment is a cluster that consists of 16 Dell PowerEdge 6650 servers interconnected with Gigabit, Myrinet and Quadrics. Each PowerEdge 6650 has two Intel XEON MP Processors running at 1.6 GHz with 512KB L2 cache, 1MB L3 cache, 4GB of DDR-RAM (double data rate RAM) memory operating on a 400 MHz Front Side Bus. The chipset of PowerEdge 6650 is the ServerWorks GC-HE, which accommodates up to sixteen registered DDR PC1600 (200Mhz) DIMMs with a 4-way interleaved memory architecture. The PowerEdge 6650 is also equipped with two integrated Broadcom Gigabit Ethernet adapters. The operating system installed for the cluster is RedHat 7.3 with kernel version 2.4.18-4smp. Note that for being able to use the Quadrics, the kernel is upgraded to a special kernel based on 2.4.18. The benchmark programs were compiled with Intel C or FORTRAN compilers. Figure 1 shows the architectural stack of our test environment.

The MPI programs we used for the experiments are the NAS Parallel Benchmark (NPB) suite. NPB is a commonly used benchmark in the High Performance Computing arena, developed by NASA Advanced Supercomputing Division. The benchmarks, which are derived from computational fluid dynamics (CFD) applications, consist of five kernels and three pseudo-applications designed to gauge parallel computing performance. Each of the programs solves a specific numerical problem [6]. The performance results are measured in Million Operations per Second (Mop/s). Since each program represents a specific part of CFD applications, from the benchmark results, one can realize the performance characteristics of the system from various aspects. For our study, we use the results of three of the eight programs, the EP, FT, and IS to facilitate our explanations.

In our experiments, we run the NPB on the test cluster by using different combinations of compute nodes and number of CPUs in each node. Three sets of testing for the three interconnects are performed separately. For each set, we run the NPB for both HT disabled and enabled configurations. Then, compare the results to show how HT affects the clusters' performances.

4. Benchmarking Results and Analysis

4.1 Cache Effect

To understand the cache effect of Hyper-Threading, FT is used, given that its performance is sensitive to the cache size. In FT, the ***3-D FFT PD benchmark***, a 3-D partial differential equation is solved using FFTs, the Fast Fourier Transform. This program performs the essence of many *spectral methods*. It is a good test of long-distance communication performance. FT requires intensive float-point operations and messages passing among processes. More importantly, FT is a cache-friendly benchmark; the large cache will facilitate better performance [7][10].

Figure 2 shows the results obtained by running FT on our test cluster with 16 nodes equipped with 32 XEON MP Processors comparing to that of a 16-node cluster with 32 XEON DP Processors. The results of the DP cluster were obtained from our prior study in [10], and both of the results are obtained on clusters with Myrinet interconnect. From the Figure 2, it can be seen that the XEON MP cluster shows improvement in performance with HT enabled, while the XEON DP cluster shows a fall in performance. The improvement for the MP cluster is primarily due to the large L3 cache of the MP Processors. Based on the analysis in [10], the drop in performance of the DP cluster was because of the considerable increase of L2 cache miss rate without L3 cache support in the DP Processor, when running FT with HT enabled. In the case for XEON MP Cluster, the L3 cache was large enough to house the memory accesses for both the logical processors sharing the caches. As a result, the increase of L2 cache misses was compensated by L3 cache hits, and the performance improved via better CPU resources utilization.

Another observation from Figure 2 is the FT performance of MP and DP Clusters is considerably close, although the difference in clock speed between XEON MP (1.6GHz) and DP (2.4GHz) is large. That again, indicates the cache is a major factor, which affects the FT performance significantly, and HT can improve the performance, if the cache size is sufficient to accommodate both logical processors.

In Figure 3, we show the performance results obtained by running FT on XEON MP Cluster for different numbers of compute nodes and different interconnects, Gigabit Ethernet, Myrinet, and Quadrics. Observed from the results, the interconnect capacity is important for FT to scale. The performance differences between the faster interconnect and the slower interconnect are larger when the node count of the cluster is increased. Slower interconnect, like Gigabit Ethernet, apparently creates the bottleneck for larger cluster with more FT processes running. Nonetheless, enabling the HT provides an overall performance improvements on all three interconnects' clusters. And, the improvements become more noticeable while running the FT on larger node count configurations.

4.2 Interconnect effect

Integer Sort (IS) performs an integer sorting operation that is important in *particle method* codes. This type of application is similar to particle-in-cell applications of physics, wherein particles are assigned to cells and may drift out. The sorting operation is used to reassign particles to the appropriate cells. This benchmark tests both integer computation speed and communication performance. This problem is unique in that floating-point arithmetic is not involved. Significant data communication, however, is

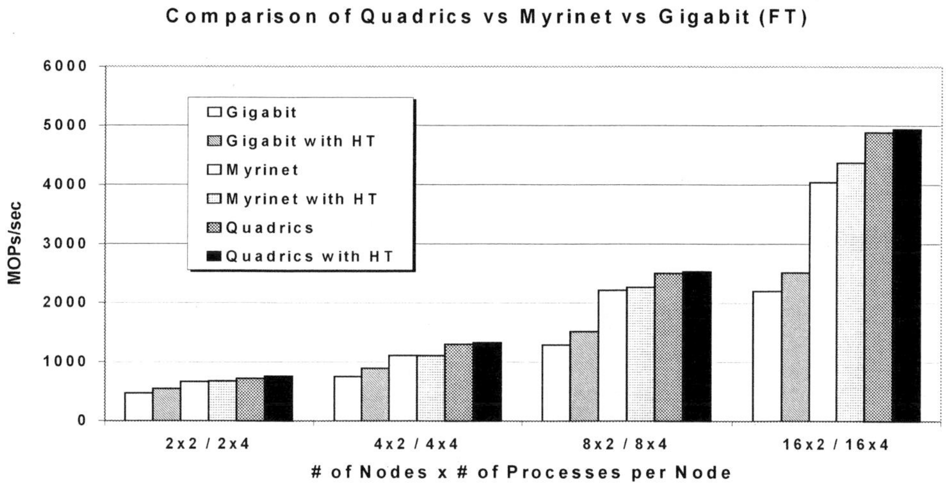

Figure 3. The FT (Class B) benchmark results for Hyper-Threading enabled and disabled for the three interconnects. Gigabit shows a larger percentage improvement from HT disabled to HT enabled.

required. Hence, IS is particularly useful for testing the communication capability of the cluster. For our study, the results of IS will show not just the communication performance for each interconnect, but also whether doubling the processes will complete the Sorting faster or the increased communication traffics will slow down the performance, when HT is on.

The communication traffic here indicates message-passing between processes, which could be inside a cluster node or among different nodes. Memory and I/O contentions both could potentially decrease the cluster performance. The Dell PowerEdge 6650 platform has a 4-way interleaved memory architecture. The high memory bandwidth helps minimize the effect of memory contention due to increased number of processes.

The IS performance results in Figure 4 show that the performances of the three interconnects are as expected. Quadrics is the best followed by Myrinet then Gigabit Ethernet. Furthermore, unlike Quadrics and Myrinet clusters, the Gigabit Ethernet cluster has the worst scalability, due to the high latency of the interconnect. Increasing the node count of the cluster running IS would not improve the performance too much for the Gigabit Ethernet configuration.

Figure 4 also shows that HT helped the IS performance slightly for Gigabit Ethernet and Myrinet configurations. However, the Quadrics configuration, despite giving the highest overall performance, did not benefit from HT as much. For applications to benefit from HT there has to be underutilized shared resources in the CPU. In the case with a very low latency interconnect such as Quadrics, the CPU is occupied doing computation. The amount of idle time a process is pending for message-passing activities is minimized. Thus, there is no performance improvement realized by enabling HT for IS in the Quadrics configuration. Furthermore, we observe a slight performance drop for large node counts, due to contention for memory and interconnect. A similar contention occurs for slower interconnects that have high latency such as Gigabit Ethernet. On the other hand, as we can deduct from the relatively lower overall performance and scalability obtained in these configurations, the system resources are not utilized to their full potential. Enabling HT helps these configurations resulting in an overall performance gain. Although contention for I/O is higher for slower interconnects, utilizing the idle CPU cycles caused by high message passing latency negates the effect of I/O contention and results in a net performance increase with HT enabled.

On the contrary to IS, the ***Embarrassingly Parallel (EP) Benchmark*** is an entirely computational-bound program. In EP, two-dimensional statistics are accumulated from a large number of Gaussian pseudo-random numbers, which are generated according to a particular scheme that is well suited for parallel computation. This problem is typical of many *Monte Carlo* applications. Since it requires almost no communication, in some sense this benchmark provides an estimate of the upper achievable limits for arithmetic operations' performance on a particular system. EP uses a combination of floating point and integer operations. Thus, HT technology enables independent EP processes to use different CPU resources in an interleaving manner. With HT enabled, EP could more effectively utilize the CPUs' arithmetic resources without being concerned with the communication overhead, which makes the performance improve significantly. This condition is

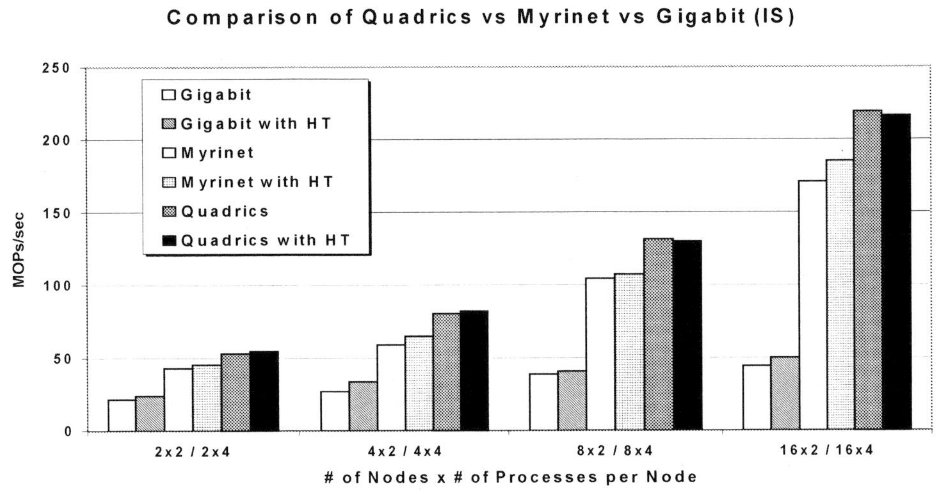

Figure 4. The IS (Class B) benchmark results for Hyper-Threading enabled and disabled for the three interconnects. Low latency, high bandwidth interconnects (Myrinet and Quadrics) outperform Gigabit by a wide margin. The Gigabit Ethernet shows unnoticeable scalability.

true regardless of the number of nodes or CPUs of the cluster. Figure 5 shows the EP performance improved linearly from two nodes to 16 nodes, as well as the constant performance gains (~40%) on HT enabled runs. Since EP has almost no communication the performance obtained on all the three clusters were near identical.

5. Conclusion

Previous studies showed that Hyper-Threading can improve the performance of some MPI applications on a HPC cluster. MPI based applications are typically run by spawning one process for each processor. This suggests spawning twice as many processes, in order to make use of HT. However, doubling the processes may cause performance degradation due to resource contentions. In this paper, we were able to focus on the cluster interconnect aspect of the cluster design by maximizing the amount of CPU cache size through the use of XEON MP Processors. This provided elimination of the cache contention effect shown in previous study for FT benchmark. We then experimented on three popular cluster interconnects; Gigabit Ethernet, Myrinet and Quadrics. Our findings from this study can be summarized in the following.

- In communication intensive applications, e.g. IS, Quadrics gives the highest overall cluster performance, however this cluster benefits the least from HT. On the other hand, the slower interconnect, Gigabit Ethernet, benefits more from HT in communications intensive benchmarks.
- Computational intensive applications with fine-tuned arithmetic operations have less chance to be improved in performance from HT, because the CPU resources are already highly utilized.
- However, if these applications are also communication intensive, such as the case with FT, the overhead and latency associated with the communications may cause the CPU resources to be underutilized. For interconnects such as Myrinet and Quadrics, this overhead is minimal since these interconnects use efficient message transfer mechanisms such as RDMA or Remote Direct Memory Access. The CPU involvement in message transfer for these interconnects is already minimal.
- Furthermore, an efficient computation intensive workload will highly utilize the CPU resources, thus HT provides little or no help. Because these interconnect also provide high-bandwidth, resource contention is also not an issue for applications like FT that exchange small size messages. Gigabit Ethernet using TCP/IP protocol has relatively high communication overhead. Even with highly-tuned applications, some cycles are spent in processing the inter-process communications (IPC) messages rather than doing computation. This causes the scalability and the overall performance of the cluster to drop. HT tends to help more in this case by claiming the underutilized resources of the CPU due to inefficient communications, and using them for computation.
- For applications that require intensive communications such as IS, enabling HT and

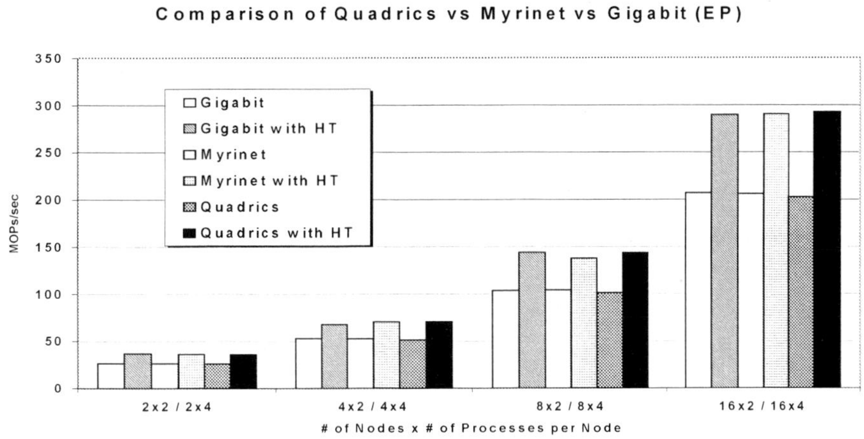

Figure 5. The EP (Class B) benchmark results for Hyper-Threading enabled and disabled for the three interconnects. The results of HT enabled configuration shows up to 40% improvement comparing to the HT disabled configuration.

doubling the number of processes in the cluster node creates I/O contention for shared memory and the interconnect subsystems. The performance degradation caused by the contention can be offset by performance increase realized by claiming underutilized CPU cycles such as the case with Gigabit Ethernet. For a very low latency interconnect such as Quadrics, the computation already occupies the CPU cycles, thus the offsetting effect of HT is minimal. This leads to a performance drop due to contention. This kind of behavior can be observed especially in higher node count configurations.

In light of these results, we can conclude that the decision whether to use or not to use HT technology in a cluster not only depends on the characteristics of the application, but also the capacities of the CPU caches and interconnect communication. Even with the same type of application, clusters with different interconnects and cache configurations may be affected differently by HT.

References

[1] D. T. Marr el al, "Hyper-Threading Technology Architecture and Micro architecture", Intel Technology Journal, Vol. 6, Issue 01, February, 2002.

[2] W. Magro, P. Petersen, S. Shah, "Hyper-Threading Technology: Impact on Compute-Intensive Workloads", Intel Technology Journal, Vol. 6, Issue 01, February 2002.

[3] J. Hsieh, T. Leng, V. Mashayekhi, and R. Rooholamini. "Architectural and Performance Evaluation of Giganet and Myrinet Interconnects on Cluster of Small-Scale SMP Servers", in the *Proceedings of Super-Computing '00*, Dallas, TX, November 2000.

[4] NAS Parallel Benchmark suite, http://www.nas.nasa.gov/Software/NPB/

[5] J. Hsieh, T. Leng, V. Mashayekhi and R. Rooholamini. "Impact of Level 2 Cache and Memory Subsystem on the Scalability of Clusters of Small- Scale SMP Servers", in the *Proceedings of International Conference on Cluster Computing*, Cluster'00, November 2000.

[6] M. Kravetz, H. Franke, S. Nagar, R. Ravindran, "Enhancing Linux Scheduler Scalability", in the 2001 Ottawa Linux Symposium, July 2001.

[7] The Linux Kernel Achieve, ChangeLog-2.4.19, http://www.kernel.org/.

[8] F.C. Wong, R.P. Martin, R.H. Arpaci-Dusseau, and D.E. Culler. "Architectural Requirements and Scalability of the NAS Parallel Benchmarks", In the Proceedings of SuperComputing '99, Portland, Oregon, November 1999.

[9] Fabrizio Petrini, Wu-chun Feng, Adolfy Hoisie, Salvador Coll, and Eitan Frachtenberg , "The Quadrics Network (QsNet): High-Performance Clustering Technology", Hot Interconnects 9, Stanford University, Palo Alto, CA, August 2001

[10] T. Leng, R. Ali, V. Mashayekhi, J. Hsieh and R. Rooholamini. "An Empirical Study of Hyper-Threading in High Performance Computing Clusters", in the *The Third LCI International Conference on Linux Clusters: The HPC Revolution 2002*, October 2002.

A Preliminary Feasibility Study of the LARPBS Optical Bus Parallel Model

René Roldán [a], Brian J. d'Auriol[a]

[a]Department of Computer Science, The University of Texas at El Paso, El Paso, Texas, 79968, USA
roldan@cs.utep.edu, dauriol@acm.org

Current and future parallel processing systems require high bandwidth interconnects to satisfy the communication demands. Optical technologies have been proposed to address the bandwidth limitation of electrical bus systems. Specifically, during the past decade, several optical bus parallel models have been proposed, together with a suite of basic and advanced algorithms. One of the more popular optical bus models is the Linear Array with Reconfigurable Pipelined Bus System (LARPBS), appearing in 1996. Since then, many publications present mostly theoretical work concerning LARPBS algorithms, and only limited comments regarding the implementation of this model have been noted. This paper assesses the realistic and practical nature of the LARPBS optical bus parallel model with respect to recent available optical technologies. An optical power and signal loss analysis for the LARPBS model is conducted. A straight forward implementation of the bus model without amplification of optical signals suggests high losses that limit the number of processors to between eight and twelve. Nevertheless, this work also suggests that variations in the architecture may lead to more practical parallel systems.

Les systèmes de traitement parallèle, présents et futurs, nécessitent une interconnectivité à haut débit qui satifasse aux besoins de communication. Des technologies basées sur l'optique ont déjà été proposées pour palier à la limitation de débit des systèmes électroniques à architecture bus. Plus précisément, plusieurs systèmes parallèles à bus optique ont été mis de l'avant au cours de la dernière décade, lesquels sont accompagnés par des algorithmes de traitement plus ou moins avancés. Un des systèmes optiques les plus connus est le "Linear Array with Reconfigurable Pipelined Bus System" (LARPBS) qui a fait son apparition en 1996. Depuis lors, plusieurs articles théoriques ont portés sur les algorithmes LARPBS, mais on y trouve peu d'informations sur l'implémentation de tels systèmes. Le présent document évalue le réalisme et les aspects pratiques dy système parallèle LARPBS à bus optique en regard des technologies optiques récentes. On y effectue une étude de la perte de puissance et de signal optique pour le système LARPBS. Une implémentation simple du système bus, sans amplifiation du signal optique, montre de fortes pertes qui limitent le nombre de processeur à un nombre variant entre huit et douze. Néanmoins, notre étude donne à penser qu'une modification de l'architecture pourrait conduire à la mise au point de systèmes parallèles plus réalistes.

1 Introduction

Current parallel processing systems require interconnections that can provide high bandwidth so as to satisfy the communication demands of a parallel system. One of the main motivations for the development and implementation of optical interconnects is to overcome the bottlenecks that electrical data buses produce due to their now relatively low bandwidth. High processing speeds of current technology have over-passed the physical limitations of electrical interconnections; in other words, in an electrical system, more data can be produced by computations than the data that can be transferred through its electrical data bus [1]. This paper focuses on optical bus technologies to overcome these limitations.

The bandwidth limitations in electrical interconnections stem from physical characteristics of the electrical conductors where the higher the frequency of the signal, the higher the loss of information. The quality of an electrical signal is frequency-dependent [1]. This characteristic does not apply to optical signals in optical fibers; there is not significant frequency-dependence loss [1]. The consequence of this is higher bandwidth for optical interconnects.

Optical interconnects can be based on one (or both) of the following two methods: a) free space interconnects and b) waveguided interconnects. The former utilizes free space (e.g. air) as the communication medium, thus the optical signals are not constrained to a waveguide. The latter utilizes waveguides (e.g. fiber) to constrain the path of the optical signal. Waveguided signals are somewhat slower than signals in free space due to the refractive index of optical fiber's material [1]. Although optical communication via either of these methods is possible, the clear majority of optical buses proposed in the literature utilize fiber for optical communication.

The Linear Array with Reconfigurable Pipelined Bus System (LARPBS) was first published in 1996 [2]. This is one of ten distinct fiber-based optical bus models that appeared between 1990 and 1998 (refer to [3] for a review of these models). Of the ten models, LARPBS appears the most popular based upon not only the number of publications that strongly relate to this model but also the extent of algorithm design, model extension and derived models from LARPBS (refer to [3] for an extensive literature review). Based upon the literature review, there appear to be three primary periods of optical bus model development: the period 1990 to about 1995 that is characterized by initial optical bus model development together with simplification attempts of such models, the period of about 1995 to about 1996 with the advance of two competitive bus models, AROB [4] in 1995 and LARPBS [2] in 1996, and the period post 1996 characterized by continued developments mostly of refinements in nature.

Despite the variety and popularity of optical buses in general, and LARPBS in particular, only limited and indeed early publications deal with the practical implementations of such parallel models. Work described in [5] lays the groundwork for optical bus implementations while the highly influential work in 1991-1994 [6,7] describe specific implementational details related to early optical bus architectures. Beyond this, we have not observed much in the way of recent efforts to consider the practical implementations of the more recent optical bus models, specifically, the LARPBS model. We do note however, that there is active work that addresses general engineering issues of optical interconnection networks in general. Also, optical technologies have advanced significantly during the past decade.

We are motivated, in part, by the claim in [2]: "...we believe that the LARPBS model is implementable and practical using current optical technology." The majority of later work on LARPBS mostly concern algorithm design and model refinements. There is therefore a need to investigate the realistic and practical modern implementation of optical bus based parallel models, specifically, the LARPBS model. For the feasibility study conducted in this paper, signal loss estimates are performed for the LARPBS model to determine the maximum number of processors that could be interconnected without the need of signal amplification. These preliminary results suggest the practical implementation, nevertheless restricted to low numbers of processors for a passive system. The results also suggest that further study and investigation is needed.

The paper is organized as follows. Related work on practical implementations conducted in the early 1990s is briefly reviewed in Section 2. A review of optical bus parallel models in general and LARPBS in particular is given in Section 3. In the spirit of this conference, a brief review of basic optics is given in Section 4 to assist less technical readers. A brief survey of optical devices suitable for optical buses is presented in Section 5. The main contribution of this paper, an estimation of the total number of processors for a passive LARPBS system appears in Section 6. Conclusions are given in Section 7.

2 Related work on Practical Optical Bus Implementations

In [6,7], the authors present two important results pertaining to optical fiber bus interconnections for a multiple processor system. First, the coincident pulse technique used for processor addressing in message routing is presented. Second, a feasibility study including power budget and scalability of such a multiple processor system is discussed. The authors specifically apply their analysis to an optical bus architecture consisting of primarily a single waveguide and using optical technologies of that period of time. In our work, we are specifically concerned with a more sophisticated optical bus model, the LARPBS [2] that appeared later, in 1996 and which incorporates architectural differences with respect to the earlier work. Furthermore, in this paper, we are particularly interested in the applicability of recent optical technologies, for example, VCSELs (Vertical Cavity Surface Emitting Lasers) and the standardization of optical carrier signals with supported data rates 10 to 40 times faster than available at the time of the early work.

In [7], results are presented that indicate in the order of 16 detectors (processors) could be supported by the system for a power margin of 20% when using 90% couplers. Also, under the assumption that the perceptible power for the photo detector could be 0.1% of the input power, results are presented that indicate that the total number of processors would be 50. These results are consistent with those we publish in this paper. Furthermore, we concur with the early observations that fiber amplifiers can be employed to extend the practical bus implementation.

3 Optical Bus Parallel Models

Several models for fiber-based optical buses have been proposed in the last two decades. One of the principal motivations is that large numbers of processors can be interconnected in linear or two dimensional topologies where the interconnect requires low power consumption without needing amplification for the signals. Other motivations include significantly increased bandwidths as well as pipelined communication. The latter is due to the physical characteristics of light when traveling in an optical fiber, i.e. unidirectional propagation and constant propagation time per unit length [8].

3.1 Brief Survey of Optical Buses

This section outlines in brief some of the important historical development of optical busses as introduction to the selection of the LARPBS for this study. The reader is referred to [9] for an excellent overview; also further details appear in [10] and historical presentations appear in [3,11].

One of the earliest forms of optical buses is the unidirectional bus where messages travel on a message waveguide from low numbered processors to high numbered processors. Three improvements made to this model include: a) the addition of a second unidirectional bus to allow communication from high to low numbered processors, b) the incorporation of coincident pulse addressing [12] induced the addition of two new waveguides, the select and the reference, and c) the incorporation of light transmission delays on the message and reference waveguides. Figure 1 illustrates a unidirectional bus with the three waveguides, but not with the second unidirectional bus.

The select and reference waveguides are utilized for processor addressing by employing the coincident pulse technique [12]. In this technique, and assuming that all three waveguides' fiber segments are all of the same length, a signal initiated on the select waveguide some delta time after a signal initiated on the reference waveguide will, if the transmission is not interfered with, reach a destination processor with the same delta time differential between the signals.

Destination addressing occurs when the transmission of reference signal is slowed in predictable amounts so that both the select and reference signals coincide at a desti-

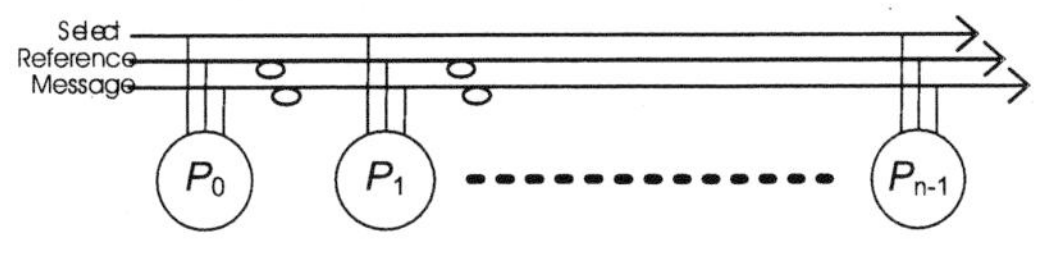

Figure 1. Unidirectional Bus with Reference, Select and Message Waveguides

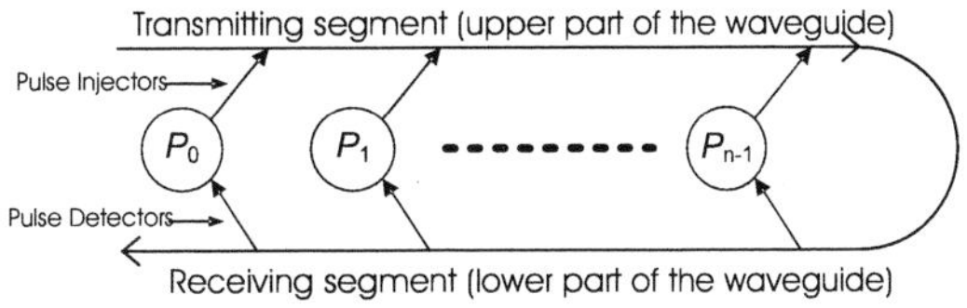

Figure 2. Folded One Dimensional Bus

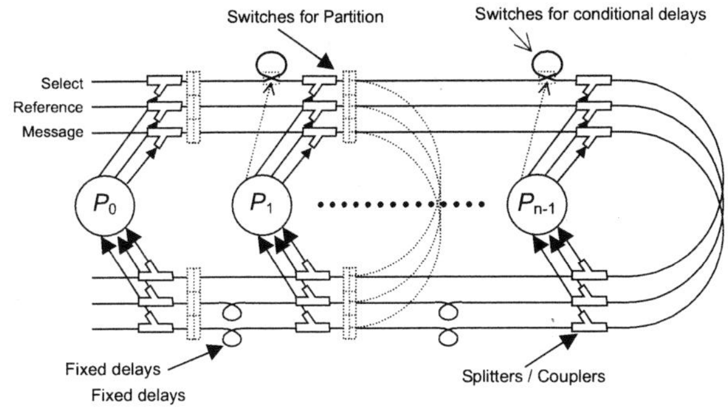

Figure 3. LARPBS -Linear Array with a Reconfigurable Pipelined Bus

nation processor (detection of the coincidence triggers the reading of the message waveguide). In Figure 1, unit delays are shown as small ovals on the message and reference waveguides. If each delay introduces an ω unit of delay, then Processor P_0 can address destination P_1 with an initial one ω time differential; P_1 can address P_3 with an initial two ω time differential, etc.

A common architecture is the folded one dimensional bus as shown in Figure 2. This configuration allows a single waveguide to communicate to all the processors in the system. Processors write messages to the upper side of the bus and read them from the lower side. Coincident pulse is often used for addressing, that is, three waveguides with delays on the reference and message waveguides *on the receiving segment only.*

A number of two and multi-dimensional optical bus architectures have also been proposed in the literature, for example, APPB/APPBS [13], RASOB [14], AROB [4] and PR-MESH [15]. In these cases, rows and columns of processors are interconnected either through processors or via optical switches. In general, these architectures conceptually extend a linear array topology. The results presented in this paper are applicable to such extensions.

3.2 The LARPBS Model

The Linear Array with a Reconfigurable Pipelined Bus System (LARPBS) [2] is a reconfigurable model of n processors identified as P_0 through P_{n-1}. LARPBS uses three folded waveguides, one for message passing and the other two for addressing. Addressing is accomplished via the coincident pulse technique. In addition to the fixed delays on the reference and message waveguides, LARPBS also includes conditional delays on the select waveguide in the transmitting segment only. This provides, in addition to the initial time differential between the select and reference signals, the option to adjust that time differential by factors of ω. For example, P_0 can address P_{n-2} by sending out a select and reference pulse at the same time, and setting exactly one of the configuration switches to delay. The reconfigurability in this model is provided by the pairs of partition switches located between each processor on both the upper and lower segments; these switches can partition the system into two subsystems with the same characteristics at any of these pairs of switches. As a consequence, the total number of subsystems can be equal to the total number of processors. Figure 3 illustrates the LARPBS model. Further details about the LARPBS model can be found in [2,8].

In the theoretical model, an optical signal is initially generated by a pulse injector while the signal is detected by a pulse detector. Photo emitters are optical devices that implement the pulse injector function and the signal is routed into the fiber bus by an optical coupler. In a similar way, a photo detector and a splitter (coupler) implement the pulse detector function. The elements in this model which contribute a loss to the signal are the following:

- three waveguides: select, reference, and message,
- (n-1) partition switches,
- (n-1) conditional delay switches,
- (n) pulse injectors per waveguide (each injector is composed of a photo emitter and a coupler), and
- (n) pulse detectors per waveguide (each detector is composed of a photo detector and a coupler).

In this paper, we confine ourselves to the feasibility of the LARPBS model [2].

4 Review of Basic Optics and Measuring Units

4.1 Refractive Index and Total Reflection

Light travels at different speeds in different transparent media where the denser the medium, the slower the speed of light. When a beam of light in a transparent medium reaches a boundary with another transparent medium, two phenomena may occur: refraction and reflection. Refraction occurs when part of a light beam passes through the

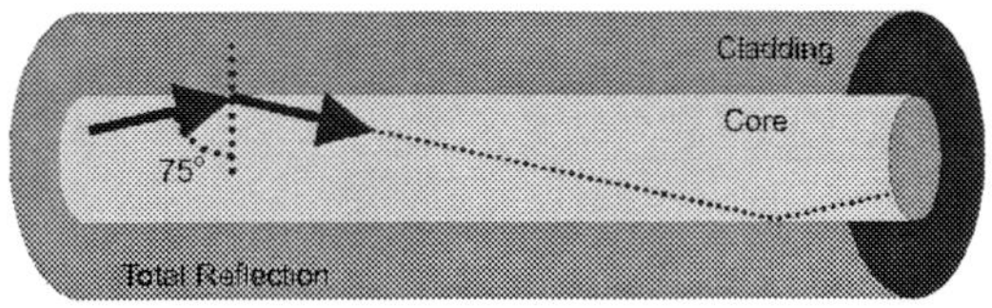

Figure 4. For Total Reflection to take place in a fiber, the minimum angle of incidence is about 75°.

other medium and suffers a deviation if the incident angle is small enough but greater than zero. Reflection occurs when part of the light beam is reflected back into the original medium. If the incident angle is sufficiently large then the phenomenon of total reflection [16,17] occurs; this means that no portion of the beam escapes from the original medium due to refraction. The amount of deviation of a beam due to refraction between free space and another transparent medium is called the refractive index (RI) of the medium. The RI indicates how dense a medium is with respect to free space in terms of light transmissibility and also is an indication of how fast light travels in that medium [16]. The speed of light in a medium is obtained by dividing the speed of light in free space, c = 299,792,458 m/s, by the RI of the medium: $v = \frac{c}{n}$ [18]. For example, if the RI for optical fiber is n=1.47 then the speed of light in the optical fiber is 203,940,447 m/s, which is about 30% slower than that in free space. Light transmission in a fiber is mostly enabled by the total reflection of light within the core due to the difference of refractive indices between the core and the cladding, as shown in Figure 4.

4.2 Gain and Loss

Any transmission line causes attenuation to the signal it carries, some of this attenuation is caused by the conductor itself when other devices also contribute to the attenuation. Devices such as amplifiers provide for a gain to the power of the signal. Optical fiber introduces a very small loss to the signal, this loss is given in dB/Km (where dB refers to decibels) [19]. The unit dB was created by the Bell Telephone Company to facilitate the calculation of the total loss in a transmission line by replacing losses given in percents or factors by their corresponding logarithms [20]. By doing this, the total loss in a transmission line can be calculated by summing individual losses given in decibels. The unit decibel is defined as follows [19,20]:

$$\mathrm{dB} = 10 \log \left(\frac{\text{Input Power}}{\text{Output Power}} \right)$$

4.3 Optical Power

Similarly to electrical power, optical power is measured in Watts (W). However in networks, powers are very small and are measured in the order of milliwatts (mW) [19] or in an equivalent but more practical unit called decibels relative to milliwatts (dBm) [19,20]:

$$\mathrm{dBm} = 10 \log \left(\frac{\text{Power in mW}}{1 \text{ mW}} \right)$$

The input power value is considered as a factor of one which can be replaced by its logarithm. By doing this the total loss in the system can be subtracted from the input power in order to calculate the output power. For example, if the input power is 9 dBm and there are losses of 2 dB and 3 dB, then the total loss is 5 dB and is subtracted from the input power to give an output power of 4 dBm. Note that losses are given in dB and powers are given in dBm, nevertheless, they can be subtracted or added directly. Also note that negative powers given in dBm correspond to values which are less than 1 mW, e.g. 0.5 mW = -3.01 dBm [19] and that a loss of 3.01 dB corresponds to a power halving whereas a gain of 3.01 dB corresponds to a power doubling [19].

Table 1
VCSEL's Powers

VCSELs	
Wavelength	Emitting Power
850 nm	10dBm
1310nm	4dBm
1550nm	2dBm

5 Survey of Optical Devices

This section describes the optical technologies available currently, that is, post 2000, which can be deployed in realizing an LARPBS system. The inclusion of this section is necessary since for two reasons: first, we identify specific technologies and standard wavelengths as eligible for a realization for LARPBS, second, we lay the groundwork for the analysis conducted later in the paper.

5.1 Photo Emitters and Photo Detectors [17,21]

There are several kinds and technologies of photo emitters: LEDs (Light Emitting Diodes), Laser Photo Diodes, VCSELs (Vertical Cavity Surface-Emitting Laser). The latter is the most appropriate for LARPBS implementation due to its special features such as low cost, low power consumption, and easy coupling to optical fiber. VCSELs are now available in the three principal wave lengths: 850nm, 1310nm, and 1550nm. VCSELs provide different emission power for each of these wavelengths. Table 1 shows the respective powers for each wavelength [22,21].

There are also several kinds of photo detectors which do not vary technologically from one to another as much as photo emitters. Also, they are available in a wider range of options. For these reasons, the principal concern is the minimum power that they can detect. The minimum power perceptible by a photo detector is about 1 μW, or -30dBm [21].

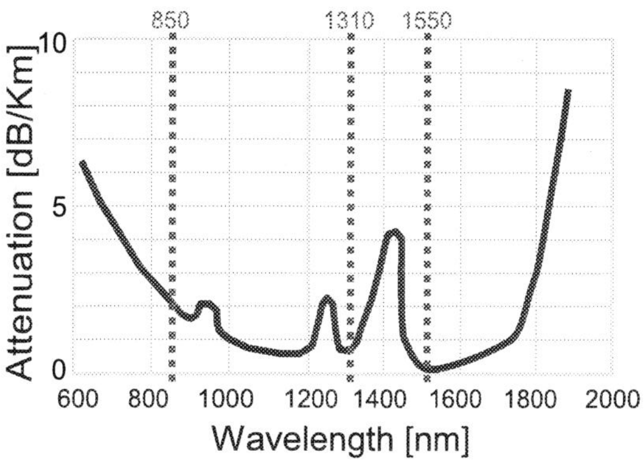

Figure 5. Fiber Loss (dB/km)

5.2 Optical Fiber

Optical fiber is the main component of an optical waveguided system; it is the communication medium through which the information is sent. The core is that part of the fiber which actually transmits the signal and whose refractive index is about 1.47. The cladding is made of a material with a smaller refractive index than the core to allow the effect of total reflection as shown in Section 4.1 and in Figure 4. Finally, the coating layer is intended for easy handling of the fiber since the size of the core and cladding are very small.

There are two main kinds of optical fiber: multimode and single-mode [16,17]. Multimode fiber is used to transmit several signals with different wavelengths at the same time while singlemode optical fiber is used to transmit monochromatic signals, that is, a single wavelength. Singlemode and multimode optical fibers differ on their core diameters, for example, singlemode has a core diameter of 10μm and a cladding diameter of 125μm whereas multimode has core diameters ranging from 50μm to 110μm.

Optical signals with different wavelengths suffer different losses in an optical fiber. Figure 5 shows a graph of signal attenuation for different wavelengths of light. Losses for the three principal wavelengths used in optical communication are given in Table 2. The minimum loss in a fiber corresponds to signals with a wavelength of 1550nm [23]. This is the ideal wavelength to use for telecommunication systems where distance and the length of the fiber are large. However for the expected scale of interconnection networks, loss due to the fiber may be negligible [1]. In particular, break even losses are calculated for lengths of approximately 5.7km or less. The vertical dotted lines, from left to right in the figure, show the chronological sequence of VCSELs as available commercially; only recently are the 1550nm emitters available.

From these three options the maximum loss in fiber occurs for a wavelength of 850nm as shown in Figure 5 and in Table 2. However since the loss of signal due to the length of the fiber is very small, a better consideration in choosing the appropriate wavelength is selecting the photo emitter that offers the maximum optical power. This extends as much as possible the interval between the emission power and the detection power. This is important so as to maximize the available power, thereby tolerating the greatest amount of transmission loss. Therefore, a wavelength of 850nm with an emitting power of 10dBm is selected.

Table 2
Loss in Optical Fiber

Loss in Optical Fiber	
Wavelength	Loss (dB/Km)
850nm	1.6
1310nm	0.65
1550nm	0.2

Table 3
Typical insertion losses in splitters [17]

Splitting Ratio	Typical Insertion Loss (dB)
50/50	3.1/3.1
40/60	4.1/2.3
15/85	8.4/0.8
10/90	10.2/0.6
5/95	13.2/0.4

5.3 Splitters and Couplers

Splitters or Couplers divide one optical path into two or more with any combination of splitting ratios.
Table 3 shows some common splitting ratios and their corresponding insertion losses.

6 Power Loss Analysis of LARPBS

This estimation of the number of processors in the LARPBS optical bus model considers the total loss of an end-to-end signal. Using the currently available devices for a wavelength of 850nm the total signal loss budget is about 40dB.

In order to carry out this analysis, it is necessary to identify where the losses occur and their respective amounts. Following from Section 3.2, the following presentation summarizes the optical components of interest with emphasis on the induced signal losses.

- Optical Fiber: Losses for 850nm wavelength are given in Figure 5 and Table 2. The loss depends on the fiber length. Either single or multimode fiber may be used, however, when using a single wavelength in LARPBS, there is no need to use multimode.

- Photo Emitters: VCSELs generating 850nm wavelengths are chosen to implement the emitters. The emitting powers are shown in Table 1. There is a

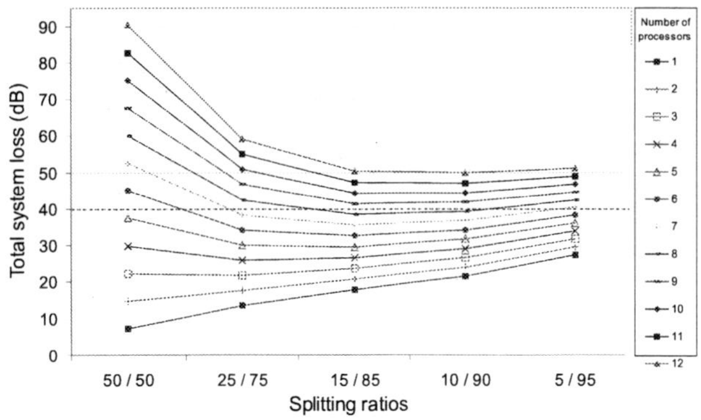

Figure 6. Number of processors vs. splitting ratios.

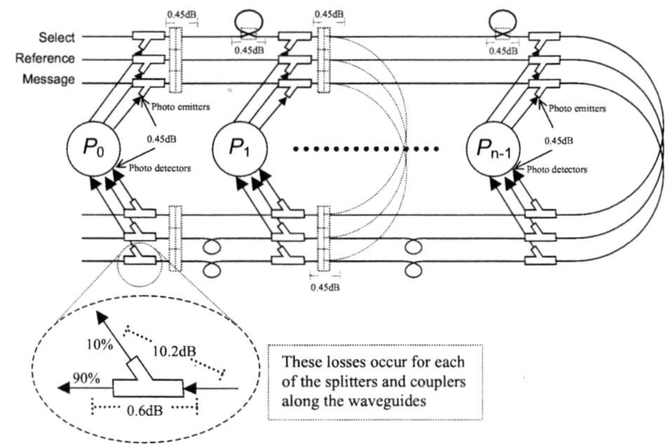

Figure 7. LARPBS signal loss.

loss that corresponds to the coupling of the VCSEL to the fiber, this loss is between 0.4dB and 1dB [21].

- Photo Detectors: The minimum perceptible power for a photo detector is about -30dBm as discussed in Section 5.1. The coupling loss is between 0.4dB and 1dB.

- Couplers and Splitters: Splitters introduce different loss depending on the splitting ratio as shown in Table 3. Figure 6 presents our analysis of the effects that different splitting ratios would have on the overall system (keeping the other parameters constant for this particular finding). Note that the power loss effect is minimal at splitting ratios 10/90 and 15/85. In the LARPBS system, this observation stems from balancing the losses along each of the out-bound paths, that is, we wish to reduce the costs along the longest path. We therefore select the 10/90 splitting ratio: 10% for the path that connects to the processor and 90% for the path that gives continuity to the waveguide. The corresponding losses for this splitting ratio are 10.2dB and 0.6dB respectively.

- Switches (for example as used for bus partitioning) either are the one-input, two-output or two-input, one-output variety. In the former, 100% of the signal is switched to the appropriate output whereas in the latter, an either-or but not both coupling occurs. Losses on the average of 0.45db occur per switch.

Table 4 summarizes the maximum range of signal loss that can be tolerated, that is, 40dB.

Figure 7 shows the LARPBS model with the expected sources of signal loss.

Table 5 summarizes the known constant sources of signal loss for one optical communication: that is, from any specific source processor to any specific destination processor The fixed constant signal loss is calculated as: 21.46dB (for an assumed 100m maximum length of an optical path).

Table 4
Range of Loss in the system

Emitting power:	10dBm
Detector power:	-30dBm
Range of loss:	**40dB**

Since the intent of this study is to determine the maximum number of processors, note that each processor is considered as an assembly composed of an injector, detector, one conditional delay switch and two partition switches. For each processor in the system then, an optical signal must pass through this assembly and is subject to signal loss. The maximum number of processors can hence be estimated by considering a bus cycle, that is, a communication from P_0 to itself.

From the range of loss, 40dB, minus the fixed loss, 21.46, the variable loss should be less or equal to 18.54. Table 7 shows some calculations on the number of processors which can give valid variable and/or total losses. The maximum number of processors is eight.

If the reconfigurability that partition switches offer is sacrificed by removing them, some loss is eliminated. In that case the variable loss corresponds to (n-1)°0.45 + (2n-2)°0.6. Table 8 shows the results when partition switches are removed. The maximum number of processors is twelve under these conditions. Recall from Section 3.2 that LARPBS is a defined architecture that includes the bus partition switches for the purposes of dynamic bus reconfigurations during operation. Our analysis here should be viewed as estimating the cost for this characteristic of LARPBS.

7 Conclusion

An optical power budget and signal losses of an LARPBS optical bus parallel computing model are considered in this study. Accordingly, it is determined that an optical signal originating at the beginning of the bus, pro-

Table 5
Fixed losses for any optical path

Fixed Losses	
Loss Localization	Amount
Emitter Insertion Loss:	1×0.45 dB
Detector Insertion Loss:	1×0.45 dB
Fiber Loss:	0.16 dB/100m
Splitters Loss 10/90:	2×10.2 dB
Total Fixed Loss:	**21.46 dB**

Table 6
Variable loss for a path with n processors

Variable Losses	
Loss Localization	Amount
Partition Switches:	$(2n-2) \times 0.45$dB
Switches for delays:	$(n-1) \times 0.45$dB
Splitters Loss 10/90:	$(2n-2) \times 0.6$ dB
Total	$(3n-3) \times 0.45 + (2n-2) \times 0.6$

Table 7
Number of processors and the corresponding losses

Number of Processors	Variable Loss ≤ 18.54	Total Loss ≤ 40
n=7	15.30	36.76
n=8	17.85	39.31
n=9	20.40	41.86

Table 8
Number of processor and corresponding losses when partition switches are removed

Number of Processors	Total Loss ≤ 40
n=11	37.96
n=12	39.61
n=13	41.26

cessor 0, is able to reach, with sufficient power, the last processor in the receiving segment, which is again processor 0. Despite the loss of signal in this passive system, the number of processors that can be accommodated is about eight when the LARPBS model is complete with all the optical devices that are required. If the reconfigurability of the model is sacrificed, then the total number of processors can be increased to twelve due to the loss reduction from the absence of partition switches.

These results are promising despite the low order of processors. In the literature, the expectations of having large, on the order of hundreds or thousands, of processors has motivated the further development of such optical parallel models, in particular, the LARPBS model. Our results clearly establish the reasonable and practical implementation of the LARPBS optical bus parallel computing model using current optical technologies. In particular, VCSELs are used in our analysis.

Since two and multidimensional variations of optical bus parallel models extend from the one dimensional case, the approach we have taken can be applied to these other models as well. Our approach can also be applied to models that incorporate multiple optical buses as well.

Despite the decade long advancements, our results are are consistent with work reported a decade ago. Differences between our work and that reported earlier include: (a) the earlier work conducted an analysis of an architecturally simplified optical bus system to the one we have considered, that is, the LARPBS model, and (b) the earlier work applied technologies at that time whereas we conclude our work with current optical technologies.

The analysis conducted did not consider amplification of optical signals, as perhaps can be done by erbium-doped fiber. Also, a study of data rates along with a BER analysis lies outside the scope of the present work. The analysis did provide the major source of signal loss: splitters. In our future work, we consider amplification and alternative detector technologies to address the limitations on the number of processors. We also intend to continue the work by considering data rates and a BER analysis.

References

1. D. A. B. Miller. Physical reasons for optical interconnection. *International Journal of Optoelectronics*, 11:155–168, May-June 1997.
2. Yi Pan and Keqin Li. Linear array with a reconfigurable pipelined bus system — concepts and applications. In H.R. Arabnia, editor, *Proc. of the International Conference on Parallel and Distributed Processing Techniques and Applications (PDPTA'96), Vol. III*, pages 1431–1441, Sunnyvale, California, USA, August 1996.
3. Marie Beltran. A safe communication model for optical buses. Master's thesis, The University of Texas at El Paso, Department of Computer Science, 2003. in progress.
4. Sandy Pavel and Selim G. Akl. On the power of arrays with reconfigurable optical buses. *Technical Report No. 95-374, Queens University, Kingston, Ontario, CANADA*, February 1995.
5. Donald M. Chiarulli, Rami G. Melhem, and Steven P. Levitan. Using coincident optical pulses for parallel memory addressing. *IEEE Computer*, 20(12):48–58, Dec. 1987.
6. D.M. Chiarulli, R.M. Ditmore, S.P. Levitan, and R.G. Melhem. An all optical addressing circuit: experimental results and scalability analysis. *Journal of Lightwave Technology*, 9:1717, 1991.
7. D. Chiarulli, S. Levitan, R. Mehlen, M. Bidnurkar, R. Ditmore, G. Gravenstreter, Z. Guo, C. Qiao, M. Sakr, and J. Teza. Optoelectronic buses for high-performance computing. *Proceedings of the IEEE*, 92(11):1701–1709, Nov.

1994.

8. Brian J. d'Auriol. Communication in the LARPBS (optical bus) model: A case study. In A. Goscinski et al., editor, *Proc. of The Fourth International Conference on Algorithms And Architecture for Parallel Processing (ICA3PP2000)*, pages 581–590, Hong Kong, December 2000.
9. Sartaj Sahni. Models and algorithms for optical and opto-electronic parallel computers. *International Journal Foundations in Computer Science*, 12:249–264, June 2001.
10. René Roldán. A fesability study for fiber-based optical bus networks. Master's thesis, The University of Texas at El Paso, Department of Computer Science, 2003. in progress.
11. L. Susan Draper. A free space optical bus system (FSOBS). Master's thesis, The University of Texas at El Paso, Department of Computer Science, 2003. in progress.
12. S.Q. Zheng, Keqin Lin, Yi Pan, and M.C. Pinotti. Generalized coincident pulse technique and new addressing scheme for time-division multiplexing optical buses. *Journal of Parallel and Distributed Computing*, 61:1033–1051, August 2001.
13. Zicheng Guo, Rami G. Melhem, Richard W. Hall, Donald M. Chiarulli, and Steven P. Levitan. Array processors with pipelined optical busses. In J. Jaja, editor, *Proc. 3rd Symposium on Frontiers of Massively Parallel Computation (Cat. No.90CH2908-2)*, pages 333–342, College Park, MD, USA, October 1990.
14. Chunming Qiao. Efficient matrix operations in a reconfigurable array with spanning optical buses. In *Proceedings. Frontiers '95. The Fifth Symposium on the Frontiers of Massively Parallel Computation (Cat. No.95TH8024). IEEE Comput. Soc. Press. 1994*, pages 273–280, McLean, VA, USA, Feb 1995.
15. Jerry L. Trahan, Anu G. Bourgeois, and Ramachandran Vaidyanathan. Tighter and broader complexity results for reconfigurable models. *Parallel Processing Letters*, 8(3):271–282, 1998.
16. Stamatios V. Kartalopoulos. *Introduction to DWDM Technology, Data in a Rainbow*. IEEE Press, 2000.
17. Force Inc., 2003. http://www.fiber-optical.info.
18. Optical Sciences Center 1630 E.University Blvd, Tucson, Arizona 85721, 2002. http://www.optics.arizona.edu/.
19. Light Reading, Inc, 2003. http://www.lightreading.com/document.asp?doc_id=6730&site=lightreading.
20. Paul H. Bock, Jr., 1994. http://www.columbia.edu/~fuat/cuarc/dB.html.
21. Honeywell, 2003. http://content.honeywell.com/vcsel/.
22. Optowell Co., 2000. http://optowell.com/homepage2/vcsel/SH85-2N001.pdf.
23. Light Reading, Inc, 2003. http://www.lightreading.com/document.asp?doc_id=3108&site=lightreading.

Efficient Broadcast on Computational Grids

Gabriel Mateescu [a] and Ryan Taylor [b]

[a] Information Management Sservices Branch, National Research Council Canada, 100 Sussex Drive, Ottawa ON K1A 0R6, Canada
E-mail: `gabriel.mateescu@nrc.gc.ca`

[b] School of Computer Scince, Carleton University, 1125 Colonel By Drive, Ottawa, K1S 5B6, Canada
E-mail: `rtaylor@scs.carleton.ca`

Collective communication operations such as broadcast, gather and reduce are potential performance bottlenecks for scientific computing software. With the advent of wide-area distributed computing and computational Grids, achieving efficient collective communication for applications running on geographically distributed computers becomes of paramount importance. We propose an efficient broadcast algorithm, that is applicable to any connected network and show that it improves the performance of the MPI broadcast operation.

Les opérations de communication inter-processus telles la diffusion (broadcast), la collecte des données (gather), et les opérations mathématiques inter-noeuds (reduce) peuvent aisément limiter la performance des codes de calcul scientifique. L'intérêt croissant que suscite le calcul géographiquement distribué de type grille rend d'autant plus primordial le développement de méthodes collectives de communication efficaces. Nous proposons ici un algorithme de diffusion efficace des données qui peut être utilisé sur tout type de réseau actif. Cet algorithme améliore la performance de l'opération MPI de diffusion.

1 Introduction

Parallel and distributed scientific computing software applications employ various forms of collective communication, such as broadcast, reduce, scatter, and gather. Collective communication is a potential performance bottlenecks, especially when the communication occurs over shared networks with large latencies. For computational Grids, achieving efficient collective communication for applications spanning geographically distributed computers is of paramount importance. We propose an efficient broadcast algorithm, that is applicable to any connected network and show that its performance is competitive with that of the MPICH implementation [1,2] of the Message Passing Interface [3].

We consider a set of networked computer resources, and represent the network as a directed graph $G = (V, E)$, where V is the set of vertices, and E is the set of edges. Vertices represent computer nodes and edges represent the interconnect. With each edge $(u, v) \in E$, we associate the weight $w(u, v) > 0$, which represents the latency of the communication from vertex u to v. A message of size m is to be sent from a designated root to all the other vertices such that: (i) for each edge $e = (u, v) \in E$, it takes the time $\Delta(u) > 0$, called the *injection time* for the node u to inject the message for delivery to v; (ii) a sender vertex can inject only a message at a time, i.e., point-to-point communication. The graph is strongly connected, i.e., for each pair of vertices $u, v \in V$, there is a path from u to v and from v to u.

The problem is to to find the *broadcast schedule* that minimizes the time at which all the vertices have the message, where the broadcast schedule specifies the vertices that each vertex sends messages to, and the order in which the sends are performed. Notice that the problem contains undirected graphs as a special case. The problem can be shown to be NP-complete [4,5]. We present here an approximate solution.

2 Related Work

The published literature on collective communication for wide-area networks [6,7] typically follows the approach of dividing the network in a hierarchy of levels, and define collective operations in terms of collective operation within the levels. Often, a simplified view of the wide are network is assumed, in which point-to-point latencies are equal.

An approach that supports general latencies has been proposed by Mandal, Kennedy and Mellor-Crummey [5]. The authors consider the special case when Δ is a constant, and employ Dijkstra's algorithm together with a broadcast schedule derived from node labeling. Our approach has some common points with the method proposed in [5]. Unlike our method, the authors build the communication tree by applying the original Dijkstra's algorithm. However, simply using Dijkstra's algorithm does not include the effect of the insertion time on the communication topology. This may produce a shortest path three that is far from the optimal communication topology, as shown by the example in Fig. 1, where all the edges have the weight of one.

The single source shortest path tree (left graph, the shortest path edges are marked with arrows) determined assuming $\Delta = 0$ has the longest path of 1. However, if Δ is included, the length of the longest path is actually $1 + 5\Delta$, since all the messages are sent by vertex 0 and there is insertion delay of Δ for each message. The tree shown on the right side (the shortest path edges are marked with arrows) has the longest path $2 + 3\Delta$, which is better than $1 + 5\Delta$, when $\Delta > 0.5$. Moreover, in the labeling stage of the algorithm, [5] uses an expensive method for computing the

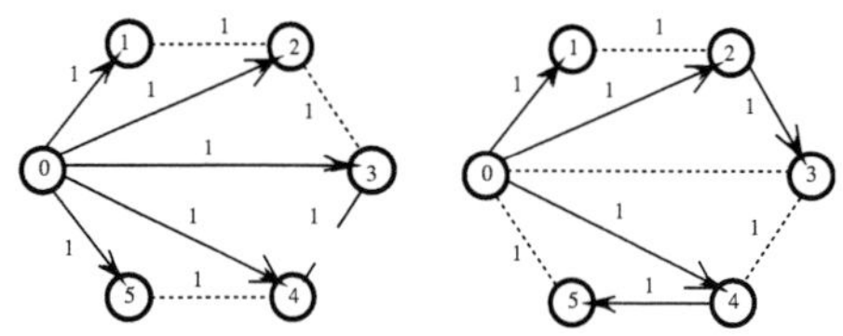

Figure 1. Single Source Shortest Path (left) is not optimal for broadcast. The broadcast schedule defined by the tree on the right side is better for $\Delta > 0.5$.

labels and the schedule, performing a level-ordering of the shortest path tree, followed by two level-order tree traversals.

3 Proposed Method

We propose a two stage algorithm for determining the schedule of the broadcast. In the first stage, a tree T is extracted from the graph G. The tree defines the communication topology such that each vertex receives the message m from its parent in T and sends the message to all its children in T.

In the second stage, we determine the order in which each vertex sends the messages along the edges of the tree T. As discussed earlier, the order affects the time to perform the broadcast because of the cost Δ of inserting a message. The order is performed in terms of a vertex *labeling* which is defined recursively as follows:

$$label(u) = \begin{cases} 0, & \text{if } u \text{ is a leaf in } T \\ \max_{1 \le i \le n} \{label(v_i) + w(u, v_i) + i\Delta(u)\} & \text{otherwise} \end{cases}$$

where n is the number of children of node u in T, $v_1, v_2, \ldots, v_n$ are the children of u, and $label(v_1) + w(u, v_1) \ge label(v_2) + w(u, v_2) \ge \cdots \ge label(v_n) + w(u, v_n)$.

The label of a vertex u gives the maximum time it takes a message sent from u to reach the vertices in the subtree rooted at u. We perform the sends from a vertex u to its children such that u sends the messages in order of decreasing label of the vertices. Choosing this order means that, for a given set of labels of the child vertices of u, the label of u is minimized.

The first stage of the algorithm is an extension of Dijkstra's single source shortest path algorithm, whereby we incorporate in the cost of the paths the cost of inserting the message. Taking into account the insertion time is critical for finding a good communication topology, as illustrated by the example given in Fig. 1. The pseudocode of the algorithm is shown in Fig. 2.

The second stage of the algorithm is implemented using a post-order traversal of the tree to compute the label of the vertices and the schedule, as shown in Fig. 3.

```
extended_single_source_shortest_path{
/*
 Inputs:
     G        = graph representing the
                network of host machines
     V        = number of vertices in G
     E        = number of edges in G
     root     = the vertex from which data
                is broadcast
     w[E]     = array of edge weights
   DELTA[E]   = array of insertion delays

 Outputs:
    dist[V]   = array holding shortest distance
                from root to every vertex
  parent[V]   = array holding the parent of each
                vertex in the shortest path tree
*/

 dist[0:V-1]  = infinity;
 dist[root]   = 0;
 parent[root] = null;

 // priority queue
 queue = init_queue(G, dist);

 while( (u=dequeue_min(queue)) != NULL ){
  // compute shortest distance from u
  // to all its neighbors in the queue
  while((v=get_next_neighbor(G,u)) != NULL){
   e = (u,v);    // edge connecting u and v

   if( (v in queue) &&
       (dist[v] > dist[u] + w[e] + DELTA[e])){
     // new minimum found for dist[v]
     dist[v] = dist[u] + w[e] + DELTA[e];
     // v is the child of u, so u incurs an
     // injection time along e = (u,v)
     dist[u] = dist[u] + DELTA[e];
     parent[v] = u;
   } // end if

  } // end while
 } // end while
}
```

Figure 2. Extended Single Source Shortest Path Algorithm

4 Modelling Real Networks

The algorithm works for any directed acyclic graph with positive edge weights and is thus able to handle all real-world networks. The network topology and the latencies (edge weights) are made available to the algorithm through external tools such as the Network Weather Service [8]. Thus, the approach proposed here can be applied to topologies that are dynamic and the global graph can be assem-

```
label_nodes{
/*
Inputs:
     u     = vertex whose label is computed
     T     = the tree determined by
             extended_single_source_shortest_path
     V     = number of vertices in T
     E     = number of edges in G
     w[E]  = array of edge weights
 DELTA[E]  = array of injection times

Output:
 label[V]  = array containing the label of
             each vertex in T
*/

 label[u] = 0;

 // return at bottom of recursion
 if ( u is a leaf in T ) return;

 // get adjacency list of u
 list = adjacency_list(T, u);

 while ( v = get_next_vertex(list) ){
  // visit all children of u
  label_nodes(T, V, v, label);
 }

 // find label of u
 //  sort adjacency list of u by
 //  decreasing label(v) + w(T,u,v)
 sort_decreasing( list, label, w);
 count = 1;
 for ( get_next_vertex(list) ){
  e = (u,v);    // edge connecting u and v
  tmp = label[v] + w[e] + count*DELTA[e];
  if ( tmp > label[u] )  label[u] = tmp;
  count++;
 }
}
```

Figure 3. Vertex Labeling algorithm

bled from querying several information services.

In other words, the graph itself is not static; instead the algorithm uses the graph that provides the most recent model of the network topology. This allows to support real networks where the latency is non-constant and non-uniform.

5 Injection Time Impact

The implementation of the algorithm uses for point-to-point communication the standard send function of MPI [3], called MPI_Send. The effect of the injection time on the broadcast time is significant when MPI_Send is used. For example, for a message size of 100000 bytes sent between two machines located about 6 miles away, the value of the measured injection time has been $\Delta = 7.3\,ms$, while the value of latency measured was $1.6\,ms$.

The injection time is larger when the function that performs the send operation returns control after some movement of data out of the send buffer occurrs (e.g., for MPI_Send) than when the function only initiates the send operation and immediately returns control (e.g., for MPI_Send [3], nonblocking *immediate* send). In particular, MPI_Send returns control when the the send buffer is free for reuse by the program. In the MPI [3] specification, MPI_Send is called a *blocking send* whereas, traditionally, a blocking send is defined as an operation that completes when an acknowledgement (such as "ready to receive message" or "message received") from a matching receive process is received. Nonblocking send functions such as MPI_Isend rely on buffering, either system or additional user area buffers. For example, a program using MPI_Isend to invoke a large number of send operations and to send large amounts of data relies on the existence of buffering space, either at the sender's or receiver's end, to hold the pending data.

Buffer space is a finite resource; the amount of buffer space depends on several factors including the MPI implelemenation and the amount of memory available on the host machines. Programs relying on the existence of buffer space may deplete the buffers and may run correctly in some conditions but fail sometimes. Hence, these programs are unsafe, unless care is taken to make sure that enough buffer space is available. To achieve safety, the use of nonblocking sends should be combined with some kind of handshaking between the sends and receives, e.g., the sender process should first wait for a *ready to receive* message from the receiver before posting the send.

Therefore, writing correct programs with MPI_Isend requires additional synchronization operations beyond waiting for the completion of the posted sends by invoking the functions MPI_Waitall or MPI_Test [3]. As the number of processors over which an MPI program is distributed increases and the distance between the processors increases (so the communication latency increases), the cost of the additional synchronization increases and the advantage of MPI_Isend having a lower injection time than MPI_Send may be offset by the additional synchronization operations required to guarantee program safety when using MPI_Isend (particularly for processors located hundreds or thousands of miles away). In addition, the smaller the message size, the smaller the difference between the injection time of MPI_Isend and that of MPI_Send.

6 Evaluation

The first stage of the algorithm has the same complexity as Dijkstra algorithm, i.e., $O(V \log V + E)$, and the second stage has $O(V \log V)$ operations. Thus, the complexity of the algorithm is $O(V \log V + E)$. While the complexity is

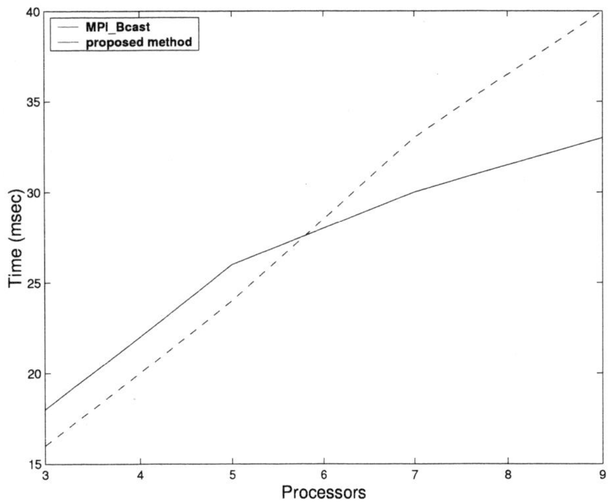

Figure 4. Broadcast time versus the number of processors for the proposed method (continuous line) and for MPICH MPI_Bcast x(dashed line)

a significant characteristics of the algorithm, the algorithm itself is executed only once at the beginning of the application and produces the broadcast schedule. The quality of the algorithm is assessed also by the improvement it brings to the wall-time of the broadcast operation.

We have compared the running time of the broadcast operation implelemted in MPICH [1,2] (the `MPI_Bcast` function) with the time given by the proposed method. In Fig. 4 we show the results on a network of five Intel workstations, four of which are dual processors, and the fifth is single processor. The workstations used in the experiment are located on different local area networks, as follows: two workstations located on a 100 Mb/s local area network, and the other three located on another local area network, with a distance of about 6 miles between the two networks. We have compared against the `MPI_Bcast` implementation of MPICH that uses the *ch_p4* device. The message size used has been of 100000 bytes. The results indicate that as the number of processors increases, our method outperforms `MPI_Bcast`.

7 Conclusion

We have introduced an efficient broadcast algorithm that is applicable to any connected network. First experiments indicate that, for a large enough number of processors, it outperforms the broadcast function implemented in MPICH. We plan to conduct more experiments, using larger testbeds and benchmarking real applications. We also intend to generalize the method along three directions: the first is to replace `MPI_Send` with a more efficient method, the second is to take into account the link bandwidth; the third is to use runtime network performance information provided by tools such as the Network Weather Service [8].

References

1. W. Gropp and E. Lusk. A high performance MPI implementation on a shared-memory vector supercomputer. *Parallel Computing*, 22(11):1513–1526, 1997.
2. W. Gropp and E. Lusk. User's guide for MPICH, a portable implementation of MPI. Technical Report ANL 96/6, Argonne National Laboratory, 2002.
3. W. Gropp, E. Lusk, and A. Skjellum. *Using MPI*. MIT Press, Cambridge, MA, USA, 1999.
4. M. R. Garey and D. R. Johnson. *Computers and Intractability: A Guide to the Theory of NP-Completeness*. W. H. Freeman and Company, New York, NY, 1979.
5. A. Mandal, K. Kennedy, and J. Mellor-Crummey. An approximate balanacing algorithm for efficient broadcast. http://www.cs.rice.edu/~anirban/acads, September 2001.
6. T. Kielmann, R. F. H. Hofman, H. E. Bal, A. Plaat, and R. A. F. Bhoedjang. MagPIe: MPI's collective communication operations for clustered wide area systems. *ACM SIGPLAN Notices*, 34(8):131–140, 1999.
7. M. Banikazemi, V. Moorthy, and D. Panda. Efficient collective communication on heterogeneous networks of workstations. In *International Conference on Parallel Processing, Minneapolis, MN*, pages 460–467, 1998.
8. Richard Wolski. Forecasting network performance to support dynamic scheduling using the network weather service. In *6th IEEE Symp. on High Performance Distributed Computing*, pages 316–325, 1997.

The Canadian Internetworked Scientific Supercomputer

Christopher Pinchak, Paul Lu, Jonathan Schaeffer, and Mark Goldenberg [a]
http://www.cs.ualberta.ca/~ciss

[a]Department of Computing Science, University of Alberta, Edmonton, Alberta, Canada, T6G 2E8
{pinchak,paullu,jonathan,goldenbe}@cs.ualberta.ca

On November 4, 2002, a Canada-wide virtual supercomputer gave a chemistry research team the opportunity to do several years worth of computing in a single day. This experiment, called CISS-1 (Canadian Internetworked Scientific Supercomputer), had three research impacts: (1) in partnership with C3.ca, created a new precedent for cooperation among Canadian high-performance computing sites, (2) demonstrated the scalability and capabilities of the Trellis system for wide-area high-performance metacomputing, and (3) produced a new computational chemistry result.

Using roughly 1,376 dedicated processors, at 20 facilities, and in 18 administrative domains across the country, approximately 3.5 CPU years of computing were completed. CISS-1 is a prototype for future research projects requiring large-scale computing in Canada. This is the first step towards making CISS a regular event on the Canadian research landscape.

Le 4 novembre 2002, un super-ordinateur virtuel pan-canadien a fourni à une équipe de chimistes l'équivalent de plusieurs années de calcul en une seule journée. Cette expérience, appelée CISS-1 (Canadian Internetworked Scientific Supercomputer)*, a eu trois impacts sur la recherche : (1) En collaboration avec le C3.ca, elle a créé un précédent de coopération entre les centre de calcul canadiens; (2) elle a démontré la mise à l'échelle et la capacité du système* Trellis *dans le calcul de haute performance sur une vaste étendue géographique; (3) elle a produit un nouveau résultat en chimie numérique.*

En utilisant environ 1 376 processeurs dédiés, sur 20 centres et 18 domaines administratifs à travers le Canada, environ 3,5 CPU-année de calculs ont été complétées. CISS-1 est un prototype de projets futurs demandant de vastes ressources de calcul au Canada. Il s'agit de la première étape visant à faire de CISS un événement régulier sur la scène de la recherche canadienne.

1 Introduction

Over the past four years, the Canada Foundation for Innovation (CFI) has partnered in acquiring $160 million in high-performance computing (HPC) equipment at over 20 sites in Canada. These resources have had a huge, positive research impact. However, this funding strategy is not amenable to creating large computing centres. For example, there is still only one Canadian academic site on the November 2002 listing of the world's Top 500 Supercomputer Sites [1]. Unfortunately, some scientific problems require computational resources greater than that of any single site (or regional consortia) in Canada.

CISS (pronounced "kiss"), the Canadian Internetworked Scientific Supercomputer, is an attempt to harness the research computing capacity in Canada to create a virtual supercomputer. Creating a nation-wide virtual supercomputer has long been a goal of C3.ca [2], Canada's national high-performance computing consortium, with support from a Natural Sciences and Engineering Research Council of Canada (NSERC) Major Facilities Access (MFA) Grant. The idea for CISS was spawned at the HPCS 2002 conference. With a CFI policy that requires each facility to make at least 20% of their resources available to external users, the timing was right to realize this vision.

Grid software packages, such as Globus [3], have the potential to meet our needs, but they require all participating sites to install and configure several software packages. Instead, we decided to use the Trellis system, developed by Paul Lu and colleagues at the University of Alberta [4], for the CISS experiment. Trellis emphasizes the use of widely-deployed software installed at the user-level, thus reducing the dependence on system administrators for extensive installation and configuration. For example, the Trellis *placeholder scheduling* model [5,6] is a simple, user-level approach to global scheduling over a wide-area network of heterogeneous resources.

The first CISS experiment, dubbed CISS-1, gave chemist Dr. Wolfgang Jäger and his research team the chance to get a new research result in a single day [7,8]. The application required up to six years of computing time. Normally, he would not tackle a problem of this size since other researchers with access to more computing power could beat him to the result.

The CISS-1 application, based on the MOLPRO software package [9], was "embarrassingly parallel" – filling in data points in a three-dimensional spatial grid. A parameter space study is the natural way to formulate the problem. This application was deliberately chosen for its simplicity, since it was felt that the logistics of getting more than 1,000 processors working together the first time would require extensive effort. It did, and even then we underestimated how time-consuming it would be!

CISS is an attempt to build the software *and* social infrastructure for a Canada-wide metacomputer (i.e., a useful aggregate of individual computer systems). Although there are still many unsolved technical problems in the metacomputing infrastructure, it may be an even greater challenge to establish a community of researchers to effectively share HPC resources. CISS-1 is just the first step towards our long-term vision. We envision CISS being utilized on a regular basis by researchers from across the country. This would be unique in the world and a tremendous opportunity for Canadian scientists to tackle problems that they previously thought were too large.

This paper is a semi-technical discussion of the motivation, implementation, and outcomes (both technical and social) of CISS. The contribution is in documenting and quantifying CISS as well as the lessons learned from the experience. Finally, we wish to acknowledge the support and hard work of a lot of people and agencies that made CISS possible, as detailed in the Appendix.

2 Trellis and Related Work

The concept of grid computing is popular these days. The goals of the Trellis project are more modest and simpler than that of grid computing. In particular, Trellis is focussed on supporting scientific applications on high-performance computing systems; supporting business applications and Web services are not explicit goals of the Trellis project. Therefore, we prefer to use older terminology—metacomputing—to reflect the more limited scope of our work. Currently, Trellis does not use any of the new software that might be considered part of grid computing, but the design of Trellis supports the incorporation of and/or co-existence with grid technology in the future.

In computing science, the dream of metacomputing has been around for decades. In various forms, and with important distinctions, it has also been known as distributed computing, batch scheduling, cycle stealing, peer-to-peer systems, and (most recently) grid computing. Some well-known, contemporary examples in this area include SETI@home [10], Project RC5/distributed.net [11], Condor [12], and the projects associated with Globus/Open Grid Service Architecture (OGSA) [3]. Of course, there are many, many other related projects around the world, including some in Canada (for example, Grid Canada [13] and the University of Victoria Grid Testbed [14]).

The Trellis philosophy has been to write the minimal amount of new software and to require the minimum of superuser support. Simplicity and software re-use have been important design principles. Trellis uses mostly widely-deployed, existing software systems so that system administrators who want to participate in CISS do not have to install new software. In fact, all that is needed to integrate a new site into CISS is for the system administrator to create a regular user account.

2.1 Overlay Metacomputers

Users often want to aggregate the computing power of a number of individual computers to get maximum job throughput and minimize makespans (i.e., time from start to finish to complete a workload). Using the Trellis software, users create an *overlay metacomputer* from a list of computers they have access to. An overlay metacomputer is like a grid or virtual supercomputer, except that the metacomputer exists entirely at the user-level and is considered an overlay because different metacomputers can be created on a per-user and per-application basis. The overlay metacomputer can be as simple as one computer, or as complicated as hundreds of computers in many administrative domains. Therefore, CISS is an overlay metacomputer of Canadian HPC systems.

2.2 Metacomputing Applications

In HPC, one often makes a distinction between *capacity* and *capability* computing. Capacity computing is centered on maximizing the throughput for a workload with multiple jobs. A large set of independent jobs is typical of capacity computing. Capability computing is centered on minimizing the turnaround time of individual jobs. Often, capability computing deals with applications that require advanced parallel algorithms, low-latency interconnection networks, high-performance input/output, or large amounts of physical memory to complete in a reasonable amount of time.

At the level of the workload, CISS is focussed on capacity computing; the goal is to complete as many independent jobs as possible. At the level of the individual jobs, CISS supports applications that are shared-memory or message-passing codes (i.e., capability computing) as long as all of the processes execute within the same machine or cluster [5,6]. But, so far, the CISS applications have all been embarrassingly parallel sequential jobs; each job is an independent data point in a parameter space.

Fortunately, embarrassingly parallel workloads are a natural and common occurrence in computational science, including chemistry, physics, discrete simulations, and bioinformatics. But, since not all workloads have independent jobs, future CISS experiments will address more sophisticated workloads, including workflow dependencies between jobs. For example, pipelines and job dependency graphs are supported by the Trellis system [15].

2.3 Issues in Global Scheduling

Metacomputers (and grids) need a system for global resource scheduling and allocation to deal with:

1. **Multiple Administrative Domains**: A global scheduler must be able to make use of resources from a wide variety of administrative domains and should do so while adhering to the local policies set out by the administration.

2. **Local Batch Scheduler Interaction**: Many HPC sites employ one or more batch schedulers to govern access to local computational resources. A global scheduler should take advantage of the underlying local batch scheduler, if it exists, by layering on top of it.

3. **Load Balancing**: A global scheduler is expected to improve performance by load balancing. Ideally, a global scheduler should provide lower makespans than any alternative methods the user has available.

2.4 Placeholder Scheduling

A placeholder is a mechanism for global scheduling in which each placeholder represents a potential unit of work. For further details, the interested reader is referred to other papers [5,6]. The current implementation of placeholder scheduling uses normal batch scheduler job scripts to implement a placeholder. Placeholders are submitted to the local batch scheduler with a normal, non-privileged user identity. Thus, local scheduling policies and job accounting are maintained.

When the job (a.k.a. placeholder) begins executing, it contacts a central server and requests the job's actual run-time parameters (i.e., late binding). For placeholders, the communication across administrative domains is handled using Secure Shell (SSH). In this way, a job's parameters are *pulled* by the placeholder rather than *pushed* by a central authority. In contrast, normal jobs hard-code all the parameters at the time of local job submission (i.e., early binding). Through the late binding of job parameters to placeholders, the global scheduler has maximum flexibility in implementing load balancing policies.

Placeholders do not require any special software, other than SSH, to be installed on individual computers. Moreover, they utilize existing normal user accounts at various sites, thereby allowing the sites to enforce per-user policies such as CPU accounting, disk quotas, and access restrictions.

2.5 TrellisWeb

TrellisWeb is an evolution of the PBSWeb system that was originally designed to simplify job submission to the Portable Batch System (PBS). TrellisWeb provides a convenient interface to placeholder scheduling to address:

1. **Resource Scheduling and Allocation**: With placeholder scheduling, global jobs can co-exist with local jobs from local users and all jobs are subject to local policies, such as priority schemes and queue structures. Additionally, zero-infrastructure placeholders can be used at sites without an underlying batch scheduler. Zero-infrastructure placeholders are, essentially, a script with an infinite loop of "get next job, compute job, and return result".

2. **Single Log On**: TrellisWeb provides a Web-based graphical user interface (GUI), or portal, with a single username/password access to overlay metacomputers.

3. **Access Control**: Placeholder scheduling and TrellisWeb use normal, non-privileged user accounts to provide a metacomputing environment. Therefore, the local site policies and access control are reflected implicitly within the system.

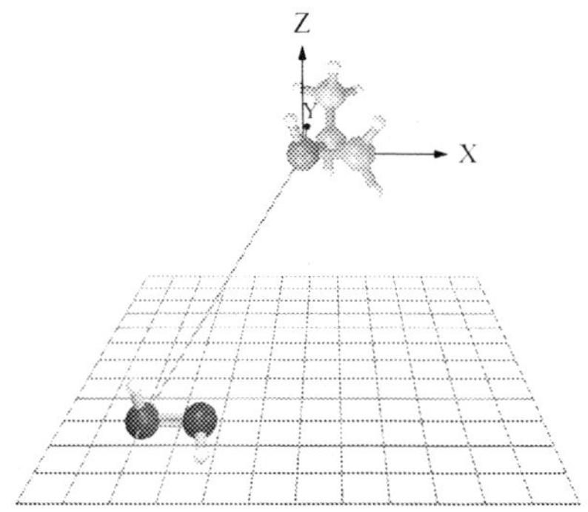

Figure 1. The "shifting" of the H_2O_2 molecule with respect to the space-fixed propyleneimine molecule.

3 The CISS-1 Application

The computational chemistry experiment was designed by Wolfgang Jäger, Aiko Huckauf, and Yunjie Xu of the Department of Chemistry, University of Alberta [8]. The chemistry application is the computational determination of chiral molecule interaction energies. The following description comes from Dr. Jäger.

"An object that cannot be superimposed with its mirror image is called chiral. Our hands are the most familiar example of such chiral objects. Image and mirror image are called enantiomers of the chiral object. Chiral molecules play important roles in nature. For example, life itself is based on single enantiomeric forms of amino acids and sugars, a fact known as "homochirality of life". Many pharmaceuticals are chiral molecules of which one enantiomer has a beneficial effect whereas the other may have severe side effects.

"At the heart of it all is chiral recognition or chiral discrimination. A handshake is possible between two left or two right hands, but not between left and right hand. On the molecular level, there is an energy difference between the interaction of, for example, the right handed form of a chiral molecule and the two enantiomeric forms of another substance.

"How can this subtle energy difference have such a profound effect in nature? The CISS-1 experiment involved computing the interaction energy of two chiral molecules at many different separations and orientations. The specific system consisted of 1,2-propyleneimine (an aziridine derivative) and hydrogen peroxide. The calculations were carried out on two different hydrogen peroxide enantiomers. An analysis of the results gives a "chiral recognition surface" that identifies the active sites of the chiral components."

To calculate the potential energy surfaces, a three-dimensional (spatial) grid was created with the fixed molecule at the centre. Calculations of potential energy between an enantiomer and the fixed molecule were performed at each point of the grid to yield the entire energy surface (for example, Figure 1). Because of the nature of the calculation, the grid may be arbitrarily dense, resulting in a potentially infinite number of points. However, the grid was chosen so as to provide adequate granularity for interpreting the potential energy surface while still being computationally feasible (even with a large number of computers participating in computing results). Each point may require several hours of computing time on a modern workstation. In computational terms, this is an ideal parallel problem which can be distributed onto as many processors as points needed and is therefore ideally suited for the CISS experiment.

The commercial product MOLPRO was used for the electronic structure calculations [9]. The computations for each single point were performed using a state-of-the-art level of theory. For this particular experiment, a single MOLPRO job requires a site-specific amount of main memory and between 0.5 GB and 1 GB of temporary disk space. On an average contemporary processor (such as an AMD Athlon CPU running at 1.3 GHz with 256 KB cache available in the Department of Chemistry at the University of Alberta), MOLPRO takes approximately four hours to compute one data point.

4 The CISS-1 Experiment

4.1 CISS-1 Environment

Porting any application to a heterogeneous set of computing platforms is always a labour-intensive and frustrating experience — CISS-1 was no exception. Some of the minor and majors issues that had to be addressed included:

- Hardware. A variety of different hardware platforms were used, each with their own set of peculiarities (see Table 1).
- Operating system. A variety of operating systems were encountered, each with their own set of peculiarities.
- Compilers. MOLPRO had particular requirements with respect to C and Fortran compilers. Often, the widely-available GNU compilers were not able to build the code correctly and we had to use either the Portland Group or Intel compilers, if available.
- Batch schedulers. CISS-1 used systems running PBS, Sun Grid Engine (SGE), and IBM's LoadLeveler. On systems that did not have a batch scheduler, we used a version of Trellis placeholders that did not depend on a local scheduler (the zero-infrastructure placeholders).
- Quotas. Many sites had explicit or implicit disk quotas which had to be removed. In many cases, we only found out about the quotas the hard way.
- Network. Some sites had firewalls or gateway nodes. Assistance was needed to communicate securely through them.
- Disk. Disk was located in different places on different systems. Some disk was local, some was shared across a storage area network (SAN). The chemistry application required roughly 1 GB of temporary storage for each job. For CISS-1, our experience was that local disk was much faster than a shared, parallel file system.
- Secure shell. Some sites used the commercial version of SSH, which turned out to have some incompatibilities with the open-source OpenSSH (e.g., the on-disk format of the public/private keys).

4.2 The Throughput Experiment

On November 4, 2002, the CISS-1 experiment combined 1,376 CPUs from 20 different HPC systems (16 different institutions, 18 different administrative domains) across Canada to cooperatively execute the computational chemistry parameter space study (Table 1) [6]. The experiment received a lot of media exposure, and the Web site received over 30,000 hits in the 24-hour period [7]. In our opinion, the most noteworthy metric of CISS-1 is the 18 different administrative domains, since that represents an unprecedented amount of (human) cooperation among Canadian HPC centres and one of the largest cross-domain metacomputers reported to date.

The CISS-1 experiment was performed as a 24-hour throughput test (i.e., capacity computing). For convenience, TrellisWeb was used to manage placeholder scheduling. Starting on November 4, 2002 at 12:00 midnight, and ending on November 5, 2002 at 12:00 midnight, placeholders were executed on the systems shown in Table 1. The two days prior to November 4, 2002 were used as a ramp-up period to finish integrating several sites and bring all sites up to full capacity, but only the computations performed during the 24-hour period will be discussed here. Several other institutions offered additional computing resources for CISS-1, but (regrettably) a lack of time prevented us from integrating them into the experiment.

A high-level overview of the throughput of the CISS-1 experiment is shown in Table 2. Performance varies from site to site because of differing numbers of processors, placeholders launched at each site, and how well-suited MOLPRO was for the particular hardware architecture at a given site. For example, since MOLPRO uses a substantial amount of temporary disk space during a computation, systems with fast, local disk drives (e.g., clusters) performed much better than systems with shared, parallel file systems.

A total of 7,593 work units (jobs) were completed by CISS-1 in the official 24-hour period.[1] The top four sites, in terms of throughput, were the CLUMEQ cluster in Montreal (`stokes.clumeq.mcgill.ca`) with 2,162 units, the cluster at Simon Fraser University in Burnaby

[1] Many more units of work were completed during the development of CISS, the ramp-up period, and after November 4, 2002. Over 27,000 units of work have been completed in total.

No.	Site	Description	Local Scheduler	PH
1	athlon-cluster.nic.ualberta.ca	x86 Linux Cluster	PBS	32
2	aurora.nic.ualberta.ca	SGI Irix	PBS	236
3	brule.cs.ualberta.ca	x86 Linux Cluster	SGE	26
4	bugaboo.hpc.sfu.ca	x86 Linux Cluster	Zero-Infrastructure	192
5	chromosome1.ocgc.ca	SGI Irix	PBS	96
6	deeppurple.sharcnet.ca	Alpha Linux Cluster	Zero-Infrastructure	22
7	driftwood.iam.ubc.ca	x68 Linux Cluster	PBS	16
8	gnome.usask.ca	x86 Linux Cluster	Zero-Infrastructure	32
9	hammerhead.sharcnet.ca	Alpha Linux Cluster	Zero-Infrastructure	22
10	herzberg.physics.mun.ca	SGI Irix	Zero-Infrastructure	20
11	maci-cluster.ucalgary.ca	Tru64 Alpha Cluster	PBS	176
12	mercury.sao.nrc.ca	x86 Linux Cluster	PBS	48
13	minerva.uvic.ca	IBM AIX SP	LoadLeveler	128
14	monolith.uwaterloo.ca	IBM AIX P-Series	Zero-Infrastructure	16
15	myri.ccs.usherbrooke.ca	x86 Linux Cluster	Zero-Infrastructure	8
16	p4-cluster.nic.ualberta.ca	x86 Linux Cluster	PBS	26
17	stokes.clumeq.mcgill.ca	x86 Linux Cluster	PBS	248
18	symphony.unb.ca	IBM AIX SP	LoadLeveler	2
19	white.cs.umanitoba.ca	x86 Linux Cluster	Zero-Infrastructure	22
20	zodiac.chem.ubc.ca	x86 Linux Cluster	PBS	8
			Total	1376

Table 1
CISS-1 Sites (PH = placeholders; typically one PH per CPU)

(`bugaboo.hpc.sfu.ca`) with 1,575 units, the various clusters and machines at the University of Alberta in Edmonton with 1,275 units, and the MACI cluster at the University of Calgary (`maci-cluster.ucalgary.ca`) with 1,065 units.

When examining these numbers, several points should be kept in mind:

1. Most sites possessed much more computing power than that used for CISS-1. Therefore, the throughput numbers should be viewed as lower bounds on the HPC resources at the various sites.

2. Unfortunate, but normal, hardware/software failures at a few sites affected their throughput. For example, a failed hard disk at the University of Calgary and a reboot at the University of Alberta led to a gradual restart of the placeholders and computations at both sites. Without the failures and reboots, several sites would have achieved better throughput. As an aside, we are fairly pleased with our software's ability to deal with faults.

3. The MOLPRO application was not substantially tuned for the architecture at each site. When possible, we used the recommended build procedures from the developers of MOLPRO, but the emphasis in CISS-1 was on the metacomputing aspects of the experiment and not on optimizing MOLPRO for each system.

Overall, CISS-1 consumed approximately 2.94 years (25738:58:40) of computing time across all sites. The mean time required to compute a work unit was approximately 3.39 hours (3:23:23). However, if we instead assume that a work unit takes approximately four hours to compute on a contemporary x86 cluster processor located in the Department of Chemistry at the University of Alberta, the total computation comes out to about 3.46 years worth of computation (7,292.94 work units at four hours per work unit). These numbers could be even better, but (as discussed above) a number of faults resulted in several hundred processors being unavailable for a few hours.

Most sites exhibit a large amount of variability (as evidenced by standard deviation σ) due to the fact that MOLPRO required a variable amount of time depending on the particular data point being computed. Other sources of variability include heterogeneous CPU clock rates (e.g., the various SGI Origins at the University of Alberta and the different Alpha-based nodes at `maci-cluster.ucalgary.ca`) and contention for shared storage systems.

Some of the systems, such as `athlon-cluster.nic-.ualberta.ca`, `brule.cs.ualber-ta.ca`, and `bugaboo.hpc.sfu.ca` had relatively steady and predictable rates of execution. Although computational ability varies among the sites, the overall rate within these sites stayed fairly consistent. This is largely due to the fact that these sites employed the use of local scratch disks present at each node (all three are clusters). In contrast, sites such as `aurora.nic.ualberta.ca` and, to some extent `maci-cluster.ucalgary.ca`, exhibited spikes in work completion due to the use of a parallel file system (as with `aurora.nic.ualberta.ca`), or

No.	Site	Number of Jobs	Total CPU Time	MeanTime Per Job	σ
1	athlon-cluster.nic.ualberta.ca	307.75	751:12:52	2:26:27	0:46:20
2	aurora.nic.ualberta.ca	437.17	4530:30:47	10:21:46	4:34:15
3	brule.cs.ualberta.ca	433.31	958:13:50	2:12:41	0:33:10
4	bugaboo.hpc.sfu.ca	1575.22	3984:29:37	2:31:46	0:36:55
5	chromosome1.ocgc.ca	136.79	1310:10:33	9:34:41	3:40:41
8	gnome.usask.ca	159.13	729:58:24	4:35:14	1:29:49
10	herzberg.physics.mun.ca	107.37	441:04:44	4:06:29	1:15:01
11	maci-cluster.ucalgary.ca	1064.61	2919:52:07	2:44:34	1:03:15
12	mercury.sao.nrc.ca	397.61	941:16:43	2:22:02	0:43:51
14	monolith.uwaterloo.ca	356.09	383:37:03	1:04:38	0:09:06
15	myri.ccs.usherbrooke.ca	73.02	161:45:13	2:12:54	0:38:28
16	p4-cluster.nic.ualberta.ca	96.56	579:38:53	6:00:10	2:47:13
17	stokes.clumeq.mcgill.ca	2162.47	5625:23:44	2:36:05	0:47:12
19	white.cs.umanitoba.ca	57.46	479:57:20	8:21:10	2:37:03
	other	228.36	1941:46:53	8:30:11	7:38:53
	Overall	7592.94	25738:58:40	3:23:23	2:40:54

Table 2
CISS-1 Throughput: Number of Jobs Completed All times are reported as H:MM:SS.

some cluster nodes sharing the same scratch disk (as with `maci-cluster.ucalgary.ca`). Because of the temporary storage requirements of MOLPRO, and because such storage is heavily used, MOLPRO jobs may contend with one another in a shared file system situation. `aurora.nic.ualberta.ca` experienced a severe I/O bottleneck at the parallel file system that resulted in high contention and high mean execution time.

4.3 CISS-2

CISS-2 was run over the Christmas holidays, from December 23, 2002 to January 2, 2003. In contrast to CISS-1, two applications were used: a molecular dynamics application from Dr. Peter Tieleman's group (University of Calgary) and a physics simulation from Dr. David Sénéchal's group (Université de Sherbrooke). Also, in sharp contrast to CISS-1, we did not request exclusive access to the computing resources; CISS-2 was designed to use whatever cycles might be available during the holidays. A subset of the sites from CISS-1 were used for CISS-2, including: CLUMEQ (at McGill University), the Hospital for Sick Children (Toronto), Memorial University of Newfoundland, Simon Fraser University, and the Universities of Alberta, Calgary, New Brunswick, Saskatchewan, and Victoria.

The CISS-2 experiment is still being analyzed. Since the machines were not dedicated for CISS-2, it is more difficult to analyze the throughput in a meaningful way. However, it is known that CISS-2 completed more than the originally-planned workload. In fact, more jobs were created and added during the experiment's time window and, in the end, CISS-2 completed almost twice the original number of computations.

5 Concluding Remarks

Although there was room for improvement, both CISS-1 and CISS-2 were successes, as judged by many metrics. CISS showed that there is a need for large-scale high-performance computing in Canada. The experiments produced new research results in computational science [8,16]. Finally, CISS achieved national and international media exposure, furthering the campaign for an increase in the commitment of funding for HPC in Canada.

Perhaps most importantly, CISS helped foster a new social infrastructure for sharing computational resources in Canada. The sociology behind the sharing of multi-million dollar facilities worked well, but it continues to need work and attention. This project convinced some of the skeptics, but not all of the skeptics. We will continue to build the cross-institution bridges and contacts required for future CISS experiments. More HPC centres can be, and must be, included for future efforts.

To ensure a successful continuation of the CISS initiative, several things have to happen:

1. CISS should become a regular event on the Canadian research calendar. Computational scientists should be encouraged to tackle problems on the scale of CISS. Whether CISS should be scheduled as a few days per month, set aside specifically for CISS, or whether it should be irregular, based on demand, remains to be seen.

2. Given the large commitment of computing resources involved, CISS should only endeavor to undertake the highest-quality research projects. This requires a proper refereeing process to evaluate the impact of the research and the need for the resources.

3. Substantially more resources need to be devoted to the CISS effort; for example, CISS could be taken

over and administered by C3.ca under the TASP program.

Worldwide, there are many, large grid computing and metacomputing projects. Computational science and high-performance computing have become vital, complementary approaches to theoretical and experimental science. When appropriate, we should borrow inspiration and technology from other projects. When it makes sense, we should develop our own approaches and infrastructure solutions. But, if Canada does not define and commit to its own strategy for HPC, we risk putting artificial limits on the imagination and innovation of our scientists.

Acknowledgments

Financial support was provided by the Natural Sciences and Engineering Research Council of Canada (NSERC), C3.ca Association Inc, and Alberta's Informatics Circle of Research Excellence (iCORE). Canada Foundation for Innovation (CFI) funding supported the acquisiton of most of the HPC resources used in this research.

References

1. TOP500 Supercomputer Sites. `http://www.top500.org/`.
2. C3.ca Association Inc. `http://www.c3.ca/`.
3. Globus Project. `http://www.globus.org/`.
4. Trellis Project. `http://www.cs.ualberta.ca/~paullu/Trellis`.
5. Christopher Pinchak, Paul Lu, and Mark Goldenberg. Practical Heterogeneous Placeholder Scheduling in Overlay Metacomputers: Early Experiences. In *Proc. 8th Workshop on Job Scheduling Strategies for Parallel Processing (JSSPP)*, pages 85–105, Edinburgh, Scotland, UK, July 24, 2002. Also published as Springer-Verlag LNCS 2537 (2003), pages 205–228. Available at `http://www.cs.ualberta.ca/~paullu/`.
6. Christopher Pinchak. Placeholder scheduling for overlay metacomputing. Master's thesis, Department of Computing Science, University of Alberta, 2003.
7. CISS – The Canadian Internetworked Scientific Supercomputer. `http://www.cs.ualberta.ca/~ciss`.
8. Yunjie Xu, Aiko Huckauf, Wolfgang Jäger, Paul Lu, Jonathan Schaeffer, and Christopher Pinchak. The CISS-1 experiment: *ab initio* study of chiral interactions. In *39th International Union of Pure and Applied Chemistry (IUPAC) Congress and 86th Conference of The Canadian Society for Chemistry*, Ottawa, Ontario, Canada, August 10–15, 2003.
9. MOLPRO Quantum Chemistry Package. `http://www.molpro.net/`.
10. SETI@home. `http://setiathome.ssl.berkeley.edu/`.
11. RC5 Project. `http://www.distributed.net/rc5`.
12. Condor. `http://www.cs.wisc.edu/condor`.
13. Grid Canada. `http://www.gridcanada.ca/`.
14. UVic Grid Testbed. `http://grid.phys.uvic.ca/`.
15. Mark Goldenberg. TrellisDAG: A system for structured DAG scheduling. Master's thesis, Department of Computing Science, University of Alberta, 2003.
16. Justin L. MacCallum, Parag Mukhopadhay, Huaqiang Luo, and D. Peter Tieleman. Large scale molecular dynamics simulations of lipid-drug interactions. In *17th Annual International Symposium on High Performance Computing Systems and Applications (HPCS)*, Sherbrooke, Quebec, Canada, May 11–14, 2003.

Appendix

We thank the scientists who helped make CISS-1 and CISS-2 a success by contributing their applications to the experiment: CISS-1: Wolfgang Jäger, Aiko Huckauf, and Yunjie Xu (University of Alberta); CISS-2: Peter Tieleman and Justin MacCallum (University of Calgary); David Sénéchal and Dany Plouffe (Université de Sherbrooke). Thank you to all of the researchers who interrupted their own work to give us exclusive use of the computational resources for CISS-1.

C3.ca's vision, support, and leadership was vital to CISS. We hope to continue and expand C3.ca's role in future experiments. We gratefully acknowledge the role that Canarie and Netera have played in high-performance networking, with respect to CISS and the MACI Project in Alberta.

We thank the authors of MOLPRO, P. Knowles and H. Werner, for permission to use their software for CISS-1.

We acknowledge the contributions of Rob Lake, George Ma, Victor Salamon, Jeff Siegel, Jeremy Handcock, Nolan Bard, Mark Lee, Vanessa Chung, Yaling Pei, and Danny Ngo to the Trellis Project.

The following people graciously committed time and/or resources to make CISS-1 and CISS-2 a success. Please accept our apologies for any inadvertent omissions.

Mark Andrews, Hospital for Sick Children; Bruce Attfield, C3.ca; Roman Baranowski, University of British Columbia; Virendra C. Bhavsar, University of New Brunswick; David Bickle, Carleton University; Kayla Bonham, University of Calgary; Jonathan Borwein, Simon Fraser University; Mehdi Bozzo-Rey, Université de Sherbrooke; Chip Campbell, Hospital for Sick Children; Colin Cherry, University of Alberta; Scott Delinger, University of Alberta; Harold Esche, University of Calgary; Darrell Fraser, Aurora College; Robert Fridman, University of Calgary; Peter Graham, University of Manitoba; Wagdi G. Habashi, McGill University; Mark Hahn, McMaster University; Jason Hlady, University of Saskatchewan; Marc La France, University of Alberta; Colin Leavett-Brown, University of Victoria; Waldemar Lysz, University of Alberta; Chris MacPhee, University of New Brunswick; Paul Masiar, C3.ca; Gabriel Mateescu, National Research Council; Gary Molenkamp, SharcNet; John Morton, University of Guelph; Fred Perry, Memorial University of Newfoundland; Doug Phillips, University of Calgary; Wayne Podaima, National Research Council; Andrew Pollard, C3.ca; Darryl Reid, Memorial University of Newfoundland; Sean Seeley, University of New Brunswick; Ron Senda, University of Alberta; Martin Siegert, Simon Fraser University; Luc Simard, McGill University; Rob Simmonds, University of Calgary; Amik St-Cyr, McGill University; Mark Thachuk, University of British Columbia; Brian Unger, University of Calgary; Alain Veilleux, Université de Sherbrooke; Chris Want, University of Alberta; Kevin Watts, University of Alberta; Norris Weimer, University of Alberta; Douglas Weir, University of Waterloo; Len Zaifman, Hospital for Sick Children.

Distributed Beagle: An Environment For Parallel And Distributed Evolutionary Computations

Christian Gagné, Marc Parizeau, and Marc Dubreuil [a]

[a] Laboratoire de Vision et Systèmes Numériques (LVSN),
Département de Génie Électrique et de Génie Informatique, Université Laval, Québec (QC), Canada, G1K 7P4.
{cgagne,parizeau,dubreuil}@gel.ulaval.ca

Evolutionary computation is a promising artificial intelligence field involving the simulation of natural evolution to solve problems. Given its implicit parallelism and high computational requirements, evolutionary computation is the perfect candidate for high performance parallel computers. This paper presents Distributed BEAGLE, a new master-slave architecture for parallel and distributed evolutionary computations. It is designed as a robust, adaptive, and scalable system targeted for local networks of workstations and Beowulf clusters. Results obtained with a plausible deployment scenario demonstrate that system performance degrades gracefully when failures occurred, while still achieving near linear speedup in the ideal case.

Le calcul évolutionnaire est un champ prometteur de l'intelligence artificielle impliquant la simulation de l'évolution naturelle afin de résoudre divers types de problémes. Etant donné son parallélisme intrinséque et ses forts besoins en puissance de calcul, Il est le parfait candidat pour les ordinateurs paralleles de calcul haute performance. Cet article présente "Distributed BEAGLE", une nouvelle architecture maître-esclave pour les calculs évolutionnaires paralléles et distribués. Celle ci est conçue pour etre robuste, adaptative, extensible et adaptée à des réseaux locaux de stations de travail de même qu'aux grappes de calcul Beowulf. Les résultats obtenus avec un scénario possible de déploiement démontrent que les performances du système se dégradent lors de pannes alors que dans le cas idéal, le gain de performance est linéaire.

1 Introduction

Evolutionary Computations (EC) [1] is a promising machine intelligence discipline involving the simulation of natural evolution on computers. It is a generic problem solving method applicable whenever solutions can be represented by some data structure and evaluated by an objective function; the so-called "fitness" function. Populations of solutions – initially random solutions – evolve over time through a sequence of processes that include (natural) selection and different genetic operations. In the end, the fittest individual is chosen as "the" solution to the problem and, although EC systems do not in general guaranty convergence to an optimal solution, they have been shown in practice to outperform other techniques as well as human experts for several hard problems [2,3].

However, this generic capacity often comes at a high computational cost, especially when the evaluation of the fitness function is time consuming, which is usually the case for non trivial problems. On the other hand, the evolution process is implicitly parallel as every individuals composing a population of potential solutions can be processed mostly independently. This paper introduces Distributed BEAGLE, an extension of the Open BEAGLE EC framework [4], where evolutionary processes can be efficiently and easily distributed on a network of loosely coupled computers.

Paper structure goes as follows. A presentation of the principal EC flavors is first conducted. Then some nomenclature is presented about the four main types of Parallel and Distributed Evolutionary Computations (PDEC). Thereafter, Open BEAGLE is summarized before introducing the *distributed* BEAGLE architecture. The paper finishes with an analysis of the merits and limitations of the proposed system.

2 Evolutionary Computations

A specific instance of an EC, an Evolutionary Algorithm (EA), can be seen as an optimization process in which a population of solutions evolves over time, to solve a given problem. The EC principles have been successfully applied to numerous situations where classical methods of optimization, classification and automatic design were not able to produce adequate solutions. EC is generally divided in four major flavors: genetic algorithms (GA), genetic programming (GP), evolution strategy (ES), and evolutionary programming (EP).

Genetic algorithms (GA) [5,6] involve the evolution of a population of individuals representing possible solutions to a problem. An individual is usually a string of symbols defined over a given alphabet, most often bits (individual = string of bits). The idea is inspired from genetic DNA that composes every living creature. The search process is made by an iterative application of genetic operators, such as crossover, mutation, and Darwinian selection operators biased toward the fittest individuals. Using this Darwinian paradigm, a population of solutions evolves until some stopping criterion is reached. Figure 1 depicts a flowchart of the general GA algorithm. GA has been widely used as a numerical method to optimize parameters of systems without having any *a priori* knowledge about the search space. Only a feedback criterion is needed to give an objective value that guides the search.

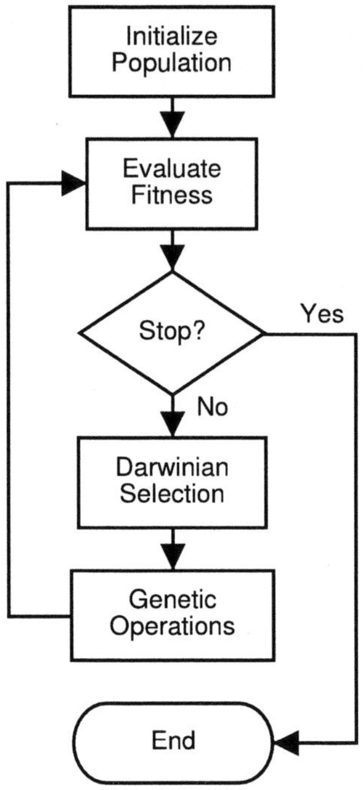

Figure 1. Classic GA Flowchart.

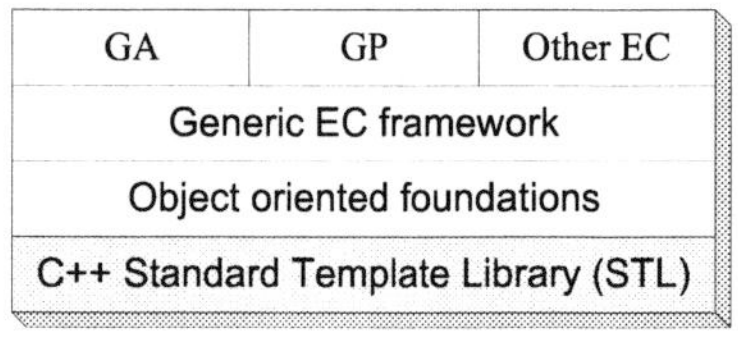

Figure 2. Open BEAGLE Framework Architecture.

Genetic programming (GP) [7,8] is a paradigm that allows automatic programming of computers by heuristics inspired from the same evolution principles as GA: genetic operations of crossover and mutation, and natural selection operation. The difference between GA and GP lies mainly in the representation used, for which GP is similar to a computer program structure. Canonical GP was first formally expressed by Koza in the beginning of the 1990s [7,9]. Koza's GP represents programs as trees, that is acyclic and undirected graphs, where each node is associated to an elementary operation specific to the problem domain. Others have experimented with different representations, such as linear programs [8] or cyclic graphs [10]. GP is particularly adapted to the evolution of variable length structures.

The evolution strategy (ES) paradigm was developed by I. Rechenberg and H.-P. Schwefel at the Berlin Technical University in the 1960s [1,11]. In ES, each individual is a set of characteristics of a potential solution. This set is generally represented as floating-point vectors of fixed length. ES is applied to a parent population (of size μ) from which individuals are randomly selected to generate an offspring population (of size $\lambda \gg \mu$). Offsprings are modified by mutation, which consists in adding a randomly generated value that follows some parametrized probability density function. The parameters of this probability density function, called the *strategy parameters*, themselves evolve over time following the same principles. To engender a new population of size μ, the best μ individuals are chosen within either the λ offsprings (approach (μ, λ)), or the μ parents and λ offsprings (approach $(\mu + \lambda)$). Modern ES can also be nested.

Evolutionary programming (EP) has been developed by L.J. Fogel in the 1960s and later by D.B. Fogel et al. in the 1990s [12,1]. EP was initially designed to evolve finite state machines and has been later extended to parameter optimization problems. The approach is more focused on the relation between parents and offsprings than on the simulation of nature-inspired genetic operators. Contrary to the three first EC flavors, EP doesn't involve the use of a particular representation, but rather a high-level evolutionary model and a representation appropriate for the problem to solve. Only a mutation operator specific to the representation is needed. To do EP, a population of μ solutions is randomly generated. Each individual of the population produces λ offsprings resulting from mutation. Then, a natural selection operation is applied to produce a new population of μ individuals. The mutation - selection process is applied iteratively until a good solution is found.

3 Open Beagle

Open BEAGLE[1] [4] is a C++ framework for doing almost any kind of EC. Its architecture follows the principles of Object Oriented (OO) programming, where some abstractions are represented by loosely coupled objects and where it is common and easy to reuse code. Open BEAGLE has a three level architecture as illustrated in Figure 2. The OO foundations are the basis of this architecture, as a high-level extension of C++, inspired by *design patterns* [13,14]. It offers basic functionalities like smart pointers and garbage collection, object allocators, standard containers, and XML readers/writers. The generic EC framework implements basic mechanisms and structures to design versatile specialized Evolutionary Algorithms (EA). It is summarized in Figure 3.

The generic EC framework comprises three main components: a vivarium, an evolution system, and an evolver. The vivarium is a container for demes of generic individuals. The individuals themselves are specified by an abstract genotype. This genotype can be instantiated to any relevant structure (in Figure 3, it is shown as a GP tree, but this is just an example). Individuals and demes can also be specialized if needed. Open BEAGLE is a multiple populations EC system where synchronous migration between

[1]The recursive acronym BEAGLE means *the Beagle Engine is an Advanced Genetic Learning Environment*, or in French *Beagle est un Environnement d'Apprentissage Génétique Logiciel Évolué*.

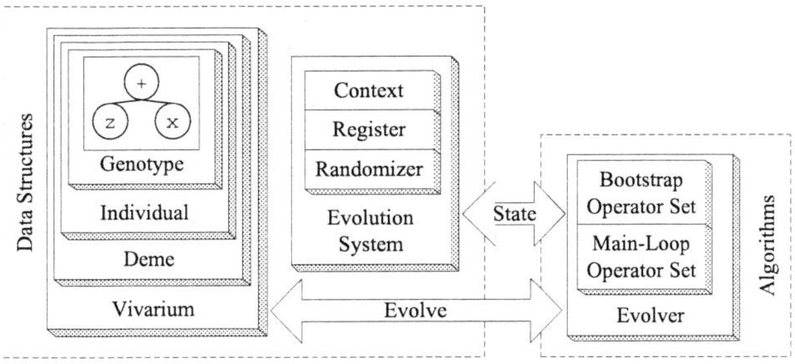

Figure 3. Open BEAGLE Generic EC Framework Architecture.

demes is possible. It takes advantages of greater diversity provided by the simulation of the island-model (see section 4) on one processor.

In the evolution system, the *context* contains the state of the genetic engine, such as the current deme and generation number. This concept is similar to the execution context of a computer. The *register* is a central repository for all evolution parameters. The evolving process itself is governed by an *evolver* that defines sequences of operations, contained in operator sets, that are iteratively applied to demes. The evolver applies the *bootstrap operator set* to initialize the first generation, and the *main-loop operator set* to the subsequent generations. For common EA, standard operators have been defined. These can be common genetic operators, such as selection, crossovers, and mutations, or more functional ones such as statistics calculation, evolution checkpoint backup, and migration operators. This approach is abstract from the evolutionary algorithm used. New algorithms can be made by plugging together standard and custom operators.

The specialized frameworks are at the top level of the architecture. Currently, only classical genetic algorithms and genetic programming frameworks have been implemented. The framework code and documentation is available on the project's Web page at http://www.gel.ulaval.ca/~beagle.

4 Parallel And Distributed Evolutionary Computations

EC is a very generic approach to solve problems. But, applying of EC to real-life problems is usually computationally burdensome, as the CPU time needed to evaluate the fitness of an individual can easily be in the order of seconds or even minutes. However, it is quite easy to exploit the implicit parallelism of EC by distributing the evolutions on several processors.

There are usually four types of Parallel and Distributed Evolutionary Computations (PDEC) [15]: master-slave with one population, island-model made of several distinct populations, fine-grained, and hierarchical hybrids.

Master-slave

Usually, this kind of PDEC has one processor which store the whole population and apply genetic operators (selection, crossover, and mutation). At each generation, the master processor distributes the individuals to slave processors for fitness evaluation. For most difficult problems, fitness evaluation is the main computation bottleneck of EA. This type of PDEC works on a global population and is a simple transposition of the evolution process on several processors.

Island-model

An island-model PDEC consists in evolving isolated sub-populations, named demes, that occasionally exchange individuals in a migration process. These algorithms are very popular in the EC community. Super-linear speedup[2] have been observed when using the island-model [16]. According to Cantú-Paz [15], however, these observations are probably the result of an additional selection pressure induced by the migration process: when the k best individuals of a given deme replace the k worst individuals of another deme, for example. Anyway, using multiple populations with migration schemes usually encourages diversity and prevents premature convergence.

Fine-grained

A fine-grained PDEC consists in evolving populations spatially distributed on processors, generally using a rectangular matrix. Ideally, one individual is assigned to each processor, which allow evaluation of all individuals in parallel. This class of PDEC is particularly adapted to massively parallel SIMD computers. The fine-grained approach is now rarely used in the EC community, as SIMD supercomputers have a low CPU power over cost ratio compared to modern Beowulf clusters [17].

Hierarchical hybrids

This class of PDEC uses an hybrid approach between master-slave and island-model. In hierarchical hybrids, sub-populations evolve on local networks, using the master-slave (or fine-grained) distribution evolution model. At a higher level, the local network populations represent demes of a global island-model. Individuals are exchanged between these demes using migration. Hierarchical hybrids tends to exploit the positive aspects of both master-slave (or fine-grained) and multiple population models.

We found three freely available PDEC systems on the Web: DREAM, ECJ, and GALOPPS. DREAM[3] (Distributed Resource Evolutionary Algorithm Machine) [18] is a peer-to-peer system based on the island-model. In DREAM, each node evolves its own population. Nodes discover the network by interacting with their neighbors. The DREAM system is targeted toward Wide Area Networks (WAN) where communication costs are high [19]. It is very scalable and robust as there is no critical entity that the system depends upon. But it has the limitations of the

[2] Super-linear speedup is observed when the processing time needed for an evolution to converge on n processors is less than $\frac{1}{n}$ the processing time needed on a single processor.

[3] http://www.world-wide-dream.org

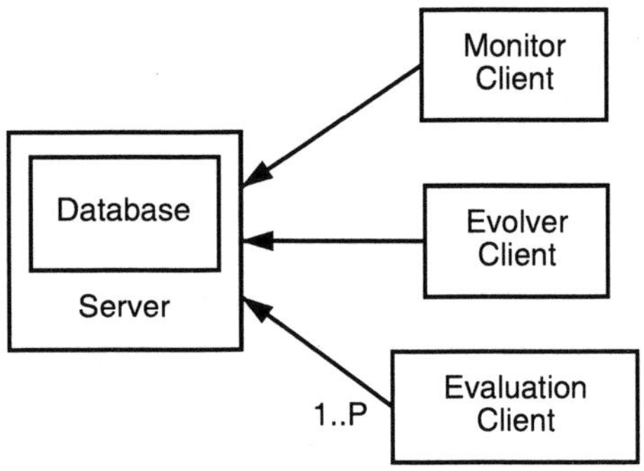

Figure 4. Distributed BEAGLE Architecture.

island-model. ECJ[4] is also based on the island-model. It is a generic EC Java-based framework that implements its PDEC using Java TCP/IP sockets. Its distribution features are not as sophisticated as DREAM, but it includes enough functionalities to be used on Local Area Networks (LAN) or on Beowulf clusters. Finally, GALOPPS[5] (Genetic ALgorithm Optimized for Portability and Parallelism System) is also based on the island-model. It is tightly linked with a specific genetic algorithms library, *S-GA*. It uses the file system to share information among processors. We are not aware of any freely available master-slave PDEC. But we know that several researchers have implemented basic master-slave architectures based on tools such as PVM or MPI.

5 Distributed Beagle

Distributed BEAGLE is an extension of the Open BEAGLE framework which allow evolution distribution on several processors. Evolutions are distributed using a master-slave model. The architecture is independent of the evolutionary algorithm used in Open BEAGLE. Distributed BEAGLE is targeted toward Beowulf clusters or LANs of workstations, where the cost of communication is relatively low.

Distributed BEAGLE comprises four main components: the database, the server, one or more evolver clients, and a pool of evaluation clients. Figure 4 illustrates the system architecture. The system works on data by separating the EC generation concept into two distinct steps: deme evolution and fitness evaluation. Deme evolution is done by evolver clients. It consists in applying several genetic and natural selection operations to evolve the deme through one generation. Once a deme has evolved, the composing individuals need to be evaluated for fitness. Fitness evaluation is done by evaluation clients. When all individuals have been evaluated, the generation is finished and the demes are ready to be evolved again. Since the computational bottleneck in EC is usually the fitness evaluation (at least for hard problems), an evolution with Distributed BEAGLE is usually conducted using a single evolution client and as much evaluation clients as possible (one per available processor).

Database

The database guarantees data persistency by storing the demes and the evolution state. This is an important element of robustness for such a software system, where computations may span several weeks or even months. Furthermore, the use of a common database separates software elements specific to EC from population storage management. Data are classified into two categories: demes that require evolution, and individuals that need evaluation. The database in Distributed BEAGLE is inspired from the distributed and persistent evolutionary algorithm design pattern [20].

Server

The server acts as an interface between the different clients and the database. The primary function of the server is to dispatch the demes to evolver clients, and the individuals to evaluation clients. The number of individuals sent to an evaluation client depends on a load balancing mechanism. This mechanism dynamically and independently adjusts the number of individuals sent to a given evaluation node based on its recent performance history.

Evolver client

An evolver client sends requests for a deme to the server, and then applies selection and genetic operations on this deme. These operations are usually specific to the implemented EC flavor.

Evaluation client

An evaluation client sends requests to the server for individuals that need to be evaluated. The number of individuals returned by the server is variable and depends on the (recent) past performance of the client. The evaluation clients are specific to the problem at hand.

Monitor client

A monitor client sends requests to the server in order to retrieve the current state of the evolution, allowing users to monitor it. This client does not modify the database content.

Load balancing

The load balancing policy is to regulate the size of individual sets in order to achieve (approximately) a constant time period between requests for all evaluation clients. For fast clients, more individuals are sent in order to lower communication latency. For slow clients, fewer individuals are sent in order to minimize synchronization overheads at the end of an evaluation cycle. The pursued time period is set during initialization and can be modified during evolution in order to optimize throughput. This design choice of Distributed BEAGLE allows efficient performances on

[4] http://www.cs.umd.edu/projects/plus/ec/ecj
[5] http://garage.cps.msu.edu/software/galopps

loosely-coupled multi-processor systems such as Beowulf clusters or LAN of workstations.

When all individuals of a deme have been distributed and after a time out proportional to the load balancing time period, individuals that have been sent to lagging nodes are automatically re-dispatched to other nodes by the server until it receives a fitness response. If duplicate answers are received, only the first one is kept and all others are discarded. This approach both reduces the synchronization time needed to finish a generation and assures general fault tolerance for the system.

A prototype of Distributed BEAGLE has been developed using a MySQL[6] database, TCP/IP sockets as the communication protocol and XML (eXtensible Markup Language) [21] for data encoding. The use of XML is inspired from lightweight XML-based protocols for distributed applications such as XML-RPC[7] and SOAP[8]. The main advantages of using XML is that messages are strongly structured, they are represented using portable character encoding, and there is a variety of XML parsers available to process messages.

6 Analysis

In classical master-slave PDEC, two main distribution policies can be used. The first, n-slaves-n-sets, separates the demes into n equal sets of individuals and then sends a set to each of the n nodes. It has the advantage of minimizing the number of client-server connections. But non homogeneous clients generate synchronization overheads as the processing of the fitness evaluation will be as fast as the slowest node. Also, if a node is removed or crashed, its associated set of individuals must be re-dispatched to another node, emphasizing the synchronization overhead. Moreover, a slave added during an evaluation cycle will not be used until the next generation.

The second distribution policy is to send the individuals one-by-one to client nodes. Using this approach, the synchronization problems are minimized and an implicit load-balancing is accomplished. Nodes can be added (or removed) dynamically with minimal overhead. But the problem that lurks is communication latency which reduces scalability of the system.

Distributed BEAGLE exploits a half-way policy where a variable-size set of individuals is sent to evaluation nodes. The speedup of such an approach can be modeled using the following equation.

$$speedup = \frac{T_s}{T_p} \tag{1}$$

where T_s is the time needed to evaluate the fitness of the demes on a single processor, and T_p is the time needed to evaluate the fitness of the same deme in parallel, using P processors. We assume here that the time required for selection and genetic operations (processed by the evolver client) is negligible. Time T_s is given by:

$$T_s = NT_f \tag{2}$$

where T_f is the time needed to evaluate the fitness of a single individual, and N is the population size. Assuming a fixed size S for the sets of individuals (i.e. complexity of the fitness evaluation is about constant over all individuals and processing nodes are homogeneous), and that the number of communication cycles C for a generation is:

$$C = \left\lceil \frac{N}{PS} \right\rceil \tag{3}$$

then time T_p can be modeled by:

$$T_p = \underbrace{CST_f}_{\text{computation}} + \underbrace{CPST_c}_{\text{communication}} + \underbrace{CT_l}_{\text{latency}} \tag{4}$$

where T_c is the transmission time needed to send one individual and receive its fitness, and T_l is the average latency of each connection (here we assume that the load on the server and the network is constant). Finally, a last term T_k may be added to equation 4 to represent the time delay associated with node failure:

$$T_p = CST_f + CPST_c + CT_l + T_k \tag{5}$$

with:

$$T_k = \begin{cases} 0 & K = 0 \\ \underbrace{(1 - 0.5^K)ST_f}_{\text{synchronization}} + \underbrace{KST_c}_{\text{comm.}} + \underbrace{T_l}_{\text{latency}} & K \in [1, P] \end{cases} \tag{6}$$

where K is the number of observed failures. The term associated with synchronization in equation 6 is given under the assumptions that each failure follows a Poisson process and occurs on average at half-way time during an evaluation cycle (i.e. at time $ST_f/2$). We neglect here slowdown associated with processors unavailability, which is likely in presence of failure. It would have greatly complicate the equations while giving no pertinent informations as the loss would be the same independently of the parameters used (i.e. the value of S).

Equipped with this model, we can now investigate some scenarios. Supposing a Beowulf cluster made of identical computers and a 100 Mbit/s Ethernet switch. We evolve populations of $N = 500000$ individuals (total) where fitness evaluation requires an average of $T_f = 1$ s. Assume that the average length of individuals (coded in XML), including their fitness, is 1 Kbyte, which may necessitate about $T_c = 1.4 \times 10^{-4}$ s to transmit over the network[9]. Finally, let the average latency per connection be $T_l = 0.1$ s (this value seems quite high but includes all connection latency, that is latency associated to networking, operating system, and program processing). Figure 5 illustrates the

[6] http://www.mysql.com
[7] http://www.xmlrpc.org
[8] http://www.w3.org/TR/SOAP

[9] This value stems from an effective network bandwidth of $\approx$ 7 MB/s.

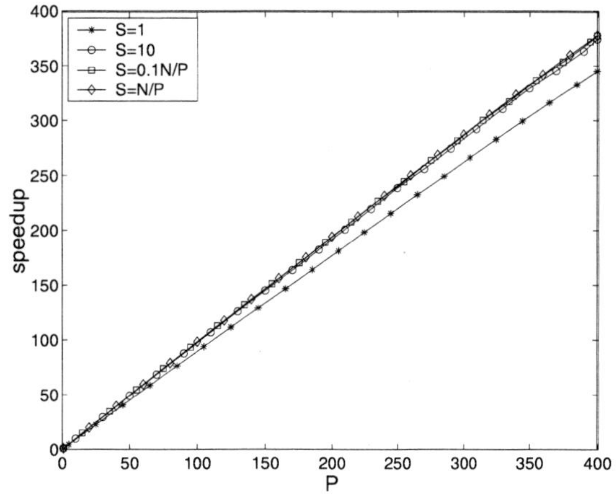

Figure 5. Speedup curves for different set sizes when no failure occur ($K = 0$). Parameters used are $N = 500000$, $T_f = 1$, $T_c = 1.4 \times 10^{-4}$, and $T_l = 0.1$.

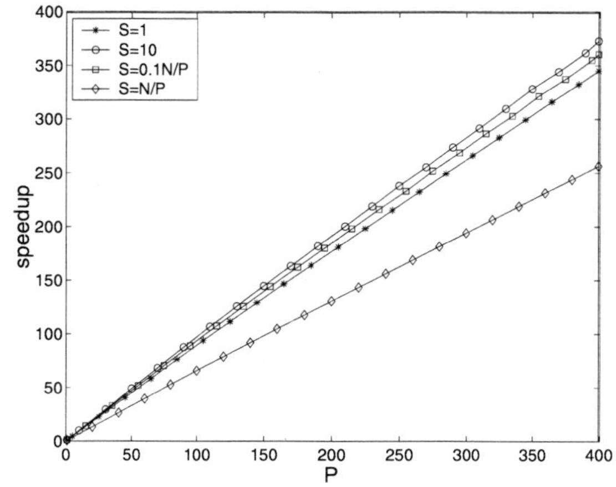

Figure 6. Speedup curves for different set sizes when exactly one failure occurs at each generation ($K = 1$). Parameters used are $N = 500000$, $T_f = 1$, $T_c = 1.4 \times 10^{-4}$, and $T_l = 0.1$.

corresponding speedup curves for different S values and without any failure. This figure shows speedup near linear (near optimal) for $S = \{10, \frac{0.1N}{P}, \frac{N}{P}\}$. For $S = 1$, however, performance degrades significantly given the large latency delay.

Now, Figures 6 and 7 show the same curves but for one and five failures respectively ($K = 1$ and $K = 5$). These Figures show that a value $S = \frac{N}{P}$ no longer achieves linear speedup, and that the intermediary value of $S = 10$ (in this scenario) makes a good compromise between efficiency and robustness. When the number of failure increases, greater loss of performance should be expected with larger sets of individuals. In any case, the second common policy of splitting the total number of individuals into equal size sets ($S = \frac{N}{P}$) is not robust to node failures nor is the first policy efficient for lagging networks. These curves illustrate that the S parameter should be adjusted dynamically in order to optimize performance. In future release this process could even be automated using an intelligent monitor client.

In the above analysis, it was implicitly assumed that the server would never be overwhelmed by the client requests. But in fact, passed a certain threshold on the number of processors, the speedup will reach an asymptote and stagnate with no further performance improvements. This implies that a connection communication time must be less than the time needed to evaluate the fitness of a single set of individuals plus the latency of a connection.

$$SPT_c \leq ST_f + T_l \tag{7}$$

and thus:

$$P \leq \frac{ST_f + T_l}{ST_c} \tag{8}$$

Now, if we set $S = \frac{FN}{P}$, that is a ratio F of the maximum size of individuals set, then the maximum number of

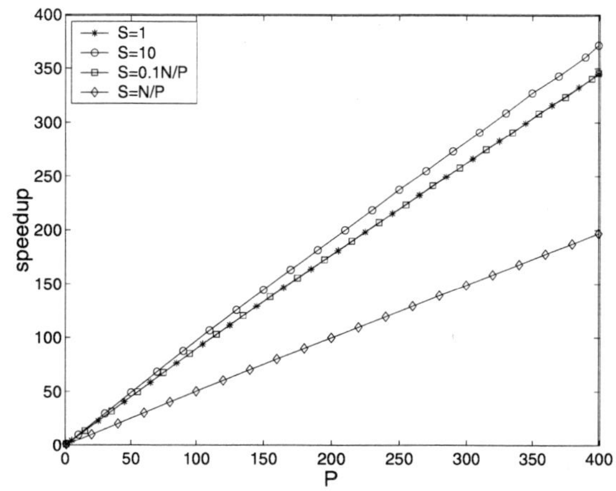

Figure 7. Speedup curves for different set sizes when exactly five failures occur at each generation ($K = 5$). Parameters used are $N = 500000$, $T_f = 1$, $T_c = 1.4 \times 10^{-4}$, and $T_l = 0.1$.

processors becomes:

$$P \leq \frac{FNT_f}{FNT_c - T_l} \tag{9}$$

With the parameters used in our scenario (i.e. $N = 500000$, $T_f = 1$, $T_c = 1.4 \times 10^{-4}$, and $T_l = 0.1$), we obtain a maximum of 7800 processors for $S = 1$, and around 7200 processors for $S = \{10, \frac{0.1N}{P}, \frac{N}{P}\}$. It goes to show that the system can scale well for a relatively high number of processors.

7 Discussion

The island-model is the PDEC that currently receives the most attention in the EC community. Here is a list of the advantages that make this distribution model attractive:

- Scales well as each node communicates only infrequently with its neighbors.
- Robust as there is no centralized control. Data are distributed among nodes; a node crash doesn't affect much the other nodes.
- Communication is asynchronous and limited to punctual migration of small set of individuals.
- Implicit uses of multidemic populations.

But the island-model also has several limitations:

- Population sizes must be tuned to roughly balance computational load of nodes.
- Evolution cannot be reproduced, as migration is asynchronous and depends on the state of the processors/network.
- Distribution of results among nodes complicates data collection and analysis.
- Not particularly adapted to networks of non homogeneous computers where availability of nodes is limited in time.
- When a node crashes, part of the global population doesn't evolve and may even be lost.

On the other hand, master-slave PDEC have also been widely used by the EC community for the following reasons:

- Simple transposition of the single processor evolutionary algorithm onto multiple processor architectures. Allows reproducibility of results.
- No information lost when a slave crashes or is unreachable by the master.
- Appropriate for networks of computers where availability is sometimes limited (i.e. available only during night time). A node can be added or removed dynamically with no loss of information.
- A centralized repository of the population simplifies data collection and analysis.

But the master-slave also has limitations that restrict their usability under some circumstances:

- May not scale as well when the master is overloaded or when the population size becomes very high.
- A crash of the master node can paralyze the whole evolution.
- Significant communication cost as all individuals are transmitted through the network.
- Synchronization overhead for lagging slave nodes[10].

[10] Assuming a generational evolutionary algorithm.

The critical failure point of Distributed BEAGLE is the server. If it crashes, the whole system comes down. But, data persistency is guaranteed by the database. Another interesting aspect of Distributed BEAGLE is the robustness over computer or network failures. If a client (slave) crashes or is unreachable over the network, the data under process is not lost.

An important design choice of Open BEAGLE is the use of a multidemic population model with synchronous migration. This is independent of Distributed BEAGLE. It separates parallel multiple populations from evolution distributed on multiple processors. As far as we know, there is no other such system currently available. We strongly believe that there is no need to evolve a separate deme on every available processor. Moreover, the size of the demes do not needs to be proportional to processor performance. Adding a degree of liberty by separating these elements enable a finer control over the evolution parameters.

8 Conclusion

This paper has presented Distributed BEAGLE, a distribution extension to the Open BEAGLE EC framework. Basically, it is a master-slave PDEC system that implements several features which enhance its general robustness and efficiency:

- Persistent database;
- Dynamically adjustable sets of individuals sent to clients;
- Redistribution of data when clients are lagging or not responding;
- Multidemic populations implemented in a processor independent way.

The Distributed BEAGLE project is still under development. We plan to make it an open source project as soon as the software will be in a stable state, with adequate testing for a beta release. It is targeted for Beowulf clusters and LAN of workstations (also for high performance WAN). It is therefore planned to transform this master-slave architecture into an hierarchical hybrid system, by adding a migration client that will exchange individuals between servers. This will transform master-slave sets into meta-island of a broader evolution environment. Finally, although the current implementation is specialized to do EC, it could possibly be transformed into a more generic framework for distributed computations.

Acknowledgments

The authors would like to thank Frédéric Jean, Jacques Labrie and Hélène Torresan for their participation in the project. This research was supported by a NSERC-Canada and FCAR-Québec scholarships to C. Gagné and a NSERC-Canada grant to M. Parizeau.

References

1. T. Bäck, D. B. Fogel, and Z. Michalewicz, editors. *Evolutionary Computation 1: Basic Algorithms and Operators*. Institute of Physics Publishing, Bristol, UK, 2000.
2. J. Beaulieu, C. Gagné, and M. Parizeau. Lens system design and re-engineering with evolutionary algorithms. In *Proceeding of GECCO 2002*, pages 155–162, New York, NY, USA, 2002.
3. J. R. Koza, M. A. Keane, J. Yu, F. H. Bennett III, and W. Mydlowec. Automatic creation of human-competitive programs and controllers by means of genetic programming. *Genetic Programming and Evolvable Machines*, pages 121–164, 2000.
4. C. Gagné and M. Parizeau. Open BEAGLE: A new versatile C++ framework for evolutionary computation. In *Proceeding of GECCO 2002, Late-Breaking Papers*, New York, NY, USA, 2002.
5. D. E. Goldberg. *Genetic Algorithms in Search, Optimization, and Machine Learning*. Addison-Wesley, Reading, MA, USA, 1989.
6. J. M. Holland. *Adaptation in Natural and Artificial Systems*. University of Michigan Press, Ann Arbor, MI, 1975.
7. J. R. Koza. *Genetic Programming: On the Programming of Computers by Means of Natural Selection*. MIT Press, Cambridge, MA, USA, 1992.
8. W. Banzhaf, P. Nordin, R.E. Keller, and F.D. Francone. *Genetic Programming – An Introduction; On the Automatic Evolution of Computer Programs and its Applications*. Morgan Kaufmann, dpunkt.verlag, 1998.
9. J. R. Koza. *Genetic Programming II: Automatic Discovery of Reusable Programs*. MIT Press, Cambridge, MA, USA, 1994.
10. A. Teller and M. Veloso. PADO: A new learning architecture for object recognition. In K. Ikeuchi and M. Veloso, editors, *Symbolic Visual Learning*, pages 81–116. Oxford University Press, 1996.
11. I. Rechenberg. *Evolutionsstrategie*. Friedrich Frommann Verlag (Günther Holzboog KG), Stuttgart, 1973.
12. L. J. Fogel, A. J. Owens, and M. J. Walsh. *Artificial Intelligence through Simulated Evolution*. John Wiley & Sons, New York, 1966.
13. E. Gamma, R. Helm, R. Johnson, and J. Vlissides. *Design Patterns: Elements of Reusable Object-Oriented Software*. Addison-Wesley, Reading, MA, USA, 1994.
14. T. Lenaerts and B. Manderick. Building a genetic programming framework: The added-value of design patterns. In *Proceedings of EuroGP'98*, pages 196–208, 1998.
15. E. Cantú-Paz. *Efficient and accurate parallel genetic algorithms*. Kluwer Academic Publishers, Boston, MA, USA, 2000.
16. D. Andre and J. R. Koza. Parallel genetic programming: A scalable implementation using the transputer network architecture. In P. J. Angeline and K. E. Kinnear, Jr., editors, *Advances in Genetic Programming 2*, chapter 16, pages 317–338. MIT Press, Cambridge, MA, USA, 1996.
17. F. H. Bennett III, J. R. Koza, J. Shipman, and O. Stiffelman. Building a parallel computer system for $18,000 that performs a half peta-flop per day. In *Proceedings of the GECCO 1999*, volume 2, pages 1484–1490, Orlando, Florida, USA, 13-17 July 1999. Morgan Kaufmann.
18. M. G. Arenas, P. Collet, A. E. Eiben, Márk Jelasity, J. J. Merelo, B. Paechter, M. Preuß, and M. Schoenauer. A framework for distributed evolutionary algorithms. In *Proceedings of PPSN 2002*, 2002.
19. M. Jelasity, M. Preuß, and B. Paechter. A scalable and robust framework for distributed applications. In *Proceedings of the CEC 2002*, pages 1540–1545. IEEE Press, 2002.
20. A. Bollini and M. Piastra. Distributed and persistent evolutionary algorithms: a design pattern. In *Proceedings of EuroGP'99*, volume 1598 of *LNCS*, pages 173–183, Goteborg, Sweden, 1999. Springer-Verlag.
21. T. Bray, J. Paoli, and C. M. Sperberg-McQueen. Extensible Markup Language (XML) 1.0 - W3C recommendation 10-february-1998. Technical Report REC-xml-19980210, World Wide Web Consortium, 1998.

A Brief Introduction to UPC

William W. Carlson[a]

[a]IDA Center for Computing Sciences, 17100 Science Drive, Bowie MD 20715
wwc@super.org

UPC is a parallel extension of the C programming language which provides programmers with a shared global address space. A descendant of Split-C [1], AC [2], and PCP [3], UPC has two primary objectives: 1) to provide efficient access to the underlying machine, and 2) to establish a common syntax and semantics for explicitly parallel programming in C. The quest for high performance means in particular that UPC tries to minimize the overhead involved in communication among cooperating threads. When the underlying hardware enables a processor to read and write remote memory without intervention by the remote processor (as in the Cray T3E), UPC provides the programmer with a direct and easy mapping from the language to low-level machine instructions. At the same time, UPC's parallel features can be mapped onto existing message-passing software or onto physically shared memory to make its programs portable from one parallel architecture to another. As a consequence, UPC has seen implementations on a variety of hardware platforms and is becoming a standard language.

UPC est une extension parallèle du langage C, qui donne aux programmateurs un accès mémoire global. UPC est un héritier de Split-C [1], AC [2], et PCP [3], et vise deux objectifs : 1) donner un accès efficace à la machine sous-jacente; 2) établir une syntaxe et une sémantique communes pour la programmation explicitement parallèle en C. La recherche d'une performance maximale fait que UPC tente de minimiser la surcharge résultant de la communication entre les processus. Lorsque le matériel permet à un processeur d'accéder à de la mémoire distante sans l'intervention d'un processeur distant (comme chez le Cray T3E), UPC donne au programmateur une correspondance simple et directe entre le langage et les instructions-machine de bas-niveau. D'autre part, les caractéristiques parallèles de UPC correspondent à des librairies de passage de message existantes ou à des appel à une mémoire partagée, ce qui rend les programmes portables d'une architecture parallèle à une autre. UPC est implémenté sur plusieurs plate-formes et est en train de devenir un langage standard.

1 Introduction

Even though latency and contention problems in large-scale multiprocessors have resulted in a general move away from uniform shared memory toward distributed memory, the shared-memory programming model retains many attractions for users of these systems. In particular, the ability to read and write remote memory with simple assignment statements is considerably more attractive than having to learn all the conventions of a message-passing library, even if the latter is portable. At the same time, the quest for performance often makes it desirable to view program data as distributed among a number of local memories. One of UPC's chief advantages as a language is that it enables programmers to exploit data locality in a variety of memory architectures. UPC does not offer programmers a silver bullet for any parallel programming task. Instead, it assumes that the programmer must think about issues of memory locality in designing effective data structures and algorithms, and it offers the programmer a reasonable means of expressing the result of the design effort.

One of the primary principles of UPC is that the presence of parallelism and remote access should not unduly obscure the resulting program. Users must be able to view the underlying machine model as a collection of threads operating in a common global address space and not worry about such details as whether the model is implemented as shared memory or as a collection of physically distributed memories. Within that model the user makes decisions about data locality and memory consistency. It is up to the compiler and runtime to ensure that the programmer's declarations of shared and private data, and strict or relaxed consistency, are implemented correctly. The programmer's job is to understand the programming model and its relation to the algorithm or application.

To create a memory model in which local data and remote data are differentiated solely by the ways in which they are declared, we have made a small number of modifications to the C language. Because the central question of data locality involves local and remote addresses, we have focused on pointers and arrays, the two C constructs which are most closely tied to addresses. The addition of keywords gives the programmer the ability to distinguish between data that is strictly private to a given thread and data that is shared among all threads in the parallel program. Arrays can be declared to be shared among the threads in a variety of different ways; the result is a flexibility in data layout comparable to that of HPF [4].

By keeping software constructs to a minimum and enabling programmers to use underlying hardware efficiently, UPC is solidly in the C tradition. Programmers can write efficient programs because they can choose how much run-time error checking and synchronization is necessary for their particular codes. At the same time, programmers need to understand the code they are writing. For example, writing a value to a remote memory location does not guarantee that another thread will get the new value when it next reads the variable unless the programmer tells the compiler that such a guarantee is necessary. The compiler is thus free to use the memory consistency mechanisms of the underlying hardware to achieve the best performance it can for the specified program.

2 Threads

In UPC, a program consists of some number of threads of computation, each of which behaves like a normal C program. They all call the program's `main()` and each ends by calling `exit()` or by returning from `main()`. In UPC programs, `THREADS` is an integer value representing the number of threads which the UPC program is using, and `MYTHREAD` is an integer value which, for each thread, is the index of that thread, between 0 and `THREADS-1`. These values are automatically available to all UPC programs.

3 Shared and Private Data

Adding shared objects to ANSI/ISO C required the addition of the keyword `shared` as a type-qualifier [5] in data declarations to distinguish between declared objects that are shared across all the threads in the system and those that are private to a single thread. Examples of shared and private declarations include:

```
/* one xp private to each thread */
int xp;

/* one xs shared by all threads */
shared int xs;

/* one int per thread, shared by all */
shared int y[THREADS];

/* one a[100] per thread*/
shared int a[100][THREADS];

/* no need to be a multiple of THREADS */
/* a total of 100 ints, shared by all */
shared int b[100];
```

3.1 Affinity

Each element of a shared object has *affinity* to a single thread. While any thread may access any element of a shared object, the thread with affinity may treat the element as private, often getting a performance boost. In the simple case of arrays ending in a `THREADS` dimension, the syntax indicates affinity; the addresses `a[100][5]` and `a[100][6]` are associated with successive threads, with "successive" meaning the next higher numbered thread, with the exception of the last thread, whose successor is thread 0.

A statement of the form

```
i = a[42][i];
```

will result in the computation of an address on thread i and a fetch from that address from thread i. Similarly, a statement of the form

```
a[i][j] = i;
```

will result in the address computation and a store to address i on thread j.

It is also possible to declare shared arrays that are blocked differently across threads.

```
shared [20] int c[100][THREADS];
```

Array `c` will be distributed among the threads so that the first 20 elements will be on thread 0, the next 20 on thread 1, and so on. Thus each thread will have the same number of elements of c as of a, but the arrangement of those elements will be different according to the blocking in the declaration for the arrays.

3.2 Pointers

In order to achieve consistency between arrays and pointers, operations on pointers to shared objects have several characteristics that differ from those of conventional C pointers. Internally, pointers to shared objects have two logically separate components, a thread number and a local address. The thread number is used to determine where the remote reference is to be done, and the local address is used on that thread as if it were in that thread's "local" view. It is important to understand a distinction in the ANSI standard term type qualifier[5]. The question is "What is shared, the pointer itself, or what it points to?" There are 4 cases:

```
/* a private pointer to a private object */
/* THREADS copies, all independent */
int *p2p;

/* a private item which points to shared */
/* THREADS copies, all independent */
shared int *p2s;

/* a shared item which points to a private */
/* single object, shared by all */
int *shared sp2p;

/* a shared item which points to a shared */
/* single object, shared by all */
shared int *shared sp2s;
```

Note that users will find the second example the most useful, but it is possible (as in all C code) to create arbitrarily complex effects by using arbitrarily complex declarators.

3.3 Casting

Whenever a pointer to shared is cast to a pointer to private, the thread number is lost. Therefore, this operation is dangerous, because the resulting pointer may point to a different object than the input pointer. However, it is useful to get a pointer to private for efficient access to the local elements of a shared array. Such casting is only allowed when the pointed-to shared object has affinity with the casting thread.

```
\begin{verbatim}
shared int x[THREADS];
int *p;
```

```
p = &x[MYTHREAD]; /* p points to x[MYTHREAD],
          but is more efficient for access */
```

Casting a private pointer to shared is not allowed in the UPC model. This design decision allows efficient implementation on a wide variety of architectures.

3.4 Consistency Model

UPC provides a hybrid, user-controlled consistency model for the interaction of memory accesses in shared memory space. Each memory reference in the program may be annotated (using a variety of approaches) to be either "strict" or "relaxed". Under strict behavior, the program executes in similar manner to a sequential consistency model [6]. This implies that the user can be sure that it appears to all threads that the strict references in a particular thread appear in the order they are written, relative to all other accesses. Under relaxed behavior, the program executes in what we term a "local" consistency model. This implies that the user can assume that it appears to the issuing thread that all shared references in that thread occur in the order they were written. Note that because each reference may be annotated, a number of models between relaxed and strict consistency are available to the user.

The general method of using these models is that the programmer will first establish a default environment by including either <upc_strict.h> or <upc_relaxed.h>. All unannotated references within functions defined after these directives operate under the selected model. The programmer then may annotate more explicitly those references to be handled differently. One method for annotating references is to declare shared variables and pointers with the type qualifiers `strict` and `relaxed`. All references to annotated variables and through annotated pointers will operate under the selected model, regardless of the default behavior in force.

3.5 Global Synchronization

UPC provides two mechanisms for global coordination of work in a program: barriers and forall loops. The barrier provided is a split-phase barrier which allows the "notify" phase to be separated from the "wait" phase with local work. This allows for increased barrier efficiency on machines with less than stellar barrier performance. The forall construct allows not only the specification of work sharing, but also the affinity of data and work assignment for increased efficiency.

3.5.1 Barriers

A barrier synchronization point in a parallel program has the effect of causing all threads to wait at the barrier until every thread has reached it. To accomplish this behavior, there are two distinct actions each thread must take: notifying all other threads that it has reached the barrier and waiting for every other thread to report its presence. Whether barriers are implemented in hardware or software on a given machine, these steps are always required and often distinct. UPC provides three statements which allow users to implement barriers: `upc_notify`, `upc_wait`, and `upc_barrier`, the final being a convenience notation which combines notify and wait. The advantage of this design is that it allows users (or compilers) to place local work between the notify and wait calls.

```
int x;               int x;
shared int *p;       shared int *p;

x = *p;              x  = *p; upc_notify;
upc_barrier;         x += local_pure_function();
*p = x;              upc_wait; *p = x;
```

The performance of the split code will be greater than that of the barrier code because the variance in arrival time at the notify point will be covered by the time to execute the local function. If the variance is less than the time taken for the local function, no processor will need to wait at the wait point.

3.5.2 Forall

The `upc_forall` statement allows programmers to describe a global loop with assignment of threads to loop indices made by the compiler and/or runtime system. It makes a fair number of assumptions about the environment of the system when the loop is executed, including that all threads enter the outermost `upc_forall` statement of a set of nested `upc_forall` statements. Users writing "SPMD" style programs should find this convenient. Because `upc_forall` is also a parallel statement, all iterations of the loop are independent and can be executed in any order desired by the compiler and runtime system. The `upc_forall` statement adds to the traditional for statement a fourth field that describes the affinity under which to execute the loop. In a typical case, the affinity expression will be an expression which occurs in the loop. Consider the following code:

```
shared float x[100], y[100], z[100];

addit() {
  int i;
  upc_forall (i=0; i<100; i++; &x[i]) {
    x[i] = y[i] + z[i];
  }
}
```

In this code, the compiler can assign tasks to threads so that `x[i]` is local to that thread. It can also detect from the data declaration that `x`, `y`, and `z` are aligned, so it can arrange to execute this code with total locality. The `upc_forall` statement has no implied barriers; if barriers are needed before or after the loop to ensure proper program execution, they need to be inserted.

4 Implementation

UPC has been implemented efficiently on a variety of multiprocessor architectures, including shared memory systems as well as distributed shared memory systems. While the details of implementation may vary considerably from system to system, the primary focus for the user should be on the semantics defined in previous sections. For example, a shared array `x` will be laid out in memory so that thread 0 will be able to access `x[0]` and `x[THREADS]` equally well. On a distributed shared memory system such as the T3E these two elements will be adjacent in the local memory of the processor that executes thread 0. On a shared memory machine the thread number may become part of a virtual address in such a way that x[0] and x[THREADS] will be adjacent on a page of physical memory in some way "assigned" to thread 0.

Acknowledgments

This paper represents the efforts of a large number of people working on the UPC team over the past 5 years. The language was designed by Eugene Brooks, William Carlson, David Culler, Jesse Draper, Karen Warren, and Katherine Yelick. Industry teams from Cray, Compaq, Computer Sciences Corp, Etnus, Intrepid, Hewlett-Packard, IBM, and SGI, and Sun have all worked on implementations of UPC. Research teams from the Arctic Region Supercomputer Center, George Washington University, The IDA Center for Computing Sciences, Lawrence Berkeley National Labs, Lawrence Livermore National Labs, Michigan Technological University, and The University of California, Berkeley have all contributed greatly to UPC's ongoing development. See the website http://www.upcworld.org for more details. The website also includes information on available libraries, implementations, documentation, and tutorials.

References

1. David E. Culler, Andrea Dusseau, Seth Copen Goldstein, Arvind Krishnamurthy, Steven Lumetta, Thorsten von Eiken, and Katherine Yelick. Parallel programming in Split-C. In *Proceedings of Supercomputing '93*, pages 262 – 273, Portland, OR, November 1993.
2. William W. Carlson and Jesse M. Draper. Distributed data access in AC. In *Proceedings of the Fifth ACM SIGPLAN Symposium on Principles and Practice of Parallel Programming (PPOPP)*, pages 39 – 47, Santa Barbara, CA, July 1995.
3. Eugene D. Brooks and Karen Warren. Development of an efficient parallel programming methodology, spanning uniprocessor, symmetric shared-memory multiprocessor, and distributed-memory massively parallel architectures. *Supercomputing '95*, 1995.
4. High Performance Fortran Forum. *High Performance Fortran Language Specification, Version 1.0.* Rice University, May 1993.
5. ANSI. *Programming Languages - C.* ISO/SEC9899, 2000.
6. L Lamport. How to make a multiprocessor computer that correctly executes multiprocessor programs. *IEEE Transactions on Computers*, C-28(9), September 1979.

SCOJO – Share Based Job Coscheduling With Integrated Dynamic Resource Directory in Support or Grid Scheduling

Angela C. Sodan[a] and Xuemin Huang[a]

[a]University of Windsor, Computer Science, 401 Sunset Ave., Windsor, ON N8Y 1B1, Canada

Grid environments currently use mere batch scheduling or assume jobs to be started immediately. We apply a combination of batch scheduling and time sharing and propose an approach which assigns certain start times and certain shares based on integrated resource management. Employing loosely coordinated coscheduling, provides good chances for latency hiding and high flexibility in executing jobs across multiple sites. Our approach takes potential slowdowns or speedups from coscheduling into consideration. We support such scheduling by a dynamic directory service. Current directory services for grid computing provide static machine descriptions plus some dynamic information like CPU load as obtained via NWS. However, in other work, we have shown that the detailed application characteristics matter in coscheduling. Furthermore, predictability is currently limited to short-term extrapolations from the recent history. We develop scheduling plans and consider site workload and application characteristics, while not disclosing such information to other users or sites. This approach enables higher-quality decisions and longer-term predictability. We demonstrate our approach on the basis of simulations and simplified real coscheduling tests, run on an SMP server.

Les environnements de type grille utilisent généralement un système d'ordonnancement (files d'attente) simple, présupposant un démarrage immédiat des travaux soumis. Nous proposons ici une combinaison de l'approche de traitement par lots et de celle des systèmes à exploitation partagée. Nous déterminons le délais avant démarrage et les ressources qui seront allouées grâce à une analyse des ressources disponibles. Avec l'utilisation du traitement par lots latéral à coordination souple, nous diminuons les effets de latence et augmentons la flexibilité dans la distribution des tâches de calcul sur un plus grand nombre de sites. Notre approche tient compte des possibles ralentissments ou accélérations du traitement par lots latéral. Pour ce faire, nous utilisons un service d'annuaire dynamique. Les systèmes d'annuaire actuellement utilisés sur grille de calcul sont basés sur une description statique des noeuds de calcul, à laquelle s'ajoute des informations dynamique obtenues via NWS, tel le taux d'utilisation des processeurs. Nos précédentes recherches démontrent que les caractéristiques propres à une application influent sur son traitement par lots latéral. On ne peut actuellement faire que des prédictions à court terme basées sur l'historique récente du traitement par lots. Nous développons la méthode de traitement par lots en lui adjoignant une analyse de l'état de charge du site visé, ainsi que des caractéristiques de l'application, le tout en évitant la diffusion de ces informations aux usagers ou sites du réseau. Cette approche améliore le processus de prise de décisions par le système ainsi que la prévisibilité à long terme. Nous illustrons notre approche à l'aide de simulations et de tests de traitement par lots latéral, le tout effectué sur architecture à mémoire partagée.

1 Introduction

The Globus grid system [5] provides services for request submission to local schedulers and for resource reservation (GARA) but does not provide an own scheduler. The assumption is that either batch space sharing (assigning CPUs/nodes exclusively) or immediate execution via time-sharing (sharing CPU resources) are applied. In the latter case, certain CPU shares may be maintained, though, through reservation with e.g. the GARA service. We focus on time-sharing aspects here but combine time sharing with a batch job scheduler which selects the jobs that are run together at the same time. We assume a task per site needing all CPU resources (i.e. we currently ignore space sharing). Furthermore, we focus on loosely coordinated coscheduling (the alternative would be gang scheduling) on shared-memory systems. The combination of admission control and time sharing has the following benefits:

- control of the multiprogramming level while not rejecting jobs which cannot currently be scheduled
- choice between time-shared and exclusive execution according to the predicted slowdown or speedup
- increase of flexibility in scheduling cross-site jobs

The further specific goals of our approach are to support:

- reservation of stable CPU rates which are not changed by coscheduling
- job start-time reservations for cross-site jobs
- estimation of coscheduling cost and predictability
- protocol which is suitable for efficient and flexible multi-site reservations
- support of combined execution of short and long jobs
- secure maintenance of detailed application characteristics and site status

We present the following solutions to meet these goals:

- using effective shares (taking slow-downs or speed-ups into account) for reservations of CPU shares

- running a two-level protocol for cross-site reservations (rough and fine), offering multiple choices via alternate scheduling plans
- keeping application characteristics and differentiating between private and public information
- providing a coscheduling-effect predictor based on integrated site-status and application characteristics
- employing priorities (set dependent on execution time)

In this paper, we present the core scheduling algorithm and investigate the detailed problems in calculating schedules. We demonstrate the scheduler based on a simulation with different workloads and some concrete coscheduling runs (to demonstrate coscheduling effects) on an SMP server.

2 Related Work

Grid scheduling imposes certain requirements. To properly partition and assign parallel programs, the allocation per node needs to be predictable. Thus, reservation of network bandwidth and CPU time are essential. Globus GARA [5] supports the assignment of certain CPU shares, assuming that a scheduler like DSRT [2] is being used. DSRT is originally designed for Multimedia and can assign certain CPU ratios per application. However, coscheduling could only be enforced with prior global synchronization to accomplish kind of gang scheduling. Furthermore, frequent flexible switching is not possible. Share-based scheduling is a currently emerging approach also for OS schedulers, e.g. in Solaris, QLinux or Linux/RT. The Solaris Resource-Manager scheduler [9] can combine flexible priority-based scheduling with share assignment. Furthermore, SUN MPI meets the requirements to run in such an environment on the basis of loose coordination [10]. This means, MPI should not arbitrarily poll for incoming communication but block after some time. Furthermore, receiving processes should get a priority boost to accomplish coscheduling. The limitation of the SUN environment is that the resource manager works per user and not per application. Qlinux allows us to define specific CPU shares per application and assign certain ratios of communication and disk bandwidth. Thus, it is more promising. However, it has not yet been employed in parallel processing and does not work in SMP systems.

Grid schedulers so far typically consider only static machine characteristics and general system status like available CPU rates or free memory space vs. the requirements of the application. The mutual effects of different jobs running together are not yet investigated. In our approach, we consider and keep the characteristics of all jobs and can (re-)evaluate them at any time. A number of grid scheduling approaches are under development but so far not really integrated with local job schedulers. The Working Group on a Grid Resource Allocation Agreement Protocol is currently addressing this problem [6].

3 The Scheduler

We assume distributed grid-job schedulers. The grid-job scheduler for the site with the job request negotiates with the grid-job schedulers of remote sites to find a suitable slot (i.e. per job the negotiation is carried out centrally). There are basically two cases:

- the job is to be run on one site and
- the job is to be run across multiple sites

The first case is relatively easy and only requires to ask different sites, find proper slots and finally select the optimal one. The second case requires to find simultaneous time slots which can be difficult to accomplish. We assume to run the application as one contiguous task per node and search for slots to schedule the application tasks at different sites at the same time. There exist other approaches (promising for loosely dependent computations) which structure the application in a series-parallel manner and run the individual tasks of the application arbitrarily as dependencies permit [8]. We discuss here local scheduling in support of global scheduling but not how the global scheduling plan is calculated (approaches like list scheduling may be applied to find globally simultaneous scheduling slots). We assume that the number of sites to be asked and the work to be possibly scheduled on them are already determined. We ignore site-to-site communication cost, which, if being different for different site choices also plays a role in the decision procedure. Possible solutions would be ranked by finish time.

3.1 The Local Scheduler

We ignore systems implementation consideration as to how existing job schedulers like LSF or PBS can be extended to support time sharing and how the grid-job layer can interact with such a scheduler. Instead, we focus on the scheduling algorithm and refer to it as the local scheduler. This scheduler combines job entry control with time-shared CPU scheduling and can allocate/reserve certain time shares. A job gets a guarantee only for a certain share. If no other job is scheduled at the same time, the share is increased up to 100%. If new jobs are submitted which are eligible to run at this time (e.g. have higher priority) and can run with the remaining un-reserved share, the shares of the currently running jobs are decreased to their reserved ones. Note that an increased share may not necessarily help a cross-site job as it is typically dependent on the computations run at other sites and the whole workload distribution is adapted to the reserved shares.

We apply backfilling [4], i.e. same-priority jobs can

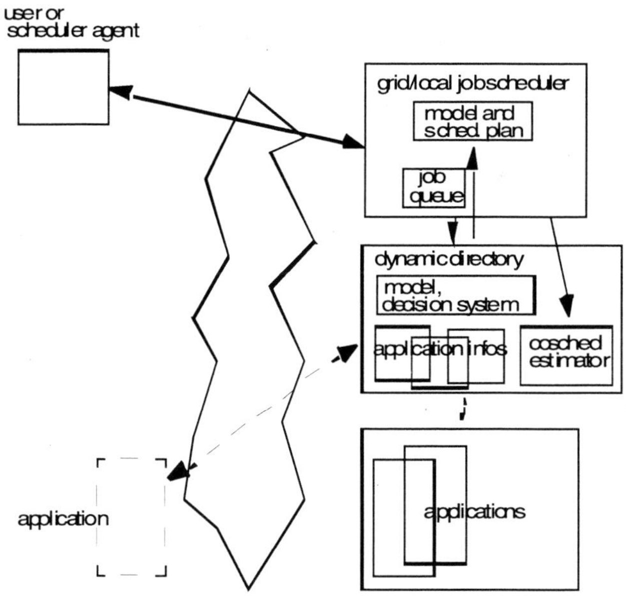

Figure 1. Scheduler and dynamic directory.

be scheduled earlier than their normal position if they can fill schedule holes without delaying other jobs (if priority is assigned other than by runtime, lower-priority jobs may be included as backfilling candidates - otherwise they are too large to fill holes anyway). Note that higher-priority jobs would anyway push other jobs backward in the job queue and therefore never occur as backfilling candidates. Note that whereas backfilling in space sharing means to fill empty space gaps, we here fill time-share space. We never give medium and large jobs a reservation for 100% of the CPU time but only for up to a certain fraction R_{max}. This is done to make it possible to get short jobs through quickly. The time share assignment may also take basic kernel activities into proper consideration (i.e. so to say, reserve a minimum share for background activities).

If a job completes earlier than its runtime estimate had predicted, the jobs behind in the queue can be moved ahead. However, fixed reservations for cross-site jobs are always kept at their scheduled time. We currently do not consider preemption which, however, would be beneficial as additional measure to increase the flexibility in scheduling and the resource utilization by filling holes in front of fixed reservations and dealing with unreliable runtime estimates.

3.2 The Basic Algotithm

SCOJO finds different slots for coscheduling and rates the quality, i.e. the performance available in these slots. Currently, we consider only the available CPU rate. However, for calculating it, we include coscheduling effects, i.e. the benefit or slowdown obtained when executing multiple applications together via time sharing. To keep guarantees for reservations despite such effects, we guarantee an *effective share* as the reservation. The actual share assigned then considers both the requested share and the slowdown/speedup. Furthermore, we decide whether time-coscheduling is meaningful at all or applications better run with exclusive resource allocation. To make these decisions, we provide a coscheduling performance model and a decision system which are further discussed in Sections 3.6 and 3.7. The different components are shown in Figure 1.

We currently mostly simulate our approach, on the basis of having implemented the core scheduling algorithm. We can also start and join real applications on the local machine (without any handling of errors etc.) to demonstrate slowdown effects in coscheduling and that the scheduling algorithm works under practical runtime conditions. The scheduler keeps a scheduling plan (which job is started when, including all reservations) in addition to a job queue. The scheduler basically considers priorities, and requested shares. Jobs with same priority are currently ordered according to their requested share (though other policies are possible like considering submission order). To prevent starvation, priorities are combined with an aging scheme (jobs are aged every T_{age} minutes). Different policies can be applied to assign priorities. We currently roughly classify job size (runtime) and assign different priorities for the classes *short*, *medium*, *large* (as some practical job schedulers do); class *special* is very short of otherwise explicitly assigned.

Cross-site jobs are not shifted even if a higher-priority job arrives or previous jobs finish earlier than expected. For cases where the discrepancy to the reserved start time becomes very high and/or there are large time slots which cannot be filled, later a protocol may be added to try a global cross-site rescheduling of the job. Or the cross-site application may be informed if more CPU time becomes temporarily available and allow it to schedule more work on the remote site.

The scheduler considers coscheduling only if one of the following applies:

- a job is scheduled cross-site and cannot take benefit of getting a higher share than it has reserved
- a job arrives which has higher priority than the currently running one(s)
- jobs have same priority, are classified as coschedulable and slowdown is below a certain limit $CoSl_{Max}$ which may be weighted by the job runtime
- there is a benefit (speed-up) from coscheduling

Furthermore, of course, in any case, the request must be compliant with the available shares. The rationale for the restricitons is that in most cases (i.e. unless long latencies such as from I/O are involved) coscheduling increases the overall execution time for the individual job. Then, overall throughput is better if running the jobs one after the other - except if a job has made a reservation. Slowdown is less critical for short and more critical for long jobs - thus relating $CoSl_{Max}$ to job runtime makes sense. Jobs may be classified as not coschedulable due to their characteristics - e.g. if needing all memory.

For all jobs in the scheduling plan, we keep references to the application descriptions, their shares etc. If remote requests consider to schedule a job, preliminary reservations are made until the remote site decides whether to use or not to use the site and which slot is preferred. We run one remote protocol after the other (i.e. we serialize the requests and they cannot interfere with each other). To protect against failure and malicious sites, the preliminary reservations expire after a certain timeout.

We never give 100% of CPU time to any job and always keep a share for urgent short tasks (for cases where already long jobs are running) and for overruns. obs that excede their reserved runtime (as a matter of the difficulty to make proper estimates) get their share reduced but can continue to run in an *overrun share* (this idea is taken from DSRT [2]). In practical usage, jobs might be preempted or terminated after a certain grace period (proportional to their runtime). Using an overrun share helps to deal with fixed cross-site reservations which cannot be shifted. Other jobs are moved to later start positions (as we do if higher-priority jobs arrive). Closely related, jobs may finish earlier, either again because estimates were not met or because a higher share became available than was reserved. This changes the start time of the following applications and requires to recalculate the schedule.

Another problem is that jobs have different runtimes and thus shares along the runtime axis can fragment time shares. Thus, we avoid this situation and first try backfilling. For all remaining time, we let the application(s) consume all resources to get a clear cut for the next job. Figure 2a) illustrates the problem. Solution c) would be o.k. but not b). Note that this clean cut is easily possible in time sharing whereas in space sharing jobs would have to be reconfigured. For a concrete scheduling example, see Figure 3.

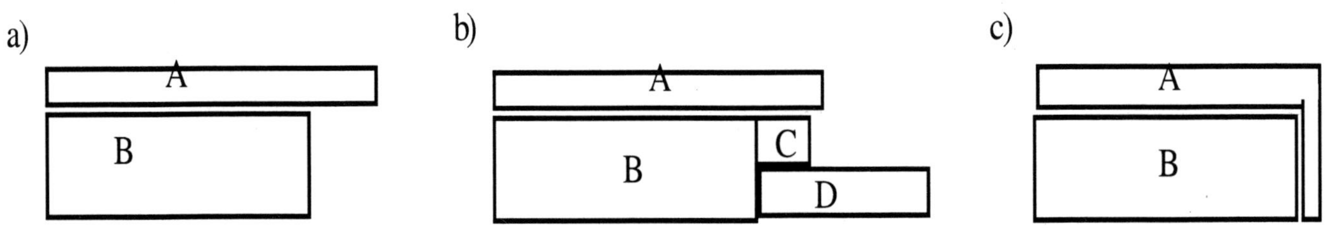

Figure 2. Basic scheduling plan (a) and two possible solutions (b and c).

3.3 The Global Reservation Protocol

We assume that global searches for proper sites are performed prior to the request as anyway accounts have to be established. This also implies that the number of sites under consideration is typically limited to a small number - likely less than 10. Furthermore, we assume that the suitability of the static machine characteristics is already checked in advance and that the runtime is estimated on the basis of a full time-share performance per site.

We propose a two-level protocol for reservation. First, remote sites can query rough load information to decide whether the site is chosen as a candidate for selection. At this stage the query has not yet any impact on the status of the site. In the next step, possible scheduling slots are identified and preliminarily reserved. This is the most costly part of the calculation as multiple plans have to be generated. At this stage, the remote site has to provide detailed information about the application characteristics and about other resource requirements than the CPU (memory, I/O etc.) The rough/fine protocol makes the selection faster if a larger number of sites is involved (otherwise the rough step can be skipped). Security and authentication would be especially important for the second step as it discloses details about the local schedule and the application.

As already mentioned, the assumption is that the requesting site collects all information about the individual different slots and decides about the final schedule. At this point a contract is made with all the involved sites about a specific scheduling slot. In detail, the steps are the following:

- *RoughLoadQuery* (*input:* estimated CPU time and requested share; *output:* earliest possible time slot)
- *FineSchedulingRequest* (*input*: detailed application characteristics, requested share, runtime estimate; *output:* possible scheduling slots and their share and start/ finish time; *effect:* preliminary scheduling plans and application characteristics kept until timeout or confirmation).

JOB_ID	PRIORITY	RUNTIME	SHARE	JOB_TYPE	SUBMIT_TIME	RES_TIME	START_TIME	FINISH_TIME	RESPONSE_TIME
1	0	300	40%	1	11:42:39		11:42:40	11:57:07	868
2	5	60	40%	1	11:43:09		11:43:10	11:46:23	193
3	5	60	20%-40%	1	11:43:39		11:43:40	11:50:02	382
4	15	10	20%	1	11:44:09		11:46:23	11:47:29	199
5	15	10	20%	1	11:44:39		11:47:29	11:48:34	234
6	15	10	40%	1	11:45:09		11:50:02	11:50:35	325
7	10	30	20%-40%	1	11:45:39		11:50:51	11:52:42	422
8	15	10	20%-40%	1	11:46:09		11:50:02	11:50:51	281
9	10	30	20%-40%	1	11:46:39		11:51:16	11:55:05	505
10	15	10	20%-40%	1	11:47:09		11:50:35	11:51:16	246
11	0	300	40%	2	11:56:49	11:57:00	11:57:07	12:12:56	966
12	5	60	40%	1	11:57:19		11:57:20	12:00:34	194

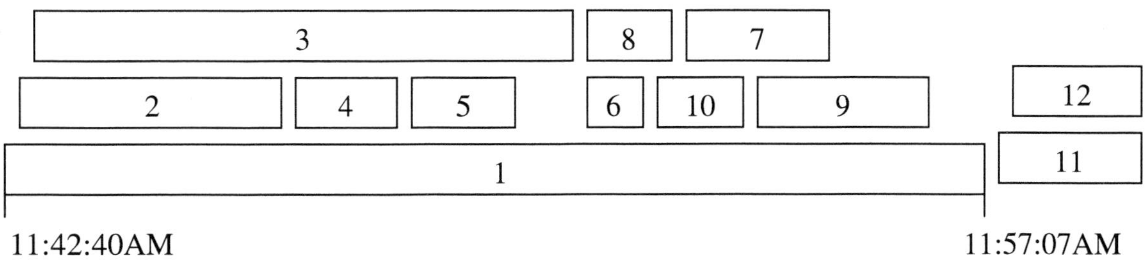

Figure 3. Scheduling example.

- *ConfirmSchedule* (*input:* slot to be confirmed; *effect:* contract agreement, certain slot/plan accepted/reserved and other preliminary plans released, application characteristics stored)
- *TerminateQuery* (*effect:* all slots released, application information removed)

Note that there is always at least one time slot available at the end of the job queue.

3.4 The Dynamic Directory

The dynamic directory keeps information about all currently running and all scheduled applications (jobs in the scheduling plan). Our dynamic directory is a significantly extended version of the rough idea described in [11]. The following information is maintained:

- owner (user)
- remote request yes/no, single-site/cross-site request
- requested share, runtime estimate (and potentially maximum usable share, notification of change yes/no)
- communication pattern (like "all-to-all", "point-to-point random", "central")
- communication frequencies/sizes
- memory, I/O, and other requirements

In the future, we intend to optionally keep distribution functions for certain parameters and to keep structured information for multiple patterns (different phases, multi-level). This includes local/remote patterns with e.g. more intensive communication locally and less intensive remotely.

Furthermore, we assume that information per user (accounting) is maintained (in a database): permitted and left overall resource usage per time interval (e.g. month); any restrictions (like access only during certain hours, e.g. night, etc.), maximum runtime per application; general priority or for certain types of user's applications; potentially performance information from previous runs (to support estimates) - as much of it is used in Maui [7].

Our design envisions a second dynamic part for the directory which can keep information during the run of the applications (like application-internal workload), see Figure 4. Standard and user-specified information may be transfered, pull and push versions be provided, and standard tools be used or specific ones be chose. The integrated service then provides the chance to combine measurements needed for several applications. Furthermore, certain information - like overall workload - may be summarized and made available to all applications vs. other more specific information be private.

We assume that general authentication would be provided by grid middleware like Globus. In addition, a special more lightweight authentication would be required to control which information is accessible to whom.

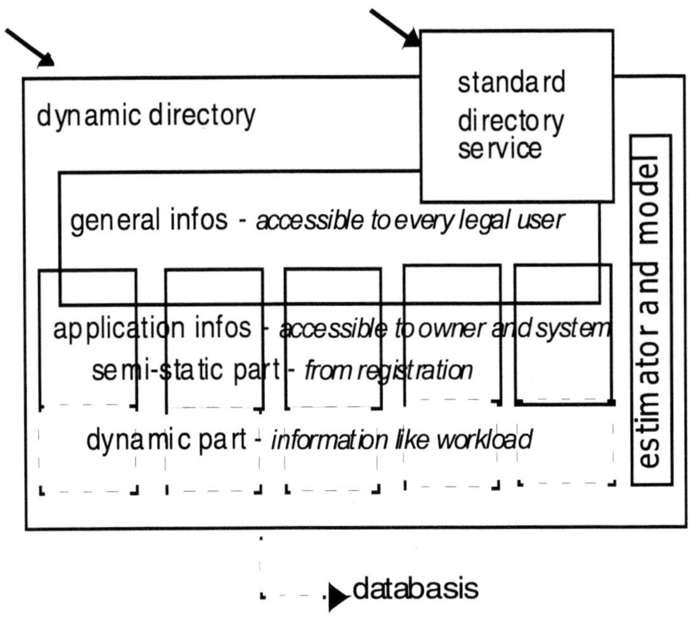

Figure 4. Dynamic resource directory.

3.5 The Coscheduling Estimator

SCOJO uses the provided characteristics of the new job and of the already scheduled jobs. For possible scheduling time slots (slots that fit the application including runtime and time share), we then estimate the slowdown or benefit, taking the characteristics of the other potentially concurrent applications into account. Slowdowns are considered acceptable only under certain circumstances and up to a certain extent. Note that a slowdown of 1.5 means that the runtime increases by a factor of 1.5. Thus, 2 applications which each need 1 hour runtime would be finished after 1 or 2 hours with average response time of 1.5 hours. With a slowdown factor of 1.5 each would have mere runtime of 1.5 hours and they would both the completed after 3 hours, i.e. average response time be 3 hours. But a slowdown of 1.5 would be well acceptable if a short application needing 1 minute can be scheduled quickly while running 1.5 minutes instead of having to wait 1 hour before being started. Benefits can be obtained from coscheduling if I/O or long-distance communication delays are involved.

For cross-site applications, the scheduler provides a list of times when jobs may be scheduled, with which effective CPU share and with which runtime. Otherwise, the best-possible slot is returned (shortest finish time). Important is that we calculate the effective share (the time contributing to the real progress of the application, i.e. not counting slowdown effects) and make sure that each application that got a share granted gets computation time of at least that amount. Thus, if an application got a share of 30% CPU time granted and due to coscheduling there would be a slowdown of 1.33, the application would be granted 40% of the CPU time to keep its effective share. The other application(s)' effective share needs to fit into the remaining share of CPU time.

Table 2. Slowdowns in different application combinations. All runs are on 9 CPUs, 80-85% idle (either directly or 93-95% and via 2 extra processes as background load from other users varies). This was done since there is always minor background load with a few percent of CPU time and 1 or 2 CPUs busy even during the night (measurements were done on our common department server). Numbers in parenthesis are granularities. Left value represents slowdown for row, right value represents slowdown for column application.

	grid-300 (1.3 msec)	**grid-1200** (27.9 msec)	**grid-2400** (116 msec)	**central** (29.3 msec)	**random** (4 msec)	**stream** (3.5 msec)	**seq**
grid-300	1.2	1.4 / 1.1	2.2 / 0.9	0.9 / 1.6	1 / 1.3	1.8 / 0.8	2.5
grid-1200		1.2	1.4 / 0.8	1.1 / 1.7	1 / 1.4	1.3 / 0.8	1.2
grid-2400			1.1	1 / 3.1	1.5 / 2.3	0.8 / 0.8	1
central				1.3	1.3 / 0.9	2.5 / 0.8	3.3
random					2	1.8 / 0.9	3.5

Modeling and cost estimation include both the application and the machine characteristics as coscheduling effects depend on the operating and the communication system. First, a rough classification is done whether coscheduling is possible or not. Next, the slowdown/speedup is estimated.

In previous work [12], we found the following application information to be relevant:

- communication pattern
- communication frequency and size
- asynchronous communication yes/no, probing yes/no
- combination of jobs being scheduled

Important cost contributions are the switching cost, the spinning cost (both in the application and in the spin daemon used in SUN MPI), and potential waiting time because of dependencies. If one process/thread of the application stays behind, none of the others may be able to make progress. Thus, a central master task cannot send out new requests before the previous results are received. Therefore, we also consider the average maximum delay. Furthermore, the probability for each cost to occur has to be taken into account. See Table 1 for a summary of cost terms. We propose the following performance model, describing the extra cost per step of the application:

Table 1. List of cost terms.

Cost Term	Explanation
T_{delay} (Env)	idle time (unused resources because of wait, dependent on other processes)
$P_{ncosched}$ (Env)	probability not to be coscheduled
T_{switch}	process switching cost
T_{spin}	spin time before descheduling
T_{slice} (T_{gran})	time slice, dependent on granularity
T_{gran}	own granularity

$$T_{cost}=P_{ncosched}(Env)*T_{delay}(Env) + P_{ncosched}(Env)*(\min\{T_{spin},T_{gran},T_{slice}(T_{gran})\}+T_{switch})$$

In our measurements with SUN MPI under Solaris with Resource Manager, we found that almost a whole CPU is occupied by the spin daemon (serving all MPI applications) and that therefore one CPU should be "reserved" for it. Furthermore, we could not take advantage of the Resource Manager as it assigns shares to users and our user-level scheduler starts all applications. We found that runtime then is not distributed fairly, i.e. equally (which is consistent with observations in [10]) but that jobs with larger granularities get a larger amount of runtime, i.e. there is an additional effect of R_{share} * $Shift_{share}$ *(Env)*. This demonstrates that true share assignment would be important for predictable performance.

4 Experimental Results

4.1 Coscheduling Effects

Table 2 shows results from coscheduling measurements. The application used are Grid (real simple heat distribution calculation, 4-neighbor communication) with different problem sizes / granularities, Central (synthetic, iterative master-slave), Random (synthetic, random point-to-point with probing). As can be seen, the combination plays a significant role. Observations are that larger granularities of one application (leading to larger time slices) have a negative effect on the coscheduled application, especially if it has strong dependencies.

In tests, we found that T_{switch} = 0.09 msec and $T_{spin} \approx 5$ msec (measured by finding a granularity in a server process from which on there is a difference between limited spinning and unlimited spinnning). T_{slice} is between 20 and 200 msec in Solaris. A rough estimate is that $P_{ncosched}$ = 1 for Grid (except to 300 which accomplishes coscheduling) and the server of Central. For Central, this does not yet explain the observed slowdown. We found a higher runtime share for the applications with larger granularities which explains why in some cases they have a speedup. (This even applied when starting the corresponding applications manually from 2 different accounts which should make the resource management effective.) The reason is probably that the waiting states of the finer-grain processes let the CPU be given to the larger-grain processes which then run for a while and get increased CPU usage. Dependency delays should not produce a slowdown of e.g. larger than 2 for Central as spinning time is relatively small vs. granularity and at worst a single task of each application is finished from the previous iteration while leaving the other CPUs idle. However, it was impossible to extract the details of this behavior (CPU scheduler) to obtain the values of our parameters, and we therefore could not verify the estimations. For our scheduler tests, we have taken the slowdowns as measured and shown in Table 2. These results are slightly better than reported in [12] because we now leave some CPU share for background load.

4.2 Scheduler Benefits

We have done several simulations to demonstrate that our scheduling algorithm works and show which benefits it has. We have oriented our tests slightly (i.e.

with respect to percentages in the different job classes though not with respect to actual runtimes which are too high for our test conditions) to the workloads measured in [3] on a distributed-memory machine (iPSC/860 at NASA AMES), Case 1, and in [1] on a DSM machine (Origin 2000 at NSCA), Case 2. We compare FCFS, mere priority scheduling (Pri), priority + coscheduling (PriCo), and priority + coscheduling + backfilling (PriCoB). Our maximum multiprogramming level is 2 (i.e. 2 jobs run at the same time). For Case 1, we have extended the simulation toward using our sample programs and running them on our SUN SMP server (Enterprise 6500 running Solaris) to check actual coscheduling behavior. However, we had to confine our experiments to equal shares for the resons explained above. Slowdowns are taken as shown in Table 2). We have simulated 36 jobs: 11% long jobs (30 min, Grid-2400), 11% medium jobs (8 to 10 min, Random and Grid-300), 16% short jobs (3 to 5 min, Grid-300 and Central), and 60% very short jobs (1 to 1.5 min, Grid-1200 and Stream). Two of the long jobs are cross-site jobs. Job submission is such that the interarrival time of long jobs is 40 min, whereas the others are equally spread. As can be seen in Figure 5, PriCoB provides the best average response time and the best relative average response time (response time in relation to job runtime). The former reduces from 45 to 25 min vs. FCFS. The latter from about 14 to about 3.

For Case 2, we have not actually run programs but fully simulated the workload, using 40 jobs and assuming that all applications have a slowdown of 1.2. We have chosen 15% long jobs (5 min), 20% medium jobs (1 min), 30% short jobs (30 sec), and 35% very short jobs (10 sec). The long jobs are submitted every 10 min followed by various mixtures of other jobs. The average response time reduces from about 5.5 min to about 3. The average relative response time from about 12.5 to about 1.8. See Figure 6. However, worth to note, the overall execution time for the workloads increased due to the slowdown effects. In Case 1, the execution times are 3:34h for FCFS and for Pri, 4:08h for PriCo and 4:29h for PriCoB. In Case 2 the numbers are 45min for FCFS and for Pri, 47min for PriCo, and 55min for PriCoB. Case 1 demonstrates that better coscheduling approaches are needed which keep the slowdown low.

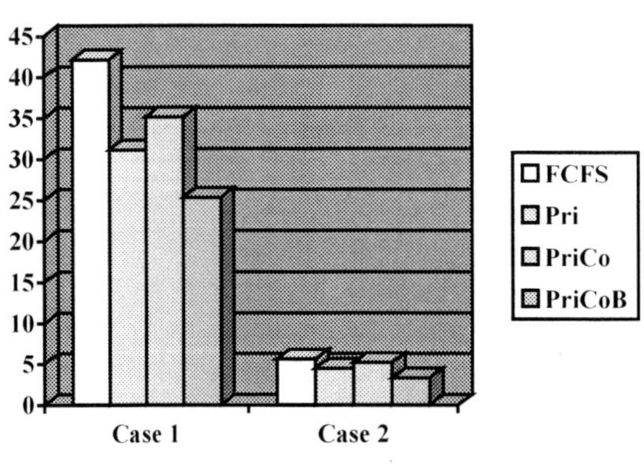

Figure 5. Average response time for Case1 and Case2.

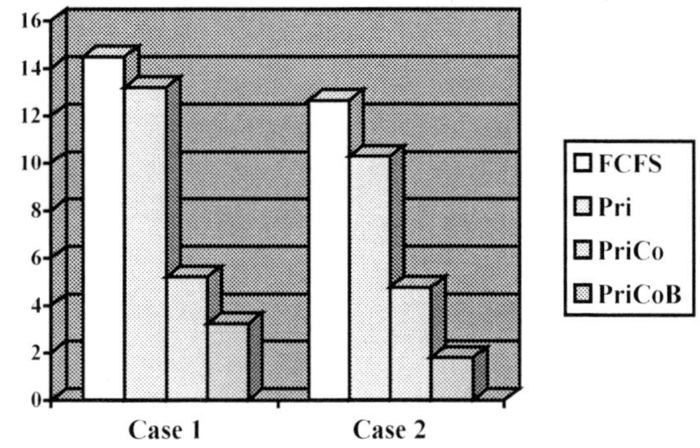

Figure 6. Average relative response time for Case 1&2.

Finally, we have simulated different share assignment and considered multiprogramming levels of 2 and 3 (Case 3). The guaranteed shares for the first 2 coscheduled jobs is 40%, leaving potentially 20% for a third job. Slowdown is set to 1.2 for all jobs if coscheduling 2 jobs (C2), and 1.3 if coscheduling 3 jobs (C3). We have simulated 40 jobs: 10% long (5 min), 20% medium (1 min), 20% short (30 sec), and 50% very short (10 sec). The long jobs were submitted every 14 min, immediately followed by medium jobs. Short and very short jobs arrived arbitrarily. Only PriCoB was tested. Figure 7 shows that the average response time drops from 6 to 3.7 min if coscheduling 3 jobs. Average relative response time is almost the same.

Thus, overall we have shown that coscheduling provides benefits, especially if the percentage of short and very short jobs in the workload is high. Furthermore, we have demonstrated that the algorithm works properly for cross-site and local reservation submissions, priorities, backfilling, shares, and slowdowns from coscheduling.

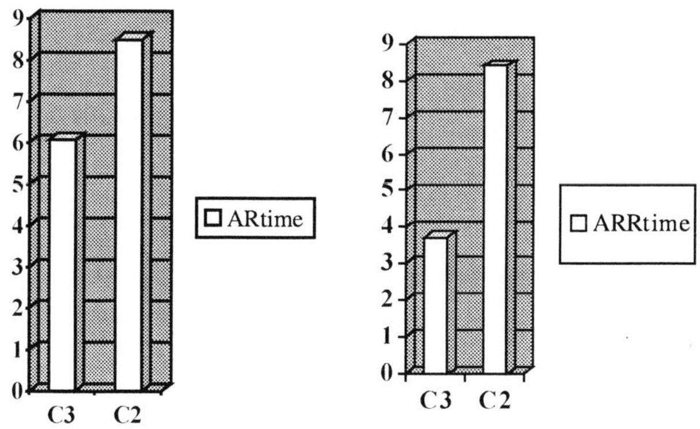

Figure 7. Average and average relative response time for Case3 with varying time shares.

We also have checked that remote requests get the proper lists of possible time slots and that the overflow share works properly (needed in Case 1 as real runs cannot be 100% accurate in time vs. estimate).

5 Summary and Future Work

We have presented a scheduling approach which is capable of making starttime and share reservations for cross-site jobs. Shares are used to coschedule applications in a predictable manner. The main contributions are that coscheduling effects are considered on a per-application and per-combination basis and that guaranteed shares are effective shares. The latter take slowdowns from coscheduling into proper consideration to keep the share reservations. We have incorporated the well-known backfilling approach from space sharing to our share assignment.

Furthermore, we base our estimations on an integrated dynamic directory which keeps information about the applications in the scheduling plan and can later be used to keep dynamic-execution information. We have implemented the core scheduling algorithm and shown that the approach works and that we can obtain better response time than with FIFO or pure priority scheduling. This applies under the assumption that workloads have many short applications.

We have demonstrated coscheduling effects between different communication patterns on sample applications under Solaris and SUN MPI. Flexible share allocation has been demonstrated via simulations. We expect share-based allocation (on the basis of systems like QLinux) to gain larger importance in the future, indicated by the fact that QoS and DSRT have found strong interest in the grid community.

As future work, the goal is to integrate our scheduling approach with Globus or Condor and a local scheduler like PBS, LSF or Maui. This means to extend the local scheduler, put the grid scheduler as a layer on top of the local scheduler and let it interact with the local scheduler.

Acknowledgements

We thank the reviewers for their valuable comments and Feng Yang for an initial directory implementation.

References

[1] S.-H. Chiang and M.K. Vernon. Characteristics of a Large Shared Memory Production Workload. Proc. JSSPP, 2001.

[2] H. Chu and K. Nahrstedt. CPU Service Classes for Multimedia Applications. Proc. IEEE Multimedia Systems, June 1999.

[3] D.G. Feitelson and B. Nitzberg. Job Characteristics of a Production Parallel Scientific Workload on the NASA Ames iPSC/860. Proc. JSSP, 1995.

[4] D.G. Feitelson, L. Rudolph, U. Schwiegelsohn, K.C. Sevcik and W. Parkson. Theory and Practice in Parallel Job Scheduling. In Proc. JSSSP, 1997.

[5] I. Foster and C. Kesselman, The Globus Toolkit. In I. Foster and C. Kesselman (eds), The Grid - Blueprint for a New Computing Infrastructure, Morgan Kaufmann Publishers, San Francisco/CA, USA, 1999.

[6] GRAAP-WG: http://people.man.ac.uk/~zzcgujm/GGF/graap-wg.html, Nov. 2002.

[7] D. Jackson, Q. Snell, and M. Clement. Core Algorithms of the Maui Scheduler. Proc. JSSPP, 2001.

[8] C. Pinchak, P. Lu and M. Goldenberg. Practical Heterogeneous Placeholder Scheduling in Overlay Metacomputers: Early Experiences, Proc. JSSPP, 2002.

[9] Solaris Resource Manager, http://wwws.sun.com/software/resourcemg, 2002.

[10]P.G. Sobalvarro, S. Pakin, W.E. Weihl and A.A. Chien. Dynamic Coscheduling on Workstation Clusters. Proc. JSSPP, 1998.

[11]A.C. Sodan, Towards Asynchronous Metacomputing in MPI, Proc. HPCS, 2002.

[12]A.C. Sodan and M. Riyadh. Coscheduling of MPI and Adaptive Thread Applications in a Solaris Environment. Proc. IASTED PDCS,2002

A Genetic Algorithm for Scheduling Directed Acyclic graphs in The Presence of Communication Contention

Yoginder S. Dandass[a]

[a]Mississippi State University, Department of Computer Science, PO Box 9637, Mississippi State, MS 39762
yogi@hpcl.cs.msstate.edu

This paper presents an algorithm for scheduling parallel applications represented in the form of directed acyclic graphs (DAGs) onto a set of homogeneous parallel processors. The algorithm utilizes a genetic algorithm to prioritize scheduling activities for a list scheduling algorithm with the primary goal of minimizing schedule length and a secondary goal of minimizing the total number of processors used in the schedule. The genetic list scheduling (GLS) algorithm presented in this paper extends existing research by considering contention for processor-to-network links during communication operations. This requires the GLS to efficiently schedule both communication and computation operations in order to reduce schedule lengths. Furthermore, The GLS presented in this paper also strives to efficiently schedule multicast operations over a virtual point-to-point topology. Schedules produced by this GLS algorithm are shown to have shorter lengths than those produced by the HLEFT and ETF algorithms that have been modified to handle communication contention and multicast communication. A parallel implementation of the GLS algorithm using the synchronous connected island model is also investigated and is shown to produce better results than the sequential implementation.

Cet article présente un algorithme d'ordonnancement d'applications parallèles, représentées par des graphes à orientation acyclique (directedacyclic graphs ou DAGs), sur un ensemble homogène de processeurs parallèles. L'approche utilise un algorithme génétique qui priorise l'ordonnancement de façon à réduire le délai d'attente et minimiser le nombre de processeurs utilisés. L'approche présentée (genetic list scheduling ou GLS) permet d'augmenter l'étendu de nos connaissances actuelles avec la prise en compte de l'embouteillage du lien processeurs-réseau pendant les opérations de communication. L'algorithme GLS doit donc ordonnancer efficacement à la fois la communication et les calculs. De plus, la variété de GLS présentée dans cet article prend en compte le plus efficacement possible les opérations de multidiffusion sur topologie réseau point à point. Cet algorithme GLS donne lieu à de plus court délais que des algorithmes HLEFT et ETF ayant été modifiés pour prendre en considération les embouteillages réseau et les multidiffusions. Une implémentation parallèle de l'algorithme GLS (synchronous connected island model) a également été expérimentée et a produite de meilleurs résultats que l'implémentation séquentielle.

1 Introduction

Parallel processing is becoming a popular approach for solving large problems whose processing requirements exceed the computational and memory capacity of individual processors. In order to make economical use of system resources, parallel applications require efficient scheduling of their computation and communication tasks in resource-constrained systems (*e.g.*, systems with limited number of processors and network bandwidth). Therefore, fine-grained scheduling and resource allocation of parallel application with the goal of increasing system efficiency has become an important area of research.

The computational requirements of the constituent tasks for many parallel applications can be estimated using analytical and empirical techniques, and the analysis of the control and data flow of these applications can provide information regarding inter-task precedence relations and communication requirements [6, 8]. This information, represented in the form of direct acyclic graphs (DAGs), can be used to construct efficient static schedules for these applications prior to their execution in production environments where minimizing runtimes is critical.

Scheduling DAGs with the goal of minimizing *makespan* (*i.e.*, schedule lengths) is known to be NP-hard in general [5]. Therefore, a number of heuristic approaches have been proposed that can produce near-optimal schedules in polynomial time [2, 9]. List scheduling (LS) is one such heuristic technique that has been extensively studied, and a large number of LS heuristics have been proposed [1, 15]. Genetic algorithms (GAs) have also been applied to solve scheduling problems and hybrid algorithms combining list scheduling with GA (called genetic list scheduling) have recently been developed [11, 12, 16].

Most LS research efforts make the simplifying assumption of having completely contention-free communication operations (*i.e.*, a point-to-point physical network is assumed). This assumption allows the list schedulers to focus on scheduling computational tasks without considering the interaction of communication operations competing for limited network resources. While a high-capacity network fabric (*i.e.*, switches and switch interconnects) may appear to be contention free, contention over processor-to-switch links cannot be disregarded when scheduling communication operations. This is because communication delays due to link contention can, in turn, delay the execution of dependent computational tasks.

This paper presents a genetic list scheduling (GLS) algorithm, that takes communication contention into account when constructing schedules from DAGs. In the face of competing computation and communication tasks, the algorithm proposed in this paper strives to optimize the scheduling of both computation and communication.

The contention free communication assumption in prior research enabled all the edges originating from and arriving at a vertex to be scheduled to occur simultaneously. This obviated the need for special handling of multicast operations. In a multicast operation, identical data appears to be transmitted from the *root* (*i.e.*, source) vertex to all recipient vertices. The GLS algorithm presented here parallelizes the logical point-to-point operations underlying the multicast operation by considering all processors that have copies of the data to be potential sources. This parallelization can significantly reduce schedule makespan as compared to schedules with serialized point-to-point multicast implementations. The algorithm presented in this paper uses an extended DAG representation in order to enable the specification of multicast edges.

The remainder of this paper is organized as follows: Section 2 provides a detailed problem definition, describes the parallel processing environment, and identifies the simplifying assumption made regarding the communication infrastructure. Section 3 provides a brief overview of LS and GLS techniques. Section 4 describes the GLS approach used in this research. Section 5 presents experimental results and analysis. Section 6 highlights key contributions and discusses of avenues for further research.

2 Problem Definition

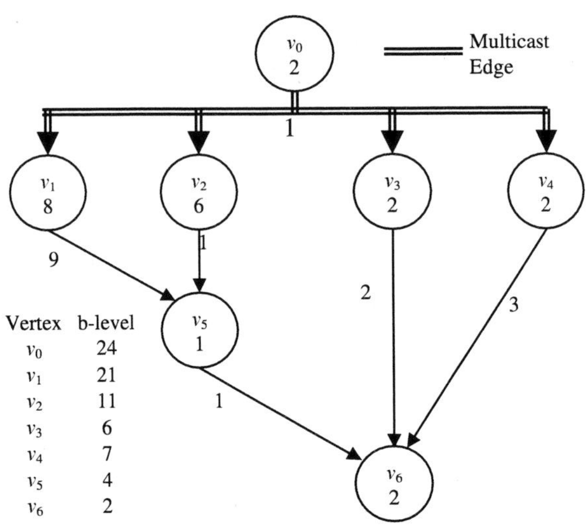

Figure 1: Hypothetical DAG and vertex b-levels

A DAG $G = \{V, E\}$ consists of a set $V = \{v_1, v_2, \ldots, v_n\}$ of n vertices and a set $E = \{e_1, e_2, \ldots, e_k\}$ of k directed edges connecting the vertices. The vertices represent computational tasks in a parallel application and the edges represent communication and precedence relations between the tasks. The ordered pair $e_i = (v_{src}, v_{dest})$ indicates that the direction of edge e_i is from vertex v_{src} to v_{dest}. In Figure 1, depicting a simple DAG, edges (v_0, v_1), (v_0, v_2), (v_0, v_3), and (v_0, v_4) are multicast edges.

The primary objective of the algorithm described in this paper is to schedule DAGs onto a parallel machine so as to minimize its *makespan* (*i.e.*, schedule length) while utilizing a "reasonable" number of processors. Of two schedules with identical makespans, the schedule requiring fewer processors is preferred.

The processor time $t(v_i)$ required to complete the computation of node v_i is given by its weight $w(v_i)$. For example, in Figure 1, $t(v_0) = w(v_0) = 2$. Because communication cost between vertices scheduled on the same processor is assumed to be negligible, the time to execute e_i is given by

$$t(e_i, p_s, p_d) = \begin{cases} 0 \text{ when } p_s = p_d \\ w(e_i) \text{ otherwise} \end{cases},$$

where p_s, and p_d are the processors on which the source and destination vertices of e_i are scheduled, respectively.

A homogeneous parallel environment consisting of identical processors is assumed for executing the parallel application. Therefore, the time taken to execute a computational task is the same on any processor. Also, a uniform network capacity is assumed over the entire parallel system. This implies that the time needed to complete a particular point-to-point communication operation is the same over any combination of source and destination processors.

Each processor is assumed to have a half duplex interface to the homogeneous virtual point-to-point network. This restricts communication to either one incoming operation or one outgoing communication operation at each processor-network link at a time. Conversely, the switched network fabric is assumed to be contention free (*i.e.*, there is sufficient network capacity available to ensure that the various communication operations do not interfere with each other). This is a reasonable assumption because high-performance switches can multiplex several messages simultaneously, and alternative routes can be used to avoid congestion.

This research also considers efficient scheduling for multicast operations over a virtual point-to-point network. Instead of using a single spanning tree-based pattern of point-to-point operations for all instances of multicast communication as proposed in [4], a GLS is used to discover the best possible schedule for the best possible set of point-to-point operations that can be used to implement each multicast edge.

This research assumes that computation and communication may be overlapped without affecting each other's completion time. In practical systems, contention over the shared system and memory busses between the processor the network interface card (NIC) during DMA operations can cause variances in communication and computation completion times. However, these variances are assumed to be sufficiently small so as to have minimal impact on the schedule.

It is also assumed that communication operations need not be tightly coupled between sending and receiving tasks (*i.e.*, the sending and receiving computation tasks need not be executing simultaneously with each other or during the associated communication operations). Given a schedule, the system initiates data transfer at the appropriate time and buffers data that cannot be immediately transmitted or consumed. Note that precedence is still observed; the destination task cannot begin execution before all incoming communication operations are completed. The overhead of buffer manipulation can be reduced through the use of efficient buffer management semantics (*e.g.*, similar to the buffer management facilities provided by MPI/RT [18]).

3 Background

3.1 List Scheduling

The fundamental LS process is the following:

1. Construct a *ready list* of vertices with no preceding vertices.
2. While vertices remain in the ready list:
    3. Prioritize the ready list.
    4. Remove the highest priority vertex from the ready list and schedule it on the processor that will allow the earliest start time for this vertex.
    5. Add the newly readied vertices to the ready list.

A ready vertex is one whose precedence constraints have been met. In typical LS algorithms, vertex priorities are determined either statically from vertex attributes before the scheduling process begins or dynamically during the scheduling process. The variety of attributes and ways in which they are applied in various LS approaches are too numerous to mention here. The survey of LS algorithms by Kwok and Ahmad [15] provides such details.

Of all LS algorithms, the *Dynamic Critical Path* (DCP) algorithm [17] appears to have the best performance over a large number of sample DAGs. However, as with most other LS algorithms, DCP assumes contention free communication and does not consider multicast operations. Unfortunately, the complex nature of DCP precludes its straightforward modification to address these issues. Therefore, in order to provide a basis for evaluating the GLS approach proposed here, two simpler LS algorithms were modified to handle communication contention and multicast edges.

The *Highest Level First with Estimated Times* (HLEFT) [1] algorithm is a simple (and consequently a fast) LS algorithm. It prioritizes vertices in the ready list in descending order of their *static b-level* attributes. The *static b-level* of a node n_i is the length of the longest path between n_i and an exit node and is computed before the scheduling process is begun.

The *Earliest Time First* (ETF) [14] algorithm exhaustively computes the earliest start time of each ready-vertex—processor pair and greedily schedules the ready vertex with the earliest possible start time first.

As depicted in Figure 2(a), the modified HLEFT and ETF algorithms produce identical schedules for the DAG in Figure 1 (although the individual vertices and edges are allocated to processors in a slightly different order). In Figure 2, rows represent parallel processor nodes and columns represent time units. Each row is divided horizontally into two halves. Gray and hatched rectangles represent vertex and edge allocations to the corresponding parallel node's processor and network link, respectively. Absence of rectangles indicates that the processor or network link is idle.

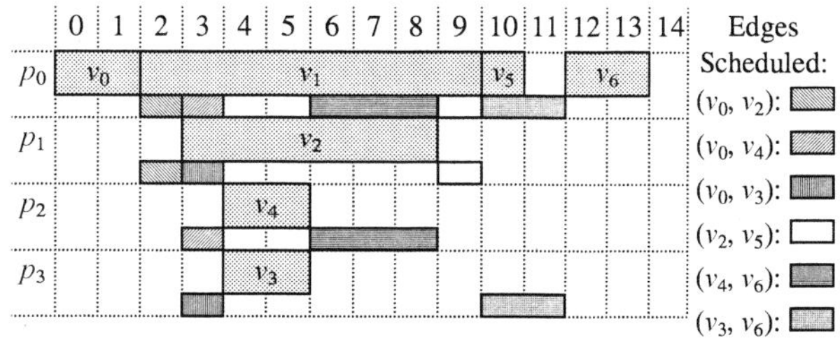

(a) Schedule created by the modified HLEF and ETF algorithms when (v_4, v_6) is considered before (v_3, v_6) while scheduling v_6.

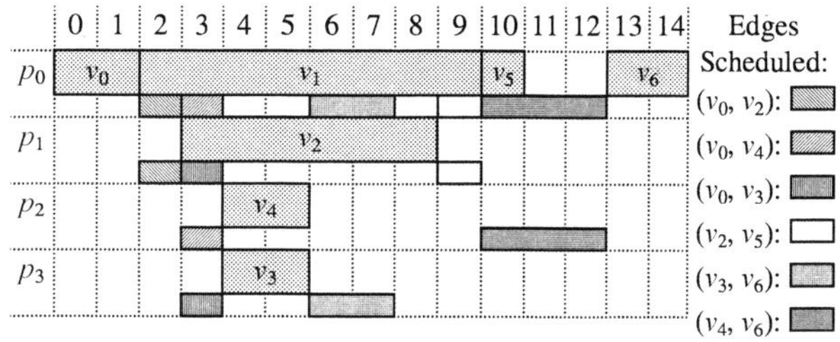

(b) Schedule created by the modified HLEF and ETF algorithms when (v_3, v_6) is considered before (v_4, v_6) while scheduling v_6.

Figure 2: Schedules produced by the modified HLEFT and ETF algorithms for the DAG in Figure 1.

Edges originating and terminating within the same processor do not consume network resources, and therefore, are not shown. Also, note that the multicast edge (v_0, v_3) originates from p_1 rather than p_0 even though v_0 is scheduled at p_0. This is because p_1 has previously received the multicast data in the form of edge (v_0, v_2) and can transmit it to p_3 while p_0 is busy with edge (v_0, v_4).

3.2 Genetic List Scheduling

GAs are optimization algorithms that are based on the principles of natural evolution. A GA iteratively evolves improved solutions by randomly exploring the solution space while simultaneously exploiting the features of the previously discovered solutions. Essentially, the GA optimizes an objective function by repeatedly selecting the "fitter" solutions (as determined by the objective function) to contribute characteristics to their progeny and by discarding the relatively poor solutions. This causes the features of the fittest solutions to remain in the population and repeatedly recombine, producing even better solutions, while the features of poor solutions disappear over time. In GLS, the LS algorithm schedules the ready vertices in the order determined by the GA and solution fitness is derived from the makespan of the associated schedules.

Several genetic operators such as selection, crossover, and mutation are used to combine features from parent chromosomes into offspring chromosomes. The selection operator is responsible for selecting fitter chromosomes for recombination into new chromosomes and for discarding poor chromosomes to make room for the new chromosomes. The crossover operator is used to combine the features of two chromosomes to form a new chromosome. The mutation operator is used to induce stochastic exploration of the search space and to reduce the occurrence of premature convergence of the GA at a local optimum. Convergence is indicated when most of the chromosomes in the population have similar features and nearly identical fitness values. When the population has converged at a local optimum, the ability of the GA to explore new areas in the search space in order to locate the global optimum is reduced. The wide variety of genetic representation schemes, selection operators, crossover operators, and mutation operators proposed in the literature precludes their detailed description here.

4 Approach

The outline of the steady state GLS algorithm investigated in this paper is as follows:

1. Generate the initial population.
2. Use list scheduling to construct a schedule in order to evaluate each of the initial chromosomes.
3. Do while the termination criteria are not satisfied:
    4. Select a genetic operator.
    5. Select chromosome(s) from the local population and apply the operator to produce the offspring chromosome.
    6. Use LS to construct a schedule in order to evaluate the offspring chromosome.
    7. Select chromosome from the local population to be replaced by the offspring chromosome.
8. Use the fittest chromosome to construct the solution schedule.

4.1 Genetic Representation

Most existing LS and GLS algorithms focus on prioritizing vertices in the ready list and can schedule the incoming edges of a vertex in arbitrary order because communication contention is ignored. However, when communication contention is allowed, the order in which edges are scheduled also impacts makespan. For example, the schedule in Figure 2(a) is shorter than the schedule in Figure 2(b) because edge (v_4, v_6) is considered for scheduling before edge (v_3, v_6) while scheduling v_6.

Each chromosome in the GLS developed in this research consists of two vectors of genes. The *vertex vector* contains a gene for each vertex in the DAG and the *edge vector* contains a gene for each edge in the DAG. Essentially, each gene uniquely identifies its corresponding vertex or edge and there are $|V|+|E|$ genes in each chromosome. The position of the vertex and edge genes in their respective vectors determines the priority of the corresponding vertices and edges used by in the LS phase of the GLS.

4.2 Schedule Construction

Given a DAG G and set of parallel nodes P, the LS component of the GLS algorithm essentially operates as described in Section 3.1. The ready list, R, consists of vertices whose predecessor vertices have been scheduled but have not necessarily completed execution. At each step, the ready vertex, $r \in R$, whose gene appears foremost in the vertex vector is removed from the ready list and is allocated to the processor that allows the earliest start time (subject to precedence constraints). Formally, the start time for r is

$$\tau_s(r) = \min\{\tau_{alloc}(r, p) : p \in P\},$$

where $\tau_{alloc}(r, p)$ is the earliest time vertex r can be allocated to processor p. $\tau_{alloc}(r, p)$ is determined as follows. Let $A(p)$ represent the list of intervals in the schedule during which vertices are allocated to processor p. Assume that the intervals in $A(p)$ are ordered according to start times. Therefore, for a_k, the kth vertex in $A(p)$, $(\tau_s(a_k), \tau_e(a_k)]$ represents the interval during which a_k is scheduled on p, and $\tau_e(a_k) \leq \tau_s(a_{k+1})$. Similarly, let $L(p)$ represent the ordered list of edges allocated to the communication link on p, and $(\tau_s(l_k), \tau_e(l_k)]$ represents the interval during which edge l_k is scheduled on p's link. Further assume that all $A(p)$ and $L(p)$ contain two sentinel intervals $(-\infty, -1]$ and $(\infty, \infty]$.

$\tau_{alloc}(r, p)$ is the beginning the first idle slot in $A(p)$, after all preceding edges of r have been allocated, that can accommodate the compute time for r. Therefore,

$$\tau_{alloc}(r, p) = \min\{\max(\tau_e(a_k), \tau_{ready}(r, p)) : a_k, a_{k+1} \in A(p), \tau_s(a_{k+1}) - \max(\tau_e(a_k), \tau_{ready}(r, p)) \geq t(r)\},$$

where $\tau_{ready}(r, p)$ is the time the last preceding edge of r is completed on p. Assuming that Q_r represents the list of all incoming edges of r,

$$\tau_{ready}(r, p) = \max\{\tau_e(q, p) : q \in Q_r\},$$

where $\tau_e(q, p)$ is the completion time for edge q with the destination vertex scheduled at p. For an as-yet unscheduled point-to-point edge q with a predecessor vertex σ_q that has been scheduled on processor s and has a completion time $\tau_e(\sigma_q)$,

$$\tau_e(q, p) = \lambda(t(q, s, p), s, p, \tau_e(\sigma_q)).$$

The function $\lambda(w, s, p, \alpha)$ returns the time when the communication operation with weight w completes from processor s to processor p and α is the earliest time that the edge is permitted be scheduled. If s and p are the same,

$$\lambda(t(q, s, p), s, p, \tau_e(\sigma_q)) = \tau_e(\sigma_q)$$

because intra-processor communication consumes no time. Otherwise,

$$\lambda(w, s, p, \alpha) = \max(\tau_e(l'_{i-1}), \tau_e(l''_{j-1}), \alpha) + w$$

when the following condition is true:

$$\underset{l'_i \in L(p)}{\forall} \underset{l''_j \in L(s)}{\forall} \min(\tau_s(l'_i), \tau_s(l''_j)) - \max(\tau_e(l'_{i-1}), \tau_e(l''_{j-1})) \geq w$$

and $\tau_s(l'_{i-1}) \geq \alpha$ and $\tau_s(l''_{j-1}) \geq \alpha$.

When edge q belongs to the set B of edges associated with a multicast group, there are several source processor choices available. Essentially the processor, s, on which the multicast root vertex, υ, has been scheduled and the set of any of the other processes, O, that have received a copy of the multicast data can be used as the edge source. Therefore,

$$\tau_e(q, p) = \min(\lambda(t(q, s, p), s, p, \tau_c(\upsilon)) \cup \{\lambda(t(q, o, p), o, p, \tau_c(o)) : o \in O\}).$$

4.3 Recombination Operators

Two different crossover operators, *ordered crossover* (OX) [7] and *vector crossover* (VX) are used in this GSL algorithm. In OX, a single crossover point is randomly selected in the vertex vector. The sequence of genes prior to the crossover point is copied from the first parent to the front of the vertex vector in the offspring chromosome. The remaining genes in the first parent (*i.e.*, following the crossover point) are copied into the offspring gene in the order they appear in the second parent. The same operation is also performed on the edge vectors to construct the offspring chromosome. In VX, the first parent contributes a complete copy of its vertex vector and the second parent contributes a complete copy of its edge vector to construct the offspring chromosome.

The mutation operator swaps the location of a pair of genes within the vertex vector, the edge vector, or a pair each from both vertex and edge vectors. One of these three mutation options is selected with equal probability.

The GLS produces good results when the probabilities of selecting the OX, VX, and mutation operators are $\pi_{ox} = 0.75$, $\pi_{vx} = 0.20$, and $\pi_m = 0.05$, respectively.

4.4 Selection

Other researchers have observed that making direct use of the objective function (*i.e.*, makespan in this case) to compute the fitness of chromosomes can lead to premature convergence [3]. This occurs when a single chromosome with a significantly better than average objective function value is repeatedly selected for reproduction, leading to reduced genetic diversity in the population. In order to prevent this situation, the rank of chromosomes, rather than their objective function values are used to compute their fitness. The rank of chromosome c is the number of chromosomes in population Ω that produce worse schedules than c. More precisely,

$$rank(c) = |\{c_i \in \Omega : makespan(c) < makespan(c_i) \vee \text{if } makespan(c) = makespan(c_i) \rightarrow processors(c) < processors(c_i)\}|.$$

In order to further reduce the ability of high ranking individuals to dominate the population, the fitness of a chromosome is made inversely proportional to the number of offspring it has produced. This results in the following fitness function, also used by Grajcar [12]:

$$\varphi(c) = \frac{rank(c)}{|offspring(c)|+1}.$$

The chromosome with the largest fitness value in a random subset of Ω is selected for reproduction. Similarly, the chromosome with the least fitness value from another random subset of Ω is selected for replacement. In the experiments reported here, selection subset sizes ranging from 2% to 10% of $|\Omega|$ worked well for populations ranging from 200 to 800 chromosomes.

4.5 Parallel Implementation

A parallel implementation of the GLS using the *synchronous connected island model* [10] is also under investigation. In this model, the parallel GLS processes operate on separate local populations and communicate synchronously to exchange the fittest chromosomes with each other periodically. This "migration" of chromosomes enhances the exploitation of high quality solutions in parallel GAs, while the relative isolation of the subpopulation enhances genetic diversity and prevents premature convergence.

The number of iterations between migrations is reduced exponentially to a specified minimum, m (*i.e.*, migrations occur after M, $M/2$, $M/4$, $M/8$, …, $2m$, m, …, m iterations). The value of M is tuned so that high-frequency migrations occur shortly before the number of iterations expected to produce results, or more realistically, the maximum allowed iterations or time elapses. This strategy emphasizes exploration of the solution space at the beginning of the evolutionary process and emphasizes exploitation of good genetic information towards the latter stages.

As suggested in [19], varying the GA control parameters in each of the N parallel GLS processes can lead to increased genetic diversity. Therefore, the mutation, vector crossover, and ordered crossover rates used in a parallel GLS process $n_i \in \{0, 1, \ldots, N - 1\}$ are given by

$$\pi_m(n_i) = 0.05 + 0.05 \times n_i/N,$$
$$\pi_{vx}(n_i) = 0.20 + 0.10 \times n_i/N, \text{ and}$$
$$\pi_{xo}(n_i) = 0.75 - 0.15 \times n_i/N,$$

respectively. This implies that the mutation rate ranges between 0.50 and 0.10, the feature crossover rate ranges between 0.20 and 0.30, and the order crossover rate varies between 0.75 and 0.60. These ranges appear to work well for the sample scheduling problems solved in the research effort.

5 Experimental Analysis

5.1 Setup

DAGs with three distinct types of structures are used in order to evaluate the performance of the GLS algorithm. The first type of DAG has an "out-tree" structure as illustrated in Figure 3(a). The number of outgoing edges from each vertex is randomly selected from a uniform distribution between one and ten. The second type of DAG has a "fork-join" structure illustrated in Figure 3(b). The width of each "fork" in the fork-join DAGs is selected randomly from a uniform distribution between two and ten. The third type of DAG has a random structure. The random DAG has eight times as many edges as vertices connecting randomly selected edges (*i.e.*, on average, each vertex has eight incident or outgoing edges).

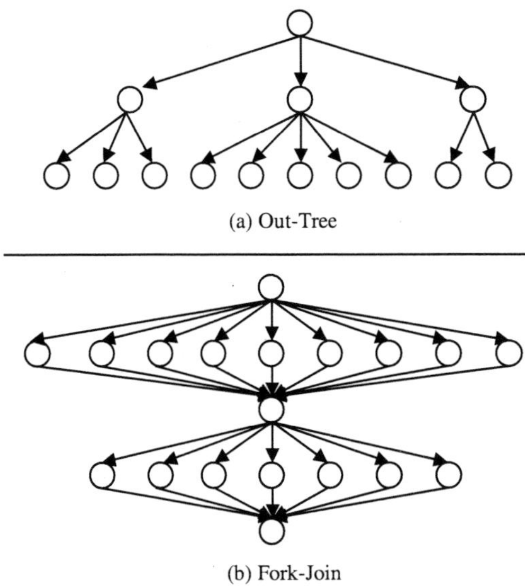

Figure 3: Sample DAG types

Six instances of each type of DAG were created. Each of these DAG instances consists of approximately 300 vertices. Within a DAG, each vertex is assigned a weight selected from a normal distribution with mean = 10 and variance = 3. Edge weights are also selected from normal distributions with a variance = 3. However, the mean of the edge distribution is set to 5, 10, or 20 at the beginning of the generation process. Additionally, in each DAG, either no edge is part of a multicast group, or all outgoing edges from every vertex are grouped into multicast groups (note that edges originating at different vertices cannot belong to the same multicast group). These combinations of structure, edge weight distributions, and multicast or non-multicast edges result in a total of 18 distinct DAGs.

In order to provide a basis for comparison, the HLEFT and ETF algorithms were also modified to handle multicast edges and communication contention. Nominally, HLEFT and ETF do not consider edge ordering when scheduling. However, because edge ordering is significant in the presence of communication contention, all inbound edges of a vertex are scheduled in descending order by weight in the modified HLEFT and ETF algorithms. While this "first fit decreasing" bin packing heuristic results in the shorter schedule of Figure 2(a), it does not guarantee optimality. Computational costliness precluded the exhaustive examination of all possible edge orderings in this research effort.

5.2 Sequential Results

A problem with GAs is that the number of iterations required to produce near-optimal results is not known *a-priori*. Indeed, for many large NP-hard problems, the precise nature of the optimal solution is unknown, and therefore, cannot be used to determine the termination point for the GA. Because of these reasons, GAs are typically executed for a fixed number of iterations or for a fixed amount of time.

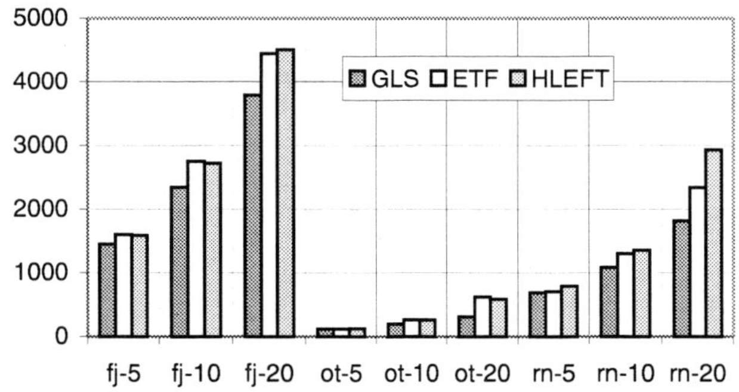

Figure 4: Schedule makespans for the multicast DAGs

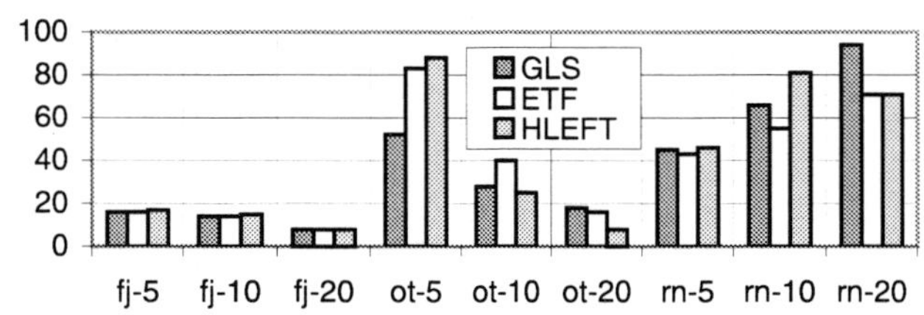

Figure 5: Schedule processors for the multicast DAGs

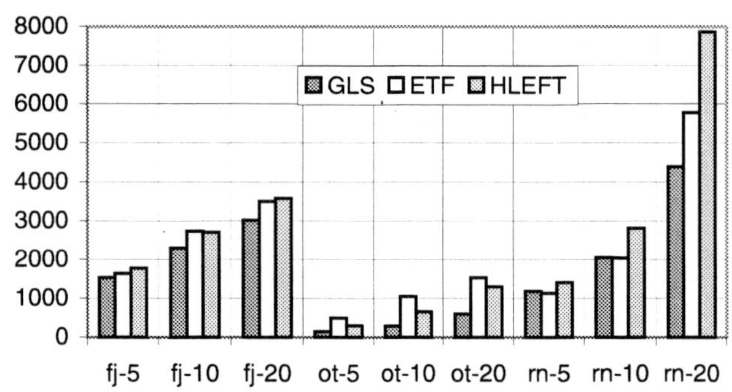

Figure 6: Schedule makespans for the pt-to-pt DAGs

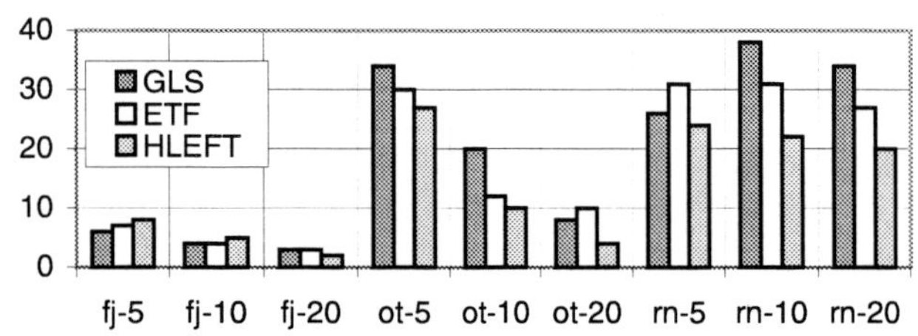

Figure 7: Schedule processors for the pt-to-pt DAGs

The large number of edges in the random DAG instances causes the GLS implementation to take a long time to construct schedules. Therefore, each GLS run was initially limited to a maximum of 9,000 iterations in order to complete the experiments in a reasonable amount of time. Also, based on results from preliminary experimentation, the population size for each GLS run was set to 600. Because of the stochastic nature of GAs, the GLS algorithm was applied on each DAG instance at least three times and the median results are reported here.

Figures 4 and 5 illustrate the makespan and number of processors, respectively, in the schedules for the nine DAGs with multicast operations. Figures 6 and 7 illustrate the makespan and number of processors, respectively, in the schedules for the nine DAGs with only point-to-point communication. In order to determine the shortest possible schedules could be produced by this GLS, the GLS was permitted to use an unlimited number of processors in the schedules.

Labels fj-*x*, ot-*x*, and rn-*x* along the bottom axis of the figures indicate the results for the fork-join, out-tree, and random DAGs, respectively. The *x* value indicates the mean edge weight in the DAG instances.

In terms of minimizing makespan for the 18 DAGs, GLS outperformed HLEFT in all instances and ETF in 15 instances. ETF did better than HLEFT in 11 instances. When the three instances for which the GLS was unable to find better makespans than ETF were re-executed without iteration restrictions, the GLS took 1,537, 3,919, and 16,464 iterations to produce shorter schedules than ETF for multicast-ot-5, pt-to-pt-rn-5, and pt-to-pt-rn-10, respectively. This highlights the problem with the probabilistic nature of GAs in that it took several attempts before the GLS was able to solve these three problems.

In general, shorter schedules should require a greater number of processors than longer schedules for the same DAG instance. However, of the 15 instances in which GLS produced shorter schedules than ETF, GLS used equal or smaller number of processors than ETF in 8 instances. Similarly, in 8 of 18 instances, GLS used fewer processors than HLEFT. This ambiguity in processor utilization results suggests that the strategy of minimizing the start time for vertices at the cost of allocating a new processor is non-optimal. This is further illustrated by the schedule in Figure 8 for the DAG in Figure 1. This schedule requires only three processors. However, none of the LS algorithms tested is able to produce this schedule.

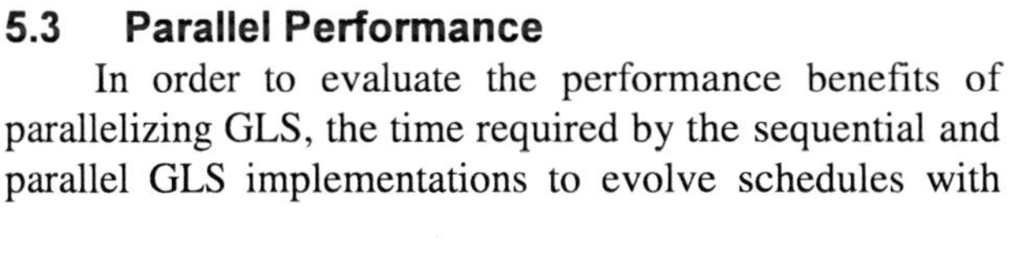

Figure 8: Optimal schedule for the DAG in Figure 1

5.3 Parallel Performance

In order to evaluate the performance benefits of parallelizing GLS, the time required by the sequential and parallel GLS implementations to evolve schedules with specific makespans is measured and compared. Speedup is given by $S = T_s/T_p$ where T_s is the time taken by the sequential implementation and T_p is the time taken by the parallel implementation. As has been observed by other researchers (*e.g.*, [13]), this strategy for computing speedup is required in order to accurately account for the benefit of using larger global population sizes and improved population diversity of parallel GAs.

Table 1 shows the speedup achieved by the MPI-based parallel GLS implementation executed on a 8-node dual 450MHz PIII cluster with a high-speed Giganet interconnect fabric. The multicast fj-10 DAG instance was used for this analysis because this DAG's structure allows a large number of iterations to complete in a relatively short amount of time. This enabled the use of challenging makespan thresholds, requiring over 50,000 iterations. Furthermore, the global population size of 9,600 was used in this experiment (*i.e.*, the local population size for each parallel GLS process was 9600/*P*, where *P* is the number of processes in the parallel GLS). Several runs of the sequential and parallel GLS implementations were performed to collect execution time data and the best results were used to compute speedup.

	Seq	P=2	P=4	P=8	P=16
Speedup		0.98	2.20	4.07	3.43
Makespan range after 80K iterations	2359-2325	2329-2290	2286-2266	2290-2232	2286-2242

Table 1: Performance of Parallel GLS

Although, these speedup figures in Table 1 are small, an analysis of the schedule makespans that resulted when each algorithm was run for 80,000 iterations demonstrates that given a fixed amount of time, the parallel version running on 8 or 16 processors evolves better schedules than the sequential GLS. The second row of Table 1 lists the maximum and minimum schedule lengths that resulted for the sequential and the various parallel configurations of the GLS.

6 Conclusions

The research presented in this paper extends existing genetic list scheduling research by considering communication contention at the processor-to-network links. This communication model more accurately reflects the behavior of processor-to-network links in the switched network technology used to deploy clusters. Therefore, the resulting schedules can be more readily realized in the scheduling of parallel applications on practical parallel systems.

In order to construct efficient schedules in the presence of communication link contention, the GA approach used in this research seeks to optimize both vertex and edge priorities for the list scheduler. Optimizing edge priorities is important because the order in which communication links are allocated to edges affects schedule makespan in the presence of communication contention. The GLS approach developed here also seeks to efficiently schedule multicast operations in the presence of communication contention.

Because of the NP-hard nature of the DAG scheduling problems, optimal solutions were not available for the large problems addressed here. However, the comparison of schedules resulting from GLS, HLEFT and ETF algorithms suggests that GLS is able to produce much better results at the cost of using significantly more time.

The probabilistic nature of GLS means that the algorithm may need to be run several times in order to find a near-optimal solution. A related problem is that it is difficult to predict how long GLS must run before a near-optimal schedule is evolved.

As expected, the parallel implementation of GLS produced better schedules in a shorter amount of time than the sequential GLS. The speedup characteristics of this parallel implementation, based on the synchronous connected island model, were disappointing. However, the parallel GLS was able to delay premature convergence and, therefore, was able to discover schedules shorter than the shortest schedule produced by the sequential GLS.

Ongoing research is focused on extending this work to construct schedules for heterogeneous environments with multiple communication links per processor. The feasibility of applying GLS in scheduling for real-time systems is also under investigation as is the optimization of the parallel GLS control parameters (*e.g.*, population size, frequency and topology of migrations, adaptive crossover and mutation rates, and termination criteria).

7 References

[1] T. L. Adam, K. M. Chandy, and J. Dickson, "A Comparison of List Scheduling for Parallel Processing Systems," *Communications of the ACM*, vol. 17, December, pp. 685-690, 1974.

[2] I. Ahmad, Y. Kwok, and M. Wu, "Analysis, Evaluation, and Comparison of Algorithms for Scheduling Task Graphs on Parallel Processors," in *Proc. of the International Symposium on Parallel Architectures, Algorithms, and Networks*, pp. 207-213, 1996.

[3] T. Bäck and F. Hoffmeister, "Extended Selection Mechanisms in Genetic Algorithms," In Proc. of the 4th International Conference on Genetic Algorithms, pp. 92-99, 1991.

[4] M. Barnett, D. Payne, and R. van de Geijn, "Optimal Broadcasting in Mesh Connected Architectures," TR-91-38, University of Texas, 1991.

[5] E. G. Coffman, *Computer and Job-Shop Scheduling Theory*, John Wiley and Sons, New York, 1976.

[6] W. W. Chu, M. Lan, and J. Hellerstein, "Estimation of Intermodule Communications (ICM) and its Application in Distributed Processing Systems," *IEEE Transactions on Computers*, vol. C-33, no. 8, pp. 691-699, 1984.

[7] L. Davis, "Applying Adaptive Algorithms to Epistatic Domains," in *Proc. of the 9th international joint conference on artificial intelligence*, pp. 162-164, 1985.

[8] D. Gajski and J. Peir, "Essential Issues in Multiprocessors," *IEEE Computer*, vol. 18, no. 6, 1985.

[9] A. Gerasoulis and T. Yang, "A Comparison of Clustering Heuristics for Scheduling DAGs on Multiprocessors," *Journal of Parallel and Distributed Computing*, vol. 16, no. 4, pp 276-291, 1992.

[10] V. S. Gordon and D. Whitley, "Serial and Parallel Genetic Algorithms as Function Optimizers," Technical Report CS-93-114, Colorado State University, 1993.

[11] M. Grajcar, "Strengths and Weaknesses of Genetic List Scheduling for Heterogeneous Systems," in *Proc. of the 2nd International Conference On Application of Concurrency to System Design, IACSD*, 2001.

[12] M. Grajcar, "Genetic List Scheduling Algorithm for Scheduling and Allocation on a Loosely Coupled Heterogeneous Multiprocessor System," in *Proc. of the 36th Design Automation Conference*, pp 280-285, 1999.

[13] W. E. Hart, S. Baden, R. K. Belew, and S. Kohn, "Analysis of the Numerical Effects of Parallelism on a Parallel Genetic Algorithm," in *Proc. of the 10th International Parallel Processing Symposium*, pp. 606-612, 1996.

[14] J. J. Hwang, Y. C. Chow, F. D. Anger, and C. Y. Lee, "Scheduling Precedence Graphs in Systems with Interprocessor Communication Times," *SIAM Journal of Computing*, vol. 18, no. 2, pp. 244–257, 1989.

[15] Y. Kwok and I. Ahmad, "Static Scheduling Algorithms for Allocating Directed Task Graphs to Multiprocessors," *ACM Computing Surveys*, vol. 31, no. 4, pp. 406-471, 1999.

[16] Y. Kwok and I. Ahmad, "Efficient Scheduling of Arbitrary Task Graphs to Multiprocessors using a Parallel Genetic Algorithm," *Journal of Parallel and Distributed Computing*, vol. 47, no. 1, pp. 58-77, 1997.

[17] Y. Kwok and I. Ahmad, "Dynamic Critical-Path Scheduling: An Effective Technique for Allocating Task Graphs to Multiprocessors," *IEEE Transactions on Parallel and Distributed Systems*, vol. 7, no. 5, pp. 506-521, 1996.

[18] MPI/RT Forum, *Document for the Real-Time Message Passing Interface (MPI/RT-1.1)*. http://www.mpirt.org, 2001.

[19] J. C. Potts, T. D. Giddens, and S. B. Yadav, "The Development and Evolution of an Improved Genetic Algorithm Based on Migration and Artificial Selection," *IEEE Transactions on Systems, Man, and Cybernetics*, vol. 24, no. 1, pp. 73-86, 1994.

Optimization of Load Balancing Algorithm Using Workload Simulator For a HPC Environment

AK Aggarwal[a], Haresh S. Bhatt[b], BK Singh[c]

[a] University of Windsor, Windsor, On., N9B 3P4, CANADA
akshaia@uwindsor.ca

[b] Space Applications Centre, Indian Space Research Organization, Ahmeadbad – 380015, INDIA
haresh@ipdpg.gov.in

[c] Space Applications Centre, Indian Space Research Organization, Ahmeadbad – 380015, INDIA
brajendra_kumar@indiatimes.com

It is difficult to devise a uniform load balancing strategy for heterogeneous distributed computing environment, designed to cater to a number of users and a variety of applications, with unpredictable arrival patterns of jobs. This paper investigates the effect of the type of workload on the performance of a load balancing algorithm by using a Workload Simulator. The Simulator helps identify various parameters for improving the performance of the Load Balancing Algorithm for different workload and resource availability conditions. The algorithm and the workload simulator have been applied along with WebDedip, a distributed computing environment.

Il est difficile de mettre au point une stratégie de répartition des ressources dans un environnement hétérogène de systèmes distribués, pour un certain nombre d'utilisateurs, une variété d'applications, et des enchaînements de travaux imprévisibles. Cet article étudie l'effet du type de charge (Workload) sur la performance d'un algorithme de répartion des ressources en utilisant un simulateur de charge. Le simulateur aide à identifier différents paramètres améliorant la performance de l'algorithme pour différentes charges et différentes disponibilités de ressource. L'algorithme et le simulateur ont été appliqués en utilisant l'environnement de calcul distribué WebDedip.

1. Introduction

A Load Balancing algorithm for a heterogeneous distributed computing environment attempts to improve the response time of a parallel or distributed application by ensuring optimum utilization of available resources. It should respond quickly to the changing workload and environmental conditions without causing much overhead. Hence it should customize its strategy as per the prevailing conditions. One method to do this is by having an efficient learning system [15,16,17,18]. Such a system requires a long history of run of load balancer and distributed computing environment involving a large number of combinations of workload and environmental conditions. Even if we have a long history of run, it may not include all the conditions, particularly those which are encountered rarely. Moreover to obtain the data for a large variety of load conditions may prove to be a costly process in terms of the systems resources. Hence we have devised a faster means of testing a load balancing algorithm. We have made a rule based fuzzy simulator [13] which generates a session with low, medium, high and burst workload conditions. These simulated sessions are given to the load balancer, which along with WebDedip [12], runs the session for 2 to N number of nodes. Each run is analyzed and corresponding changes are suggested for the load balancer to optimize its performance. These studies have identified a method of detecting important parameters for variable load conditions. We have used the method to work out the important parameters for two types of load conditions.

Various scheduling optimization algorithms [1,2,3,4] are discussed in the literature. Tang *et al.*[1] have given an optimization scheme for static job scheduling. They use a centralized load balancing policy like us, but allow round robin job dispatching and multiple processes simultaneously while we run one process at a time. The weighted workload allocation scheme introduces the reallocation strategy to get the performance benefit in terms of session duration and to accommodate high priority applications. We are able to avoid the need for separate weighted workload allocation scheme and job dispatching scheme by using a waiting queue and a prediction mechanism. The Simulator generates a real world scenario and obtains a workable load balance policy, rather than a set of fixed mathematical optimizations, consistent with the complexity and dynamic nature of the heterogeneous environment.

Various workload simulators [5,6,8,9,10] for testing are discussed in the literature. They are used for application and environment specific simulation. Incase of the generic distributed processing environment like WebDedip, it is supposed to handle, nearly simultaneously, a large variety of applications. We have developed a simulator [13] for testing the WebDedip Load Balancer under controlled and reproducible conditions. It uses rule based fuzzy probabilistic randomization for simulating distributed processing applications.

2. Backround

Several distributed computing environments, providing different types of tools to the developer, have been developed. Many scientists have worked on improving the efficiencies of such environments. Ease of use, is the parameter which is normally untouched by most of the scientists. WebDedip [12], developed under a research project at Gujarat University, Ahmedabad, India, is the environment which was developed with ease of use as the core theme to support HPC users like physicists, mathematicians, civil engineers, etc. Initially, the performance issues were not addressed. Later, a hybrid application centric load balancer [11], consisting of 6 algorithms, a heuristic and a normalization process, was developed for optimizing the performance.

Testing and tuning of such a load balancer is always a complex and challenging task. It is very difficult to get the required number of nodes as well as different applications for testing. Hence a rule based fuzzy simulator [13] was developed to generate a variety of sessions with different applications. The simulator was used extensively to test the load balancer. It was observed during testing that the performance of the load balancer can be improved a great deal by choosing the parameters appropriately.

3. Goal and Issues

WebDedip load balancer uses a variety of algorithms and rules. Furthermore, it supports the multi-user environment. This is achieved at the cost of overheads, while handling sessions having a number of distributed applications, with different characteristics. The basic aim of the WebDedip load balancer is to improve the session throughput and to manage requests with different priority levels. Furthermore, WebDedip does not postpone an application beyond a certain limit to improve throughput. We aimed at optimizing such a complex algorithm to improve the performance and efficiency.

4. Load Balancer Complexity

We need to understand the WebDedip load balancer before proceeding further.

WebDedip uses a deterministic approach for normalizing the heterogeneous nodes into few classes to reduce the node (class) assignment complexity for an application. Each application has different processes connected to each other through Task Flow Graph (TFG). The critical branch of TFG is taken as the baseline to assign the class to each process. Other branches can be delayed to optimize the resource allocation until it doesn't cross the baseline. It has process completion and application completion predictors that use different permutations of available resources versus requirements. The load balancer uses dynamic sliding window technique, while assigning a class to reduce the complexity of permutations. Applications outside the sliding window, are placed in different FIFO queues based on priority. However, queues are reshuffled to optimize the session throughput. Simultaneously it increases the priority of the applications, that are delayed, to restrict the delay to predefined limits.

WebDedip load balancer is a pseudo dynamic design that applies a set of rules and algorithms on predefined events.

5. Load Balancer Improvement Model

We developed a simulator [13] to simulate a variety of sessions with different characteristics to test the efficiency of the load balancer. The session may be in low, medium, high or burst mode of loading. Each session was repeatedly submitted to the load balancer, at a time, varying 2 to 35 nodes of the WebDedip environment. Application of each case of each session was submitted to the load balancer dynamically (when it was expected to arrive) using threads and sockets.

Load balancer analyses all applications of a session for a case (say 5 nodes) and dynamically assigns the resources to all the processes of all applications. It generates the node allocation graphs and expected session completion time. A throughput graph for each session is generated based on the results available for 2 to 35 nodes.

All sessions were submitted one after another in the same manner. Three critical parameters affecting the performance are identified on the basis of node allocation graphs and session throughput graphs

6. Defining Performance Parameters

The First parameter for load balancer is 'Requirement Factor'. It is defined as the time required by any application on a new node in terms of fraction of session duration. If its value is kept high, then it may happen that in spite of having resources, we may not be using them. If its value is kept low, then overhead associated with inducting new resources may exceed the advantage of occupying resources for a small period of time.

The second parameter is 'Level of Branch delay'. It is defined in terms of number of other nodes whose allocation needs to be altered by dependent as well as subsequent processes (may be of other applications also) of a process to accommodate another process ahead of it on a given node. If its value is higher, then load balancer overhead may increase more than the advantage gained by accommodating another process ahead. This is because the Branch Delay algorithm is implemented by recursive procedures. A higher value of 'Level of Branch delay' means less possibility of Branch delay. This would mean a number of small time intervals, during which the node remains unutilized, may be there after load balancing.

The third parameter is 'Depth of Reallocation'. It is defined in terms of time duration up to the end of allocation window [11], within which all the processes of all the nodes need to be reallocated to accommodate a new application. Optimization of this parameter is required to minimize session completion time. If its value is higher, then load balancer overhead will increase for reallocating nodes and other resources. Moreover some application may get delayed more than their allowable duration. If it is less, then wastage of resources occurs.

7. Results and Discussion

We have taken only two types of sessions i.e. Medium load session and High load session to test and optimize our load balancer. We have not simulated the Light load session since it does not benefit much through load balancing. These test sessions are generated by a Fuzzy simulator. We have generated more than 50 sessions of each type for our exhaustive testing. A typical simulated Medium load session and High load session are shown in Figure 2 and Figure 3 respectively.

These sessions are given to the load balancer which gives a set of load balanced sessions for 2 to 35 number of nodes. The whole philosophy is shown in Figure 1. Figure 4 and Figure 5 show the Percentage CPU utilization and normalized session completion time for a typical set of values of optimization parameter i.e. 'requirement factor' increased by 5 percent,' Level of Branch delay' is increased to 3 nodes and 'Depth of Reallocation' is increased by 20 percent.

As shown in Figure 5, Percentage CPU utilization is, in general, quite less for a Medium load session as well as for a High loaded session even for two nodes. The reason for this behavior is the arrival pattern of the applications. During some time interval within a session, there may be very less load or no load at all, even for High loaded sessions.

For less number of nodes, Percentage CPU utilization is less in case of Medium load session as the session may have less load intermittently or no load at all. In general, a High load session will have sufficient load all the time. Hence for this case percentage utilization will be more for less number of nodes.

Gradient of Percentage CPU utilization curve is more in case of High load session, as load balancer will assign the load optimally for less number of nodes. But as the resources increase, it will try to occupy new resources even for a very short duration. Induction of a new system for very short duration will decrease Percentage CPU utilization sharply, as most of the capacity of newly inducted node remains unutilized. In general, when the level of requirements is low, no new systems should be inducted into the system, as it increases network data transfer overhead, the overheads of managing resources of newly inducted system, polling overhead etc.

In Figure 4, Normalized session completion curve saturates earlier for Medium load session because a Medium load session requires less resources. Average node requirement for a given type of session is expressed in terms of the minimum number of nodes required to complete the session for a given session duration. It can be obtained from Normalized session completion curve. It is equal to the number of nodes at the starting point of saturation of the Session completion time curve. The system shows remarkable improvement when the number of available nodes is closer to the average node requirement. Improvement is less in case of scarcity as well as abundance of resources.

As shown in Figure 5, an increase in 'requirement factor' will not only increase CPU utilization for a given number of nodes but it also increases session completion time. Its effect is more pronounced on a High load session for the reason explained earlier in conjunction with Gradient of Percentage CPU utilization curve. If the 'Level of Branch delay' is increased, the CPU utilization increases and Session completion time decreases. Similarly when 'Depth of Reallocation' increases, the session completion time decreases and CPU utilization increases. The effectiveness of parameters 'Level of Branch delay' and 'Depth of Reallocation' is high for Medium load session as a High load session requires extensive recursive calls or reallocation causing excess overhead to load balancer.

Interdependency between optimization parameters is also observed. For example, reallocation becomes quite frequent when optimization parameter 'Depth of reallocation' is more than 40 percent of the allocation window length in the reallocation algorithm. First this parameter was decided in terms of remaining session duration. After experimentation we made it dependent on allocation window length as well. This works fine for both the sessions. Similarly branch delay algorithm responds slowly when the value of optimization parameter 'Level of branch delay' is raised by more than four levels. Hence the load balancer takes unusually large time for such cases. This becomes comparable to the average process duration for a given session. Hence we decided to restrict the value of this parameter to four.

8. Conclusion and Future Scope

We have carried out exhaustive testing using more than 100 sessions for our optimization. The simulated environment has enabled such a testing in a short duration. Otherwise such an exercise would require many days of work on about 35 nodes for each session in actual production environment.

During this exhaustive and rugged exercise, we could fix more than 85 programming bugs to improve the load balancer accuracy. We had to carry out eight major modifications in the algorithm to improve the efficiency and performance. We have improved the performance of the load balancer by 17%.

We have identified three parameters for improving the session through put. These should be usable for other similar algorithms also. It is only by using optimized values of these parameters, that a load balancer may be able to achieve an optimum throughput. We are also working to address the optimization of burst mode and priority management cases.

We are in the process of interfacing our optimized load balancer with WebDedip in production environment. We wish to conduct sample testing for verifying the optimization effectiveness in production environment.

References

1. Optimizing static job scheduling in a network of heterogeneous computers *Xueyan Tang; Chanson, S.T.* Parallel Processing Proceedings. 2000 International Conference on, 2000, Page(s): 373 –382
2. *Haddad, E.,* Real-time optimization of distributed load balancing, Parallel and Distributed Real-Time Systems, 1994. Proceedings of the Second Workshop on , 1994 Page(s): 52 –57
3. Cherkasova L., Ponnekanti S.R., Optimizing a "content-aware" load balancing strategy for shared Web hosting service, Modeling, Analysis and Simulation of Computer and Telecommunication Systems, 2000. Proceedings. 8th International Symposium on , 2000 Page(s): 492 –499
4. Hamidzadeh B., Lau Ying Kit, Lilja D.J., Dynamic task scheduling using online optimization, Parallel and Distributed Systems, IEEE Transactions on , Volume: 11 Issue: 11 , Nov. 2000 Page(s): 1151 –1163
5. Kao W.I., Iyer R.K., A user-oriented synthetic workload generator, Distributed Computing Systems, 1992., Proceedings of the 12th International Conference on, 1992, Page(s): 270 –277
6. Gomez M.E., Santonja V., A new approach in the modeling and generation of synthetic disk workload, Modeling, Analysis and Simulation of Computer and Telecommunication Systems, 2000. Proceedings. 8th International Symposium on, 2000, Page(s): 199 –206
7. Wen-Sheng Wang, Dujmovic, J.J., Mathews W., A tool for performance measurement of NT networks, Modeling, Analysis and Simulation of Computer and Telecommunication Systems, 2000. Proceedings. 8th International Symposium on, 2000 Page(s): 281 –288
8. Jean-Marc Saglio and José Moreira, Oporto: A Realistic Scenario Generator for Moving Objects, Found in: 10th International Workshop on Database & Expert Systems Applications pp. 426, September 1999.
9. Darko Marinov, Davor Magdic, Aleksandar Melenkovic, Jelica Protic, Igor Tartalja, Veljko Milutinovic, Scowl: A Tool for Characterization of Parallel Workload and its Use on Splash-2 Application Suite, Found in: 8th International Symposium on Modeling, Analysis and Simulation of Computer and Telecommunication Systems pp. 207, August 2000
10. P. Mehra and B. Wah, Synthetic Workload Generation for Load Balancing Experiments, IEEE Parallel and Distributed Technology: Systems & Applications , Volume: 3 Issue: 3 1995, pp 4-19.
11. Bhatt H. S., Singh B.K., Aggarwal A.K., Application centric load balancing based on hybrid model, International conference for advance computing and communication ADCOM-2001, organised by IEEE and ACS India, Dec. 2001, Page(s): 231-238
12. Bhatt H.S., Aggarwal A.K., web enabled client-server model for development environment of distributed image processing, Proceedings of international conference on meta computing, GRID-2000, pp 135-145
13. Aggarwal A.K., Bhatt H. S., Singh B.K., Rule-based Fuzzy Simulator for testing Load Balancing Algorithms, transmitted for publication.
14. Gopal, S., Vajapeyam, U., Load balancing in a heterogeneous computing environment, System Sciences, 1998, Proceedings of the Thirty-First Hawaii International Conference on, Volume: 7, 1998, Page(s): 796 -804 vol.7
15. Mehra P., Wah B.W., Adaptive load-balancing strategies for distributed systems, Systems Integration, 1992. ICSI '92., Proceedings of the Second International Conference on, 1992, Page(s): 666 -675
16. Koch T., Rohde G., Kramer B., Adaptive load balancing in a Distributed Environments, 1994, Proceedings of 1st International Workshop on Services, 1994, pp 115 –121
17. Gil-Haeng Lee, Wang-Don Woo, Byeong-Nam Yoon, An adaptive load balancing algorithm using simple prediction mechanism, Database and Expert Systems Applications, 1998. Proceedings. Ninth International Workshop.1998 Page(s): 496 -501

18. Chin Lu, Sau-Ming Lau, An adaptive load balancing algorithm for heterogeneous distributed systems with multiple task classes, Distributed Computing Systems, 1996., Proceedings of the 16th International Conference on, 1996,Page(s): 629 –636
19. Joshi B.S., Hosseini S.H., Vairavan K., A methodology for evaluating load balancing algorithms, High Performance Distributed Computing, 1993., Proceedings the 2nd International Symposium on, 1993, Page(s): 216 –222
20. Sarje A.K., Sagar G., Heuristic model for task allocation in distributed computer systems, IEE proceedings-E, vol. 138, no. 5, SEPTEMBER 1991, Page(s): 313-318
21. Chulhye Park, Kuhl J.G., A fuzzy-based distributed load balancing algorithm for large distributed systems, Autonomous Decentralized Systems, 1995. Proceedings. ISADS 95, Second International Symposium 1995, Page(s): 266 –273

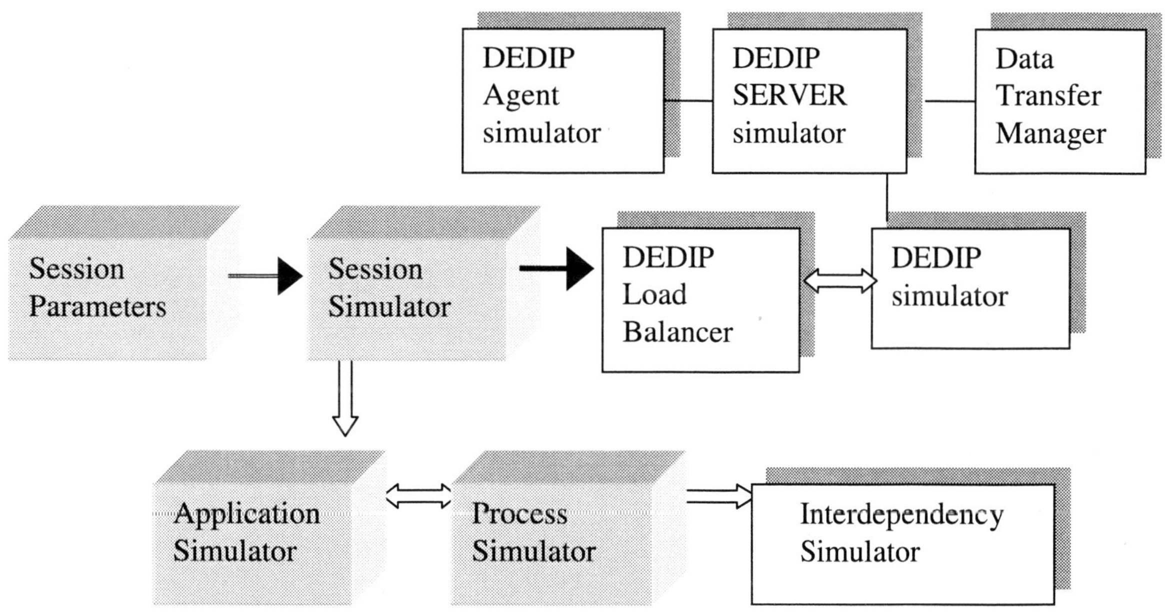

Figure 1: Simulator model for testing DEDIP load balancer

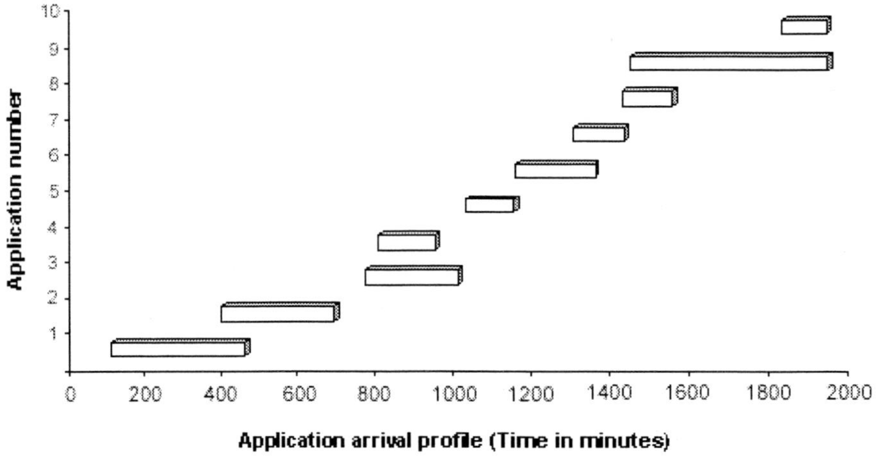

Figure 2: Simulated Application distribution for a medium loaded session

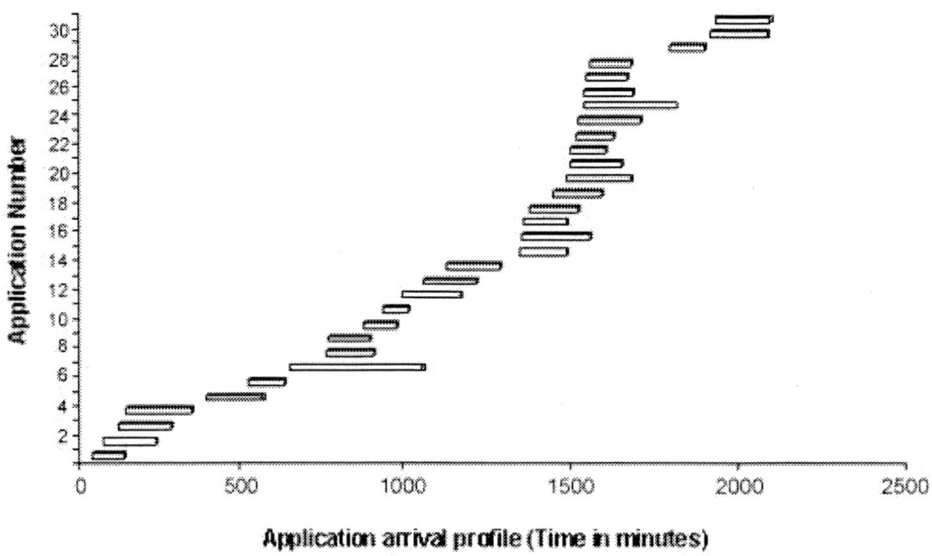

Figure 3: Simulated Application distribution for a heavily loaded session

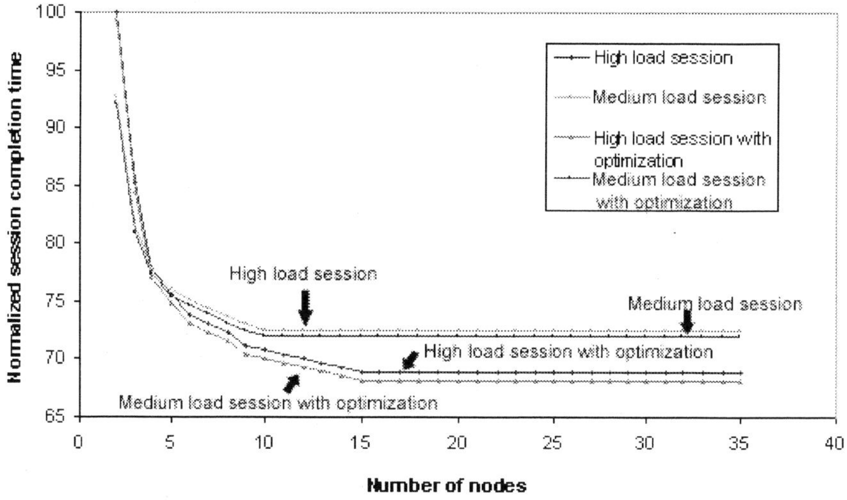

Figure 4: Normalized Session completion graph

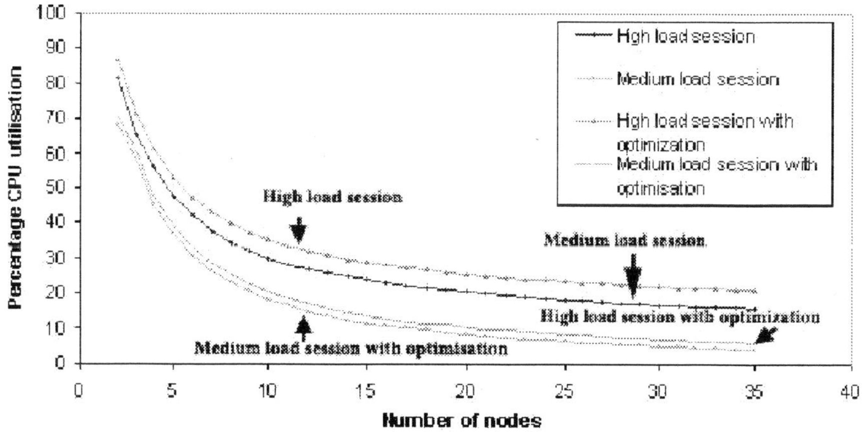

Figure 5: Percentage CPU utilization graph

Part III : OSCAR
Partie III : OSCAR

Open Source Cluster Application Resources (OSCAR) : design, implementation and interest for the [computer] scientific community.

Benoît des Ligneris[a]*, Stephen Scott[b], Thomas Naughton[b] Neil Gorsuch[c]

[a]Centre de Calcul Scientifique, Université de Sherbroke, Québec, Canada

[b]Computer Science Group, Oak Ridge National Laboratory, Tennessee, USA

[c]NCSA, University of Illinois at Urbana-Champaign, Illinois, USA

The Open Source Cluster Application Resources (OSCAR) project is the founding working group of the Open Cluster Group (OCG). The OCG is an informal group of people dedicated to making cluster computing practical for high performance computing and more recently, clustering in general (high availability, diskless). OSCAR is a package that makes it easy to build clusters for high performance computing. Everything you need for a cluster – installation and configuration, maintenance, [parallel] programming, queuing system, scheduler – is included in OSCAR.

In this article we will present a brief history of OSCAR, the actual components of OSCAR as well as the design and implementation proposal for OSCAR 2.1 and beyond.

Le projet OSCAR, Open Source Cluster Application Ressource, constitue un groupe de travail du Open Cluster Groupe (OCG). L'OCG est un rassemblement informel d'individus dont le but est de faciliter l'installation, l'utilisation et la maintenance de cluster dédiés au calcul haute performance. Récemment, cet objectif a été étendu au clustering en général : cluster de haute disponibilité et cluster sans disque. OSCAR est donc une suite logicielle qui facilite grandement la création et l'administration de clusters. Tout ce qui est nécessaire à ces objectifs : installation, configuration, maintenance, programmation parallèle, système de gestion de travaux, programmateur est inclu dans la suite OSCAR.

Dans cet article, nous présenterons une courte histoire du projet OSCAR, les composants actuels de OSCAR ainsi que l'évolution préssentie de OSCAR pour les version ultérieures.

1 Introduction

Cluster computing is the "new" way of doing parallel computing. From the modest creation of this field with the Wiglaf project [1,2] to the huge supercomputers that are now built, a wide range of new problems can be addressed and solved. The price and as a consequence, the accessibility of supercomputers is going down as the ratio power/price of commodity hardware (PC components) drops.

There are several cluster distributions available [3–11], of which, OSCAR is a very popular choice for clustering today [12]. There have been slightly less than 85,000[2] downloads of the software, which shows sound indication that the project has good stability and a large user base. OSCAR is not specific to a particular distribution and is not, as such, linked to any Linux vendor. The current offering has support for Red Hat and Mandrake Linux and efforts within the group are investigating support for SuSE Linux.

OSCAR provides a cluster computing solution, including development of a set of tools for cluster installation and management[3]. The focus of the development is "best cluster practices", taking the best of what is currently available and integrating it into one package. This focus offers the user the ability to get a cluster up and running with standard tools in a timely fashion.

*Corresponding author : benoit@des.ligneris.net

[2]Number based on a snapshot taken January 28, 2003.

2 History

A complete history of the project has already be published [13]. OSCAR was created in April 2000 (first OSCAR meeting) because, it was apparent that the assembly of a cluster was challenging for some and often tedious by all. Although reference material was available [14], each cluster was an experiment in itself and cluster builders had to download, compile, buy, and test a large variety of software and hardware components. Moreover, technological evolution (hardware and software) was happening fast and as a consequence cluster computing was a perpetual (re)invention of the wheel.

After this first meeting the group decided to choose "best practices" for High Performance Computing (HPC) clusters. The open-source solutions for each component were identified and work began on the software stack. This work is still in progress as detailed in Table 1. A primary objective of the OSCAR working group is to make the installation, configuration and management of modest sized clusters easier.

OSCAR is the first project set forth by the Open Cluster Group (OCG). The OCG is an informal group dedicated to making cluster-computing practical for high-performance computing research and development While membership to the OCG is open to anyone, it is directed by a steering committee with committee positions up for election every two years. Currently, the steering committee is made up of representatives from IBM, Indiana University, Intel,

Release	Date	Distribution(s)
2.1	2002-12-12	RedHat 7.2, 7.3, IA64 Mandrake 8.2, 9.0(exp)
2.0	2002-11-20	RedHat 7.2, 7.3, IA64 Mandrake 8.2
1.4	2002-09-30	RedHat 7.2, 7.3, IA64 Mandrake 8.2
1.3	2002-07-15	RedHat 7.1, 7.2 Mandrake 7.2(exp)
1.2.1rh72	2002-04-12	RedHat 7.2
1.2	2002-02-11	RedHat 7.1
1.1	2001-08-03	RedHat 7.1
1.0	2001-02	RedHat 6.2

Table 1
OSCAR software release history. Experimentally supported distributions are marked with '(exp)'.

MSC.Software, National Center for Supercomputing Applications (NCSA), and Oak Ridge National Laboratory (ORNL) [3].

3 Overview

The installation of a computing cluster typically involves the installation and configuration of a *headnode*, which in turn provides services to the compute nodes. Once the headnode has been setup the compute nodes must be "built". This latter portion is where a great deal of time and effort is often duplicated unnecessarily. OSCAR assists with the headnode configuration and then builds the compute nodes based upon a user specified description of the desired software packages. This build and configuration greatly reduces the effort and expertise necessary to setup a cluster.

3.1 Installation

In order to use OSCAR one simply does a standard 'Workstation' install with a supported Linux distribution and architecture, see also Table 1. The distribution RPMs should be copied to a default directory for use during the node image build phase. The user is then able to download, extract and start the OSCAR install wizard.

A graphical user interface (GUI) is available to assist with the installation. This GUI based OSCAR wizard consists of several steps that the user walks through in sequence to perform necessary operations to obtain a masternode (node executing wizard) and a set of compute nodes. The necessary headnode services are configured during this process as well as the number of nodes and what software to install on the cluster.

The heart of the OSCAR installation is the construction of a logical node "image"[4] (SIS image see Section 4.1) that contains a base operating system, plus the selected cluster software packages. The cluster nodes are defined (IP address, etc.) and associated with an SIS image. Then each node network boots (via a floppy or PXE), exchanges identification information (MAC address), is remotely formatted and installed based upon the SIS image. This entire cluster installation process is managed by OSCAR and therefore greatly reduces the expertise and time required to build and configure a cluster.

3.2 Design

High performance computing software evolves very rapidly and, as a consequence, the OSCAR framework has to be able to do frequent releases in order to provide, at a given time, a snapshot of the best known methods for building, programming, and using clusters. This strong requirement leads to a distributed architecture based on OSCAR packages. The OSCAR framework includes some core utilities as well as the core packages that have to be installed on every OSCAR cluster. Once this is done, a collection of additional packages can be downloaded and installed that provide functionality to the cluster.

With this modular design, packages can be updated independently of the core utilities and core packages. Additional flexibility to this model is provided by the Oscar Package Downloader (see also: Section 3.2.1), which allows for multiple repositories so that each package maintainer can provide package updates. The OSCAR toolkit is freely redistributable and therefore requires all distributed packages to conform, each organization is free to setup their own OSCAR repository for internally developed (i.e. not free) software.

This distributed system allows the OSCAR community to efficiently manage contributions from every interested developer : each organization has the complete control of the packages they maintain. Functionality can be added and bugs can be fixed every time it is necessary without affecting functionality of other packages. Regular check points are made so that all packages remain compatible : this correspond to a major OSCAR release (as specified in Table 1).

3.2.1 Modular Packaging

The modular packing facility enables OSCAR to install and configure software that has been dropped into a prescribed directory format. The packages are based upon the RedHat Package Manager (RPM) system and allow for additional scripts for cluster configuration. The OSCAR packages are basically the RPM-ized software plus an XML meta file describing the package and various installation criteria, e.g. where to install the software: server, clients, both. The OSCAR packaging API allows authors to provide additional documentation as well as tests to validate the installation.

A selected set of packages are "included" with OSCAR and others are available from remote locations. The OS-

[3] For more information on OCG and its working groups see, http://www.openclustergroup.org/

[4] This is in contrast to a binary "bit" image, e.g. as used by the dd utility.

CAR Package Downloader (OPD) is similar to the Perl CPAN utilities for acquisition of packages from remote repositories. This capability enables package authors to provide updates and/or packages that might have restrictions prohibiting direct inclusion in OSCAR. Once the OSCAR packages are obtained they are added to the list of available software for installation on the cluster.

4 Components

The common software packages that are installed on High Performance Computing Clusters (HPCC) are bundled with OSCAR. A small set of packages are "core" or required to support the base OSCAR framework. This core set of software is used for the installation and configuration of the cluster.

This section discusses the four major groups of cluster software found in OSCAR. The *Core Infrastructure and Management* facilities as mentioned above are required and tasked with the installation and configuration of the cluster. The *Administration/Configuration* packages are essential for cluster maintenance [5]. The remaining two sections summarize the HPCC and Security packages.

4.1 Core Infrastructure/Management

Environment Switcher

A standard issue with system administration is management of a user's environment. This includes things like which implementation of MPI is the default for users. These defaults should also be easily modifiable on a per user basis. Typically this environment management is performed by manually modifying ".dot" files, e.g. *.bashrc, .cshrc*.

The Environment Switcher tool, or simply Switcher, provides a clean mechanism to manipulate system- or user-level defaults through a command-line interface [15]. This allows for cluster administrators to set a system default, e.g. MPI = lam-6.5.7. Then a user has the option of accepting system defaults, checking for other available software and selecting an alternative at the per user basis, e.g. MPI = mpich-1.2.4. Again, these environment changes are via the Switcher command-line interface and do not require the user to manually edit files.

Switcher extends the Modules tool by making the environment settings persistent upon subsequent shell invocations. Another feature of switcher is that environment is maintained across non-interactive shells, e.g. rsh/ssh.

C3 - Cluster, Command and Control

The C3 power tools offer a command-line interface for cluster system administration and parallel user tools [16]. They are the product of scalable systems research being performed at ORNL [17,18]. The tool set includes commands to execute (`cexec`) across the entire cluster (or a subset of nodes) in parallel. The scatter/gather (`cpush/cget`) operations are also available. The C3 power tools have been developed to span multiple clusters. This multi-cluster capability is not fully harnessed by OSCAR currently but is available for administrators or standard users.

C3 is used internally throughout the OSCAR toolkit to distribute files and perform parallel operations on the cluster. The OPIUM tools (see Section 4.2) use C3 as well to provide clusterized user management tools, e.g. `useradd`. Since C3 enables standard Linux commands to be run in parallel, administrators can use the tools to maintain clusters. A common example is the installation of a Red Hat RPM software package across the cluster using for example `cexec rpm -ivh foo.rpm`.

SIS - System Installation Suite

OSCAR uses the System Installation Suite (SIS) to perform the initial installation of the compute nodes [19]. SIS is based upon the popular *SystemImager* tool. The *System Installer* and *System Configurator* tools extend SystemImager by adding a description based image construction interface and dynamic configuration facility, respectively.

The OSCAR wizard leads the user through the creation of a SIS image. This image is a "virtual node" having all the software contained on the cluster node(s). The nodes boot and copy an install script over the network that partitions and formats the hard disks, and then copies all software to the newly configured disk. The installation of the compute nodes is done automatically and after the nodes build and reboot they are accessible via the network.

SIS can be used beyond the initial installation to maintain a cluster by making modifications to the image and synchronizing the cluster nodes to transfer the changes. This image based cluster management is also useful for maintaining diskless clusters and used by the Thin-OSCAR working group, (see also: Section 5.1).

ODA (OSCAR DAtabase)

The ODA package is used by the OSCAR wizard and OSCAR packages to store and retrieve data. It uses the mySQL database as the underlying database engine. ODA adds user and program friendly interfaces for database access, and the capability to expand database commands in various ways, and for administrators and programs to define new database commands. These definitions are themselves stored in the database, and allow OSCAR and ODA to provide a database API that hides the details of the database. Each OSCAR package can define and modify it's own set of database commands that all OSCAR packages can use, allowing each OSCAR package to provide it's own database API. The package specific definitions can either be statically supplied by OSCAR packages, or created dynamically by the packages. Initially, the ODA package populates the database with various cluster information and static information supplied by each OSCAR package.

[5]Note, most of the "core" tools are as well used for cluster administration and maintenance.

4.2 Administration/Configuration

A number of tools are provided to assist cluster administration, including the previously mentioned SIS and C3 packages. The OSCAR Password Installer and User Management (OPIUM) utility synchronizes user account files across the cluster. The standard user add and delete commands are wrapped to be cluster aware. The Kernel-Picker tool allows one to substitute a given kernel into the SIS image prior to building nodes.

OSCAR also helps with the configuration of standard cluster services, such as Network File System (NFS) to share the user `/home` filesystem across the cluster. This enables users to easily access their files from any of the cluster nodes. The Network Time Protocol (NTP) service is also setup to keep a consistent time throughout the cluster as well as syncing the headnode to one of the atomic clocks on the Internet. Another useful configuration that is performed by the Loghost package is to forward system log (syslog) entries from compute nodes to the headnode. This centralization is helpful when trying to maintain a cluster.

4.3 HPC Services/Tools

Ganglia Monitoring System

Ganglia offers a scalable monitoring system with both command line and GUI based access tools. The base system as configured by OSCAR includes a monitor daemon on each node and a server on the headnode gathering the information. The system communicates over a multicast channel using XML as the data format language. Metrics such as CPU usage and uptime as well as identification information like OS version are added to the multicast stream. These metrics can be extended if desired to include further data.

The monitoring system offers a very nice web based GUI to browse historical data and view usage information for the cluster. The command line interface provides access to machine cpu load, which can be used to for creating host files if working outside a batch scheduling system.

HDF5 (Hierarchical Data Format)

HDF5 is a general purpose library and file format for storing scientific data. The data can be grouped into hierarchical user-defined structures with various datatypes and attributes. There are a variety of datatypes available, including compound and user-defined datatypes. The library is intended for users working with large files, theoretically in the terabyte and greater range.

Parallel Libraries

The message-passing libraries of PVM (Parallel Virtual Machine)[20] and the MPIs [21], LAM/MPI [22] and MPICH [23], provide the requisite capability in the OSCAR environment that enables one to take advantage of this distributed computing environment for the creation of parallel distributed programs. The OSCAR distribution tracks the most recent release of each of these packages and provides the necessary configuration at installation for the above libraries. There is no modification of the standard library package provided by each of these groups; OSCAR is only a repackaging of the standard library distribution with the addition of the cluster configuration/installation automation. OSCAR enjoys an inside track to the LAM/MPI and PVM packages, as core members of the OSCAR team are also members of these two parallel library teams.

OpenPBS/MAUI

The Portable Batch System, OpenPBS [24] is a flexible workload management system. It operates on networked, multi-platform UNIX environments, including heterogeneous clusters of workstations, supercomputers, and massively parallel systems. The OSCAR package includes several useful enhancements (node failure "support", support of more than 500 nodes, ...).

The default scheduler included with OpenPBS is a simple First In First Out (FIFO). Therefore, the more advanced MAUI [25] scheduler is included with OSCAR and setup as default. MAUI is very powerful and offers numerous advanced features, many of which go beyond the default OSCAR configuration. Numerous scheduling policies are supported as well as dynamic priorities, node reservations and fairshare.

4.4 Security

Clusters are under increasing attacks through outside networks. Providing cluster security is especially important for private research and even, in certain case sensitive (military, ...) research. Most of the provided OSCAR tools were not built with security in mind. The preferred networking model for clusters uses a private network for the cluster with limited outside access. The use of private network for securing the cluster from the outside world, strong encryption whenever possible (OpenSSH [26]) for internal and external communication as well as general usage of local firewalls (Pfilter[27,28]) both on the master node and on the regular nodes provide, we believe, a secure clustering solution. OSCAR configures both ssh and the core packages to use ssh within the cluster for communication wherever possible. This also provides secured logins into the cluster from outside. Pfilter is configured to provide packet filtering firewalls on each machine in the cluster. The firewalls are configured to allow unrestricted network communication between machines in a cluster, prevent all but a few types of authorized methods of outside access to the cluster, and allow complete unrestricted access from within the cluster to outside network resources.

Pfilter

Pfilter provides configurable packet filtering firewalls [27,28]. Pfilter is installed on each system as a system service that can be started, stopped, and restarted. Easy to understand, high level configuration files are "compiled" by Pfilter into packet filtering ruleset command files. Pfilter also handles multiple network interfaces, allowing one machine to be a packet forwarding firewall for machine that are "behind" it on a private network, allowing the protected machines to access the outside network in a safe manner. It can also provide pseudo interfaces for protected hosts, allowing the protected hosts to be visible from the outside network.

OpenSSH

Access to a cluster is typically from remote locations (not the console). The Secure SHell (SSH) enables users to connect to the cluster in a safe manner. The open source implementation, OpenSSH, is configured and used by the default OSCAR configuration. The authentication and encryption schemes incorporated can be scaled for less or more stringent security needs. The usage is similar to that of telnet and rsh/rlogin with the provided security masked from the user.

5 Future

Since, the first OSCAR release in early 2001 there have been approximately eight major releases. Each of these releases has seen OSCAR evolve and improve. The current development path includes an overhaul of the base installation harness. This MetaMenu tool is being designed to provide a state-machine facility that will allow developers to more easily modify and extend installation and maintenance procedures.

Another goal is to enhance the OSCAR maintenance facilities. This includes the ability to both add, delete and update software from a uniform interface. This will include both the OSCAR packages as well as standard system updates. The OSCAR package itself is also going to be rebundled to allow for simpler upgrades between releases. The Linux Standards Base (LSB) is now being supported by most major distributions. Current OSCAR plans are to embrace this standardization for better multi-distribution support.

The scalability of OSCAR and its components is also being investigated. This may be an opportunity for the various OCG working groups to interact and extend current cluster practices.

5.1 Thin-OSCAR

The Thin OSCAR work-group [29] was created in Summer 2001 to specifically analyze and solve problems that will arise while adding diskless support to OSCAR clusters. The current implementation use the SIS image and create an initial RAM disk that contain a minimal Linux system. Users programs (/usr), OSCAR binaries (/opt) and users directories (/home) are exported via NFS.

The long term goals of the Thin OSCAR work-group are to support systemless nodes (i.e. nodes without any system on disk), heterogeneous clusters that are constituted of nodes with disk and system, systemless nodes as well as diskless nodes. Finally, Thin-OSCAR would like to provide several clustering solution by including cutting edge kernel with specialized clustering solutions for instance OpenMOSIX, BProc, LTT as well as distributed filesystems dedicated to clustering (e.g. cluster).

5.2 HA-OSCAR

The High Availability OSCAR working group was established in Summer 2002. This group is tasked with looking into and developing techniques to provide high-availability for both general purpose high-performance cluster computing as well as for special interest groups such as the telecommunication and defense industries. This group is presently studying the problems associated with achieving high-availability to determine the cost of implementing such operations. A reliability-modeling project is presently under way with preliminary findings presented in [30] submitted to this conference. Other efforts are underway including the development of tools for reliability estimation and the study and subsequent improvement of the various system infrastructure and framework to enhance self-healing and failure management. The long-term goal of this group is to develop a complete, cost effective, and open source solution to the high-availability problems associated with high-performance cluster computing.

6 Conclusion

OSCAR is a very powerful package that allows anyone interested by clustering and/or parallel programming to quickly and easily deploy a medium-size cluster. The modularity of OSCAR allows computer scientist, researcher and companies using computer science to easily develop new cluster concepts without being encumbered by installation, configuration and maintenance details. This is a big step toward general use of clustering in all areas of research as present-day commodity hardware is perfectly capable. This is the primary goal of the OSCAR working group.

Acknowledgments

We would like to thank the other OSCAR developers for their time and efforts in making such a sound clustering toolkit. Special thanks to Jeff Squyres who has done a wonderful job as 2002 OSCAR Chair, while managing an extremely militant schedule.

References

1. T. Sterling, D. Savarese, D. J. Becker, J. E. Dorband, U. A. Ranawake, and C. V. Packer. BEOWULF: A parallel workstation for scientific computation. In *Proceedings of the 24th International Conference on Parallel Processing*, volume I, Architecture, pages I:11–14, Boca Raton, FL, August 1995. CRC Press.
2. Phil Merkey. Beowulf, Introduction - History - Overview, May 1998. Revised May 2000. http://beowulf.gsfc.nasa.gov/overview.html.

3. Open Cluster Group: OSCAR Working Group. OSCAR: A packaged cluster software for High Performance Computing. http://www.OpenClusterGroup.org/OSCAR.
4. SCore Cluster System Software, http://www.pccluster.org.
5. Scyld Beowulf Scalable Computing, http//www.scyld.com.
6. MSC.Linux, http://www.msclinux.com.
7. NPACI Rocks Cluster Distribution, http://rocks.npaci.edu.
8. Scalable Cluster Environment (SCE), http://www.opensce.org.
9. ClusterMatic, http://www.clustermatic.org.
10. Cheos – LLNL, http://cheos.llnl.org.
11. KA-Tools, http://ka-tools.sourceforge.net.
12. Poll: *What Cluster system (Distribution) do you use?*, 233 votes (Feb. 01, 2002). Other 24%, OSCAR 23%, Score 15%, Scyld 12%, MSC.Linux 12%, SCE 6%, http://clusters.top500.org.
13. Richard Ferri. The OSCAR revolution. *Linux Journal*, (98), June 2002. http://www.linuxjournal.com/article.php?sid=5559.
14. Thomas Sterling, John Salmon, Donald J. Becker, and Daniel F. Savarese. *How to Build a Beowulf.* MIT Press, May 1999.
15. Env-Switcher, http://env-switcher.sourceforge.net.
16. Cluster Command & Control (C3) power tools, http://www.csm.ornl.gov/torc/C3.
17. M. Brim, R. Flanery, A. Geist, B. Luethke, and S. Scott. Cluster Command & Control (C3) tools suite. In *To be published in, Parallel and Distributed Computing Practices, DAPSYS Special Edition*, 2002.
18. Al Geist et al. Scalable Systems Software Enabling Technology Center, March 7, 2001. http://www.csm.ornl.gov/scidac/ScalableSystems.
19. System Installation Suite (SIS), http://www.sisuite.org.
20. Parallel Virtual Machine (PVM), http://www.csm.ornl.gov/pvm/.
21. Message Passing Interface (MPI) Forum, http://www.mpi-forum.org.
22. LAM/MPI: Implementation of MPI, http://www.lam-mpi.org.
23. MPICH: Implementation of MPI, http://www-unix.mcs.anl.gov/mpi/mpich/.
24. Portable Batch System (OpenPBS), http://www.openpbs.org.
25. MAUI Scheduler, http://supercluster.org/maui/.
26. Secure Shell (OpenSSH), http://www.openssh.org.
27. Network Packet Filter, http://pfilter.sourceforge.net.
28. Neil Gorsuch. PFILTER in OSCAR - Industrial Strength Cluster Firewalls in an Open Source Environment. In *To be published in, OSCAR2003 Conference*, May 11-14, 2003.
29. Benoît des Ligneris and Francis Giraldeau. Thin-OSCAR : Design and future implementation. In *To be published in, OSCAR2003 Conference*, May 11-14, 2003.
30. C. Leangsuksun, L. Shen, H. Song, S.L. Scott, and I. Haddad. The Modeling and Dependability Analysis of High Availability OSCAR Cluster System. In *To be published in, HPCS2003 Conference*, May 11-14, 2003.

OSCAR Cluster Administration With C3

Brian Luethke[a], Stephen Scott[a], Thomas Naughton[a]

[a]Oak Ridge National Laboratory

The Cluster Command & Control (C3) tools developed at ORNL provide the ability to treat the cluster as a single entity. That is, a single command may be issued that will affect the entire cluster, or a specified subset of the cluster, in a predictable and controlled manner. This paper is a "hands-on" discussion of system administration of an OSCAR cluster using the C3 tools. First is a brief overview of the C3 tools and their configuration, next is a discussion of the use of C3 tools for cluster administration within an OSCAR cluster, and the discussion ends with a coverage of C3 use outside the standard scope of the OSCAR environment.

Les outils Cluster Command & Control (C3) développés au Laboratoire National d'Oak Ridge (ORNL) fournissent les capacités de traiter un ordinateur de type cluster comme une entité unique. Ainsi, une simple commande pourra affecter l'ensemble du cluster ou un sous-ensemble déterminé de celui-ci, de manière reproductible et controlée. Cet article est une introduction pratique à l'administration d'un cluster OSCAR en utilisant les outils C3. Premièrement un bref apperçu des outils C3 et de leur configuration sera présenté, suivi d'une dicussion sur l'emploi des outils C3 pour administrer un cluster OSCAR. La discussion se terminera par un exposé sur l'emploi des outils C3 en dehors du projet OSCAR.

Introduction

In a rather short time, clusters have gone on from the poor-man's super-computer to become the defacto standard in super-computing. With the advent of the Open Source Cluster Application Resources (OSCAR) cluster distribution, it has become easy for those desiring super-computer power to exploit computing clusters to satisfy this need. However, with scores of individual machines wired together as one, the need to deal with these machines as a single entity becomes even more important. The Cluster Command & Control (C3) tools developed at ORNL provide this ability – to treat the cluster as a single entity. That is, a single command may be issued that will affect the entire cluster, or a specified subset of the cluster, in a predictable and controlled manner. While somewhat similar to parallel shell environments, C3 differs in that it provides its core functionality as an extensible framework that may be used to derive other parallel tools for both the command line as well as embedding in user applications. This paper is a "hands-on" discussion of system administration of an OSCAR cluster using the C3 tools. First is a brief overview of the C3 tools and their configuration, next is a discussion of the use of C3 tools for cluster administration within an OSCAR cluster, and the discussion ends with a coverage of C3 use outside the standard scope of the OSCAR environment.

Overview

The C3[1][2] tools suite consists of ten general use tools: *cpushimage*, *cshutdown*, *cpush*, *crm*, *cget*, *cexec(s)*, *ckill*, *clist*, *cname*, and *cnum*. The cpushimage and cshutdown are both system administrator tools that may only be used by the root user. The other eight tools may be employed by any cluster user for both system and application level use. A brief description of each core C3 tool follows – detailed information may be found on the web site and in their respective man pages.

- The **cexec** command is the C3 general utility tool as it may execute any command on each cluster node (parallel shell). If serial execution is desired (useful for debugging a cluster or if an interactive command is run) then **cexecs** should be used.
- The **cget** command retrieves files from each cluster node and deposits them in a specified directory on the local machine. To differentiate files from one another, the node's IP or hostname and cluster name are appended to the filename.
- The **ckill** tool runs the standard Linux kill command on each cluster node for a specified process name. Unlike Linux kill, ckill must use the process name (similar to the Linux killall), as the process ID may be different on each node. Root has the ability to ckill by user / process name pair. Root may also use signals to do a broad based kill.
- **cpushimage** enables the sys-admin to push a cluster node image across cluster nodes with the option to reboot. Cpushimage makes use of SystemImager[3] and SIS[4] to accomplish image transfers.
- **cpush** may be employed by both standard users and root to copy files.
- **crm** is a clusterized version of the standard Linux rm, for file/directory removal.
- **cname** translates node name into a C3 position index value.
- **cnum** takes a range argument and returns the node names of those positions – no range returns all nodes.
- **clist** returns a list of clusters and their type.

C3 File Format

Since OSCAR[5][6] will generate a valid C3 configuration file it is not important to fully understand the C3 configuration file. As long as all updates to the configuration of the cluster are done through OSCAR, little editing of the C3 configuration file should be needed in normal operations.

The default location of the C3 configuration file is `/etc/c3.conf`. C3 allows the use of alternate configuration files through a command line option. Through the use of the configuration file it is possible to use C3 to administrate multiple clusters, but that is beyond the scope of OSCAR. If you are interested in a full explanation of the C3 configuration file please see the *c3.conf(5)* man page.

OSCAR will generate a configuration file using one line per compute node (C3 also allows the use of ranges to specify nodes in the configuration file). The following would be a typical configuration file for a four node OSCAR cluster:

```
cluster oscar_cluster {
  node0
  dead remove_this_for_zero-indexing
  node1
  node2
  node3
  node4
}
```

Figure 1

The general format of the c3.conf file is; first a cluster tag followed by the cluster name signifying the beginning of a cluster definition block. In this case the cluster name is oscar_cluster. This is the default name OSCAR supplies for the cluster. The cluster name is followed by an opening curly brace, "{". The next line is the head node specification; OSCAR will generate this from the head nodes hostname (this is required to be the internal interface of the cluster). Because C3 uses the position of the node in the configuration file for node identification on the command line, it is important to maintain position within the configuration file. OSCAR adds the line "`dead remove_this_for_zero-indexing`" resulting in one indexing for the command line. If you would rather have zero indexing remove this line. The dead tag tells C3 to remove the node from execution at run time while maintaining its position in the configuration file. When a node is temporarily offline use the "`dead`" tag to remove it from execution. The list of nodes follows, one per line. Lastly the cluster definition block is closed by a closing curly brace, "}".

It is important to note that C3 is capable of managing multiple clusters from a single configuration file. Each cluster is in it's own cluster definition block with the same format as above. If using C3's multiple cluster capabilities and using the OSCAR add/delete node interface, be aware that OSCAR will replace the c3.conf file with a new version having only the OSCAR cluster in the file. This will require you to manually add the clusters outside of OSCAR back into the file.

Command Line Interface

All commands in C3 follow the same general format: *command [options] [machine definitions] arg arg….* The *command* is the command being run (cexec, ckill, etc). *Options* are the C3 command options specific to each command. The options may be viewed by either referring to the commands respective man_page or using the --help option with each command.

The *machine definitions* block allows specifying a subset of the given cluster from the command line. Please refer to Figure 1 for the following discussion when referring to a configuration file. The first part of the machine_definition section is the declaration of which cluster you wish the command to be executed on, followed by a colon, and then the node ranges you wish to execute on. For example, "*oscar_cluster:*" would refer to the cluster in Figure 1. You may also specify the first cluster in the configuration file (the default cluster) by the use of a colon, ":". If no cluster is specified then C3 will execute on the first cluster in the configuration file and every node in the cluster. The default OSCAR configuration will only include one cluster. Ranges may be specified as a list of single and multiple node numbers as follows: "*:1-2,4*" will execute on the nodes in position 1, 2, and 4 of the configuration file. In figure 1 this would correlate to node1, node2, and node4. Notice that the head node does not participate in the execution of a C3 command nor does it occupy a position in the configuration file. Had the dead node line been removed then the first node would be in the 0'th position resulting in the following: "*:0-1,3*". You may also explicitly state the cluster to execute on – for example "*oscar_cluster:2-4*". Lastly each argument required for the respective command must be supplied.

For an example, we will run "*hostname*" on node2 and node4 using "*cexec :2,4 hostname*". To execute on all nodes of the default cluster we would use "*cexec hostname*".

While this is outside the scope of OSCAR, C3 easily extends to execution on multiple clusters by adding multiple cluster definition blocks to the c3.conf file. The following would restart sshd on several clusters:

```
# cexec  torc: xtorc: :  service sshd restart
```

For full documentation on the command line and running multiple clusters see the c3.conf(5) and c3-range(5) man pages.

System Administrator Use of C3

Nearly any operation a system administrator can do on a single machine can be extended into a cluster wide application. Below are several examples of common tasks in everyday maintenance of a cluster. This is not a comprehensive list of the capabilities of C3, but is intended to show the concepts involved.

Managing Services

Managing services is one of the most common operations a system administrators may do. For example, restarting the sshd server on each machine may be required if either a change in policy is required or sshd has become unstable. For this example we will be enabling X11 forwarding on the cluster. First, retrieve a copy of one of the nodes sshd_config file:

```
# cget :1 /etc/ssh/sshd_config  .
```

This will retrieve the sshd_config file from only the node in position one (node1 in our example) to the local directory renaming it *sshd_config_oscar_cluster_node1*. Edit this file to allow X11 forwarding (see the sshd man page for details). Next this file needs to be distributed to the cluster:

```
# cpush ./sshd_config_oscar_cluster_node1 \
> /etc/ssh/sshd_config
```

Cpush is a general file scatter operation, it copies the source file (first file on the command line) from the local machine to the destination on each of the compute nodes using rsync. Once each node's configuration file has been updated you need to restart the service:

```
# cexec service sshd restart
```

Process Management

Another operation that is very useful is the maintenance of processes in general. In this example there is a user, *sgrundy*, who has spawned too many processes and is creating a high load on the compute nodes. The process the user started is called "c_model". Using C3, root would kill this process with:

```
# ckill --user sgrundy c_model
```

The first thing to note is that ckill does not use a process id, as this will be different on each compute node, but uses the process name. In this respect ckill is much more similar to the Linux killall command. Ckill also kills every process of that name running on the compute nodes under the given user name. Only root may specify a username other than itself (by the use of the –u option). Root also has the ability to kill all processes regardless of the username by specifying "–u ALL" as one of the options. For example, assume that someone has compromised several user accounts and has started several processes that attempt to crack some other user accounts with a process called "cracker". In order to kill every instance of this program root would do the following (using a signal 9 to immediately terminate the process):

```
# ckill -u ALL -s 9 cracker
```

Log Files

It can sometimes be difficult dealing with compute node log files, both because of the amount of information present and the location of their respective log file. C3 can simplify the task of dealing with error logs and system reporting in many cases. For example, */var/log/messages* is one of the standard logging files in Linux. With C3 there are several ways of dealing with these log files depending on the amount of information and the type of information you need. The first example shows someone trying to ascertain when the above mentioned intruder logged into the compute nodes and compare them to the login times on the head node. First you would need to determine his login times on the head node by grepping the local log file for his name (this assumes he did not obtain root access on the cluster and remove such information).

```
# cat /var/log/messages | grep sgrundy
```

Next you want to execute the same command on each compute node. There are several ways of doing this depending on how you want your output formatted. In the first example all processing is done on the compute nodes:

```
# cexec 'cat /var/log/messages |grep sgrundy'
```

It is important to note that the pipe, "|", is inside the single quotes, thus keeping the local shell from interpreting the pipe. In the second example all the processing is done on the head node:

```
# cexec cat /var/log/messages |grep sgrundy
```

This will output /var/log/messages on each compute node, C3 will sort the output, then grep the contents on the local machine. Unfortunately this will not display which node the output is from. While these views are easy for a person to read it is not ideal for another script or program to read. If you need this information in a pipe friendly format then use cexec with the --pipe option as follows:

```
# cexec --pipe cat /var/log/messages \
> |grep sgrundy
```

Since each line is prepended with the cluster name and node name processing the command locally, as was done in the second example, will still be readable.

See Appendix 1 for example output of all the cexec examples.

User Tasks With C3

OSCAR NFS mounts the user's /home directory on the cluster. However, it may not always be in the user's best interest to run their application over NFS. C3 greatly eases running processes with a local file system. Assuming that the user wishes a data file (data.bin) to reside completely on the local storage of each compute node this is easily accomplished by either a cpush or a cexec. For the initial move a cexec would be best used in the following manner:

```
$ cexec cp ~/proj/data.bin /tmp
```

Since cpush uses rsync[7][8] to only move changes of a file across the network, subsequent changes made to the data file would be better handled by cpush:

```
$ cpush ~/proj/data.bin /tmp
```

If the changes are small and data.bin is a large file the reduction in time can be significant.

Distributed processes may also produce local data making the problem similar in scope to the system administrator task of parsing log files. The user can easily use cget to gather all their data from the compute nodes to the head node of the cluster:

```
$ cget /tmp/output.txt .
```

C3 Outside of OSCAR

There are instances where C3 is helpful to do operations that are beyond the scope of OSCAR. OSCAR leverages Red Hat's RPM system to simplify package management. One of the characteristics of the RPM system is that all package names must be unique. There are "work arounds" that modify the name to allow for multiple instances of effectively the same package, e.g. Python (v1.5) and Python2 (v2.x). Regardless, there are times when system administrators would like to add software without using RPMs because of this naming limitation or possibly the software is not available in RPM form. At these times, it is necessary to go outside the OSCAR framework and use standard source archives, i.e. "tarballs". On a cluster this requires a few extra steps but can be greatly simplified by using the C3 tools. Additionally, the Env-Switcher tool that accompanies OSCAR can be leveraged.

The following sections summarize the Env-Switcher tool and provide details on how to use C3 & Env-Switcher to add software to OSCAR clusters from standard source tarballs.

Env-Switcher

Env-Switcher, or simply Switcher [9], is a tool to manage environment settings and is based upon Modules [10]. Switcher enables an administrator to cleanly manipulate system wide tags that are used to setup user environment, e.g. PATH, PVM_ROOT. Switcher allows you to selectively load items into the environment, which helps when managing mutually exclusive packages. The canonical example is the situation where multiple MPI implementations are installed on a system. The switcher modules allow for a system wide default, but also enable users to select an alternate version from the pool of available MPIs.

```
 # Show available MPI's on system
$ switcher mpi --list
lam-6.5.7
mpich-1.2.4

 # Show current default
$ switcher mpi --show
system:default=mpich-1.2.4
system:exists=true

$ which mpirun
/opt/mpich-1.2.4/bin/mpirun
```

Switcher enables the system wide default to be overridden at a per user basis. The user would set an alternate MPI implementation by setting the *mpi* tag as follows:

```
$ switcher mpi = lam-6.5.7
```

Switcher changes take effect on subsequent shell invocations and the environment is maintained across non-interactive shells, e.g. rsh/ssh.

These available *tags*, e.g. lam-6.5.7, mpich-1.2.4, are setup manually by the administrator (or by OSCAR) via a module file. These module files state what environmental changes are necessary for the package. Switcher is smart enough to undo these modifications as needed[1]. The full format is beyond the scope of this article but much can be gleamed from a simple example. A source listing of the

[1] The actual shell modifications are performed by the Modules tools.

mpich2-0.91 module file is given in Appendix 2[2]. The actual environment modifications for the package are lines 20 & 21. This is used the in the next section when discussing the MPICH2-0.91 installation from source tarball.

The "*tarball example*"

The source tarball method of software distribution is fairly standard and often includes an *Autoconf* and *Make* facility. The following example shows the installation of a development version of MPICH [11][12] onto a running OSCAR cluster from source tarball.

Once the software has been downloaded and extracted the software is compiled and built as a standard user.

```
$ tar -zxvf mpich2-0.91.tar.gz -C /tmp
$ cd /tmp/mpich2-0.91
$ ./configure --prefix=/opt/mpich2-0.91
<<Cut output, configures successfully>>

$ make
<<Cut output, builds successfully>>
```

At this point the software has been configured and compiled and is ready to be installed. After becoming root (via `su`) the software is installed into the */opt/mpich2-0.91* directory.

```
 # Become the SuperUser for install
$ su -
# cd /tmp/mpich2-0.91
# make install
```

Since, the compute nodes have the same hardware configuration this compiled/installed result can simply be archived, `tar`'d, and pushed, `cpush`, to all nodes in the cluster[3].

```
# cd /opt
# tar -cvf /opt/mpich2-0.91.tar mpich2-0.91/
<<Cut output, archives successfully>>

# cpush /opt/mpich2-0.91.tar  /opt
```

The archive is extracted on the compute nodes using the change directory flag "-C" to place the output in `/opt`. Single quotes surround the `cexec` command.

```
# cexec 'tar -xvf /opt/mpich2-0.91.tar -C /opt'
```

This puts the software on all nodes and we are now ready to create the Switcher module file as shown in Appendix 2. This file can reside anywhere but it is commonly placed in a "share/" directory under the package's directory. The file is named whatever the *tag* should display, e.g. *mpich2-0.91*. Therefore in this case the directory structure and file would be "/opt/mpich2-0.91/share/mpich2-0.91". This is created on the head node and mirrored on the compute nodes.

```
# mkdir /opt/mpich2-0.91/share
# cexec 'mkdir /opt/mpich2-0.91/share'
# vi /opt/mpich2-0.91/share/mpich2-0.91
<<Add contents as shown in module example>>

# cpush /opt/mpich2-0.91/mpich2-0.91
```

Finally, to make Switcher aware of the new software a new tag name must be added, *mpich2-0.91*. The `switcher` command is executed on the head node and compute nodes so the changes appear in the respective Switcher configuration files.

```
# switcher mpi --add-name mpich2-0.91 \
> /opt/mpich2-0.91/share --silent --force

# cexec 'switcher mpi --add-name \
> mpich2-0.91 /opt/mpich2-0.91/share \
> --silent --force'
```

At this point `switcher mpi --list` will display "mpich2-0.91" as one of the available MPI implementations on the cluster. This approach of C3 and Switcher could also be automated on development clusters to offer "cvs" or "devel" snapshots, e.g. *lam-cvs* or *pvm-devel*. The available commands and syntax for Switcher are available in the SWITCHER(1) manual page.

Remote Administration

Another benefit of C3 is it's remote cluster administration capabilities. Through the use of C3's configuration file it is possible to control a cluster from your desktop with the same interface and power that you would have using C3 locally. The basic requirements are that the person has login access to the head node of the remote cluster and that C3 is installed correctly – OSCAR takes care of last part for you. Next you would follow C3's installation procedure outlined in the install section of C3 documentation on your desktop. Next is the setup of the c3.conf file. For this example, you will use what is referred to as an indirect remote cluster. This is essentially a pointer to the head node of the cluster. No information about the layout of the cluster is stored locally, C3 will determine the layout of the cluster from the head node. For example, assume a user wishes to remotely access the cluster in Figure 1, the indirect remote configuration file

```
cluster torc {
       :garm.csm.ornl.gov
}
```

Figure 2

---

[2] This was manually added and adapted from the existing LAM and MPICH module files included with OSCAR.

[3] The software can be built on the individual nodes by `cpush`'ing the "mpich2-0.91.tar.gz" tarball to the nodes and performing the commands using `cexec`.

in Figure 2 would be used on the local machine.
Cluster is a key word denoting the beginning of a cluster block, *torc* is the name of the cluster (any name is acceptable). The line ":garm…" signifies that the cluster is an indirect remote cluster. "garm…" is the external interface name of the head node of the clusters (the DNS name – it could also be an IP address). All of the commands shown work in the exact same manner as previously described – from the command line point of view it is impossible to tell if a cluster is remote or local.

Conclusion

This paper provided a number of examples using the C3 tools for cluster administration and operation tasks both within the OSCAR framework and outside the normal scope of OSCAR. While this paper is not intended to serve as a comprehensive list of uses for C3, it does show a number of significant uses for the tool suite and it is intended to provide examples on which the reader may build their own C3 derived works. The C3 development team at ORNL is in the process of writing a more comprehensive documentation set for the use of C3 for the administration and operation of machines ranging from single cluster -to- federated clusters (multi-clusters) and also for single workstations with a single point of administration. Look for this document on the C3 web site in the near future.

References

[1] M. Brim, R. Flanery, A. Geist, B. Luethke, and S. Scott Cluster Command & Control (C3) tools suite. In *To be published in, Parallel and Distributed Computing Practices, DAPSYS Special Edition,* 2002.

[2] "C3", http://www.csm.ornl.gov/torc/C3/

[3] "SystemImager", http://www.systemimager.org/

[4] "SIS", http://sisuite.org/

[5] Thomas Naughton, Stephen L. Scott, Brian Barrett, Jeff Squires, Andrew Lumsdaine, and Yung-Chin Fang. The Penguin in the Pail – OSCAR Cluster Installation Tool. In *Proceedings of SCI'02: Invited Session – Commodity, High Performance Cluster Computing Technologies and Application*, Orlando, FL, USA, 2002.

[6] "OSCAR", http://www.OpenClusterGroup.org/OSCAR

[7] A. Tridgell and P. Mackerras. The rsync algorithm. Technical Report TR-CS-96-05, Australian National University, Department of Computer Science, June 1996.

[8] "rsync", http://samba.anu.edu.au/rsync/

[9] "Env-Switcher", http://env-switcher.sourceforge.net.

[10] John L. Furlani and Peter W. Osel, "Abstract Yourself With Modules, In *Proceedings of the 10th Large Installation Systems Administration Conference (LISA'96)*, pages 193-204, Chicago, IL, September 29 -- October 4, 1996.

[11] W. Gropp, E. Lusk, N. Doss, and A. Skjellum. A High-performance, portable implemntation of the MPI message passing interface standard. *Parallel Computing* 22(6):789-828, September 1996.

[12] "mpich", http://www-unix.mcs.anl.gov/mpi/mpich

Research supported by the Mathematics, Information and Computational Sciences Office, Office of Advanced Scientific Computing Research, Office of Science, U. S. Department of Energy, under contract No. DE-AC05-00OR22725 with UT-Battelle, LLC.

APPENDIX 1

Use of quotes with cexec.

cexec 'cat /var/log/messages |grep sgrundy':

```
[root@node0 test]# cexec 'cat /var/log/messages |grep sgrundy'
************************ local ************************
processing node  node1
processing node  node2
--------- node1---------
Mar 11 18:23:01 node1 sshd[1073]: Accepted publickey for sgrundy from 10.0.0.50 port 32805 ssh2
Mar 11 18:23:01 node1 sshd(pam_unix)[1073]: session opened for user sgrundy by (uid=0)
Mar 11 18:23:01 node1 sshd(pam_unix)[1073]: session closed for user sgrundy

--------- node2---------
Mar 11 18:23:01 node2 sshd[1208]: Accepted publickey for sgrundy from 10.0.0.50 port 32806 ssh2
Mar 11 18:23:01 node2 sshd(pam_unix)[1208]: session opened for user sgrundy by (uid=0)
Mar 11 18:23:01 node2 sshd(pam_unix)[1208]: session closed for user sgrundy
```

cexec cat/var/log/messages |grep sgrundy

```
[root@node0 test]# cexec cat /var/log/messages |grep sgrundy
Mar 11 18:23:01 node1 sshd[1073]: Accepted publickey for sgrundy from 10.0.0.50 port 32805 ssh2
Mar 11 18:23:01 node1 sshd(pam_unix)[1073]: session opened for user sgrundy by (uid=0)
Mar 11 18:23:01 node1 sshd(pam_unix)[1073]: session closed for user sgrundy
Mar 11 18:23:01 node2 sshd[1208]: Accepted publickey for sgrundy from 10.0.0.50 port 32806 ssh2
Mar 11 18:23:01 node2 sshd(pam_unix)[1208]: session opened for user sgrundy by (uid=0)
Mar 11 18:23:01 node2 sshd(pam_unix)[1208]: session closed for user sgrundy
```

cexec --pipe cat /var/log/messages |grep sgrundy

```
[root@node0 test]# cexec --pipe cat /var/log/messages |grep sgrundy
local node1: Mar 11 18:23:01 node1 sshd[1073]: Accepted publickey for sgrundy from 10.0.0.50 port 32805
ssh2
local node1: Mar 11 18:23:01 node1 sshd(pam_unix)[1073]: session opened for user sgrundy by (uid=0)
local node1: Mar 11 18:23:01 node1 sshd(pam_unix)[1073]: session closed for user sgrundy
local node2: Mar 11 18:23:01 node2 sshd[1208]: Accepted publickey for sgrundy from 10.0.0.50 port 32806
ssh2
local node2: Mar 11 18:23:01 node2 sshd(pam_unix)[1208]: session opened for user sgrundy by (uid=0)
local node2: Mar 11 18:23:01 node2 sshd(pam_unix)[1208]: session closed for user sgrundy
```

APPENDIX 2

Listing of module file: ***mpich2-0.91***

```
#%Module -*- tcl -*-
#
# MPICH modulefile for OSCAR clusters
#

proc ModulesHelp { } {
  puts stderr "\tThis module adds MPICH to the PATH and MANPATH."
  puts stderr "\tHence, the mpicc, mpiCC, mpif77, and mpirun commands"
  puts stderr "\tthat you run will be from MPICH."
}

module-whatis   "Sets up the MPICH environment for an OSCAR cluster."

# Don't let any other MPI module be loaded while this one is loaded

conflict mpi

# It's real simple.  Append to the PATH and to the MANPATH.

append-path PATH /opt/mpich2-0.91/bin
append-path MANPATH /opt/mpich2-0.91/man
```

The PFILTER Firewall Compiler for Clusters

Neil Gorsuch[a]

[a]*NCSA, University of Illinois, Urbana, Illinois*

Linux clusters range from tiny to huge, but all sizes can benefit from effective firewalls. Stateful packet filtering firewalls can provide excellent security from network attacks, but are difficult at best to set up and maintain. When packet filtering is combined with packet forwarding, NATTING, and pseudo interfaces, a single machine can provide firewall protection for a private network of machines, while allowing the protected machines to have complete access to the general networks, and can allow the protected machines to be visible at general network addresses while maintaining firewall protection for them. This paper will discuss an open source, easily configurable packet filtering compiler system for clusters that can provide all these benefits.

Les grappes d'ordinateurs de toutes tailles ont avantage à comporter un coupe-feu. Les coupes-feu dynamiques offrent un excellent niveau de sécurité contre les attaques par réseau, mais il n'est pas facile de les configurer et d'en effectuer l'entretient par la suite. Lorsqu'on combine les techniques de filtrage et de réacheminement des paquets, de traduction d'adresses de réseau, ainsi que l'interfaçage réseau virtuel, il est possible d'utiliser un seul ordinateur coupe-feu pour protéger un réseau privé comportant plusieurs ordinateurs, lesquels conservent un accès complet au réseau externe. Cet article présente une application à code source libre facilitant la compilation de règles de filtrage de paquets pour la protection réseau d'une grappe d'ordinateurs.

1 Introduction

Packet filtering is the process of examining each network packet as it comes into or through a device, and either allowing, dropping or rejecting the packet based on various factors such as the source and destination addresses and port numbers, and whether the packet is the start of new connection attempt. Packet filtering can block all incoming network connection attempts except for the ones that are explicitly allowed. This prevents computer configuration mistakes allowing an insecure network service from being accessed by mistake.

Stateful packet filtering keeps track of each network communication sequence of packets, and provides for simpler, easier to setup and maintain, and more secure firewalls.

All cluster machines that can receive packets from outside the cluster should either have their own packet filtering installed, or a common firewall machine should filter all packets going in and out of the cluster

Using packet filtering to set up a firewall on a computer system is difficult at best, being similar to writing programs in assembly language. A method is needed for system administrators to setup and maintain good packet filtering firewalls without having to learn the intricacies of packet filtering commands.

2 Security Layers

To provide effective cluster security, multiple security layers should be provided. Cluster network security layers should ideally consist of: router filtering, network stack protections, IP masquerading and NATTING, packet filtering, disabling unused network services, TCPwrappers, and configuring applications.

2.1 Router Filtering

If possible, routers should be set up to block various types of unwanted packets, including: all source spoofed packets, all packets claiming to be coming from an RFC1918 "private" address that arrive from a public network, all packets coming into the cluster going to most privileged ports except for a few explicitly allowed ports, and all packets destined for various "problem" high ports such as X or NFS. Redirect, echo request, timestamp request, timestamp reply, address mask request, and address mask reply ICMP packets coming into the cluster should be dropped.

Some routers lack these filtering capabilities, while others are difficult to program. Because routers cannot typically track connections, outside attackers can sometimes craft special network packets to bypass router filtering.

2.2 Network Stack Protections

The Linux kernel has a number of attributes that help with network security which can be turned on or off through entries in the /proc directory tree. Some of the more useful features are: source spoofing prevention, disabling of ICMP redirect packets, and syncookie attack protection.

2.3 IP Masquerading and NATTING

If some of a cluster's nodes are only connected to a private cluster network, and it is desired for the nodes to be able to access outside network resources, a machine needs to forward network packets between the private cluster network and other networks. To maintain the privacy of nodes with no direct outside network connection, they should be assigned IP addresses that are not directly accessible outside the cluster. RFC 1918 reserves the IP ranges 10.x.x.x, 172.16-31.x.x, 192.168.x.x that cannot be routed across the Internet. To allow hidden cluster nodes to access outside network resources, the machine doing packet forwarding needs to provide IP masquerading. This alters all packets being forwarded from a hidden cluster node to an address outside the cluster to appear as if they came from the forwarding machine. Packets coming back in as part of a masqueraded connection are translated and forwarded to the appropriate hidden cluster node. NAT (Network Address Translation) is this process of modifying the addresses within the packets as they are being forwarded. Setting up IP masquerading requires special packet filtering rules.

2.4 Packet Filtering

Packet filtering is one of the most effective security layers, because it affects all network communication, intercepting network packets before they are passed up to application programs.

Linux kernels from version 2.4 on can track active network connections packet by packet. This is called stateful connection tracking. In addition to filtering which network connections are allowed to start and proceed, stateful packet filters can block all packets that are not part of a valid ongoing network connection. This prevents attackers from passing specially crafted packets into high network ports.

The main drawback of packet filtering is that it is difficult to configure. BSD derived operating systems use the netfilter command to control packet filtering, while Linux systems use the ipfw, ipfwadmin, ipchains, or iptables commands to control packet filtering. Without special tools, scripts consisting of many commands have to be hand-coded and maintained. It is difficult for non-experts to find adequate information to allow them to produce scripts that provide secure firewalls.

2.5 Disabling Unused Network Services

The most straightforward method of reducing network vulnerabilities is to disable incoming network services. Any unused or unnecessary incoming network services should be disabled. Most of them can be disabled using the linuxconf program. A few of them need to have their entries commented out in the /etc/inetd.conf file. Unfortunately, earlier versions of Linux and some network services in current Linux versions, do not follow this model. They can be inadvertently turned on and it is not always obvious that this has happened.

2.6 TCPwrappers

Newer versions of Linux support TCPwrappers, which adds another layer of application level filtering. This is accomplished through inetd with the files /etc/hosts.deny and /etc/hosts.allow controlling access for each network service. Unfortunately, some network services cannot be filtered this way.

2.7 Application Layer Filtering

Some server applications can be set to block access to certain addresses, or to allow access only to certain addresses. This feature should be used wherever possible. For example, the exporting of NFS shares can be to a limited list of machines and addresses, with or without write access.

3 Packet Re-Writing

Linux and other operating systems can modify network packets as they pass through a system. This is a more sophisticated type of NAT and can yield some very useful results. Since this is controlled through the packet filtering rules, a packet filtering compiler needs to control this.

3.1 Host Aliasing

Consider a firewall machine that has multiple network interfaces and that is acting as an IP masquerading firewall for one of the interfaces. In some cases it is advantageous to be able to access one or more of the machines that are on the private network through a public address. However if the access method desired for more than one of the machines is through the same type of service, a method is needed to have those machines appear as if they were also on the public network, with only outside connections to the desired services being passed on the private address of the machines. This allows one firewall machine to act as a gateway for a number of hidden machines behind it, with all of the firewalling and packet filtering protection only needing to be set up on one machine.

A classic example of this is a development laboratory. There might be a dynamic mix of machines or clusters that are constantly being rebuilt and that don't need the administrative overhead of setting up firewalls on each one every time they are rebuilt. But they all need to be accessible from the public networks through a security communication channel such as SSH. With host aliasing, this needs to only be set up once on the laboratory's firewall machine.

3.2 Packet Redirection or Forwarding

Sometimes packets need to be re-written and sent to a different destination than intended. One example of this would be having all outgoing packets that are destined for web servers being redirected to a proxy web server on a local machine.

4 Packet Filtering Details

Linux kernels use "chains" of packet filtering rules to filter packets. Each filtering rule has a set of matching conditions and an action to take if the packet is matched. Some of the conditions that packets can be matched by are source address, destination address, source port, destination port, TCP flags, type, MAC address, length, throttling limits, specific byte patterns, and the user id of locally generated packets. Some chains are pre-defined and always exist; others can be defined or deleted by the user. Rules can be added to any chain, and any chain can have all it's rules flushed from it. Packets can traverse more than one chain.

Linux version 2.4 and later kernels support integrated connection tracking and stateful inspection. This adds more ways to match packets, based on whether they are new packets, packets that are part of an existing connection, or packets logically related to an existing connection. In addition greatly increasing security, this also vastly simplifies filtering rulesets.

A script that controls packet filtering is difficult to set up. The cluster administrator would like to specify something like "block every incoming connection attempt except for SSH to machines 1 and 2, and allow all cluster machines to access the outside network. To do this safely requires a script that is dozens of lines long with many commands, and setting up various network stack parameters by writing into the /proc directory tree. Packet filtering scripts are akin to an assembly language. For things to run correctly, "glue" code has to be added.

What system administrators need is a method to "compile" packet filtering firewall scripts that requires no knowledge of packet filtering configuration commands. Given this need, it was decided to implement a packet filtering compiler.

5 Firewall Compiler Requirements

The following requirements were determined for a packet filtering firewall compiler.

Firewall packet filtering rules should be specified in a high level language. The filtering language should be independent of iptables, ipchains, netfilter or whatever other packet filtering commands are actually used to implement the firewall. The compiler shall be designed so that any Unix variant that has commands to configure packet filtering can be supported.

The firewall compiler shall convert a text configuration file consisting of high level filtering language directives into a complete firewall implementation that includes all commands to modify appropriate kernel network stack parameters to provide added security.

A GUI shall be provided that modifies the same firewall text configuration file. An administrator may go back and forth between editing the firewall text configuration file and using the GUI, with changes done by one method being reflected in both.

The compiler defaults should allow no incoming network connection other than those that are specifically enabled.

The compiler defaults should allow all outgoing network connections.

On Linux, the compiler should be installed as a system service so that a firewall can be enabled or disabled with the /sbin/chkconfig command, and started, stopped, and restarted with the /sbin/service command. Every time the compiler is "started" or "restarted", the firewall configuration file should be re-compiled. When the compiler is "stopped" it should turn off all network packet filtering, letting all packets be accepted. The /sbin/service command shall also support a "status" command, and a "chains" command to list the packet filtering chains currently in effect.

The compiler should be available as binary and source rpms, and as a source tarball that a "make" then "make install" will install correctly.

The compiler should be implemented using an interpretive language. The compiler itself should never need to be compiled and linked as a binary image. The compiler rpm shall be of the "noarch" type, and not tied to any particular hardware platform.

The firewall filtering language should be reasonably free form, and support comment lines, and comments at the end of lines.

The firewall filtering language should allow for sequences of network packet matching, with each successful match allowing the packet to be accepted, dropped, or rejected.

The firewall filtering language should support defined constants whose values cannot be changed once they are set, and symbolic variables that can be redefined and changed. Constant and variable values should consist of strings.

The firewall filtering language should support macros that can be expanded with parameter substitution.

The firewall filtering language should support conditional blocks.

Multiple network interfaces have to be supported per machine.

Each network interface shall be able to be marked separately as being attached to either a trusted network where no filtering is done for connection attempts from that network, or marked as being on an untrusted network where all connection attempts to the host machine shall pass through the filtering rules.

One or more network interfaces can be marked to have packets forwarded by using IP masquerading NAT. All machines attached to interfaces so marked shall have access to public networks through the firewall machine.

One or more machines attached to a network interface that is marked as being firewalled by IP masquerading NAT shall be able to be aliased onto an address on another network. For each aliased machine, a pseudo interface shall be created with it's own separate address. Each pseudo interface shall be able to have it's own filtering rules that are specific it's address, and connection attempts from the outside that are allowed will be forwarded/translated onto the real address of the aliased machine on the private network. Outgoing connections from aliased machines will be translated so that they appear to be originating from the machine's pseudo address.

The compiler shall support connection tracked flexible packet forwarding.

The "glue" code parts of the compiled output should be user configurable through text files.

Network services to be allowed and/or blocked should be able to be defined in user modifiable text files.

Network services should allow for more complex allowing and/or blocking, including embedded shell script fragments.

At present, all of the requirements except the GUI have been met. The GUI is in development.

6 PFILTER – a Firewall Compiler

The firewall compiler that was developed is called PFILTER (Packet FILTER). It was decided to implement PFILTER in the PERL language. There are better interpretive languages available, but none are so widespread as PERL. The main PFILTER program is installed as a PERL executable program at /usr/sbin/pilter. The remainder of the executable program is stored as included PERL files in the /usr/lib/pfilter directory. Included files were chosen instead of the more traditional perl modules to insure that PFILTER functions are placed in a more secure directory, and because the functions are very specific to PFILTER and generally not of use to other programs.

PFILTER is an open source project hosted on SourceForge, see http//sourceforge.net/projects/pfilter/

6.1 Ruleset Files

The PFILTER executable program is designed to do as little as possible. Instead, PFILTER uses built-in files called ruleset files to do most of the work of compiling output scripts. The ruleset files are editable text files that can be modified or added to by system administrators. Heavy use is made of conditional text blocks and macros. This design was chosen for the following benefits:

PFILTER determines which packet filtering system is in use such as iptables or ipchains or netfilter. Setting a constant value to indicate which type of system is in use, conditional blocks and macros in the ruleset files are used to generate compiled code for all the different types of systems. This allows for easily adding complete new types of packet filtering systems by simply adding a few macros and some glue code text.

Almost all of the "glue" code that is put in the compiled output is specified in the ruleset files. This allows for a vast amount of flexibility, and support for many types of Unix variants.

New types of network services to be filtered on or off are defined in ruleset files. This allows system administrators to add new types of network services to be supported.

Because network services to be filtered on or off are defined by macros, they can embed shell script fragments in the compiled output code, allowing for filtering services such as NFS which dynamically allocate port numbers.

Because of the built-in constants, variables, conditions, and macros, the main firewall configuration file can be quite sophisticated, and will allow the same configuration file to be used throughout a cluster.

Compiled output scripts shall be optimized, with redundant or impossible combinations of packet filtering sources and destinations not being written to the output scripts.

The compiled output scripts shall include verbose comments explaining what each script line does. The configuration source lines that cause generation of output script lines shall be included as comments immediately above their generated output.

6.2 The PFILTER Firewall Language

The PFILTER firewall configuration is defined in the /etc/pfilter.conf file. Comments start with either the # or % characters and can be complete lines. Comments that start with the % character are not copied to the compiled output script, while comments starting with the # character are copied to the output script when appropriate. All directives and keywords are case-insensitive.

6.2.1 Constants and Variables

Named constants are defined like this:

%constant%   constant_name   strings ...

A constant's value will be set to everything after the name but not including any comments at the end of the line.

Trying to redefine a constant with a new value produces an error. Variables are defined like this:

%variable% variable_name strings ...

Variables can be re-defined any number of times. To substitute a constant or variable value, simply insert it with % characters on each side. For example, these lines:

%variable% var b c
%constant% const d e f
a %var% %const% g

will expand into this:

a b c d e f g

There are a number of constants that are defined by PFILTER during each compilation.

6.2.2 Macros

PFILTER supports macros with named parameters. When a macro is expanded, temporary variables that match the macro's parameter names are created just for that expansion block. Macros are heavily used when generating the compiled firewall output script. As an example, these lines:

%macro% compute-node management-node
 # compute node compute-node
open ssh from %domain%
open tcp 1024:65536 from %cluster%
open tcp 0:1023 from %management-node%
%endmacro

%compute-node% node17 mgmt12

would expand to this:

 # compute node node17
open ssh from %domain%
open tcp 1024:65535 from %cluster%
open tcp 0:1023 from mgmt12

Macro definitions and invocations can be nested.

6.2.3 Conditional Blocks

Blocks of text or single lines can be conditionally included in the output based on any of the following types of conditional expressions:

%ifdef name is true if constant/variable is defined
%ifndef name is true if constant/variable is undefined
%if string = string is true if strings match
%if string != string is true if strings do not match
%if string is true if the string is non-blank

Conditionals can either surround a block of lines, or only affect one line. If the conditional expression is at the beginning of a line, the lines following that up until a line that starts with %endif are included in the output if the condition is true. If the end of line is a conditional expression, that line will be included in the output if the condition is true. The conditional expressions and any possible %endif lines are not included in the output.

6.2.4 Protocols, Ports, and Network Services

Some directives include lists of protocols, ports, or network services. These lists can include any of the following, separated by spaces or tab characters: a protocol and then one or more port numbers, port ranges, and network service names, network service name without a proceeding protocol.

Network service names are defined in four ways. First, a matrix of protocols, ports, and matching service names are parsed from the /etc/services system file if it exists. Second, some symbolic names are defined by the iptables and ipchains commands, but it is not advisable to use those, since newer versions of those commands might change or remove symbolic names. Third, network services can be defined in the either the main firewall configuration file or in one of the firewall ruleset files as a simple constant. For example, scattered in the ruleset files are these lines:

%define service-x-protocols-ports tcp udp/6000:6063
%define service-ping-protocols-ports icmp/8
%define service-ssh-protocols-ports tcp/22

This defines the network service *r* as responding to both TCP and UDP ports ranging from 6000 to 6063, defines the network service *ping* as responding to ICMP packets of type 8, and defines the network service *ssh* to respond to TCP port 22. A service name defined in this way overrides any definitions in the /etc/services file. In the case of the *SSH* ruleset entry, the /etc/services lines that define the SSH service as being both TCP and UDP ports 22, are over-ridden, so that when the configuration file says:

open ssh

it will only open TCP port 22 and not open UDP port 22. The last way a network service can be defined is with a pair of PFILTER macro definitions. This allows for opening and closing of network services to involve shell script fragments, or to do anything else that isn't just a list of TCP and/or UDP ports or ICMP types. For example, one of the ruleset files includes these segments:

```
%macro service-multicast-open source destination
# Let all multicast packets through from %sources%.
# The destination is always 224.0.0.0-239.255.255.255.
# This method is used because multicast packets are
# identified by their destination address.
 %open_protocol_port% %source% 224.0.0.0/4 ANY
ANY
%endmacro

%macro service-multicast-close source destination
# Block all multicast packets from %sources%.
# The destination is always 224.0.0.0-239.255.255.255.
# This method is used because multicast packets are
# identified by their destination address.
 %close_protocol_port% %source% 224.0.0.0/4 ANY
ANY
```

%endmacro

This segment defines how to open or close multicast packets going through the firewall. If someone puts this line in their /etc/pfilter.conf configuration file:

open multicast from mydomain.com

then the compiled output script will include directives that will accept packets from mydomain.com going to anywhere in the address range 224.0.0.0/4.

6.2.5 Network Addresses

Network addresses can be specified as simple IP addresses, IP address ranges, DNS host names, or address ranges that include DNS host names.

6.2.6 Directives to Open/Close Access

To allow or block incoming network connections, these directives are used:

OPEN protocols-ports-services [from source(s)] [to destination(s)]
CLOSE protocols-ports-services [from source(s)] [to destination(s)]

If no source addresses are specified, incoming connections to the specified protocols-ports and/or services are allowed (or blocked) from any address. When no destination addresses are supplied, the connections are allowed or blocked going to the firewall machine. Destination addresses can be specified for other machines if the firewall machine is receiving and forwarding packets to the other machines.

6.2.7 Directives for Interface Attributes

The following directives specify attributes of network interfaces. They all take one or more network attribute directives, followed by one or more network interface names as.

FILTERED or UNTRUSTED – all network connection attempts coming from these interfaces are packet filtered to determine if the connections should be allowed.

UNFILTERED or TRUSTED – all network connection attempts coming from these interfaces are allowed, without any packet filtering.

PRIVATE or PROTECTED – interfaces marked this way are presumed to be on a private network that is being protected by the firewall machine. IP masquerading and NAT are applied to all outgoing connections coming from these networks.

PUBLIC or UNPROTECTED – interfaces marked this way are not being protected behind the firewall machine.

6.2.8 Directives to Setup Host Aliasing

To set up host aliasing, where a machine on a protected network is made to be partially accessible on a public network, this type of directive is used:

ALIAS pseudo real [ports-protocols-services] [from source[s]]

For example, if a machine named private1 on a protected network needed to have it's SSH server accessible from machines in mydomain.com, which has a 16-bit mask, appearing to be at public address public1, a line like this could be used:

ALIAS public1 private1 ssh from mydomain.com/16

Ports/protocols and/or services to be passed through do not have to be listed on the line that defined the ALIAS mapping, they can be listed elsewhere. The line above could also have been done like this:

ALIAS public1 private1
OPEN ssh from mydomain.com/16

6.2.9 Directives for Packet Forwarding.

To set up packet forwarding/re-writing a line like this need to be included:

FORWARD protocols-ports-services [FROM source[s]]
*[TO destination[s]] ONTO forwarded-desistination-address *
[forwarded-protocols-ports-services]

A list of protocols/ports and/or services, possibly matched by where they are coming from and/or going to, will be translated to instead go to the forwarded-destination-address, possible being translated to a different group of protocols/ports/services.

7 Conclusion

The first method of network security to be installed should be packet filtering. This will block access from outside the cluster to all but needed services while allowing the cluster to access the outside freely. With tools such as pfilter, it is straightforward to generate packet filtering firewalls with ipchains/iptables rule sets.

Thin-OSCAR : Design and future implementation

Benoît des Ligneris [a] [b]*, Michel Barrette[a], Francis Giraldeau[ab], Michel Dagenais [b]

[a]Centre de Calcul Scientifique,
Université de Sherbrooke, Québec, Canada

[b]Département de génie informatique,
École Polytechnique, Montréal, Québec, Canada

A description of the actual status of the thin-OSCAR project will be made. Future development of the project will be detailed and desired functionality will be exposed. We will then determine and analyze the interactions that are needed with the different components of OSCAR.

Une description du statut actuel du projet thin-OSCAR sera faite. Enfin, les grands axes de développement du projet seront discutés ainsi que les fonctionalités additionnelles souhaitées. Une analyse des interactions requises avec les différentes composantes d'OSCAR sera proposée.

Introduction

While OSCAR [1] has been conceived for clusters with disk(s) since its very first version, diskless (and systemless) support was a feature that lot of people expected. The Center for Scientific Computing [2] (CCS) has built several clusters without disk [3]. We tested OSCAR and were easily convinced of it's quality and professionalism especially compared to our own home-made scripts. We decided to use OSCAR for our diskless cluster and then transfer our diskless expertise to the OSCAR project. The thin-OSCAR [4] work-group was created to specifically analyze and solve problems that will arise while adding this diskless clusters support.

We will first define essential notions for a diskless cluster. Then, the actual implementation of thin-OSCAR will be exposed. We will expose a « road-map » for the development of thin-OSCAR. Interaction with OSCAR will be detailed so that features can be discussed, prioritized and eventually added to the OSCAR framework.

1 General definitions

This section presents some useful notions from a node perspective and several existing technical solutions for diskless support.

1.1 Node Definition

We planned to support several types of nodes, from nodes without disk to nodes with at least a disk dedicated to the cluster. In this section, we will define the node thickness levels.

1.1.1 Diskless nodes

Diskless nodes are well named : they have no disk. The main consequence is that the node has no functionality to boot without the presence of a network mechanism to initiate the boot process and then provide necessary permanent storage (disk) over the network. This kind of node is generally found in dedicated diskless clusters and in network terminals [5]. However, nodes with disks can be considered diskless when, for security or practical reason, the disk cannot be used. This can be the case in a GRID environment where cluster nodes are workstation during the day for instance. It allows nodes that are not used in a cluster to be very rapidly integrated into a cluster without any alteration of the "main" operating system stored on their disk.

Diskless clusters maybe more efficient, affordable and reliable than clusters with disks. Limitations on the type of computation that can be made on this kind of nodes exist : intensive I/O applications could be executed on such nodes but obviously, will not scale well and slow down each calculation to the point it is extremely inefficient. It will even crash the master node, if the protocol used is not robust enough.

In order to limit or even avoid I/O intensive tasks on this kind of node, a special property must be defined so that the queuing system can manage efficiently those nodes (property proposed name : `diskless`).

1.1.2 Systemless nodes

Those nodes have a file (swap file, temporary storage), a partition (swap, temporary storage) or a complete disk dedicated to the cluster ; they don't contain a disk bootloader, and boot from the network. There is large variety of nodes and no more formal definition is necessary.

This type of node is complicated to manage and special precautions must be taken : some useful data may already be stored on the disk (even alien operating systems) and because they are not completely diskless, the disk has to be accessed with care, especially when installing the node (initialization of the swap file, copy/rsync of directories, formating of partition). If those nodes have swap space and temporary storage, then they have no particular property for the queuing system, otherwise they will have the same property as the diskless nodes (`diskless`).

*Corresponding author : benoit@des.ligneris.net

1.1.3 Diskfull nodes

Those nodes have dedicated disks for the cluster. This is the only type of node currently managed by OSCAR. Management of nodes can be done entirely within the OSCAR framework : installation from scratch of the nodes, including hard disk formating, or update of the image (via the C3 [6] command **cpushimage** command).

1.2 Diskless and systemless clustering solutions

Several solutions exists to boot a node without disk. We will not discuss here the different booting mechanisms (PXE, floppy, ...) but the different models that exist so that nodes can be functional.

The main idea behind diskless solutions is that disks are useless for numerous types of calculation. Because network is a prerequisite in order to have a cluster, you can get rid of disk by using a network boot process. Moreover, disks are a point of failure, and because you must store nodes data onto permanent storage, like SAN, disks on nodes brings only trouble.

1.2.1 Root-NFS model

To the best of our knowledge, this is the oldest solution. The NFS protocol is very robust and can be used, if the kernel supports it, to initialize and run a system directly from the network. It does not solve the first step (i.e. how to transfer the initial kernel !) but, along the years, this method proved its viability and reliability [3].

Its main drawback is a scaling problem that is common to all clusters that share files with the NFS protocol (`/home` is generally exported and used like a distributed resource among the nodes). As a consequence, if computations make intensive I/O usage, network will be exclusively used by the NFS protocol, and then, the cluster will be paralyzed and finally crash the system (NFS server), depending on the quality of the NFS implementation.

A common solution to this problem is to use a dedicated network exclusively for the transport of information for permanent (NFS) storage. However, it does not solve the inherent NFS problem : server is central and NFS (network) load can't be distributed. While this problem wasn't very important when building small clusters, nowadays, it is a very important problem as clusters are commonly built with more than 1000 nodes.

In that respect, diskless clusters have the same problem but it occurs on a smaller scale because NFS is more heavily used. The complete root file system of each nodes resides on the NFS server. Only /opt and /usr are common (and read only). As such, diskless nodes are not good candidates for large root-NFS based clusters.

1.2.2 Ramdisk model

With this approach, a minimal ramdisk containing a completely functional Linux system is uploaded to the client. It's root device is in RAM. Once this is done, it can mount NFS partitions or any distributed file-system partition in order to access programs and users data. Once this is done, some RAM is used by the root-RAM-disk (see [10] for a more complete description of the process). The typical footprint of the minimal ram disk is $20MB$ and it involves either recompiling your kernel or making some root-raid-ramdisk.

The main interest of this approach is that the transfer of the initial ramdisk can be multi-casted so that booting a cluster can be very fast (this is not possible with NFS). Another advantage is that the connection with the file server can be lost and the node will still be up and running correctly (as the `/var` partition is included in the ramdisk).

1.2.3 Network Block Device (NBD) model

This is a relatively new distributed file system, compared to NFS (first version around 1997) [11, 12] that seems very interesting for clusters. NBD devices cannot be shared unless readonly but they can be duplicated and, as a consequence, load balancing and even redundancy can occur so that the network will be used much more efficiently. It allows much better scaling : you can add a NBD device on another file server so that your network does not saturate as you add nodes to your cluster. The team isn't aware of any clustering solution that use this file system.However, replacing NFS is definitely needed so that a better scalability can be achieved.

1.2.4 Single System Image Model

This is a whole new class of clustering. It doesn't need to be diskless but this model supports diskless clusters naturally. The idea behind those implementations (e.g. [13–16]) is to simplify both the administration and usage of clusters. It is the same idea behind SMP computers : the whole cluster appears as a single resource with lots of CPU and RAM. Efficient algorithms allow either queuing or load balancing. Several clustering distributions exist that are built with diskless nodes in mind and function very well with disks (for swap, temporary storage or distributed file-system).

2 Actual Implementation

The actual implementation of thin-OSCAR is very simple and is more a proof of concept than anything else. It is based on Ram Disk model. The script is a non-interactive Perl script **oscar2thin.pl** which operates in a serial way, transforming step after step a regular systemimager image into a RAM disk for diskless operation. Then, files are moved to their relevant location (`/tftpboot`) and some configuration files are modified on the server so that NFS export and PXE operations are adapted for the diskless cluster. We will examine each of these steps.

While the implementation details of those steps are expected to change, general ideas are expected to stay as development progresses, adding more user-friendliness and options in the process. Therefore, it seems interesting to detail those functions.

2.1 Image creation

We provide some reduced-size image into OSCAR in the `oscarsamples/Mandrake-8.2-noX-i386.rpmlist` and `oscarsamples/Mandrake-9.0-noX-i386.rpmlist` which are rpm lists with a minimum number of RPMs : no Xfree86 and no compiler on the node. This image list can certainly be reduced but those files are a good starting point.

2.1.1 Blank image creation

Loopback device support has to be available on the system (master node) where this script is executed. "loop" is the module that enable the loopback device support. The script creates a traditional `ext2` file-system as a loopback device. The size of this partition has to be defined otherwise it is $80Mb$ which should be sufficient in most cases. Note that this maximum size will not be used in RAM (Ramdisk uses only their exact size) nor be transfered via the network (the image is compressed in the process). This file-system is then mounted in a temporary location called image directory.

2.1.2 Image copy and customization

The relevant directories are copied from their systemimager image location to the image directory : `/bin`, `/boot`, `/dev`, `/etc`, `/home`, `/lib`, `/mnt`, `/proc`, `/root`, `/sbin`, `/var` (some of the copied directories are empty). The directories `/usr` and `/opt` are created : they will be used as mounting point for the NFS exported file-system.

The `/etc/fstab` file is then generated in the image directory and contains the `/dev/ram0` device as its root mount point, the `/home` is mounted via NFS (standard OSCAR) and the `/opt` and `/usr` directories are NFS mount points from the systemimager image directory on the server.

Networking capabilities are then generated (mainly `/etc/sysconfig/network-scripts/ifcfg-eth0` which is configured via DHCP).

2.1.3 Image cleaning

This step is interesting because it allows us to reduce considerably the image size. At this step, two optimizations are made. First, we delete the modules directory (at least $10Mb$ in recent Linux distributions) and the RPM database (no further RPM operation on the node).

2.1.4 Server "configuration"

The `/etc/hosts` file is copied in the image directory, `/var/spool/pbs/server_name` and `/var/spool/pbs/mom_priv/config` generated in the image directory so that PBS will be functional on the nodes.

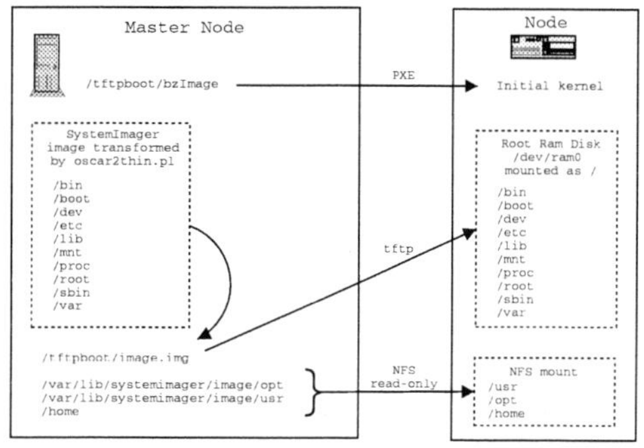

Figure 1. Master node and node scheme

2.1.5 Image compression, installation, PXE and NFS configuration

The image is then unmounted, compressed (because default kernel can uncompress ramdisks on the fly) and copied in the `/tftpboot` directory so that it can be transfered by TFTP. The default configuration file for PXE is created (`/tftpboot/pxelinux.cfg/default`) so that PXE loads the kernel `/tftpoot/bzImage` and the ramdisk we just created.

The `/etc/exports` is adjusted so that all the systemimager image is exported (read only) to the cluster net with a given subnet mask. `/home` is exported read-write to the same network.

3 Development road-map

The main goal of the thin-OSCAR work-group is to add diskless and systemless support to the OSCAR clustering framework. As a consequence, support for all the models (root-NFS based, NBD based and single system image based) of diskless and systemless nodes is expected. This will lead to profound modification or at least strong interactions with some core components of OSCAR that we will try to anticipate in the next section. This road-map is a more detailed version of the `oscar-package/ROADMAP` file.

3.1 Kernel discussion

For the moment, you need to compile your own kernel (sample configuration file provided in the `sample/ramdisk.cfg` file). We plan to distribute some kernels with the thin-OSCAR package. It is the simplest solution as we can not provide support for any installation and configuration. General NIC will be supported (eepro100, rtl8139, ...) and, of course, configuration file provided so that exotic hardware can easily be supported (with a kernel recompilation).

Modular kernel is another possibility that is already used in LTSP [5]. The potential number of modules needed by a diskless node is small : network adapters and (distributed) filesystems are the two main classes of necessary drivers. Moreover, we will focus our development effort on nodes with i586 or higher and PCI bus. Only the necessary modules will be included in the image in order to keep the image small. Other modules can be accessed via a distributed file system and only those from the two mentioned classes (NIC and filesystem) are indispensable for the successfull network boot of the node.

Because we will distribute our kernel, we will be able to add support for very different clustering solutions :

- root-NFS, ramdisk or NBD based diskless/systemless nodes
- distributed file systems (lustre, XFS, ...)
- automatic load balancing (openMOSIX)
- trace capability (Linux Trace Toolkit)
- real-time Linux (RTAI)

3.2 version 0.0-0.5 : Proof of concept

This is the actual version of thin-OSCAR.

3.2.1 Features

- All nodes DHCP
- Homogeneous cluster only : all nodes share the same image
- Monolithic kernel only
- Sample kernel configuration file provided

3.2.2 To-do

- Add a button in the OSCAR wizard for making thin-OSCAR nodes
- Pre-compiled kernel (1 standard, 1 SMP) with the most common NIC drivers built-in.
- Distro independence : most of what the **oscar2thin.pl** script is doing right now is very distro-dependent. We want to be distro independent and will certainly write a distro abstraction layer in the process.

3.3 0.5-1.0 : OSCAR integration

- Well tested and functional version for complete diskless cluster
- Support for mixed cluster : **C3** interaction !
- Storage of node information in order to provide heterogeneous cluster support (each node can use a different kernel or a different image). SIS integration ?
- Command Line Interface :
  - Creation of a complete diskless cluster with a simple file having the following information : MAC,IP,node name,KERNEL,SISIMAGE
  - Automatic collection of all MAC address : completely automatic install

3.4 1.0-1.5 : Heterogeneous cluster support

- Meta-definition of diskless model (name of model, kernel to use, SIS image to use, DISK usage [none, /tmp, /var, /home, ...], modules to keep [drivers/net], configuration file generator in order to fill configuration files [/etc/X11/XF86config-4, ...].

The aim of this step is to support heterogeneous clusters : disk/no disk, swap file, swap partition, /tmp storage, distributed /home, ...

3.5 2.0 : long term objective / wish-list

- provide last generation kernel for diskless nodes with precompiled utilities (openMosix, LTT, lustre, coda, ...) so that tests can easily be made and other types of clusters can be supported.

4 OSCAR interaction

In this section we will examine what kinds of additional features are needed by OSCAR to support thin-OSCAR. When possible, the actual component of OSCAR that is involved will be identified and some solutions proposed. Some items are more important than others and this will help us to prioritize OSCAR and thin-OSCAR development.

4.1 Storage of additional thin-OSCAR information : OSCAR Database

As explained in the first section of this article, there is several kind of nodes and the ultimate goal of thin-OSCAR is to support all the nodes. Nodes properties have to be carefully determined. As it can be used by several OSCAR packages, this data should be organized in a relational database of well defined structure and format. While OSCAR Database provides a database abstraction and a permanent storage area for OSCAR packages, all the common information has to be organized and a GUI has to be created to enter this data (MAC address, model, ...).

In order to support diskless and systemless clusters, the installation process of an image has to be refined. Indeed, systematic format of hard disk prior to installation has to be avoided.

4.2 Image diffusion and build : systemimager ?

This is one of the steps made by the **oscar2thin.pl** script. As we use mainly SIS information and certainly redo (very crudely) what SIS is already doing (namely network and file-system configuration), maybe a kind of integration should occur in order to ease the development of both SIS and thin-OSCAR.

4.3 Cluster Management : C3

C3 is a core component of OSCAR and it works very well with nodes with disk. In order to support diskless (and systemless) clusters, the **C3** tools have to be aware of diskless nodes. Several commands have to be modified :

- **cpush** Instead of remote copying the file, the file has to be copied in the relevant SIS image directory
- **cpushimage** A new initial RAM disk has to be regenerated and nodes using this image has to be rebooted
- **crm** has to remove files in the SIS image directory

Morevover, warning should be send to the user because he can't modify a single node : those actions will affect the group of nodes that use the altered image.

4.4 Different kinds of nodes

This is a crucial point. Currently, nodes can be "personalized" only with the selection of different rpmlist for them. However, in practice, there is one (or two !) file available for each distribution. We need a more complete way of managing different kinds of nodes.

A mechanism to store, distribute and manage node "profiles" has to be created within OSCAR. The potential of this point is very important for the openness of OSCAR. Here are some arguments in favor of OSCAR node modelization :

- Separation of the master node in several nodes in order to achieve a better scaling : dedicated NFS server, dedicated PBS server, dedicated monitoring server, ...
- Cluster hierarchy : OSCAR currently supports two levels of nodes (one master and several nodes). For large clusters, this is not suitable and we should be able to add at least one level. However, implementing one additional level is not much more difficult than adding a general node abstraction layer.

Conclusion

Useful definitions of nodes were exposed : diskless, systemless and diskfull. Then some techniques for diskless and systemless clustering were briefly reviewed. Finally, the goals, actual implementation and future development of thin-OSCAR were exposed.

The last part discussed interactions with OSCAR, OSCAR modifications and finally new OSCAR features that are needed in order to fulfill the thin-OSCAR goals. Even if this is a written article, most of what is exposed here is open for discussion and not carved in stone !

Acknowledgments

We would like to thank Michel Barrette, Mehdi Bozzo-Rey and Sean Dague for valuable discussion. All this work was possible thanks to the existence of the Center for Scientific Computing of Sherbrooke University [2] and its enthusiastic acceptance of the Open Source model.

References

1. Open Source Cluster Application Resource (OSCAR) http://oscar.sf.net/
2. Centre de Calcul Scientifique, Université de Sherbrooke http://ccs.usherbrooke.ca/
3. Development, installation and maintenance of Elix-II, a 180 nodes diskless cluster running thin-OSCAR, M. Barrette, M. Bozzo-Rey, C. Gauthier, F. Giraldeau, B. des Ligneris, J.-P. Turcotte, P. Vachon, A. Veilleux, submitted to HPCS2003.
4. thin-OSCAR work-group. Support for diskless and systemless cluster for OSCAR http://thin-oscar.ccs.usherbrooke.ca/
5. Linux Terminal Server Project http://www.ltsp.org/
6. Cluster Command & Control (C3) power tools, http://www.csm.ornl.gov/torc/C3
7. NFS-Root mini-HOWTO http://www.tldp.org/HOWTO/mini/NFS-Root.html
8. TFTP standard (RFC 1350) ftp://ftp.rfc-editor.org/in-notes/rfc1350.txt
9. System Installation Suite website http://www.sisuite.org/
10. Root Raid in Ram How-To, Mehdi Bozzo-Rey, Michel Barrette, Benoît des Ligneris submitted to HPCS2003 (2003).
11. Network Block Device project page http://nbd.sourceforge.net/
12. The Network Block Device, *Linux Journal*, 73, may 2001 http://www.linuxjournal.com/article.php?sid=3778
13. Scyld Beowulf Scalable Computing http://www.scyld.com/
14. Beowulf Distributed Process Space http://bproc.sourceforge.net/
15. Single System Image Clusters (SSI) for Linux http://openssi.org
16. openMOSIX http://www.openmosix.org/

Root Raid in Ram How To

Mehdi Bozzo-Rey[a], Michel Barrette[b], Benoît des Ligneris[c], Francis Giraldeau[d]
Centre de Calcul Scientifique, Université de Sherbrooke, Québec, Canada

[a]mbozzore@physique.usherb.ca

[b]mike@ccs.usherbrooke.ca

[c]benoit@des.ligneris.net

[d]giraldeau@hermes.usherb.ca

Sherbrooke University is involved in the development and support of diskless clusters. The approach use a regular Linux system with a minimal ramdisk as its root device. In order to support different kind of kernel without fancy compilation options we used the software RAID capacity of the kernel to mount an array of RAID-0 RAM disks, before the actual loading of the operating system. Once the real root file system is mounted, the loading of the operating system can then be done in numerous way (TFTP, wget, NFS, ssh, ...) and the diskless node can operate even when the network is down or the so called master-server is unavailable. We will present in this article all the necessary steps to build your own ramdisk based diskless or systemless node.

L'Université de Sherbrooke est impliquée dans le développement et le support de grappes dont les noeuds de calcul ne possèdent pas de disque rigide (grappe sans disques). Ce type de grappe utilise un système d'exploitation Linux standard avec un système de fichiers minimal résidant en mémoire vive. Nous telechargeons ce système via différents protocoles de communication (Trivial File Transfer Protocol (TFTP), Network File System (NFS), ssh, ...), afin d'assurer à chaque noeud de calcul une plus grande autonomie en cas de panne réseau ou d'inaccessibilité du serveur maître. Afin d'assurer la compatibilité avec différents noyaux Linux standards, nous utilisons la capacité du noyau Linux à gérer les réseaux redondants de disques indépendants (RAID, Redundant Array of Independant Disks) pour monter un réseau RAID-0 de disques virtuels en mémoire vive, afin d'y installer le système d'opération.Nous présentons dans cet article les différentes étapes nécessaires à l'élaboration d'un noeud de calcul sans disque. Nous présentons dans cet article les différentes étapes nécessaires à l'élaboration d'un noeud de calcul sans disque.

Introduction

By using a minimal Linux system loaded in RAM, we can achieve a much better scaling than « traditional »root-NFS based clusters [1]. With this minimal system in RAM, nodes do not depend on the network for their general operations. NFS is still used for general applications so that they are served on demand from a read-only partition which reduce the NFS traffic.

We will examine in details the different steps necessary for the support of a root file system in RAM. We will also specify some interesting points relevant to the support for RAM disk in the kernel, how to create from scratch the initial ramdisk, propose some way of obtaining the ramdisk we created from a disk (for testing) and then from the network. Finally, we will show how to support generic kernel (with small 4Mb ramdisk) by mounting a software RAID-0 array of ramdisk.

1 Kernel recompilation

It is not the goal of this document to explain in great details how to compile a kernel. Some very pertinent information already exists [2]. Please refer to it if something goes wrong.

1.1 Kernel compilation 101

- download : `http://www.kernel.org/`
- configuration interface : **make xconfig**
- **make dep** ; **make bzImage**, and if you enabled the loadable module support **make modules, make modules_install**

1.2 Necessary options

If you want to support modules you can do it. We will see how to support modules in our initial ramdisk (NIC driver, RAID, file-system, ...) but it is easier to start with a monolithic kernel.

It is necessary to select the initial ramdisk support. We will then be able to specify it size (4Mb by default). Support for the loopback device is also necessary.

1.3 Essential documentation

If the kernel sources are symlinked (or directly installed) in `/usr/src` then some files are very interesting and you should refer to them for up to date documentation (especially if you use another kernel version : kernel evolution can be very fast and some adjustments to the instruction given in this article can be necessary).

- `/usr/src/linux/Documentation/devices.txt`
  This is the complete list of defined devices with corresponding minor and major numbers (in particular, `/dev/ram` and Myrinet devices).
- `/usr/src/linux/Documentation/initrd.txt`
  Complete description for the initial ramdisk support.

- /usr/src/linux/Documentation/ramdisk.txt
  How ramdisk support is working.

2 Initial ramdisk creation

The initial ramdisk is a minimal installation of Linux that has to be used for several reasons (one of them is the installation of modules necessary for the normal operation of a regular Linux box : NIC, file-system, RAID, ...). As such, it has to include a shell, some utilities as well as all the libraries used by the binaries you want to use in this minimal system.

We will not detail how to make a suitable system for embedded systems [3] and how to use some minimal library [4] to reduce the memory footprint. In modern computers, RAM is not so expensive and while we will use generic techniques to obtain a small ramdisk, we wanted to be fully compatible with all existing applications (Open Source or commercial ones).

2.1 Which files to include ?

One of the great virtue of open source software is the availability of others work. We will first examine a regular `initrd` from your preferred Linux distribution. We made our experimentation on Mandrake 8.2 but it will work on any distributions that support ramdisk (it has to be selected explicitly for Debian and you will certainly have a warning if you never did that before).

The generic location of the initial ramdisk is `/boot`. In this directory you will find files with name starting with `initrd` and those are the actual initial ramdisks. For Mandrake 8.2 it is `initrd-2.4.18-6mdk.img` and we will use this name as reference for our example of operation.

The kernel can uncompress ramdisks on the fly. Ramdisks are generally a compressed image of a Linux file-system so that transfer time is minimized. In order to actually browse through this image and then modify it, add .gz extension : **mv initrd-2.4.18-6mdk.img initrd-2.4.18-6mdk.img.gz**, uncompress it with a **gunzip initrd-2.4.18-6mdk.img.gz**, create a `/mnt/initrd1/` directory and then mount this image using the loopback device with the following command : **mount -t ext2 -o loop /tmp/initrd-2.4.18-6mdk.img /mnt/initrd1/**.

Then, if you go into the `/mnt/initrd1/` directory, you will see a similar structure than the one presented figure 1.

```
- bin/
- dev/
- etc/
- lib/
- loopfs/
- proc/
- safedev/
- sysroot/
- sbin/ → bin/
```

Figure 1. Structure of an initial ramdisk

This is almost a « complete »functional Linux system. The `sbin/` directory point to the `bin/` one because at this early stage of the boot process system commands and user commands are the same : the initial ramdisk at this stage is in single user mode.

2.2 Which binary to install and how to find the linked libraries ?

As mentioned previously, we won't compete to make the smallest linux distribution but only examine which tools are mandatory.

The number of binaries will be kept small so that we don't end up with a huge initial ramdisk. We will choose only low-level binaries and sometime some binaries that are useful for the debugging of ramdisk experimentation. Once you have a working system, you can remove those debugging tools.

Binaries are usually linked against a certain number of libraries. This is a great feature that allows binary programs to be small and only include the functionality they have to provide. Binary programs can be compiled statically in which case they include the libraries. This is not generally done by distributions because it produce huge executables, and you don't want to have several copies of the same library on your hard drive, you want to optimize your space (as well as upgrade only one file when there is a library [security] update !). An interesting fact is that we are working the opposite way for an operational cluster, in this case we don't want to install the mathematical libraries on every node, but just on the « compilation node », users compile statically their application, so it can run in a calculation node. In our ramdisk image we will use the tools provided by the distribution and include the necessary libraries too.

In order to find which library is used by each binary, we will use the **ldd** tool. **ldd** prints shared library dependencies of the program given in argument. For instance **ldd /bin/cat** will produce an output similar to the one presented figure 2.

```
libc.so.6 => /lib/libc.so.6 (0x40028000)
/lib/ld-linux.so.2 => /lib/ld-linux.so.2 (0x40000000)
```

Figure 2. Example of ldd usage

In order to save you some time, we provide a complete list of the binaries that are necessary as well as the libraries dependencies (all this was done on a Mandrake system). The list of binaries is presented figure 3 and the corresponding libraries figure 4.

2.3 The linuxrc file

This script is the first one executed at boot. Don't forget to make it executable. Also, it may need to be added explicitly into your boot loader like this :

```
init=/linuxrc
```

- bash : interactive shell
- cat : useful to read /proc, /proc/mdstat for instance
- cp : to copy file (move files too with rm)
- gzip : compression / uncompression utility
- insmod : module loader
- ls : useful for debugging
- modprobe : automatic module loader
- mount : to mount a file system
- rm : to remove some files and directory
- tar : useful when retrieving any tape archive
- umount : unmount a file system
- pivot_root : change root

Figure 3. Typical binaries to include in the initial ramdisk, in the `bin/` directory

- libcom_err.so.2
- libc.so.6
- libdl.so.2
- libe2p.so.2
- libext2fs.so.2
- libpthread.so.0
- librt.so.1
- libtermcap.so.2
- libuuid.so.1

Figure 4. Library dependencies, typically in the `lib/` directory

This script has to be very simple because very few commands are available. One example is given figure 5.

The root is switched by the use of the **pivot_root** command. The old root (initrd-2.4.18-6mdk.img) is put into /initrd of the new root (tiny_system.img). As a consequence that the old root is contained into the new root.

This method is the simplest one. It is strongly recommended to use it to replace the old method that consist of setting a specific string into `/proc/sys/kernel/real-root-dev` because it may not be supported in future kernel release.

In the following section, we will describe more precisely how to create devices and where to found relevant documentation on this subject.

2.4 Building a tiny system image

The complete procedure is detailed in the kernel documentation [6]

This image will be run on the computer after the boot process : it will become the new root.

How to build it :

1. Creation of the root tree in a temporary directory
2. Create, format (ext2) and mount the initrd ramdisk
3. Creation of the necessary devices and copy of the necessary files

A script doing those operations is presented figure 6.

It is mandatory that the kernel support the « loopback block devices ». It is preferable to build first the structure of the ramdisk so that no space is lost when we create the file-system. Of course, if you use a compressed file system, this is not very important as the compression will reduce any unused space to a very small size because there is a repetitive structure of "zeros" (don't **dd /dev/urandom** in order to create your initial ramdisk or you will have some trouble !). The first initial ramdisk must fit into a 4Mb partition because, at this time, it is not possible to have more space unless you compiled a specific kernel.

```
#!/bin/bash

# Default Path
export PATH=/bin:/sbin

# Mount the /proc file-system
mount -t proc /proc /proc

# Mount the disk (read-only) to retrieve
mount -t ext3 -o ro -o nocheck /dev/hda1 /mnt/hda1

# Copy the model in ram, uncompress on the fly
cat /mnt/hda1/tiny_system.img.gz | gzip -dc > /dev/ram3

# Unmount the disk
umount /mnt/hda1

# Mount the new root
mount -t ext2 -o ro -o nocheck /dev/ram3 /mnt

# let's unmount /proc and change the root
# The old root is placed into /initrd of the new root
umount /proc && cd /mnt && pivot_root . initrd

# Get rid of the original console device file still
# in the initrd
exec </dev/console >/dev/console 2>/dev/console

# Pass ctrl to the normal init script of the new root
exec /sbin/init 3
```

Figure 5. `linuxrc` example.

```
# Make the {bin, etc, lib, dev, initrd, loopfs,
# proc, safedev, sysroot, sbin } dir
mkdir -p essai_initrd/bin [ ... ]

# Image creation and mount
dd if=/dev/zero of=image bs=1024k count=4
mke2fs -F -m0 image
mount -t ext2 -o loop image /mnt/toto
cd /mnt/toto/dev

# Make the devices
mknod [ ... ]
```

Figure 6. Script : How to make an image.

2.4.1 Creation of devices

Devices are special files with a definition given by the kernel. We will use the user-land tool available to create the devices : **mknod**. The command has numerous options, please read its **man** page for more information. Basically it has the following syntax : **mknod name type major minor** where the type can be **b** for block device, **c, u** for a character device and **p** for a FIFO relay.

For instance, in order to create the device corresponding to `ram0` we will use the following command : **mknod ram0 -m 660 b 1 0**. For more information about device type, major and minor numbers please consult the kernel documentation[7]. In most distributions, the **MAKEDEV** command is available. This script will create or delete devices in `/dev` so that you don't have to manually create each of them. Devices creation or deletion are grouped together (for instance std, ram, cpu, ...).

All those groups are defined in the `/etc/makedev.d` directory. Inside this directory, the `00macros` defines the permission for devices. All other files are definitions extracted from the kernel documentation that will create each group of devices with the correct permissions for a typical Linux system.

In our case, we are only interested in essential devices. The minimal list with a short description of each device is given figure 7.

- `console` : In order to have a display to the screen (5, char, 1).
- `tty#` : Virtual consoles. In order to have multiple screen on the same video output (4, char, #) and (5, char, 0) for the current TTY device.
- `md#` In order to use meta-disk (RAID) device (9, block, 0 or 1) for `md0` or `md1`.
- `null` The black-hole device.
- `ram#` Ramdisk. (1, block, #)

Figure 7. Devices that have to be present in the initial ramdisk (major number, type, minor number)

In order to have a functional system, some symbolic links have to be created : `ram`→`ram1`, `ramdisk`→`ram0`, `systty`→`tty0`.

In order to create all of those devices, we used a short script presented figure 8.

```
liste="0 1 2 3 4 5 6 7 8 9 10 11 12 13 14 15"
for i in $liste; do mknod ram$i -m 660 b 1 $i; done
mknod null -m 660 c 1 3
mknod tty -m 666 c 5 0
liste1="0 1 2 3 4"
for i in $liste1; do mknod tty$i -m 666 c 4 $i; done
mknod console -m 666 c 5 1
for i in $liste1; do mknod md$i -m 660 b 9 $i; done
```

Figure 8. Script : How to make devices.

Once this is done, we've got a functional minimal system and we can try to boot our system with it.

3 How to load a complete system image from a disk

We will first review several ways to do an image for a complete system and then, in order to test our work, examine how to load the image from a regular disk. In the next section, we will examine how to download the image from the network.

3.1 How to make a [diskless] image ?

In our first cluster called Elix, we made the images ourselves from a minimal installation of Linux. Now, this step is completely automated, thanks to the System Installation Suite[8] and the OSCAR[9] integration of this tool. The thin-OSCAR work-group[10] has been created to automate completely the server configuration for diskless nodes, the image creation and the transfer of the diskless image to the node.

3.2 Proof of concept

In order to transfer the image, we will just use the `linuxrc` file given figure 5. In this file, we mount the regular hard disk and then copy this minimal system in the ramdisk after the archive extraction. Then we change the « official »kernel root by running the command **pivot_root**.

The compression of the image is not strictly speaking necessary. We can either uncompress the image on the fly or use an uncompressed image. The last solution is the more interesting while debugging your system because it allows you to easily update your mounted image without never being out of sync from your uncompressed image.

4 How to transfer an image from the network

For the network part, we have two ways to proceed, including or not the necessary drivers in the kernel. We choose the second case : building a modular kernel with his modules collection ; we don't want to compile a collection of monolithic kernels for an heterogeneous cluster and as we have to use modules.

Once this first step is done, there are several ways to get the image, here is a non exhaustive list :

- PXE This can be used with regular NIC supporting PXE (very common nowadays) by including lines like those one **DEFAULT bzImage_2.5.30_nfs3** and then **APPEND initrd=thinimage.img.gz devfs=nomount root=/dev/ram0**.
- archive (**tar**), compression (**gzip**) of the repertory containing the image → transfer via **wget**, **tftp**, **scp** followed by **gunzip**
- **rsync** (with or without ssh) of the repertory containing the image
- creation of an ext2 file containing the image → transfer via **wget**, **tftp**, **scp** and **dd** on the fly on the device in RAM

After having tested different ways to create, modify, and transfer the image, we came to the conclusion that the most reliable way is the combination of ext2 file and **dd** on the fly. This technique is presented in the complete `linuxrc` file in figure 10.

5 Boot from the network and usage of a RAID-ram device

In this section, we will add a refinement and build a RAID device with some ram disks.

5.1 Creation of RAID disks in RAM

In order to create a RAID ramdisk we will use the **raidtools** package [11]. The definition of the RAID device is defined in the `/etc/raidtab` file. Don't forget that `/dev/ram0` is already used by the initrd, so you can't use it to build your raid array in `/linuxrc`. In order to create a RAID device in RAM with 4 ramdisks in it, please see figure 9.

```
raiddev         /dev/md0
raid-level      0
chunk-size      64k
persistent-superblock 1

nr-raid-disks 4
device      /dev/ram1
raid-disk 0
device      /dev/ram2
raid-disk 1
device      /dev/ram3
raid-disk 2
device      /dev/ram4
raid-disk 3
```

Figure 9. `/etc/raidtab` example : 4 ramdisk for one RAID array.

You can then manipulate your RAID array (in ram) exactly like a regular partition (once you created it). Some example of typical manipulation on your disk array :

- **mkraid /dev/md0** or **raid0run /dev/md0** : creation of the disk array
- **mke2fs /dev/md0** : Format the disk array
- **mount -t ext2 /dev/md0 /mnt/raidram** : Mount the disk array

In our case, their is no persistent super-block and the `/etc/raidtab` has to be altered by changing the fourth line for this one :

```
persistent-superblock 0
```

You can notice that we use in our scripts the command **raid0run /dev/md0**, which is the command to start up old (super-block-less) RAID0/LINEAR arrays. This is just a symlink to the binary **mkraid** in the raidtools package.

5.2 Integration of the necessary binaries, libraries and modules

As any tools that we want to include in our initial ramdisk, we have to include some binaries and the libraries that they use. We need the `raid0run`, as well as the additional libraries `libcrypto.so.0`, `libssl.so.0` and for instance, the network module `eepro100.o`. The additional files required by those new utilities are `/etc/raidtab` and the RAID device `/dev/md0`.

5.3 Module loading and RAID in ram technique integration

The complete `linuxrc` file is given figure 10.

6 Conclusion

We have exposed and tune all the Linux boot process so that we can control effectively the root device. In the first part, all the necessary steps to support large ram disks and transfer the initial image have been reviewed. In order to support kernel with default compilation options (16 disks of 4 Mb, and modules), we created a RAID file-system in RAM so that larger images (up to 64 Mb) can be loaded within this framework with any module necessary for the NIC. This work has been done for generic diskless support and will be used by the thin-OSCAR project to support effectively diskless clients for OSCAR without the need to recompile a new kernel. We have tested the R^3 How-to on several distributions (Mandrake 8.2, 9.0, Red-hat 7.1, Debian Woody and SID) and two architectures, IA32 and IA64 (for Raid Ram only).

Acknowledgments

We would like to thank HP Canada for the IA64 (Itanium2) they sent to us for testing.

References

1. NFS-Root mini-HOW-TO
   http://www.tldp.org/HOWTO/mini/NFS-Root.html
2. The Kernel How-to
   http://www.tldp.org/HOWTO/Kernel-HOWTO.html
3. Embedded Linux Consortium
   http://www.embedded-linux.org/
4. μlibc, a C library for embedded systems
   http://www.uclibc.org/
5. Software-RAID how-to
   http://www.tldp.org/HOWTO/Software-RAID-HOWTO.html
6. Kernel Documentation on initrd
   /usr/src/linux/Documentation/initrd.txt
7. Kernel Documentation on devices
   /usr/src/linux/Documentation/devices.txt
8. System Installation Suite
   http://www.sisuite.org/
9. Open Source Cluster Application Resource(OSCAR)
   http ://oscar.sf.net
10. Diskless support for OSCAR
    http://thin-oscar.ccs.usherbrooke.ca
11. raidtools download (documentation inside)
    http://people.redhat.com/mingo/raidtools/

```
#!/bin/bash

# Default Path
export PATH=/bin:/sbin

#Mounting the /proc file-system
mount -t proc /proc /proc

# Creation of the RAID ramdisk
insmod /lib/raid0.o
raid0run -a

# Network initialisation

#Loading appropriate module(s)
insmod /lib/sunrpc.o
insmod /lib/lockd.o
insmod /lib/nfs.o
insmod /lib/eepro100.o
echo "Step loading network module END"

#Loading module for dhcpcd
insmod /lib/af_packet.o
echo "etape af_packet.o END"

#Running dhcpcd
dhcpcd
echo "DHCPCD END"

#Verifying if the eth0 adapter is working
ifconfig

portmap -v &
# Download the RUN image and copy it in the raid device
mount -t nfs -o nolock 10.0.1.100:/tftpboot /mnt
cat /mnt/thinimage_RUN.img.gz | gzip -dc > /dev/md0

killall -9 dhcpcd
killall -9 portmap
umount /tftpboot

# Mount the md0

echo "Mounting md0"
if mount -t ext2 -o ro -o nocheck /dev/md0 /mnt; then
  echo "Mounted"
else
  error="Cannot mount, RAID and/or network problems?"
fi


# Pivot the root, umount /proc

echo "Unmounting /proc, changing root from"
echo "initial ram disk to md0 root"
if umount /proc && cd /mnt && pivot_root . initrd; then
  echo "Root changed"
else
  error="Problem using the new root"
fi


# Get rid of the original console device file still
# in the initrd
if exec </dev/console >/dev/console 2>/dev/console; then
  echo "Console switched"
fi

# Pass control to the normal init script in the raid root
exec /sbin/init 3
```

Figure 10. Complete functional linuxrc file for RAID in ram, loadable NIC support and network retrieval of the image

Development, installation and maintenance of Elix-II, a 180 nodes diskless cluster running thin-OSCAR

Michel Barrette[a] , Xavier Barnabé-Thériault[a], Mehdi Bozzo-Rey[a],
Carol Gauthier[a], Francis Giraldeau[a], Benoît des Ligneris[a*],
Jean-Philippe Turcotte[a], Patrick Vachon[a], Alain Veilleux[a]

[a]Centre de Calcul Scientifique,
Université de Sherbroke, Québec, Canada

A short presentation of the first diskless cluster developed at Sherbrooke University physics department (Elix) will be made. Then we will present the development of Elix-II, a 180 nodes diskless cluster installed and managed with the Open Source Cluster Application Resource (OSCAR) framework. The need to support diskless cluster for OSCAR lead us to create the thin-OSCAR workgroup, we will present the specific requirements for this particular architecture type (diskless and systemless) for Beowulf clusters. Some examples of scientific problems that can be solved on a diskless cluster will also be given.

Une brève présentation du premier cluster sans disque réalisé au département de physique de l'Université de Sherbrooke, Elix, sera faite. Ensuite, nous présenterons Elix-II, un cluster sans disque de 180 processeurs installé et maintenu à l'aide du projet Open Source Cluster Application Ressource (OSCAR). La nécessité d'adapter le projet OSCAR aux systèmes dans disques nous a poussé à créer le groupe de travail thin-OSCAR. Nous présenterons les prérequis pour ce genre d'architecture (sans disque-dur ou sans système sur le disque-dur) ainsi que des exemples de problèmes scientifiques qui ont été résolus sur les clusters sans disque Elix et Elix-II.

Introduction

Diskless clusters are a recent evolution of the general Beowulf idea which consist of removing all computer parts that are not directly useful for scientific computation. Hard-disks are useful for data storage but not directly for computation. Specifically, disk access time is very slow compared to RAM access time and even slower compared to cache access time. Some very successful data-mining company [1] decided, for efficiency reason, to have all their database in RAM and therefore prove the viability of the RAM-based approach on a very large scale (more than 10.000 nodes).

We use the same approach for scientific computing and we wanted to prove, on a smaller scale, that diskless cluster is a viable solution for numerous type of numerical problems that can be used in a large variety of scientific fields.

The Scientific Computing Center [2] of Sherbrooke University developed a unique knowledge and experience relative to diskless clusters. The first diskless cluster we built, Elix (1999) will be presented from a hardware and software perspective. This cluster is used for solid state physics computations that will be briefly presented.

For our most recent cluster, Elix-2, we decided to use the OSCAR [3] framework that brings us « the best known methods for building, programming, and using clusters ». The realization of Elix-II will be detailed from a hardware perspective (realization of our own blades, out of band node power management system, ...) and software perspective. Our implication in OSCAR grew to the point that we are now core members of the OSCAR work-group. We created and lead the thin-OSCAR [4] workgroup in order to address the specific problems of supporting diskless and systemless nodes inside the OSCAR framework.

*Corresponding author : benoit@des.ligneris.net

1 Elix

This is the first Linux cluster in Sherbrooke University. The project was started at the end of 1998.

1.1 Hardware organization

A bunch of standard desktop boxes were purchased and interconnected with standard 100 Mb Ethernet network. The first phase was 16 boxes of dual Pentium-II 400 MHz whereas the second phase was 30 boxes of mono Pentium-III 667 MHz and a dual Pentium-II 400 MHz as a server for a total of 64 CPUs usable for calculation into 46 nodes.

Figure 1. Picture of the Elix Rack with nodes

1.2 Software implementation

We used the standard rootnfs mechanism [5] to boot our diskless client from a dedicated server that is used as NFS server, PBS server (no calculation on the server), DHCP and TFTP [6] server. The boot process for a node is presented figure 2.

For each node, we duplicated completely all files on the server so that they have all their complete file-system available via NFS except for the `/usr` directory that was common to all nodes and mounted in read-only mode. The `/home` directory was also common to each nodes but, as it's the case for user files, this directory was readable and writable by all clients. The total size of a node image (without the `/usr` and `/home` directory) was around 40 Mb. The `/usr` directory for the nodes size was less than 200 Mb.

The only delicate part of this cluster was the boot and reboot process (it happens often because power failures are frequent at Sherbrooke University and the UPS for the whole cluster provides only a few minutes of additional uptime). Indeed, the **tftp** server we used was not optimized for high-performance and it was impossible to boot the 46 nodes at the same time.

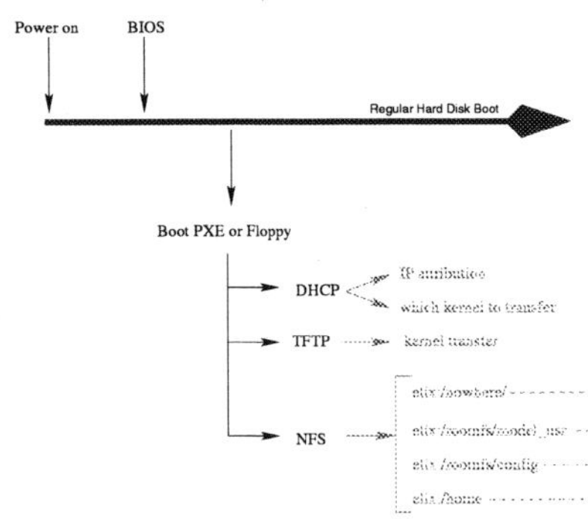

Figure 2. Boot process of an Elix node

1.3 Scientific problems solved

The Elix cluster has been used extensively by professor Tremblay's team to solve numerous problems relative to quantum state of matter [7–9] and to quantum computing [10, 11]. Quantum Monte Carlo simulations were the main numerical tool but simulated annealing and other computationally intensive algorithms were used. The Professor Senechal's team [12, 13] uses Elix for Cluster Perturbation Theory (CPT) and extensive sparse matrix inversion (Lanczös method, see, e.g. [14]) as well as for postprocessing.

Table 1 summarize the number of people that used the Elix cluster at the physics department from it's early beginning up to now. The table 2 gives the aggregated statistics (per group) from march 2001 to the end of December 2002.

Study level	Number	Year(s)
Undergraduate students	5	2000 - 2002
M. Sc. Students	5	2001-2002
Ph. D. Students	4	2000-2002
Post Doctoral Fellows	3	2002
Professors	2	2000-2002

TAB. 1
Usage of Elix cluster (people)

Group	Usage (CPU-hours)
A.M. Tremblay's group	135110
D. Senechal's group	140971
Other	12794

TAB. 2
Usage of Elix cluster (hours) from march 2001 up to December 2002

Numerous results of these scientific calculations were presented at several international conferences. Also, the Elix cluster was a key tools for the Master's thesis of three students. A patented technology has been developed using numerical computation made on the Elix cluster. Moreover, it gives the occasion to others students (experimentalists and theoreticians alike) to try and develop several numerical intensive programs that would not have been useful otherwise because of huge calculation time and scarcity of computing resources for experimentalists.

While we could believe that the Elix usefulness would come to an end abruptly with the coming of its bigger and more efficient successor, Elix2, the cluster is still used by postdoctoral fellows, graduate and Ph. D. students and therefore has shown an exceptional longevity for a computing resource. The cluster will be upgraded soon to more powerful processors.

Another side effect of the presence of the Elix cluster is that the numerical computation course (for undergrad students) is now given on Linux workstation so that students are now more efficient than ever on any Linux cluster as they are more familiar with the operating system and all the excellent open source tools available for programming. Most of theorists students that are the core users of Elix work under Linux so that they can test their programs on their workstation and then use the cluster to do the massive computation.

All in all, we can conclude that the Elix cluster gave access to very efficient and cost effective computing resource. The total cost of the cluster, including cooling system, research, development and installation is evaluated to 90.000 $ (Canadian). The cost per CPU is around 1400 $ (CA). The diskless cluster did not limit that much the range of problems that were addressed and a wide range of numerical simulation has been made : optimization (simulated annealing, quantum Monte-Carlo, matrix inversion, numerical treatment (FFT, fit, integration, ...), finite differences and finite elements. The only tasks that can't, of course, run on a diskless clusters are I/O intensive tasks requiring a disk per node.

2 Elix-2

With the great success of the Elix cluster, from a scientific, sysadmin and « builder of cluster » point of vue, the creation of its successor, called Elix2 was decided. This new cluster was funded by professors Tremblay (Sherbrooke University) and Nelson (Bishop's University). The total number of node will be 180. For this bigger cluster, we decided to look at the available tools for cluster installation and management.

OSCAR was tested and seemed to be able to fulfill our needs. It's image management system (the System Installation Tools) was something we did not have and each image creation was a (painful) manual step (basically, tries and errors until it works !). We had some kind of remote node execution but the simplicity and power of the C3 tools seduced us. Finally, OSCAR uses PERL for it's internal work (as well as shell scripts) so we know, because OSCAR was an open source project, that we will be able to code any missing features.

The next step was to add support for diskless nodes for OSCAR and this lead us to create the thin-OSCAR workgroup. Elix2 is the model for a bigger and already funded project (the Mammoth project) that will have more than 1000 nodes. Elix2 is a proof of concept for the Mammoth project and, while we use thin-OSCAR internally, we plan to submit all the written code to peer review by integrating it's functionality into OSCAR.

2.1 Hardware organization

The first Elix was built with standard desktop boxes with their floppy disk (we did not know PXE well by the time of Elix creation). This time, we decided to get rid of floppy drives and, because no more space was available in the Elix room, we decided to use a more compact vertical blade solution. This solution allows us to put more computers per square foot and, as a consequence, reduce the total cost of ownership of the cluster.

All this work was done in cooperation with the RITTAL [15] company that help us from the early stage of design, prototype and final system.

2.1.1 Blade design

While a lot of clustering companies sell blades, they are not particularly cost effective. When we made our calculations for the best performance/cost ratio, the home-made blade solution was definitely the winner. In order to do that, we designed an aluminum plate able to hold the motherboard (standard ATX or micro ATX) and a regular size power-supply. Those components are very cost effective and that is the main reason for our choice. We had some trouble designing a clean way to fix the power supply and we decided to produce custom components only for this specific part.

The front panel of the blade is also in aluminum and has all the slots (network, power, ...) accessible so that maintenance of nodes can be made very easily : the only operation required to access all those slots is to open the rack door. A picture of an assembled blade is presented figure 3.

Figure 3. Picture of a Elix2 blade

2.1.2 Rack Design

As mentioned previously, RITTAL helped us to design the rack. Each rack holds 3 stages of blades that are then placed back to back. The total capacity of a rack is then 36 (3 stages, 6 by stage, back to back) with room available at the bottom of the rack for network hardware (switch HP4000 , 40 100 Mb ports with GB up-link). We use hardened power-bar (8 outlets, 20A) to power all the nodes and the switches. A picture of second stage of the first rack is presented figure 4.

Figure 4. Picture of the Elix-2 Rack

2.1.3 Out of band node power management

This particular feature, developed with the CEGEP of Sherbrooke [16], allows us to remotely switch the power of any given node. In order to have this control on remote nodes, two contacts have to be made on the power supply. Then, each node can have three power states : automatic (i.e. controlled by the out of band node power management system), always on or always off (i.e. no out of band node power management). As a consequence, it is possible to switch on or off a node manually (for security reason) or remotely with the out of band control system. At the time of this writing, the out of band management system is a prototype and has to be installed on the production cluster. However, all power supply has been linked to the control system so that the only requirement on installation will be to plug the out of band control system into the nodes slots.

2.2 Software organization

All the installation process is based on OSCAR [3] and the server is strictly identical to a regular OSCAR server. We were very pleased to use the System Installation Suite [17], which is a core component of OSCAR, in order to build nodes images. Of course, we did not use the regular installation process, we wrote a script that allows us to transform a regular image into a minimal ramdisk, that is then transferred to the node via NFS. The detailed procedure of how to build a root ramdisk and even a root-raid-ramdisk is explained in another article presented at this conference [18].

2.2.1 OSCAR diskless : proof of concept

One of the big advantage of diskless clusters is, of course, the removal of the only mechanical component of a regular system : the hard disk. The removal of a moving part, which is one of the major cause of node failure in regular clusters, provides the global cluster with a better availability. Another major advantage of diskless and systemless cluster is the easier manageability of the whole cluster. All the files are located on a so-called master node and are transferred via the network. Update of nodes can be made « live » from the master node and all gets updated at the same time (reboot of node is only necessary when updating kernel or because of power failure). It is harder for entropy to grow in diskless or systemless clusters because all the nodes share exactly the same image. In clusters with disks, it is necessary to rebuild nodes frequently to make sure that all nodes are up, running and responding when doing any update (we had some bad experience of this entropic behavior with our IBM-SP3 of 64 nodes).

2.2.2 thin-OSCAR working group : design an implementation

On the old Elix cluster, there was no bundled software solution that makes an easy way to install, use and maintain diskless clusters. Now, the team uses thin-OSCAR as the development framework for Elix II. This solution is now available for the advantage of all the open source and scientific community. See the thin-OSCAR web site for additionnal information.

Acknowledgments

We would like to thank Intel for their generous donation and technical help. The RITTAL company was very helpful for the design and implementation of our home-made blade and specific rack needs.

References

1. Google Search Engine
`http://www.google.ca/press/highlights.html`
2. Sherbrooke University Centre de Calcul Scientifique
`http://ccs.usherbrooke.ca/`
3. Open Source Cluster Application Resource (OSCAR)
`http://oscar.sf.net/`
4. thin-OSCAR work-group. Support for diskless and systemless cluster for OSCAR
`http://thin-oscar.ccs.usherbrooke.ca/`
5. NFS-Root mini-HOWTO
`http://www.tldp.org/HOWTO/mini/NFS-Root.html`
6. TFTP standard (RFC 1350)
`ftp://ftp.rfc-editor.org/in-notes/rfc1350.txt`
7. B. Kyung, S. Allen, A.-M. S. Tremblay, Pairing fluctuations and pseudogaps in the attractive Hubbard model, Phys. Rev. B 64, 075116/1-15, 2001
8. B. Kyung, J.S. Landry, D. Poulin, A.-M.S. Tremblay, Comment on "Absence of a Slater Transition in the Two-Dimensional Hubbard Model, submitted for publication `cond-mat/0112273`
9. B. Kyung, J.S. Landry and A.-M.S. Tremblay, "How antiferromagnetic fluctuations both help and hinder d-wave superconductivity", submitted for publication
10. A. Blais, "Quantum network optimization" Phys. Rev. A 64, 022312 (2001).
11. A. Blais and A.-M.S. Tremblay, Effect of noise on geometric logic gates for quantum computation, Accepted in Phys. Rev. A
12. D. Sénéchal, D. Perez and M. Pioro-Ladrière, The spectral weight of the Hubbard model through cluster perturbation theory, Phys. Rev. Lett. 84 (2000) 522-525.
13. D. Sénéchal, D. Perez and D. Plouffe, Cluster Perturbation Theory for Hubbard models, Phys. Rev. B 66, 075129 (2002)
14. Exact diagonalization methods for quantum systems H.Q. Lin and J.E. Gubernatis Computers in Physics, vol. 7, no 4, Jul/Aug. 1993, p. 400.
15. RITTAL Canada : web site
`http://www.rittal.ca/`
16. Remote Power Management of cluster nodes, to be published.
17. System Installation Suite website
`http://www.sisuite.org/`
18. Root Raid in Ram How-To, Mehdi Bozzo-Rey, Michel Barrette, Benoît des Ligneris submitted to HPCS2003 (2003).

Integration of the LAM/MPI environment and the PBS scheduling system

Brian Barrett[a*], Jeff Squyres[†], Andrew Lumsdaine[†]

[a]Open Systems Laboratory, Indiana University
{brbarret,jsquyres,lums}@lam-mpi.org

The growth of cluster computing as a viable option for high performance computing has lead to the development of a comprehensive software stack for these machines, including cluster scheduling, parallel environments, and scientific libraries. OpenPBS or PBS/Pro is often used for scheduling, with LAM/MPI or MPICH used for parallel communication. This paper details the integration of the PBS scheduling and resource managing infrastructure with the LAM/MPI parallel run-time environment. The integration provides a cluster with several features that, although commonly available on traditional supercomputers, have been conspicuously missing in cluster computing environments: fast job startup, proper resource cleanup, and detailed accounting.

La forte croissance de l'informatique distribuée sur une architecture de type cluster dans tous les domaines du calcul haute performance a conduit au développement de différentes couches logicielles dédiées à ces machines comme la soumission de travaux, la gestion des travaux, des environnements parallèles et au développement de nombreuses librairies scientifiques. OpenPBS ou PBS/Pro sont très souvent utilisés pour la soumission de travaux alors que LAM/MPI ou MPICH sont utilisés pour les programmes parallèles. Dans cet article, nous détaillerons l'intégration du système de gestion de travaux PBS avec l'environnement d'exécution parallèle LAM/MPI. Cette intégration apporte de nombreuses fonctionnalités supplémentaires au cluster qui ne sont habituellement disponibles que sur les superordinateurs traditionnels. Ces fonctionalités faisaient jusqu'à présent défaut aux clusters : démarrage rapide des travaux, nettoyage adéquat des ressources et comptabilité détaillée des ressources utilisées.

1 Introduction

In recent years, the use of commodity hardware for high performance computing has grown dramatically. Commodity hardware, a fast network, and a small software stack present a complete clustering solution. With the advent of packages like OSCAR [1] and Scyld [2] to assist in installing software on the cluster, clusters have proven to be inexpensive, easy to build, and provide a formidable computational resource.

A common practice for clusters is the use of PBS[1] for batch scheduling of user jobs, combined with either an MPI [5,6] implementation or PVM [7,8] for a parallel run-time environment. Commonly used MPI implementations on clusters are LAM/MPI [9,10] and MPICH [11,12]. Both of these MPI implememntatoins by default use `rsh` or `ssh` to provide remote process startup.

Each of these software components is of high quality, but unlike traditional supercomputer stacks, cluster software tends to be poorly integrated. The MPI implementation and the batch scheduler do not interact, leading to a number of issues for both systems administrators and end users.

This paper presents a solution for integrating PBS and LAM/MPI. LAM/MPI is a freely-available, open source implementation of the MPI standard. The implementation includes all of MPI-1.2 and large portions of MPI-2, including dynamic process control, one-sided communication, C++ bindings, and MPI I/O (through ROMIO [13,14]). The project is currently developed by the Open Systems Laboratory at Indiana University and is available under a BSD-like license.

The remainder of this paper is structured as follows: Section 2 presents the motivations for this project, detailing the shortcomings of existing integration between PBS and MPI implementations. Section 3 presents a high-level overview of the architecture of both PBS and LAM/MPI. The integration architecture is presented in Section 4. Future work and suggested improvements for both LAM/MPI and the PBS interface are suggested in Section 5. Finally, results of the implementation are provided in Section 6 and conclusions are presented in Section 7.

2 Motivation

As discussed in the introduction, commodity clusters running MPI jobs with PBS for batch scheduling face a number of challenges. Current usage requires a parallel application to start as shown in Figure 1 - either `rsh` or `ssh` is used for remote job startup. Specifically, the MPI processes started on remote nodes "escape" PBS's tracking abilities, due to standard Unix process behavior (remote MPI processes are not the children of any PBS control / monitoring process). Because PBS is unaware of processes executing on remote nodes, it is unable to properly free resources at the end of a job's execution. Further, it is unable to provide adequate usage accounting numbers, providing only wall-clock time for a particular job.

A number of solutions have appeared for these problems, mostly as the result of sites sharing scripts written to solve a problem seen on their cluster. "Clean-up"

*Work supported by a Department of Energy High Performance Computer Science fellowship

†Work supported by a grant from the Lilly Endowment

[1]PBS, the Portable Batch Scheduler, was commercialized after development for NASA. There are currently two versions of PBS under development: OpenPBS, which is available at no cost, and PBS/Pro, which is a commercial product from Veridian Software. In this paper, we use "PBS" to refer to both OpenPBS [3] and PBS/Pro [4].

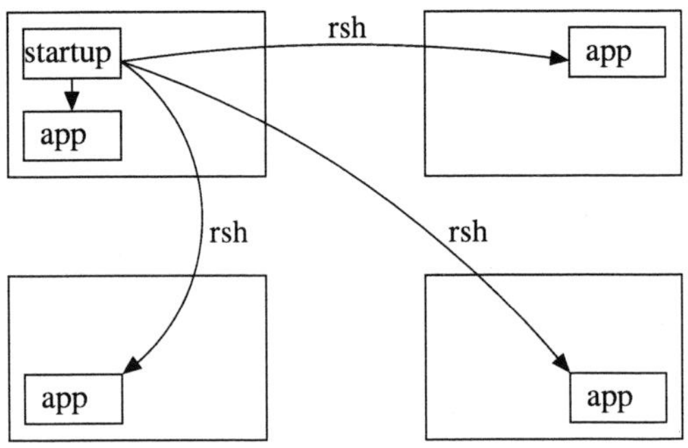

Figure 1. Starting a parallel application using `rsh` or `ssh`. PBS is only able to track resource utilization on the node from which the application is started.

scripts to kill processes remaining after a job ends are common of many PBS installations. In order to disallow users from bypassing the batch system, shell access is limited by a number of ingenious mechanisms, including modifying `/etc/passwd` on the client node to toggle the user's shell from `/bin/false` to a real shell upon scheduling by PBS. The myriad of possibilities dramatically increases the complexity of installing and maintaining such a cluster. Note, however, that none of these kinds of solutions provides accurate accounting statistics. At best, the wall clock time of the job multiplied by the number of CPUs can determine approximate CPU usage.

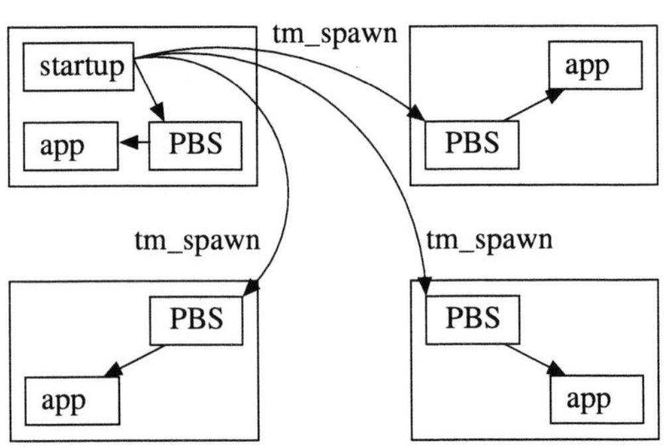

Figure 2. Starting a parallel application using PBS's TM interface. PBS is able to track resource utilization for the entire application.

PBS provides an interface, referred to as the Task Management (TM) interface [15], for job control in the PBS environment. PBS's TM interface is a subset of the PSCHED interface [16]. The PSCHED API aimed to provide a complete interface for parallel job and resource management. Utilizing the TM interface results in an application startup similar to that shown in Figure 2. All processes started by the TM interface remain under PBS control, allowing both resource cleanup and process accounting.

By modifying LAM/MPI to utilize the TM interface, we are able to provide a comprehensive job control facility under PBS. The integration allows LAM/MPI to:

- Start run-time environment without the use of `rsh` or `ssh`
- Provide guaranteed cleanup of resources
- Enable PBS to collect accounting information from all processes in the MPI application

As a side-effect, the startup time of LAM/MPI under PBS was dramatically reduced, even for small numbers of nodes.

3 Systems Overview

This section presents the general architecture of both LAM/MPI (Section 3.1) and PBS (Section 3.2), with a focus on issues that affect integration.

3.1 LAM/MPI

LAM/MPI is designed with two major layers, the LAM layer and the MPI layer, as shown in Figure 3. The LAM layer provides a framework upon which the MPI layer executes. The LAM layer provides a complete message passing service as well as process control, remote file access, and `stdio` forwarding. The MPI layer provides the MPI interface and an infrastructure for direct communication with high-speed networks.

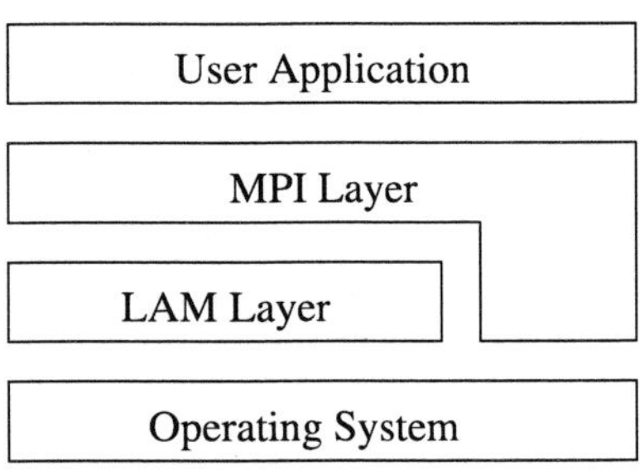

Figure 3. The layered design of LAM/MPI

LAM utilizes a user-level daemon to provide many of the services needed for an MPI run-time execution environment. The daemons are started at the beginning of an execution session using the `lamboot` command, a process often referred to as "booting LAM." At the end of an execution session, the daemons are killed using the `lamhalt` command. The network of daemons is referred to as the LAM run-time environment. Figure 4 depicts booting the LAM environment using `rsh`.

The LAM daemons provide process control for all MPI jobs executed under LAM/MPI. `mpirun` launches an MPI

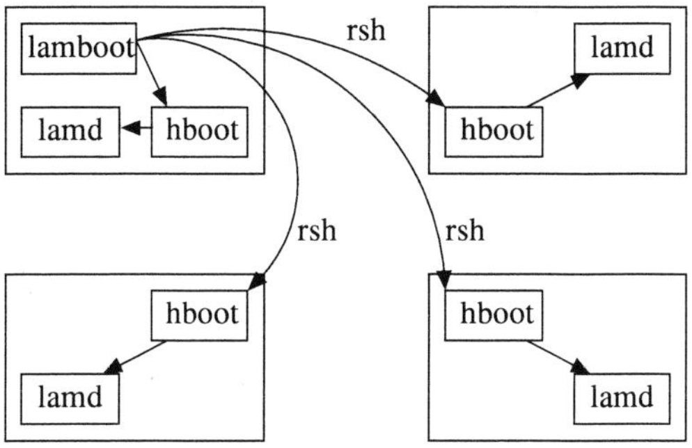

Figure 4. Booting of the LAM environment using `rsh`. The `lamd`s are the user-level daemons used by LAM. `hboot` provides start-up assistance for the LAM daemons.

application by sending a request to the daemons, which then `fork()/exec()` the user's application. At the end of the application's life, the daemons are notified of the process deaths through the standard Unix `SIGCHLD` mechanisms. Additionally, the daemons are able to stop execution of an MPI application running under the environment through the use of `kill()`.

3.1.1 System Services Interface

The development version of LAM/MPI has been redesigned to provide a plug-in module framework for various services provided by the LAM infrastructure. This framework, the System Services Interface (SSI), is composed of a number of "kinds" of plug-ins, each of which provide a single service to the MPI implementation. Modules are chosen at run-time, either by the SSI infrastructure or the user, allowing a particular version of LAM/MPI to support multiple underlying infrastructures. Currently, there are SSI interfaces for booting LAM, for the MPI device-dependent communication layer, and for MPI collective communication algorithms.

At present, there are two implementations of the boot SSI interface: RSH and TM. The RSH boot module allows the traditional `rsh`[2] booting mechanism. The TM boot module supports any batch scheduler that conforms to the PSCHED API, although PBS is believed to be the only scheduler with such support. Only one boot SSI module can be used to boot LAM – the run-time environment must either be booted entirely using TM or entirely using RSH. Although the user is free to specify a specific boot module, the SSI infrastructure can generally automatically select the most appropriate module at run-time.

3.2 PBS

PBS is composed of three components: the scheduler, server, and a per-node control daemon (referred to as the Machine Oriented Mini-server, or MOM), as shown in Figure 5. The scheduler provides job-to-node mappings and handles queue management. The server handles communication between components as well as accounting logs. There is generally one scheduler and one server per cluster. The PBS MOM executes on every node in the cluster and provides a number of health and process control features. The MOMs provide a heartbeat mechanism for the server so that jobs are not allocated to unresponsive nodes. The MOMs are also used by the server and TM interface for job startup.

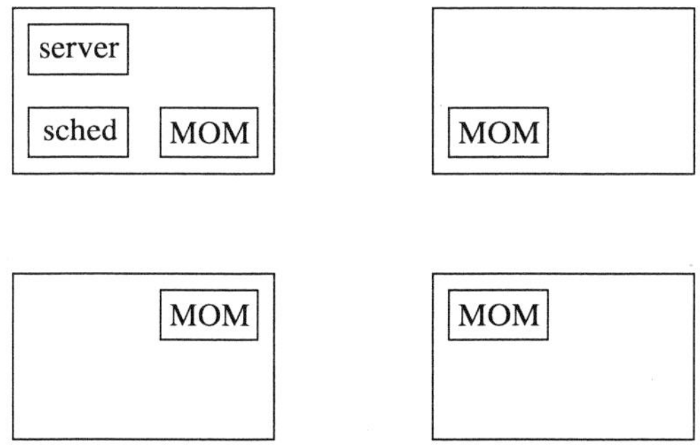

Figure 5. Architecture of a cluster running PBS. The MOMs are responsible for monitoring activity on each node and job startup. The scheduler allocates resources to jobs and communicates with the server, who is responsible for job startup, shutdown, and accounting logging.

PBS defaults to scheduling jobs on a per-node basis. However, PBS can use the concept of a Virtual CPU (VCPU) for per-CPU scheduling. The mapping between physical CPUs and VPCUs is arbitrary and set by the system administrator. Since PBS can not influence the OS scheduler on a cluster node, the mapping is simply a guideline. The concept is useful, however, for providing hints to the layers above PBS about how to schedule processes within a single job.

3.2.1 The TM Interface

The PBS implementation of the TM interface, provides a number of services for LAM's TM boot module, including remote or local process start-up (`tm_spawn()`), job node assignments (`tm_nodeinfo()`), and resource information for a particular node (`tm_rescinfo()`). `tm_spawn()` and `tm_rescinfo()` are both asynchronous events.

`tm_spawn()` starts a single process on a node specified by a `tm_node_id`. The spawned task is started by the relevant MOM, allowing PBS to track resource utilization for the spawned process and all its children. To allow resource accounting, if the `tm_spawn`ed process exits, all children of the spawned process are immediately killed by the MOM on that node.

[2] `ssh` or any other remote process command with a similar interface may also be used.

In order to examine the execution environment, TM provides `tm_nodeinfo()` and `tm_rescinfo()`. `tm_nodeinfo()` provides a list of `tm_node_ids` – one for each VCPU allocated to the job. The `tm_node_ids` only have meaning within the current job and have no direct mapping to IP addresses or hostnames. Using `tm_rescinfo()`, it is possible to obtain the hostname that corresponds to a particular `tm_node_id`. `tm_rescinfo()` provides all the information normally provided by `uname -a` in a platform-independent format. From this, a hostname that will resolve across the cluster can be obtained.

4 Implementation Architecture

The integration of PBS and LAM/MPI involves three types of changes: implementation of the TM boot module (Section 4.1), improvements in the general LAM infrastructure (Section 4.2), and PBS-specific modifications that fall outside the TM boot module (Section 4.3).

4.1 The TM Boot Module

The traditional RSH booting mechanism, shown in Figure 4, consists of the following steps:

1. Parse hostfile and allocate nodes
2. Use `rsh` to start `hboot` on each node
3. `hboot` starts LAM daemon on each node
4. LAM daemons connect to `lamboot`, providing location information
5. `lamboot` broadcasts location information

`hboot` is responsible for starting the LAM daemons each node. It parses a configuration file to determine which applications to start, closes `stdout` and `stderr`, starts the applications, and exits. The configuration file may specify more than one application to start; using `hboot` allows multiple remote processes to start with only one call to `rsh`. Due to the overhead of `rsh`, this can greatly reduce boot time. Once the applications have launched, `hboot` exits, allowing `rsh` to complete.

The functionality of `hboot` is largely irrelevant in a PBS environment. Remote job startup with TM is significantly faster than with `rsh`, so the overhead of multiple calls to `tm_spawn()` per node is negligible. The configuration file can be parsed on the booting node rather than on each node. More importantly, `hboot`'s early exit causes PBS to kill all children of `hboot` as soon as it exits. Such behavior is obviously not desirable. Since `hboot` is largely rendered irrelevant in a PBS environment, the parsing functionality that it provides was moved into a library call; the `hboot` command is not utilized in the TM boot module.

The booting process for the TM boot module is shown in Figure 6. `lamboot` is run, often with no arguments. A hostfile is not needed, as LAM will obtain a list of target hosts from PBS. `lamboot` initializes the TM boot module, which initializes the TM interface. The TM boot module obtains a list of `node_ids` from PBS and uses `tm_rescinfo()` to find all the unique hosts in the list. If a hostname appears more than once, PBS has scheduled more than one VCPU on that host, and LAM will set its internal CPU count accordingly.

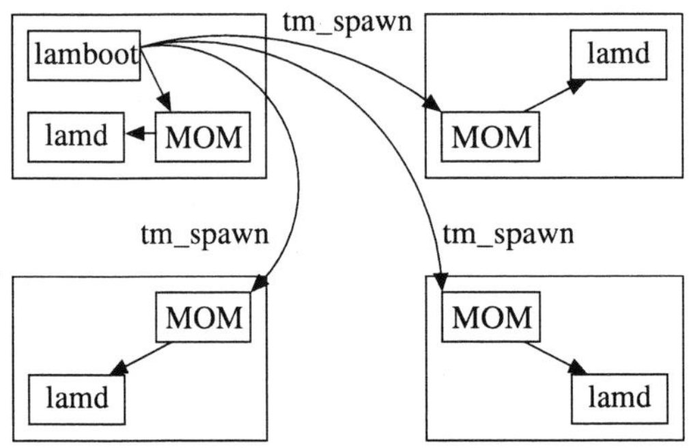

Figure 6. Booting of the LAM/MPI environment using PBS. `lamboot` calls `tm_spawn()` to directly execute the LAM daemons (`lamds`).

The boot configuration file is then parsed to determine which processes to start in order to form the LAM run-time environment.[3] The TM boot module then calls `tm_spawn()` once per process per node. `tm_spawn()` returns an event handle to allow the starting application to poll for a success / failure in startup. However, the TM boot module ignores the event handle. The call-back in the next phase of booting will ensure that all processes started up correctly, so there is no need collect the events from PBS. The asynchronous nature of `tm_spawn()` means that LAM is able to start multiple processes in a parallel fashion, something that it is not capable of doing with the RSH boot module.

Once all the LAM daemons are started, the TM boot module behaves exactly like the RSH boot module. The LAM daemons each send their location to information to `lamboot`, who then broadcasts this information back out to all LAM daemons. At this point, the boot process is complete and the TM boot module is closed. `lamboot` returns and the user is able to run MPI jobs in the environment.

4.2 LAM Infrastructure Improvements

As a result of work on the TM boot module, some changes were made to LAM that are applicable in environments outside of PBS. The changes are enabled by default, regardless of which boot module is used. The notable changes are automatic resource cleanup if the LAM daemons receive a `SIGTERM` and proper usage of the `$TMPDIR` environment variable.

[3] Normally, this is just one processes: the `lamd`.

While PBS provides a guaranteed process cleanup, other resources may still be left in use by MPI applications. In particular, it is possible for temporary files and System V semaphores to remain if TM prematurely kills a LAM/MPI run-time environment. PBS provides a "warning" of impending death by sending a `SIGTERM` to all processes in a job. A short time period later, PBS forcibly kills all remaining processes with `SIGKILL`. By catching the `SIGTERM`, the LAM daemons are each able to launch a small cleanup process (`tkill`) that ensures that all LAM processes are killed, all System V semaphores used by LAM are freed, and all files and directories are deleted. The `SIGTERM` / `SIGKILL` procedure is a common way to "warn" processes they should exit. Therefore, it was felt that such functionality would be useful for cleanup outside of PBS environments.

PBS/Pro 5.0 also provides a `$TMPDIR` environment variable for every job that points to a unique temporary space for that job. The temporary space exists for the duration of the job and is removed during job post-processing. By utilizing the `$TMPDIR` directory, LAM is able to ensure all files are removed, even in the case of a malfunction by the LAM daemons. In addition, the `$TMPDIR` is standard UNIX practice, and therefore applicable outside of PBS environments.

4.3 Other Changes

The only PBS-specific modification to LAM that is not contained in the TM boot module is in the naming of LAM's temporary directory. As PBS defines the `$PBS_ENVIRONMENT` variable in all jobs, if LAM detects this variable, the unique PBS job ID is appended to the directory name. Since the directory name is used throughout LAM (not just in the boot modules), it did not make sense to add the functionality only in the boot module. In addition, there is support for other naming schemes that do not have their own boot module at this time.

5 Improvements

The TM boot module is largely feature complete. A small number of issues remain, mainly related to scalability on large clusters (Section 5.1). There are a number of restrictions placed on the environment, due either to LAM or PBS design decisions (Section 5.2). Finally, there are some issues with the TM interface that unnecessarily complicated the implementation of LAM's TM boot module (Section 5.3).

5.1 Remaining Work

The TM boot module still requires testing on large clusters. While there are no apparent limitations in the TM boot module that do not exist in the RSH boot module, only testing can verify the ability to run on hundreds of nodes.

There is also a problem of node failures during boot – the TM interface is not designed to handle failures during run time. The only practical solutions for LAM in the case of failure are to either give up on booting and let the user attempt to restart the job (which PBS may be able to do automatically) – or to start the run-time environment on a subset of the nodes, those that remain alive. This means that the MPI universe would be smaller than requested, which may cause problems for some applications. Abort-on-failure is the is current behavior, as it appears to follow the "law of least astonishment" [17].

5.2 TM Boot Module Restrictions

The TM boot module does place some restrictions on the user of LAM/MPI that do not exist in the RSH boot module. With the RSH boot module, LAM/MPI can be installed in different places on each machine, as long as the LAM executables can be found in the `$PATH`. This scheme allows users to achieve multi-architecture support through the use of intelligent path settings. TM, however, requires that the full path to the executable be given to `tm_spawn()`, so LAM must be installed in the same place on all nodes in the cluster. Multi-architecture support is therefore more difficult on a filesystem shared across all nodes in the cluster. However, the common case for PBS installations is a cluster of the same architecture, so this limitation is not seen as unworkable.

LAM/MPI's RSH boot module allows booting with different usernames on each node. This functionality is not explicitly available in the TM boot module, as `tm_spawn()` does not provide a way to specify a username. As PBS does not appear to be able to create a job using different usernames on different nodes, this is not a limitation in LAM/MPI, but a design decision in PBS.

5.3 TM Improvements

Implementing a run-time environment startup infrastructure using the TM interface presented a number of challenges. Some of the challenges, such as the killing of all children of `tm_spawn()`ed processes, exist for technical reasons and cannot be avoided. Other aspects of the TM interface present issues for implementors of middleware, but do not appear to exist for any technical reason. For example, the TM interface is not well-suited for multiple-CPU execution. In order to map TM `tm_node_id`s to actual nodes, the application must parse a node information string to get the hostname, then do hostname comparisons. A format where this information was returned directly would be beneficial to application writers.

The requirement that `tm_spawn()` be given a full path name also presents problems in some situations. While homogeneous clusters will not experience problems with the requirement that a full path be provided, heterogeneous clusters will require more careful planning. A `tm_spawn_multiple()`, similar in functionality to MPI_SPAWN_MULTIPLE, would also be useful. This was suggested in the PSCHED API, but was not implemented in PBS's TM API.

6 Results

The implementation of the TM boot module enables process accounting and resource cleanup in a PBS environment. As a side-effect of the implementation, boot time was drastically decreased compared to `rsh` or `ssh`

All testing was performed on an OSCAR 2.1 cluster running Red Hat 7.3. Version 3.0.7p8 of the Maui scheduler, combined with OpenPBS 2.3.16 provided batch scheduling services. LAM/MPI was built from a CVS snapshot from January 30, 2003. The server node is a dual 1Ghz PIII machine with 512MB of RDRAM. The 8 compute nodes are single 1.4Ghz P4 machines with 756MB of PC133 SDRAM. The system is connected via 100MB ethernet and MDDS copper Myrinet 200, although the Myrinet was not used in any of the tests. The user account used for testing used the `tcsh` shell, with a `.tcshrc` that contained a single statement setting `$PATH`. SSH keys were setup using the default OSCAR mechanisms.

6.1 Process Accounting

The use of the TM interface enabled process accounting for the entire job. With `rsh` or `ssh`, process resources are only logged on a single node. However, with the TM interface, such control is now possible. Using the accounting logs provided by the PBS server, CPU time and memory usage can be tracked, in addition to wall-clock time. Figure 7 provides resource information for the execution of test program that executes a computational kernel for approximately 90 seconds.

Boot	Nodes	Wall Clock	CPU	Mem
RSH	1	120s	111s	4396kb
TM	1	120s	119s	4396kb
RSH	8	100s	93s	4960kb
TM	8	108s	600s	16296kb

Figure 7. Accounting information from PBS, comparing a job run on 1 node and 8 nodes for a process with no run-time communication and requiring approximately 90 seconds of CPU time.

6.2 Resource Cleanup

Through both the use of the PBS MOMs to start applications and the `SIGTERM` handling in the LAM daemons, LAM is able to properly return resources to the system after job execution. Testing was done under a number of scenarios, including PBS ending a job because resources (such as wall-clock time) had expired. In all cases, the environment was properly cleaned by the LAM infrastructure.

6.3 Improved Boot Performance

The TM boot module is able to quickly and efficiently bring up the LAM run-time environment on a homogeneous cluster of workstations. As shown in Figure 8, the startup time is drastically reduced compared to the RSH boot module, using either `rsh` or `ssh`. There are two reasons for the decrease. First, `rsh` must authenticate every time a remote process is launched, whereas the MOMs only authenticate at startup. Second, the TM boot module is not forced to serialize job startup. The system is capable of sending control messages out serially, but does not wait for the response before sending the next control message.

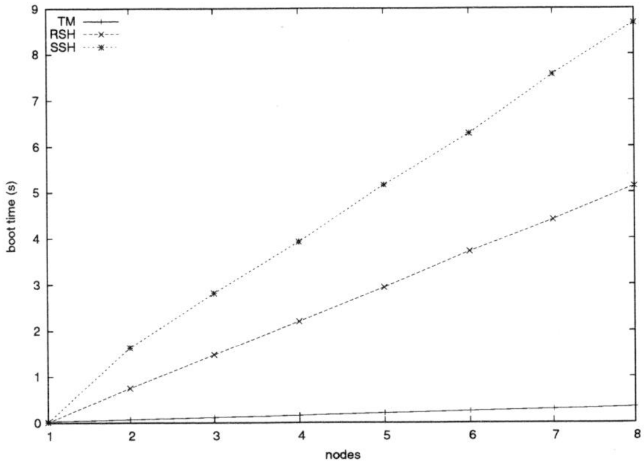

Figure 8. Startup time for LAM/MPI using SSH, RSH, and TM.

7 Conclusions

The ability of LAM/MPI to start jobs using the TM interface of PBS provides a number of important features. It removes the dependency of LAM/MPI on `rsh` or `ssh` in a cluster environment. Job startup time is greatly decreased. More importantly, the system is able to provide guarantees that resources are returned to the system at the end of a PBS job. Accounting is also enabled, proving usage statistics other than simply "wall-time."

Although the modification of LAM/MPI to better integrate with PBS is another step towards clusters providing the same feature set of traditional supercomputers, other parallel environments must still be modified to use the TM interface. Only when parallel environments provide this functionality can systems administrators remove the myriad of kill scripts and login controls from their systems.

The TM boot module and all modifications to the infrastructure that grew out of the project are currently available in LAM's CVS tree. Anonymous, read-only access is available for users wanting to utilize the latest features in LAM/MPI. The TM boot module is also scheduled to be included in the upcoming LAM/MPI 7.0 release. More information on the project can be found on the web:

`http://www.lam-mpi.org/`

References

1. Open Cluster Group: OSCAR Working Group. OSCAR: A packaged cluster software for High Performance Computing. http://www.OpenClusterGroup.org/OSCAR/.
2. Scyld Beowulf Scalable Computing, http//www.scyld.com/.
3. Portable Batch System (OpenPBS), http://www.openpbs.org/.
4. Portable Batch System (PBS/Pro), http//www.pbspro.com/.
5. Message Passing Interface Forum. MPI: A Message Passing Interface. In *Proc. of Supercomputing '93*, pages 878–883. IEEE Computer Society Press, November 1993.
6. Al Geist, William Gropp, Steve Huss-Lederman, Andrew Lumsdaine, Ewing Lusk, William Saphir, Tony Skjellum, and Marc Snir. MPI-2: Extending the Message-Passing Interface. In Luc Bouge, Pierre Fraigniaud, Anne Mignotte, and Yves Robert, editors, *Euro-Par '96 Parallel Processing*, number 1123 in Lecture Notes in Computer Science, pages 128–135. Springer Verlag, 1996.
7. Al Geist, Adam Beguelin, Jack Dongarra, Weicheng Jiang, Robert Manchek, and Vaidyalingam S. Sunderam. *PVM: A Parallel Virtual Machine*. Scientific and Engineering Computation Series. MIT Press, 1994.
8. J. Dongarra, A. Geist, R. Manchek, and V. Sunderam. Integrated PVM Framework Supports Heterogeneous Network Computing. *Computers in Physics*, 7(2):166–75, April 1993.
9. Greg Burns, Raja Daoud, and James Vaigl. LAM: An open cluster environment for MPI. In John W. Ross, editor, *Proceedings of Supercomputing Symposium '94*, pages 379–386. University of Toronto, 1994.
10. The LAM Team. *Getting Started with LAM/MPI*. University of Notre Dame, Department of Computer Science, `http://www.lam-mpi.org/`, 1998.
11. W. Gropp, E. Lusk, N. Doss, and A. Skjellum. A high-performance, portable implementation of the MPI message passing interface standard. *Parallel Computing*, 22(6):789–828, September 1996.
12. William D. Gropp and Ewing Lusk. *User's Guide for* `mpich`*, a Portable Implementation of MPI*. Mathematics and Computer Science Division, Argonne National Laboratory, 1996. ANL-96/6.
13. Rajeev Thakur, William Gropp, and Ewing Lusk. Data sieving and collective I/O in ROMIO. In *Proceedings of the 7th Symposium on the Frontiers of Massively Parallel Computation*, pages 182–189. IEEE Computer Society Press, February 1999.
14. Rajeev Thakur, William Gropp, and Ewing Lusk. On implementing MPI-IO portably and with high performance. In *Proceedings of the 6th Workshop on I/O in Parallel and Distributed Systems*, pages 23–32. ACM Press, May 1999.
15. OpenPBS 2.3.16. *TM(3) (manpage)*, May 1997.
16. The PSCHED API Working Group. PSCHED: An API for Parallel Job/Resource Management, November 1996.
17. Geoffrey James. *The Tao of Programming*. Info Books, Santa Monica, CA, 1987.

The Modeling and Dependability Analysis of High Availability OSCAR Cluster System

Chokchai Leangsuksun[a], Lixin Shen[a], Hertong Song[a], Stephen L. Scott[b], Ibrahim Haddad[c]

[a]Department of Computer Science, Louisiana Tech University, Ruston, LA 71272, USA
[b]Computer Science and Mathematics Division, Oak Ridge National Laboratory, Oak Ridge, TN 37831, USA
[c]Open Systems Lab, Ericsson Corporate Unit of Research, Town of Mont Royal, Quebec H4P 2N2, Canada

With over 85,000 downloads to date, OSCAR is the most widely used, freely available, open source software stack for the building and maintaining of high performance computation clusters. The desire for a high availability cluster computing solution is presently coming from two directions. First, traditional high performance computing clusters are growing in size beyond that which one can reasonably expect an application to complete prior to a hardware failure. Second, there is a growing demand for the use of high performance computing systems as platforms for mission critical or highly available computing. In this paper, the current OSCAR cluster computing system is presented. Reliability oriented and architectural features are then introduced to render a high availability OSCAR environment. Continuous Time Markov Chain models are then built and applied to these two systems; the classic OSCAR and the high availability OSCAR. Based on these models, the dependability of the two systems is analyzed and compared. The results show that the high availability path is reasonable and will significantly improve the availability of OSCAR cluster system.

Avec plus de 85000 téléchargements jusqu'à maintenant, OSCAR est la suite logicielle gratuite à code libre la plus utilisée pour l'installation et l'entretient des grappes de calcul de haute performance. La demande pour des grappes de calcul de haute disponibilité provient de deux tendances. Primo, les grappes de calcul de haute performance traditionnelles augmentent en taille, et l'on ne peut plus raisonnablement espérer compléter un calcul distribué avant que ne survienne un bris matériel. Secondo, il y a croissance de l'utilisation des systèmes de haute performance en tant que systèmes vitaux, ou encore en informatique de haute disponibilité. Dans cet article, nous décrivons l'environnement OSCAR. Nous lui ajoutons ensuite de nouvelles fonctions de fiabilité permettant d'obtenir un environnement OSCAR de haute disponibilité. Des modèles Continuous Time Markov Chain sont ensuite mis au point et appliqués à deux ensembles: la version classique de OSCAR et la version haute disponibilité de OSCAR. En se basant sur ces modèles, on analyse et compare la sécurité de fonctionnement de ces deux ensembles. Les résultats montrent que l'option haute disponibilité est intéressante et améliore notablement la stabilité de l'environnement OSCAR.

1. Introduction

Open Source Cluster Application Resources (OSCAR) [1, 6, 7] is a fully integrated, easy to install software package designed to facilitate the creation and operation of a Linux cluster for high performance computing. It has been widely used for building and maintaining Beowulf clusters, which are the fastest growing architecture choice for high-performance parallel computing systems [2]. High-performance systems are also in growing demand as platforms for mission critical applications. In many cases, high availability (HA) requirement becomes as critical as high performance. We anticipate that for OSCAR to be adopted for use in mission-critical and enterprise environments such as telecommunications or the defense industry will require the addition of high availability features [3].

From the HA view point, the current OSCAR release is not suitable since its system reliability components are exposed to multiple single points of failure. These failure rates will dominate the availability of the entire system. In order to increase system reliability, high availability requirements will be applied to several of these key components. One solution is to build redundancy in the system. Duplicating key components will significantly improve the availability of the redundant components and that of the whole system. However, the overall price/performance ratio of the system will most likely rise in direct relationship to the introduced redundancy and therefore may compromise the cost-conscious advantages of the Beowulf cluster system. It is also very possible that system redundancy will introduce additional system overhead, which will in turn reduce overall performance thereby reducing the price/performance ratio even further.

Dependability analysis demonstrates whether or not the HA requirements will be met without building an actual system during the design stage. It provides a good insight for examining the reliability characteristic of these systems. Continuous Time Markov Chain (CTMC) [6] is a useful modeling formalism for dependability analysis of computer systems. It can easily handle many of the interdependencies and dynamic relationships among the system components [4].

In this paper, we introduce reliability-oriented requirements and architecture that will render a high availability OSCAR cluster system. We then demonstrate the HA-OSCAR reliability improvement via CTMC technique. In the following section, we will discuss the architectures of the OSCAR cluster system and the proposed HA-OSCAR cluster system. Section three (3) describes the corresponding CTMC models for the two systems and is followed by their dependability analysis. The paper is ended with concluding remarks and a discussion of future work.

2. System Architecture

Before diving into the dependability analysis, system characteristics are investigated. We first examine the current OSCAR architecture and its anatomy. Our goal is to identify the potential single-point-of-failure components. This will provide an opportunity to introduce system level redundancy to produce a high availability initiated improvement over the existing OSCAR cluster framework. However, only a brief description of the proposed architecture is provided here. Additional HA-OSCAR details may be found in [3].

2.1 Oscar Cluster Architecture

Figure 1 shows the architecture of an OSCAR cluster system supported by the current release (i.e. release 2.1, at the time of writing). Each individual machine within a cluster is referred to as a node. There are two types of nodes: server node (also called "head node") and client node (also known as "computing node" or simply "node"). The server node is responsible for providing service requests and routing appropriate tasks to client nodes. A client node is primarily dedicated to computation. The present OSCAR cluster architecture consists of a single server node and a number of client nodes, where all the client nodes contain somewhat homogeneous hardware. The server node and client nodes all communicate on a private Ethernet network not exposed to the outside world [2]. To provide cluster access to the external network, the server node is dual ported with a second network interface card connected to the outside world via a public network address. The server node file system is NFS mounted, contains the home directories of all users, and runs various service-providing servers, such as the PBS queue system and MAUI scheduler. Each client has a complete local copy of the operating system and other software, with the exception of aforementioned NFS mounted users' home directories on the server storage.

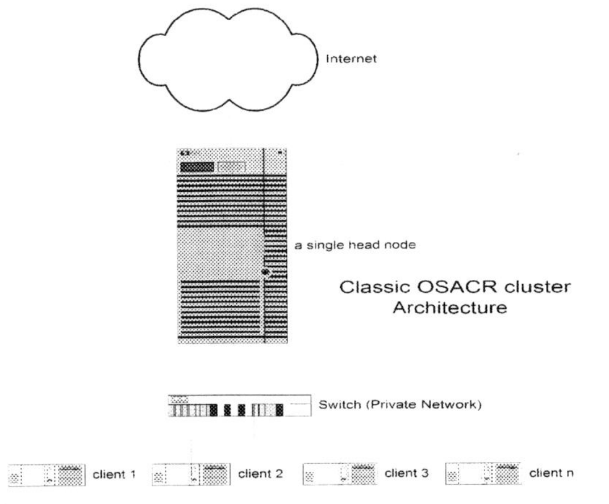

Fig. 1. Architecture Supported by Current OSCAR Release

2.2 HA OSCAR Cluster Architecture

The OSCAR working group of the Open Cluster Group continues to update the packages in OSCAR to ensure that it represents the best-known practices for building, using, and managing clusters [1]. The current release of OSCAR is not suitable for mission critical systems as it contains several individual system elements that are a single-point-of-failure. In order to support HA requirements, clustered systems must provide ways to eliminate single-point-of-failures. This will then allow them to be considered for adoption in environments that require high reliability and high availability such as the Telecommunications industry, Network or Application Service Providers (ASP), National Security, Military, etc.

Hardware duplication and network redundancy are common techniques utilized for improving the reliability and availability of computer systems. To achieve an HA-OSCAR cluster system, we must first provide a duplication of the cluster head node. There are different ways for implementing such an architecture, which includes Active-Active, Active-Warm Standby and Active-Cold Standby [7]. Currently, the Active-Active configuration is the model of choice since both head nodes can be simultaneously active to provide services. The dual master nodes will run redundant DHCP, NTP, TFTP, NFS and SNMP servers. In the event of a head node outage, all functionalities provided by that node will fail-over to the second redundant head node and will be served at a reduced performance rate (i.e. in theory, 50% at the peak or busy hours).

An additional HA functionality to support in HA-OSCAR is that of providing a high-availability network via redundant Ethernet ports on every machine in addition to duplicate switching fabrics (network switches, cables, etc.) for the entire network configuration. This will enable every node in the cluster to be present on two or more data paths within its networks. Backed with this Ethernet redundancy, the cluster will achieve higher network availability. Furthermore, when both networks are up, an improved communication performance may be achieved by using techniques such as channel bonding of messages across the redundant communication paths.

Figure 2 shows the HA-OSCAR cluster system architecture. Each of the duplicate server nodes is connected to the external network by two or more different links. These redundant links will keep the system connected to the external environment if one of the network systems should fail. Inside the cluster connectivity, on the private network, each server node is separately connected to two switches and each client node is connected to both switches providing two redundant switching fabrics via the Ethernet connections.

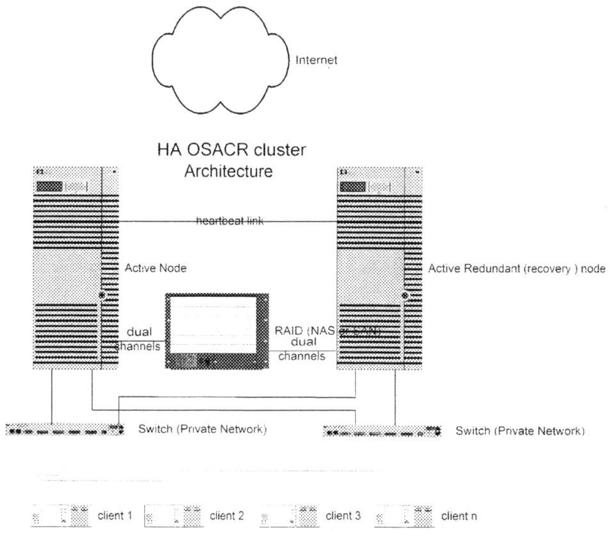

Fig. 2. A HA OSCAR Cluster System

3. System Model

Based on our previous study [8], we select the state-space model for reliability improvement evaluation. Our analysis focuses on servers and switches that dominate cluster availability.

We made several assumptions to reduce the size of the state-space as follows:

- Time of failure for each component is exponentially distributed, with the parameters being λ_{SV} for the servers and λ_{SW} for the switches, respectively.
- Failed components can be repaired.
- Times to repair a server and switches are exponentially distributed with parameters μ and β.
- When the system is down, no further failure can take place. Hence, for OSCAR cluster, when the server is down, no further failure can take place on the switch. Similarly, when the switch is down, no further failure can take place on the server. For the HA-OSCAR cluster, when both servers are down, no further failure can take place on the switches. Likewise, when both switches are down, no further failure can take place on the servers.

The following section contains more details regarding each of the OSCAR system models.

3.1 Classic OSCAR Cluster System Model

The CTMC model corresponding to the OSCAR cluster system is shown in Figure 3. At the state 1, both server nodes and switches are functioning properly. The transition to state 2 occurs if a server node has a failure and the transition from state 1 to state 3 occurs when a switch has a failure. The system will be available for service in state 1, and will be unavailable for state 2 and state 3. The system goes from state 1 to state 2 when server failure occurs at rate λ_{SV}, and from state 1 and to state 3 when switch failure occurs at rate λ_S. After server recovery at rate μ, the system is back in state 1 from state 2. Moreover, after switch recovery at rate β, the system is back in state 1 from state 3. Ultimately, we must try to keep system in the state 1 as long as possible.

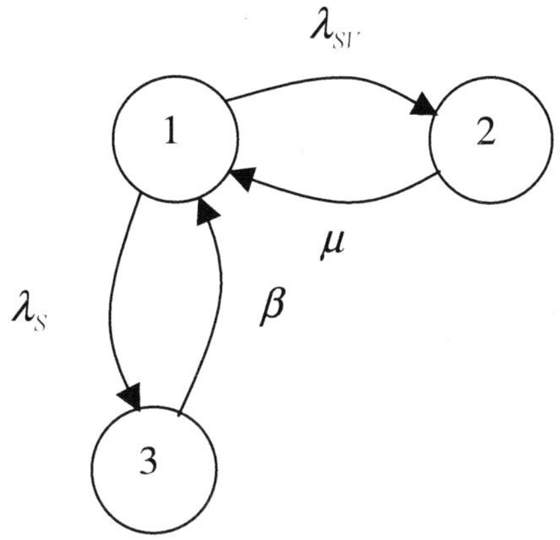

Fig. 3. CTMC for Current OSCAR Cluster System

3.2 HA OSCAR Cluster System Model

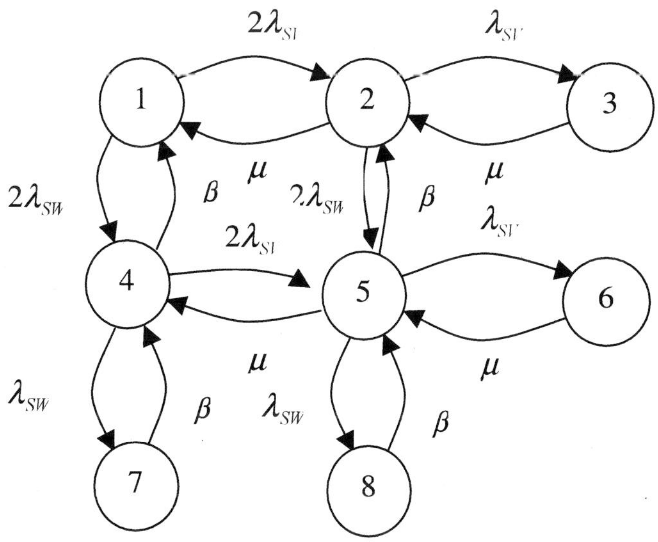

Fig. 4. CTMC for HA-OSCAR Cluster System

The CTMC model corresponding to HA-OSCAR cluster system is shown in Figure 4. The states and their corresponding system status are shown in Table 1. The system will be available for service in states 1, 2, 4 and 5, and will be unavailable during states 2, 6, 7 and 8. The system goes from one state to another at the rates mentioned in the corresponding arrow lines in Figure 4.

Table 1. System Status

State Number	Number of Servers (Up)	Number of Switches (Up)	System Status
1	2	2	Up
2	1	2	Up
3	0	2	Down
4	2	1	Up
5	1	1	Up
6	0	1	Down
7	2	0	Down
8	1	0	Down

4. Availability Analysis

Let π_i be the steady-state probability of state i of the CTMC. They will satisfy the following equations:

$$\pi Q = 0$$

and

$$\sum_{i \in \Omega} \pi_i = 1$$

where Q is the infinitesimal generator matrix [5]. Let U be the set of up states, the availability of the system A is

$$A = \sum_{k \in U} \pi_k$$

4.1 OSCAR Cluster System Analysis

We compute the steady-state probabilities by balance equations, and finally we have the steady-state availability

$$A = \pi_1 = \frac{1}{E} \qquad (1)$$

where

$$E = 1 + \frac{\lambda_{SV}}{\mu} + \frac{\lambda_{SW}}{\beta}.$$

4.2 HA OSCAR Cluster System Analysis

We compute the steady-state probabilities by balance equations, and finally we have the steady-state availability

$$\mathrm{A} = \pi_1 + \pi_2 + \pi_4 + \pi_5$$

$$= \frac{1 + \frac{2\lambda_{SV}}{\mu} + \frac{2\lambda_{SW}}{\beta} + \frac{4\lambda_{SV}\lambda_{SW}}{\mu\beta}}{E} \qquad (2)$$

where

$$E = 1 + \frac{2\lambda_{SV}}{\mu} + \frac{2\lambda_{SW}}{\beta} + \frac{2\lambda_{SV}^2}{\mu^2} + \frac{2\lambda_{SW}^2}{\beta^2} + \frac{4\lambda_{SV}\lambda_{SW}}{\mu\beta} + \frac{4\lambda_{SV}^2\lambda_{SW}}{\mu^2\beta} + \frac{4\lambda_{SV}\lambda_{SW}^2}{\mu\beta^2}$$

4.3 Comparison and Example

For a hypothetical system, we assume that $\lambda_{SV} = 0.001$ hr^{-1}, $\lambda_{SW} = 0.0005\ hr^{-1}$, $\mu = 0.5\ hr^{-1}$, *and* $\beta = 1.0\ hr^{-1}$. By formula 1 and 2, we can calculate the availability of the system. The availability for OSCAR cluster is 0.996, and the availability for the HA-OSCAR cluster is 0.99999. The downtime of the two systems in a year is 39.2 hours and 4.45 minutes, respectively. Typically, a high-availability system is one that has a downtime that does not exceed "five-nines" or 0.99999.

5. Conclusions and Future Work

Through the analysis and comparison of the theoretical dependability of OSCAR and HA-OSCAR cluster systems, we are able to conclude that the availability of HA-OSCAR cluster systems can be significantly higher than that of OSCAR cluster systems without going through the actual cluster construction process. This encouraging result has convinced us to pursue an experimental development of a prototype HA-OSCAR system infrastructure. We plan to explore additional ways to extend the availability, robustness and reliability of an HA-OSACR system already in development. We expect that a successful HA-OSCAR implementation will spur an increased adoption of OSCAR in the enterprise and mission-critical computing environments.

6. References

1 The Open Cluster Group, *OSCAR: A packaged Cluster Software stack for High Performance Computing*, http://www.openclustergroup.org/

2 S.L. Scott, T. Naughton, B. Barrett, J. Squyres, A. Lumsdaine, Y.C. Fang, and V. Mashayekhi, *Looking Inside the OSCAR Cluster Toolkit*, Dell Power Solution magazine (online and printed editions), http://www.dell.com/us/en/esg/topics/power_ps4q02-oscar.htm, November 2002.

3 I. Haddad, F. Rossi, C. Leangsuksun, S. L. Scott, *Telecom/High Availability OSCAR Suggestions for the 2nd Generation OSCAR, Technical Report TR-LTU-12-2002-01*, Computer Science Program, Louisiana Tech University, December 2002.

4 J. Muppala, M. Malhotra, K. S. Trivedi, *Markov Dependability Models of Complex Systems: Analysis Techniques, Reliability and Maintenance of Complex Systems*, S. Ozekici (ed.), pp. 442-486, Springer-Verlag, Berlin, 1996.

5 K. S. Trivedi, *Probability and Statistics with Reliability, Queuing, and Computer Science Applications*, John Wiley and Sons, New York, 2001.

6 http://www.ee.duke.edu/~kst

7 P. S. Weygant, Cluster for high availability: a primer of HP solutions, 2nd ed., 2001, Hewlett-Packard Company, Prentice-Hall, Inc.

8 S. Lixin, and C. Leangsuksun, Techniques for System Dependability Evaluation, *Technical Report TR-LTU-09-2002-01*, Computer Science Program, Louisiana Tech University, September 2002.

Efficient and Accurate Tracing of Events in Linux Clusters

Michel Dagenais[a], Richard Moore[b], Robert Wisniewski[c], Karim Yaghmour[d], Thomas Zanussi[e]

[a]Ecole Polytechnique de Montreal

[b]IBM Linux Technical Center

[c]IBM Research

[d]Opersys Inc.

[e]IBM Linux Technical Center

The Linux Trace Toolkit is a low overhead, accurate, extensible tracing infrastructure for Linux systems. It is used extensively for embedded systems and is included in all major Linux distributions targeting embedded systems. It was recently optimized and expanded to offer per CPU lockless tracing and near clock cycle level accuracy, making it suitable for high performance SMP systems. Further work is underway to manipulate several traces side by side, typically collected on parallel systems within a cluster, and to allow custom trace analysis plugin modules. This makes the Linux Trace Toolkit particularly suited for performance analysis and debugging of high performance SMP clusters. Indeed, it can collect unobtrusively and most accurately any needed information directly from the operating system or the applications and offers a convenient offline graphical display and analysis tool.

Le projet Linux Trace Toolkit est une infrastructure précise utilisant très peu de ressources additionnelles permettant d'enregistrer les évèmements d'un système Linux. Ce programme est très utilisé dans les système embarqués et est inclu dans toutes les grandes distributions Linux dédiées aux systèmes embarqués. Il a été très récemment optimisé et amélioré pour fournir des enregistrements sans verrouillage et par processeur à une précision de l'ordre du cycle d'horloge du processeur, ce qui le rend intéressant pour les système haute performance de type SMP. Des travaux additionnels sont en cours pour manipuler plusieurs traces collectées sur un cluster et pour permettre une analyse facile des résultats à l'aide de modules additionnels dédiés à l'analyse. Ceci rend Linux Trace Toolkit particulièrement intéressant pour l'analyse et le déverminage d'applications parallèles sur cluster. En effet, il est possible de récupérer sans verouillage et avec une grande précision tous les évènements produits par le système d'exploitation et par les applications puis de les analyser et de les afficher de manière graphique une fois les traces effectuées.

1 Introduction

Several tools may be used for performance analysis. Coverage analysis tools [1] obtain a precise count of instructions executed in a program, a strong indication of the processing time required. Profilers [2] use sampling at regular time intervals to statistically determine the time spent in each function. Some profilers use hardware performance counters [3] to obtain program counter samples correlated to metrics other than CPU time, for instance cache misses, mispredicted branches or pipeline stalls. For CPU intensive applications, these tools produce useful and reasonably accurate measurements.

However, this may not be sufficient for applications, or portions thereof, where interactions between one or more processes and the operating system impact significantly the performance. In many cases, resources managed by the operating system may indeed strongly affect the performance. This includes disk heads scheduling, I/O buffer cache, virtual memory management, signal delivery, interprocess communication, network I/O and locking.

Tracing all system calls for one or more processes may be achieved through the Linux *ptrace* system call, for instance using *strace* or *GDB*. This is often helpful to understand the interactions between the processes and the operating system. However, in many cases, the timing is changed significantly, producing grossly inaccurate performance data and even changing the behavior of asynchronous processes.

2 The Linux Trace Toolkit

The Linux Trace Toolkit (LTT) [4] offers a low overhead detailed trace of all significant operating system events. Every time a system call, interrupt, scheduling change or other important operating system event occurs, a few bytes are written to a trace buffer. In contrast, the ptrace interface requires two or more context switches for each event, and has only access to system call and signal events. When the trace buffer is full, tracing continues in another buffer while the first buffer is copied asynchronously to disk. The trace daemon, responsible for writing the trace buffer to disk, has shared memory access to the in kernel trace buffer, thus avoiding any buffer copying in memory.

The resulting performance allows full tracing of a system with heavy interactive load (which is very demanding for the tracing system) with an overhead of less than 5% [4]. The Linux Trace Toolkit has been used successfully to study the performance of the Linux virtual memory subsystem and of many real time applications in embedded Linux systems.

The Linux Trace Toolkit is currently being enhanced in

several ways, and is becoming even better suited for high performance Symmetric Multi-Processor (SMP) systems and clusters. The enhancements recently completed or under way are described in the following sections.

2.1 Functionality Layering

The Linux Trace Toolkit is currently distributed as a separate patch to apply to the Linux kernel, thus requiring downloading the Linux kernel source and LTT, and recompiling the patched kernel. It has been submitted for inclusion in the Linux Kernel since it is very useful in its own right, and it could serve as an efficient underlying tracing mechanism for other existing applications such as printk and Evlog [5].

While all these applications need to efficiently accumulate trace information and communicate it to a user level daemon, their different scope may motivate different choices in terms of event creation API, trace format, time granularity and notification mechanisms. For this reason, a new *data relay* file system, *relayfs*, was created to handle in a generic way the creation, buffering and delivery of data between the kernel and a user level daemon.

When a *relayfs* object is created in the kernel, buffers are allocated and a new filename becomes visible in the *relayfs* filesystem. The *relayfs* object is then used to write data as needed. Whenever a buffer start or buffer end is encountered, the relayfs object activates callback functions. These functions are specified at creation time and may be used to write any application specific (e.g., LTT, Evlog) buffer start and buffer end data.

The file associated with a *relayfs* object may be opened by a user level daemon, subject to usual file access permissions. The opened file may then be used in one of two modes. Read events from the file one by one, blocking or non-blocking. Memory map the file and thus obtain shared memory access to the trace buffers as well as notification each time a buffer is full.

Relayfs offers all the functionality required by LTT, yet is equally applicable to other logging or tracing systems such as printk and Evlog. Indeed, the exact trace format, time granularity, or number of buffers per CPU is unspecified at this level.

2.2 Minimizing Contention in SMP Systems

The latest stable release of LTT used a single set of tracing buffers, used by all processors in a SMP system, and protected by locking. This was replaced in the development version by lockless, per CPU, trace buffers. When an event arises on a processor, space is reserved in the associated trace buffer using an atomic operation, and the event data is written to the reserved space. If the process is interrupted before writing the data, the space in the buffer remains properly reserved, and any other event created gets space allocated sequentially in the trace buffer. Thus, there is no blocking lock involved, and tracing is allowed everywhere, even in interrupt routines.

Events created on different processors within a SMP system are written to separate, per CPU, trace buffers. No global locking is therefore necessary and cache conflicts are avoided, unlike with shared trace buffers.

2.3 Time granularity

The latest stable release of LTT uses the real time clock (gettimeofday) as timestamp for each event. The cost of calling gettimeofday is non negligible and its time granularity is limited. The development version now directly reads the processor cycle counter, if available. Cycle counters are fast to read but may reflect time inaccurately. Indeed, the exact clock frequency varies with time as the processor temperature changes, influenced by the external temperature and its workload. Moreover, in SMP systems, the clock of individual processors may vary independently.

LTT corrects the clock inaccuracy by reading the real time clock value and the 64 bits cycle counter periodically, at the beginning of each block, and at each 10ms. This way, it is sufficient to read only the lower 32 bits of the cycle counter at each event. The associated real time value may then be obtained by linear interpolation between the nearest full cycle counter and real time values. Therefore, for the average cost of reading and storing the lower 32 bits of the cycle counter at each event, the real time with full resolution is obtained at analysis time.

2.4 Tracing at all Times

LTT currently starts tracing when enabled by the tracing daemon, and the trace is obtained when filled event buffers are written to disk. There are many difficult to diagnose problems which occur at other times and cannot easily be traced using the current version of LTT.

Boot time tracing will be obtained by allocating a static buffer to receive events until the tracing facility itself is properly initialized. The events will then be copied from the static buffer to the regular LTT buffers.

Similarly, when a system crashes, the tracing daemon does not have time to save on disk the events in the yet unfilled tracing buffer. Yet, those are often the most interesting events for the system engineer. By integrating LTT to the Linux Kernel Crash Dump facility [6], it will be possible to recover from memory the unfilled buffer upon the soft reboot following the crash.

Transient problems are another difficult category to study. Enabling tracing for long periods of time incurs a reasonable system overhead, but the disk space required for the trace soon becomes prohibitive, as it may reach 1MB/s. The solution is to periodically overwrite the trace data, only keeping the last few minutes or the last hour. Whenever the transient problem is encountered, the tracing may be stopped before overwriting the events associated with the problem just noticed.

2.5 New Events

Event types in LTT are currently defined as packed C structures in the kernel, and accessed using corresponding structure definitions in the LTT visualiser. Custom event types may be defined at run time using a textual description, but creating custom events is slightly less efficient than builtin event types. Adding new builtin event types requires modifying and recompiling both the kernel and the LTT visualiser.

In development is a simple event type description format, used at kernel compilation time to generate the needed event type declarations. The same description is used at runtime by the LTT visualiser to properly interpret event types in traces. Checksums are used to verify that the event type descriptions provided to the trace visualiser are those used in the kernel which generated the trace to visualise.

This new scheme even allows dynamically loaded modules to define new event types, or new versions of event types.

2.6 Adding Analysis Tools

As it became more widely disseminated, LTT has been used for many new applications. In each case, new event types and new specialised computations were required. Examples include the detailed analysis of process elapsed time (e.g., 3.56s waiting for process X, 1.24s waiting for page faults on file Y...) and a study of average block device queue length and processing time. Under development is a tool to correlate traces from several communicating nodes within a cluster.

Each specialised analysis requires the insertion of new code in the LTT visualiser main processing loop, a software development and maintenance nightmare. To solve this problem, the visualiser is being rearchitected. The new modular design allows dynamic loading of modules and provides hooks at numerous places to let the modules perform conveniently the desired computations. Furthermore, a hierarchical *property* table is associated with each important object in the visualiser (trace, process, CPU, device...). This way, modules can store and accumulate computed statistics as needed during the trace processing phase, and print the results at the end, all using generic hooks. This keeps the modules completely decoupled from the visualiser.

3 Discussion

The Linux Trace Toolkit is widely used in embedded Linux development. It can already provide very useful information for performance measuring and understanding in high performance SMP distributed systems. As the new discussed features are completed, it will become even more accurate, less intrusive and easier to use in high performance SMP distributed systems.

Tracing systems have existed in the past. The distinguishing feature of LTT is the freely available source code of both the operating system and the tracing tool. Not only can LTT benefit from contributions of the community, it enables its interoperability with other useful tools like Dynamic Probes [7] and the Linux Kernel Crash Dump facility [6]. Moreover, it is possible to add tracepoints anywhere in the Linux kernel and thus obtain precise traces for any desired event in Linux.

References

1. Gcov a test coverage program, 14 March 2003. http://gcc.gnu.org/onlinedocs/gcc-3.2.2/gcc/Gcov.html.
2. Gnu gprof, 14 March 2003. http://sources.redhat.com/binutils/docs-2.12/gprof.info/index.html.
3. Oprofile, 14 March 2003. http://oprofile.sourceforge.net/.
4. Karim Yaghmour and Michel R. Dagenais. Measuring and characterizing system behavior using kernel-level event logging. In *Proceedings of the USENIX Annual 2000 Technical Conference*, pages 13–26, San Diego, California, USA, June 2000.
5. Linux event logging for enterprise-class systems, 14 March 2003. http://evlog.sourceforge.net/.
6. Linux kernel crash dumps, 14 March 2003. http://lkcd.sourceforge.net/.
7. Dynamic probes, 14 March 2003. http://www-124.ibm.com/developerworks/oss/linux/projects/dprobes/.

Effective HPC Hardware Management and Failure Prediction Strategy Using IPMI

Richard Libby[a,i]

[a]HPC Technical Marketing Engineer, Intel Corporation; OSCAR Working Group, OSCAR Steering Committee
rml@hpc.intel.com

Intelligent Power Management Interface (IPMI) defines common interfaces to "intelligent" hardware used to monitor a server's physical health characteristics, such as temperature, voltage, fans, power supplies and chassis. These capabilities provide information that enables system management, recovery, and asset tracking which help drive down the total cost of ownership (TCO) and increase reliability in today's HPC market. The new interfaces in IPMI v1.5 facilitate the management of rack-mounted HPC servers and systems in remote environment over serial, modem and LAN connections. New capabilities combined with the remote management functionality allow HPC IT managers to manage their servers and systems, regardless of system health, power state or supported communication media. IPMI compliant servers essentially eliminate the need for external hardware to perform the same function, thus saving costs. This paper will introduce the specification, the benefits of IPMI with respect to HPC and other clusters and how it could be used to generate alarms to a monitoring system before hardware failures become severe enough to cause cluster failure.

Intelligent Power Management Interface (IPMI) définit une interface pour du matériel "intelligent" utilisé pour surveilleur les caractéristique de fonctionnement d'un serveur comme la température du processeur, la tension aux bornes de la carte mère, la vitesse de rotation des ventilateurs et du chassis. Ces sondes fournissent l'information nécessaire pour gérer ces systèmes, les remettre en fonction et la surveillance du matériel ce qui aide à réduire le coût total d'acquisition et à augmenter la disponibilité du système. Les nouvelles interfaces définies dans IMPI v1.5 facilite la gestion des serveurs montés sur cabinets (racks) grace à une gestion à distance via un cable série, via modem ou encore via un réseau local (LAN). De nouvelles fonctionnalités, jumelées à l'accès à distance de celles-ci, permet aux administrateurs de gérer au mieux leurs serveurs et autres systèmes et ce sans aucune perte d'information liée à une perte de communication, une défaillance matérielle ou encore même une panne de courant. Les serveurs conformes à IPMI éliminent la nécessité de recourrir à une solution matérielle extérieure offrant des services équivalents, ce qui contribue également à réduire les coûts. Nous introduirons dans cet article les spécifications ainsi que l'intérêt d'IPMI dans un environnement de type cluster dédié au calcul haute performance ainsi que la manière dont IPMI peut être utilisé pour déclencher des alarmes avant qu'une panne se produise et ne paralyse tout le cluster.

Introduction

If we were to look at what hinders large scale cluster deployments, only a handful of barriers come to mind. There is, of course, always the barrier of limited bandwidth, be it in the front side bus, the interconnect or any other form of I/O. Others include space, power, cooling, monitoring and management. This paper will focus on monitoring, management and predictive analysis: essentially overall HPC health and 'sickness prevention'. Intelligent Power Management Interface (hereafter referred to as IPMI) is an abstracted hardware layer that provides power control, alerting, sensor monitoring, Field Replaceable Unit (FRU) storage, Sensor Data Record (SDR) storage, customization, configuration all through multiple methods of secure access. The total cost of a hardware and software package has come down from US$30/node to sub US$10, making management a viable solution to reduce the total cost of ownership (TCO).

The IPMI specification itself is a mere 450 pages, and the other supporting documents (four of them [Reference section: C, D, F & H], plus 23 referenced documents or RFCs) make for a good, long weekend of reading. This paper is a brief summary on how to use IPMI to get the most out managing large scale HPC deployments, and be able to use it to predict failures before they happen, thereby reducing the TCO of the entire system. The assumption is made in this paper that IPMI is implemented with strict consideration to the specifications.

Power Control

Hardware management of large scale HPC deployments today is quite possible if you have access to many people, infinite resources, or a magic wand. Since most of us have either none of these (in the case of the magic wand), or limited amounts of them (in the case of many people and infinite amounts of money), managing large scale deployments of anything is quite a chore. What do we really mean by 'managing?' Most think of managing a cluster as isolated systems: hardware and software. I would submit that it is a combination of both. If hardware fails, so does software. If software fails, hardware becomes a really expensive room heater. So, management becomes the ability to control software by looking at hardware as one failure point, or have the software control the hardware if thresholds increase beyond set limits. These control methods include powering off a server, powering on a server, resetting a server, and obtaining status of the power condition.

Resetting the server from a remote location seems trivial to most. "Why not just execute a command such a remote 'init 6' (Soft reset)?" or something similar depending on the operating system some might ask. Ah, but what happens if the operating system is hung? Oh, just send one of your people down and hit the reset button. In the case of the TeraGrid[i] project, that may not be possible since there are at least four sites where the HPC might be at. So, a system reset function has gone from being a trivial action to a not-so-trivial action. Using IPMI, a system reset is trivial with a mere command.

Powering on and off a system is not quite as trivial to achieve. Sure it is, you say. You go out and purchase a network power switch, and spend about US$500.00 in the process. Ok, so you _can_ achieve power control this way, but not cost effectively in a large scale HPC deployment. Let's say for example, that at best you could control eight machines with one network power switch. At US$63 per outlet, 256 outlets would cost you US$16k, 512 outlets would cost US$32k and 1000 outlets would cost US$63K. This adds only a little to the overall cost, but hey, if it is offered with an IPMI compliant server, you could use this additional money to purchase more servers. There's more on powering on and off, but it will be covered in another section.

In addition to being able to reset, power on and off, having the ability to query the server power status is also valuable. Instead of having to force power off (if on and vice versa), potentially losing a job or data, you can query to see if the server's power is on or off. This seems rather trivial at times, but in some instances when there is no OS available and the server is not in any proximity to you, it is nice to have this feature.

Lastly, one nice control feature is telling the UID light what to do, and how long to do it for. This is the little blue light found on the front and rear of most servers that turns on to identify it from other servers in cases of large scale HPC build-outs.

Alerting

Power control is essential, but from a predictive failure analysis standpoint, alerting is the driving force of determining if any one point of the HPC is suffering. Think of the alerting component as pain identification. This identification breaks down into event filtering, trapping (via SNMP), and policy management. Some aspects will not be mentioned fully, as they will be covered in other sections.

Without going into too much depth, when the Baseboard Management Controller (BMC, a.k.a. the service processor) observes an event that occurs (see sensor section for types of events that might be interesting), it logs it into non-volatile space into a Server Event Log (SEL). Events generated either externally or internally are run through a filter within the BMC that can perform actions based on policies (more on policies later). These types of events might indicate impending danger of catastrophic events on any one machine, or in more serious cases, could indicate rack-wide implications, such as a fire. The ability to filter events combined with policy management gives the HPC administrator a powerful tool in predicting impending failure.

One of the keys to being able to predict (and later analyze) whether there is an impending failure, is knowing about it. The trapping component forwards on messages via SNMP to a "Health Master" that could look at the event (and compare it against a set of policies), determine if it was critical enough to ruin jobs on that node, and take appropriate action(s).

Policies can be set up to read either discrete or threshold-based values and define an action based on the type of event it is. For example, if a server in your HPC had a fan failure, the most likely thing you would see from an end user point of view is to hear the other fans ramp up. That action is an event that was driven by the BMC through a policy that was set either by a factory setting, or specified by an administrator programmatically. Once the other fans were ramped up to compensate for the missing fan, alerts can be trapped and sent via any number of methods to the "health master," which in turn, can determine (possibly by it's own set of policies) if the event warrants moving data or jobs from one machine to a spare. Data can be recorded and analyzed later for recurring trends or even external environment conditions that might be causing failures. One example of this might be as follows: One rack might be sitting directly under a cooling source. The racks adjoining it would read higher ambient chassis temperature, and show skewed temperature data, but with the information, a stealthy sysadmin could correlate the HVAC 'on' times with a drop in ambient temperature inside the rack that gets hit with a blast of cool air. Although this condition in and of itself is not bad, one set of servers in the HPC might run faster due to being slightly cooler and cause other bottlenecks.

Common Sensor Model

So, what can IPMI in its present state touch and feel? Presently, it includes voltage, temperature, fan speeds, and presence.

Servers based on IPMI give the ability to monitor voltages on the baseboard and power supply. In cases where there is a lot of solar spot activity, this data could be useful. For example, too many voltage changes, and memory might start to have single bit errors, and too many of those might generate a multi-bit error that is not recoverable. From an industrial and commercial perspective, if the server suffered this, jobs would either be lost, or potentially have silent data corruption. Having the ability to monitor and log this data could be useful to see if there were external environment conditions that would impact server stability. In this particular example, a sysadmin might want to spec out Telco grade hardware that runs on DC power, thereby eliminating the external condition and increasing reliability.

With the tight thermal tolerances these days, a fan failure in server chassis can result in a catastrophic loss, especially in the smaller form factors (i.e. 1U). Having the ability to monitor fan speeds can greatly increase the chance of keeping jobs that are running on one member of the HPC and moving them to another, provided the event deems it worthy of doing so. This does not just include chassis fans, but can be expanded to include processor, memory, and hard drive bay fans.

Temperature is a key aspect to monitor for predicting failure in an HPC. Logging events, using stats to show trends, and reacting to generated alerts are the ways to decrease a sysadmin's possibilities of downtime. It will also increase the ability to determine external environment conditions that would affect HPC performance, since heat is a critical aspect.

The last aspect of the common sensor model is the ability to detect presence. At times it would be nice to detect if the server chassis lid was opened. The system might log an entry into the SEL based on chassis intrusion. This might be useful information later on to determine causes of ambient temperature changes, or even to determine what time the processors and memory disappeared out of the best server.

Access Methods

Ok, so we are able to monitor all these cool things on our server, but how does the sysadmin or developer _*really*_ get to them? There are multiple methods to get the information you need from an IPMI-based server. They include KCS, LAN, serial, modem, I^2C, IPMB and ICMB. None of these methods will be discussed in too much detail here due to space and scope constraints.

One of the most common methods to get to the BMC is through an interface called Keyboard Controller Style (KCS). For IPMI laymen, this means a driver that is loaded and controlled through the OS. This is the preferred method to access the Intelligent Power Management Bus (IPMB), but certainly not the only one, and certainly in cases where the OS has gone south for the winter.

If the OS does go south, another nice method is using the Remote Management Control Protocol (RMCP) over the LAN. IPMI-based servers have 3.3 volts standby power that provides the BMC with enough juice to live on. With the cost of network interface cards (NIC) coming down, and many board manufacturers placing them on their server boards, this becomes the avenue on which to send UDP packets directed to port 623 that can issue IPMI commands. This becomes a close second to the KCS in that it replaces legacy serial concentration servers, allowing the sysadmin or IT manager to spend their ~US$50K (for every 40 ports and ~US$1.2M for 1000 servers) elsewhere on the HPC.

Other methods of access include direct serial using a serial concentration server. The downside to this interface is the cost for the serial concentration server. One nice feature worth mentioning in a Linux environment is Serial Over LAN (SOL). This allows the HPC sysadmin to enable serial redirect and have it piped over the network interface, thereby eliminating the need for a Keyboard-Video-Mouse controller (KVM). Costs are exorbitant and cabling becomes a nightmare for large scale HPC deployments. (Other features include private management bus (private I2C bus), and ability to add above board remote management cards.)

One nice feature of IPMI is the ability to forward information on to other IPMI compliant servers. Essentially, each IPMI server can become a proxy to relay messages to another IPMB through the Intelligent Chassis Management Bus (ICMB). A sysadmin or network architect could design an ICMB network (really an RS-845 multiport serial bus) that would allow up to 64 nodes per network. Management packets could be routed over this network instead of tying up the LAN channel, or in cases when the LAN was down, routing over ICMB. RS-845 also allows broadcasts, so the sysadmin could invoke a broadcast to a bank of servers. Imagine it, a command that said: "hello rack of servers, shut down."

Authentication

All the methods of access are excellent to have, but how are they protected against intrusion? This section briefly discusses the channel privilege levels and encryption methods used to authenticate to the BMC.

There are four privilege levels to the BMC as defined by the IPMI specification: callback, user, operator, and administrative.

Callback is essentially irrelevant these days. It calls only a predefined number via a modem. It also only supports enough commands to initiate a callback. If the user is not at that location, then callback is not highly useful.

One nice channel privilege is called user. It would allow subsystems to monitor HPCs without being intrusive, and potentially lethal from a job perspective. Think of this privilege as 'sensor snag' only—essentially read-only or only benign commands are allowed. From a predictive analysis perspective, this level would give alerting mechanisms with the peace of mind that power control could be assigned to alternate members of the HPC.

Occasionally though, job scalability demands delegation of authority, but not total relinquishing of control. In these cases, the operator privilege level should be chosen. It has all commands available to administration, except configuration commands that can change the behavior of the out-of-band interfaces.

And then you have full rights—administrative privilege level. This privilege allows for full control over an IPMI-based server. In simple "health master" implementations, this would be the preferred privilege level to use. One quick word of caution: an administrative privilege level can even disable the channel they are coming in over...

Encryption is tied closely to authentication. There are basically three main points to remember on IPMI encryption. The first is that passwords can be sent clear-text, so from a security standpoint, it is something to consider. The second is that whatever the user initiates as an encryption algorithm is what will be returned, provided it falls into the third category. That is that there are generally two supported encryption algorithms, MD2 and MD5.

Field Replaceable Units (FRU)

An enterprise-class system will typically have FRU information for each major system board (e.g. processor board, memory board, I/O board, etc.). The FRU data can include information such as serial number, part number, model, and asset tag. What is this really good for in a failure prediction situation? Well, the "health master" could be programmed such that it could detect that a remote server's part is going to have a failure (let's just say overheating CPU), look up the part in a parts database, and alert the sysadmin which part they need to take with them to service the unit, what the unit serial number is, and possibly when it was last serviced. It would minimize downtime. By the way, FRU information can even be available when the system is powered down. Another useful example of FRUs being used is automated remote inventory. "IPMI does not seek to replace other FRU or inventory data mechanisms, such as those provided by SM BIOS, and PCI Vital Product Data. Rather, IPMI FRU information is typically used to complement that information or to provide information access out-of-band or under 'system down' conditions."[ii]

Sensor Data Records

IPMI was created with extensibility and scalability in mind. Unfortunately, with that capability comes a myriad of different components that can be monitored and controlled in different fashions. Sensor Data Records (SDRs) provide system management software the ability to retrieve information from the platform, and automatically configure itself to meet the capabilities of the platform—essentially an abstraction layer.

SDRs exist primarily to describe to server management software what a sensor configuration should look like, and to tell software to pay special attention to certain sub functions. SDRs are mostly not available to end users, but could potentially, especially if purchasing a board and chassis separately. For the most part, SDRs are made specifically for certain configurations of board/chassis combinations.

SDRs also define thresholds and actions based on those thresholds. For example, there might be an upper critical threshold on a board thermal sensor, and that might be tied via an SDR to an action of ramping up fans if excessive heat was detected. From a failure prediction standpoint, the "health master" could detect these changes, and ramp fans accordingly. This is just one small case, but you can see that the permutations get quite large with more servers in your HPC. What kind of sensor types are there? Two main categories exist—analog or digital, or fan, voltage, temperature. SDRs tell the BMC what the sensor type is in order to know how to process it (i.e. analog fan situation: you actually get a voltage back when polling it. The software will need to convert it via a mathematical function (a slope function: logarithmic, square root, quadratic, sin and many more defined in the IPMI spec.)

Realistically, the types of information that SDRs can store configuration on are: CPU sensors, chassis intrusion, power supply monitoring, fan speeds, fan presence, board voltages, board temperatures, bus errors, memory errors, and even possibly ASF progress codes (where the subsystem is in coming up—essentially a POST code). "Sensor Data Records are kept in a single, centralized non-volatile storage area that is managed by the BMC. This storage is called the Sensor Data Record Repository (SDR Repository). Implementing the SDR Repository via the BMC provides a mechanism that allows SDRs to be retrieved via 'out-of-band' interfaces, such as the ICMB, a Remote Management Card, or other device connected to the IPMB. Like most Intelligent Platform Management features, this allows SDR information to be obtained independent of the main processors, BIOS, system management software, and the OS."[iii]

System Event Log

Every IPMI compliant server has a System Event Log (SEL) which is a centralized, non-volatile repository for all events generated. Think of this not only as a BMC journal. Any authenticated user can enter a SEL entry.

Common events that might be stored are reboots, processors offline, memory (both single and multiple bit) errors, sensors that go beyond set thresholds, PCI parity errors (PERR), Non-maskable interrupts (NMI), and many more. The "health master" could periodically poll select system event logs from the HPC, and determine if there are potential problems that could be coming down the wire, and mitigate a response to those problems.

Alerting is done off the SEL as well. When an event is written to the SEL, it is checked against policies and threshold values, and performs actions based on those policies. Too much of a health conscious sysadmin could put in place tighter thresholds, and decrease the possibility of downtime, while at the same time possibly risking more time checking out false alarms. A truly health conscious sysadmin would determine standard thresholds to work with safely, while keeping in mind that a false alarm here and there might keep them on their toes and possibly prevent a catastrophic failure on a node (or more in some cases).

Clearing the SEL is possible as well, in fact, once a SEL is queried and data is stored on the "health master", it is advisable to clear the SEL. The main reason for this is that if the SEL fills up, new entries are dropped. This could cause a sysadmin to miss critical events that could lead either to extensive downtime, or a catastrophe.

Configuration

IPMI gives such flexibility that many aspects can be configured to fit the end-user's needs.

These parameters include: BMC policies, LAN configuration (such as static or dynamic IP address, mask, and gateway), privilege levels, alerting functions (such as whom to forward alerts to), sensor polling rates, etc.

Imagine for a moment that your "health master" detects that it one of the nodes in the HPC is going down due to some failure, and you are able to retrieve the critical data off the hard drive. When you bring up a spare node in it's place, you can dump the hard drive data back down, right? Sure, but what about BMC configuration? This is where IPMI shines through if implemented properly. With most IPMI compliant servers today, a sysadmin can retrieve the BMC information. But stuffing it back onto another machine is a little trickier, especially if it is over the LAN interface.

QUESTIONS USERS MIGHT ASK

A few questions might remain in the reader's mind still after this brief whetting. One such question might be, "What is the relationship or difference between IPMI and Alert Standard Forum (ASF)?" "While somewhat of an oversimplification, ASF may be considered to be scoped for 'desktop/mobile' class systems, and IPMI for 'servers' where the additional IPMI capabilities such as event logging, multiple users, remote authentication, multiple transports, management extension busses, sensor access, etc., are valued. However there are no restrictions in either specification as to the class of system that the specification can be used. [(i.e.)] you can use IPMI for desktop and mobile systems and ASF for servers if the level of manageability fits your requirements."[iv]

Another might be, I don't have IPMI capable servers today, can I add in an IPMI card? The short answer to that question is possibly, but it depends on your server base board. Provided it has an interface to IPMB, the possibilities increase. But, the best thing to do is to weigh the costs associated with not having IPMI (as mentioned earlier—no KVM, network power switch, serial concentration server) and see what benefits it can bring to predict an impending failure before it happens.

Summary

The key to using IPMI for failure prediction analysis is the polling and listening software, and how intelligent it is at analyzing the data to make predictions as to where problems lie.

As most HPC sysadmin's know, one large scale cluster deployment barrier is management, monitoring, fault isolation and failure prediction. IPMI enables a sysadmin a great way to reduce the TCO of HPCs by monitoring overall HPC health and 'prevent sickness' by providing an abstracted hardware layer that provides power control, alerting, sensor monitoring, Field Replaceable Unit (FRU) storage, Sensory Data Record (SDR) storage, customization, configuration all through multiple methods of secure access—all through software.

Call to action

When writing RFQs, make sure to include IPMI as a required feature in order to reduce TCO and increase manageability in HPC deployments.

References

A. *Alert Standard Format v1.0 Specification*, ©2001, Distributed Management Task Force. http://www.dmtf.org

B. *The I^2C Bus And How To Use It*, ©1995, Philips Semiconductors. This document provides the timing and electrical specifications for I2C busses.

C. *Intelligent Chassis Management Bus Bridge Specification v1.0, rev. 1.2*, © 2000 Intel Corporation. Provides the electrical, transport protocol, and specific command specifications for the ICMB and information on the creation of management controllers that connect to the ICMB. http://developer.intel.com/design/servers/ipmi

D. *Intelligent Platform Management Bus Communications Protocol Specification v1.0*, ©1998 Intel Corporation, Hewlett-Packard Company, NEC Corporation, and Dell Computer Corporation. This document provides the electrical, transport protocol, and specific command specifications for the IPMB. http://developer.intel.com/design/servers/ipmi

E. *Intelligent Power Management Interface Specification v1.5; rev. 1.1*, ©2002 Intel Corporation, Hewlett-Packard Company, NEC Corporation, and Dell Computer Corporation. http://developer.intel.com/design/servers/ipmi

F. *IPMI Platform Event Trap Format Specification v1.0*, ©1998, Intel Corporation, Hewlett-Packard Company, NEC Corporation, and Dell Computer Corporation. This document specifies a common format for SNMP Traps for platform events.

G. *Proposal for Callback Control Protocol (CBCP)*, draft-ietf-pppext-callback-cp-02.txt, N. Gidwani, Microsoft, July 19, 1994. As of this writing, the specification is available via the Microsoft Corporation web site: http://www.microsoft.com

H. *Platform Management FRU Information Storage Definition v1.0*, ©1999 Intel Corporation, Hewlett-

Packard Company, NEC Corporation, and Dell Computer Corporation. Provides the field definitions and format of Field Replaceable Unit (FRU) information.
http://developer.intel.com/design/servers/ipmi

I. *RFC 1319, The MD2 Message-Digest Algorithm*, B. Kaliski, RSA Laboratories, April 1992.

J. *RFC 1321, The MD5 Message-Digest Algorithm*, R. Rivest, MIT Laboratory for Computer Science and RSA Data Security, Inc. April, 1992.

K. *System Management BIOS Specification*, Version 2.3.1, © 1997, 1999 American Megatrends Inc., Award Software International, Compaq Computer Corporation, Dell Computer Corporation, Hewlett-Packard Company, Intel Corporation, International Business Machines Corporation, Phoenix Technologies Limited, and SystemSoft Corporation.

L. *System Management Bus (SMBus) Specification*, Version 2.0, ©2000, Duracell Inc., Fujitsu Personal Systems Inc., Intel Corporation, Linear Technology Corporation, Maxim Integrated Products, Mitsubishi Electric Corporation, Moltech Power Systems, PowerSmart Inc., Toshiba Battery Co., Ltd., Unitrode Corporation, USAR Systems.

M. *The TeraGrid Project*, National Center for Supercomputing Applications, San Diego Supercomputer Center, Argonne National Laboratory and Pittsburgh Supercomputing Center; http://www.teragrid.org

N. *Wired for Management Baseline Version 2.0 Release*, ©1998, Intel Corporation. Attachment A, UUIDs and GUIDs, provides information specifying the formatting of the IPMI Device GUID and FRU GUID and the System Management BIOS (SM BIOS) UUID unique IDs.

O. Glossary of terms

Term	Definition
BMC	Baseboard Management Controller
CMOS	In terms of this specification, this describes the PC-AT compatible region of battery-backed 128 bytes of memory, which normally resides on the baseboard.
Diagnostic Interrupt	A non-maskable interrupt or signal for generating diagnostic traces and 'core dumps' from the operating system. Typically NMI on IA-32 systems, and an INIT on Itanium™-based systems.
EFI	Extensible Firmware Interface. A new model for the interface between operating systems and platform firmware. The interface consists of data tables that contain platform-related information, plus boot and runtime service calls that are available to the operating system and its loader. Together, these provide a standard environment for booting an operating system and running pre-boot applications.
FRB	Fault Resilient Booting. A term used to describe system features and algorithms that improve the likelihood of the detection of, and recovery from, processor failures in a multiprocessor system.
FRU	Field Replaceable Unit. A module or component which will typically be replaced in its entirety as part of a field service repair operation.
Hard Reset	A reset event in the system that initializes all components and invalidates caches.
HPC	High Performance Computing, commonly computationally intense.
I^2C	Inter-Integrated Circuit bus. A multi-master, 2-wire, serial bus used as the basis for the Intelligent Platform Management Bus.
ICMB	Intelligent Chassis Management Bus. A serial, differential bus designed for IPMI messaging between host and peripheral chassis. Refer to [ICMB] for more information.
I/O	Input / Output. Typically refers to I/O subsystems such as PCI (and variants), memory, and CPU buses.
IPM	Intelligent Platform Management.
IPMB	Intelligent Platform Management Bus. Name for the architecture, protocol, and implementation of a special bus that interconnects the baseboard and chassis electronics and provides a communications media for system platform management information. The bus is built on I^2C and provides a communications path between 'management controllers' such as the BMC, FPC, HSC, PBC, and PSC.
NMI	Non-maskable Interrupt. The highest priority interrupt in the system, after SMI. This interrupt has traditionally been used to notify the operating system fatal system hardware error conditions, such as parity errors and unrecoverable bus errors. It is also used as a Diagnostic Interrupt for generating diagnostic traces and 'core dumps' from the operating system.
MD2	RSA Data Security, Inc. MD2 Message-Digest Algorithm. An algorithm for forming a 128-bit digital signature for a set of input data.
MD5	RSA Data Security, Inc. MD5 Message-Digest Algorithm. An algorithm for forming a 128-bit digital signature for a set of input data. Improved over earlier algorithms such as MD2.
PEF	Platform Event Filtering. The name of the collection of IPMI interfaces in the IPMI v1.5 specification that define how an IPMI Event can be compared against 'filter table' entries that, when matched, trigger a selectable action such as a system reset, power off, alert, etc.
PERR	Parity Error. A signal on the PCI bus that indicates a parity error on the bus.
PET	Platform Event Trap. A specific format of SNMP Trap used for system management alerting. Used for IPMI Alerting as well as alerts using the ASF specification. The trap format is defined in the PET specification. See [PET] and [ASF] for more information.
POST	Power On Self Test.
RFQ	Request for Quote.
SDR	Sensor Data Record. A data record that provides platform management sensor type, locations, event generation, and access information.
SEL	System Event Log. A non-volatile storage area and associated interfaces for storing system platform event information for later retrieval.
SERR	System Error. A signal on the PCI bus that indicates a 'fatal' error on the bus.
Soft Reset	A reset event in the system which forces CPUs to execute from the boot address, but does not change the state of any caches or peripheral devices.
TCO	Total Cost of Ownership. All of the possible costs involved in the purchase, installation, management, support and use of the IT infrastructure within an organization throughout a product's life cycle, from acquisition to disposal.

FIGURES

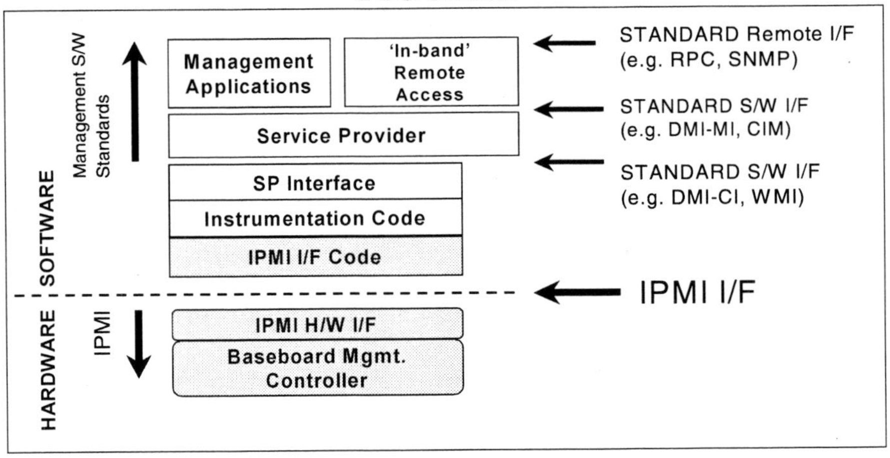

Figure 1 IPMI and the Software Management Stack[v]

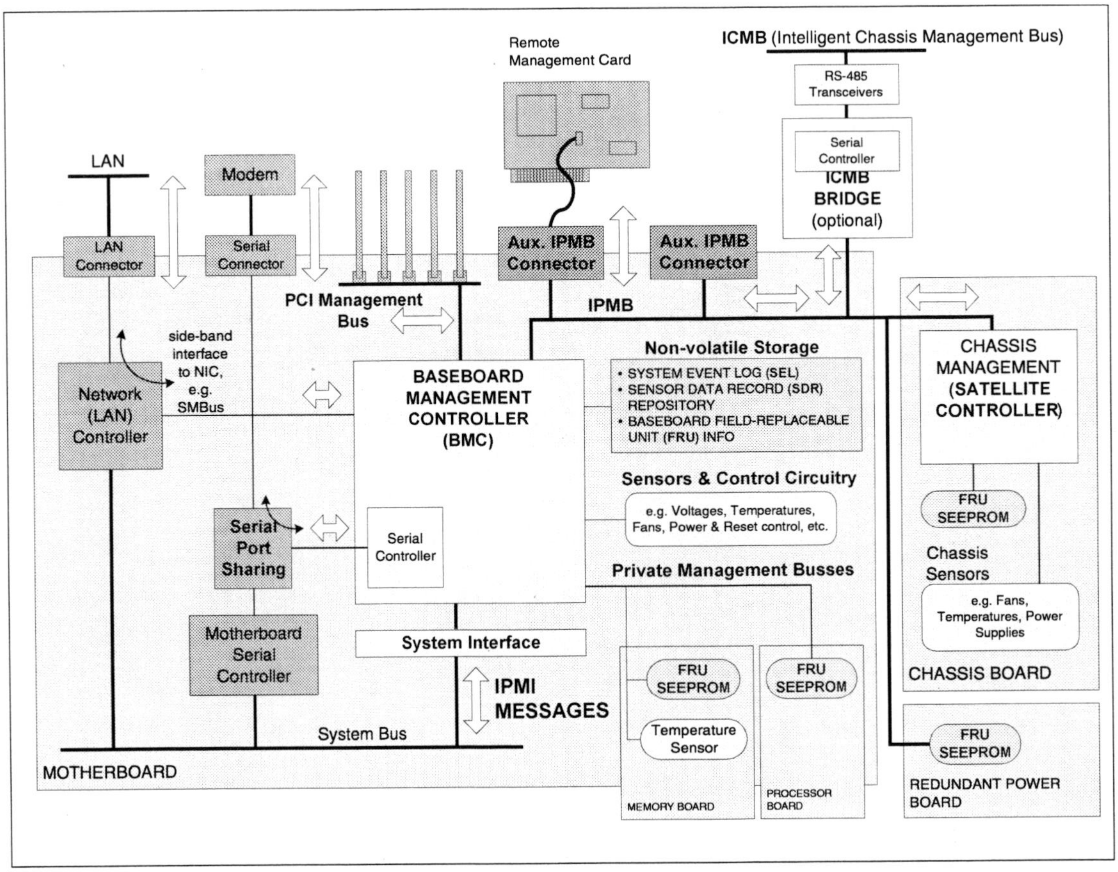

Figure 2 IPMI Block Diagram[7]

---

[i] NCSA, SDSC, ANL, PSC http://www.teragrid.org
[ii] IPMI Spec. v1.5, ©2002 Intel et. al. Sec 1.6.11
[iii] IPMI Spec. v1.5, ©2002 Intel et. al. Sec 1.6.9
[iv] IPMI Spec. v1.5, ©2002 Intel et. al. Sec 1.6.20
[v,7] IPMI Spec. v1.5, ©2002 Intel et. al.

Part IV : TUTORIALS
Partie IV : TUTORIELS

An Evaluation of Globus and Legion Software Environments

M.A.R. Dantas[a], J.N.C. Allemand[b], L.B.C. Passos[b]

[a]Department of Informatics and Statistics (INE), Federal University of Santa Catarina (UFSC), 88040-900, Florianopolis, Brazil
[b]Department of Computer Science (CIC), University of Brasília (UnB), 70919-970, Brasília, Brazil

In this article we present a case study comparison of the implementation characteristics of two software environments which are well known in grid computing configurations. We evaluate the performance of these environments during the execution of parallel distributed MPI tasks. Therefore, first we consider some concepts of the grid paradigm and then we present a comparison between the two software environments. Our case study is based on the *Globus* and *Legion* environments, because these two research projects are in more developed stage when compared to others research initiatives. Our experimental results indicate that the grid computing approach can be interesting to execute parallel distributed MPI applications with a performance improvement.

Dans cet article nous présentons une étude comparative des caractéristiques d'implémentation de deux environnements logiciels bien connus dans le monde du calcul distribué sur une "Grille" (GRID computing). Nous évaluons la performance de chacun de ces environnements pendant l'exécution en parallèle de tâches MPI distribuées. Une introduction des concepts entourant les calculs distribués sur une "Grille" est présentée, suivie de l'étude comparative des deux environnements logiciels, Globus et Legion, ces derniers étant les plus avancés dans le domaine. Nos résultats expérimentaux montrent que l'utilisation de la "Grille" peux s'avérer intéressante pour l'exécution d'applications parallèles MPI avec une certaine amélioration des performances.

1. Introduction

Advances in the communication and computer technologies are providing to an applications programmer access to a large quantity of computer resources distributed in wide area networks. As [Bak00, Buy01] mentioned, it is possible to image that many users´ problem can be solved without the requirement of a local supercomputer.

In this context, we base our goal to build a *grid computing environment* which could represent a global infrastructure of hardware and software. This environment can provide users with a reliable access and low cost to share distributed resources. This concern is expressed by many other research groups (e.g. [Bak01, Gri99, Fos01a, Bes97, Fos99]). We can consider a *grid computing environment* as an infrastructure because in many aspects this paradigm represents the gathering action of resources, information and people which are widely distributed. As a result, it is necessary the use of a complex software environment to manage this configuration and also provides a useful computer power to application programmers.

Many research initiatives [Bru98a, Bru98b, Fos01b] are in advanced stage, providing several software tools which can represent the right answer for a grid configuration. In this paper, we present a case study performance evaluation considering the *Globus* and *Legion* software environment to execute parallel distributed MPI tasks. Therefore, in section 2 we describe some characteristics of these two software packages. The research grid environment used in this paper is introduced in section 3. Implementation aspects of the two software environments and our experimental results, executing parallel distributed MPI applications, are presented in section 4. Finally, in section 5 we present our conclusions and future work.

2. Software Characteristics

In section we address a brief overview of the *Globus* and *Legion* environments. Our target is to present some important components and their functions in these powerful grid tools.

2.1 Globus

The Globus software environment [Fos98c, Fos97b] is a project developed by Argonne National Laboratory (ANL) and University of Southern California. In this paper we use the version 1.1.4 of the Globus software package because this release provides support to MPI applications. The Globus environment is composed by a set of components implementing basic services to resource allocation, communication, security, process management and access to remote data [Fos97b, Glo00].

The resource allocation component of the Globus environment (GRAM - Globus Resource Allocation Manager) is the element that acts as an interface between global and local services. Application programmers use the GRAM element, through the gatekeeper software portion which is responsible for the user authentication and association with a local computer account. The mechanism to identify users of the grid is based on a file called map-file. In this file exists information about authorised users of the grid configuration. Any requirement for resource should be translated to the Resource Specification Language (RSL).

Communication in the Globus environment is performed using a communication library called Nexus [Fos94a, Fos94b]. This component defines low a level

Computer Name	**AIX 1**	**AIX 2**	**AIX 3**	**AIX 4**
Operating System	AIX 4.3	AIX 4.3	AIX 4.3	AIX 4.3
Processor	PowerPC_604 233 MHz	PowerPC_604 233 MHz	PowerPC_604 233 MHz	PowerPC_604 233 MHz
Memory RAM	256 MB	128 MB	128 MB	512 MB
Hard disk	Two disks of 9 GB	Two disks of 4 GB	Two disks of 4 GB and one 2 GB disk	Two disks of 4 GB and one 2 GB disk
Software Environment	*Legion*	*Globus*	*Globus*	Legion

Table I: The grid environment configuration

API to support high level programming paradigms. Examples of high level programming paradigms supported are message passing, remote procedure call and remote I/O procedures. The information about the system and the grid configuration are management by a component called Metacomputing Directory Service (MDS) [Fit97, Fos97a,Ste98].

An important aspect of the Globus software environment is the security. This software tool employs the certificate approach, which is carried by a CA (Certificate Authority) using the protocol Secure Socket *Layer* (SSL) [Fos98a, Fos98b].

2.2 Legion

The Legion software environment is a system object oriented which is being developed since 1993 at University of Virginia. This environment has an architecture concept of grid computing providing a unique virtual machine for users´ applications. The approach of the Legion is to have some important concepts of a grid configuration (e.g. scalability, easy to program, fault tolerance and security) transparent to final users [Cza98].

In the Legion, every entity such as processing power, RAM memory and storage capacity is represented as objects. Objects communicate with each other using services calls to a remote mechanism [Cza98, Leg01]. The security component of the Legion, as the others elements of this software, is based on an object. The application programmer specifies the security related to an object, where it is defined which type of mechanism is allowed [Leg01]. In addition, the Legion provides some extra basic mechanism to ensure more security. The May I method is an example. Every class should define the method May I, which check for a called object the related allowed access.

The traditional system file is emulated in the Legion environment through the combination of persistent objects with the global information of object identification. This approach simplifies the manipulation of files to application programmers. In addition, it is allow to users to add fault tolerance characteristics to applications using rollback and recovery mechanisms [Cza98].

3. The Grid Environment

After providing some characteristics of the Globus and Legion software tools, in this section we present our grid configuration environment. It is important to mention that all the machines were in the same laboratory. However, using a *Ethernet Layer 3 Switch* we were able to have the abstraction of a WAN (Wide Area Network) inside this box. In other words, this equipment could prove the abstraction of a distributed resource environment for our experiments.

Our configuration environment was formed by four IBM RS/6000 workstations connected using an *Ethernet Layer 3 Switch.* The decision to use the RS/6000 was based in the fact that we are planning to connect an IBM supercomputer SP4 to the grid configuration. In addition, it is interesting to mention that we have used before some IBM-PC machines running Linux. We have previously information about some problems with the AIX operating system. Therefore we decide to learn about the software environments in an open source operating system.

Table I shows the configuration environment of our *grid.* The environment could be considered heterogeneous once some elements, as memory and disk capacity, were different.

4. Evaluation of the Environments

After understanding and using both software environments, with a special attention to the concepts of wide distributed resources and passing through some problems related to AIX operating system, we were able to configure the *grid* environment for experiments. In this section, we are going to present comments about the use of two software environments and our results executing parallel distributed MPI tasks.

4.1 General Aspects of the Environments

The *Legion* software provides a homogeneous view of the *grid* to the application programmer. The environment uses its own tools to create the homogeneity. The procedure to install the software does not represent any

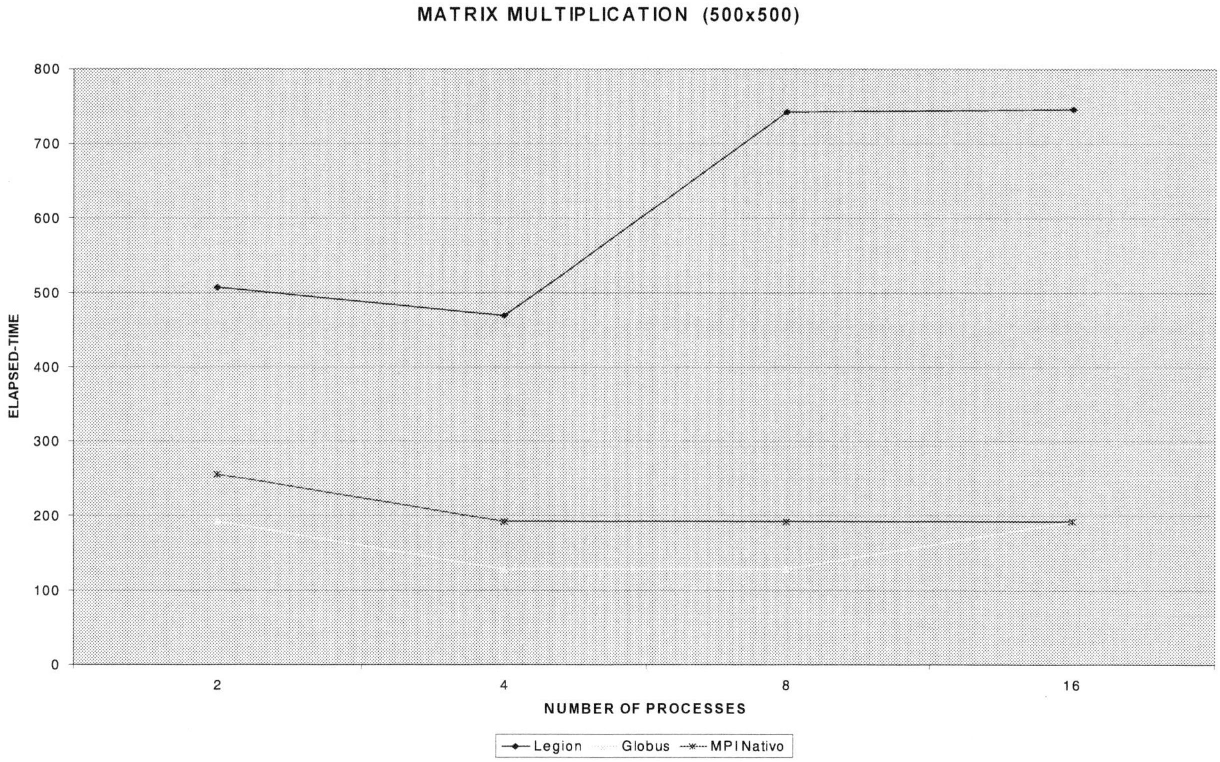

Figure 1: Execution of the parallel MPI code on Globus and Legion Environments

problem, because the application programmer needs only to uncompress binary files and execute some script files. However, for the AIX environment it is necessary more information then those available from the software documents. We fixed some problems using our background on AIX and exchanging several e-mails with other AIX systems managers. The *Legion* concept of file system represents an advantage of the environment. The *Legion* file system presents a unique identifier for each object. This approach provides application programmers the facility to access files widely distributed only using their names. In other words, the users only use the name of the file, which can be storage in a local or remote machine. On the other hand, we have verified some problems with the package. As a first problem, we can mention the necessary installation of the entire environment when the *bootstrap host* has a power failure. The *bootstrap host* is responsible for the domain control. Another drawback of the environment is the low communication rate between objects. The paradigm of the *Legion* is to be a *framework environment,* where users can develop their own tools, such as security and fault tolerance facilities. This freedom can represent some flexibility to any developers group. However, it does not allow the use external tools.

The *Globus* approach allows users to use existing system available tools and have a uniform interface to the gird environment. Interesting features of the *Globus* environment are related to the security and to the autonomy of the configuration. The system has an infrastructure based on X509 certificate [Fos98a, Fos98b] and the use the mutual autentification. On the other hand, one drawback of the software is the scalability, which can be understood as the capability to add new resources and new sites. When considering new facilities application programmers are required to have account into all new hosts.

4.2 Experimental Results

The next stage of our research work was the implementation of a parallel distributed application. We decided to use a parallel matrix multiplication using the MPI message-passing library. The *Globus* environment has a tool called MPICH-G2 to execute the application. On the other hand, the *Legion* has an internal tool called *legion_mpi_run* for executing MPI applications. As we mentioned before, because of the *Legion* framework, it was required some fixes on our MPI original code using the *Legion libraries.* Our results represent the average elapsed-time of twenty executions.

Figure 1 shows the comparison to execute a 500 x 500 matrix multiplication MPI parallel code in the Globus and Legion environments. As we have mentioned before, the low communication rate between objects is responsible for the low performance of the Legion environment.

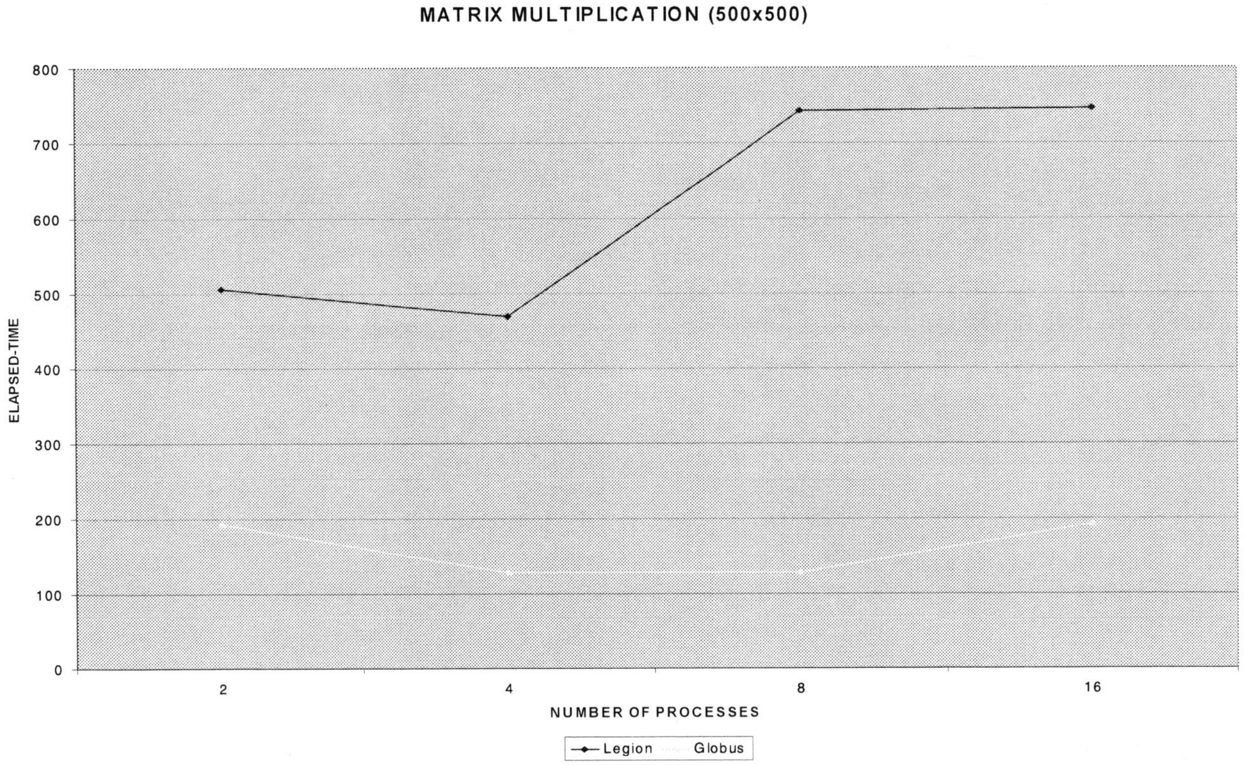

Figure 2: Execution of the parallel MPI code on Globus, Legion and MPICH

Our second experiment was configured using the native *MPICH* and comparing with the two software environments. The MPICH package is an implementation of MPI library and we considered the version mpich-1.2.2.3. Figure 2 presents results of parallel matrix multiplication of Globus, Legion and MPICH. This graphic show that the Globus scheduling mechanism can represent an interesting feature.

5. Conclusion and Future Work

In this research work we have presented the implementation characteristics of the *Globus* and *Legion* software environments. In addition, we have evaluated these two environments when executing a parallel distributed MPI application.

Globus and *Legion* are important tools to configure grid configurations. The *Globus* environment has presented a more robust features, because the software includes security and fault monitoring mechanisms together with many others services. On the other hand, because it is an object-oriented package the *Legion* environment is more efficient to present the grid abstraction. This software is a *framework* and it is not a finished tool. However, we believe that *Legion* can address those users who are expecting a grid configuration that can be customised for their organisations.

One direction as a future work for this research is to understand how these two grid environments can perform under heterogeneous operating systems (e.g. Linux, Irix, HP-UX and Solaris). As we notice in this work, several problems can appear to an application programmer when using these packages. Another future path is to develop a friendly interface (e.g. via *browser)* to present the grid environment to users. As we have presented in [Dan02], users can be awarded of the available resources in the grid environment. This approach should be easy as an ordinary interface used on an operating system (e.g. Linux or Windows) to display resources available in the local computer.

Acknowledgements

The first author was funding by the Brazilian National Research Council (CNPq). The Grid environment used in our experiments comes from collaboration between UnB-CiC/TECSOFT-DF.

References

[Bak00] Baker, M., *Cluster Computing Trends*, Physics Seminar, Liverpool University, http://www.dcs.port.ac.uk/~mab/Talks/Liverpool00/ , May 2000.

[Bak01] Baker, M., *Technologies for MultiCluster/Grid Computer*, Cluster 2001,

Newport Beach, http://www.dcs.port.ac.uk/~mab/Tutorials/ Los Angeles, EUA, 2001.

[Bes97] Bester, J., Foster, I., Kesselman, C., Tedesco, J., and Tuecke, S., *Gass: A Data Movement and Access Service for Wide Area Computing System,* In 7 (1997), ftp://ftp.globus.org/pub/globus/papers/gass.pdf.

[Bru98a] Brunett, S., Davis, D., Gottschalk, T., Messina, P., and Kesselman, C., *Implementing Distributed Synthetic Forces Simulations in Metacomputing Environments,* In Proceedings of the Heterogeneous Computing Workshop (Mar. 1998), ftp://ftp.globus.org/pub/globus/papers/sf-express.pdf.

[Bru98b] Brunett, S., Czajkowski, K., Foster, I., Fitzgerald, S., Johnson, A., Kesselman, C., Leigh, J., and Tuecke, S., *Application Experiences with the Globus Toolkit.,* In Proc. 7th IEEE Symp. on High Performance Distributed Computing (July 1998), IEEE Computer Society Press, ftp://ftp.globus.org/pub/globus/papers/globus-apps.pdf.

[Buy01] Buyya, R. e Baker, M., *Emerging Technologies for MultiCluster/Grid Computing,* www.cacr.caltech.edu/cluster2001/program/abstracts/buyya.html, 2001.

[Cza98] Czajkowski, K., Foster, I., Karonis, N., Kesselman, C., Martin, S., Smith, W., and Tuecke, S, *A Resource Management Architecture for Metacomputing Systems.,* In The 4th Workshop on Job Scheduling Strategies for Parallel Processing (Mar. 1998), IEEE-P, pp. 4-18, ftp://ftp.globus.org/pub/globus/papers/gram97.pdf.

[Dan02] Dantas, M.A.R,J.G.C Lopes, T.G. Ramos, *An Enhanced Scheduling Approach in a Distributed Parallel Environment using Mobile Agents, In Proc. 16th Annual International Symposium on High-Performance Computing and Systems,* Moncton, Canada, 2002, IEEE Computer Society Press.

[Fit97] Fitzgerald, S., Foster, I., Kesselman, C., von Laszewski, G., Smith, W., and Tuecke, S., *A Directory Service for Configuring High-performance Distributed Computations,* In Proc. 6th IEEE Symp. on High Performance Distributed Computing (1997), IEEE Computer Society Press, pp. 365-375, *ftp://ftp.globus.org/pub/globus/papers/hpdc97-mds.pdf*

[Fos01a] Foster, I., Kesselman, C. e Tuecke, S. *The Anatomy of the Grid : Enabling Scalable Virtual Organizations,* www.globus.org/research/papers/anatomy.pdf, 2001.

[Fos01b] Foster, I., *Grid Technologies & Applications: Architecture & Achievements,* Computing in High Energy and Nuclear Physics 2001 - CHEP'01, Pequim, China, September 2001, http://www.ihep.ac.cn/~chep01/paper/10-047.pdf.

[Fos99] Foster, I. e Kesselman, C.;*The Grid: BluePrint for a new computing infrastructure,* Morgan Kaufmann, 1999.

[Fos98a] Foster, I., Kesselman, C., and Tsudick, S. T.G., *A Security Architecture for Computational Grids,* In Proc. of the 5th ACM Conference on Computer and Communication Security (Nov. 1998), ACM Press, ftp://ftp.globus.org/pub/globus/papers/security.pdf

[Fos98b] Foster, I., Karonis, N. T., Kesselman, C., and Tuecke, S.., *Managing Security in High-performance Distributed Computations,* Cluster Computing 1, 1 (1998), 95-107, *ftp://ftp.globus.org/pub/globus/papers/cc-security.pdf*

[Fos98c]Foster, I., and Kesselman, C., *The Globus Project: A Progress Report,* In Proceedings of the Heterogeneous Computing Workshop (Mar. 1998), ftp://ftp.globus.org/pub/globus/papers/globus-hcw98.pdf

[Fos97a] Foster, I., and von Laszewski, G., *Usage of LDAP in Globus,* TR, ANL, 1997, ftp://ftp.globus.org/pub/globus/papers/ldap_in_globus.pdf.

[Fos97b] Foster, I., and Kesselman, C., *Globus: A Metacomputing Infrastructure Toolkit,* International Journal of Supercomputer Applications 11, 2 (1997), 115-128, ftp://ftp.globus.org/pub/globus/papers/globus.pdf

[Fos94a] Foster, I., and Tuecke, S. , *Nexus: Runtime Support for Task-parallel Programming Languages,* ftp://ftp.globus.org/pub/globus/papers/nexus_paper_ps.pdf, TR, ANL, 1994.

[Fos94b] Foster, I., Kesselman, C., and Tuecke, S., *The Nexus Task-parallel Runtime System,* In Proc. 1st Intl Workshop on Parallel Processing. Tata McGraw Hill, 1994, pp. 457-462, ftp://ftp.globus.org/pub/globus/papers/india_paper_ps.pdf.

[Glo00] The Globus Project, *Globus Toolkit 1.1.3 Sytem Administration Guide*, University of Shouthern California, http://www.globus.org, December 2000.

[Gri99] Grimshaw, A., Ferrari, A., Knabe, F., Humprey, M.; *Legion: An Operating System for Wide-Area Computing*, 1999.

[Leg01] University of Virginia, *Legion 1.8 System Administrator Manual*, http://legion.virginia.edu, 2001.

[Ste98] Stelling, P., Foster, I., Kesselman, C., Lee, C., and von Laszewski, G. , *A Fault Detection Service for Wide Area Distributed Computations,* In Proc. 7th IEEE Symp. on High Performance Distributed Computing (July 1998), IEEE Computer Society Press, ftp://ftp.globus.org/pub/globus/papers/hbm.pdf.

Providing Cluster Environments with High-Availability and Load-Balancing

M.A.R. Dantas[a], R.M. Alvim[b], F.L.L. Grossmann[b]

[a]Department of Informatics and Statistics (INE), Federal University of Santa Catarina (UFSC), 88040-900, Florianopolis, Brazil
[b]Department of Computer Science (CIC), University of Brasilia (UnB), 70919-970, Brasília, Brazil

[a]*mardantas@computer.org*

Cluster environments are usually provided at a low cost with an interesting performance when compared to parallel machines. However, some aspects of clusters configurations should be tackled to improve the environment to execute real applications. In this paper we present a framework in which we join functions of high-availability and virtual server to enhance services for application programmers using a cluster environment. Our results indicate that this approach can improve successfully this distributed system to execute real applications.

Les grappes d'ordinateurs sont généralement peu dispendieuses, et donnent accès à une performance intéressante lorsqu'on les compare aux ordinateurs parallèles classiques. Mais, sous certains aspects, le processus de configuration de ces grappes doit être amélioré pour y permettre l'exécution d'applications courantes. Dans cet article, nous présentons un cadre qui combine des fonctions de haute disponibilité avec l'utilisation d'un serveur virtuel, dans le but d'améliorer les services accessibles aux programmeurs en environnement grappe. Les résultats que nous obtenons indiquent que cette façon de faire peut améliorer sensiblement la capacité d'une grappe à exécuter des applications courantes

1. Introduction

Nowadays we cannot image any organization working without its computational systems even for a few minutes. A computational system not working for any fraction of time can represent an enormous lost for the organization. A redundancy approach it is necessary to avoid any risk to stop the computational system. The concern with this issue can be exemplified by IBM [1] and Microsoft [2,3], the two companies are already providing some features of reliability for their cluster solutions.

On the other hand, there are some researches on the open software arena. The idea is to demonstrate that open source solutions can provide interesting cost-efficient functions to cluster configurations. Examples of these environments are the *high-availability* (*HA*) [4,5] and *Linux virtual server projects* (*LVS*) [6,7].

The goal of the *high-availability project* is to provide a software package where a user can define one machine as a shadow of another computer. In other words, if any problem occurs with the first computer the second machine acts as a mirror, working in the same fashion as the original machine. This approach provides to programmers a more reliable environment to execute their applications.

The *virtual server* addresses the load balancing of a cluster configuration providing an even distribution of the workload among all machines of the environment. During an ordinary period of the cluster environment execution many requests are received to execute many tasks. Therefore, an element of the cluster could be in charge to redirect all the incoming tasks to the appropriate computers. An appropriate computer is a machine that has a low workload index. However, this approach has a drawback on the central element, which is responsible for redirects the tasks. This central function cannot work properly if the computer presents a failure.

In this article we present our research integrating functions of the *high-availability and virtual server projects.* Our target is to provide to application programmers the facility of virtual server with high-availability characteristics. This approach can enhance the vulnerability of the central element for distributing the workload, providing to programmers a reliable configuration. In section 2 we present some function characteristics of the *high-availability* and *virtual server projects.* Section 3 shows our cluster configurations and in section 4 we present some experimental results of the integration. Our conclusions and final comments of the research work are presented in section 5.

2. High-Availability and Virtual Server Projects

2.1 High-Availability (HA)

The high-availability project targets to provide reliability in distributed environment providing a shadow of one computer on a secondary machine. There are two important concepts when we consider especially the Linux High-Availability (LHA), these are the virtual address IP and the heartbeat [4]. The first concept (virtual address IP) means that the IP address is linked to a service and not to a certain host. During an interval of time, for example, services can be provided in computer **A**. In other interval of time, computer **B**, which is the backup service of computer **A**, can provide the same services because computer A presents hardware problems. In a cluster we can have many virtual IPs services, where each IP can be linked to one or more services [4]. The heartbeat concept is a process responsible for monitoring all services in a high-availability environment. The concept also provides the intranet services communications executing the message passing among servers [5]. Therefore, the heartbeat is the element that decides which server will be responsible for assuming a certain virtual IP address. The LHA works with deamons on both servers. After initializing the Linux, the heartbeat is initialized and checks if the servers are working. The virtual IP is created on the primary server and the machine exchange continuously messages. The procedure of message exchanging is used for check the availability of the servers.

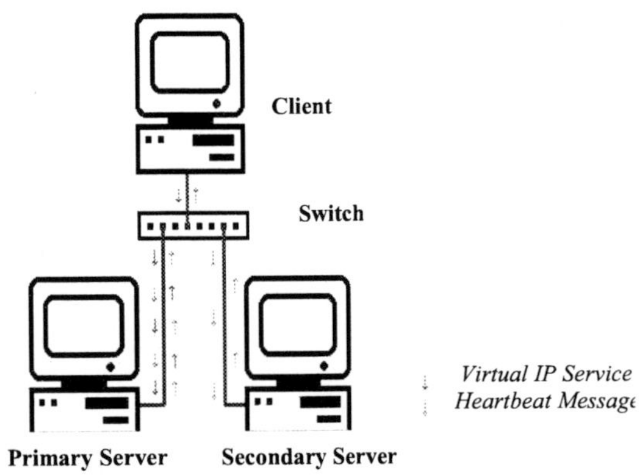

Figure 1. High-Availability working characteristics

Figure 1 shows the high-availability working characteristics, where three machines called *client, primary* and *secondary server* exists. The computer called *client* receives request of services for the cluster environment. The primary server receives the service of the virtual IP. On the other hand, the secondary server receives the messages from the heartbeat.

In the cluster environment we usually specify an interval of time that is valid for the messages exchange for the heartbeat function. When the interval is reached the high-availability software understand that the server of a specific service is out-of-order. Therefore, the secondary machine assumes all the tasks providing services, which were executing on the primary server. The approach of messages passing is not stopped because the primary server can run properly and assume all the services again. This is an example situation when the primary server returns to work.

2.2 Virtual Server (LVS)

The project call *Linux Virtual Server (LVS)* [6] is designed as an abstraction where inside a cluster environment only one computer can provides services to all incoming requests. This central host is called *virtual server*. An external host requesting services to this host *suppose* that all the tasks will be execute by this central node. However, the *virtual server* has two parts: one *load balancer* and others *n computers*. The function of the *load balancer* is to receive the external work requests and then to distribute among the others *n computers* of the *virtual server*. Reading the IP datagram, the *load balancer*, decides in which computer the task will execute. The external node does not know that another computer is executing the incoming request [7].

The main target of the *virtual server* approach is to prove high performance and high availability for distributed applications executing in the cluster. These two aspects are reached by the load balancing and redundancy functions. The first function executes a workload among the *n computers* of the configuration. The second feature it is provided by the *n computers* available in the cluster.

Figure 2 represents the *Linux Virtual Server* (LVS) working characteristics. This figure shows the *load balancer* and the others *n computers* (*Real Server*). We can consider an example in which a cluster is connected to the Internet. In this case incoming requests are received from the Internet through the *load balancer* and then it is distributed to each available computer of the cluster.

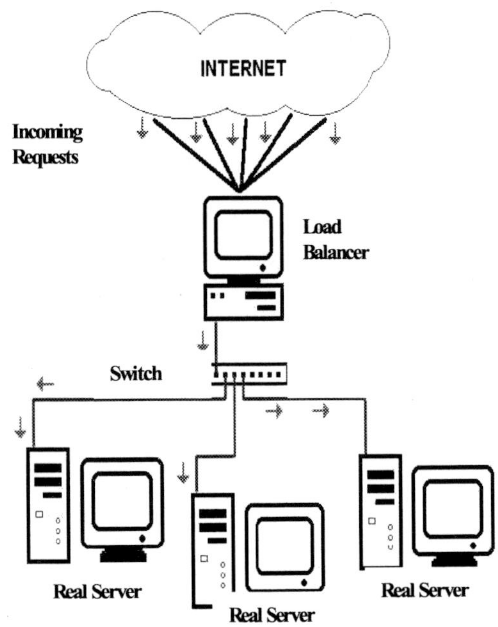

Figure 2. Linux Virtual Server working characteristics

In a virtual server environment the software responsible for monitoring and distribution of the tasks is called *ldirectord* [6,7]. Running into the *load balancer* this process uses the exchange of messages to identify computers to execute specific tasks and if all the *n computers* are working as expected. In the case of failure in a computer this machine will not receive any task before it shows that is working in a normal condition. After working as expected, the computer that had the failure is again inserted into the cluster to execute requests. The *ldirectord* can implement several scheduling policies for the load balancing. The usual, but not the unique, is the *round-robin* approach. Using this approach each machine of the cluster has a weight to execute a task (or service). In other words, this weight translates to the *load balancer* if a computer can execute *n* times more services than another computer.

Another important process in the *virtual server* configuration is the *IPVSADM.* This process execute in the *load balancer* providing vital information such as the cluster configuration and which tasks are executing in which computer.

3. Cluster Configuration

The cluster configuration used for our experiments is form by conventional IBM-PC machines executing the Linux operating system. This environment can be considered an interesting environment because it is an ordinary heterogeneous cluster configuration that is common in several laboratories.

The cluster configuration characteristics are presented in table I.

Processors	**Pentium 100-100-233-233-233**
Memory (Mbytes)	**32-32-64-64-64**
Operating system	**Linux 6.0 kernel 2.2.17**

Table I. Cluster configuration

4. Experimental Results

After understanding interesting features of the *high-availability* and *virtual server projects* we decided to extend the functionality of these environments, therefore we decide to integrate the two approaches. It is clear that the *load balancer* as a central element of the cluster receiving requests, it is a point that can occurs a failure. In this case, all the interesting functions of the cluster environment cannot be translated as a useful work.

In figure 3 we present our suggestion for integrating the HA and LVS functions for a cluster configuration. A secondary *load balancer* is connected to the cluster using the *high-availability* paradigm. This second *balancer* uses the *heartbeat* functions to monitor the primary *balancer.*

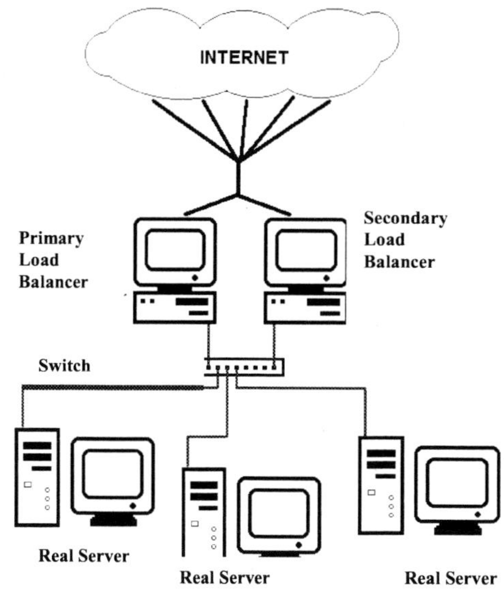

Figure 3. Integrating HA and LVS functions

All experimental results present in this section are based on our change of the cluster configuration. Therefore, we have created several study case situations to verify if our approach works as expected. Figure 4 shows the IP addresses and names used for our experiments. The integrated environment is form by the *load balancer.* The primary *balancer was* called *Laico Z* and the secondary as *Laico Y.* On the other hand, the *n computers* used were called as *Laico 2, Laico 3* and *Laico 4.*

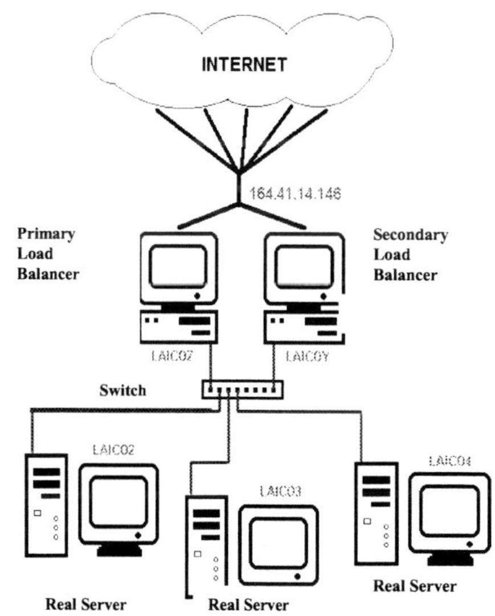

Figure 4. The integrated environment

In figure 5 we present a monitoring view of the cluster (using the IPVSADM) in which shows that all the *n computers* are working with the same weight and executing 5 processes.

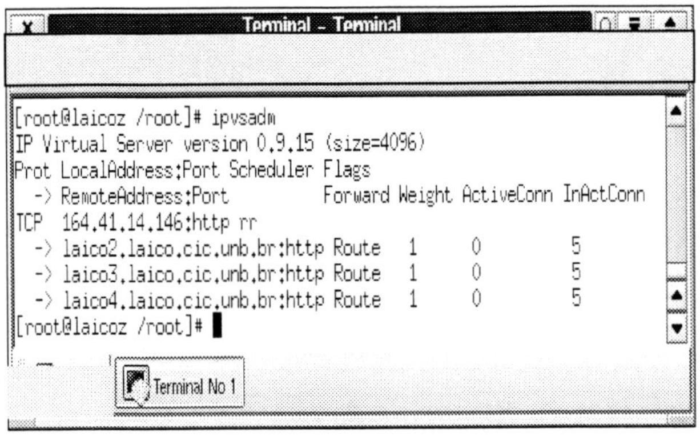

```
[root@laicoz /root]# ipvsadm
IP Virtual Server version 0.9.15 (size=4096)
Prot LocalAddress:Port Scheduler Flags
  -> RemoteAddress:Port          Forward Weight ActiveConn InActConn
TCP  164.41.14.146:http rr
  -> laico2.laico.cic.unb.br:http Route   1      0          5
  -> laico3.laico.cic.unb.br:http Route   1      0          5
  -> laico4.laico.cic.unb.br:http Route   1      0          5
[root@laicoz /root]#
```

Figure 5. Cluster with all servers working

As a first study case example we have simulated a problem in the Laico 2 computer shutting down this machine, as illustrated in figure 6. Just after shutting down the computer we have used the IPVSADM monitoring tool to evaluate the configuration status. In the figure 7 it is possible to verify that the Laico 2 is not available to provide services to the cluster configuration.

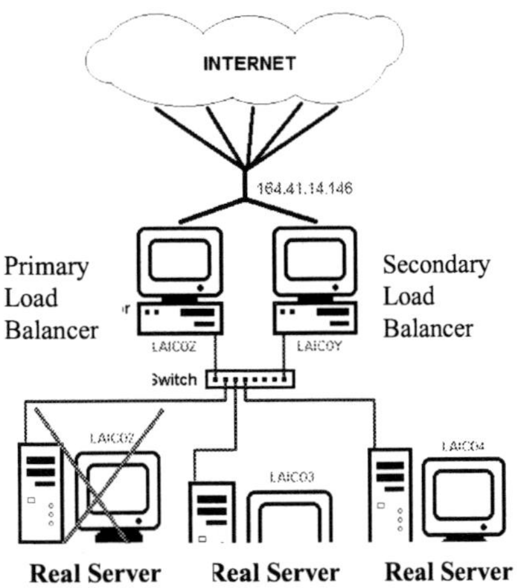

Figure 6. A study case without a machine Laico 2

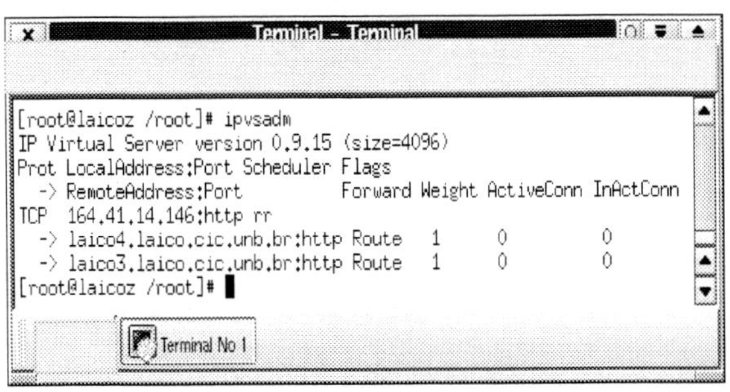

```
[root@laicoz /root]# ipvsadm
IP Virtual Server version 0.9.15 (size=4096)
Prot LocalAddress:Port Scheduler Flags
  -> RemoteAddress:Port          Forward Weight ActiveConn InActConn
TCP  164.41.14.146:http rr
  -> laico4.laico.cic.unb.br:http Route   1      0          0
  -> laico3.laico.cic.unb.br:http Route   1      0          0
[root@laicoz /root]#
```

Figure 7. Cluster without Laico 2 services

A few minutes later we decide to start up again the Laico 2 computer and verify how the cluster configurations would be presented. Figure 8 represents an output of the IPVSADM a few moments after Laico 2 works.

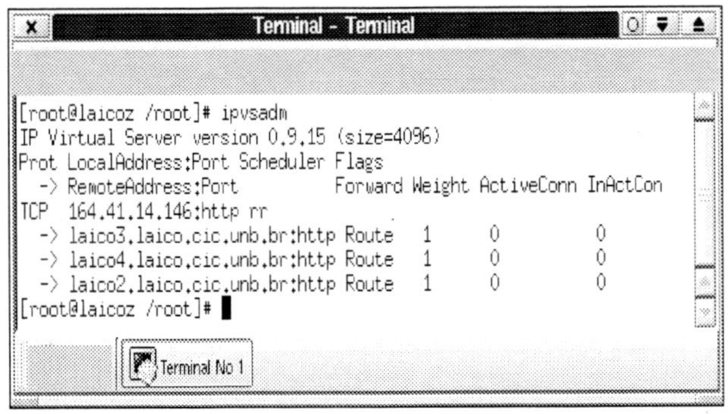

```
[root@laicoz /root]# ipvsadm
IP Virtual Server version 0.9.15 (size=4096)
Prot LocalAddress:Port Scheduler Flags
  -> RemoteAddress:Port          Forward Weight ActiveConn InActCon
TCP  164.41.14.146:http rr
  -> laico3.laico.cic.unb.br:http Route   1      0          0
  -> laico4.laico.cic.unb.br:http Route   1      0          0
  -> laico2.laico.cic.unb.br:http Route   1      0          0
[root@laicoz /root]#
```

Figure 8. Cluster with Laico 2 services working

Another case situation that we have created was to simulate a failure in the primary *load balancer* (called as Laico Z). Before the simulation we have verified the status of the secondary *load balancer (*called as Laico Y). Figure 9 shows the status of the Laico Y computer before the failure on the primary server. This figure shows that no work has being assigned to this machine. The *heartbeat* is executing as expected. In other words, the computer is active but not executing any external task.

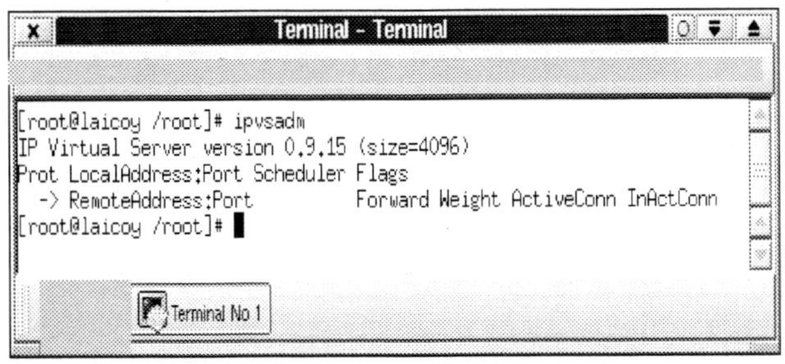

```
[root@laicoy /root]# ipvsadm
IP Virtual Server version 0.9.15 (size=4096)
Prot LocalAddress:Port Scheduler Flags
  -> RemoteAddress:Port          Forward Weight ActiveConn InActConn
[root@laicoy /root]#
```

Figure 9. IPVSADM executing in the second load balancer

Figure 10 represents a failure in the primary *load balancer* (Laico Z). The expected situation is that the secondary *load balancer* (Laico Y) should take action to execute all the external tasks, which were running in the primary load balancer.

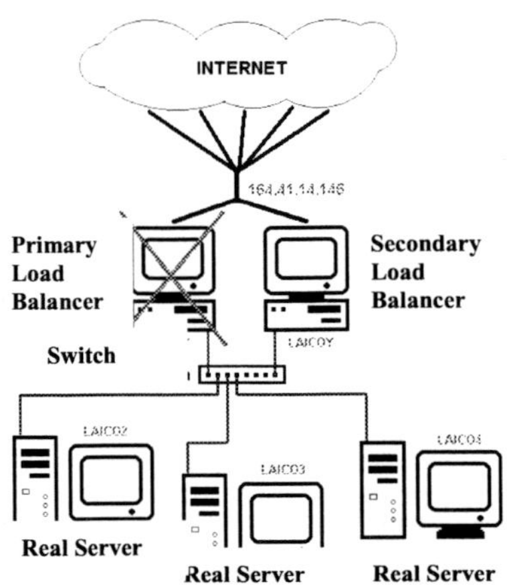

Figure 10. The primary load balancer presents problem

In the figure 11, we present the result of the IPVSADM monitoring tool, where it is possible to see that all the n computers of the configuration are under the secondary load balancer (Laico y) domain.

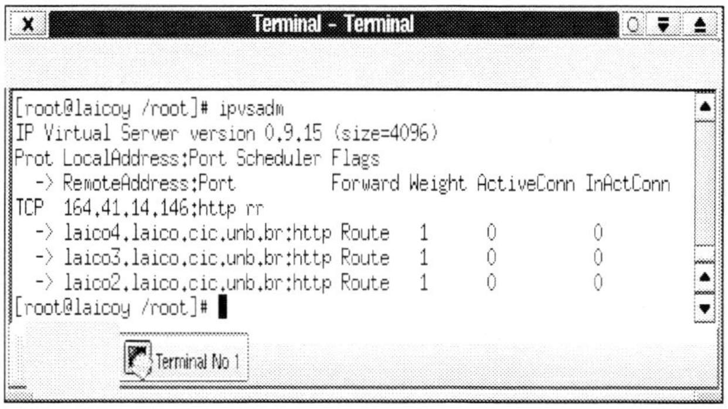

Figure 11. IPVSADM executing in the second load balancer

After a few minutes we have returned the normal situation, where the Laico Z is working without failure and this machine is the primary *load balancer*. Our case study is presented in figure 12 where the domain of the *n computers* is now under the Laico Z responsibility.

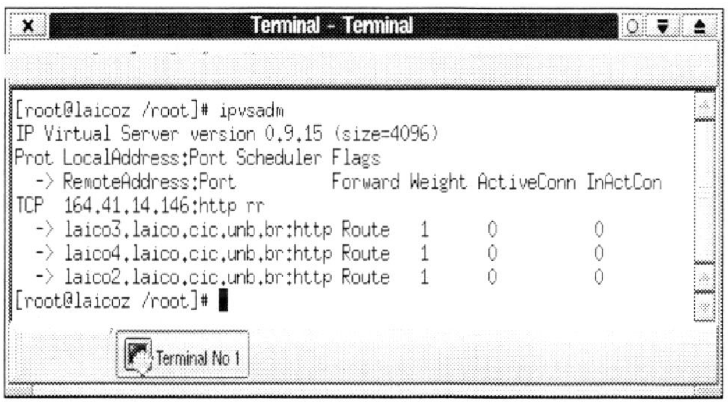

Figure 12. IPVSADM executing in the primary load balancer

In parallel with the primary *load balancer* activity, figure 13 shows that the secondary *load balancer* (Laico Y) is not more responsible for the domain.

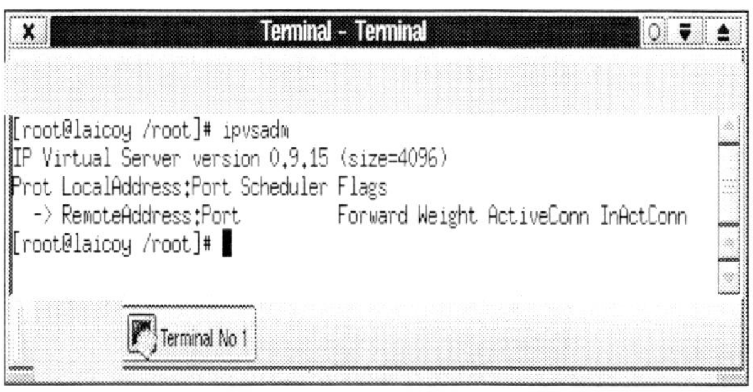

Figure 13. IPVSADM executing in the second load balancer

5. Conclusions and Future Work

The several experiments illustrated in our study cases indicate the integration success of HA and LVS. Integrating the *high-availability* and the *virtual server functions* for a distributed cluster can represent to this environment an interesting reliable configuration to execute several applications.

As a future work we are planning to submit the cluster environment to execute hundred thousand requests at the same time. Our goal is to verify how the load balancer works when millions of incoming requests are coming. In addition, it is interesting to use the integrated approach in a grid configuration where many failure problems occur and the number of requests is enormous.

Acknowledgments

The first author's work was partially funded by the Brazilian National Research Council- CNPq (300874/006). The Computer environment used was from the LAICO laboratory and it was supported by the PROJECT INEG/CNPq-UnB.

References

[1]IBM,http://www.ibm.com/servers/eserver/pseries/solutions/ha/hans.html, 2002.

[2] Microsoft, http://www.microsoft.com/windows2000/technologies/clustering/default.asp, 2002.

[3] Martin, Peter (p.martin@ies.uk.com) e Cronin, John (jsc3@havoc.gtf.org), 05/07/2001, http://www.microsoft.com/SERVICEPROVIDERS/solutions/haoview.asp, 2001.

[4] High Availability Project, http://www.Linux-HA.org, 2002.

[5] Milz, H., "HA-HOWTO" http://www.ibiblio.org/pub/Linux/ALPHA/linux-ha/High-Availability-HOWTO.html

[6] Linux Virtual Server Project, http://www.Linuxvirtualserver.org, 2002.

[7] Mack, J., "LVS-HOWTO", http://www.linuxvirtualserver.org/Documents.html#manuals, 2001.

Author Index
Index des auteurs